PRODIGAL
SOLDIERS

How a Generation
of Officers
Born of Vietnam
Revolutionized
the American Style
of War

PRODIGAL SOLDIERS

James Kitfield

BRASSEY'S

Washington • London

Brassey's Editorial Offices: Brassey's Order Department:
22883 Quicksilver Drive   P.O. Box 960
Dulles, Virginia 20166   Herndon, Virginia 20172

Brassey's books are available at special discounts for bulk purchases for sales promotions, premiums, fund-raising, or educational use.

Library of Congress Cataloging-in-Publication Data

Kitfield, James.
        Prodigal soldiers / James Kitfield.
        p.   cm.
        Originally published: New York : Simon & Schuster, 1995.
        Includes bibligraphical references (p.   ) and index.
     ISBN 0-671-76925-1 (casebound.)—ISBN 1-57488-123-X (pbk.)

     1. Military art and science—United States—History—20th century.
2. Unified operations (Military science)   3. Vietnamese Conflict,
1961–1975—Veterans.   I. Title.
        [UA23.K526   1997]
        355'.00973'09045—DC21   97-15273
                                                                        CIP

Designed by Karolina Harris

Softcover Edition
10 9 8 7 6 5 4 3

Printed in the United States of America

In memory of my mother, Ruste Murray Kitfield, who
set me upon this adventure eyes dancing over the rim
of the first book she ever read me, and remained
throughout the journey my fiercest defender and
gentlest critic.

Acknowledgments

THERE are a number of people without whom this book could not have been completed. Though she could not be here for its publication, my mother, Ruste Kitfield, was my most prized critic and cheerleader. Eleanor Evans was a source of constant support and encouragement throughout, and deserves special thanks, as does my sister, Allison Kitfield.

As my editor at Simon & Schuster, Gary Luke originally saw the worth in this idea, and shepherded it through the long and arduous path to publication with equanimity and keen insight. Thanks also to my agent, Gail Ross.

My friends and colleagues at *Government Executive* magazine and *National Journal* Inc. were also essential to making this project possible, especially editor and publisher Tim Clark; the rest of the staff, for graciously accepting my frequent absences; Steve Hull, for lending his valued editorial guidance; Isobel Ellis, for always dropping everything whenever my frequent technological crises erupted; and John Fox Sullivan, for his support.

This is essentially a story about those in uniform, and without the willing cooperation of scores of service members, active duty and retired, it could not be told. Many of their stories are directly reflected inside, but some are not. My thanks to the service chiefs who consented to interviews and gave guidance: Gen. Gordon Sullivan, Adm. Frank Kelso, and Gen. Tony McPeak. Others I am indebted to include Adm. Ron "Zap" Zlatoper, Gen. Dave Barrato, Colonels Bill Schwetke, John LeMoyne, Burt Tackaberry, Steve Turner, Pat O'Neal, Boots Boothby, Moody Suter, and Ed Clements.

prodigal son *Bible:* a son who journeyed into a far country where he wasted himself with riotous living, yet who was welcomed back warmly on his homecoming in repentance: Luke 15:11–32

> *For this my son was dead,*
> *and is alive again;*
> *he was lost, and is found.*

The human heart is the starting point of all matters pertaining to war.

—Maréchal de Saxe, *Reveries on the Art of War* (1732)

All historically important armed forces have developed their own distinctive operational style. For example, historians agree that the Roman style of warfare fitted well the objectives of the Senate and the People of Rome, and of the Roman Emperors. . . .

There is emerging a distinctive American style of war, a style that is essentially joint, drawing on the unique capabilities of each service via centralized planning and decentralized execution. This jointness, plus an amalgam of surprise, discriminate use of overwhelming force, high op tempo, and exploitation of advanced technology, has led to a whole new order of military effectiveness. This is the "revolution in military affairs" that certainly figured in the Soviet decision to end the Cold War.

—From a letter by the late Gen. William DePuy to Gen. Colin Powell

 # An AUSA Institute of Land Warfare Book

The Association of the United States Army, or AUSA, was founded in 1950 as a nonprofit organization dedicated to education concerning the role of the U.S. Army, to providing material for military professional development, and to the promotion of proper recognition and appreciation of the profession of arms. Its constituencies include those who serve in the Army today, including Army National Guard, Army Reserve, and Army civilians, the retirees and veterans who have served in the past, and all their families. A large number of public-minded citizens and business leaders are also an important constituency. The Association seeks to educate the public, elected and appointed officials, and leaders of the defense industry on crucial issues involving the adequacy of our national defense, particularly those issues affecting land warfare.

In 1988, AUSA established within its existing organization a new entity known as the Institute of Land Warfare. ILW's mission is to extend the educational work of AUSA by sponsoring a wide range of publications, to include books, monographs, and essays on key defense issues, as well as workshops, symposia, and since 1992, a television series. Among the volumes chosen as "An AUSA Institute of Land Warfare Book" are both new texts and reprints of titles of enduring value. Topics include history, policy issues, strategy, and tactics. Publication as an AUSA Book does not indicate that the Association of the United States Army and the publisher agree with everything in the book but does suggest that AUSA and the publisher believe the book will stimulate the thinking of AUSA members and others concerned about important defense-related issues.

Contents

Part III: 1981–1986

Part IV: 1989–1992

Prologue

IN a hollow trough carved by long-forgotten rains, the sound began as a distant thrumming in the still air and increased steadily until even the sheep began to shuffle restlessly. Two young boys stopped their playing long enough to search the cloudless sky, shading their eyes against the harsh glare.

The voracious rhythm of the noise continued to grow until it seemed for an instant to swallow even the light, and then the shadow passed through the wadi and was just as quickly gone. The bedouin shepherds tending the flock looked on passively. Their forefathers had watched the marshaling of other armies with similar stoicism, continuing with their nomadic lives long after all traces of the great battles and the generals who fought them had been swept from that unforgiving land, from Alexander the Great at Arbela to Montgomery at El Alamein. All relegated to the history books. Only the bedouin still remained.

Continuing its long journey south, the Blackhawk helicopter passed over a vast, featureless landscape. Far out to the left toward the Persian Gulf a blue haze obscured the horizon, and tiny oil derricks marked the hidden treasure that had brought fantastic wealth and now again the threat of war to that barren region. The helicopter's shadow skimmed over road junctions choked with military traffic and disappeared into irregular encampments shrouded with camouflage netting. In the distance numerous convoys were revealed by the shimmering dust clouds that hovered around them as they snaked across the desert floor. For hundreds of miles, the desert was on the move.

It was an army unlike any yet seen in that region, even by the bedouins and their ancestors. Certainly it bore little resemblance to those the United States had fielded in the past or was likely to field again in the conceivable future. Swelled by the final, decade-long standoff of the Cold War, it represented a military machine so massive and technology so complex that many of its individual elements had never been tested together even in exercise, much less in war. For better or worse, it was an army that had been revolutionized from the bottom up and reformed and reorganized from the top down. Its ranks were filled by volunteers, professional soldiers who had never seen combat led by combat veterans who had known bitter defeat. Above all else, the army that was massing on November 14, 1990, from points all around the globe was an unknown entity.

From ground level, the massive force had a dangerously loose and ungainly feel to it. If there was a master plan guiding all of the seemingly haphazard movement and lethal weaponry, it was not readily apparent to someone standing in the clattering bowels of the machine, trying to direct traffic at a dust-choked intersection in a vast track of featureless desert. It would be easy to believe that the view from the helicopter passing just overhead would be much better, might even reveal the grand scheme that made sense of all this.

Somewhere down there Maj. Gen. Barry McCaffrey had a son. The thought didn't consume him, but as he looked down from the speeding Blackhawk and surveyed the vast force that was stacking up for hundreds of miles behind his 24th Infantry Division, neither was it ever very far from his consciousness. Somewhere out there a first lieutenant led troops of the 82nd Airborne just as his father had twenty-five years earlier.

McCaffrey had told his wife that the 82nd was stationed safely to the south, knowing the opposite to be true. As many times as Jill had willingly sent him to war on foreign battlefields as a young man, sending Sean had proven altogether more difficult. Now their daughter Tara, a second lieutenant in the Army's nursing corps, was hoping to be deployed to Saudi Arabia. Funny, even Sean had balked at the idea of his sister joining this fray, figuring two McCaffreys in a potential war zone at one time was plenty. And Jill, whose jokes about being a crazed warrior wife revealed a woman who loved the Army at least as much as her husband, was discovering that when it came to Sean and Tara, she was just another mother worried for her children.

In the early days of the crisis, Sean and the rest of the men of the 82nd served as a ridiculously fragile trip wire for Iraqi armored forces massed at the Saudi border. McCaffrey smiled at the thought of his son's letters and his upbeat enthusiasm, full as he was of stories about facing down unseen armored divisions in the desert with handheld antitank weapons and paratrooper machismo. The plan was all but suicidal, even calling for cutoff paratroopers to swim out to Navy boats in the Persian Gulf after they had blunted Saddam's initial assault.

It was vintage 82nd Airborne, recalling a poster that one of McCaffrey's brigade commanders had in his office back at Ft. Stewart, Georgia. On it was a picture of a mud-splattered and unshaven GI in World War II, a bazooka in his hand and a cigarette clenched insolently in a jutting jaw. The setting of this actual incident, the caption clarified, was the Ardennes forest, when American forces were in routed retreat before German panzers in a counteroffensive that would become the Battle of the Bulge. A tank commander had hastily stopped his track to ask the soldier for directions.

"You looking for a safe place to park that thing?" the GI asked.

"I sure am," the tank commander replied.

"Well, pull it in right behind me, 'cause I'm the Eighty-second Airborne, and this is as far as the bastards are going."

Yet an uneasiness had crept over McCaffrey as he read his son's letters. In the boy's thirst for adventure and excitement at the prospect of combat there was a mirror image of the father as a young man, and for just a moment it served to reflect the unfathomable gulf of experience that now yawned between them. McCaffrey knew that Sean and many like him might soon be asked to blindly leap that chasm. He also understood in a way that his son couldn't the utter capriciousness with which fate would decide who made it to the other side.

Barry McCaffrey filed it away and concentrated instead on the landscape that sped underneath his helicopter. He would compartmentalize the worry, because that's what generals did. As a division commander, one of only eighteen in the Army and a small handful in Saudi Arabia on the eve of war, he had nearly twenty-six thousand soldiers to think about, each one a son or daughter, husband or wife, father or mother. You could care about them and even love them, but you sure as hell couldn't avoid sending them into harm's way. That was the pact he had made pinning on the stars, an extension of the one he had made more than twenty-five years earlier pinning on lieutenant's bars.

The mantle of long command had weighed differently on each man who was even then traveling like McCaffrey to a briefing in Daharan. Some it gave a chilly aloofness where they had had none as young men, others it saddled with bombastic tempers. The bad ones it could make bullies. More than a few it left with a disregard for their personal safety that bordered on recklessness. In McCaffrey's case, there was a palpable intensity that no one who came into contact in Saudi Arabia with the wiry general with the close-cropped gray hair and dark eyes failed to notice. There are those who were judged as measuring up short under that gaze who will never forget. But a war was looming, and McCaffrey knew there were worse sacrifices to be made than his popularity.

Nor did he doubt that they were on the eve of war. McCaffrey focused again on the summons he was answering from Gen. H. Norman Schwarzkopf, fancying that he could almost hear the cameras of history whirring in his ear instead of the familiar whine of the Blackhawk's twin engines. In a way that was unmatched in practically any other of society's endeavors, he had sweated and bled and fought his way ahead for his entire working life to perform precisely this task at a defining moment in his nation's history. They all had, each and every man who was converging by land, sea, and air on an officers' club in Daharan, Saudi Arabia.

The stakes were the highest they'd been in more than twenty years, when all of them had heard the summons as young men. And perhaps only those who had answered that call before understood the razor's edge they all now walked between success and ignoble catastrophe. Certainly Schwarzkopf, a Vietnam veteran who had also been second-in-command in the controversial Urgent Fury operation in Grenada, understood it well.

So much depended on the plan, McCaffrey thought. Had the troops on the ground but known it, the general in the Blackhawk had only a slightly clearer picture than they did of the strategy now shaping the largest deployment of U.S. forces since Vietnam. To date, the operation had been largely reactionary, and even at the level of the division staff, there had been a jerky, piecemeal feel to it.

As part of the rapid-reaction force assigned to the Pentagon's Central Command, which had responsibility for this region, the 24th Infantry Division had arrived in early September on fast sealift ships and immediately deployed north on the left flank of a Marine regiment. It would have been a near thing had the Iraqis attacked in those first days, and all the intelligence reports of their configuration at that time pointed to an offensive. Only recently had McCaffrey begun to breathe easier, confident that there was enough firepower in place to repel any advance into Saudi Arabia.

So he's really going to do it, McCaffrey thought. President Bush's announcement a few days earlier that he was increasing the size of the U.S. force in Southwest Asia by 150,000 troops to open an "offensive option" had been interpreted at home as a dangerous step on the path to war. For commanders in the Persian Gulf, it was more than that. A force of nearly 400,000 was simply too large to sustain in that barren land at the end of a five-thousand-mile umbilical cord, especially when the summer heat began its relentless assault, turning life in the desert into its own fight for survival. Either George Bush or Saddam Hussein would have to blink in this showdown, or there would almost certainly be war by spring at the latest.

Without saying as much, Secretary of State James Baker had underscored that point the week before on a visit to troops in the midst of an eight-country, week-long trip to confer with coalition members. His publicly stated goal was to discuss with the coalition partners how, when, and against what targets military force would be used to force Iraq out of Kuwait. Many of the senior military leaders had laughed at press accounts of Baker approaching a young woman sergeant to shake hands and being given some unsolicited advice. "Time is being wasted," twenty-nine-year-old Lisa Jones told him curtly. "Let's do something or go." If the secretary of state was taken aback, he wouldn't be the first person surprised by his initial encounter with the face of America's brash, all-volunteer army. If McCaffrey read the signs right on the likelihood of war, Saddam Hussein himself might catch on too late to some fundamental changes that had taken place.

Even in America they were largely an unknown quantity. Every newspaper article or CNN report confirmed that, but the thought was still astounding for many of those in uniform old enough to remember the draft Army, and growing up as children in the wake of World War II, when everyone seemed to have a direct link to the military and "What did your father do in the war?" was guaranteed to prompt wildly exaggerated playground war stories. Vietnam had cut that link for an entire generation, as it has severed so many of the traditional ties that bound the military to society at large. Now a generation of Americans had grown up in relative peacetime with only the most casual knowledge of and interest in the military.

Even for those who had studied the evolution of America's all-volunteer force from the beginning, who understood intuitively that it was unlike any army this country had ever sent to war, were apt to find this disconnect unsettling. McCaffrey had studied it long and hard and to an extent that would have surprised many of his countrymen who seemed to expect only cigar-chomping reactionaries to wear stars.

So much had been written of Schwarzkopf's 170 genius-level IQ, and the fact that he had studied T. E. Lawrence's *Seven Pillars of Wisdom* and kept *The Kingdom*, Robert Lacey's history of Saudi Arabia, on his nightstand; that he was fluent in French and German, liked Pavarotti as well as Willie Nelson, was a fan of ballet and opera. Schwarzkopf was generally admired as one of the great characters and commanders of the Army, but it was almost as if the public were surprised that a four-star general was even well-read, much less well-rounded.

McCaffrey had long studied the vital link between the United States and its armed forces, first as a student and then as sociology instructor at West Point, then as a master's student in civil government at American University, later at the Army Command and General Staff College, the National Defense University, and Harvard's National Security Program. Over the years, he had even acquired his father's unshakable faith in the good judgment of the American people. Yet it took a certain leap of faith to devote your life to the service of a society that so steadfastly exercised its democratic right to have only a casual acquaintance with its armed forces. Never mind that it happened to be the most powerful armed force in the world. A casual acquaintance, that is, until now.

How else to explain the apparent surprise of the populace at the maturity and forthrightness of the young troops in the field, or the fact so many of them were women or blacks or high school graduates or reservists or two-career military couples? Or the fact that the generals who came to the world from briefing rooms in Riyadh and the Pentagon seemed to defy some maniacal, *Dr. Strangelove* image?

Combat was the only true test of both weapons and soldiers, and most of those in the Gulf had never been fired in battle or fired at in anger. Maybe they were the same brave but ill-prepared American troops that had been bloodied early at Kasserine Pass in North Africa, in Task Force Smith in Korea, in the Ia Drang Valley in Vietnam. Maybe the weapons were no better than the headlines implied. Perhaps they would get bogged down in a bloody war of attrition with dug-in Iraqi divisions.

Yet what of the largest peacetime defense buildup in history, and two tumultuous decades of sometimes agonizing self-appraisal? Had those who had decided to stick it out in uniform really learned nothing in all that time? Some of those making the journey that day to an officers' club in Daharan couldn't shake the feeling that the image the public carried of the military was frozen in a darker time, though no doubt it had been reinforced over the years by debacles in Iran and Beirut, and many a misstep in developing the high technology on which so much now depended. For those who lived through the darkest of those days, however, it almost seemed as if they had witnessed a revolution that no one else had noticed.

Or perhaps nothing had really changed after all. McCaffrey was by nature optimistic, and while the trait had served him well in his career, he sometimes felt he had to step back and view things more analytically. Perhaps the changes had not been as dramatic as they seemed from the inside. So much depended not only on what the military had learned from the defeat of Vietnam but also on what the civilian leadership and the country as a whole had taken from the experience.

If any of them had gotten it wrong, then he knew exactly how the briefing Schwarzkopf was summoning them to would go. They would engage the Iraqis defending the Kuwaiti border to demonstrate to Saddam Hussein U.S. resolve. If he didn't withdraw, they would gradually escalate, announcing that they were willing to up the ante as required. For fear of offending the Saudis or threatening the fragile coalition, they would forgo direct attacks inside Iraq. Horrified by the mounting casualties such a plan would insure, Americans would take to the streets by the hundreds of thousands, protesting the war and vilifying the military for being mired in it.

The Blackhawk lurched as it shifted from forward flight to the more precarious hover of a hummingbird, setting down on the sticky tarmac of Daharan International Airport. McCaffrey knew that was a worst-case scenario, yet he sensed acutely how much could now go wrong. Schwarzkopf was about to brief them on an offensive plan for war, and there was no endeavor of man's more complex, fraught with risk, or unforgiving of timidity. The labors of countless people over the past two decades would be judged largely on what transpired in the next hour. Everything now depended on the plan.

McCaffrey didn't wait for the help that is immediately offered to any general in uniform, hopping out of the helicopter as soon as it hit the ground. His father, Lt. Gen. William McCaffrey, who had retired as inspector general of the Army in the early 1970s, told the story of a general who came to accept the fawning attention of subordinates as his due. So much so, in fact, that one day when that help failed to materialize in time, the general walked right into a plate-glass door, confident to the last moment that someone would surely step forward and open it for him. Maj. Gen. Barry McCaffrey had been accused of knocking down a few doors, but he had yet to walk into one.

No stars or bars, no entry. Nearly all of the men who filed past security in the hallway into the officers' club at Daharan were in their fifties or early sixties, and they entered without the usual entourage of aides. Had their uniforms been blue pinstripe instead of primarily chocolate-chip desert fatigues, it might have been a board-of-directors meeting or the drawing room of an exclusive men's club. As businessmen they would have been more fit than most, their hair cut a little shorter, and for the size of the corporation they ran, they were grossly underpaid. Each could also be said to have worked his way up from the mail room.

No women were in attendance, for that was part of the bottom-up revolution that had begun in the 1970s and had yet to reach the level of this unique fraternity. These men had been career military when the country still relied on women in uniform primarily as a nurses corps, and the draft as a nearly inexhaustible manpower pool. Many of them were former classmates, if not at the service academies then at some level in the steep pyramid of military schools and courses they each had climbed.

There was also this: almost without exception, each of those present had as a young man gone off to fight the same war, or different wars in the same place. They had lost friends and innocence early and in equal measure, and they had been the keepers of those memories ever since. Usually the voices from the past were the merest whispers, but at times they could still speak loudly to convictions on how wars should be fought and what was worth dying for. In that sense the officers' club at the Daharan Air Base was more crowded than the casual observer might have thought.

Despite the underlying current of suspense in the room, the greetings as the generals milled about the folding tables and chairs were heartfelt and generally upbeat. Without having to put it into words, each man knew exactly what was riding on this briefing.

In many ways Schwarzkopf was a contradiction, though one with which most of those present were familiar either personally or through reputation. A thoughtful man with a mercurial temperament, quick both to mirth and explosive anger, he was fully capable of shooting the messenger bearing bad news and at the same time worrying incessantly about his troops in the field. However, the number one responsibility of a four-star field general was to inspire other generals, and it was that role which would be tested in the next hour.

At that moment Schwarzkopf held greater power and authority than any other U.S. field commander in modern times. The expansive Goldwater-Nichols defense reforms passed in 1986 had seen to that. Alarmed by the bombing of the Marine barracks in Beirut and the operation to rescue American students in Grenada—the one revealing the unresponsiveness of a Byzantine command chain and the other the continued inability of the armed services to work smoothly together—Congress had streamlined the command chain and strengthened the joint commanders who ruled over all of the services, in this case Central Command commander in chief Schwarzkopf, and above him Gen. Colin Powell, chairman of the Joint Chiefs.

Part of Schwarzkopf's unprecedented authority and influence was evident in the presence in the room of Lt. Gen. Fred Franks, and the announcement days earlier that his entire VII Corps would be deploying to the desert from Germany in the coming months. When Powell had visited Saudi Arabia three weeks earlier to discuss an offensive war plan, Schwarzkopf insisted that he would need to double his forces before going on the offensive, and he wanted the VII Corps. Schwarzkopf felt that Washington had begun talking offense far too quickly.

Powell had fully agreed with Schwarzkopf's request for a doubling of his forces, even going so far as to expand it. At a defining moment, destiny and luck had conspired to place these two unlikely men at the helm of an organization over 2 million strong—one the nation's first black chairman of the Joint Chiefs, the other the brash and unpolitic commander of the United States' newest war-fighting command—and neither one was about to be pushed into war before they were ready to deliver a decisive blow.

The three heavy divisions of VII Corps were among the best equipped and trained in the Army, and they anchored the NATO defense. Schwarzkopf's counterpart in Europe, Gen. Jack Galvin, supreme allied commander, Europe, had instructed his commanders to respond to every communication from Central Command with an emphatic "Yes. Now what's the question?" Pulling VII Corps out of Germany would have been unthinkable, however, before the collapse of the Warsaw Pact a year earlier. It was yet another indication to the men in the room that they were at a rare cusp in history, riding a wave of Cold War military spending and suddenly free of many Cold War constraints. It was a high-water mark for the U.S. military, and Saddam Hussein had revealed an almost uncanny penchant for poor timing when he chose that moment to swim against the tide.

As a field commander on the precipice of war, Schwarzkopf in particular was feeling the weight of the unprecedented responsibility he now bore. To those close to the burly general, it was obvious that he was beginning to fray under the incredible pressure, becoming even more volatile than usual. That group included two men who stood together in the briefing room, Lt. Gen. Charles Horner and Lt. Gen. John Yeosock, the senior component commanders for the Air Force and Army, respectively. Old friends and now roommates in Saudi Arabia, they had in the mid-1970s been classmates along with Colin Powell at the National War College. All three had played on the softball team together. As the direct conduits of Schwarzkopf's orders to their respective services, Horner and Yeosock were both among his closest advisers and the first to feel the lash of his considerable temper.

Chuck Horner's penchant for always having a good joke or story on hand probably explained why Schwarzkopf would sometimes seek Horner out for much-needed levity during his blackest funks, which were coming more frequently now. He was probably the closest person in that room to the CINC, though Horner felt that Schwarzkopf was too volatile for anyone who worked with him to get truly close.

How are we going to do this? Horner wondered to himself, mentally going over the unprecedented complexity of his air campaign. If it came to war, Horner also knew that he was personally going to send a full squadron of pilots against one of the most heavily defended targets in the world, naked except for an untried technology called stealth. If it didn't work, if somehow the Iraqis saw that his young emperors had no clothes, then Horner would have their blood on his hands, too. And he didn't know if it would work. Like so much of the technology they now depended on, stealth was a wild card in a game of Cold War poker whose stakes were so high that no one had ever dared play. Now he was going to bet everything on it. It's in God's hands, Horner told himself yet again. Just have faith.

When McCaffrey entered the room, he scanned it rapidly, taking a quick mental roll call and noting a number of contemporaries whom he had known for practically his entire professional life. Some longer. There was Creighton Abrams, son of the legendary Army chief of staff after whom the Army's state-of-the-art M-1 Abrams tank was named. Their fathers had run in the same circles since World War II and had served together in Vietnam. Though the announcement that the Army's VII Corps would be deploying to Saudi had only come days earlier, he saw his lifelong friends Freddie Franks, VII Corps commander, and Bush Funk, commander of the 3rd Armored Division. He also recognized Walt Boomer, the senior Marine Corps commander in the Gulf. He and McCaffrey had been classmates together at Harvard's National Security Program. The slight, straight-backed Marine next to Boomer was Mike Myatt, commander of the 1st Marine Division that was even then deployed on the right flank of his 24th Division.

Their two divisions were the tip of the spear now blunting any Iraqi advance, and McCaffrey and Myatt had come to know each other in the preceding months as they met repeatedly, along with Myatt's assistant division commander Brig. Gen. Tom Draude, to iron out force boundary issues and coordinate counterattack plans. There, too, was Snuffy Smith, the admiral in command of the Battle Group America and a former classmate of McCaffrey's at the Capstone course, a high-powered, six-week program that was mandatory grooming for all officers promoted to general or flag rank.

On the way to his table, McCaffrey spotted the name tag for Maj. Gen. Binney Peay before an empty chair, and he quickly grabbed it and placed it next to his own. He and Peay, commander of the 101st Airborne Division, had become friends while serving together as brigade commanders in the 3rd Infantry Division in Washington State during the early 1980s, a friendship solidified in the crucible of the National Training Center, the Army's high-tech training center for armored forces in the middle of the Mojave Desert, where they had teamed to fight the center's vaunted Soviet-style Opposing Force, or OPFOR. The friendship between the outgoing McCaffrey, who never shied from the spotlight, and the more reserved Peay was well-known amongst their subordinates. Secretly, some even worried that the natural competition between them might color their judgment in the months ahead.

As Schwarzkopf began his briefing, McCaffrey watched him intently. Schwarzkopf was himself a former commander of the 24th Infantry Division, and the two had crossed paths a number of times over the years. McCaffrey's wife even remembered Schwarzkopf from Berlin, where she was a teenage Army brat and all her girlfriends could talk about was the handsome young lieutenant and general's aide who dated all the terribly sophisticated "older" women in their twenties. Though he had never personally witnessed Schwarzkopf heave subordinates physically out of his office, McCaffrey knew him well enough not to doubt tales of his legendary temper. The "Bear," as some called him, had even leaned on McCaffrey pretty heavily during some recent briefings. Yet there was also an unquenchable spirit behind Schwarzkopf's fire that, at least in McCaffrey's mind, made him fun to be around.

Different generals filled the mantle of command differently and were in turn shaped differently by its demands. If being rough on staff was a sin, probably few in the room would care to throw the first stone, least of all McCaffrey. While known to be personable with troops in the field, McCaffrey could also strike fear into a staff, inspiring the joke that the fastest way to become a captain in the 24th was to join the general's staff as a major.

Behind Schwarzkopf, a large map board was covered with a protective cloth. After confirming that he had indeed called all of his commanders together to brief them on the operational plan to liberate Kuwait, the CentCom commander motioned for his aides to remove the covering. All eyes stared as the plan that was to shape so many of their lives from that moment on was unveiled for the first time.

There was a deafening silence.

It was overwhelming. As Schwarzkopf began identifying with his pointer the various units represented by attack arrows of the map, the unprecedented scope of the operation came into sharp focus for the entire room. The plan covered an area roughly the size of Pennsylvania. The air campaign would strike directly into Baghdad, attacking not only Iraqi centralized command-and-control, but also its nuclear and chemical-weapons plants and production facilities. The Marines and Saudi forces would thrust straight into Kuwait and perhaps mount an amphibious landing.

By far the boldest aspect of the plan, however, was a sweeping "left hook" maneuver deep into Iraqi territory by two entire Army corps. If successful, and no army in history had ever moved a force that size over three hundred miles on the time lines Schwarzkopf was reciting, the move would flank the Republican Guard divisions in Kuwait and cut off all avenues of retreat. It was classic AirLand Battle doctrine the Army had developed in the late 1970s and early 1980s—combined and coordinated assault, maneuver, deception, deep strike—only on a grand scale.

After letting the implications of the plan sink in and taking a few questions, Schwarzkopf recalled wrapping the meeting up thus in his biography, *It Doesn't Take a Hero:*

"For our country we dare not fail. We cannot fail, and we will not fail. Anybody in here who doesn't understand that, get out of the way. Any questions? Okay, good luck to you. You know what needs to be done."

As he listened to Schwarzkopf finish, Maj. Gen. Mike Myatt kept going back to something the CINC had said earlier about training and preparing their troops for the worst. To do any less, Schwarzkopf had said, would be a disservice to the parents who had given each man in that room the privilege of commanding their young sons and daughters. Exactly right. We aren't taking the enemy for granted this time, thought Myatt. We'll let our troops know that they're in this together until the job is done.

The briefing had left McCaffrey slightly stunned. He was part of the flanking force, and his mind was already starting to race over a logistics problem the war colleges would call a potential war-stopper, yet he had one overriding thought: We're not going to fight a war of attrition, or a limited war. It was a revelation. He saw now that the Army was going to play to its strengths and the enemy's weakness. By God, we learned. We learned.

When he turned to his friend Binney Peay, whose division would be by his side in the flanking maneuver, there were tears in McCaffrey's eyes. Peay just nodded his head in confirmation: "That's it, Barry. That's what we'll do."

Similar shorthand conversations and knowing glances swept around the room at the end of the briefing, voices from a shared past mingling with those of the present to fill in for all that wasn't said. We'll be ready, a clear mission, we're in this together, the country's behind us this time, only one way home, we cannot fail. *Never again.*

They were prodigal sons all, and the reckless journeys of their youth had ended in the unthinkable, an American defeat in war. Vietnam wasn't theirs alone to embrace, but it had robbed them of the homecoming without which any soldier is lost. Now after two decades of painful self-appraisal they were being offered a chance at redemption.

A few months later, Barry McCaffrey stood in a small circle of commanders on the eve of war. It was a somber moment, and each man was alone in his thoughts.

"You know," McCaffrey broke in to alleviate the tension as soldiers will, "one of us is bound to bite it on this campaign."

Brig. Gen. Terry Scott, the assistant division commander of the 24th and a former airborne commander who had been wounded in Vietnam, fixed McCaffrey with a crooked West Texas grin that would have brought Saddam Hussein little comfort.

"Yeah, well, I'd rather freaking bite it tomorrow than have to go back and explain for the next twenty years how we screwed this one up."

Part I

1: Duty, Honor, Country 1965–66

O N a mild spring night in 1965, the switchboards blinked crazily in Fayetteville, North Carolina. Phones were ringing in apartments, bars, bowling alleys, and strip joints, all part of a well-rehearsed but unseen network that was stretching out over the entire town. The conversations that resulted rarely lasted more than a sentence or two. The recipients quickly kissed their wives good-bye or threw a gutter ball or drained the last of their beer, and after making another short phone call they were gone. That's how word went out that the 82nd Airborne's Division Ready Force was on Alpha Alert.

Nowhere was that phone call more eagerly awaited than down Corregidor Court on Fort Bragg, a neighborhood of tidy red-brick buildings with white awnings and dark shutters, an architectural style much favored in officers' quarters built after World War II. Ever since the 82nd's first Division Ready Brigade had been activated days earlier for a growing crisis in the Dominican Republic, Lt. Barry McCaffrey's footfalls had echoed on the hardwood floors as he paced the small town house.

After hanging up the phone, McCaffrey looked at his wife's expectant expression. "That's it. We're going," he said with a smile.

Jill McCaffrey wondered whether she should try to hide the relief she felt. For days Barry had been working himself into the worst funk she had witnessed during their short marriage. If she had to hear him plaintively declare one more time that he knew he wouldn't get to go, Jill was afraid she'd scream. Secretly, she had even prayed that her husband would get sent to combat.

After seeing her husband off to war for the first time, Jill McCaffrey reflected that he was still the same impetuous boy who had asked her to marry him on a blind date two years earlier. They had met in Washington, D.C., where both of their fathers were stationed in the summer of 1963. Jill had recently broken up with her boyfriend, and while she was home on break from the University of Missouri, a girlfriend had offered to set her up with a West Point cadet she had met at the Ft. Meyer swimming pool.

Graced with delicate good looks and a self-confident, almost mocking smile that could turn some boys her own age into stammering teenagers again, Jill Faulkner certainly didn't feel she *needed* a blind date. She did just fine getting her own dates, thank you very much. Still, she was only home for a few weeks and had always found the notion of the man in uniform romantic. As an Army brat who had seen a bit of the world, Jill also had a hard time imagining herself hooked to a college boy in Missouri and maybe ending up a veterinarian's wife in Chillicothe.

That first night Barry McCaffrey had taken her to the Bolling Air Force Base officers' club, a well-known gathering spot for the thousands of service members stationed around Washington, and the women anxious to meet them. Barry's many stories about life at West Point had been irreverent and funny, and Jill had been relieved that he wasn't one of those spoony cadets with the spit-and-polish bearing and inflated sense of their own importance.

Yet compared to the college boys she knew, the young cadet had an earnestness and sense of direction that had impressed Jill. He seemed to know exactly where he was headed and what he wanted, and before the night was over, what he apparently wanted was to marry Jill.

She had laughed and told Barry that the very idea was silly. Yet in truth Jill Faulkner hadn't found it so preposterous. If the audacious cadet was serious, there was a man she thought she could love. Certainly there had been nothing particularly flippant in his expression. Amused perhaps, but also determined. If he was so interested, Jill had told Barry McCaffrey, he would just have to ask her out again and see how things went. That night when she came home, however, Jill told her mother that she had just met the man she was going to marry. Four days later when Barry proposed yet again, she had accepted.

During the following year, Jill visited Barry at West Point several times. She had even accompanied him to his Ring Hop in 1964 in West Point's cavernous mess hall, stood under the giant ring with Barry after accepting his class ring with the familiar inscription *Duty, Honor, Country.*

By the time Barry graduated in June of 1964, Jill's family had already moved to Newport Beach, California. He drove across the country nearly nonstop in his cherished navy blue Pontiac LeMans with leather upholstery and four-on-the-floor. They were married on June 8 in the chapel at the El

Toro Marine Base. Standing next to her father and Barry, the bride had felt the rush of elation of someone who, for at least that moment, had been given exactly what she wanted out of life.

After she later joined Barry at Fort Benning, Georgia, where he underwent his initial infantry training, the couple had packed his few belongings into the LeMans and driven north towards Fayetteville, North Carolina, home of the 82nd Airborne. As the sun-splashed fields gave way to Southern pine forests dark with dusk, Jill McCaffrey had felt almost intoxicated by the uncertainty and hidden promise that seemed to stretch before their lives, the forks in the road ahead always hidden just out of sight. Now Barry had disappeared around an unseen bend called the Dominican Republic. Within a year he would be gone again, this time to someplace called Vietnam.

As 1st Lt. Barry McCaffrey hit the cot in his bachelor officers' quarters outside of Saigon in October of 1966, he felt the refrigerated air pleasantly dry the sweat on his skin. The clammy heat outside refused to relent even in the early evening, sucking the energy out of you in a furtive embrace. Though he felt the kind of weariness far out of reach of a single night's sleep, McCaffrey decided to write Jill a letter. After being sent to South Vietnam as an adviser, his second deployment to a foreign battlefield in the space of a year, Barry had fallen into the habit of writing home nearly every day.

The fatigue alone wasn't as bad as Ranger School, where there were no airconditioned bachelor officers' quarters (BOQ) and sometimes the first thing that woke you up was the impact of your head hitting a tree or the ground during a night march. After a nap he might even head for the roof of the Rex BOQ, tell lies with some of his buddies over sweating bottles of beer. Right now, however, he wanted to try to capture some of the weird essence of what he was feeling, a mixture equal parts exhilaration, fear, and exhaustion. When he got back, he might save the letters as a diary.

Lying on his cot, McCaffrey could identify the moment his life detoured down the path that led to a BOQ in Saigon. It had been nearly midnight on a December night in 1959, and most of his classmates at Andover Prep School had already left for the holidays. The next day he had planned to take the train to Charleston, South Carolina, where his father was serving as commandant of cadets at the Citadel.

With the Andover dormitory almost deserted, McCaffrey had put *Bolero* on his stereo and turned the volume up loud. A steady snow had fallen that night, covering the campus like a shimmering white veil. He had listened to the music and watched as the thick flakes swirled into the lamplight outside and disappeared. Though he had been accepted as a premed major at Johns Hopkins for the following year, Barry McCaffrey had realized at that moment that he missed the Army he had grown up in.

If the change in career ambitions had come as something of a revelation to Barry McCaffrey, however, it had been an even greater surprise to his parents. While his father did not try to talk Barry out of it, neither did he offer to pull any strings to help his son get accepted to West Point. Nor did Barry ask.

Gen. William McCaffrey was devoted to the principle that Barry should choose his own career. As chief of staff of the 92nd Division in Italy during World War II, the senior McCaffrey had watched as his division commander encouraged his own son's interest in the Army, first steering him to West Point and then into company command in the infantry branch where promotions were plentiful during the war. The son was leading that company up the Rhone Valley when a German sniper put a bullet between his eyes. William McCaffrey had vowed then never to tell his own son, or anyone else for that matter, what to do with his life.

Barry had instead turned to his mother for help in getting into West Point, and he had eventually been sponsored by South Carolina's Sen. Olin Johnson. Initially, McCaffrey had bucked against a system so rigid and unyielding—so *unfair*—and the fourth-class plebe system had bucked back harder with a thousand barbs of humiliation honed to perfection since West Point was established by Thomas Jefferson over 160 years before. Nor had the upperclassmen apparently been amused by the somewhat all-knowing smile on the face of the wiseass "smack" who seemed to think everything was so funny.

After what was a generally hellish first year, however, McCaffrey had begun to warm to many aspects of cadet life and West Point. He had found something deeply satisfying about watching the transformation of his class from a bunch of frightened plebes to the precision unit that marched across the green expanse of the Plain in their dress grays on parade days. Everything about West Point also emphasized the greater good of the corps over the needs of the individual, speaking to a higher purpose. It had struck a cord in the young McCaffrey.

"Your mission remains fixed, determined, inviolable—it is to win our wars," a frail, eighty-two-year-old Gen. Douglas MacArthur had told the assembled corps of cadets at West Point in a valedictory speech that had brought tears to Barry McCaffrey's eyes. "From your ranks come the great captains who hold the nation's destiny in their hands, the moment the war tocsin sounds. The long gray line has never failed us. Were you to do so, a million ghosts in olive drab, in brown khaki, in blue and gray, would rise from their crosses thundering those magic words: duty, honor, country."

For all its proud and stubborn adherence to tradition, however, West Point had been buffeted by changes that were sweeping the country in the early 1960s. The year McCaffrey had graduated, the sweeping Civil Rights Act of 1964 had been passed into law. McCaffrey's father was one of the white officers who had led a division of black soldiers in World War II, and since then the Army had slowly been integrating. Barry could remember black soldiers coming to the back door of their house and being told by his father to use the front door in the future. Yet only two black cadets were in his graduating class, and in its 160-year history West Point had graduated only fifty black cadets. The idea of a female cadet was still laughable.

Vietnam had remained a favorite topic of conversation among McCaffrey's cadet class their final two years, and most of the cadets hoped the conflict would last long enough for them to graduate and serve a combat tour. Many of them recalled June 6, 1962, when on the eighteenth anniversary of D day, Pres. John F. Kennedy had also come to West Point and outlined a new mission for an Army that some claimed was all but obsolete in an era of nuclear weapons.

"I know that many of you feel, and many of our citizens may feel, that in these days of the nuclear age, when war may last in its final form a day or two or three days before much of the world is burned up, your service to your country will be only standing and waiting. Nothing, of course, could be further from the truth," said Kennedy.

The type of conflict the president foresaw was "new in its intensity, ancient in its origin—war by guerrillas, subversives, insurgents, assassins, war by ambush instead of by combat, by infiltration instead of aggression, seeking victory by eroding and exhausting the enemy instead of engaging him. These are the kinds of challenges that will be before us in the next decade if freedom is to be saved, a whole new kind of strategy, a wholly different kind of force, and therefore a new and wholly different kind of training."

Yet while the conflict in Indochina had certainly broadened since Kennedy spoke at West Point, and others had flared up in Latin America, there was little sign of the "wholly different" kind of Army that he had invoked, with new kinds of training and strategies. Indeed, the service that Barry McCaffrey had inherited upon graduation just a year earlier was very much his father's Army, solidly rooted in World War II and Korea.

It was a disciplined but unsophisticated force that worked six-day weeks, kept its rifles in unlocked platoon bays, and required its officers to get a weekend pass to go off posts overseas. It was an Army where the draftees tended to keep their noses clean, do their two years, and get out, and the old-timer sergeants and crusty lifers sometimes slept off Saturday night in the stockade. If it happened to cost them a few stripes or bars, that was a badge of respect among fighting men. An experienced Army, it relied more on mentoring than formal training and was anchored by a solid noncommissioned-officers corps that had successfully broken in many a buck private and cherry lieutenant.

To go along with its experience, the Army also had the all-American arrogance of the perennial winner, a supreme confidence in the righteousness of its ways. Its leaders were committed to pile on aggressiveness and massed firepower, set-piece battles, and overwhelming logistics because these were the same blunt-force tactics that had eventually turned the tide in World War II and Korea. Beyond basic military skills, the emphasis was on discipline and obedience. It was an Army sensitive to outside criticism and intolerant of it from within its lower ranks.

While the constrained budgets and single-minded focus on nuclear forces during the Eisenhower years had seriously sapped the Army's strength, the U.S. Army had never won in the past on its readiness to go to war anyway. Far from it. Losing early battles was something of an Army tradition, tragically established at places like Kasserine Pass in North Africa and on the Korean peninsula with Task Force Smith. Rather, the Army relied on the ability of a relentless industrial machine and massive manpower pool to keep it in a war long enough for its dogged determination and aggressiveness to wear an opponent down.

The Army's attitude was cocky and can-do, and that was both its greatest strength and a potentially fatal weakness, for it masked a certain blindness. It was a confidence untempered by great introspection, and condescending toward potential adversaries, especially those in far-off Third World jungles. In that, too, as in so many other ways, the Army was a mirror image of the nation itself.

In Saigon, Barry McCaffrey was forming his own opinion on the fighting caliber of the Vietnamese, which he knew bore little resemblance to the popular image back home of an undisciplined and even primitive fighting force. He had already spent three months in-country serving as a member of an Army advisory group attached to a South Vietnamese Airborne battalion. If they seemed unsophisticated by American standards, they were also tenacious and determined fighters.

The general consensus inside Army ranks was that ARVN (Army of the

Republic of Vietnam) units were as hopelessly inept as the Viet Cong were overmatched. The attitude, as one general put it, was, "You little guys get out of the way; here come the Americans and we'll show you how it's done." Though the original reason for establishing the U.S. Military Assistance Command, Vietnam (MACV), had been to advise the South Vietnamese armed forces, with American troops taking over more and more of the fighting in 1966, the exact role of the ARVN in this new "strategy" was unclear.

For a young lieutenant recently of the 82nd Airborne, the Vietnamese Airborne were the epitome of the swashbuckling paratrooper ethic. In Saigon they slept in comfortable quarters and cut a dashing figure in the nightclubs. But as a national reaction force, they could be alerted at any time, and on some nights the battalion was rounded up in bars in the early hours of the morning and whisked by helicopter to a free-fire zone up-country, finding itself hunkered down in a bitter struggle for survival only hours after chatting up Cholon mama-sans over cool ones. There was a certain schizophrenia to that type of warfare. Even for a U.S. paratrooper, Vietnam near the end of 1966 bore little resemblance to anything being taught in the military schools and conventional training programs back home.

While the U.S. team attached to the ARVN unit called themselves "advisers," it soon became clear to McCaffrey that these seasoned combat veterans were not looking to him for advice. Rather, he and the rest of his team were their lifeline to American air and artillery support, as well as helicopter resupply and evacuation. At first they had watched McCaffrey closely, just trying to figure out if he might get them killed. A green young lieutenant, especially if he thought he knew it all, could prove a deadly liability.

Yet the young American paratrooper with the quick smile and cool demeanor under fire had quickly won their confidence. It helped that Barry McCaffrey was part of an experienced adviser team, and eager to learn fieldcraft from the ARVN paratroopers. While he might sometimes question their tactics in his mind, it was obvious that they could pick up signs of enemy activity in the field of which he was only dimly aware.

McCaffrey quickly learned how to dig a firing position for the night with enough overhead support to stop an incoming mortar round, where to set up bamboo markers on a battalion perimeter as a gauge to call in artillery, when to roll out of field hammocks and head for the foxhole before even the first mortar round or attack wave was launched. It got to the point that McCaffrey could tell if they would be hit that night just by watching how the ARVN paratroopers dug in.

He had also learned that the night is to be feared, and that there was no feeling on earth better than crawling out of a foxhole at the light of dawn dripping tears, sweat, and sometimes blood, overwhelmed by the sheer exhilaration of survival. It was the job of national reaction units such as the ARVN paratroopers to respond to setbacks on the battlefield, and the pace of those operations was behind the weariness that had begun to seep into McCaffrey through every pore.

Even before realizing that he had fallen asleep, McCaffrey was swinging himself up after being tapped on the shoulder. "Where we going?"

"Big doings all the way up near the DMZ from what I understand. Someplace near Dong Ha."

Even among the ARVN paratroopers in Saigon, the northernmost tip of I Corp near the border between North and South Vietnam had an eerie reputation. The roughly two hundred square miles of jagged mountain ranges and deep ravines existed in a sort of primordial dark age, a lost world where the sunlight rarely penetrated and unnamed species of animals were said to roam. Nearly the only human inhabitants of the area not forced there by the war were montagnard tribesmen, dark-skinned, aboriginal highlanders who were favored by the Special Forces as trackers. The undergrowth on the jungle floor in some sections of northern I Corps was said to be so thick that stranded units sometimes had to call in bombing strikes to cut a path.

For nearly the entire year, the U.S. Marine Corps had been playing a deadly game of cat and mouse with North Vietnamese regulars along the DMZ. The infiltration into the area of the ten thousand men of NVA Division 324B had generated considerable concern at MACV headquarters in Saigon, where planners worried over a full-scale, Korean-style invasion across the DMZ.

The continued presence of such a large-scale enemy unit enticed the Marines into establishing a series of permanent fire bases along the DMZ. MACV commander Westmoreland viewed them as sentry posts guarding against increased infiltration by major NVA units. The leadership in Hanoi, however, saw them as isolated outposts, scattered across some of the most remote and inhospitable land in all of Vietnam, north or south. In that view, they were perfect bait for the favored NVA tactic of attacking to cripple but not to kill, then waiting in ambush for the inevitable relief forces.

As the light began to fade the next evening, Barry McCaffrey stopped a moment to look out into the middle distance, then returned to his digging with renewed urgency. The hill commanded a wide view of the Ben Hi river valley, which straddled the DMZ, the mist-shrouded highlands giving way in lush shades of green to marshy coastal lowlands. Just out of range, North Vietnamese officers in khaki-drab uniforms were clearly visible as they gestured to mortar teams scrambling to set up for the night's work. It was the first time McCaffrey had ever actually clearly seen the enemy he was fighting.

The plaintive cries of their own wounded and dying filled the perimeter, the new reality of a ripped and mangled body evoking a note of such anguished surprise that McCaffrey could almost wish for the mortars to start so he wouldn't have to listen. He dug harder to drown out the sound. Their two ARVN battalions had flown into the Marines' fire-support base at Dong Ha that morning and had been in contact with the enemy from the moment they left the base's barbed-wire perimeter. The resistance had stiffened the closer they got to the "Z," until there was no going forward and no getting back. Just to his right McCaffrey could hear the frantic scrape of his Vietnamese radioman's shovel, digging, digging. The hunters had become the hunted.

Somewhere near the landing zone his sergeant Rudy Ortiz lay with scores of other wounded, hit so many times that McCaffrey couldn't count. Good old Rudy. McCaffrey stopped digging for a moment, listening to a drumming in his ears that could have been his own heart pounding. No, there it was again, the distinctive rotor-thud of a helicopter. Another medevac helicopter was going to try to get in.

As the sound came closer, automatic-weapons fire erupted from around the base of the hill and was quickly answered from inside the perimeter as everyone tried to lay down covering fire. It was "Mike Mike," a mad minute of fire, and everyone traded in his shovel for the blessed relief and rapid-fire retort of an M16 on full automatic. When the pandemonium abruptly died, however, and leaves from overhead branches floated down before their eyes like confetti, there was no sound of rotors. A handful of helicopters had been shot down already trying to evacuate their wounded, and with night coming on, McCaffrey knew that would be the last. There would be no extraction by air.

Sometime after midnight, the sporadic fire around their perimeter died down and was replaced by an eerie stillness, the quiet in McCaffrey's foxhole broken only by the crackle of static from the field radio. It was pitch-dark outside. Then he heard it. The noise was distinctive, the hollow retort like a large stone being dropped down a deep well. Instantly it was answered by hundreds of identical retorts echoing around their perimeter, putting them in the center of a huge void that seemed to suck the air out of McCaffrey's lungs. There would be no ranging rounds.

Somewhere behind their foxhole he vaguely heard the shout go up, as if in a dream. McCaffrey could almost visualize the mortar fusillade as it hurtled through the blackness in a fine arc, the apex somewhere far above their heads. They would have about thirty seconds. His mind thought about everything and nothing all at once as he sat in that eternal moment between the lightning bolt and the deafening thunder.

They were supposed to disappear by sunrise, those were the rules of the game. If you lasted through an all-night mortar pounding, managed somehow to avoid being blown up, overrun, shot, or bayoneted, then you goddamn well got to crawl out of your foxhole at first light to drink in the unbelievably sweet elixir of survival. The promise of that momentary triumph over death had helped McCaffrey preserve his sanity through the long night's journey into the abyss.

They had come like wraiths out of the night, the darkness somehow lending substance to their high-pitched, disembodied voices as they charged time and again. The worst was not the fighting but the fear that came afterward, as they listened to the excited chattering of the NVA picking over the bodies of anyone who had been caught outside the contracting perimeter. Four times during the night McCaffrey had been forced to stop treating the wounded to pick up his weapon to direct counterfire at the human waves, until he couldn't pick up his rifle anymore and realized he had been hit by the mortars. During one of the assaults McCaffrey had taken the .45 automatic off his dead captain and continued to fire with one hand.

At least in the past, they had always melted away at the first threat of light and the portent of American firepower to come. Barry McCaffrey peered out his firing position at an overcast dawn, and the morning mists that hung in pockets across the valley. A muzzle flash disturbed the hedgerow some seventy meters outside their perimeter, and impacts crisscrossed his position, cutting the radio antennae in half. McCaffrey sprawled against the dirt wall just where the shrapnel had entered his shoulder the night before, crying out at the jolt of searing pain.

Almost as much as anything that had happened in the last twelve hours, the fact that the North Vietnamese had stayed to fight in broad daylight hit McCaffrey hard. It was a break from one of the few established laws of a badly deranged universe, and he knew it boded ill for those left surrounded inside that shaky perimeter.

His entire adviser team was dead or wounded, the enemy fire having cut down a third of their task force. Outside his position McCaffrey could see clouds obscuring some of the surrounding mountaintops. Far too low a ceiling for the Air Force to get under, even if they were inclined to risk it. Two World War II–vintage B-57s had already been shot down trying to keep the NVA at bay. A Marine tank column sent to rescue them had been turned back, and the latest radio report from a prop-driven L-1 reconnaissance plane that had gamely peaked through the clouds reported thousands of NVA reinforcements streaming across the river, some dragging wheeled artillery pieces and machine guns.

Within a short time the radio crackled to life again. McCaffrey recognized the voice of his American major back at Dong Ha. Everyone in the task force who could still walk was instructed to break into small groups and attempt to exfiltrate through the NVA lines at nightfall.

If they were going to break into small groups, he would have to figure out who was left. During a slackening in the fire, McCaffrey again bolted out of his foxhole and made a run for the nearest firing position. Everywhere he stopped, it was the same story. Four out of five company commanders had been killed or wounded. The battalion commander had reportedly been hit repeatedly and couldn't be moved. Crawling between foxholes in that intimate embrace with the ground known only to the soldier under fire, McCaffrey nearly bumped helmets with 1st Lt. Bill Barron, another American adviser.

"Ya know something, Barry," Barron had said in the deliberate tones of south Georgia. "If we don't get out of here, we're all going to be killed."

McCaffrey looked at his friend and tried to think of something encouraging to say. A tear had squeezed out of his friend's eye, leaving a white streak down his dirt-stained face. McCaffrey just nodded his head.

Back in his firing position, while Barry tried to raise a naval gunfire liaison, the Vietnamese battalion executive officer came over and sat down outside his foxhole. McCaffrey could only stare up at him incredulously, trying to make sense of his suicidal nonchalance. French-educated Captain Truong was an engineer before the war, and McCaffrey had come to respect him in the short time they knew each other.

"Lieutenant McCaffrey, have you gotten the same word that I have, that we're to break up into small units and try and escape?" Captain Truong said, peering into the firing position from his exposed perch outside.

"Yes, sir, I have."

"Well, you know the honor of the Vietnamese Airborne is at stake," Captain Truong said. Why was he taking off his helmet and replacing it with the red beret? Looking around at the other scurrying figures outside his position, McCaffrey saw that all of the paratroopers had now traded their helmets for the signature berets of the South Vietnamese paratrooper. He wasn't even sure he caught what Captain Truong had just said.

"Sir?"

"I said we're forming up the battalion for an attack. It's time to die now."

McCaffrey nodded. No time now to stop and untangle it. The lines between desperation, bravery, and fatalism had somehow become hopelessly entangled. A tremendous sense of relief flooded over McCaffrey at the thought that he could still fire his captain's .45 automatic with his one good arm. Must call in some artillery or we won't have a chance, he thought. Always a chance.

When the ranging rounds found the enemy perimeter, the ARVN bugler sounded the charge. McCaffrey scrambled out of his foxhole and began running crouched down, then standing up as his body uncoiled with the blessed relief of action. Lots of explosions were tearing into the NVA positions, momentarily covering the charge. The sound of guns firing was everywhere, and voices shouting, his own and others. As they got closer, he could see some of the NVA in the first line of hedgerows turning and running, but there would be thousands of others behind them.

The NVA were surely unprepared for a desperation charge right into the teeth of their assault, but cornered animals will turn on their attackers. If not for the lumbering Air Force AC-47 gunship that banked under the cloud cover in the midst of the melee at that desperate moment, it would have been but a short setback for the North Vietnamese force. Between the troops fleeing the forward positions and those running up to reinforce from the rear, however, nearly an entire battalion of NVA regulars were caught in the open by "Puff the Magic Dragon," a relatively new addition to the arsenal developed specifically to lend close-in fire support to beleaguered units, night or day. Its three 7.62mm Gatling guns began spitting out a tracer-laden hail of bullets at the rate of eighteen thousand slugs a minute.

The month that followed Dong Ha was the happiest in Lt. Barry McCaffrey's young life. In the mornings he would walk the decks of the medical ship USS *Repose*, breathing deep of the sea breezes and feeling the sun slowly melt the ache in his bandaged body. During the afternoon he played shuffleboard with some of the other patients, sometimes beating them with only his one good arm. After dinner each night, he watched as the sun extinguished itself into the South China Sea in a palette of color almost excruciating in its splendor. The simplest pleasures once taken for granted—the touch of a warm sea breeze on his face or the taste of a cold beer—carried a delight so keen that it sometimes brought tears to Barry McCaffrey's eyes.

Back in Saigon and Washington, D.C., a debate was raging about the progress of the war. Westmoreland believed that spoiling attacks against NVA and VC main-force units such as the one McCaffrey's ARVN battalion had participated in near the DMZ had pinned the enemy to remote border areas and away from the densely populated coastal cities. With the number of U.S. troops in Vietnam climbing rapidly, Westmoreland believed the war of attrition was grinding the enemy down, and he requested additional troops for a final effort the coming year that would break the enemy's will to fight.

Although he was only a young lieutenant ignorant of geostrategic politics, Barry McCaffrey knew something about the will of the Vietnamese. Indeed, many of the commanders and troops in the ARVN Airborne had themselves come out of North Vietnam, and some of them had fought the French. At night, ARVN commanders could sometimes be heard talking to their counterparts in the North over an open radio frequency. Sworn enemies fighting on different sides of the war, they may nevertheless have grown up in the same village and spoke the same dialect. Some Vietnamese would discover over an open radio network at night that they were fighting and killing their own cousins, and still they fought on.

As he finished his second beer of the night on the deck of the *Repose*, Barry McCaffrey decided to go below and write his wife a letter. Ever since Dong Ha, he had been writing almost every day again. He thought back on that day and what a near thing it had been. McCaffrey figured he knew something about the will of the Vietnamese all right. In two months time McCaffrey would receive the Distinguished Service Cross, the nation's second-highest award for valor, for his actions at the DMZ. But somehow it wasn't about glory or adventure anymore. What Barry McCaffrey thought most about was how glad he'd be to get home and see his wife and young son.

2: Barnstormers 1965–66

AS he milled about the processing point in San Francisco, Air Force captain Chuck Horner reflected once again on the emergency orders in his hand. They had arrived only a few days earlier, while Horner was on temporary duty in Orlando, Florida, doing what comes naturally for fighter pilots on the road, which was drinking and chumming and drinking some more. The orders were so urgent that he had been told to fly home immediately despite being woozy from an evening of partying with the true fighter-jock brethren.

Chuck Horner wasn't particularly distressed by the surprise orders to Thailand. Unexpected travel was one of the reasons he loved the Air Force, which Horner still viewed more as a temporary ticket out of rural Iowa than as a career. Certainly his was not a military family, at least not in the traditional sense.

His father, Everett Horner, did possess a pugnacious streak that had first revealed itself after he joined up to fight Pancho Villa in Mexico as a fifteen-year-old. Horner's grandmother had interceded in that adventure by pulling his father from his tent and out of the Army literally by his ear. When World War I began, his father had been old enough to enlist on his own, however, which he did in time to be sent to France and gassed by the Germans. Though a lawyer with a wife and four children, Everett Horner had again reenlisted in the Army as a master sergeant at the outbreak of World War II.

Still, it wasn't a hunger for combat that had enticed Chuck Horner into the Air Force, so much as it was a yearning to see beyond the flat Iowa landscape that had formed the boundary of his world since he was a boy growing up in Davenport and Des Moines. Horner knew that his former classmates at the University of Iowa would even then be heading to work in their tidy Midwestern towns, preparing for another day on the middle-management treadmill.

As a twenty-nine-year-old captain, however, Horner had *seen* things. He had stood watch at the gateway between East and West, whiling away the chill hours of an all-night nuclear alert in Turkey with a doomsday weapon strapped to the bottom of his F-105 aircraft. Like every fighter pilot, Horner had also confronted death, brushing close to it and escaping only to witness friends caught in its fiery embrace.

In an Air Force operational squadron in the early 1960s, sudden, violent death was an occupational hazard. In some units pilots were dying at the rate of nearly two a week. Nor was the violent-death epidemic restricted to the Air Force. A study the Navy was compiling at that time would show that over a twenty-year career, its fighter pilots would face a 23 percent chance—nearly one in four—of dying in an aircraft accident. That didn't count death by decidedly nonaccidental means, such as being shot down by a determined enemy. It was a lifestyle apt to change how a young man thought about his future in a way that had everything to do with the live-for-today bravado of fighter pilots.

Strapping yourself to rockets for combat at speeds faster than sound itself required a diamond-hard core of confidence that the uninitiated found dazzling to behold. Formed by the incredible pressures of hundreds of hours in the cockpit, it was a confidence impervious to the normal doubts and laws of averages that chip away at less developed psyches. No, if anything, Chuck Horner was excited to be heading to Thailand and on the eve of his first combat tour.

As he finally made it up to the processing desk in San Francisco, Horner's suspicions were aroused when a processor tried to issue him a rifle and a helmet. Part of the fighter-pilot creed dictated that the true brethren not flinch when asked to fly down a gauntlet of enemy antiaircraft fire, but no one said anything about crawling through the mud wearing a steel pot.

"Hey, wait a minute, you've got the wrong guy," Horner protested. "You see this flight suit? I'm a *fighter pilot.*"

While he waited for his plane, Horner had time to kill. The papers were filled with accounts of Cassius Clay's improbable first-round defeat of Sonny Liston, the fastest knockout on record in a heavyweight title bout. Los Angeles Dodger Don Drysdale had pitched a one-hitter, snapping a seven-game winning streak by the St. Louis Cardinals.

Indeed, in the late spring of 1965, everything seemed possible in America. The news section was filled with reports of Pres. Lyndon Baines Johnson fervently pushing his Great Society programs to eradicate poverty. The Senate had just passed the Voting Rights Act by a lopsided margin. In the most one-sided contest over such legislation since the days of the Marshall Plan, the Democratic leadership in Congress pushed through LBJ's bountiful foreign-aid plan, authorizing a $3.67-billion export of the Great Society. Meanwhile, Gemini astronaut Maj. Edward H. White was poised to make America's first walk in space.

There was simply no feat so daunting nor problem so intractable that it couldn't be mastered by the country's almost breathless enthusiasm and confidence. At home and aboard, around the world and even in space, America was taking on all challenges.

The weather was stifling when Horner arrived in northern Thailand along with two other pilots. Capt. Roger Myhrum was a friend and fellow pilot from the 4th Tactical Fighter Wing, and Lt. Col. Bill Redemis a Korean War veteran they had met on the flight to Bangkok. The tactical Air Force was peopled by many pilots who had been rushed through pilot training to fill cockpits during Korea and World War II. If they were not exactly the barnstormers that answered the call in World War I, they were close in spirit.

Horner remembered the near-weekly fistfights between his wing executive and operations officers at his first operational squadron in Lackenheath, England. The executive officer had actually been one of the first pilots sent to Vietnam, the better to escape the authorities after he punched the face of a police officer who had the temerity to stop him for speeding.

While many of these older, experienced pilots seemed a throwback to a bygone era, they had more than distinguished themselves during the Korean War. The Air Force had produced no fewer than thirty-eight aces with five or more MiG kills apiece in Korea. In the end, they were shooting down MiGs almost as fast as the Koreans and Chinese could get them in the air, registering roughly a twelve-to-one advantage in aircraft destroyed to those lost. There was no reason to believe that Vietnam would be any different.

The Korat Royal Thai Air Force Base north of Bangkok turned out to consist of a runway and a cluster of dilapidated wooden shacks with corrugated-tin roofs. Collecting their duffels, the pilots entered an unpainted wooden hut that served as headquarters for the 388th Tactical Fighter Wing. Inside the command room, sunlight poured through gaps in the wooden-slat wall like the bars of a cage.

Looking over from a flight chart, an action officer gave them the once-over. "So who're you guys?" They introduced themselves without igniting the faintest flicker of recognition. "Yeah," said the officer, "so what'd you come over for?"

Actually, the question was not as inane as it initially sounded. In the middle of 1965, Air Force units based in Thailand had no permanent command structure. In fact, the mere presence of the bases at Korat and Takhli was kept secret from the public at the request of the Thai government. Squadrons from various air wings were simply rotated in and out, and nearly everyone was on a temporary tour of duty of only a few months. While in Thailand, squadrons came under the operational control of the 2nd Air Division headquartered at Tan Son Nhut airfield in South Vietnam.

Horner and Roger Myhrum passed along their orders, which explained that they were there primarily to augment the wing's planning staff and help develop air tasking orders. The operations officer told them to get squared away in quarters and come back later. Outside, they were led to a clearing between shacks by a Thai workman, who motioned for them to set their things aside. After dropping their duffels in the dust, Horner and Myhrum watched incredulously as a Thai work team appeared and, while they waited, began hasty construction of the quarters that would serve as home for roughly the next six months.

After depositing their belongings in their newly minted quarters, which somehow managed to look old and decrepit already, the two decided to seek out the one place where fighter pilots worldwide know they can get the no-bullshit lowdown. There they would find out everything they needed to know about this war in Indochina that the tight-assed briefers would be afraid to say in front of their bosses.

The officers' club on Korat was actually another shack with a splintered wooden bar, where they immediately secured two ice-cold, jumbo bottles of Sing Hai beer. Horner was delighted to find that Capt. Bill "Black Bart" Barthelmous was also stationed at Korat. Horner and Barthelmous had gone through pilot training and gunnery school together, where Black Bart had earned a reputation as the bachelor most likely to succeed with the women.

As one of the heavy rains that regularly deluge northern Thailand in the late afternoons drummed loudly on the tin roof, Horner and Myhrum sat in the midst of a growing group of pilots. Many were just back from missions and ready to unwind. Eventually the rain broke and the light began to fade while crickets chirped in the fresh night air, and still the men sat huddled together, making strange looping motions with their arms over a growing cluster of empty beer bottles.

The pilots at Korat were part of an initial tide of Air Force personnel flooding into air bases throughout Southeast Asia in mid-1965. By the end of the year, five hundred Air Force aircraft and twenty-one thousand personnel would be stationed at the eight major air bases in South Vietnam alone.

The opening of the floodgates had come earlier that year, when President Johnson had finally agreed to the systematic bombing of military targets in North Vietnam. Code-named Rolling Thunder, the "measured and limited air action against selected targets in North Vietnam" followed nearly a year of mostly ineffective tit-for-tat air reprisals by Air Force, Navy, and South Vietnamese (VNAF) aircraft.

Not only had the policy of tit-for-tat reprisals failed to deter North Vietnam, but by the early summer of 1965, Ho Chi Minh's government seemed tantalizingly close to the goal for which it had sacrificed and struggled for nearly twenty years. A ferocious Viet Cong offensive launched that spring had convinced nearly everybody, including President Johnson, that the North was poised for a final blow. Short of a massive deployment of U.S. ground troops, the air campaign was widely viewed as the only thing standing between an already shaky South Vietnamese government and absolute collapse.

Yet the conflict in the skies above North and South Vietnam was hardly the one for which the Air Force had been preparing since Korea. Most of the flying and nearly all of the officially sanctioned training in the Air Force revolved around the nuclear-delivery mission. The creation of the atomic bomb, in fact, had reduced the tactical fighter force to an afterthought in Air Force planning.

In the early 1960s fighter pilots thus felt like an endangered species within their own service. To justify their existence, even fighter aircraft such as the F-105 were tasked with nuclear-bomb delivery. Because they would be flying in at low level to avoid Soviet air defenses, and a standard approach would put them directly in the path of an atomic backblast, fighter pilots constantly practiced overflying their targets and releasing their bomb *skyward*, peeling off in the opposite direction while it arced toward the ground. While nuclear delivery was a tricky maneuver requiring a deft touch, Chuck Horner doubted that it would prove much use in Vietnam.

According to the F-105 pilots at Korat, very little had gone according to plan or expectation since the very first Rolling Thunder mission on March 2. That mission to take out an ammunition depot at Xom Bang, thirty-five miles north of the DMZ, had represented the first combat for some of the pilots sitting at the table with Horner, and it had left an indelible mark that was easy to read in their faces. The pilots had been told, they said, to expect relatively light and ineffective antiaircraft fire, and it was probably the last official word they had accepted without a grain of salt and an ounce of derision.

Instead of light resistance, they had arrived in the third wave of airplanes to find the sky crisscrossed by orange tracers and the smoke trails from crippled aircraft. The mission timing had been completely disrupted, with the pilots in the third wave arriving only to find those in the second still swarming over the target. In that first, chaotic mission over a single target, six U.S. aircraft had been shot down.

When squadron commanders from Thailand had flown to 2nd Air Division headquarters at Tan Son Nhut to complain bitterly about planning that would put so many aircraft over a target so close together, they had been gently rebuffed by Air Force lieutenant general Joseph Moore. While sympathetic, the 2nd Division commander said that in their zeal to honor the president's wish for "limited" air strikes, Pentagon planners had hog-tied the operation with restrictions.

Not only was Washington sending down detailed target lists, but they were also specifying the day and sometimes hour of attack, the types of weapons that could be used, in some cases even the *approach* aircraft could take to the target! If a mission was canceled because of factors that Washington had somehow overlooked—like bad weather—then it could not be rescheduled without first clearing it with the Pentagon. The White House was clearly obsessed with the idea that nothing be done that might draw China or the Soviet Union into the Vietnam conflict.

While some of the restrictions had been relaxed after complaints made it up the chain of command all the way to the Joint Chiefs of Staff, the pilots clearly chaffed under a command hierarchy that left the men doing the fighting and dying in operational squadrons almost no control over their own destiny. There were plenty of other complaints: about air staff officers in Saigon who were trained in strategic-bombing theory and ignorant of the most fundamental knowledge of fighter aircraft and conventional bombing tactics; about the vulnerability to ground fire of the F-105, with its non-self-sealing fuel tanks; and especially about the jungle fungus that was spreading through the ranks of American pilots like moss on a dead log.

Horner awoke the next day already clammy with sweat and suffering a splitting hangover. No one had bothered to mention that formaldehyde was used as a preservative in Sing Hai beer, and the resulting headaches were practically epidemic at Korat. Both he and Roger Myhrum reported to the squadron air-planning staff and were immediately put to work helping develop air-tasking orders from the target lists sent down from Saigon.

Typically orders would come out the day before a planned strike, and the planning staff would often work late into the night breaking them down and translating them into specific instructions for each of the air wing's three squadrons. These fragmentary orders, or "frags," included specifics such as scheduled times, number of aircraft, and weapons load. It didn't take Horner too many late-morning debriefings to discover that the pilots weren't exaggerating about the command-and-control muddle.

The focus of the Rolling Thunder campaign had shifted toward trying to sever North Vietnam's lines of supply below the twentieth parallel. Primary targets were bridges, ferries, major highway routes, and rail lines. While the bombing had met with considerable success, the North Vietnamese were proving adept at taking advantage of U.S. restrictions, keeping convoys hidden in population centers during the day, for instance, knowing pilots were forbidden to strike them for fear of causing civilian casualties.

By far the most frustrating problem for pilots, however, was the target restrictions. Often they would be sent to strike suspected "truck farms" or other transportation facilities and find that the North Vietnamese had already moved them. Because they were strictly forbidden to hit secondary targets not cleared by the Pentagon, pilots would often have to bomb forests that clearly masked no weapons or enemy, referring to the exercise as "making toothpicks."

Yet target recommendations from pilots returning from missions in Thailand had to climb a convoluted command-and-control flowchart. First they were relayed to Air Force general Moore, the 2nd Air Division commander ostensibly in charge of air forces in Vietnam. Moore himself served two direct bosses, Army general William Westmoreland, commander of the Military Assistance Command, Vietnam, and the commander of the 13th Air Force back in the Philippines. Anxious to get into the action but unwilling to relinquish its independent grasp on its bombers, Strategic Air Command in Omaha had retained operational control of the B-52s, which had begun flying missions into South Vietnam out of Anderson Air Force Base in Guam.

Target recommendations from Thailand that made it past 2nd Air Division were sent to Honolulu, headquarters of the commander in chief (CINC) of Pacific Forces. There the staff had to settle increasingly acrimonious disputes between the Air Force and Navy carriers at "Yankee Station" in the South China Sea over who got to hit the relatively paltry targets that the Pentagon doled out, neither wanting the other to fly more missions. This continued the traditional rivalry between the two services that was usually played out in Washington over funding. In Southeast Asia, however, it was greatly exacerbated by the tensions of war, overlapping command structures, and poor communications between aircraft carriers and Air Force headquarters near Saigon.

Once target recommendations were forwarded from CINCPAC to Washington, they were reviewed by the Joint Chiefs of Staff and civilians on the International Security Affairs staff, who reported to Secretary of Defense Robert McNamara. Here, too, a bitter rift was growing, with the JCS stridently arguing that the "progressive squeeze" that characterized the bombing campaign in the summer of 1965 was not working, and that only a greatly expanded and more aggressive air blitz would break North Vietnam's will.

Secretary of Defense and former Ford Motor Company president Robert McNamara was caught between the Joint Chiefs on one hand, and the influential voices of presidential advisers who argued for a more cautious and gradual approach, chief among them Assistant Secretary of State William Bundy. For his part, McNamara tended to surround himself with statisticians and systems analysts who broke the air war down into its most minute components, incrementally ratcheting up or down the numbers of sorties flown, bombs dropped, and targets approved in their search for the winning equation.

Recommendations that cleared the Pentagon were sent to the White House, where they were further reviewed by a select policy group that met for lunch every Tuesday afternoon. Each request was graded by a set of four criteria, including its military significance, risks to pilots and planes, the danger of civilian casualties, and the risk of widening the war. At the head of the table sat President Johnson himself, who liked to brag to reporters that "I won't let those Air Force generals bomb an outhouse without checking with me first."

Not all of the command-and-control problems, however, originated in Washington, D.C. Air Force and Navy commands squabbled constantly about jurisdiction over targets and areas. Because they were never able or willing to coordinate their command-and-control and tactics, planners at 2nd Air Division headquarters eventually carved North Vietnam into inviolate service zones. On more than one occasion, F-105 pilots at Korat would spot a military convoy heading south, but because it was in a "Navy zone," they were not allowed to attack. By the time an attack order could be issued out to carriers sitting at Yankee Station in the South China Sea, the convoy would have long since disappeared.

The strain and frustrations of fighting such a war predictably began to show on the Korat pilots. The worst were the ones who had been shot down and rescued, a group whose number grew each week. The closed cockpit of a fighter jet is a warm and secure place, the pilots hooked to the nourishment of oxygen and information by cords running to their masks and helmets, everything almost liquid in its sense of weightlessness. Bailing out meant getting ripped from that protective womb by a nitroglycerin charge, frequently flaying knees, elbows, and shoulders on the rim of the cockpit on the way out, and then hitting "the wall" of air outside at hundreds of miles an hour.

Those who survived ejection and didn't break their neck in a tree or drown in a rice paddy on the ground were then left to wonder for hours and sometimes days whether their immediate future held a rescue helicopter, an indefinite stint in the "Hanoi Hilton," or worse, much worse. Horrifying tales abounded about the fate of pilots who fell into the hands of enraged villagers. The last rescued pilot Chuck Horner had talked with had sworn he was fine, yet was shaking so hard he could hardly get a drink to his mouth without spilling the whole thing. No one mentioned it.

Soon enough Horner and Myhrum were flying missions roughly every other day to give their colleagues badly needed rest, and filling in on the air staff in between. Before the end of a full week they would have been hard pressed to say what month it was, much less the day of the week. Both soon discovered that combat at Mach speed warps time as well as sound, endless hours of tension preceding moments of infinite terror followed by everlasting relief and the perpetual tug of exhaustion. It was rock around the clock, with each day dawning promising the full pendulum swing of human emotion.

Loathing was in there, too, at least for Horner, especially those frozen moments of lucidity when he saw himself before God with the blood of countless strangers on his hands. Life at Korat tended to season a pilot so fast that you didn't realize when you had acquired the same strung-out look that had you worried about your buddies, at least not until someone was in your face strongly suggesting a little R&R in Bangkok. Until then, however, no one had to ask himself what he had accomplished that day before surrendering to sleep. One just had to live with it.

Alternating staff work with combat missions gave Chuck Horner a unique perspective. One of the primary lessons that flying combat drove home was how woefully unprepared they were for conventional bombing missions. During training a pilot could qualify for dive-bombing by dropping a string of bombs within a 280-foot circle. Compared to that, hitting a small expanse of bridge or a moving truck in Vietnam was like trying to thread a needle while dodging flak and checking over your shoulder for MiG pilots with murder in their eye.

Flying combat also quickly drove home to Horner how the countless restrictions and convoluted rules of engagement that seemed merely petty and infuriating on the ground could assume the shape of an almost cosmic stupidity from the air. Their charts were covered with red circles designating zones that were out-of-bounds to attack, including one describing a ten-mile radius around Hanoi, and another a four-mile radius around Haiphong harbor. In "prohibited zones" stretching thirty miles outside of Hanoi and ten miles outside of Haiphong, they could fire on antiaircraft batteries only in self-defense, and then only if they were not located in populated areas. There was another restricted zone stretching thirty miles south of the Chinese border.

Of all the restrictions, the one that pilots could least understand were the ones barring strikes against North Vietnamese MiG bases and surface-to-air-missile (SAM) sites. While restricting attacks on air bases and missile sites where Soviet and Chinese military advisers could become collateral casualties might seem like a perfectly logical exemption from the perspective of a White House situation room, it looked like something altogether different for a pilot in the cockpit of an F-105 jinking low-level at six-hundred knots an hour trying desperately to shake a MiG off his tail.

As for the SAMs, American pilots had been aware of their existence since the previous April, when reconnaissance photographs revealed a site under construction fifteen miles southeast of Hanoi. Within a month, two more sites had been discovered. Aware of the danger presented by SAMs ever since 1960, when a Soviet missile shot down a U-2 high-altitude reconnaissance plane piloted by Francis Gary Powers, the Air Force and Navy commanders had immediately asked for permission to take out the sites. Because no SAM had yet been launched at an American aircraft, however, policymakers in

Washington apparently believed the SAM sites were just another move in the game of bluff, counterbluff they were playing with the Soviets. Request denied.

The situation changed irreversibly on July 24, 1965, when a Soviet-model SA-2 surface-to-air missile shot down an Air Force F-4 Phantom operating out of Thailand. Because it had a lethal range as high as sixty thousand feet and could track a target at more than twice the speed of sound, the SA-2 threatened to deny American pilots medium and high altitudes, forcing their attacks down to low altitudes where they were vulnerable to everything from antiaircraft batteries to small-arms fire. Realizing that SAMs could no longer be ignored, Washington agreed to a onetime-only strike at the two sites suspected of firing at the F-4.

Up until that point, it had been easy for Horner and the rest of the Air Force pilots to blame civilians in Washington almost solely for the various screwups in the air campaign, as well as its inability to decisively turn the tide in the war raging in South Vietnam. The restrictions placed on the air campaign probably did render moot heated debate in Washington over whether air power alone could prove decisive in the war. Traditionalists pointed out that short of delivering nuclear weapons, air power had failed to be decisive in Hitler's blitz of London in 1940, and again in Allied bombing of Germany and Japan later in World War II. Air-power proponents argued that advances in technology were tilting the balance of military power inexorably into the air arm.

From the beginning of the conflict, however, Secretary of Defense Robert McNamara rejected recommendations by the Joint Chiefs for a massive, coordinated bombing campaign directed at all ninety-four targets on the JCS master target list. Given the spotty early results of Rolling Thunder, McNamara and others doubted that a bombing campaign could shake Hanoi's will while the possibility of victory on the ground remained. He also believed that the dangers of drawing the Soviet Union or China into the war with an all-out air blitz, or forcing these traditional antagonists into closer cooperation against the United States, outweighed the potential benefits.

Yet the "progressive squeeze" that had characterized Rolling Thunder up to that summer went against every instinct in the American military psyche. After Korea, the Joint Chiefs were already highly suspicious of civilian theories on limited warfare. The increasing civilian influence on the conduct of the conflict in Vietnam was only heightening those feelings, with the chiefs arguing that a gradually escalating bombing campaign punctuated by frequent halts only gave the enemy time to prepare and repair his defenses.

As it was being fought in 1965, the Vietnam War was thus not destined to provide an answer to the argument on the impact of air power. After some soul-searching that followed the events of July 27, however, pilots in Thailand knew that not all the blame for shortcomings in their ability to wage conventional war from the air could be conveniently shifted onto Washington. It struck much closer to home than that.

The buzz of excitement that filled the briefing room gave way to a polite quiet as the strike mission was outlined, and then to an almost dumbstruck silence. That was the sound of doubt spreading through the room, and it instantly quelled the elation the pilots had initially felt at finally getting a crack at the SAM sites. As the plan was laid out, sixteen F-105s from the 12th Squadron at Korat would split into two groups, one to launch a diversionary attack and the other to strike at SAM Site 6, forty miles west of Hanoi on the Black River. At the same time, another sixteen F-105s would depart Takhli for SAM Site 7 on the nearby Red River. The aircraft were to break into flights of four each and come in at the targets at low level along identical courses.

They don't know how to do this, Horner thought with an almost numbing sense of unreality. The pilots had already learned that sending successive flights down the same chute gave North Vietnamese antiaircraft gunners a chance to fix their altitude and direction. Because the Red and Black rivers converged at a point near the two targets, there was also a danger of the two attacks running into each other head-on if the timing slipped. In the unimaginative, "bomber stream" tactics Horner was sure he recognized the hand of the Strategic Air Command planners who had driven so much of his own training as a young pilot.

Some of the young captains went so far as to make an unauthorized call to 2nd Air Division headquarters after the briefing, wondering who the idiot was that thought up this nightmare. They were curtly put in their place, which was to fly the missions, not plan them. As for Horner, both he and Roger Myhrum were scheduled for staff duty, so they would not be flying on the mission. After putting the air crews to bed, they both worked through the night to prepare the aircraft for the mission. During the early-morning hours, Horner's gnawing suspicion that the planners in Saigon had no idea how to attack a SAM site became a nauseating certainty.

They kept changing the weapons load. No sooner would sweating ground crews finish arming the Thunderchiefs with 750-pound bombs than a call would come in from Saigon to change it to rockets and napalm. Later a call instructed them to download the rockets and reload the bombs. By the time a third call rescinded the second order and instructed them to reload the rockets and napalm, dawn broke over the flight line to reveal a scene of utter confusion, ground crews running frantically about and arguing over weapons carts. With pilots climbing into their cockpits, some stopping to exchange words with the squadron chaplain, Maj. Bill Hosmer realized that two of the F-105s in his flight had been caught in the switch and were armed only with their 20mm cannons. The control tower told him to launch anyway.

Groggy from not having slept the entire night, Horner just stared at the staff officer a moment when he and Roger Myhrum were asked to fly for two pilots who had reported in sick. As Horner squeezed into the F-105 cockpit, weighted down by a G suit, a fifty-pound parachute, and a survival vest containing a two-way radio, flares, and a .38 revolver, the sense of unreality grew. Funny the things you think about at a time like that. As Horner was cleared for takeoff by the tower and noted the comforting sensation of g forces enveloping him as the Thunderchief blasted down the runway, it suddenly occurred to him that his last meal was a hastily eaten liver sandwich. Chuck Horner hated liver.

Crossing into North Vietnamese airspace, Horner listened to the sound of his steady breathing and the muffled whine of the jet engine. Almost by rote reflex, his fingers flipped through the sequence of switches on his cockpit panel that activated the bomb-release mechanisms and electronic countermeasures gear. Switching the radio over to the predetermined strike frequency, he heard the flight leader's voice directing them to begin their descent into the winding river valley far below. As the four jets dropped below the ridge line into single-file formation just a few hundred feet above the water, the banks and river melted into a liquid blur of green and sparkling silver splashing against the canopy. Horner heard his breathing quicken at the familiar sensation of ground rush. Half a mile ahead the river disappeared around a sharp bend.

"Buick One is in the water!" crackled over Horner's headphones. The call signs for aircraft based at Korat were all Detroit nameplates. Suddenly the strike frequency was alive with shouts and nervous chatter. Just like that, someone down already. The flight lead disappeared around the bend in the river, and Horner banked his own F-105 sharply. Leveling off, his hand gripped the control like a vise. The narrow corridor ahead was filled with black cloudbursts, burning aircraft trails, and orange tracers streaming. A firepower demonstration and they were flying right through it, the bright muzzle flashes winking angrily from the banks as they streaked whizzing past.

"Percy's hit!" blasted in Horner's ear just as he saw the smoke-engulfed aircraft of Capt. Bob Purcell rear up out of the corner of his right eye and exit the gauntlet in flames. His heart fluttered against his ribs like a caged bird, explosions bursting overhead as he coaxed the aircraft lower, lower. They were coming in under the 37mm flak now, and Horner worked his rudder pedals, control stick, and throttle simultaneously to keep the aircraft on its target run as it was buffeted by the turbulent air. The aircraft ahead popped up over the SAM site and Horner quickly tried to line up his optical aiming device as the explosions rocked the target. Something wasn't right, the timing felt off, and as he pulled back on the control stick and pickled off the napalm, he glanced quickly at his airspeed. Six hundred and forty knots! Way over the 365-knot delivery limit for napalm. Dammit!

Lighting up the afterburner as he pulled out, the g forces pushing his helmet into the back of the seat, Horner banked in time to see Capt. Frank Tullo's aircraft just behind him careen out of the river gauntlet trailing a hundred-foot tongue of flame. He never saw a parachute.

After the flight regrouped and headed back for base, the radio remained mostly quiet. Each pilot was left to his own thoughts. For Horner's part, the seed of unreality that had been planted at the previous day's briefing had blossomed into dark disbelief. The Korean War vets who had trained him had always said that only a war would truly reveal what kind of air force they were. Horner didn't even want to think about what the Black River disaster implied.

As they neared Korat, a pilot broke over the radio network and requested a visual inspection of his aircraft. Horner recognized the voice of Black Bart Barthelmous. The next voice he heard was that of Jack Farr, the operations officer:

"You're okay underneath."

"Roger that," replied Barthelmous. "Give me a once-over from above." Because the North Vietnamese antiaircraft gunners couldn't swing the big 37mm batteries low enough, many of the aircraft had been hit from shrapnel exploding over the pilots' heads. As Farr maneuvered his F-105 directly over Barthelmous, his voice broke in excitedly:

"Holy shit, Bart! You've got—"

No one who witnessed them would ever forget the next few seconds. With his flight controls apparently damaged by shrapnel, Bill Barthelmous's aircraft suddenly careened straight up into the F-105 giving him the visual inspection. Jack Farr was killed instantly in the collision. Barthelmous's broken body was eventually found beneath a partially opened parachute in the rice paddy where he drowned.

Between Takhli and Korat, six aircraft were lost in the SAM raid on the

Red and Black rivers. Besides Barthelmous and Farr, Walt Kosko was reported missing in action and never found. Captains Bob Purcell and Kile Berg were captured and would wait out the remaining long years of the war in a roach-infested cell in Hoa Lo Prison, derisively dubbed the Hanoi Hilton. No one at Korat knew what had happened to Capt. Frank Tullo, who had gone down in flames.

The day after the strike, Gen. Hunter Harris, the four-star commander of Pacific Air Forces, arrived at Korat in his personal plane to get a full debriefing on the SAM raid. As his aircraft taxied to a stop, the pilots and base personnel at Korat stood at attention at the runway apron. When the door opened, however, it was not the spit-and-shine visage of Harris that first emerged, but rather the blood- and vomit-caked figure of their friend Frank Tullo, a toothy grin lighting his dark if disheveled features. As it turned out, Tullo had been rescued in the most far-flung search-and-rescue (SAR) mission yet attempted in the war. Like a good pilot, he had dutifully stayed up late into the night drinking to the health of the helicopter pilot who saved him. The next day he had simply hitched a ride home with General Harris, somewhat the worse for wear.

Eventually, Chuck Horner and a few others would go through Bill Barthelmous's legendary address book, sending letters to all those listed to tell them that Black Bart would not be writing anymore. There was one woman, however, whose name Barthelmous had not listed in his little black book nor included in his macho tales of conquest. They would find out later that Barthelmous already had his papers in to leave the Air Force so he could marry her and settle down. His buddies in Korat first became aware of this secret life of Bart's when they received a wanted poster with Barthelmous's picture on it, with the caption, "Have you seen this man? My fiancé hasn't written in three weeks."

As for the raid itself, when the poststrike reconnaissance photos had been developed, the pilots learned that they had been the victims of a clever ruse. After shooting down the Phantom on July 24, the North Vietnamese had removed the real SAMs, concentrating every available antiaircraft battery in the region around sites with dummy cardboard missiles. And then they had patiently waited for three days to spring the trap, as if they knew exactly how and when the Air Force would strike. Six aircraft had been lost bombing a decoy.

Days after the SAM strike, on July 29, 1965, *The New York Times* carried a front-page article detailing the costly raid, under the headline "U.S. Raids 2 Missile Sites in Vietnam, Wrecking One; Johnson to Speak Today." It was the second part of the headline, however, that dominated conversation around coffeepots and in the myriad alcoves that carve the Pentagon into countless fiefdoms. After a week of intense, closed-door discussions with his top military and foreign-policy advisers on Vietnam, Pres. Lyndon Johnson had called a news conference for twelve-thirty P.M. that afternoon.

With nearly everyone expecting some escalation given the worsening crisis, most speculation centered on whether the president would ask Congress for a joint resolution authorizing him to call up the reserves, as Kennedy had done during the Berlin crisis in August of 1961, or whether he would bypass Congress and issue an executive order declaring a state of national emergency. Either move would allow for a mobilization of the reserves, but only with a joint resolution by Congress would the secretary of defense likely have authorization to extend present tours of service as well. Men in uniform whose tours were up were apt to take a hard look at their career objectives if they knew they were about to be sent off to fight a war, especially those who were drafted in the first place.

Most in the military's senior leadership believed that a call-up of the reserves and full military mobilization was the only move that made sense. Get the American people behind the effort, get in big and get the job done, and get the hell out. Just the commitment to action implicit in a mobilization sent a powerful message and had eventually helped convince the Soviet Union to back down during the Berlin crisis.

Lyndon Johnson's instincts and a number of trusted aides, however, were cautioning him that a full mobilization for war could prove a political time bomb. Already, some of the president's former colleagues in Congress were complaining about the likely political fallout of a reserve call-up. When McNamara had recently returned from a trip to South Vietnam and endorsed Gen. William Westmoreland's request for forty-four battalions of combat troops as the only way to stave off defeat in the South, LBJ had held a series of high-level meetings with his top military and foreign-policy advisers. Just after noon on July 29, 1965, the president appeared on television screens before 28 million Americans to inform them on the outcome of those deliberations:

"I have today ordered to Vietnam the Airmobile and certain other forces, which will raise our fighting strength from seventy-five thousand to one hundred twenty-five thousand men almost immediately. Additional forces will be needed later and they will be sent as requested." Even as Lyndon Johnson depicted America as a final shield protecting fledgling democracies from Asian communism, members of the 1st Air Cavalry Division were loading their equipment onto ships for transfer to Vietnam. Army leaders knew that the requests for additional forces were already in, and that the open-ended deployment would approach nearly two hundred thousand by the end of the year.

Stating that the deployment would require the Selective Service to double the draft, from seventeen thousand a month to thirty-five thousand, President Johnson let fly the blow that would knock the collective breath from the military.

"After this past week of deliberations, I have concluded that it is not essential to order reserve units into service now. If that necessity should later be indicated, I will give the matter careful consideration and I will give the country due and adequate notice. . . ."

Even for the handful of men in uniform who knew the president's plans in advance, the announcement was stunning in its implications. The war would be won or lost on the ground in Vietnam, and it would be fought largely by an Army divorced from one of its fundamental sources of support. Diminished by four years of cost-cutting under McNamara, the services were already stretched thin in terms of equipment, spare parts, and especially manpower. Mounting a war now without a full mobilization meant they would have to cannibalize their other commands around the world of men and matériel, especially the Seventh Army in Germany. And from that moment on, until the president either reversed himself and mobilized the country or withdrew forces from Vietnam, the experience level and readiness of the armed forces would steadily decline.

World War II veterans such as Army chief of staff Gen. Harold Johnson also understood that a principle was at play that was even more important. They would be going to war without the declaration of a national emergency and all the urgency and sense of national purpose that implied. General Johnson had already vowed to personally write the parents of every soldier killed in combat in Vietnam, and at the end of most days he could be found at his desk, poring through personnel files, absorbed in his grim task.

Yet perhaps more than any other role model, the West Pointers of Johnson's generation had been molded in the image of George Catlett Marshall, a general, former secretary of state, and Nobel Prize winner who preached the absolute sanctity of the military's subordination to its civilian masters. How to know when principle dictated that you personally could no longer follow that lead?

A new generation of young officers looking for their own role models would never forgive Harold Johnson and many of his contemporaries for not taking the step that the chief of staff almost made that day, resigning rather than seeing his men placed in an untenable position. For a man as heavily principled and torn by the war as Harold Johnson, who would eventually become overwhelmed by trying to write letters to the parents of as many as five hundred dead soldiers a week, the scorn was but a dull reflection of his own. Johnson later reportedly confided in a colleague that he never forgave *himself* for not resigning that day.

3: I Corps 1965–66

THEY would sleep in the field by night in a state of semiconsciousness and by day slog through rice paddies in stifling heat. The only break from the constant patrolling came when they gathered together for battalion-sized operations. Ever since they'd waded ashore back in March of 1965, the Marines had simply patrolled in ever-expanding concentric circles around their established enclaves at Da Nang, Phu Bai, and Chu Lai. Mostly they encountered only the stony stares of local villagers and the occasional well-concealed booby trap or hit-and-run sniper attack.

It was a routine that enervated Marine Corps lieutenant Tom Draude in a way he hadn't thought possible. The worst was the trip-wire tension created by the constant threat of booby traps. The VC were old masters at disguising these deadly calling cards. Mangled by an unseen enemy, the Marines longed for someone to swing back at.

The northernmost of the four military districts that subdivided South Vietnam was a land of sandy beaches and marshy river valleys, giving way to rolling hills farther inland. Torrential rains of the summer monsoon turned the area into a tropical steam bath that rusted equipment and could practically rot a uniform off your back. Time in I Corps drained you like a disease, and more than once Tom Draude had to shake himself out of a sort of walking dream.

The son of immigrant parents, his father a German steamfitter who dodged the kaiser's army by settling in Illinois, his mother the daughter of immigrants who escaped poverty in Ireland, Draude had inherited a working-class ethic and the kind of patriotism that takes nothing for granted and asks for little in return. He fit perfectly in the Marine Corps.

The idea of the Naval Academy had come in Tom Draude's junior year in high school. Someone had loaned him Leon Uris's *Battle Cry*. The hero was a Naval Academy graduate and Marine Corps officer named Huxley. Draude had put the book down and seen his future with a clarity reserved for seventeen-year-olds with romantic dreams, and he had seen it through with a young man's determination. He had become a Naval Academy graduate and a Marine Corps officer, and now he was on his first combat tour. Because that's what the Marine Corps was, a band of fighters.

It was all he'd heard from the moment he first put on the uniform three years ago after graduating from the Naval Academy in Annapolis; the Marine Corps fights. We're not pretty, we don't do parades, we fight. Most of the senior noncoms and officers at the level of captain or above were combat veterans from Korea or World War II, and they pounded that message home until it became a sort of mantra to the almost mythical esprit de corps of the tightly knit Marines.

As his gunnery sergeant told Draude on practically his first day on the job, "Lieutenant, you should have been with us in Korea, that was a fight to behold."

"Sure, Gunney, but I was just ten years old at the time," Draude had protested.

"Well, Lieutenant," the sergeant had replied with a smile, "you could have lied about your age."

Yet few of them had envisioned the type of fighting the Marines encountered in I Corps. Perhaps it was fitting that the Marines, the first to land in Vietnam in force and be exposed to its deprivations, the jungle rot and patrol fatigue, would be among the first to realize that a conflict without clear fronts or even a well-defined enemy would prove rife with moral ambiguity and frustration.

In fact, even identifying the enemy had proven maddening. Intelligence indicated that the Marines were in a hotbed of Viet Cong activity, with an estimated fifteen hundred hostile troops within a two-day march of Da Nang. Yet when they swept through villages that revealed unmistakable signs of a recent Viet Cong presence, the enemy had often melted into the surrounding countryside or joined the throngs of frightened civilians.

Absent a clearly articulated strategy coming out of Gen. William Westmoreland's headquarters in Saigon, which was still developing a war-fighting plan for the tens of thousands of troops flooding into Vietnam, the Marines had begun ad hoc experiments in pacification and population control. Working with American advisers and ARVN units, they established a "civic action policy," helping to coordinate relief efforts from private organizations such as

CARE, and offering villagers the services of their medical officers.

The Marines had also made headlines with a controversial incident at Cam Ne, a village with communist ties going back to the French Indochina War. With orders to burn the village down if fired upon by the enemy, the Marines proceeded to do just that after taking small-arms fire from Cam Ne. The scene of a Marine setting fire to a thatched-roof hut with his cigarette lighter while a peasant stood crying nearby was captured by a young television correspondent named Morley Safer, and the footage soon appeared on Walter Cronkite's *CBS Evening News*. The wave of indignation that image ignited worldwide had come as an early warning to the Marines that there was a darker side to the counterinsurgency conflict heralded by former president Kennedy as the struggle of the future.

That autumn Draude's company was chosen to establish a combat outpost south of Chu Lai near the Tra Bong River. He was actually relieved by the orders. They talked about it often, how a heavy sense of indolence already seemed to pervade the rear area, with its NCO shows and growing trappings of "little America." It would take more than Bob Hope to keep him from going stir-crazy in the rear. For all its hardships and deprivations, the field was where Draude felt most like a Marine.

Humping brought with it a breath of clarity that swept away the doubts that lingered in the rear like fog. What were they accomplishing? Why were they there? Stripped to its most basic elements, they were there to secure the countryside and put a thorn in the side of the VC. The intent was to stay alive in the process. It was tested almost immediately just north of the Tra Bong.

Though they didn't know it at the time, Draude's company had established itself right on a main supply route of the Viet Cong. During the first week, he was awakened by the sound of Claymore mines and heavy fire. A main-force battalion of Viet Cong had penetrated their perimeter and overrun a section of their position. After a pitched firefight that lasted much of the night, the Marines seized the ground back. As the sun rose the next morning, ground mists receded to reveal a grisly scene of death, trees and brush splattered with blood and the ground littered with both American and Viet Cong bodies. There was little question that the guerrillas knew whom they were fighting and sensed that the war was shifting irrevocably into the hands of the Americans. While searching through the enemy dead, the Marines found pamphlets in Vietnamese that carefully spelled out in phonetic lettering the English required to take American prisoners.

Over the next few months, Draude acquired a grudging respect for the Viet Cong soldiers. Not only were they fierce fighters, but they were masters at deception. Frequently, the Marines would attack what appeared to be dug-in Viet Cong only to receive flanking fire at the last moment. They had expended their artillery preparation on dummy positions that the VC had dug during the night even though they were no doubt exhausted. After the fire of his anger burned itself out, mostly Draude was left with a cold admiration for his foe and his deceptive tactics.

The Marines were learning, but it seemed to Draude as if the lessons all came at precious expense. As they continued to play a deadly game of cat and mouse with the Viet Cong battalion whose supply line they had blocked, the casualties in his company mounted steadily. When the company commander was wounded in one engagement, Draude was promoted to captain and took his place. For thirty days he commanded the company without another officer or a first sergeant, doing all the administrative work as well as commanding in the field. By the time a new lieutenant arrived, Draude made sure to have a little talk with him.

"Look, just because you're new and these other men have been shot at, that doesn't mean they know it all," Draude told the green officer. "You just do your job, and don't worry about any heroics." Within twenty-four hours Draude had written the man into the unit diary, assigned him a slot in the company, marked him up for hostile-action pay, and dropped him off the unit roll as wounded in action. Welcome to the 'Nam.

Even in the early months of the deployment, dealing with the constant replacements became Draude's most daunting challenge. In contrast to earlier wars, troops in Vietnam were being rotated individually into and out of units in twelve-month cycles according to their personal DEROS (date of expected return from overseas). It was difficult to know how to get these green replacements accepted into a band of men whose bonds were already forged in the heat of combat.

Draude tried the buddy system, assigning new guys to someone with experience so they weren't ostracized. Before he had a chance to go through that routine with one new replacement, the company found itself in a fierce firefight, and Draude saw the young lance corporal off by himself, an unknown quantity from which the other men unconsciously shrank under fire. He ran over to the man.

"Don't worry, Corporal Martin, you just hang in there and we'll get you through this!" Draude had shouted over the noise and confusion. Though he forgot about the incident, the young corporal came to Draude later to offer his thanks.

"It was no big deal, Corporal," Draude had said when reminded.

"It was a big deal to me, sir," the young Marine replied. "Don't you understand? You knew my name. *You knew my name.*"

Draude was both shocked at the Marine's words and dumbfounded by the simplicity of it. Can that be all that it takes? he wondered. Here was a teenager who had since proven himself willing to lay down his life for Draude's company, and all he needed in return was the assurance that first day that if he had been killed, somebody would have known who he was. Yet under their new replacement system, it was becoming increasingly hard to guarantee a Marine even that he wouldn't die among strangers.

When a *Newsweek* reporter visited Draude's company in the field one week, he sat down with the young company commander and asked what he had learned about fighting the Viet Cong, and what was the key to success from a grunt's ground-eye view. Time and again, Draude explained, his company revisited a village only to find that a hamlet chief who had previously cooperated with them had been murdered by the Viet Cong. Yet rather than establishing a stable presence in the villages, the Marines were increasingly ordered by MACV headquarters to conduct major, far-flung "search and destroy" operations. "I believe if we could just get the people on our side, we might be all right," Draude told the reporter.

By March of 1966, Capt. James "Mike" Myatt, company commander of the 1st Battalion, 4th Marines, could practically tell without asking when a commander or one of his own men was about to rotate out of South Vietnam. It was just about the time they started to show signs of knowing what the hell they were doing. There were telltale indicators, like a battalion commander sniffing out an ambush and refusing to impatiently order Myatt's company down one of the fast-track trails so favored as VC kill sacks, or a Marine smearing a booby-trap trip wire with black greasepaint to hide it from "Charlie" and give him back some of his own bitter medicine. Oh, yeah, fieldcraft was a sure sign that someone was getting short all right.

As part of the first contingent of ground troops to deploy to South Vietnam to protect the air base at Da Nang back in May of 1965, Myatt was also one of the last of that original group still in-country. He thus witnessed firsthand the full effect of the new rotation policy the Pentagon instituted for Vietnam.

Somewhere in the transition from technological high ground to the primeval jungles of Vietnam, it seemed, the military strategists had lost sight of a fundamental truth of war: combat was not just a particularly toxic form of shift work to which soldiers could be rotated in assembly-line fashion. Men in battle did not fight for a paycheck, the flag, or apple pie. They did not fight for Mom. They fought and died for each other.

The constant reshuffling was wreaking havoc with that critical bonding of men under fire. The individual replacement system was actually a refinement of the point system adopted in Korea, where American soldiers accumulated points for time served in combat units. Facing a limited war with nearly unlimited resources and mobility, the Pentagon devised the DEROS-based system to counter the "combat fatigue" that had afflicted some units in both World War II and Korea.

A number of prominent military psychiatrists who had served during World War II, however, warned that thrusting random replacements into combat units would have catastrophic consequences, arguing that it would be better to pull units out to regroup. Experience had shown that constant, helter-skelter rotations could disrupt the crucial bonding that men experience under fire, ties that help emotionally anchor them in the brutal tempest of war. The Pentagon, however, stuck with DEROS, for it had other advantages besides limiting combat exposure. By keeping each soldier's tour of duty in South Vietnam to 365 days, it helped discourage pressure in the United States to "bring the boys home."

Only a month from rotating back home himself, Myatt often wondered at the constant shuffling and turmoil that characterized his battalion in the spring of 1966. Looking around, he hardly recognized a single face from the unit he had trained with back in Hawaii. Instead of the brothers in arms he had fought, suffered, and bled with for nearly a year, he saw instead a seething crowd of new acquaintances constantly fed by the replacement turnstile, a mishmash of short-timers, middle-distancers, and what they were already calling FNGs—fucking new guys. And every one of them had mainly time on his mind.

It was unrecognizable as the Corps he had wanted to join ever since he was a kid and his cousins worked as barbers at Camp Pendleton, California. Watching them shear the young teenagers, the first and most visible chisel stroke in the painstaking process of sculpting Marines, he had dreamed of sitting in that chair one day. So after graduating with a degree in physics from Sam Houston State in Huntsville, Texas, Myatt had decided to postpone his career with NASA for a four-year stint with the Marine Corps. The close-knit camaraderie of the Marines he joined on his first assignment with the 1st Marine Brigade in Hawaii, where tours lasted three years and the crusty noncoms seemed blasted out of the volcanic earth itself, had prompted Mike Myatt to consider making a life in the Corps.

The first disruptions caused by the individual replacement system began only a few months after they had arrived at Chu Lai. Because they could not afford to have an entire battalion reach its DEROS date and leave in mass, officials moved rifle companies such as Myatt's around so that the rotation date of personnel within a battalion would be staggered. Later in the fall came the constant rotation of individual replacements for casualties and those on sick leave.

Myatt soon discovered that it took weeks for the new replacements to acclimate themselves even to the weather and routine in the field, and many more weeks of training to fuse to the point where their squads and platoons could operate as a smoothly functioning whole, without anyone having to stop and ask questions or make a potentially fatal mistake in the field. In the meantime, each new group of replacements further diluted the company's experience, the lifeblood of an infantry line company.

In January, the first of the rotational humps had begun, and Myatt felt the full impact while watching a third of the remaining men with whom he had deployed pack their bags. Another third left the following month. Watching those friends and familiar faces leave, Myatt wondered why his commanders couldn't see what this was doing to the fabric of the Marine Corps. Maybe if he had been allowed to pull his company out of combat to train with each new wave of replacements, get acquainted in the rear rather than on the battlefield, it might not have seemed so disruptive. But he wasn't. Instead, on March 17, Myatt was ordered to form up with a wave of week-old replacements for a battalion-sized operation dubbed Oregon. Sometimes in the midst of all the shuffling it seemed as if the only constant were the ever-watchful Viet Cong.

The battalion commander for Operation Oregon was the fourth Myatt had served under since arriving in South Vietnam. With each of the services pouring forces into South Vietnam for what surely promised to be a short conflict given the amount of American troops and firepower streaming into the country and the early successes, the Pentagon decided that commanders would rotate through units every six months. That would give the maximum number of officers combat-command experience, practically a guaranteed ticket to fast-track promotions. It was, as one general later put it, almost as if the services were using Vietnam to train officers for the next war, as opposed to fighting the one very much at hand.

The morning of March 20, Myatt and the rest of his company stood stamping their feet to shake out the chill of a heavy mist. The battalion was to be inserted by helicopter into a target area in the coastal plains just north of Phong Dien to clear a pair of hamlets where intelligence placed part of the Viet Cong 802nd battalion. Two hours they waited, muttering, eyeing the evil fog, until finally the order was given to load up. Inside, the Hueys were caverns of whirling noise and wind that drowned out most conversation. As the helicopters swept under a low cloud ceiling, Myatt saw a marshy coastal plain dotted with flooded rice paddies and small streams and inlets. A few miles to the left the horizon was broken by the clearly visible ribbon of Route 1, the main north-south artery in northern I Corps. Just to the right was Pha Tam Giang bay. Beyond that the sea.

As they approached the landing zone, Myatt felt a jolt and the helicopter pitched crazily, pulling hard left. Everything inside clenched like a fist as they half-expected to feel rather than hear the familiar, sickening thud of bullets hitting the underside of the aircraft.

"Hot LZ! We have a hot LZ," the pilot shouted into his radio set.

The helicopters pulled back out of range of the antiaircraft guns. Soon, Marine Corps aircraft swept in under the clouds to strafe and bomb the area and soften up the landing zone. Charlie knew they would be coming now, the worst omen of all.

Just after noon the helicopters finally touched down, and Myatt's Alpha Company poured out in liquid motion, everyone running for cover to secure a perimeter around the landing zone. It always felt better once you were moving. There was no firing, and after Company B landed without incident, Myatt's company was instructed to advance on a small tree-shrouded hamlet of straw huts some eight hundred meters away. Myatt gave the order and the Marines began to move, fanning out and picking their way across the rice paddy that surrounded the village.

What was Charlie up to? The antiaircraft positions meant he had something to hide, but where? Someone to Myatt's left shouted, "VC!" and then he heard a burst of automatic-weapons fire from his company. He just made out two black pajama figures running into heavy brush beside the village.

Then all hell broke loose. The village erupted into an angry, flickering nest of muzzle flashes as Myatt saw two of his Marines go down in a spray of water, and everyone dove behind the rice-paddy dikes. Over the din, Myatt heard the unmistakable growl of heavy .50-caliber machine guns. This was no band of stragglers. They were pinned down in a kill sack. As he tried to raise the battalion commander on the radio, Myatt heard the wet impact of the .50-caliber slugs tearing right through the earthen dike, saw a Marine's head explode in a red mist.

Shell bursts from mortar fire began to probe their positions, and the screams of wounded and dying Marines lent their voices to the incredible din of battle. Myatt was hoping that Bravo Company would maneuver around and flank the village, but he soon saw that they were ordered up into the rice paddies just on his left flank. He couldn't believe it, but once in place, both companies were ordered to push ahead directly into the withering fire.

Their advance was halted again when one of Bravo's Marines tripped a mine. They were in a minefield. After repeated attempts to break forward met only with more casualties, Myatt was finally given the okay to fall back. His company was in pandemonium. Squad leaders who should have been able to communicate with their men with simple hand gestures were forced to try to yell over the roar of battle at their new replacements. Dragging and carrying their wounded and dying, the two companies waded back under covering fire from artillery batteries.

Unknown to the Marines, three infantry companies from the VC 892nd battalion, including one heavy-weapons group, had carefully camouflaged heavily fortified bunkers with straw huts. The hamlet was then surrounded with barbed wire and a minefield, and carefully calculated fields of fire were laid out. The VC had then simply waited for the Americans to come to them.

Late that afternoon, Myatt shook his head in confounded amazement when they were ordered again to attack into the teeth of the VC defenses. The battalion commander was apparently convinced that air strikes and naval gunfire had sufficiently weakened the resistance, and he had reinforced the decimated Alpha and Bravo with a third company. Myatt simply couldn't believe that there would be no attempt to flank the enemy, and he would instead have to again order his men into a no-win slugging match, fighting in the muck of rice paddies against a well-dug-in foe. It was the most unimaginative kind of attrition warfare.

By nightfall Myatt felt a weariness and anger that was beyond exhaustion. The Viet Cong had repulsed their continued assaults, and the attack was finally called off. The next day the Marines took the hamlet against only minor resistance. Under the cloak of darkness, the main VC force had abandoned the hamlet, their mission accomplished.

In shifting strategies in 1966 to avoid direct confrontations with the superior firepower and mobility of American forces, North Vietnamese general Vo Nguyen Giap had set as a goal the destruction of American morale. He called for his forces to kill or disable fifty thousand American troops, whenever possible with hit-and-run tactics. After the battle for an obscure hamlet, Giap was closer to his goal by a factor of fifty-six young Marines.

The Marines had forty-eight confirmed enemy dead and eight prisoners to show for what had become one of the battalion's fiercest and bloodiest engagements. All of the casualties of Operation Oregon, which lasted four days, fell in the watery rice paddies surrounding Ap Chinh An. Forty-five were wounded, many seriously. Myatt and the other company commanders had to collect the dog tags of eleven Marines who would never return to their families, some of whom they didn't even yet know by name.

By way of explanation, the battalion commander, Lt. Col. Ralph Sullivan, pointed out that they had encountered a seasoned and well-trained foe. "The tactics they utilized were not uncommon to good soldiering," he said. What struck some of the more experienced Marines was the notion that this would come as some sort of revelation. What about our training? thought Myatt. What about our tactics?

4: Find, Fix, Destroy 1966

THE monsoon rains were falling so heavily in August of 1966 that Army major Jack Galvin could see the other helicopters in his air assault trailing wakes as they sliced through nearly solid sheets of water. The 1st Infantry Division had been hopping around War Zone C north of Saigon for months looking for fights, conducting air-mobile searches for the elusive 9th Viet Cong Division.

Air assaults, mobile searches, movement to contact, movement for the sheer sake of movement. Even on the sketchiest intelligence, 1st Infantry units would clamber into their helicopters and move out. With the concept of air-mobile operations by helicopter still in its relative infancy, the commander of the 1st Infantry wanted a division that was mentally mobile, and being airborne undeniably facilitated that mind-set. Whenever an enemy main-force unit was located during searches, they would pour as many battalions into the fight as quickly as possible, piling on and destroying the enemy with superior American mobility and firepower. In 1966, the timbre of U.S. war fighting in South Vietnam was being tuned in the famed Big Red One.

After the helicopters landed along a sodden jungle riverbank, the 1st Brigade encircled a suspected enemy base camp and a brief firefight erupted. As the brigade operations officer, Galvin was responsible for calling in air and artillery support for the operation. The division's artillery support tactics were to pour rounds into a "fire box" that surrounded the engagement, hoping to catch unseen enemy forces either reinforcing or withdrawing into the jungle. It sometimes worked, but the tactic also chewed up a lot of Vietnamese countryside. The 1st Division soon earned a reputation for an especially liberal use of firepower, a tactic that alienated many South Vietnamese yet was also increasingly coming to characterize U.S. operations.

When the firing stopped, there was considerable grumbling. Advance units discovered that most of the enemy had escaped their encirclement. The fact was, the 9th VC was proving more elusive than anyone had expected, and frustrations and tempers were running high in 1st Infantry ranks in the soggy month of August. As corpsmen loaded casualties into the helicopters, Galvin wondered once again why the hell they were crashing around the jungle to get into a bayonet fight with these guys, rather than setting up ambushes on infiltration routes and letting the Viet Cong walk into them.

"Why don't we try ambushing him for a while, since he's the guy who's trying to take over the country," Galvin tentatively argued back at the Tactical Operations Center, broaching what had become a sore subject.

"Why don't you wait until you've been around long enough to see that's not the way to go," a staff officer shot back. "We're the ones with the firepower and the mobility." The man's expression filled in for what was left unsaid, which was that only a wimp would even make Galvin's suggestion.

A slight man with glasses and a rumpled look, Jack Galvin certainly didn't look the image of gung ho airborne. In fact, Galvin was an anomaly in more ways than one. The son of a Massachusetts bricklayer, he had dreamed of becoming a cartoonist. He made it as far as art school, then the money had started running out, and Galvin joined the National Guard as a way to earn some extra cash. The application to West Point had been a lark suggested by his sergeant.

After becoming the first in his family to graduate college, however, Galvin went on to complete his master's degree. He even wrote a book on the American Revolution. From the beginning of his Army life, however, he most thrived on the responsibility thrust on young line officers. Before he made captain, Galvin had already commanded two airborne rifle companies. Now he was getting a chance to serve in combat with the Big Red One. Jack Galvin seemed launched on a stellar Army career.

The 1st Infantry had a well-earned reputation for being a tough fighting unit. Word had it that the division operations officer, Col. Al Haig, had as a battalion commander in the division perfected some new night-ambush techniques. Col. Paul Gorman, Jr., who commanded a battalion in Galvin's 1st Brigade, was a noted combat veteran from the Korean War, where he had reportedly fought in the famed retreat from the Yalu River. Galvin had noted that the quiet and unassuming Gorman was missing the ring finger from his left hand. At West Point, where Gorman had taught, it was rumored that the Chinese had overrun his position, and mistaking Gorman for dead, had cut the finger off to get his Academy ring.

Of course, divisions took much of their reputation from their commanders, and the 1st Infantry's was known as one of the toughest and most savvy officers in the Army. Already he had been in Vietnam for two years, serving in the influential position of Gen. William Westmoreland's director of operations at MACV headquarters in Saigon. It was while at MACV that the general had helped develop the tactics coming to govern U.S. operations, and he was intent on making the 1st Infantry Division the key instrument of "search and destroy." Before the end of August 1966, however, Jack Galvin would have reason to wish he had never met the legendary Maj. Gen. William DePuy.

DePuy had grown up on the Depression-blighted banks of the James River in North Dakota, the only child of a country banker of French Huguenot descent, and a mother with Scotch-Irish roots whose family emigrated from Canada. It was a land of long, bitter winters and short summers, frequently plagued by locusts and drought. The people of Jamestown, many of them German and Scandinavian immigrants, tended to reflect the land they had settled: simple, straightforward, rugged.

Fascinated by the military, the young Bill DePuy had enrolled in ROTC during an undistinguished career at South Dakota State College. If World War II hadn't interrupted his plans, DePuy would probably have followed his father into banking.

As a young officer, DePuy had joined the 357th Infantry Regiment of the 90th Division. The traumatic weeks that followed the D-day landing of the 90th on Utah Beach, when the poorly trained and untested division fought the Germans across the hedgerows of France, scarred DePuy for life.

In that short time, the fighting chewed the 90th up at a stunning rate. Casualties in some infantry units of the 90th Division such as DePuy's ran higher than *300 percent*, and the life expectancy of a lieutenant commanding a rifle platoon was just over two weeks. Two division, two regimental, and three battalion commanders were relieved during the fighting, and only after officers who were promoted in the field assumed command did the division's fortunes improve.

Before the war in Europe was over, DePuy would earn a reputation as an officer coolheaded in combat and courageous, and he would win three Silver Stars. There were also stories of a tough son of a bitch who one night went so far as forcing his men into boats at pistol point for a contested crossing of the Saar River.

Steeped in those experiences of World War II, William DePuy had arrived at MACV headquarters in Saigon while the deployment of U.S. troops was still a stopgap measure to blunt the Viet Cong offensives. Beyond that, the Army lacked a clear doctrine for fighting a counterinsurgency war. DePuy, Westmoreland, and the MACV staff thus began working to develop a plan that would play to the Army's traditional strengths of aggressiveness, mobility, and overwhelming firepower.

The strategy called for major U.S. operations to "find, fix, and destroy enemy forces and base areas." In a division of labor, ARVN units would be shifted to the role of clearing small bands of Viet Cong out of areas after these large-scale "search and destroy" operations were completed. Under search and destroy, the brunt of the fighting would thus shift inexorably to the Americans.

Gen. William DePuy was well aware of the controversy surrounding those aggressive tactics. During three weeks of bloody and desperate fighting in the remote Ia Drang Valley in October 1965, the 1st Air Cavalry had engaged and eventually routed three NVA regiments, but Americans officially killed in action numbered 240, with many more wounded. Army chief of staff Gen. Harold Johnson clearly thought that he was sending the 1st Division out to practice counterinsurgency, clearing areas, securing villages, pacifying the countryside through civic-action programs. DePuy was of a different mind, however, and he was confident that his search-and-destroy operations were consistent with the intent of his direct commander, Gen. William Westmoreland.

Officers in the 1st Infantry Division were expected to reflect DePuy's hunger for action. "I will never, ever hear again over the radio, 'I'm pinned down. I'm breaking contact.' I hear it, that officer is relieved immediately," DePuy told the gathered officers of the Big Red One right after taking command. "You're never pinned down. Period."

The 1st Infantry Division's area of operations was largely jungle, where traditional Army doctrine of taking high ground or flanking maneuvers meant little. The name of the game in Vietnam, as DePuy saw it, was thus to make contact with the enemy, and that often required sending small units out to probe so as not to scare off the Viet Cong. At that point he meant to use superior American mobility and firepower to close in and destroy the enemy. Unfortunately, only roughly half of the time did firefights last long enough for the U.S. troops to call in tactical air and fire support and thus bring their superior firepower to bear.

For the small probing units that made initial contact, search and destroy frequently meant stumbling into a kill zone, then falling back and defending for dear life. Patrolling in inaccessible terrain, fighting at a time and place of the enemy's choosing, they were often cut off in remote areas until help could eventually arrive. While the tactic kept the 9th VC Division largely on the defensive in the jungles and away from populated areas, the cost in lives of 1st Infantry soldiers was high.

In April, those baiting tactics resulted in nearly an entire company being wiped out in the battle of Xa Cam My in Phuc Toy Province. The after-action report of that battle listed thirty-six killed and seventy-one wounded in "Charlie" Company, or a casualty rate of 80 percent. Shortly after the bloody Easter battle, Chief of Staff Gen. Harold Johnson had visited DePuy at his headquarters in Lai Khe. "You know," Johnson warned DePuy, "the American people won't support this war if we keep having the kind of casualties suffered by Charlie Company."

While DePuy agreed that it was regrettable, he was undeterred. If they were going to be aggressive with search and destroy, he felt that episodes like Phuc Toy were probably inevitable. Aggressive commanders thus prospered in the 1st Infantry under DePuy, and the division became a magnet for talented officers.

For those officers who didn't see things DePuy's way, however, or who he believed revealed a lack of the right stuff for combat, the 1st Infantry Division was a notorious career-breaker. Remarkably, in a single year in command he would relieve seven battalion commanders and many more division staff officers. In such matters, Gen. William DePuy had supreme confidence in his judgment, and it was little tempered by self-doubt or introspection. In that, too, as in so many other ways, he was at least an imperfect reflection of the Army whose fortunes and his would be so fatefully intertwined in the decade to come.

From the brigade command helicopter, Maj. Jack Galvin was trying to make sense of a radio network flooded with frantic voices. A cavalry troop commander sounded as if he might have cracked, and a platoon leader was plaintively calling for help: "I'm the only man left in the platoon." One battalion commander had apparently been killed, and Col. Paul Gorman was urgently requesting an air strike. A company commander on the division net kept repeating that he was in contact with something big.

It was an entire Viet Cong battalion of more than five hundred soldiers. This time the first U.S. patrol had walked into the middle of its bunker complex in heavy jungle, and the occupants were at home. A company had immediately gone in to try to rescue the patrol, and a battalion to reinforce the company. Then much of the 1st Infantry had piled into the fray, attempting to encircle and crush the heavily engaged VC battalion.

Paul Gorman's battalion, the 1st of the 26th Infantry, came in from the south. "Goony" Wallace's 1st Battalion, 16th Infantry, came across country from Lai Khe. Elmer Pendleton's 2nd of the 28th Infantry came in from the north to block the VC escape. And as the units tried to pull their ragged noose around the neck of the Viet Cong, savage fighting erupted.

As his helicopter circled above the melee, Galvin listened as Colonel Gorman urgently repeated his request for a napalm strike. Speaking over the command radio network, Galvin told the battalion commander to pop a smoke marker. When he thought he had the spot, Galvin directed the air strike on coordinates just south of the smoke. Moments later 7th Air Force aircraft made a low pass, napalm canisters tumbling out of their underbellies. Galvin noted with alarm that the smoke had already drifted, mingling above the treetops with the smoke of combat so that he had lost Gorman's position.

In the clearing below, Paul Gorman was poring over a map. Some of the soldiers in the area, however, had looked up at the sound of aircraft and watched the napalm pods as they were jettisoned. It looked as if it was going to be a close call. Sailing above their heads, one of the canisters hit a large tree and did an almost ninety-degree turn in their direction. The next instant the entire clearing was swept by a blinding fireball that incinerated the map right out of Paul Gorman's hands.

From the sense of uncertainty he felt watching the smoke marker drift, Galvin suspected that he had screwed up badly. That sinking fear was apparently confirmed when at the initial explosion of napalm below, Gorman's radio immediately went dead. Maj. Jack Galvin felt nauseous at the thought that he had called an air strike down on top of his own battalion and probably killed Colonel Gorman. Galvin also remembered that August 25, 1966, was Paul Gorman's thirty-ninth birthday.

A few days later, the battleground looked like a scene from an uncharted ring of hell. Acrid smoke still hung in pockets in the tree boughs, and many of the bodies wore charred, frozen masks of death. Green, rubberized body bags lay in rows. Jack Galvin was helping to count the enemy dead and police up the area. While casualties had been high on both sides, the main force of Viet Cong had escaped their encirclement in the confusion of battle.

After initial reports that the errant napalm strike had killed as many as forty 1st Division soldiers, it turned out the blast had apparently cost some prisoners their lives, but apparently none of the American soldiers. Paul Gorman was not seriously hurt. There was that much, at least, for Galvin to be thankful for.

While he was surveying the horrifying scene, a senior officer came up and told Galvin to add forty-five dead VC to his count. When asked from where, the man distractedly indicated an area that Galvin had already counted.

In a war with no front and with few decisive battles with major enemy units, McNamara's Pentagon had devised a series of statistical indicators such as body counts to chart progress. Some of the American troops felt body counts came uncomfortably close to turning them into bounty hunters. In fact, once punched into computers and displayed on bar graphs and briefing charts, indices such as body counts could be construed as showing marked progress in a war where none really existed.

Looking around the clearing and at his senior officer, Galvin knew that he was being asked to help make this battle look like a success. Whatever it was that had happened there on August 25, Galvin couldn't bring himself to see it as a success.

"Sir, I counted those bodies already," said Galvin.

"Not the ones I'm talking about," the man replied. "Now call them in."

Jack Galvin handed his superior officer the radio handset. "No, sir. You can call them in."

Maj. Gen. William DePuy was not a man given to mea culpas. Later he would profess, however, that his biggest surprise of the war was the will of the Viet Cong and the North Vietnamese to continue fighting despite the terrible punishment the U.S. military inflicted on them. He was also surprised at their uncanny elusiveness and ability to meter out casualties until the odds were no longer in their favor, and then to melt away into the countryside or across the Cambodian border where the United States allowed them sanctuary.

The frustrations of fighting an enemy who was usually deciding whether or not there would even be a fight was growing, and some of the seeds of that bitter enlightenment were undoubtedly planted on August 25. DePuy remembered it simply as "the day I presided over this very gory and unsuccessful operation. The VC made monkeys of us."

Jack Galvin would also long remember the Battle of August 25th. The day after the body count, he was summoned by a senior officer and summarily fired. Apparently the dismissal had the full support of General DePuy.

"Major, this combination is simply not working out. You've got to go," the man said.

Galvin felt as if he had been kicked in the stomach. One screwup on an air strike, and he was being told point-blank that he didn't have what it took to lead men in combat.

"Go where, sir?"

"Major Galvin, I'm telling you that there's no place for you in the First Infantry Division."

After having fought for nearly forty straight days with the division, Galvin felt drained and traumatized as he left. He had never thought of himself as a failure before, and it was going to take some getting used to. Of one thing he was reasonably sure. There was no way an Army officer could recover from this.

5: Red River Rats 1967

THE jagged, cobalt blue mountains that ring Nellis Air Force Base and separate nearby Las Vegas from the desolate expanse of the Great Basin to the north were tipped with fire. Only in rising and setting did the sun bleed any color into the desert. Night brought a bone-chilling darkness made even deeper by the flinty sparkle of countless stars, and by day the sun drained the landscape of everything but a white, opaque heat. Only in the brief interlude between the two extremes was the full palette of the desert revealed.

Watching the sunrise while he sipped hot, weak coffee, Capt. Chuck Horner felt his stomach start to sour at the prospect of the coming day. A line of F-105s were taxiing cautiously down the flight line outside the window of the mobile control shack, their hulking shapes outlined in the half-light. As he looked on, ready to grade landings and make sure none of the student pilots somehow overran the runway and took out a crap game in one of the juke joints that surrounded the base, it occurred to Horner that he hated instructing almost as much as he loved flying.

Normally he would have been in better spirits, for Horner stood on hallowed ground. To the casual observer the area was habitat primarily to the family of poisonous sacks—from the Great Basin rattler and desert iguana to the horny toad and the hairy tarantula. But this was also the undisputed home of the North American fighter pilot.

While others looked north across the Great Basin and saw the most inhospitable stretch of nowhere in the Northern Hemisphere, Air Force pilots saw

God's own gunnery range. They realized instantly that little havoc they could wreak on this land could compare with the desolation that had been heaped on by His hand. All of the Air Force legends who stalked MiG Alley during the Korean War had learned their moves out over the Great Basin—John Boyd, Ed Negrowsky, Fredrick "Boots" Blesse—all of them.

No, it wasn't the posting to Nellis, but rather the instructing that was bothering Chuck Horner. Teaching a particularly talented student was gratifying, but it didn't make up for the others. The bad ones or the simply slow brought out Horner's temper, and he would just as soon not have to confront this side of himself on a daily basis. No matter how many times he swore a silent oath of patience, sooner or later he found himself shouting and screaming at them, then feeling bad about it later. And given the rate they were rushing student pilots through training in May of 1967, there was really no time to separate the good from the bad. That would be left to the war.

In the year he had been an F-105 instructor pilot at Nellis, they had washed out a grand total of one pilot. That contrasted with Horner's own class of 1959, from which half the class failed to make the cut. The kid who flunked out in 1967 had been a hopeless stick man, but that was no longer enough to deny a pilot a cockpit. The instructors had eventually washed him out on a medical discharge and probably saved his life, and the healthy ones who had no business in the cockpit they sent off to die. It seemed like a crazy way to run a war, at least to Chuck Horner. And sometimes without warning the anger just bubbled out of him.

Finding themselves embroiled in an extended conventional war for which they had not planned, both the Air Force and the Navy had struggled since 1965 with acute shortages in everything from bombs to aircraft. Because they required eighteen months and roughly $100,000 to train, however, pilots were by far the most difficult shortage to fill. The problem became even more acute after the Defense Department modified its DEROS system so that a combat pilot would rotate home after flying one hundred missions or serving a year in Southeast Asia, whichever came first. That served the dual purposes of cutting the stress for pilots who were in some cases flying as many as two missions a day, and also diluting the "Bring our boys home" chorus that was steadily growing in volume.

Fighter pilots such as Horner initially accepted the rationalization that to fill the immediate gap early in the war, the services had to pluck qualified pilots from anywhere they could find them. After a time it became clear, however, that this was just another ticket-punching exercise, a chance to give everyone a crack at the only war going and fill out the résumé. Much as the Army had decided to rotate officers through combat commands every six months to maximize their chances for advancement, so, too, was the Air Force shuffling just about every pilot who could read an eye chart through Vietnam. So along with running abbreviated training courses for absolutely green student pilots, the fighter instructors at Nellis were also giving brief orientation instruction to pilots transitioning from bombers, tankers, and military transports, as well as slow-flying reconnaissance aircraft.

What really burned the fighter-pilot brethren was that with few exceptions, none of them could return for a second tour in what was essentially a fighter-bomber war until everyone else had had a chance to go at least once. From the viewpoint of the exalted fighter-pilot psyche, that was analogous to giving a crash course in race-car driving to bus drivers, commuters, and students with learning permits, then sitting in the pits while they ran the Indy 500. God knows Horner had volunteered to go back every chance he got and had just about worn out his welcome at the assignments desk back at Tactical Air Command headquarters at Langley Air Force Base, Virginia. The answer was always the same: they needed him at Nellis to pass on his combat experience to the young student pilots.

Yet Horner knew that the training going on at Nellis bore little if any resemblance to his combat experience, even had he time to share it. In fact, two years into the war the Air Force had done little to alter its fighter-pilot training syllabus, except to streamline it. The policy that air-to-air training between different types of aircraft was too dangerous, which had seemed merely bureaucratic folly before the war, assumed an almost cosmic absurdity given that in the last four months of the previous year 192 Air Force planes were intercepted by decidedly dissimilar MiGs piloted by North Vietnamese with murder in their eyes.

For combat veterans, the absurdity gave the flight line a *Through the Looking-Glass* atmosphere, as if it were a reflection of a world where the Air Force really wasn't in the midst of a real war. Units alerted for deployment to Southeast Asia, for instance, had to certify that they were combat ready by qualifying for *nuclear bomb* delivery, the pilots practicing releasing the bomb in a fine, useless arc while they flew in the opposite direction. Try that in Vietnam with a 750-pounder and the pilot would be lucky to hit the right province. Meanwhile, given the abbreviated length of training courses, they were shipping new pilots off to war without ever having dropped a real bomb or having fired a live air-to-air missile. It was to be on-the-job training in combat, where fates other than a second chance awaited every slipup.

That left Horner and the other combat veterans trying to explain the unexplainable to the uninitiated; how the incredible pressures of aerial combat would transmute even the most fundamental tasks, as surely as g forces inside the cockpit could put an elephant's foot on your forehead and render impossible the simple act of lifting your flight helmet off the headrest. The problem was that few of the new pilots had time to master even the fundamentals.

Outside the mobile control center, the young pilots were going through touchdown/takeoff cycles, their wheels hardly hitting the ground before a blue flame spat out of the rear of the F-105 fuselage, thrusting it back into the air with a deafening roar that rattled the windows. Amidst the racket, Horner didn't notice that he had been joined by Al Lamb until he saw the pilot sidle up with a cup of coffee and a grin.

Horner knew that Lamb had just returned from Thailand to teach at Nellis's Fighter Weapons School, a sort of postgraduate school for fighter pilots. He used the opportunity to pepper Lamb with questions about how the war was going, especially for his Thailand-based friends. Though none of what he heard particularly surprised Horner, it took his mind off the day's instruction that lay ahead.

Ever since the first ill-fated attack on the SAMs that Horner had flown on back in the summer of 1965, the Air Force had searched for an effective counter to the growing legion of surface-to-air missiles supplied to North Vietnam primarily by the Soviet Union. They now surrounded key targets around Hanoi like quills on a porcupine's back. Added to the threat from MiGs and especially radar-controlled antiaircraft gunfire, the high-flying SAMs effectively denied the Air Force a reasonably safe attack profile. If pilots came in high, they often found themselves jettisoning their bomb loads prematurely to try to outmaneuver the missiles, and if they flew in low, they were vulnerable to conventional AAA fire, still the most dangerous threat to pilots. And whether high or low, pilots constantly had to crane their necks checking their tail for MiGs.

The most effective answer to date had been a recently modified aircraft designed specifically to search out and destroy SAM sites. The Air Force called it the Wild Weasel. These twin-seat F-105s were stuffed with electronic countermeasure (ECM) equipment and armed with Shrike air-to-ground missiles, whose radars were capable of honing in on a SAM radar. After the ECM equipment detected a SAM site, the Wild Weasel pilot was supposed to swoop in and launch a Shrike down its radar beam. Soon the North Vietnamese caught on to the tactic, however, and would only turn their radars on at the last minute before launch. At that point it became a deadly game of cat and mouse between SAM missile operators and Wild Weasel pilots, with the difference between the hunter and the hunted decided within the space of a few seconds of reaction time.

Because they were the first in on a strike mission and the last out of the target area, loitering over enemy air defenses while offering themselves as live bait, Wild Weasel pilots had a notoriously short life expectancy in 1967. In fact, because they were flying the bulk of the bombing strikes around Hanoi, F-105 "Thud" pilots in general were considered an endangered species even among Air Force fighter jocks. The new definition of an optimist, Lamb explained to Horner, was a Thud pilot who quit smoking because he was afraid of dying of cancer.

"Hell, I'd do anything to get back over there myself," Horner said in what had become a rote lament.

"Well, we're going through Weasel pilots so fast that my boss at the Weapons School has carte blanche over assignments," said Lamb, looking at Horner inquisitively. "But do you really want to go back over that bad?"

Horner glanced out the window, saw a student glide in for a passable landing while others taxied for takeoff. Almost without bidding his mind started to calculate the odds. Even as a Wild Weasel pilot, Horner knew, he had a much better chance of surviving than the young men he was supposed to be training for war in this assembly line. There was nothing rehearsed in his reply as he turned back to face Al Lamb.

"You bet I do."

Back at Korat, Horner hardly recognized it as the dilapidated collection of shacks he had first visited two years earlier. The hut that had originally been their officers' club was now used as a storage shed behind the new club. The twenty-man life raft that had served as their swimming pool had been replaced by the real thing, and all of the new barracks were air-conditioned.

Horner was even more surprised at the increasing number of the "River Rats"—the Air Force pilots who hopped the Red River on the way to targets near Hanoi—who were failing to make the return crossing. After suffering two years of sustained bombing, the North Vietnamese had made the Red River delta area surrounding Hanoi and Haiphong arguably the most heavily defended plot of real estate on earth.

Because virtually all of its strategic targets were clustered in this relatively small area, Hanoi was able to spin a tightly woven web of air defenses around itself and wait for the inevitable swarm of flies. The hills and surrounding delta lowlands bristled with over 7,000 antiaircraft guns, and between 120 and 180 mobile SAM missile launchers, most of them carefully camouflaged as clumps of trees.

Nor did the spider wait in the center of the web, but rather he roamed the perimeter in the form of a force of roughly one hundred MiGs. The increasing success of the MiG force was a growing concern, as North Vietnamese pilots became more experienced and aggressive and were flying against U.S. Air Force squadrons whose own experience level was constantly diluted by the influx of new pilots.

At the beginning of the air war Air Force pilots were shooting down four MiGs for every one of their aircraft lost, but by 1967 that ratio had dropped to the point where the Americans were losing one plane for every two MiGs they shot down. Both were a far cry from the days of the Korean War, when U.S. pilots logged twelve kills for every aircraft they lost.

The North Vietnamese had been helped appreciably by the introduction of the new Soviet-built MiG-21, a supersonic fighter armed with heat-seeking missiles that was more than a match for the F-4 Phantom, a fast but heavy Navy aircraft that was originally designed for rugged carrier takeoffs and landings. Phantom pilots also soon discovered that their AIM-9 air-to-air missiles, designed primarily for interceptors whose mission it would be to shoot down the Soviet's clumsy nuclear bombers, turned far too slow to be of much use in a close-in "knife fight."

Thus the percentage of U.S. aircraft losses attributable to MiGs continued to grow, from 3 percent in 1966 to 8 percent in 1967, headed for a high of 22 percent in the first three months of 1968.

The nearby base at Takhli was suffering the worst, and its pilots were riding the kind of bad-luck streak that could make Horner think twice before joining them at the bar, lest some of that evil karma rub off. It got so bad that a group of pilots from Takhli were forced to travel to Korat to borrow some Wild Weasels because all of theirs had been shot down. One pilot said that of the fifteen F-105 pilots who had shipped out with him to the 345th Tactical Fighter Squadron at Takhli, eight had been shot down within a few months of their arrival.

Horner was stunned to hear from the Takhli pilots that they were still flying primarily low-level tactics. Low-level attacks eliminated the SAM threat and minimized an aircraft's exposure over a target, and the ground rush gave pilots an illusion of security. But they exposed pilots to every man, woman, and child with an automatic weapon, and the North Vietnamese had quickly learned to throw up a wall of lead over an attack route and just let the pilots fly into it.

As for Chuck Horner, he remembered what low-level tactics had cost his squadron on the first SAM raid back in 1965, and it still left a bitter taste. What he couldn't understand was why after two years, some wing commanders still hadn't adjusted their tactics. At least the commander of Korat, Gen.

Bill Cheresell, insisted that his pilots fly medium-altitude attacks and trust to the new electronic jamming equipment that had been developed to thwart the inevitable surface-to-air missiles.

Meanwhile, whenever another experienced pilot from the old fighter Mafia was taken out, it chipped away further at the cloak of invincibility that Horner and the rest wrapped themselves in. Without that protection they were naked and vulnerable to all the normal fears and self-doubt, and given their line of work, there was simply no room in the cockpit for that particular baggage.

The younger ones who didn't make it back could easily be explained away as having lacked experience or training, or some undefinable something that was key to the righteous fighter-pilot psyche, but not so Jim "White Fang" Hardney or Don Hammond or Black Bart Barthelmous or Boots Boothby or a growing list of others. It was enough to keep you up at night.

The worst was the story behind his friend Jim Hardney. The two of them had flown together with the 4th Tactical Fighter Wing back at Seymour Johnson Air Base, North Carolina, and had transitioned to the Wild Weasel together before returning to Thailand. "White Fang" Hardney had been one of the good ones.

As the story came back to them, White Fang and his electronic weapons officer, or EWO, had ejected safely only to be captured by NVA regulars outside a small hamlet in North Vietnam. After roughing them up, the soldiers let the villagers form a gauntlet between the pilots and the Russian helicopter that was their ticket to the Hanoi Hilton. The EWO made it through and could only watch helplessly as the villagers stoned Jim Hardney to death.

Anyone lucky enough to be rescued after being shot down had made a significant withdrawal from a pilot's good-fortune account, and it was apt to change the way he viewed the rest of his stay in Thailand. The worst were the ones shot down early in their tours, with only a handful of missions under their belt. All they had to do was some simple arithmetic on their chances of making it to a hundred missions, and it always seemed to equal Ain't No Way.

One Thud pilot in Horner's wing had been shot down on his ninetieth mission, and when the helicopters brought him back, he was shaking and twitching so bad he was blurry. Just looking at him close was enough to make Horner rub his eyes. The pilot fortified himself so heavily for the final nine missions that a couple of times they had to help him up the ladder into his cockpit.

Watching the man practically disintegrate before his eyes, Horner had decided that the hundred-mission ceiling was as misguided as the rest of this war. It was one more numerical twitch, an end in itself in a war seemingly without end. But by God they had means galore: megasorties, massive strike packages, maximum production all around.

Whether you were short, long, or in-between, there was no question in any pilot's mind where he stood on the sliding scale of missions completed and months served, or that the overriding concern was simply to live long enough to see a calendar full of Xs. If anyone actually remembered coming over here to win a war, they were keeping a low profile. Sometimes it seemed as if it were just one more goal that had been sacrificed on the altar of numerology.

Not that the statistics weren't impressive. As 1967 was drawing to a close, the Air Force had more than sixty thousand personnel operating out of sixteen major air bases in Thailand, South Vietnam, and Guam. By the end of the year they would have dropped a total of 864,000 tons of bombs on the tiny country, or nearly 70 percent more than was dropped in the entire Pacific theater during World War II.

While their relentless bombardment had undoubtedly taken a heavy toll on North Vietnam's impoverished people and their economy, the pilots were also beginning to feel some of the arm weariness of the fighter whose opponent simply refuses to go down. And perhaps the most fitting symbol of that tenacious defiance was the Dragon's Jaw bridge.

The F-105 pilots at Korat had been attacking that span across the Song Ma River since April of 1965, trying to sever a vital link in North Vietnam's supply chain to the south. Despite hundreds of airplanes being sent against it in the intervening two years, however, blasting it with over ten thousand tons of explosives and scorching the surrounding area until it resembled nothing so much as a moonscape, still the Dragon's Jaw stood. The Dragon's Jaw would stand as a testament to North Vietnam's tenacity until 1972, when it would finally be destroyed by one of the new laser-guided "smart bombs."

What also hadn't changed significantly in the minds of the pilots were the myriad restricted zones that were off-limits to their attacks and the stinginess with which the White House seemed to dole out additional targets over North Vietnam. Hanoi was still mostly off-limits, and a similar restricted zone surrounded the harbor of Haiphong, through which most Soviet supplies to North Vietnam flowed. While they had inflicted massive destruction on North Vietnam's own war-making capability, as long as routes to apparently unlimited external supplies remained unimpeded, it really didn't seem to matter.

Unable to shut down the enemy's war-making infrastructure or staunch his supply lines, pilots in Thailand found themselves locked in a life-or-death struggle of attrition with North Vietnamese air-defense forces. And the Air Force was finding the North Vietnamese around Hanoi every bit as tenacious and willing to absorb incredible amounts of punishment as their comrades fighting U.S. ground forces in South Vietnam.

The bombing restrictions, the increasing losses of friends, the constant fatigue—all of it fed a growing sense of futility and frustration among the pilots. For Horner and many of the others, the war and the way they were fighting it had simply ceased to make any sense. And in the vacuum of logic, a certain lawlessness had crept in.

In Horner's case, the lawlessness manifested itself in a private war against a set of searchlights near Hanoi. The night before they had hit a series of ammunition dumps north of the city and, on the way back, had been painted by a bank of North Vietnamese searchlights and the inevitable arcing stream of tracers from nearby AAA sites. The searchlights weren't on the target list and Horner hadn't stopped to check if they were in a restricted zone. Rather, he had pulled his F-105 into a steep dive toward the bright lights.

Because they relied on a radar beam, his Shrike missiles had been useless, and Horner had already used up all his bombs. He had had to rely on his 20mm cannon to strafe the site. Caught blind in its glare, however, Horner had finally been forced to pull out of his dive before his gun could snuff out the lights, and he had just missed a cliff. That night he planned to have a surprise ready for the searchlight crew.

Thinking about the night's mission, Horner looked across the air-conditioned room he shared with his EWO, Dino Regalis. As usual, his partner was unwrapping a care package from his parents back in Chicago, and Horner could already smell the familiar pungent aroma of garlic. The two of them together smelled like a walking garlic pizza thanks to the recycled air in their room and had become the butt of many a joke from the other pilots on how it would take a pretty sorry bloodhound to miss them if they were ever unlucky enough to be downed over North Vietnam.

Knowing they were due for a preflight briefing on the night's mission soon, Horner told Regalis he'd see him in the briefing room. On the way he walked out to the flight line to have a chat with the crew loading the airplanes with armament.

He watched them go through their well-orchestrated routine for a few minutes.

"Hey, Chief! How about loading me a Sidewinder on the outboard station," Horner shouted.

"You bet, Captain," the crew chief replied instantly. If it occurred to the ground crew to wonder why a Wild Weasel pilot would want a heat-seeking missile that wasn't specified in the weapons load for that night's mission, they didn't let on.

As they were flying in inky darkness at twenty thousand feet on the way back from the bombing run, Horner took a slight detour over Yen Bai, where the searchlights had caught them the night before. If anything the night missions enhanced the sense of womblike isolation of the cockpit, and a lot of the pilots didn't like flying them. After the adrenal rush of the bombing mission, the loudest noise was the sound of Horner's breath in his face mask, beating time to a racing pulse. When he judged he was in the right area, Horner lit up the F-105's afterburner and held on as he banked the aircraft in a wide circle.

There they were! Alerted by the noise, the enemy ignited the bank of searchlights, probing the darkness with searing white tendrils. Again Horner nudged the stick over and the F-105 dropped out of the night sky directly toward the lights. Horner knew from the pitch in the Thunderchief's scream and the g-force pressure that they were coming in at a very steep angle of attack, and the aircraft vibrated and shuddered through the stick as the lights searched frantically for this new intruder. The beam of light caught him in its glare, blinding him, but still Horner dove. He had to make sure they were close enough for the heat-seeking AIM-9 Sidewinder to lock in on the light source. The aircraft shook violently, and finally he pickled off the missile and immediately pulled back on the stick with all his might.

Climbing out of the cockpit back at Korat, his flight suit soaked through, Horner reflected that the night's little vendetta was probably the dumbest thing he had pulled in his career. Dumber even than the time he had flown under his flight leader at Lackenheath just as the man was getting airborne, a stunt that had him practically brushing the runway with the belly of his F-105. Dumb as dirt.

The ground crew, however, was delighted. They were all back slaps and conspiratorial grins, and when they saw that Horner and Regalis had fired the AIM-9, they presented them with a bottle of Scotch. Horner didn't have the heart to tell them that he didn't even drink Scotch.

At the debriefing with the "Operations Annies" who collected data on each mission, Horner made no mention of the AIM-9 or the detour to Yen Bai. It was a little game that many of the pilots were playing now when they didn't want to get too specific about the targets that they really attacked.

"I released my armament at four thousand five hundred feet over the assigned target, doing four hundred fifty knots on a forty-five-degree dive angle," Horner repeated in a well-rehearsed litany. Even as he was mouthing the lie, it occurred to Horner that he didn't care anymore. You couldn't qualify it as a great victory, but it was something. Some son of a bitch had tried to kill him and his friends, and Horner had gotten to him first. Anyway, why should he feel bad? The first casualty of a war that made no sense was integrity.

6: Prodigal Soldier 1968–69

THE bungalow on Fernleaf in Corona del Mar that Barry and Jill McCaffrey had rented stood in a neat row of similar houses, the small, manicured yards and freshly painted fences bespeaking the comfortable wealth that the Newport Beach area was attracting out of Los Angeles in the fall of 1968.

They had chosen the area so Jill and the children could be close to her parents, who had retired to Newport before the aerospace executives and land speculators drove real estate prices forever out of the reach of a retired Army officer on a government pension. Even at that moment, Jill's father had the car running outside ready to drive Barry to the airport.

They had been through this before, and as Jill helped Barry gather his things, she tried to affect the old nonchalance. For the third time in almost as many years, she was sending him off to war. The first time, in what seemed like another life, she had literally prayed that he not be left behind.

Jill thought about their short life together, and about young Sean and Tara, who had hardly gotten to know their father. She thought about how her love for the vagabond Army life had diminished before the pervasive sense of uncertainty that now threatened to envelope them. She thought about answered prayers.

"I'll probably make you a rich woman after all," Barry McCaffrey said, and Jill laughed in spite of herself. With high jinks or low humor, he could always make her laugh. Yet the young couple knew that everything was different this time. Now that the moment had come to say good-bye again, all they could do to ward off the dread was to laugh about Barry's life insurance.

They had already talked it out in their matter-of-fact style, for it was the one discussion that no young infantry officer and his wife could avoid in

1968. In retrospect it almost seemed as if the United States' involvement in Vietnam and McCaffrey's West Point class had begun a sort of inevitable confluence in 1964, like two trains approaching on the same track in slow motion, the war beginning its massive escalation just in time for the West Point graduates to become the junior-grade officers who would, among the officers corps at least, bear the brunt of the war.

By 1968 catastrophe seemed imminent. Casualties for the first half of the previous year had suddenly nearly doubled, to an average of 816 Americans killed in action per month. That mounting death toll was fed in part by meat grinders such as Hill 875, where on Thanksgiving of 1967 U.S. troops were ordered time and again to take a hill of heavily fortified bunkers in the face of withering enemy fire, with a resulting toll of 158 American dead and 402 wounded; or Hills 861 and 881, equally worthless real estate that cost the Marine Corps nearly 200 dead and 800 wounded. The U.S. military's aggressive tactics of confronting the enemy wherever he could be found, on practically any terms, was reaping an increasingly bitter crop in American casualties.

Back home, Army wives kept mainly to themselves, playing bridge and raising kids, and wincing as if from a physical blow at every unannounced knock on the door. It had gotten to the point where no one dropped by a friend's house without calling first, lest their footsteps be mistaken for those of a priest and a stranger in uniform. By 1968, the lives of a lot of their friends had been shattered by the reverberations from that knock on the door.

It was a lifestyle apt to make a couple frank beyond their years. If he was killed, Barry McCaffrey would insist, Jill would be sad for a while, and then she would remarry and be happy again. And very rich thanks to his life insurance, at least by the standards of a young couple living with two children on an Army captain's salary. It was part of the pact that Jill had signed just as surely as her husband, and she would have to live up to it.

Yet it had never been like this. The young wives of 1968 who had no war to go off and fight, and no office on a military base to retreat to, lived lives suspended between an Army to whom they were wedded and a society that was becoming ever more strident in its rejection of the conflict and everything and everyone associated with it. Among their own generation Army wives of a certain age were outcasts. Certainly Jill McCaffrey had begun to feel that estrangement acutely, and it had made her not a little bitter.

What bothered Jill was not that her life seemed so separate and apart from others of her generation. It wasn't even so much the protests against the war spilling off college campuses into city streets all across the nation, though they were certainly getting more militant. No, what bothered Jill the most were the looks of dumbfounded amazement on the faces of young Southern Californians when they learned what her husband did for a living. How could anyone as seemingly normal as you, those shocked expressions would shout, be married to someone stupid enough to be sent to Vietnam?

Local draft boards were routinely granting deferments for college, for religious beliefs, even for those with "family hardship" or "critical occupational skills." Everyone knew there were also a host of ingenious ways to fail the preinduction physical exam, so many in fact that fully one-quarter of all prospective conscripts were disqualified for medical reasons. Certainly as a last resort, enlistment in the National Guard or Reserve was a surefire, if not totally convenient, avenue to avoiding Vietnam. Then, of course, there were the ethical issues to consider. Which was your husband, the young Southern Californians seemed to imply with their smug questions, mentally or morally deficient?

The only ones whom Jill found the least bit supportive were friends of her parents who had fought in World War II and Korea. At least their concern seemed sincere. Yet for all their words of kindness offered over cocktails during backyard barbecues, Jill knew that none of their children, the scions of Newport Beach affluence, would face the kind of parting that she and Barry were even then trying to make easier on each other.

Looking at her husband, his lean, angular face set off by the crew cut, she detected little of the mischievousness that usually lurked close to the surface of those dark Irish features. *Damn you*, she thought, you're going to make me a widow.

Having already been wounded in combat twice and decorated with the country's second-highest award for valor during his first tour in Vietnam as an adviser to the South Vietnamese Airborne, Barry McCaffrey was under no obligation, implied or otherwise, to return now. But then January 31, 1968, had changed everything. Launched in the early-morning hours to coincide with the Tet holidays, the explosive offensive by the Viet Cong and their North Vietnamese allies had badly shaken the Army and stunned the entire country. Just months before, Lyndon Johnson had recalled General Westmoreland to Washington to reassure an increasingly restless country that a victory was in sight. "I am absolutely certain that whereas in 1965 the enemy was winning, today he is certainly losing," an ebullient Westmoreland had told reporters at the National Press Club. "We have reached an important point where the end begins to come into view."

Instead, what came into view was the horrifying onslaught of Tet. Night after night McCaffrey had sat riveted in the glare of his television, watching the siege of the American embassy in Saigon, the shelling of General Westmoreland's headquarters, and the coordinated attacks on major cities, small hamlets, and military bases throughout South Vietnam.

Back channels, the military grapevine, buzzed with sometimes contradictory tales of how close Saigon had come to falling, or how the media had missed the real story that the Viet Cong had been dealt a blow during Tet from which they could never recover. There were stories of confusion and recriminations at the top command levels.

Throughout the turbulent spring and summer of 1968, McCaffrey had continued to watch and listen with a growing sense of unease. Tet had been followed in quick succession by the announcement that Lyndon Johnson would not run for reelection, and the assassination of Martin Luther King Jr., a tragedy that led to National Guard and regular Army troops battling rioters in fire-strewn ghettos around the country.

America's long-simmering racial tensions were coming to a boil both in society at large and inside the Army, and it couldn't have struck the military at a more vulnerable time. McCaffrey already knew something about Vietnam, and he was learning a lot about the Army as a microcosm of society, reflecting its strengths and sometimes magnifying its weaknesses. The conclusion he came to was that the Army was in dire trouble.

Barry McCaffrey reviewed his decision a last time, starting from what he knew and working backward. He knew that he was a good infantry soldier, and that he could not sit in a classroom droning on about military theory while the Army was engaged in this desperate struggle halfway around the world.

Yet the stories that now reached him through the Army's informal grapevine of friends and former classmates were nothing like the siren's song of adventure and glory that had nearly driven him to distraction as a young lieutenant, though somehow the effect was no less compelling. They were more like a constant voice in his ear that he couldn't silence, speaking simultaneously to his fears and his sense of duty, whispering about unfinished business.

Barry remembered his brother-in-law Dave Ragin, who even as a cadet at the Citadel had dreamed of one day becoming a general. Instead, Dave became the Army's first recipient of the Distinguished Service Cross in Vietnam, an award he received posthumously after being killed in an ambush in 1964. Ever since he himself was a plebe, Barry McCaffrey's view of his Army career had seemed to fade out around the rank of captain. Now, here he was, a captain flying back to Vietnam to take command of a company of the famed 1st Cavalry Division, and his vision of where his Army career was taking him still didn't stretch out much further. He had just caught up to it.

Sensing a familiar agitation, McCaffrey hugged his wife and quickly gathered up his gear. Her father was waiting. If the usual breeze was still blowing outside, he couldn't feel it as he stepped out the door, and the glare from an dazzling blue sky almost made him feel dizzy. Halfway to the car the voice was still there like a hot breath in his ear, and McCaffrey slowed and then put his bags down. And there in the groovy California sunshine, the same young man who had whooped with joy at the prospect of his first combat deployment, who had driven up the East Coast with a car full of boisterous paratroopers to volunteer for his first tour in Vietnam, this prodigal soldier bent slowly down and vomited all over the spotless sidewalk.

Nights in the jungle were filled with such a cacophony of chirping, snuffling, and buzzing that sometimes the loudest noise, the one that woke you up wide-eyed with a catch in your breath, was the sound of silence. Except for occasional forays to the rear for R&R, a tour with the 1st Cav was a shotgun marriage to the field, and Bravo Company had come to embrace nights in the wild highlands like sleep with a murderous spouse. It wasn't the tossing or turning or snoring that bothered you, but beware the stillness.

First Sgt. Emerson Trainer was awake before he willed it, and for a moment he lay still with his ears straining. Soon, however, he heard the comforting sounds of a camp beginning to stir to life. The silence he had imagined for a moment had been just one more trick in a jungle that had an inexhaustible supply, and each one could swallow you.

You're too old for this, Trainer thought, painfully aware that a thirty-nine-year-old first sergeant qualified as ancient. Vietnam had proven a foot soldier's war, and by 1969 the mounting casualties had decimated the noncommissioned officers corps, the seasoned heart of the Army's infantry. Those who weren't wounded or killed were turned around so fast to second or third tours that many of the lifers were opting out as soon as their reenlistments were up, unwilling to face another separation from their families. A Korean War veteran, Trainer was himself on a second tour in Vietnam in the space of a year.

It was the inevitable result of Lyndon Johnson's steadfast denial of requests by the Joint Chiefs that they be allowed to tap into the unused pool of experience in the National Guard and Army Reserve. Rather than mobilize the country for this war, they had relegated it to a steadily dwindling cadre of regular Army officers and noncoms and a constant influx of young teenagers. If anything, the new Nixon administration was even less inclined to consider a reserve call-up. The intent now was to hand the war over to South Vietnam through "Vietnamization" and begin troop withdrawals later that year.

The Army, meanwhile, was discovering that it could draft bodies, but it couldn't draft experience. Many staff sergeants in Vietnam in 1969 were thus no more than twenty-one years old, fresh graduates of the Non-Commissioned Officers Academy. The age of the average draftee in Vietnam, meanwhile, was only nineteen, significantly younger than the bulk of soldiers who had fought America's earlier wars. Trainer and his captain were practically the only two people in their company of roughly 125 troops who were regular Army as opposed to draftees, or for that matter were over the age of twenty-five. The thought of it depressed him. Despite having worn the uniform for twenty years, Emerson Trainer increasingly felt like a stranger in his own Army.

Many of the young draftees he led had grown up watching the demonstrations against the war for the past four years and had come of age in the midst of the expanding drug culture. In the field that was rarely a problem, and they fought as bravely as any group of young Americans ever had. But too many of those confined to rear-area bases fought off the boredom getting high and getting into trouble. Trainer could picture them, the indecipherable "dapping and rapping" handshakes of the black troops, the glassy-eyed stare of the reefer heads. It was in those sprawling rear-area bases, with their air-conditioned messes and movie theaters, that Trainer had the hardest time avoiding the question of exactly what the Americans were still doing in Vietnam.

Though the sun wasn't yet up, enough light came from above that as he lay in the jungle and looked up, Trainer could see the multilayered canopy of branches and leaves outlined above like rafters in some ancient cathedral. Just then the voice of the company commander was heard as he made his usual morning rounds. Trainer had declined a scheduled assignment to the rear largely because of his captain, whom he considered one of the scrappiest commanders he'd ever met. There were just some men you didn't leave in the middle of a fight.

"All right, fellas, it's another beautiful morning in Vietnam," the voice of Capt. Barry McCaffrey was heard throughout the camp, and many of the men had to suppress smiles as they crawled out of their blankets. "It looks like another good day to go out there and kill for God and country!"

·   ·   ·

On the morning of February 19, 1969, the three platoons of Bravo Company were spread out in a cloverleaf formation to insure that the entire company could quickly collapse in on and assist any platoon that came under fire. All of the men of the 2nd Battalion, 7th Cavalry, wore a patch depicting a saber raised for the charge. It complimented the distinctive yellow-and-black shoulder patch worn by everyone in the 1st Air Cav Division, with its horse's head in the right corner.

No insignia was worn with more pride in South Vietnam in 1969, when the 1st Cav became the first division to have fought in all four tactical zones in the country. Indeed, the tactics of the 1st Cav were built around the helicopter and mobility the way the 7th Cav was designed around the horse, and the joke around the outfit was that some of the flamboyant commanders would just as soon be leading a horse charge.

That kind of nose for trouble and yearning for engagement, however, rarely went unrequited for long in Vietnam. For weeks the 1st Cav Division had been fighting a blocking action against one of three NVA divisions as they moved down a series of jungle trails called the Surgis Jungle Highway. Their mission was to fight a series of holding actions, slowing the North Vietnamese advance and hopscotching backward by air to get in front of the enemy again. The time that North Vietnam had chosen for the coordinated series of attacks, and the size of this main force, left no doubt that Hanoi was intent on reestablishing the initiative in the war and disrupting Vietnamization. In the 1st Cav they called the interdiction mission simply "Tet '69."

The Surgis Jungle Highway was actually a trunk of interconnecting roads and trails funneling from the Cambodian frontier south toward Saigon, and the North Vietnamese and VC had long been at work on it. Camouflage netting hid most of the places where the network was exposed to the air, and the entire system was laced with hidden bunker complexes. In some cases they were empty and meant only to offer advancing units cover from surprise air and artillery strikes. Others were hidden away from the main trail network and contained supplies and arms caches. These were usually well guarded. The problem for the 1st Cav units was that they almost never knew whether the tenants were home or not, or in what force, until they stumbled on top of a complex.

First Sgt. Emerson Trainer was picking his way slowly through the dense underbrush in one platoon, stopping occasionally to bend down and search the jungle ahead from one knee. Sometimes a bunker that was invisible from head level could easily be spotted near the ground, where the North Vietnamese had cleared a field of fire for unsuspecting American patrols. That's when Trainer heard the staccato crack of an M16 rifle nearby, followed by a noise that had the entire platoon grabbing facefuls of dirt.

"*Bddrraaappppp!*" "*Bddddrraapppppppp!*" Not even the new recruits had to be told that the discordant sound was not one of theirs, but rather the distinctive belch of a Russian-made RPD light machine gun.

After monitoring the radio and realizing that the lead platoon had come under fire from hidden bunkers, Trainer and the rest of his platoon silently moved in on their flank. Falling in behind cover beside the first platoon, he saw the bodies of two Viet Cong in a small clearing. As he peered around a tree in the dappled light, bullets impacted on the mulchy ground nearby, and Trainer saw a tongue of lethal flame licking from within the dark mouth of a bunker. They would have to take him out. Trainer's breath was ragged in the suddenly stifling heat, and he felt himself tighten inside at the prospect of what came next.

The key was to identify all the bunkers so they were not surprised by flanking fire. Already the still air crackled and sizzled with automatic-weapons fire as if from an electric charge, and the acrid smell of cordite stung in men's nostrils. They would have to pin the bunker down, pouring in suppression fire long enough for someone to get close enough to toss in a fragmentary grenade. It was just a matter of who the charged electricity of combat ignited first, short-circuiting the complex neural network of survival instinct that would normally shut a man down a step before he dashed across the street in front of oncoming traffic or rushed a machine-gun nest.

Trainer leaned around the tree and squeezed off a burst of the M16 on automatic. As he jerked back behind cover, he caught movement out of the corner of his eye. An NVA troop carrying a machine gun had run from concealment and dropped into a bunker on their flank. Suddenly, just like that, they were in trouble.

Even before Trainer could order his men to move, another movement on the flank caught him by surprise. Then he was up emptying his rifle at the firing bunker for suppression, yelling over the din for his men to do the same. Sprinting through the trees to the right toward the flanking bunker was the captain himself, a grenade in his hand.

As he leapt on top of the bunker, McCaffrey's figure was almost obscured by a shower of foliage loosened by enemy fire, yet he tossed the grenade in the rear entrance and quickly leapt off. He might as well have tried tried to run through a monsoon squall without getting wet. A muffled explosion sent billowing smoke and dust out of the mouth of the bunker.

Trainer knew that he and the rest of the men would willingly follow the captain anywhere precisely because he led rather than commanded and always did more than his share as a rifleman. Still, every man in combat was as superstitious as a witch, and it never hurt morale to have a lucky commander. It was just like the men all said. Capt. Barry McCaffrey was their lucky charm.

As he stood partly obscured in the lengthening shadows of the landing zone, McCaffrey heard the familiar rotor-chop of the helicopters. The sound was hooked to so many emotions that were impossible to describe, but sometimes just that distant thrumming in the air was enough to bring tears to men's eyes. Those whose DEROS dates had arrived would cling to those helicopters like drowning men to a life raft. They had already evacuated the wounded from this afternoon, and McCaffrey stood very still on the edge of the LZ and waited for the new replacements to arrive.

When they had returned to the LZ earlier, McCaffrey had been happy to see the 1st Air Cav's commander, Gen. George Forsythe, already there, nervously chain-smoking and pacing the area. The wiry general, a veteran of both the island campaigns in the Pacific and the Normandy invasion in Europe during World War II, had even lent a hand in helping load the wounded into waiting helicopters. McCaffrey knew the man was there to show support for the company, and it was a point of leadership that McCaffrey appreciated. Occasionally the general would even fly in a case of cold beer for them after a patrol.

The first Huey hovered into the clearing and quickly discharged its passengers, everyone around the landing zone shielding their eyes against the stinging backwash of the rotor blades. McCaffrey watched as his first sergeant collected the new men. Looking into the wide-eyed faces of the young draftees, some of them hardly old enough to shave, he wondered for a moment how these boys from Brooklyn, Des Moines, and Pottstown all managed to find themselves in this jungle clearing so far from home. McCaffrey thought he could guess.

They were the three-time losers of an invisible system whose odds were stacked in someone else's favor. There were a hundred ways to avoid the draft, from medical, school, and religious deferments to the National Guard. Yet these soldiers had taken their chances and been unlucky enough to get a low lottery number, unlucky to be sent to Vietnam, and unlucky to be assigned to an Army combat-infantry unit. That was about as unlucky as you could get.

In the end they could have bolted to Canada and hadn't, and there was something noble in that. McCaffrey had come to know them as just solid boys from middle America who were used to saying "Yes, sir" when told to do something by their dads, their coaches, the police. Or by the U.S. Army. They hadn't volunteered for this fight, and he doubted very much whether they believed in it. Yet if by the time the sun came up the next morning he hadn't convinced this disoriented group of young men that they were part of a family that was willing to die for them, then B Company would be weaker for their arrival, not stronger. And the only way McCaffrey knew to gain their trust was to level with them.

"Men, the fact is you are going to get hit in this company. The only real question is when, and how bad," McCaffrey told them, his words registering in their expressions like a slap in the face. He paused a moment to let it sink in.

"The good news is that if you work your asses off, pay close attention to everything First Sergeant Trainer and I tell you, we will send you home alive. And you probably won't be badly maimed."

McCaffrey knew even as he spoke that it sounded gruesome to the replacements, but after more than seven months in the field he had lost his penchant for subtlety. The fact was that after only a few weeks as B Company commander, McCaffrey was the *senior* company commander in the brigade in terms of time in position. The rest had been killed, wounded, or relieved. One company had been through two commanders in nearly as many weeks. That was why he was still in command of a company past the usual six-month rotation point, and McCaffrey knew the casualty figures were even worse for platoon and squad leaders. It was all a matter of time, and for rifle company troops in the 1st Air Cav in 1968–69, time was not on your side.

After Emerson Trainer led the replacements away to their platoons, McCaffrey felt drained in a way that he had never experienced in his life. He was physically tired, but that was just one ripple in a pool of near spiritual exhaustion. Those boys were his responsibility, in McCaffrey's mind the best America had to offer, and this war was surely going to kill or maim them. Just as it had cut down so many that came before, including his brother-in-law in what already seemed like a different life.

So many of the others he had joined the Army with back in 1964 were now quitting in droves, and maybe they were right. Sometimes late at night he would get in discussions with the young lieutenants in his company about why they were still fighting when the country, the newspaper and television reporters, even the religious community back home had all turned against the war and those who waged it.

"I'm not fighting for America, I'm fighting for the U.S. Army," McCaffrey would stubbornly tell them, not as a provocation but because under the circumstances it seemed the only logical explanation for why he and the rest of them should risk their lives the next day.

An image from the top of the bunker that afternoon intruded on his thoughts. He could clearly see the impacts of the bullets bursting in dust clouds at his feet, everything coming back in almost dreamlike detail. There were the faces of the two Viet Cong he had shot with his .45-caliber pistol at nearly point-blank range the month before, the steady parade of faces of his own wounded he had sent back in helicopters. Can't think about all that. Barry McCaffrey knew that he was on an emotional roller coaster, and the thing to do now was to try to hang on.

Sound traveled strangely under the triple canopy. Sometimes the snap of a twig would seem to carry for miles, and at others a nearby firefight would sound muffled and distant, the noise baffled by jungle rot and refracted at strange angles by foliage so dense even sound seemed unable to penetrate. Even so, from the steady fusillade of automatic-weapons fire that echoed through the jungle late on the morning of March 9, McCaffrey knew immediately that they had stumbled into a major engagement. It sounded as if someone had stuck his head inside a giant wasps' nest.

Less than an hour earlier First Sergeant Trainer's lead patrol had reported finding signs of a recent enemy bivouac. McCaffrey guessed they'd caught up with the former occupants.

"Dorsey! Raise First Sergeant Trainer's platoon," he called to his radio operator.

The answer was quick in coming. The platoon was pinned down, with multiple casualties, Sergeant Trainer among them.

The bunker complex was the largest they had seen. By the time the platoon McCaffrey was leading reached the outskirts, the lead patrol was so many scattered bodies cringing behind cover, stranded by a fusillade of fire from three directions. A kill sack. To get Trainer and the rest of them out of there, they would have to take out one of the flanking bunkers and then work through the others one by one. Crawling forward through the underbrush, they heard the bullets zipping through the leaves and chipping bark just over their heads. Between machine-gun bursts, the cries of their own wounded.

McCaffrey waited until all three platoons were on line for suppression fire, then he concentrated on a bunker just to their front that he judged to be the linchpin. They had done this plenty of times before; there was a procedure. Because the NVA juxtaposed the bunkers at odd angles so they could offer each other supporting fire, there was no pretty or painless way to take them out. But it could be done.

With their own wounded scattered among the bunkers, they would have to hold the artillery. Pour on the suppression fire, get close enough to frag them with a grenade. The deadly tongue of flame spat again, the mouth of the bunker becoming something animate and dangerous, an object of fear and hate. Rattle of M16 fire to the left, then one of his men tossed a grenade directly through the gaping mouth into the soft guts of the bunker. Before they could even cover their heads for the expected explosion, however, the grenade was hurled back, landing directly in their midst. Everyone scrambled and rolled in a different direction trying to escape the shower of hot shrapnel.

Ears ringing, McCaffrey continued to crawl away to the periphery of the bunker's field of fire, looking up in time to see another grenade tossed into its yawning maw. Again it was immediately thrown back in their direction. Cover up, hear the explosion, feel the rain of grenade fragments as they splatter the forest and appear as red splotches torn in men's backs, legs, arms. A fight to the death.

McCaffrey was up and running in a crouch, yelling for cover, the woods erupting in a torrent of supporting fire. The top of the bunker seemed to dissolve into a cloud of dust as his foot hit it, small explosions everywhere, leaves and twigs falling like a shower of confetti from just overhead. He tossed the grenade in a hole in the backside of the bunker and leapt off in the same motion. A muffled explosion and then a cloud of dust and gore vomited out of the bunker.

With the bunker gone they were able to reach the wounded in Trainer's patrol. They were cut up bad, Trainer himself hit in the neck with a shot or fragment. Neck wounds could be bad. *You will get hit.* But could he really keep them alive? As the wounded were evacuated, McCaffrey began assembling the company for an attack on the rest of the bunker complex. Their own men out of the way, he called in an artillery strike on the complex and ordered his men down. The forest was soon filled with explosions hammering through the complex, and choking, blinding smoke.

As soon as the barrage ended, McCaffrey signaled to the company bugler, who was lying behind a tree. Lifting the horn to his lips, he blew a deep-throated charge that echoed eerily in the forest, reminiscent of ancient battles in that timeless place. Even for McCaffrey it was unnerving. At the sound, the men of B Company stood and advanced on the next bunker with McCaffrey at their lead, their rifles firing on automatic. They had a procedure for this.

As they approached, the bunker was silent, and McCaffrey decided that the artillery had already taken it out. There was so much smoke. Then a deafening muzzle blast of machine-gun fire burst in his right ear. Something that sounded like a sledgehammer hit the radio operator in the helmet and knocked him down beside McCaffrey, then he felt something rip the pistol from his hand and the canteen off his back. Why was the angry retort of gun-fire coming from his right? He had to get out of the line of fire, away from the sickening wet sounds of impacts all around him, but for some reason every time he tried, his nose just kept mashing into the dirt.

McCaffrey decided to sit up. Through the haze of confusion, he stared without comprehension at two white bones that were protruding from what should have been his arm, blood spewing in time to the frantic beat of his heart. The sight froze him, and even though the muzzle blast continued to erupt only a few feet away, he couldn't take his eyes off what had been his arm. Then he felt something or someone jerk him by his web gear, dragging him back, back, until he slid down into a shallow ravine.

McCaffrey watched as the medic who pulled him to safety applied a blood expander, designed to stabilize blood pressure until a transfusion could be administered, and offered a constant patter of encouragement to take his captain's mind off the fact that his arm had been very nearly blown off and was hanging by a strip of bloody meat. McCaffrey attempted to issue orders to organize the company into a defensive position to await reinforcements. Soon, however, he felt himself starting to drift into shock. As he closed his eyes, it seemed the only thing he could hear, louder even than the nearby din of battle, was the sound of helicopters above the treetops somewhere nearby. Though McCaffrey didn't know it at the time, the man who was scheduled to replace him as company commander was riding in one of those heli-copters.

The last thing McCaffrey told his men was to evacuate the other wounded first. Torn and bloody men lay scattered everywhere in the narrow ravine, as medics ran from one to the other trying to staunch with makeshift bandages the life that was seeping out of them onto the damp jungle floor. Someone joked in a quavering voice that the captain was just trying to play it safe, knowing that the first wounded to rise up through the forest canopy in "jungle penetrators" might draw the most enemy fire. The humor was a good sign. They were fine men.

After the sling stretcher carrying Capt. Barry McCaffrey disappeared through the hole in the forest roof, all joking and most talking in the clearing stopped. They had seen how much blood he'd lost, knew it would be a touch-and-go thing, yet it was even more than that. As their captain had lain waiting for his helicopter, two B Company men had died and the wounded kept piling up. Morale was a funny thing. Back in a stateside garrison or mili-tary school it was something talked about mostly in the abstract, but out here morale was palpable and real, and you could almost feel it being sucked out of that clearing from above by the receding rotor-thud of the helicopter.

• • •

The back-channels cable notifying him that his son had been gravely wounded found Lt. Gen. William J. McCaffrey at Carlisle Barracks, Pennsylvania. He was not really surprised. The Army had an informal network through which senior officers whose sons were killed or wounded were notified first, and in 1969 it was humming with traffic. The sons of a lot of generals were in the military trying to prove themselves worthy of their fathers' names and reputations, and that was perilous work in Vietnam. Reading the cable, the senior McCaffrey realized he'd been half-expecting the news.

After calling his wife, he dialed his daughter-in-law's number.

"Jill, this is Bill McCaffrey. I'm afraid Barry's been seriously wounded."

There was a moment of silence on the line.

"Is he on his way home?" Jill asked.

"Yeah. . . . Jill, the doctors say he may lose his left arm."

"Is he wounded anyplace else?"

"No, but they—"

Before Bill McCaffrey could finish relaying the doctor's prognosis on his son, his voice was cut short on the other end. He had been dreading having to make this call; perhaps that was why he was so momentarily stunned. All the way from the other side of the country, he could hear the unmistakable sound of his daughter-in-law shouting with joy.

After she hung up, Jill McCaffrey realized how convinced she had been that her husband would die in Vietnam. She never expected to see him again. Now her father-in-law must think her mad, cheering the news of his being wounded. Somehow it just didn't matter. Barry was coming home alive from Vietnam, and Jill couldn't bring herself to give a damn whether he had one arm or two.

Vietnam. It seemed now like a malignant shadow that had darkened their entire marriage, threatening their lives together, leaving her to raise their children alone, making Barry a stranger to the baby daughter he had never even seen. But it hadn't killed him. Immediately Jill went around the house mentally preparing to leave. Though she would miss having her parents close by, she wouldn't be leaving many friends behind nor a community that she felt any part of. That was something else Vietnam had taken away.

Without knowing exactly why, Jill McCaffrey went to the bureau and opened the drawer where she kept all of Barry's letters. As she sat down with the entire stack, each bearing the unmistakable imprint of the Army Post Office, Jill remembered how anxiously she had awaited their almost daily arrival.

The ones from his earlier tour had reflected the eagerness of a gung ho second lieutenant, and that enthusiasm of being a soldier had never completely left him. Yet long ago it had become mixed with a growing sense of weariness that seemed to seep through the pages of his more recent letters. Jill had decided that if her husband was killed, she would save those letters from Vietnam as a memorial so that when they were old enough, the children would get a better sense of the father they had never really known.

Almost before she realized she was doing it, Jill found herself tearing up the letter she was holding. *Vietnam.* Then she picked up another letter and tore it into shreds. Methodically now, she began going through the entire stack, shredding the painful memories one by one. *Vietnam. Vietnam. Vietnam.* After she was finished, Jill McCaffrey collected all the pieces into a pile and burned them.

7: Wounds 1969

BY the fall of 1969, Barry McCaffrey was well enough to continue his rehabilitation on an outpatient basis between operations. He and Jill rented a small garden apartment in Silver Spring, Maryland, in a complex occupied mostly by hospital staff and the families of patients at nearby Walter Reed Army Hospital in Washington, D.C., which for the McCaffreys had become the center of a badly skewed universe.

While the nation's capital had become the key battleground for a society that at times seemed determined on tearing itself apart over Vietnam, at Walter Reed those whose bodies had been mangled by the war were consumed by the tortuous ordeal of trying to slowly piece their lives back together.

Though the doctors had just managed to save Barry's arm, they cautioned that it would take multiple operations over a period of years for him to regain meaningful use. Whether he lost the arm or was forced to leave the Army, however, it was impossible to feel sorry for yourself for long on the orthopedic ward at Walter Reed in 1969. No matter how bad you had it on ward one, you could always find someone who had it much worse.

Despite the ravages of the war and the edge of desperation to some of their antics, Jill felt that Barry's fellow patients at Walter Reed were some of the healthiest men she knew. The sight of the ward-one gang policing itself up along the path back to the hospital after a night of drinking at the officers' club, leaning on one another, wheeling back the unconscious, filling in the missing pieces for each other to make a somewhat wobbly whole, was a familiar one around Walter Reed.

What Jill McCaffrey could not understand was the virulence with which Barry's other friends and former West Point classmates were suddenly denouncing the Army. The antiwar movement was reaching critical mass in the fall of 1969, and it was threatening to rip the Army apart. Many of Barry's former West Point classmates and Army buddies who were leaving the service passed through Washington, D.C., to join the protests. Because Lt. Gen. William McCaffrey had taken over as the Army's key coordinator of troop backup for civil disturbances in the capital, Barry and Jill were acutely aware that his father could be forced to order troops against the protest crowds containing their friends and even overnight guests. Such was life in the nation's capital in 1969.

Yet despite the obvious tensions, there was an undeniable air of excitement that fall. They were at the center of tumultuous events that were reshaping society. Many of McCaffrey's best friends from West Point were already in the city, some on Pentagon assignments, others to file requests for early resignation with the Army's personnel office. Barry wasn't particularly bothered either way.

Even his former first sergeant Emerson Trainer was retiring. After the bloody fighting in the bunker complex, Trainer had returned to B Company only to be badly burned in an accident while clearing a landing zone. Soon after his recovery, Trainer was put on orders to return to Vietnam by an Army desperate for experienced sergeants. After talking it over with his family, Trainer had done exactly what most sergeants did when confronted with a third tour to Vietnam. He quit.

The truth was that Barry McCaffrey had also privately begun to consider leaving the Army. Still, he felt a lasting kinship with the young men and former cadets with whom he had shared so many tribulations at West Point, and with the brothers in arms he had served with since. So on one particularly busy weekend in Washington, Barry and Jill decided to have a dinner party for a number of his former West Point classmates who were gathered in Washington.

The party started out largely as a high-octane success. Barry was annoyed rather than angry when he returned from the kitchen with drinks at one point and caught the unmistakable aroma of marijuana. After Vietnam the odor of dope was a familiar one, often smelled while passing by doorways or around blind corners in rear-area bases. Scanning his living room, it suddenly struck McCaffrey that of the West Point alumni present, a majority were either getting out of the Army or had already left. Only he and one other classmate were still on active duty, and most of McCaffrey's action took place under a surgeon's scalpel.

They all knew and accepted that some of those present were in Washington to testify against the war the next day before Congress, part of a group called Veterans Against the War. A classmate who was staying as their houseguest that night, along with his wife and two children, was quitting the Army. Still another had already left and was in Washington attending law school. They were all but unrecognizable as the group of idealistic cadets who had shared so many dreams and aspirations just five years earlier.

Not surprisingly, much of the conversation centered on Vietnam and the antiwar protests. Most agreed that they were in the midst of losing a war that the country no longer supported. There was talk of Nixon's pledge to abolish the draft and shift to an all-volunteer force, a position many considered ridiculous given the Army's sagging popularity. The papers were also filled with reports on the case of Lt. William Laws Calley, Jr., a former infantry combat officer whom the Army had accused of murdering as many as 109 Vietnamese civilians.

When Barry McCaffrey's houseguest began to explain his reasons for leaving the Army, the man's wife broke in with the comment that would shatter the friendships around that table for nearly twenty years, before many of them even fully realized how truly brittle the war had made the ties that once bound them.

"Well, I think Kevin should get out of the Army because he's not a killer," the woman said to Jill McCaffrey, making it sound to all in the room like an accusation. "And there's certainly no shame in that."

The conversation at the table momentarily collapsed into a stunned silence before anyone could retrieve it, as the former brothers in arms cast worried sideways glances at each other. Presently someone tried to soften the blow with some tactful equivocations, but they hardly registered. Barry McCaffrey had stolen a glance at his wife, and he knew there was trouble. Not normally one for making a scene, Jill McCaffrey burst into tears and abruptly ran into the next room. Barry knew instantly that the former classmates gathered around the table had lost something that might never be recovered. When conversation finally did resume at the table, it seemed so forced that he could almost have preferred the silence.

That evening in bed, Barry McCaffrey cradled Jill in his good arm, trying in vain to still the sobs that wracked her body. Jill could not understand why so many of their friends who were leaving the Army had to turn around and spit on those who remained behind, and Barry was not sure he understood it himself.

If someone had asked him, McCaffrey would have claimed to be a Kennedy liberal, as concerned about social injustice and people's feelings as anyone. He had grown up in an Irish Catholic family with Depression-era values. Yet it seemed that nothing he stood for mattered except that he was in the Army, and that made him the enemy. You had to be either for the war or against the Army. Somewhere the country had lost its middle ground.

As Lt. Gen. William McCaffrey watched the steady stream of humanity file down Pennsylvania Avenue in the face of a gusting north wind, he was thankful once again that he'd thought of the buses. The intelligence he'd received was that some protesters were going to try to sack and burn the White House, and Bill McCaffrey was inclined to take the threat seriously.

It was dusk on a clear but wintry November 15, 1969, and looking down the block from his command post, McCaffrey shook his head again at the sight of the fifty-seven buses lined up bumper to bumper to form a barricade between the presidential mansion and the protest marchers. What must it look like to the man in the Oval Office, his view obscured by this makeshift barricade? Like a besieged settler behind circled wagons, that's what.

Days earlier four separate bombs had exploded in government buildings in New York, and two men had been arrested attempting to place bombs on Army trucks at a New York armory. The night before, riot policemen had to use tear gas to rout thousands of demonstrators who attempted to march on the South Vietnamese embassy.

For a West Point graduate who had helped lead an American division through Italy in World War II and had landed in Inchon, Korea, with Gen. Douglas MacArthur, it was heartbreaking to see armed Army troops deployed on the streets of the nation's capital, protecting the president from his own people. But the elder McCaffrey didn't blame the Army. Because of all the tangible and intangible enforcement mechanisms that supported the chain of command, the Army was the last guarantor of civil order in a society coming unraveled.

Five years of a war they should never have entered in the first place in McCaffrey's opinion, and this was where it had taken them. He had watched the war wear down his friend Harold Johnson, the former Army chief of staff. The officers who had risen rapidly through the ranks during World War II were generally a close-knit group, and those who had not double-dated as cadets at West Point had probably served with one another at some point. McCaffrey believed Harold Johnson's selflessness had been turned into a weakness by former defense secretary Robert McNamara, a man he viewed as intellectually arrogant and disdainful of those in uniform.

The burden of their generation of officers, McCaffrey felt, would be to try to explain why they had never stood up together and said this is wrong and we can't go along with it any longer. In Bill McCaffrey's mind, Lyndon Johnson and Robert McNamara's burden would be explaining how they could send the military to fight a war that they never rallied the country to support.

Bill McCaffrey looked out again over the throngs of people still pouring down the parade route, waving banners against the war and flashing their fingers in the V sign for peace. It looked as if the largest mass march ever in the nation's capital was going to remain a mostly peaceful affair. McCaffrey knew that some of Barry's friends and former classmates at West Point might well be in the crowd strolling before the command post before turning south toward the Washington Monument.

Bill McCaffrey also knew that his son was troubled about his future in the Army, and whenever they discussed it over dinner, the senior McCaffrey tried to take the long view. The Army was entering a difficult period just as it had after every war, when most of the men in uniform were sent home and pay and promotions dried up, and those that remained retreated to their Army posts and locked the gates behind them.

Though he never said as much directly, Bill McCaffrey did not believe his son would really be happy outside the Army. The nice thing about the Army, he frequently commented, was that you could leave your wallet and your wife with your coworkers for a year and return to find neither disturbed. Just watch your medals.

That was the Army Bill McCaffrey had grown up in and knew, peopled by those more interested in glory than in glorifying wealth. They were the kind of people he liked being around. Bill McCaffrey still felt it was the best place for his son. In the end, however, he believed the matter would be decided by his daughter-in-law. If Jill tired of Army life, Barry would almost certainly get out.

Bill McCaffrey also sensed that the postwar period the Army would enter after Vietnam would prove more difficult than most. In months he was scheduled to deploy to South Vietnam to take command of all Army forces in the theater and help MACV commander Gen. Creighton Abrams complete the long, arduous process of bringing nearly half a million troops home. Each week he received briefings on the situation in South Vietnam by Pentagon, State Department, and CIA experts. Every indicator pointed to the fact that an Army that was configured to fight the Russians on the plains of Europe just five years ago had begun to come unglued in the fetid jungles and delta swamp of Vietnam.

Never get involved in a land war in Asia. It was a lesson the military schools had hammered into every general officer of their generation. McCaffrey couldn't believe that anyone who had seen the human-wave assaults of the Chinese during the Korean War could have forgotten it.

As the shadows of dusk began to lengthen in Washington, bringing with them a biting chill, Gen. William McCaffrey's field radio crackled. It seemed a militant splinter group was pelting the nearby Justice Department with rocks and bottles and had even run the Viet Cong flag up the building's flagpole. The police were going to try to handle it, but troops should be on standby.

McCaffrey was reminded of something Creighton Abrams had said in a phone call from Saigon the previous year, before McCaffrey had received his recent orders to join Abrams in Vietnam and bring the Army home. The Johnson administration had been teetering, and across the country cities burned in uncontrolled rioting. "Bill, you will never know what it is like to be a commander responsible for four hundred thousand men in a theater halfway around the world when the government at home starts to come apart on you," Creighton Abrams had lamented. Soon the wind carried the faint, eye-watering bite of tear gas to his command post near the White House, and it occurred to Bill McCaffrey that Abrams had been wrong.

8: A Pitiless Folly 1970

"WHAT do you mean I don't have a battalion? I'm supposed to be going to Europe," Lt. Col. Jack Galvin said, trying to check his temper. If Galvin ever needed proof that his maverick ways had earned him an invisible black mark on his résumé, it was written all over the face of the paper shuffler at the Army Bureau of Personnel in Washington, D.C. He recognized it as one of the faces who had tried unsuccessfully to thwart his getting a battalion command in Vietnam the year before. Now he was trying to screw him out of battalion command in Europe.

With the Army lacking a formalized selection process for promotions and assignments, Galvin was beginning to understand that an old-boy network of officers rotated in and out of the personnel office where they could steer choice assignments and thus promotions to each other and their favored patrons. They ran the machine, deciding who was among the "in" crowd of officers destined to get ahead. Galvin was clearly not on their list.

"Oh, you're going to Europe all right, but not to command a battalion," the personnel bureaucrat told him, obviously enjoying this. "We have you listed for a staff job."

Galvin wheeled around and walked out before doing something he might regret. The man was screwing him out of a battalion command, and he couldn't do a damn thing about it. A year earlier he might have quit over the incident and had indeed come within a few days of handing in his resignation from the Army. Combat command in 1969, however, had forever cured Jack Galvin of the self-doubts that had haunted him after the DePuy debacle, when he was fired from the Big Red One following the gory battle of August 25, 1966.

After what he had seen and accomplished with the 1st Battalion of the 1st Air Cav Division during the past year, Galvin felt vindicated in his initial fears over where their scorched-earth tactics and body-count mentality were taking the Army. If many senior officers seemed somehow oblivious to the fact that the Army had gotten it horribly wrong in Vietnam—the tactics, the training, the leadership—then Galvin considered them part of the problem.

Before arriving at the 1st Cav, Galvin had been mired in a public-affairs job in which he culled newspaper reports on the war and condensed them for weekly Pentagon briefings. Many of his cohorts blamed the media for dwindling public support for the war, and certainly the Army was confronted by an overwhelming barrage of criticism. His superior had even warned Galvin that his press summaries were too negative, as if his sugarcoating published editorials and newspaper articles would somehow make things better.

As far as Galvin was concerned, the media was being falsely maligned for its coverage of Vietnam. The Army had somehow lost any ability for introspection or honest self-evaluation, Galvin felt, and seemed far too eager to simply blame the messengers. At a low point, Galvin had thus filled out his separation papers.

One thing that helped change his mind was a temporary assignment to assist in the compiling and writing of a secret bureaucratic history of the Vietnam War that became known simply as the Pentagon Papers. The classified report, commissioned by Robert McNamara, traced Western involvement back to the French occupation and outlined all the major decisions behind U.S. involvement. Ironically, the man who enlisted Galvin's help on the project was Col. Paul Gorman, the cerebral former battalion commander with the Big Red One whom Galvin had very nearly killed with an errant air strike on August 25, 1966.

As he reread the history of the United States' deepening involvement in the quagmire, it seemed that a critical step on the path democracies followed into war had been skipped with Vietnam. Without a declaration of war or a mobilization of the national will through a reserve call-up, Jack Galvin believed they had forsaken the "Gold Star" mothers. He clearly remembered growing up during World War II, when nothing was more revered than a family displaying a Gold Star flag in their window, signifying that they had lost a son in battle. There were no gold stars and precious little national condolence for the mothers of more than forty-five thousand Americans killed in Vietnam by 1969.

If the Pentagon Papers helped convince him that the civilian leaders had badly erred, Galvin's tour as a battalion commander in the 1st Cav was ample proof that the military leadership had much for which to answer. He had witnessed firsthand the genesis of the aggressive search-and-destroy tactics in the Big Red One back in 1966. No matter how well intentioned that policy had been three years earlier, the more Galvin understood about the war, the more convinced he was that the enemy had turned those tactics in its favor in a carefully modulated war of attrition.

Apparently MACV commander Creighton Abrams had come to the same conclusion. After taking command from Westmoreland the year before, Abrams had ordered a shift away from their large-scale search-and-destroy operations. The emphasis in 1969 had been on shielding the population centers and "pacifying" the countryside through constant patrols, while ultimately military responsibility was passed to the South Vietnamese through Vietnamization.

Working on the division staff for the 1st Cav at Phuoc Vinh, however, Galvin had been hard-pressed to find evidence that the Army's fundamental approach to the war had changed. He vividly remembered stepping outside the operations center into the darkness each night just to watch the fireworks. Like clockwork, a Viet Cong sapper team would lob a few rounds from one side of the base, then the entire perimeter would erupt in an orgy of blind counterfire.

Watching as streams of tracers and rocket fire poured into the dark jungle surrounding the base in a deafening fusillade, nearly every weapons station within the perimeter of Phuoc Vinh firing on full automatic, Galvin was always reminded of Joseph Conrad's "Heart of Darkness." For the former West Point English professor, the "mad minute" of fire recalled the scene of Belgians repeatedly emptying their rifles into the impenetrable jungle wall in the Congo, spooked by a distant scream from the dark shadows, holding at bay shapeless fears. "I've seen the devil of violence, and the devil of greed, and the devil of hot desire; but, by all the stars! these were strong, red-eyed devils, that swayed and drove men . . . ," wrote Conrad. "But as I stood on that hillside, I foresaw that in the blinding sunshine of that land I would become acquainted with a flabby, pretending, weak-eyed devil of a rapacious and pitiless folly. How insidious he could be."

In his initial assignment as the intelligence officer for the 1st Cav Division, Galvin had flown to Saigon each week for a briefing at the headquarters of the corps commander, II Field Force, Lt. Gen. Julian Ewell. There in his command bunker, Ewell kept a giant map of the entire corps area, with a black mark indicating the position and relative movement of every single platoon in the largest Army combat command in Vietnam. Ewell enforced a rule that each platoon had to move at least fifteen hundred meters a day, regardless of terrain or mission. It was the same "movement for the sake of movement" philosophy that Galvin had seen in the Big Red One, only if anything it made far less sense given the change in their tactics toward pacification and withdrawal. Nor had he ever seen such micromanagement of field units.

One of the first orders Galvin had issued on receiving command of the 1st Squadron, 8th Cavalry, was to ignore the imperative to move fifteen hundred meters each day. Hacking and slashing your way through fifteen hundred meters of jungle was a full day's work, and frequently the payoff was to stumble into an enemy kill sack. As an intelligence officer for nearly six months, Galvin had closely studied the enemy's trail complexes, and he carefully set his companies out in ambush along trails he knew were frequently traveled. Ewell was reportedly furious that the 1st Battalion did not log the requisite fifteen hundred meters each day. The only thing that saved Galvin from a severe reprimand had been the fact that the North Vietnamese and Viet Cong kept stumbling into his ambushes.

Predictably, not everyone had been enamored of a bookish-looking maverick who liked doing things his own way. Galvin would never forget one colonel, a brand-new brigade commander, who ordered Galvin's battalion to launch a frontal assault on a suspected enemy concentration at dusk, outside the range of supporting artillery. Long and bloody experience in Vietnam had taught commanders that outside the protective umbrella of their artillery, the Army ceded their critical advantage of superior firepower. There indeed had been a "rapacious and pitiless folly."

Knowing his men would pay for it with a scene of desperate horror, Galvin had refused the direct order. He knew it had been a court-martial offense, but that tour had never been about promotion or career enhancement. The country had backed into a police action and found itself in a protracted war, and the Army had never regained its equilibrium. Perhaps it was fitting that only in an act of insubordination did Lt. Col. Jack Galvin find personal vindication. He was fit to lead men in combat after all.

In a parting shot, the irked colonel had put a notation in Galvin's fitness report guaranteed to catch the notice of the personnel bureaucrats back in Washington searching for black marks. Lieutenant Colonel Galvin, his commander wrote, puts consideration for his men before that of the mission. Jack Galvin knew the comment was meant as a blistering condemnation of his leadership skills. Yet he was more proud of that fitness report than the Distinguished Service Cross, the Silver Star, or any of the other medals and campaign ribbons he brought back from Vietnam.

Galvin was frequently reminded that a lot of talented officers were equally as worried as he about what was happening to the Army. The question was whether there were enough of them to somehow make the service see that it needed to change. Certainly Galvin's feeling that he wasn't alone in that fight was bolstered when his name surprisingly surfaced on the list to attend the Army War College. That was a sure sign that someone believed he was worth grooming for higher command. Once on campus at Carlisle, Galvin also learned of a groundbreaking study by two lieutenant colonels on leadership and professionalism in the service. As much as anything else, that seminal study convinced a group of maverick officers that they were in a struggle for the Army's soul.

As Washington, D.C., began its descent into the dog days of summer in early July 1970, two young lieutenant colonels fumbled with a defective viewgraph in the army chief of staff's conference room at the Pentagon. The large room was dominated by an elongated mahogany conference table around which gathered much of the Army's senior leadership. The various name tags around the table read like a roll call of the service's most coveted command and staff positions, many of them in town for the annual Army Commanders Conference.

At the head of the table in the position of honor sat chief of staff Gen. William Westmoreland, the signature gray hair and dark eyebrows that had become familiar to the entire country distinguishing him from the others present. The visages of various former chiefs stared down sternly from portraits on the wall, lending their collective weight to the almost oppressive air of authority in the room. Indeed, most of the emperors of the Army were assembled, and as soon as the young lieutenant colonels finished stuffing sugar packets under the missing wheel of the view-graph cart, the business of explaining how they had no clothes could commence.

Perhaps they were cocky or just naive, but neither of the lieutenant colonels, Walt Ulmer or Mike Malone, was particularly nervous about being the messenger of bad news. At first glance they were an odd couple. Ulmer, the Army War College faculty member, was probably the more intellectual of the pair. He had a flair for conceptualizing solutions for complex problems.

Malone was a down-to-earth former Army brat who could crawl into the trenches with the enlisted troops and speak their language, yet whose molasses-thick accent and Southern witticisms veiled a shrewd mind with a quick grasp of scientific data that complemented his degree in psychology. As they prepared for the briefing under the not-altogether-gentle gaze of their audience, however, these two junior officers with little else in common felt bound by the kinship of those about to stand up for an unpopular truth.

The Army War College study they were about to brief, which had consumed them for the past four months, had been commissioned by Westmoreland himself. Indirectly it was yet another repercussion of the My Lai massacre. Publicly, Westmoreland blamed the personnel policies forced on the Army during Vietnam as the root cause behind the incident. Barred from tapping into the pool of seasoned officers and noncommissioned officers in the reserves, and faced with college deferments for many potential leaders, the Army had been forced to lower its quality standards to fill its junior-officer and noncom ranks.

Nor was My Lai the only incident that had called into question the moral compass from which the Army's officer corps took its heading. In another well-publicized case, a team of Army Green Berets had been charged with murdering a double agent; the sergeant major of the Army, the top noncom in the service, had been implicated in a scandal involving misuse of military-club funds; and the provost marshal general, the top cop in the Army, was convicted for illegal activities. Westmoreland had thus tasked the Army War College to investigate the moral and ethical backdrop that would allow such an array of incidents to occur, though many senior leaders still considered them aberrations.

To get a feel for the Army's moral and ethical bearing, Ulmer and Malone had led a team of War College students and faculty in interviewing roughly 450 officers, primarily at the captain, major, and lieutenant-colonel level, men not unlike Barry McCaffrey or Jack Galvin and thousands of other officers. The team's behavioral-science experts told them that above that level, persons in any organization generally tended to be more satisfied with the status quo.

What they had discovered had not surprised either Ulmer or Malone, but they were not so optimistic as to assume the same could be said for the rest of the men in the chief of staff's conference room. If nothing else, Westmoreland's consistently upbeat projections about the progress of the war and state of the Army in general, which continued unabated, indicated a certain lack of honest communication between the leadership and the junior ranks. Ulmer and Malone's *Study on Military Professionalism* was about to blast open those lines of communication.

The fact was that the Army leadership had instituted, or allowed to be instituted, a system of statistical measures that had almost nothing to do with winning a war, yet had come to mean everything in terms of getting an officer promoted to his next whirlwind assignment. Numbers had become an end in themselves and a crutch on which inexperienced officers leaned in rating themselves and their subordinates. To the rank and file, it seemed as if nothing was too sacred to be sacrificed on the altar of numerology, whether the statistics tracked enemy killed, miles trekked, villages "pacified," or soldiers reenlisted and AWOL. And the senior leadership present in that conference room had stood by for five years, seemingly oblivious to the rampant corruption that system had spawned.

That was essentially the message that Walt Ulmer and Mike Malone brought to Westmoreland's conference room. As Malone surveyed the room, he wondered how these generals were going to take the news that an Army whose officer corps professed allegiance to the ideals of duty, honor, and country had somehow seen them twisted into me, my ass, and my career.

As the senior War College faculty member on the study, Walt Ulmer led off the briefing with a summary of the *Study on Military Professionalism.*

"Gentlemen, a scenario that was repeatedly described to us during our interviews for this study includes an ambitious, transitory commander, marginally skilled in the complexities of his duties, engulfed in producing statistical results, fearful of personal failure, too busy to talk with or listen to his subordinates, and determined to submit acceptably optimistic reports which reflect faultless completion of a variety of tasks at the expense of the sweat and frustrations of his subordinates."

Someone's hand slapped the mahogany table hard and flat, jarring everyone in the room. Ulmer was all but expecting the eruption, but it startled him from the text just the same.

"That's not the goddamn Army that I know!" a three-star general proclaimed, half-rising out of his chair and looking up and down the table for support. Ulmer and Malone exchanged glances.

Finally another three-star general spoke up from across the table.

"Yeah, well, apparently that's the goddamn trouble. Now why don't you sit down and listen and let them finish."

Ulmer reiterated the degree of dissatisfaction in the junior ranks, where he described a clear, pervasive perception that not only was there a lack of professional skills at the senior-officer level, but that incredible pressures sent down the chain of command seemed to originate from an overriding concern for self-advancement. Even in a war zone, senior officers would often blow in, demand flawless operational readiness and fitness reports for their six-month tours despite the fact that the Army was staggering under the weight of a drawn-out and unpopular war, and then blow out for their next assignment.

The resulting pressures had created a conviction on the part of many junior officers that they had to be dishonest—to falsify AWOL rates, reenlistments, court-martial figures, body counts, even the incidence of venereal disease—to advance themselves. In truth, between 1967 and 1970, AWOL rates in the Army had increased by 70 percent, and desertion rates by 144 percent. The subtle message junior officers received, however, was that you could get ahead in this man's Army, or you could be honest about those shortfalls, but that you sure as hell couldn't do both.

Months ago they had been tasked to go out into the Army ranks and return to tell it like it was, and against all odds Ulmer and Malone had done just that. No one had to explain to them that briefings like the one they were giving could make or break a career in the Army, and both could feel this one beginning to turn against them on some unseen pivot.

Ulmer went on to lay the blame for the ethical morass within the officer corps directly on the Army's shoulders. There was no evidence, he said, that the present climate could be blamed on the public's reaction to the Vietnam War, the rapid expansion of the Army, or growing antimilitary sentiments. Furthermore, the pervasiveness of the climate indicated that the problems would probably not correct themselves short of dramatic action on the part of the Army leadership.

Finishing the briefing, Ulmer checked off many of the study's thirty-one recommendations, suggesting some be acted on immediately and others more gradually, and still others be considered for further study. As he well knew, nearly every recommendation gored a sacred ox in the herd of one of the generals present.

Career patterns should be rethought, Ulmer said, with command assignments lengthened to eliminate ticket-punching; the personnel management system should be reformed, with centralized command selection and promotion boards at Army headquarters to eliminate nepotism; required courses on professional ethics and interpersonal communications should be introduced at all service schools; it should be recognized that performance is not necessarily susceptible to statistical measurement; and initiative and learning by mistake should be encouraged rather than a "zero defects" mentality.

As he read through the list, Ulmer thought again about the philosophical framework behind the recommendations. Both he and Malone shared a strong conviction that the most powerful tool for changing an Army that was so clearly in need of reform was the military school system. It was an all-American trust in the almost transcendent power of education for personal and professional betterment.

The military's parallel school structure indeed made it virtually unique among major institutions and corporations in America, where change and direction usually came as edicts from the top down. Not only was the Army too massive and unwieldy to respond in lockstep with any directive, especially given its myriad competing interests, but the study being briefed had shown beyond a doubt that many officers had lost faith in the leadership at the top.

Yet the military's parallel education system, outside of the direct operational control of any particular command and straddling the divide that had so obviously developed between the rank and file and the Army leadership, presented an entirely different path for changing the Army's culture. That process could begin as early as the service academies, work through the service-branch schools, the Command and General Staff Colleges, the War Colleges, and finally even at the joint-service National War College. If they could just convince those present that the Army needed radical change, begin that process at the service schools, and then promote people fairly based on those expectations and values.

The first step, however, was critical, which is why it lay at the very top of the study's recommendations. The Army had to face up to how bad things had somehow gotten, which meant admitting to and airing its faults. Thus the first of the thirty-one recommendations was that the study itself be disseminated throughout the officer corps, not only to alert senior leaders to potential problems in their commands, but also to assure the junior officers on whose back any meaningful reform would rest that the Army was coming to grips with its problems. In fact, Ulmer found the intense concern in the junior-officer ranks for the breakdown in standards and ethics to be a cause for optimism, and perhaps the study's most important message. Distrust and discouragement had not yet given way to apathy and cynicism.

After Ulmer was finished, General Westmoreland sat with a stunned expression. "I just can't believe that," he kept repeating, looking askance at the faces around the conference table. Though the two colonels gave the chief credit for instigating the study and not kicking them out of the room outright given its implications, it seemed to them that Westmoreland was nevertheless practically in a state of shock.

Immediately a heated discussion broke out around the conference table about whether or not the study should even be released. Some supported immediate dissemination, but a number of generals warned that the press would have a field day with it and reminded Westmoreland that the Army was already taking intense fire from the media. Why give them more ammunition to shoot us with?

When Ulmer and Malone were dismissed from the conference room, the generals were still discussing whether to release the study or bury it under a "need to know" classification in the War College archives. The next day Ulmer and Malone were told that Westmoreland had directed his staff to study possible implementation of their recommendations, but he had ordered the study itself to be "close held." They could brief their findings at the military schools, but the chief had decided that the study's findings were too explosive to release at that time.

While they understood the chief's reasoning, both Ulmer and Malone felt that Westmoreland was making a serious blunder. Without the study to provide a framework and context, the recommended changes would likely be seen as disjointed and piecemeal. If key recommendations were adopted, such as reforming personnel management and promotion and establishing ethics classes at the military schools to discuss the impact of such things as body counts and six-month officer rotations, they still felt the healing process could begin for the Army.

For the thousands of junior officers who had heard about the study via the service's informal grapevine, however, word that Westmoreland had locked it away only added to their sense of estrangement from the Army's senior leadership. The Army had entered Vietnam with the arrogance of the perennial winner, and faced with impending defeat and a fusillade of unfamiliar criticisms, it seemed to be retreating deeper and deeper into denial.

In an annual assessment of the Army after the study was classified, Westmoreland wrote, "Your Army today is a dynamic organization, proud of its tradition and accomplishments, optimistic about the future, and confident about the direction in which it is moving." Whatever Army Westmoreland thought he was commanding from the Pentagon, it bore little resemblance to the one many officers in the field were struggling to salvage from growing racial strife, drug abuse, insubordination, officer fraggings, desertion, and a losing war.

9: Yankee Station 1971

ON Yankee Station in the South China Sea, Comdr. Stan Arthur scanned a bulletin board on the USS *Hancock*, wondering what the movie would be that night. Ever since serving on a board that screened all movies sent out to the fleet during his last shore duty, Arthur liked to keep a watchful eye. One film that almost made it through the system was set in the pre–Civil War South, complete with interracial rape and seduction scenes. In the fall of 1971, that kind of entertainment aboard a U.S. Navy ship could lead to mutiny.

Arthur was actually happy to be back at sea. On a deployed aircraft carrier, it was easier to keep people busy and to deal decisively with the racial tensions and the general disaffections simmering in the fleet. Shore duty was another matter.

Back at Lemoore, California, where Arthur had run a thousand-man maintenance shop, the sailors had engaged in rip-roaring finger-pointing exercises with their officers almost daily. Chief of naval operations Adm. Elmo Zumwalt, Jr., was trying desperately to cope with an increasingly rebellious rank and file by liberalizing what were seen as the more egregious regulations. Zumwalt's "Z-grams" were blanketing the fleet like confetti, each one abolishing an old regulation, whether it was the prohibition against growing beards or restrictions on hair length. The problem was that the sailors were getting wind of the changes before Arthur and waving Zumwalt's Z-grams under his nose and demanding to know why the skipper was dragging his feet on changing the regs.

At least on a combat deployment there was a sense of shared purpose, and less of the us-versus-them attitude that was becoming increasingly prevalent in the Navy. Watching as a group of replacement pilots landed aboard the *Hancock* that fall, however, Arthur wondered if they would find the situation at Yankee Station an improvement of their lot in life.

Normally they would bring the green pilots on gradually, take them on a few "low-threat" missions to work the kinks out of their necks and get their heads on an easy swivel. With the beginning of the dry season that October, however, North Vietnam had begun massing troops and supplies in its southern panhandle, and pilots reported seeing an average of one thousand trucks a night pouring down the Ho Chi Minh trail. Sensors had begun picking up major activity across the DMZ. Something big was in the works.

The U.S. response was a major increase in air strikes. Under the terms of the Paris talks, they were still only allowed to make "protective reaction" strikes if one of their reconnaissance aircraft was fired upon. The number of such strikes in 1971 had doubled from the previous year, however, after North Vietnam shifted air defenses south to cover the buildup around the DMZ.

Not only were the North Vietnamese routinely firing at recon aircraft with SAMs along the Ho Chi Minh trail but they had also spent the years of the bombing lull busily reconstituting their entire air-defense network. Four MiG airfields had been constructed south of Vinh. In the last three weeks of the year, no less than ten U.S. aircraft would be shot down. By this point the photo-recon missions were little more than bait, one more pretense in a war built on them. In the briefing room aboard the *Hancock* the recon pilots sat in the back and were hardly noticed. The emphasis was on the counterstrikes by A-4 Skyhawk pilots who flew escort.

As the executive officer of Attack Squadron 164, Arthur hated having new pilots apprentice on the kinds of missions they were flying. He had transitioned to the A-4 Skyhawk fighter late after first piloting twin-prop S-2 cargo aircraft, so he knew what it was like to be looked on as a potential weak link in a combat squadron. In fact, his inability to get assigned to single-seat fighters in naval flight school had almost prompted him to quit the Navy.

As much as anything else, the thought of what his father would think about his giving up had kept Stan Arthur in the Navy. When he was born, his father, Holland Stanley Arthur, was a second class machinist mate on a repair ship in San Diego. Some of Stan's first memories were of watching aircraft fly off the old *Lexington* and *Saratoga* with his father near their home. From the age of five, he had dreamed of flying fighters off the deck of an aircraft carrier.

With a father who was career Navy, Arthur had plenty of opportunities growing up to stoke that dream. He was only six years old and in the hospital in Hawaii with appendicitis when the family left the island by ship just before the Japanese attack. His father had already been sent to the Caribbean to repair ships damaged by German U-boat attacks, and lacking a sponsor on the island, the family had been evacuated back to the mainland.

Stan Arthur had never forgotten his father's reaction when he announced his intention of quitting high school and enlisting in the Navy. That was the course Holland Arthur had once chosen, and it had taken him twenty-three years to rise to become a Navy lieutenant, his rank on retirement from the Philadelphia Naval Shipyard. Not only was his son going to finish high school, Holland Arthur had insisted, but he also persuaded Stan to apply for a Navy ROTC scholarship to Miami University in Oxford, Ohio. Now Comdr. Stan Arthur was fast approaching his five hundredth combat mission, and hoping that his perseverance didn't outdistance his run of luck.

Arthur knew that his volunteering for a fourth combat deployment was tough on his wife, Jenny Lou, and their four kids. Just how difficult it was on the home front had not become obvious to Arthur until he had returned from his last deployment. A friend had stopped by their quarters at the Fleet Weapons Training Center, Lemoore, California, to warn Stan that he was causing a stir by driving his midnight blue sedan around the base at night. It turned out his Plymouth was almost identical to the base commander's car. Everyone who saw Arthur drive up at night feared that it was the commander coming to tell them a loved one would not be coming home from Vietnam. How many times Jenny Lou must have watched the commander's car drive by with dread in her heart, praying that he not pull into their driveway.

Yet his wife never threw it in his face. She understood that it was what Stan felt he had to do. Each time he boarded ship, Stan Arthur was convinced that they were finally going to win the war on that deployment. But as he sat at Yankee Station in late 1971, it was getting harder and harder to believe. That was another reason his heart went out to the young pilots just arriving on their first combat deployments.

Briefing a large Alpha Strike in the ready room aboard the *Hancock*, Stan Arthur thus picked out one of the greenest young lieutenants to be his wingman. Over an intercom, the tower ordered pilots to man their airplanes. All the men in VA-164 grabbed their gear and scrambled out of the ready room. Once on deck they sprinted to their Skyhawks, their flight suits rippling in the wind and the jet wash of nearby aircraft. Arthur checked over his shoulder to see a young pilot hesitating.

"Skipper, why is everyone running?" the new lieutenant shouted.

"Because that's the way we do it!" Arthur said, exasperation evident in his voice. He looked over his shoulder to assure himself that the kid was indeed hustling to his aircraft. Leave it to a cherry pilot to ask a stupid question. As his aircraft taxied slowly into line and Stan Arthur caught his breath, however, the thought occurred to him, Why *are* we in such a hurry?

The Skyhawks descended on their targets that day only to find them totally obscured by low-hanging clouds. As they circled hoping for a break in the cloud cover, the weather closed in around them. Soon threat-warning indicators revealed that North Vietnamese missiles were in the air, seeking out the Skyhawks with their radars. Stan Arthur always believed that if you could spot a SAM, you could outmaneuver it. You couldn't see one in a cloud bank, however, and with a full load of armament the Skyhawks were sluggish even to experienced hands. Finally, Arthur ordered the strike to abort.

On the way back Arthur spotted an enemy airfield sitting just outside the target area, and he radioed to the carrier asking for permission to attack it as a secondary target. Predictably the reply was negative. Once they were "feet wet," Arthur was thus treated to the sight of his attack cell having to jettison perfectly good bombs into the ocean.

Adding to his frustration was the fact that many of their targets had an eerily familiar ring. Perhaps he had been at this for too long. The transportation network that Arthur had helped destroy on earlier deployments as part of the Rolling Thunder campaign had been painstakingly rebuilt during the long lull in bombing that had begun in 1968. Bridges had been reconstructed, roads repaired, and fuel pipelines replaced. Now they were risking their lives to try to cover the same ground all over again.

When Arthur successfully completed his five hundredth combat mission soon after, the event was major news on Yankee Station. Reporters were flown out to the *Hancock* to talk with this fighter pilot who had successfully tempted the fates five hundred times. When asked his thoughts on the occasion, Arthur couldn't hide his frustration.

"Well, it's kind of discouraging. I'm back to digging holes within a few miles of the place where I flew my first bombing mission." Arthur's luck had held. Like so many other U.S. servicemen, however, he had exhausted his faith in the struggle. Somewhere between one and five hundred, Stan Arthur quit believing they would win the war in Vietnam.

10: Coming Home 1971–72

LT. Gen. William McCaffrey stopped outside his air-conditioned hooch on a Saturday morning, looking around for a moment and letting himself adjust to the heat. Even in September of 1971, Long Binh was an impressive base. A former plantation roughly thirty-five miles north of Saigon, it had once been home to two separate headquarters staffs and the men of two full divisions, well over forty thousand troops in all. The headquarters staffs remained, along with the post exchange, the expansive mess halls, the officers' club, the air-conditioned officers' quarters, and the massive hospital where surgeons had saved his son's arm, and probably his life.

As he walked across the massive compound, returning the salutes of soldiers, noticing some of the nonstandard dress, the beards and bandannas, McCaffrey felt once again that it was one of the mistakes the Army had made. They had erected this enormous infrastructure of bases throughout the country where senior officers and support units lived in relative luxury, while the line troops fought for survival in mosquito-infested jungles, eating C rations and sleeping under ponchos in the rain. No wonder grunts termed them REMFs—rear-echelon motherfuckers.

It was one of the many changes that had swept through American society in the 1960s that the Army had ignored at great risk. Back in the days of the polo-playing officer corps of World War II, West Pointers had been encouraged to think of themselves as the elite, officers and gentlemen who were *supposed* to live better and apart from enlisted men.

Yet American society had changed, and McCaffrey had to admit that perhaps the Army had been slow to take notice. Troops were no longer prepared to accept that they were second-class citizens in their own Army, black soldiers in particular. Bill McCaffrey was inclined to see it their way. He knew from talking to Barry that his son's experience as a rifle-company commander had borne little resemblance to life at Long Binh. Perhaps if the generals and other senior officers had been living in tents, swatting at bugs, and avoiding ambushes in Vietnam from the beginning, they might have been in a bigger hurry to get this damn thing finished.

As it was, they were only then pulling out in earnest from a war that had dragged on longer for America than any other in that century. From 450,000 the year before, McCaffrey well knew that by the end of the year there would be less than 185,000 troops still left in-country.

The Army in Vietnam was clearly in a race against time. Tactically they were pulling out too fast for anything like an orderly transfer of responsibility to South Vietnamese forces. After the invasion of Cambodia the year before provoked the most violent outburst of antiwar protest since the war began and led to the shooting of Kent State students by National Guard troops, support at home had plummeted even further. Finally, the political dimensions of the war had totally eclipsed the military aspects.

Having been forced to cede the initiative and any true sense of mission, the Army was fighting an increasingly desperate rear-guard action while support for the troops back home continued to erode. The job of Bill McCaffrey, Creighton Abrams, and the other senior leadership was to get the Army home before the growing rebelliousness and disenchantment of the troops led to outright rebellion, or the Congress and the American public cut them adrift altogether.

Although they had been classmates together at the Army War College, McCaffrey had come to know Creighton Abrams best in the last year and half working under him. In that time, his admiration had grown for the thoughtful, serious general who they all believed was destined to become the next chief of staff of the Army. The fact that Abrams had been running essentially an infantry/cavalry war for the past three years was all the more impressive, McCaffrey thought, given his background as one of Gen. George Patton's crack armored officers during World War II, and the man in the lead tank of the first column to relieve surrounded men of the 101st Airborne Division in Bastogne during the Battle of the Bulge.

Ever since the beginning of the war, when he had served as vice chief of staff, Abrams had questioned Westmoreland's big-unit strategy and search-and-destroy tactics. By the time he took over following Tet in 1968, however, the pressures to bring the troops home had probably doomed Vietnamization. The withdrawal had hence proven an agonizingly difficult juggling act, where Abrams continued to exhort his commanders to prepare their forces to leave, while at the same time pleading for patience from Washington, D.C. Privately, Abrams would lament to his closest associates that no one would ever fully understand the goddamn mess Westmoreland had left him in Vietnam.

Every Saturday morning Bill McCaffrey flew to MACV headquarters in Saigon for a briefing on the pacification effort, and as the ground below shifted in color and texture from the lush green hues of the countryside to the scarred and muddy sprawl on the outskirts of Saigon, he marveled at how the helicopter had come to shape nearly everything the Army did. Six years earlier the very idea of a heliborne division such as the 1st Air Cav had seemed radical to many in the Army, and now helicopters were practically as ubiquitous in Vietnam as the jeep was in earlier wars. McCaffrey wondered if it wasn't another revolution they had failed to fully anticipate, this time driven by technology.

In the previous wars McCaffrey had fought, if a commander wanted to observe a firefight or direct a rifle company, he had to approach by jeep or on foot. That simple law of logistics not only held down micromanagement of field commanders but it placed senior officers who did venture to the front at the same risk as the foot soldiers themselves. Intuitively, every officer knew that soldiers appreciated leaders who endured the same deprivations and took the same risks as they were asked to do.

The helicopter had changed all that in Vietnam. His son Barry might be locked in a struggle to the death in some jungle, and hovering in relative safety hundreds of feet above the treetops, his entire chain-of-command up to division could be monitoring the radio net and directing the fight. And when the firefight was over, they would all fly back to secure and relatively luxurious rear-area bases while Barry and what was left of his company would be stuck in the jungle.

This growing gap in Vietnam between the hardships and deadly risks of war borne by junior and senior officers was evident in the casualty statistics. During the Second World War, 77 Army colonels died in combat, one for every 2,206 men thus killed; throughout the Vietnam War, only 8 colonels were killed in action, one for every 3,407 men. In all, between 1966 and 1971, 36 million helicopter sorties were flown in Vietnam. There were obvious advantages to the level of command-and-control and mobility the helicopter had given them. McCaffrey just wondered whether they had fully come to grips with all the corresponding changes in the character of war-fighting that the helicopter had presaged.

The command center in MACV headquarters in Saigon was a spacious room whose walls were covered with map boards. As McCaffrey entered and took his seat, he nodded to Abrams, noting that the CIA station chief, Army corps commander, and Navy and Air Force component commanders were already present for the Saturday briefing.

The briefer began by rating various areas in the country according to the Hamlet Evaluation Survey, a computerized scheme for grading every hamlet on a letter scale beginning with A. The grades were given based on a variety of arcane statistical measures, from the number of orphanages assisted, the number of students who attended classes given by CIA-sponsored Revolutionary Development teams, the dollar amount of civil-action projects ongoing, to the number of days the village headman felt safe enough to sleep at home. Based on the letter grades, the Hamlet Evaluation Survey, originally the brainchild of deputy ambassador for pacification Robert Komer, established that a vast majority of the hamlets, with more than 90 percent of the population, were "pacified."

As he listened and scanned the faces of the other officers present, General McCaffrey felt the same sense of astonishment the briefings always gave him. What complete and utter nonsense! Yet while he blamed the whole system on McNamara's penchant for "systems analysis" and its voracious appetite for statistical data, the fact was that the former secretary of defense had long since retired. Where was the service backlash against this mania for often meaningless statistical minutiae?

McCaffrey knew that the Air Force component commander would surely leave the briefing and use its findings to direct air strikes in support of local ARVN forces; the Navy commander would adjust his river patrols in the Delta based on its findings; and the Army corps commander would use it to adjust his sweeps. Somehow, the system had anointed often meaningless statistics with life-and-death import.

Nor were they all even operating off the same page of instructions. While Abrams had nominal authority over forces inside South Vietnam as the "unified" commander, in fact true control still resided in disparate commands scattered around the world. As opposed to McCaffrey's past experiences—in Korea, when Gen. Douglas MacArthur's authority was unquestioned in the theater, or World War II, when the Army had de facto charge of the war against Germany and the Navy in the fighting against Japan—command in Vietnam remained a tangled web.

Naval air strikes, for instance, were still directed by Pacific Command headquarters in Hawaii. While the Air Force component commander had authority over tactical forces in South Vietnam, frequent B-52 bomber strikes were still ordered by Strategic Air Command headquarters in Omaha, Nebraska, and were routinely out of sync with pacification efforts. Some U.S. advisers complained that they spent nearly all their time doing bomb-damage assessment of B-52 strikes that they had neither requested nor wanted.

Bill McCaffrey knew that it would take only one concerted attack by the Viet Cong and the 90 percent–plus pacification figure would drop by half and the briefers would trip over themselves scrambling back to their map boards and computer readouts to adjust the numbers. General McCaffrey, meanwhile, had his own method for deciding whether an area was pacified. He would fly out to a provincial capital and ask the local American adviser to drive him to this or that village. If the man ran screaming to the other side of his jeep, then McCaffrey knew the village wasn't pacified. It worked every time.

The higher you climbed in rank in the Army, Bill McCaffrey reasoned, the more the excitement and danger of war you felt as a young man disappeared until mostly what was left was the hard work. That and the unpleasantness. Of those two there was never a shortage.

McCaffrey had recently returned from Pleiku, where he had investigated the shooting of a young lieutenant recently graduated from West Point. As he had pieced the incident together, the green officer had only just taken command of a platoon and had ordered some recalcitrant troops to join the unit on patrol or spend time in the stockade. Four of the men, who ran drugs for the unit and happened to be black, pulled their weapons and gunned the lieutenant down in front of the entire platoon. The incident included elements of several problems with which McCaffrey had been struggling for the past year, namely fraggings, epidemic drug use, and rising racial tensions.

Fragging was perhaps the most insidious side effect of the jaundiced stalemate and troubled withdrawal from Vietnam. Having more than doubled between 1969 and 1970, the incidence of enlisted men trying to murder their officers with "fragmentation" grenades or other means had continued to increase in 1971 despite the dramatically shrinking size of both the U.S. garrison and the mission.

Many fraggings went unreported and showed up only as combat fatalities or accidental discharges. Bounties as high as $10,000 were sometimes offered by disgruntled troops for the murder of an overaggressive officer fighting a war no one believed in any longer. That or some other grievance, real or imagined. Fraggings were all the more insidious because they could be the first step in breaking down the hierarchy of command on which everything now depended.

Meanwhile, black soldiers were becoming increasingly militant in their opposition to institutional racism in the Army, especially those who had been energized by the civil rights movement back home. In the early years of Vietnam they had served in the front as infantrymen and suffered battle casualties well out of proportion to their representation in the ranks and in the rear they were far more likely than their white counterparts to be delegated lowskilled jobs. Tensions had reached such a fever pitch that some bases were all but separated into armed camps of "bloods" and "whites."

Especially in rear areas, drug use had also become nearly epidemic. One

Defense Department study that year indicated that fully 50 percent of American troops in Vietnam were drug users, with marijuana the escape of choice. Black-market prices for heroin, opium, cocaine, and amphetamines were also dirt cheap, however, and those hard narcotics were readily available.

With the perpetrators from the fragging incident already in jail, Bill McCaffrey relieved the battalion and company commanders in the case, both of whom should certainly have known about the drug ring. The incident left him with a hollow feeling, not unlike his first reaction to the initial investigation into My Lai, which he had conducted. In World War II they couldn't even get most American troops to shoot at the enemy, and here some of them were killing women, children, and their own officers.

To the problems of drugs and racial tensions, McCaffrey was ready to add another that he knew the Army would have to deal with sooner or later. While his heart went out to the vast majority of young troops in Vietnam who still did exactly what was asked of them under rotten circumstances, the Army had finally scraped the bottom of the manpower bucket so long that they were coming up with an increasing number of criminals and thugs.

Bill McCaffrey had been around long enough to take the long view of the Army's fortunes, and it gave the general an unflappable air. The way he figured it, the Army had gone through down cycles before, and it was entering another one. The country would eventually help the service right itself. The important thing was to focus on doing your duty, and in his case that had been spelled out succinctly by Army Secretary Stanley Resor when McCaffrey was given this job of deputy commander of the U.S. Army in Vietnam. *Bring the Army home.*

But was the country and the rest of the Army prepared for the soldiers they were sending back? McCaffrey was often reminded of Abrams's comment a few years earlier that it was impossible to imagine what it was like trying to command a half million men in a foreign theater of war while the government back home was coming apart on you. Now he had a much better idea of what Abrams had been talking about.

Part II

1973-
1980

11: Days of Rage 1973

WHILE it brought the end of America's direct involvement in the war in Vietnam, 1973 was a moment of reckoning for the U.S. military. There were those in uniform who blamed the defeat solely on mistakes made by the nation's civilian leadership, and they saw little reason for dramatic change. Others believed nothing short of radical reform was needed. Not an officer who persevered through those dismal days was untouched by that fundamental struggle over the soul of their service. For some officers, the battles joined during what was arguably the lowest point ever in the military's fortunes would help shape not only their services' future but their own.

Certainly 1973 was a defining moment for Lt. Col. Colin Powell. After his first week in command of the 1st Battalion, 32nd Infantry Regiment, 2nd Infantry Division, in South Korea, Powell was practically dead on his feet. Even on a good day, the 2nd was well below its authorized manpower, and there were very few good days in Korea. Indeed, by nearly every indication, the division was teetering on the brink of armed anarchy on foreign soil.

Racial tensions were so high that bars in the nightlife district downtown frequented by black enlistees were considered too dangerous for officers and were de facto off-limits. Mostly command in the 2nd was an unending series of confrontations over insubordination, drug use, and racial slights. That combustible mixture finally erupted into a full-blown race riot one night when a gang of black soldiers tried to kill the base provost marshal.

That was enough for the rangy division commander, Gen. Hank Emerson. After the riot was under control, he assembled his brigade and battalion commanders and laid down Emerson's Law. Pacing before them, the tall, gangly general with the hawklike nose was seething. They were going to take back the division, he told the assembled officers, and they were going to do it the old-fashioned way.

"Touchy-feely" counseling sessions where privates advised their officers how they should be treated were herewith suspended. From that point forward, officers were to awaken their men at four A.M. and run them so hard that they would be too tired to make it back to their bunks at night, much less make trouble. There were going to be no further racial problems because that was an order. Discrimination would likewise not be tolerated.

Beginning that night, Emerson continued, battalion commanders would abolish segregated areas on and off base. Those assembled were to drive downtown and into off-limits areas of the nightlife district, and if anyone so much as touched an officer, Emerson would bring the whole division down there and clean the area out.

Before the officers fell out, he left them with one final instruction. There were some absolute bums in the 2nd that no amount of leadership would turn around, he said. "If you've got any of these bums in your unit," said Emerson, "throw them out. I don't care what kind of discharge you give them, but put them on a plane and get them out of here."

No one was more relieved to hear Emerson's tirade than Powell. He had hardly slept in days. Shortly after he reported for duty the riot had broken out, and he had personally gone to the provost marshal's office to identify the men from his unit. In one night, Powell had locked up nearly thirty soldiers from the 1st Battalion. Among them were some of the nastiest thugs Powell had yet encountered in the U.S. Army.

Many of the men on the rolls were alumni of Project 100,000, one of Lyndon Johnson's Great Society programs designed to "rehabilitate the subterranean poor" by funneling underprivileged and unemployed youth into the military. By lowering the minimum intellectual and physical standards for inductions, recruiters had brought more than three hundred thousand men into the military under the program since it was first initiated back in 1966.

Many of the Project 100,000 inductees could neither read nor write, however, and few things made officers more nervous than having men armed with automatic weapons under their command who were unable to even read their general orders. Many officers had seen their share of the Project 100,000 recruits in Vietnam, where a Pentagon study later revealed their "attrition-by-death" rate was nearly double that of Vietnam-era veterans as a whole.

Now many of those less able soldiers had worked their way into the noncommissioned officer corps, where they were responsible for training and leading new recruits. In other words, the leveling effect witnessed in Vietnam that had pulled training and operations down to the lowest common denominator had now been institutionalized.

The Pentagon had also forced the Army to admit as much as 25 percent high school dropouts. Studies had long shown that students who could not successfully complete high school were far more likely to present discipline problems than graduates and were only about half as likely as graduates to complete their first tour. It was against that backdrop of many cynical and less able noncoms leading increasingly substandard recruits that the Army was confronted with a festering racial crisis.

For Colin Powell, who had not been in a line unit since returning from his second tour in Vietnam back in 1969, the state of the operational Army came as a rude shock. Like so many officers, Powell had taken time off upon his return home from the war to go back to school, almost as a way to regroup. He had been wounded on both combat tours, first by stepping into a punji-stick trap back in 1963, and during the second tour in a helicopter accident. Those experiences were actually less disturbing to Powell, however, than the nagging sense during much of his final tour that whatever purpose they had had for fighting the war had somehow drifted away from them by 1969.

The transition from warrior to bystander at a social revolution had been disconcerting for Powell and many of his contemporaries. Some days he had sat in the student lounge on the campus of George Washington University with watering eyes as tear gas wafted through the window from antiwar demonstrations.

Powell told himself that so much of it had nothing to do with the Army, and he focused on his schoolwork and becoming close again with his wife, Alma, and his children. His third child, Annemarie, was born, and the Powells bought a new home in the Washington area. More and more, Powell found himself turning away from society and toward family and friends in uniform.

After earning his master's degree in business administration, Powell had accepted a Pentagon staff position working for the influential assistant vice chief of the Army, Gen. William DePuy. While much of the Army was fighting or coping with Vietnam, DePuy had been assigned to look at how the Army could reorganize and resize itself in the war's aftermath. The feisty general had done so with his usual fervor, and pretty soon the group of bright, hard-charging junior officers he had assembled around him became known as DePuy's fair-haired boys.

While working for DePuy, Powell had been awarded a coveted White House Fellowship and had moved to the Office of Management and Budget for a year, where he caught the eye of the director, Caspar Weinberger, and his deputy, Frank Carlucci. Significantly, both men would later become secretaries of defense and remember the bright young officer who had interned in their office. The period of mingling in the upper echelons of power in Washington had fascinated Powell and put his career on the fast track. It had done little, however, to prepare him for Korea.

The Army was in far worse shape in 1973 than was evident from Washington, D.C. The whole of the 2nd Division, for instance, was understrength, and Powell's battalion had less than half of its authorized officers and troops. Many of the men who were on the rolls, meanwhile, were shacked up downtown with local villagers or whacked-out on drugs. And then there was the electric undercurrent of racial tension.

Powell, the son of Jamaican immigrants and a child of Harlem and the South Bronx, was no stranger to prejudice or racial insult. He remembered being turned away at a hamburger joint in Columbus, Georgia, back in the early 1960s when he was stationed at Fort Benning. Negroes, he was told, had to use the back door. While he was in Vietnam on his first tour in 1963, his wife and baby daughter, Linda, had stayed with his in-laws in Birmingham, Alabama, when Bull Connor was turning cattle-prod-wielding cops and attack dogs loose on civil rights marchers.

But Powell was first and foremost an Army officer. It would never occur to him that justice and racial equality would flower in an environment of near anarchy. He had first noticed serious racial tensions arising in Army ranks during his second Vietnam tour back in 1968, the same year Martin Luther King, Jr., had been assassinated. For many blacks it had been the defining moment of an era of rising expectations.

In one year three of the men most closely associated with the civil rights movement and the Great Society passed from the national scene—Lyndon Johnson, an embittered casualty of Vietnam, and Robert Kennedy and Martin Luther King, Jr., victims of assassins' bullets. Many black Americans would look back at 1968 and especially the death of King as the high-water mark, the spot where the great wave of hope that swelled with the civil rights movement and the Great Society programs hit the breakwater of bigotry and prejudice in America, receding in a tide of frustration and rage.

Some of the white officers in his division at that time had approached Powell about the racial unrest, as if this young black officer somehow had instant answers to the problem of prejudice. There were no easy answers. What Powell had instead was a knack for command and faith in strong leadership principles. In that respect, General Emerson's approach rang true to Powell: do not tolerate discrimination in your unit and do not let soldiers use it as a pretense for insubordination.

Though there were valid complaints about the Army's lack of promotions for blacks and unequal punishment meted out to black soldiers, there were also unmistakable signs that the Army was trying to change. Magazines targeted to black and other minority-group soldiers were increasingly appearing in the base Stars and Stripes bookstores, just as the post exchanges were displaying cosmetics, records, and other products oriented toward black soldiers. Minorities were also depicted more frequently in training manuals and other official literature.

The Army was beginning to address the shortage of black officers by stressing to promising soldiers that officer candidate school was a path into the officer corps outside of college ROTC programs and the Military Academy. West Point officials had also begun actively recruiting more black cadets, and the previous year had seen forty-five enter the Academy.

There was also an increasing emphasis on racial sensitivity seminars—or "rap sessions"—that the Army had been prescribing. Many of the troops approached them reticently, but it wasn't long before real grievances began to surface. A white soldier from the South might plaster Confederate flags all over his room and wonder why his black roommate got so bent out of shape about it. A black soldier could play his soul music turned up full blast and take offense when asked to turn it down. Both black and whites might bristle at walking by a group of Hispanic soldiers speaking Spanish and laughing, wondering just what was so freaking funny.

Listening to soldiers argue over these slights, some real and others imagined, many officers began to realize that the troops had never even sat down at lunch next to someone of a different race, had no idea what their views were on music, clothes, or haircuts. Like so many Americans, they had grown up in segregated neighborhoods and schools. If the Army could somehow get through this period, laying out all these antagonisms on the table and forcing everyone to confront them, then the service might put the racial hurdle behind it before the rest of society.

The problem was making it through the transition. Some of the officers simply couldn't handle the situation. Emerson was forced to relieve one battalion commander who had totally lost control of his unit to a group of radical black activists. Initially, some of the ringleaders for the activists had approached the officer and promised that they could take care of the racial problems in his battalion if only he would do what they said. As soon as the man consented to the devil's bargain, he had essentially relinquished control of his unit. Powell was determined not to let that happen in the 1st Battalion.

He was tested soon enough, however, when Emerson broke up the antagonists and dispersed the ringleaders throughout the division. One of them landed at the 1st Battalion, which Powell became aware of when his sergeant major knocked on his office door.

"Sir, you ain't gonna believe what just showed up on our doorstep," the sergeant major said with a worried look on his face.

Looking out the door, Powell recognized Private Odom, known to be one of the division's worst troublemakers. He decided the best thing to do would be to give the man a little rope. Sure enough, Powell learned within a week that Odom was organizing clandestine meetings with other black soldiers in the battalion. Powell had the sergeant major order Odom to report to his office.

When he walked in, Odom was Mr. Congeniality.

"Sir, I'm glad you called for me, because I've been wanting to talk with you," Odom said in a voice that somehow reminded Powell of a snake-oil salesman.

"Oh, really," Powell said. "What about, Odom?"

"Well, sir, you've got problems here. Yes, sir, you've got real problems in this battalion. I've been talking to some of the brothers, and I've been talking to some of the white folks, and I think I can help you out."

Lt. Col. Colin Powell possessed an open, almost guileless face that could be misleading. At times, a look of utter seriousness of purpose could pass over it like a shadow, sharpening the features and reminding you of the imposing presence of this muscular, six-foot-one commander. Odom glimpsed that shadow. As Powell continued to study him, he stammered on.

"Yes, sir, so I wanted you to know I'm really delighted to be here so I can help you out. I think we'll get along fine."

"Oh, we're going to get along fine, you little squirrel ass," Colin Powell finally replied. "Because you're leaving tonight."

"Sir? Leaving where?"

"You're out!" Powell grabbed a sheaf of papers on his desk and tossed them to the soldier. "Here's your discharge papers. You're out of the Army as of tonight. I've got three guys waiting outside this office to escort you to the airport. You so much as blink at them, and I'll have you thrown in jail. And then you'll never leave the Army. Now get out of my office. You ain't helping nobody around here."

When word of the incident spread through the 1st Battalion, and it became clear that the colonel wasn't going to be coerced, the insubordination problems and racial tensions began to subside. With the worst of the division's discipline problems under control, Emerson encouraged his officers to motivate the troops with various competitions such as "combat football" and "combat baseball," cohesion-building exercises that were the best substitute for the realistic training they couldn't afford to conduct on a regular basis. Remedial reading and writing classes were established, as were tae kwon do lessons, and soldiers were encouraged to take night classes and get their high school diplomas.

Powell watched as the confidence and self-assuredness of his troops steadily grew, and young kids who had never achieved anything in their lives began to see themselves as winners. Gradually, he began to reinstate some of the "touchy-feely" rap sessions. To his amusement, Powell learned that his tough line with the troublemakers had actually earned him the respect of most of the black troops, who took to calling him "Bro P.," Brother Powell.

Like many officers in 1973, Powell viewed the approaching end to the draft as the country turning its back on the Army, and he suspected that they would be in trouble for years because of it. But helping to turn around the 2nd Division of the 32nd, and seeing even these troubled troops respond to rigorous training, education, and a little creative leadership, gave Powell not only renewed confidence in his ability to command, but also faith that the Army would eventually right itself. During a period when the Army was on the defensive at home as it had rarely been in its modern history, Colin Powell traveled to a strange land and had what he would remember as perhaps the most satisfying year in his career.

12: All Volunteer 1973

THE aircraft shuddered as it rose through rough air toward its cruising altitude. From the window, Capt. Barry McCaffrey could see the white-capped peaks of the Colorado Rockies recede beneath them. The severe landscape was such a contrast to the lush, rolling hills of the Hudson River Valley where he lived. Behind the granite battlements of West Point, McCaffrey and his family were safely sequestered from the turbulence that was rocking the rest of the Army as surely as the mountain airflows were rattling the drink cart. Or at least so Barry thought.

Settling back into his seat, he reflected that the presentation he had just given at the Air Force Academy in Colorado Springs went better than expected. He had been invited to deliver a paper on the future role of women in the military to an annual conference of what were called the "Young Turks," a selected group of young officers from each of the services. Gatherings where senior leadership could tap the feelings in the junior ranks had become common as the services continued trying to mend the cracks in trust that had developed up and down the command hierarchy during the war.

With the Equal Rights Amendment having just passed the previous year, the whole issue of women entering the workforce in nontraditional jobs was very much on the social agenda. It was social science in the most fundamental sense, and exactly the sort of issue that intrigued Barry McCaffrey. Perhaps that was the problem.

In his presentation, McCaffrey had had the audacity to suggest the obvious, or at least what passed for it in his eyes. From his earlier work with the office of the special assistant to the Modern Volunteer Army, he knew that all of the services were committed to dramatically increasing the recruitment of women to help fill the ranks of an all-volunteer force. Of course they did it at the persistent arm-twisting of civilian Defense Department officials, but it was a commitment none the less. For the Army, that translated into plans to double the number of women between 1972 and 1977.

Given the reaction of many in uniform, however, it almost seemed as if no one wanted to come to grips with the fact that without a major expansion of women's roles in the military, the all-volunteer effort might be doomed. Then again, McCaffrey knew from his heated discussions with his father and others that nothing would please the majority of the Army's senior leadership more than the end of what many considered this all-volunteer "madness." Yet like it or not, the draft would cease later that year, precisely on July 1, 1973.

In addition to his library research for the paper, McCaffrey had interviewed the director of the Women's Army Corps (WAC), as well as a number of social science experts. His recommendations to the conference included discontinuing the WAC, integrating women into the Army mainstream, and allowing them to compete for jobs in all military occupations save those related to direct combat, which he defined as anything at the combat brigade staff or lower. The presentation received enthusiastic applause at the conference, and McCaffrey was feeling pretty pleased with himself.

Before the plane had even cleared the Rockies, however, he was approached in his seat by two lieutenant colonels that he recognized from the Academy.

"McCaffrey, if that presentation is published, you will regret the day that you ever committed those thoughts to paper," one of the colonels warned. McCaffrey searched the faces of the senior officers.

"I think it would be very ill-advised to publish that paper," agreed the other.

As it turned out, the advice was not only heartfelt but prescient. Once McCaffrey was back at West Point, Maj. Gen. William Knowlton, the West Point superintendent, summoned him. Knowlton was livid about the presentation. The paper was conspicuously absent from the conference proceedings where the other presentations were reprinted, and clearance was later even denied by the Freedom of Information Office. When his father got wind of the paper, he would barely talk to Barry for weeks.

Not for the first time it occurred to McCaffrey that the Army was swirling in an eddy of social currents over which it had little control and about which it had virtually no understanding. The role of women in America was being redefined, blacks were rebelling against the institutional racism prevalent in so much of society, and drug use was becoming a shared experience for nearly an entire generation. A scandal was even brewing in Washington over a break-in at the Watergate that threatened to topple the president, and with him perhaps the last vestige of respect for authority in America.

The position teaching social studies at the Military Academy was meant to be a sojourn of sorts while Barry and Jill healed the emotional wounds of the war, which were proving even slower to mend than the physical. Jill had little interest in anything that happened outside of the Academy gates. Barry hadn't found out until much later that she had destroyed all of his letters from Vietnam, which he had hoped to compile into a diary. That topic remained a raw nerve between them as yet too sensitive to touch.

As for his work at West Point, ever since Barry had first become involved in the matter of the all-volunteer Army, controversy had been a constant if unwelcome companion. Thinking back to how he had become entangled in what for the Army was likely to prove the defining issue of the era, Barry McCaffrey sometimes couldn't believe how naive they had all been.

It had begun with an unexpected phone call back in February of 1971. McCaffrey had recognized the voice on the other end immediately. He remembered a pinched look of worry on a gaunt face leaning over his hospital bed in Long Binh, and the figure of a general helping to load the wounded in isolated jungle clearings. There was the radio call sign that had dropped through triple-canopy on a lifeline of static and rotor thud: "Gary Owen Six."

Lt. Gen. George Forsythe Jr., McCaffrey's former commander in the 1st Air Cav, had called to ask him to join a team of hard-charging young officers being put together to transition the Army into an all-volunteer force. Barry immediately agreed. Forsythe had always been a soldier's soldier, and McCaffrey had decided long before the phone call that he'd follow him anywhere.

Since returning from his successful tour as commander of the 1st Air Cav Division back in 1969, Forsythe had been awarded his third star and proceeded on to a number of high-profile positions. It had seemed clear to many observers that he was well on track to one day join the elite cabal of four-star generals at the top of the service's vast pyramid of command. What was less clear was why Forsythe would want to sidetrack his career, even if only temporarily, to take on a task as utterly thankless as the volunteer-Army effort.

It was no secret that the regular officer corps generally despised the all-volunteer idea. The draft had been a fixture in military plans since the beginning of World War II, when military ranks were swelled by both plumbers and Princeton Ph.D.s, sharecroppers' sons and the scions of wealth and position. During Vietnam new entrees through the draft averaged 950,000 men annually. The idea to abruptly close that spigot was thus viewed as purely political maneuvering on the part of the Nixon administration in an attempt to dodge the virulent antidraft backlash at the military's expense.

The issue struck to the very heart of the relationship of men in uniform to the society they served. The idea that national service was a moral responsibility and the bedrock of patriotism was deeply embedded in the military psyche, as was the belief that the country's armed forces should have a breadth that spanned all strata of American society—regional, racial, and socioeconomic.

Few if any questioned that the inequities in the draft needed reforming. There were profound fears, however, that a volunteer force would become disproportionately skewed toward minority or lower-income recruits or attract too many trigger-happy psychos or become such a haven for society's rejects that public support for the military would continue to degenerate, isolating them further.

There was little comfort in what was largely regarded as the rubber-stamping of the idea by the Gates Commission, which was assigned by President Nixon to study the issue. Nor were many officers comforted by Defense Secretary Melvin Laird's assurances that "long range . . . we do not foresee any significant difference between the racial composition of the all-volunteer force and the racial composition of the nation." Charges that it would be dominated by low-income youth were likewise "false and unfounded claims."

Accustomed to a captive audience of draftees, the Army and the other military services were thus to be thrown into the open market in the bitter aftermath of Vietnam, vying for the services of one of the most antiauthoritarian and rebellious generations in modern American history. At the same time, many of their most promising young career officers were resigning their commissions, and some were all but spitting on the Army on their way out.

Climbing out onto this limb when he took over as special assistant to the Modern Volunteer Army (SAMVA), Gen. George Forsythe, Jr., reported directly to Westmoreland and outside the normal command channels. Forsythe's charter had been simple: develop a master plan to increase the Army's attractiveness as a career and thus raise to the maximum extent possible the number and quality of volunteer enlistments. It's doubtful that Forsythe, who had fulfilled nearly every officer's ambition by commanding a division in combat, had ever undertaken a more daunting mission.

Forsythe was a hardheaded Montanan, however, and where most of his contemporaries had seen a thankless assignment, he discerned an opportunity to fundamentally reform the Army. Like a number of senior leaders, he had been deeply disturbed by a sense of drift in the Army. Forsythe saw an undue emphasis on spit-shine image and "Mickey Mouse" rules over true substance, not to mention a general lack of trust between the senior leadership and the junior officer and enlisted ranks. Nothing bothered him more than the rigid, authoritarian style of command so many officers seemed to favor, erecting a stony formality between themselves and the soldiers they were supposed to lead. By supplying the Army with an unending stream of draftees and requiring little accountability in return, the draft encouraged a system that took the soldier for granted.

When Forsythe assembled SAMVA's small staff of handpicked officers, most of them at or below the level of lieutenant colonel, he thus made a willingness to consider any idea the hallmark of the all-volunteer effort. The Army had to counter its overwhelmingly negative image in the media of a ponderous and monolithic bureaucracy, he felt, and prove that it was finally ready for meaningful change. We're going to lead the Army out of the dark ages and into the twenty-first century, Forsythe would tell his team, and no idea that might help us get there will be ignored.

Forsythe had broken the SAMVA's focus down into three basic areas. First they would address creature-comfort issues such as decent barracks, food, and pay. In other words, they would break the habit of taking draftees for granted and learn for the first time to truly take care of their people.

Secondly, they would help create the kind of job challenges recruits so obviously yearned for by waging war on the nitpicking regulations and stressing instead such things such as adventure training and increased autonomy for the junior officer and enlisted ranks.

Finally, professional leadership would be heavily emphasized, with Forsythe working closely with Lt. Cols. Walt Ulmer and Mike Malone at the Army War College, who were putting the finishing touches on a follow-up to their groundbreaking professionalism study entitled *Leadership for the 1970s*.

The group's proposed improvements were to be introduced on a test basis as part of Project Volar (for "volunteer army"), an effort initially involving four experimental posts where base commanders were given wide latitude and extra funds to implement Forsythe's recommendations as they saw fit.

Those had been heady days for Barry McCaffrey, working for his old commander on the Army of the future. The group of young officers Forsythe had gathered reflected their leader's bias toward officers with command experience and included the Army's drill sergeant of the year, as well as Lt. Col. Pete Dawkins. Dawkins was a legendary former cadet and first captain of the West Point class of 1959, and a winner of the Heisman Trophy and a Rhodes scholarship. Each day those Young Turks came to work eager to recast the cultural and social mores of the Army to make them relevant to a new generation of Americans, and they had been encouraged to believe everything was in play.

All their work had reflected an emphasis on innovation and lack of formality. They gleefully gored some of the Army's most sacred cows, working in small groups and passing their ideas up to General Forsythe, hastily written on bits of paper. In many ways, those innocuous scraps of paper represented a clean break with the old Army of Barry McCaffrey's father.

Ideas that eventually made it into practice as part of the Volar experiment had included transitioning to an eight-hours-a-day, five-days-a-week work schedule; eliminating Saturday-morning inspections; allowing longer hair; turning hated KP duty over to civilian workers; dividing open barracks into more private two-men rooms; putting beer machines in barracks; abolishing five A.M. reveille as well as weekend bed checks and curfews; doubling pay; and creating enlisted men's and racial-harmony councils for the airing of grievances to higher command.

To kick off the Project Volar experiment, the Army had also launched an intense radio and television advertising campaign proclaiming, "The Army Wants to Join You." Piqued by the novelty of this newly progressive and user-friendly Army, reporters had flocked to Volar bases and for the first time in memory filed scores of generally favorable stories.

Under the headline "The New Army: A Mix of Business and Pleasure," the *Detroit News* had written of enlisted clubs featuring bikini-clad go-go dancers. "It's Definitely NOT the Same Old Army," proclaimed the *Washington News* under a story that quoted a Volar base commander as bragging that his officers spent more time listening to soldiers than did the officers of any outfit in the Army. *The Wall Street Journal* reported on a program at Fort Jackson, South Carolina, where recruiters allowed potential recruits to sample Army life for three days without obligation, and of *Easy Rider* recruiters, young enlisted men with modish haircuts who roared into towns on powerful motorcycles to promote the new Army. Company commanders free to design much of their own training, it had been reported, incorporated snow skiing, white-water rafting, and drag races with fifty-ton M-60 tanks into their weekly training regimen.

A number of the Volar bases had reported reductions in AWOLs, an increase in reenlistments, and a decline in court-martials, and the experiment was expanded to twelve bases. Meanwhile, Barry McCaffrey and the rest of the officers in SAMVA had continued to brainstorm, occasionally showing a willingness to thwart tradition that shocked even some of their own members.

One idea that initially struck McCaffrey as almost laughable was that officers would salute their subordinates, rather than the other way around. *Of course.* That would accentuate the fact that the officers and noncoms were really there to serve the soldiers! The *Army* wants to join *you.* When he realized the group was actually serious about recommending the idea, however, McCaffrey had threatened to quit. That was one change he simply couldn't picture trying to explain to his father.

In the end, Forsythe had vetoed the idea, and McCaffrey was convinced that an embarrassment of staggering proportions had been averted. What he hadn't grasped at the time but was soon to discover, however, was that many officers in the Army viewed the entire Volar experiment with exactly the same mixture of dumbfounded astonishment and horror.

That realization had come later in 1972, when McCaffrey was tapped to take part in a campaign designed to promulgate the lessons of Volar. With the experiment ready to be briefed to operational commands, McCaffrey and the rest of his team were sent out to teach the rank and file about the "new Army," and what positive steps they needed to take to grow beyond outdated policies.

The feeding frenzy of recriminations and pent-up frustrations that greeted those briefings had been like a collective slap in the face. McCaffrey and the rest of the team were stunned at the time. Many of those officers were trying to keep a lid on bases that were on the threshold of anarchy, however, and suddenly into their midst come prancing the liberal crazies from the volunteer-Army office who have been trying to turn the Army into some kind of permissive day camp. Beer in the barracks? We've got drugs in the fucking barracks! Coffeehouse rap sessions? We've got dapping, rapping, and black-power salutes, not to mention race riots! Empowerment? We've got goddamn insubordination and mutiny!

It was like that at every stop, and after a few such spleen-venting sessions the sergeant major on McCaffrey's team had approached him in tears to say he couldn't continue. Of all the various echelons of the Army, the noncommissioned officers' corps was perhaps most resistant to the changes proposed during the seminars. With their ranks already decimated by the war and on the defensive over discipline and AWOL problems, many noncoms viewed the greater empowerment of junior officers and permissiveness toward enlistees as a direct threat to their authority.

After clearing it with Col. Robert Elton, his team leader, McCaffrey had let the sergeant major leave the seminar team with no mark against him. Hell, it was clear the Army had failed miserably to sell even the mid- and senior-level officer corps on the overriding vision behind the volunteer-Army effort. He could hardly blame a noncom for not understanding the bigger picture. The truth was that McCaffrey had also been shocked by the overwhelmingly negative reaction that greeted them at every base.

By the late spring of 1972, General Forsythe had decided that there would be no fourth star in his future. He had still been ardently committed to the principles of the all-volunteer Army. Every day, however, had brought fresh evidence that having once rid themselves of the albatross of the draft, the Nixon administration and some factions in Congress were perfectly willing to let the Army carry the weight of an all-volunteer force alone. In truth, there was also ample evidence that Forsythe and his group were trying to lead the Army where it had not been ready to follow.

To Forsythe, it also seemed clear that the administration was far more interested in keeping a return to conscription off the political agenda than in throwing its political weight or financial support fully behind the all-volunteer effort. His frustrations boiled to the surface in a remarkable close-held memo he wrote to the Army's General Staff, in which he openly questioned the sincerity of his civilian commander in chief.

"The White House continues to stand somewhat aloof and unconcerned, leaving the Army in the position of appearing to be the author of the all-volunteer Army concept," wrote Forsythe. "The President must have appreciated the need to persuade the Congress, the nation, and especially [the Army itself] that his goal is serious, sound and worthy."

The internal response to "The Army Wants to Join You" campaign had also increased Forsythe's frustrations over resistance to his reforms within the Army itself, and the failure of the Army leadership to successfully sell the all-volunteer effort within their own ranks. He had been well aware that most of his colleagues bristled at the slogan, viewing it in Forsythe's words as "a blatant capitulation to radical fads and rejection of Army tradition." Indeed, that summed up how the senior officer corps viewed most of SAMVA's work.

The inability to get senior-level backing to effectively sell the modern volunteer-army concept came to a head for Forsythe in what he would later call the "Rose Garden" meeting. Having already worked the back channels, Forsythe had gone into the meeting of the general staff fully expecting to get an unequivocal endorsement for the modern volunteer-Army effort once and for all. Instead, Westmoreland had gotten what Forsythe later described as an equivocal look on his face when it came time for officially approving the plan and had asked the other generals present for their opinions. He had been met with silence and averted glances. Not long afterward, Forsythe had resigned after more than thirty-two years in the Army.

A loyal soldier who truly loved the Army, Forsythe never publicly groused about his experience at SAMVA. Probably the closest he came to revealing his true disappointment and concern came in an op-ed he wrote in *The Washington Post* in January of 1972, the same month that SAMVA's role in guiding the all-volunteer effort was officially deemphasized.

"Many of the Army's older soldiers . . . contend that they have spent a lifetime learning how to run the Army and do not intend to change now to satisfy 'political expediency,'" Forsythe wrote. "Like so many other persons, we seniors of the U.S. Army sometimes have trouble accepting and dealing with youthful idealism. It does not salute by reflex, does not obey blindly.

"I am not sanguine about our institution's ability to change its attitude quickly. Ponderous bureaucracy makes it difficult. . . . Yet the American Army's appeal cannot be only to those young men whose hopes have already been crushed by circumstance. Armies have historically attracted the disillusioned, especially in peacetime. Now the Army's health depends to a certain extent on how many young men with hope and zest and idealism it attracts."

When the country was finally willing once again to consider the military as a respectable profession for its young idealists, the Army would be ready with many of SAMVA's recommendations in place and institutionalized, including more decent living conditions and work hours, a commitment to racial equality in terms of advancement, a growing emphasis on challenging training over potato-peeling and guard duty, and a command mind-set confident enough not to confuse a higher degree of personal dignity for its younger soldiers with a threat to its authority.

Coming as it did during one of the most volatile periods in modern American history, however, the message behind the "Army Wants to Join You" campaign was too much for the old guard to swallow. The willingness to change probably brought the Army some precious time until the American

public was ready for a reconciliation with its military. In the meantime, however, there was something of the desperate suitor in the appeal that many
proud men in uniform simply could not abide. So they shot the messenger.

We were so naive, Barry McCaffrey thought. The rude reception of his
"Women in the Army" paper at West Point had reminded him of the
boundless enthusiasm of those early days with the Modern Volunteer Army
effort, and the team's eventual disillusionment. Even at West Point, the very
wellspring of idealism that General Forsythe used to stress as the future hope
of the Army, the cadets sensed the Army was somehow rudderless and drifting. They read it in the front-page headlines of *The New York Times* that they
were required to memorize each morning.

Hell, thought McCaffrey, the country had just lost a war and the senior
leadership of the Army couldn't even seem to come to grips with the fact!
Whenever he felt the sense of frustration and even shame begin to build,
McCaffrey simply reminded himself that a revolution was going on in society
that was far bigger than the Army.

Though the stay at West Point had begun as a sort of respite after his stint
with SAMVA and the creative-leadership seminars, it would eventually last
four years and nearly change the course of McCaffrey's career. If there was an
air of convalescence to this tour of duty, however, it was more spiritual than
physical. The surgeons at Walter Reed had finally completed their battery of
operations, and Barry had regained most of the use of his arm.

Nor was he agonizing over whether or not to stay in the Army. He had
come close to leaving in 1969, had even interviewed with the FBI. He knew it
was a decision that Jill would have supported. But somehow it seemed like
the wrong time to quit the Army, when it was down. Looking at the vulnerable state of U.S. forces and the emerging dominance of the Soviet-led Warsaw Pact in Europe, McCaffrey also felt that the country might need the
military sooner than many people seemed willing to admit or cared to believe. Instead of resigning, he had thus completed the master's program in
civil government at American University, and that had meant a further commitment to the Army of at least a few years. So far he had not looked back.

The truth was that as a father only recently past thirty years old, the veteran of three combat tours, and an Army brat as well as a child of the 1960s,
Barry McCaffrey had been drawn to the intellectual ferment that churned
behind the peaceful stone facade of West Point in 1973. That had been at
least part of the motivation of returning to the Military Academy to teach.
Within the halls of military academia at least there still echoed the constant

murmur of debate as long-held traditions were reexamined and argued, and there was a sense that change was brewing.

Barry McCaffrey also knew that the West Point assignment would be good for his family. While Vietnam had left him with so many unanswered questions that he was willing to ponder nearly any point of view if it brought some illumination on the war and how it had affected others, Jill McCaffrey had been affected in a different way. The years of worry, the long separation, the fear and the subsequent hospitalizations stretching over two years, all had scarred her as surely as Barry. Ever since the disastrous party in 1969, McCaffrey had watched as her initial hurt and outrage had turned to a cooler and longer-lasting sense of alienation.

In that sense the West Point campus was perfect. Returning to the picturesque bluff overlooking the wide Hudson River had rekindled the memories of the couple's whirlwind courtship seven years earlier when Barry was a senior. The building where he taught social sciences flanked the green expanse of the Plain, the site of seemingly countless formations and parades for which Barry McCaffrey had mustered in a different, far simpler life.

Yet for all its outward calm, West Point had not escaped the seismic shocks rocking the rest of the Army. When McCaffrey compared the cadets in his social science class and their experiences at the Academy to his own just a decade earlier, his heart went out to these confused young men. The Army's agonized and well-publicized withdrawal from Vietnam had seemed to mock all of the tenets upon which the cadet experience was founded, outlined in the "Bugle Notes" handbook that each plebe received on entering West Point and literally etched in granite on the benches that lined the footpaths atop Trophy Point—Dignity, Loyalty, Discipline, Courage, Integrity.

In stark contrast to McCaffrey's class, when these young men left the walls of West Point behind, they immediately changed into their civilian clothes. The whole Army was like that, desperate to blend innocuously into the crowds off base lest they be identified as cadets or soldiers. Sometimes when he stood at the front of his social science class trying to answer questions posed by the cadets, Barry McCaffrey sensed that he was seeing a whole generation of Army officers at risk.

If the tenor of the West Point student body in 1973 was mainly one of confusion, however, it did not differ greatly from the overall atmosphere in the faculty ranks or at the Academy as a whole. The young faculty members, many of them Vietnam veterans and fresh out of graduate school, were themselves questioning some of the traditions of the Academy and railing against what they saw as the emphasis by traditionalists on spit and polish over substance.

Barry's former classmate Dave Barrato, for instance, had returned to West Point about the same time as McCaffrey to serve as a tactical officer and counselor to a cadet company. Old "Barrachi" was back from his second tour in Vietnam, one of which he spent as the operations officer for a Special Forces company, and his first assignment was to count the number of shoe trees in his cadet company. A Purple Heart and Bronze Star recipient, and his first bonding experience with the cadets he was supposed to mentor was to count their shoe trees!

Barrato had begged his superior officer not to humiliate him in front of the new cadets with such a ridiculous task, but to no avail. Sure enough, the cadets had stared at him with barely disguised disdain as he crawled through closets rummaging amongst their shoes. It was the same cult of numerology that had prevailed in Vietnam, where common sense was gleefully sacrificed on the altar of meaningless statistics.

The social science department where Barry McCaffrey taught was one of the most liberal on campus, and there were frequent debates in the faculty lounge on such issues as hair length and whether or not dope smoking was any worse than the older generation's taking an occasional drink. While West Point was somewhat buffered against the more serious drug problems that were filtering back onto operational Army bases from Vietnam, it offered no protection from the turbulence caused by disillusioned young officers returning to the United States from the war. The same divisiveness and acrimony that McCaffrey had seen rip at the fabric of his own West Point class and greet the creative-leadership seminars was thus painfully evident on campus.

In the previous eighteen-month period more than thirty young officers had resigned from teaching posts at West Point. Sometimes Dave Barrato proclaimed that it was a miracle they didn't all get the hell out. While he didn't quit, however, many officers did, and some could not resist venting their considerable frustrations to those who stayed behind. It was Barry McCaffrey's disastrous party of 1969 still being played out four years later, and try as they might to understand, those who still carried the Army's tattered banner were left each time with a stinging sense of betrayal. And none had shaken the collective psyche of the West Point faculty harder than the resignation to national fanfare of Maj. Josiah Bunting.

Sy Bunting's résumé seemed to reflect the pedigree of a warrior-statesman: Virginia Military Academy first captain, Rhodes Scholar, staff officer with the 9th Infantry Division in Vietnam's Mekong Delta, West Point history instructor. The previous year Bunting had even published a well-received novel about Vietnam, *The Lionheads*, which depicted the unchecked careerism of officers so enslaved "by the almighty body count" that they undertake an un-necessarily risky mission that costs the life of a young private.

Like so many promising young officers of his generation who had ago-nized over the decision to abandon their military careers, however, Bunting apparently felt the need for a public catharsis. The difference was the level of national media attention he commanded, and the smugness with which he dismissed his former colleagues at West Point.

Referring in an interview with *Family Magazine* to the social sciences de-partment at West Point as "a repository of liberalism with a small 'l,'" Bunting went on to say that at Oxford he had become something of an "in-tellectual snob." "I began to think myself not temperamentally equipped for the Army. . . . I see a lot of nuances and subtleties that many Army officers don't see."

The interview predictably sparked howls on campus, especially within the social sciences department. Though he would probably have found much common ground with Bunting over a beer at South Post Tavern outside the main gate, McCaffrey was enraged at this public depiction of West Point as some sort of plebeian backwater. This major who unabashedly laid claim to general-officer ambitions had spent his entire tour in Vietnam in a rear-area staff job. McCaffrey doubted that Bunting had ever heard a shot fired in his direction in anger. Bunting claimed to have sought command of a rifle com-pany, but having been wounded three times in combat in three successive tours, McCaffrey was not inclined to give him the benefit of the doubt. A true desire for combat in Vietnam rarely went unrequited. Privately, he sus-pected that Bunting was one of those intellectuals who believed that he was somehow above being killed in action.

McCaffrey felt the same lingering sense of hurt and betrayal at Bunting's comments that he had had after his disastrous party. Former brothers in arms continued to turn on one another with internecine rancor, reopening wounds that would take far longer to heal than many of them had initially believed. At the center of those thrashings and self-recriminations, however, was a fun-damental struggle over who would remain to guide the post-Vietnam mili-tary, and what they could possibly make of it.

13: Last Act 1973

"BABY killer!"

Lt. Gen. William McCaffrey tried to hurry through the usual throng of protesters outside his Pentagon entrance, but there was no escaping the woman's shrill voice. She followed him all the way down the walkway scream-ing. Though he was not normally given to outbursts, something inside snapped on this morning, and Bill McCaffrey whirled around and confronted his accuser.

"Lady, I've fought three wars and put my life on the line trying to prevent madmen from killing people like you!" McCaffrey's outburst was met with an uncomprehending look of contempt.

"Make love not war!"

Braving crowds of protesters had become a morning ritual for those who worked in the Pentagon. Whereas McCaffrey had returned home from previ-ous wars to outpourings of public support and even parades, his homecom-ing celebration from Vietnam with his mother and sister had been interrupted in a Boston restaurant when a number of patrons hissed at his uniform. A few even approached his table and cursed McCaffrey before his own mother.

Soon after he reached the spacious Pentagon office of the army inspector general, McCaffrey's phone rang. He could guess who was on the other end. Normally he looked forward to talking with Gen. Creighton Abrams, but not on this particular morning. After serving together for two and a half years in Vietnam, the two generals had fallen into an effortless relationship where Abrams never had to tell him what to do, and in turn McCaffrey didn't bother the chief of staff of the Army with needless questions.

"Yes, sir."

"Bill, it's Abe. I just received your report on the support center you in-spected." McCaffrey had recently returned from a trip to investigate an ad-ministration center in the Midwest. He discovered that the center had thousands of letters of inquiry from various commands that they hadn't got-ten around to processing, a fact that he had dutifully noted on the IG form under the section headed "Minor Deficiencies."

"Bill, I have just one question," Abrams said. "If you see a backlog of thou-sands of unanswered letters of inquiry as minor, exactly what would you con-sider a major deficiency?"

Not for the first time, it occurred to McCaffrey that he was one of the worst inspector generals the Army had ever had. After finishing his conversation with the chief of staff, he reflected that what was really bothering him had little to do with the episode over the backlog of unanswered letters.

McCaffrey had anticipated that the role of the inspector general would be to act as a sort of a benevolent ombudsman, someone who could help commands anticipate and thus avoid problems. Yet buffeted by problems from nearly every direction, the Army was beginning to turn a self-critical eye on many of its long-held traditions and practices, and it was using some of the same "systems analysis" techniques popularized by McNamara. Increasingly, the Inspector General's Office was expected to act almost as an internal investigations unit responding to "hot lines" and exposing wrongdoing, and McCaffrey was uncomfortable leading such a crusade.

Having resisted altering even the most disastrous policies throughout the Vietnam War, the Army was entering at war's end one of the most turbulent periods in its history. Clearly, the dramatic changes shaking the service's foundations would dismantle many of the traditions that had come to define the Army for officers of Bill McCaffrey's generation.

Raised on the precepts of national service, for instance, few of them believed the experiment with an all-volunteer force could or should work. Having it forced on them by the president precisely at the moment they were held in the lowest esteem by their country was viewed by most as a bitter betrayal. To them it was no way to run an Army, but rather further indication that American society was abandoning the principles and values that had made it great in the first place.

For Bill McCaffrey, the decision to retire was made early one morning when he awoke to the realization that he had no interest in braving the protesters and going to work that day as the Army's inspector general. While he had found joy in command, there was none in acting as the Army's designated gadfly, exposing further symptoms of the service's abundant ills. Creighton Abrams encouraged him to stay another year in hopes of getting a fourth star, but McCaffrey had received a promising job offer on the outside, and he decided then and there to accept it. That same day he tendered his letter of resignation. McCaffrey was at least glad that Creighton Abrams had been chosen to guide the Army through such a dark period.

Yet Bill McCaffrey did not despair for the Army. It was the same after every war: the country sent everyone home, vowed never to fight another war, and then when the inevitable war came along, brave young Americans would soak the soil of some foreign land with their blood for sheer lack of preparation. If the cause was desperate enough and the country committed, the

Army would eventually turn the tables out of determination and on the strength of the country's wonderful industrial engine.

Many of them had witnessed that cycle personally. At the beginning of World War II, many of McCaffrey's West Point classmates joined the American II Corps under Gen. Dwight Eisenhower to fight against Rommel's Afrika Corps at Kasserine Pass. Though wearied from their battles with the British, the more experienced Germans had delivered a stunning defeat to the II Corps, sending them into a fifty-mile retreat and costing them nearly 6,300 men.

That lack of preparation nearly cost them the war in Korea. A good friend and West Point classmate of Bill McCaffrey's had borne the initial brunt of that folly when he led the ill-fated Task Force Smith against the North Koreans. Charles Bradford Smith was ordered to take roughly 400 men up-country with little warning, and within six hours they had been overrun and routed by North Korean armored units. Only about seventy of the men of Task Force Smith survived the debacle.

Assuming his son stayed in the Army, Bill McCaffrey knew that it might even be left up to Barry to do the bleeding and dying in some future Task Force Smith, just as he had bled and nearly died in Vietnam. Much now depended on the judgment and foresight of his peers such as Creighton Abrams and the others approaching the end of their careers. The last act of the proud officers of World War II would be as caretakers to an Army reeling from its first-ever defeat. Still, he had faith that the Army would rebound from this low point in its fortunes, just as it had throughout the country's long history. Bill McCaffrey always took the long view.

"Goddamn it, Malone, what in the hell is happening out there!" Gen. Creighton Abrams barked into the telephone, and was initially met with silence. The chief of staff of the Army was well into what his staff privately termed his "King Crab" mode, and in that mood he was not a man to provoke. Specifically, Abrams was referring to what was happening at the U.S. Army Command and General Staff College at Fort Leavenworth, Kansas, but his exasperation might well have encompassed the entire U.S. Army.

What was happening out there was that the service was reeling on nearly all fronts, or in the words of an internal analysis conducted by the BDM Corporation at the behest of the Pentagon, the Army was "close to losing its pride, heart, and soul and therefore [its] combat effectiveness."

Most recently, Abrams was hearing complaints from a number of general officers who had been invited to attend a little soul-searching session on professional ethics and integrity with the students at Leavenworth, where midlevel officers are groomed for command staff jobs. The generals had come away stunned by the intensity with which the students reviled the present system and its "careerism," and by direct association apparently the generals whose careers it had most notably advanced.

Col. Mike Malone, by then a permanent faculty member at the Army War College and well-known throughout the Army for his groundbreaking work on the professionalism and leadership studies, had also been invited to attend the seminar at Leavenworth. At one point a young captain had stood up and described to the generals present an abysmal situation in an unnamed division where the command hierarchy created such pressure for glowing fitness reports that evaluations were routinely falsified. One of the generals on the stage interrupted the young officer, saying that would never have happened in his division. And in front of the College faculty, an assembly of his peers, and a lineup of generals, the young captain had replied, "Sir, that was your division."

They still thought you could dictate readiness and morale, thought Malone, as if in punishing the officers whose units didn't measure up by withholding promotions you somehow got at the underlying problems, when what you really got were officers willing to bring you good news or none at all.

The clearest indication of the Army's progress in the intervening three years was that young captain and others like him, junior officers more concerned about the way things were than how their superiors would like to see them portrayed. That was why the Army's school system continued to hammer away on the issue of professionalism and ethics, even while many operational commands were more concerned with their immediate crises.

Knowing all this, Malone carefully weighed his reply to Abrams's brusque question about what exactly was going on at the Command and General Staff College. "Sir, suppose you or the other generals went out to Leavenworth to speak about ethical and moral issues facing the Army, and you met with *apathy* instead of anger?" In fact, Abrams did travel to the Command and General Staff College to speak to the same class of students only a month later, and he left giving them and the continued emphasis on military professionalism and ethics by the school's commandant, Lt. Gen. Jack Cushman, an unqualified vote of support.

Creighton Abrams was destined to serve as Army chief of staff for only two years, but his ascendancy to that position during one of the Army's darkest hours was a fortuitous event. The noted World War II armor commander, who spearheaded the relief of the surrounded 101st Airborne Division at Bastogne during the Battle of the Bulge in World War II, was roundly respected and well liked by his contemporaries.

In making a string of fateful decisions in 1973, Abrams would rely heavily on a hard-earned reputation for straight talk and irreproachable integrity, both in dealing with Congress and in pushing sweeping reorganization and reform through the Army bureaucracy. Given the pace of the reforms he helped launch in 1973, it was almost as if Creighton Abrams sensed that his time was running out.

Abrams was visited in his spacious Pentagon office one afternoon in the spring of 1973 by Gens. Donn Starry and John Vessey. All three men were alumni of the 3rd Armored Division in Germany, where Starry had served under Abrams as a young lieutenant. Vessey was one of the few soldiers ever to climb from buck private to general.

Starry and Vessey had not dropped by the chief's office on a social visit. As the director of Manpower and Forces in the Army's Force Development Office, Starry was responsible for crunching the Army's personnel numbers, and he had discovered that the people numbers simply didn't add up to the number of divisions the service was claiming on paper. They all knew that the Army was in a demobilization freefall, with its manpower cut in half in just four years, from 1.6 million to less than 800,000. The service was down to thirteen divisions on paper, making it the smallest Army the United States had fielded since before the Korean War. Starry told Abrams that he calculated that the service could actually field just twelve divisions, and only four of those were rated as combat ready. The Army was simply less than the sum of its parts.

Abrams told Starry and Vessey that he would discuss the issue with Secretary of Defense James Schlesinger, and he left it at that. In reality, the chief of staff was concerned less about how large an Army, and more about what kind of an Army.

Already it was clear that many of the military's concerns about the all-volunteer force, which had been so perfunctorily dismissed by the Gates Commission, were indeed well-founded. For instance, when the Army had tried limiting high school dropouts to no more than 30 percent of recruits, recruiting shortfalls had quickly developed. Meanwhile, the proportion of black recruits was soaring, on a path to comprise about 20 percent of the total enlisted strength by the end of the year, and the numbers would reach an unprecedented high of 37 percent before the end of the decade. That was nearly triple the national average of roughly 13 percent blacks in the general population.

The reduction in draft authority had also led to the recruitment of women at a pace that far outstripped initial projections. In 1972, for instance,

Abrams had committed to doubling the number of women in Army ranks by 1978. After the Army met with better than expected success in attracting women recruits, he would increase that projection by a factor of two in 1973 to compensate for shortfalls in recruiting men. Unexpectedly, women recruits were also far more likely than their male counterparts to have high school diplomas, helping the Army to counter a growing "quality" problem.

Their fears were coming true. Rather than reflecting a broad cross section of American society, the initial figures suggested that an all-volunteer force was becoming racially skewed and economically disadvantaged, raising the specter of a permanent military underclass. That might just institutionalize the injustices of the Vietnam-era draft, when it was disproportionately the sons of the disadvantaged who fought and died, and the war dragged on for years before a middle-class backlash finally forced a day of reckoning.

With so few of the sons and daughters of the privileged or perhaps even the middle class held at risk by committing such an army of the disenfranchised, might not civilian leaders be tempted into military adventurism in the future? These fears, nagging at Abrams in the spring of 1973, led him to formalize one of the most fateful policies of his short but eventful tenure as chief of staff. Even while the country was cutting the tie that most securely bound it to the military by ending the draft, Abrams quietly cemented a little-understood bond between the Army and the "citizen soldier" that went back to the minutemen of America's colonial militias. Inside the Pentagon, the deal became known simply as the Golden Handshake.

The close relationship that had developed between Creighton Abrams and Secretary of Defense James Schlesinger was the subject of considerable speculation within Pentagon circles. A Harvard graduate, former director of strategic studies at the RAND Corporation, and former director of the CIA, Schlesinger was viewed suspiciously by some in the senior ranks, who saw him as aloof and elitist. For some reason, however, Schlesinger and Abrams had hit it off from the beginning, and the pipe-puffing Schlesinger and cigar-chomping Abrams met regularly on Saturday mornings for smoke-shrouded brainstorming sessions.

After one of these meetings, Abrams called Don Starry on the phone and outlined what later came to be known as the Golden Handshake agreement. For his part, Abrams secured a commitment from Schlesinger for an increase in Army divisions—the massive, 16,000-person-plus building blocks of the fighting Army—from thirteen to sixteen. Schlesinger received assurances that the Army would fill those extra divisions and necessary support units from its present manning pool of roughly 765,000 soldiers. Starry knew better than most that such a plan would stretch Army manpower impossibly thin.

What Abrams had in mind, however, was a wholesale transfer of many support missions into the reserves, and integration of reserve combat units into active divisions, creating a total fighting force more reliant on reserves than any other in modern times. With many in the Army worried that the service had been robbed of a critical link to middle America with the end of the draft, Abrams was in a stroke tightening its grip on the state militias and military reserves around the country, and by direct association with both the governors across the land and the U.S. Congress.

The name given to that policy was Total Force, and it had first been broached by the man most responsible for Abrams becoming chief, former secretary of defense Melvin Laird. To Secretary of Defense Schlesinger the concept made sense on grounds of efficiency and cost savings. Estimates in 1973 indicated that an Army Reserve unit could be maintained for anywhere from one-half to one-sixth the cost of a similar active unit, and Abrams would clearly have to eliminate duplication of roles between the active and reserve units to find the manpower for his three extra divisions. For the Army, Abrams's unilateral decision to commit the Army to fielding sixteen divisions without an increase in overall strength was stunning for the degree to which it did make the active Army dependent on the reserves.

In shifting as much as 70 percent of its combat service support into the reserves, the active Army would be ceding its ability to sustain itself in anything beyond the most temporary large-scale deployments. And because reservists would be primarily responsible for manning the seaports, airports, and rail stations to transport Army units in the first place, a reserve call-up would be needed on practically the first day of any crisis.

More troublesome still was the relationship between the active forces and the reserves, which was predictably at an all-time low. At the best of times active-duty commanders tended to view their reserve counterparts as amateurs and "weekend warriors." The history of reserve mobilizations was likewise fraught with cautionary tales. A Congressional Budget Office study revealed, for instance, that those reserves mobilized for Korea were rated only between 40 to 45 percent combat ready, and some reserve units mobilized for the Berlin crisis took up to a year to become operational.

In the direct aftermath of Vietnam, there was also seething animosity in the active Army toward reserve ranks, which were seen as riddled with draft dodgers. Now Abrams was telling the Army not only that it would be unable to fight a future conflict without the direct help of these reserve support units, but also that it would be fighting alongside reserve combat units.

By making reliance on the reserves so profound that the Army could not function without them even in the early days of a major crisis, Abrams was also fundamentally limiting a president's flexibility in committing military forces. Even activating the reserves temporarily required a presidential proclamation, a politically charged move guaranteed to spark intense debate on Capitol Hill and in governors' mansions across the country, where control of the National Guard resides short of a national emergency. Committing them to a theater of operations for longer than 180 days required the direct approval of Congress.

Because of the nature of the reserve structure, National Guardsmen and Army and Air Force Reservists are also generally older than their active-duty counterparts, and mobilizing them meant abruptly depriving families across the country of husbands and fathers. It was exactly the type of polarizing debate and national hardship that Lyndon Johnson had hoped to avoid by not ordering a major mobilization of the reserves during Vietnam.

No one close to Abrams doubted that front-loading that day of national reckoning was exactly what he intended by committing so heavily to the Total Force policy. The armed forces had been sent off to fight a protracted war in Vietnam without the will of the country mobilized behind them, and to Abrams and many other officers of his generation the myriad mistakes and tragedies of the war seemed to spread from that fateful decision like cracks in a shattered windshield.

Tragically, Creighton Abrams would be stricken by terminal cancer the next year, and the Army would lose the rarest of officers, a soldier-statesman. His final days would not be troubled, however, by lingering concern that the Army would once again be sent off to a distant war without the support of the American people. Abrams said as much to Don Starry and any other officer who cared to listen: "They're *never* going to take us to war again without calling up the reserves."

14: Epiphany 1973

DON Starry was in a hotel room in England when his telephone rang. As head of the Army's Armor Center at Fort Knox, he was making a tour of British training grounds along with Brig. Gen. Robert Baer, the manager of the Army's fledgling project to develop a new tank. Both men had brought their wives along for a little sight-seeing. Even as Starry motioned to his wife that he would answer this late-night call, however, he sensed that their little excursion to Europe might be coming to an end. Hearing General Abrams's voice on the other end all but confirmed that suspicion.

"Don, it's Abe. I've just been able to get permission for you and Baer to go to Israel. You're going to have to send the ladies home, along with your aides. It'll just be the two of you."

They were orders Starry had been anxious to hear. The entire U.S. Army knew an intelligence bonanza was waiting to be exploited on the battlefields of the Golan and Sinai. Clearances, however, were nearly impossible to come by. It seems the United States Army was about to reap a little payback for sending its own badly needed equipment to the Yom Kippur War meat grinder in Israel's desperate hour of need.

The interest of armor experts at Fort Knox and the Malinovsky Tank Academy in the Soviet Union had been intense ever since the end of the Yom Kippur War in October 1973. In nature, the predator and his potential prey are constantly testing one another, and their fight for survival thus stays fairly even. During the long years of the Cold War arms race, however, both sides were essentially kept in separate cages. In the Yom Kippur case, the Arab predators had used Soviet-supplied arms and classic Soviet tactics, while the outnumbered Israelis relied largely on arms from the United States and Britain. Thus in a microcosm of a war in Central Europe, the wild beasts of armored warfare were uncaged for Yom Kippur on a scale unmatched in nearly three decades.

The first, shocking lesson was evident after only a matter of days. The lethality of modern conventional weapons had made the battlefields of the Middle East a far more dangerous place than battlefields in earlier wars. With double the muzzle velocity of their World War II predecessors, tanks had roughly a fifty-fifty chance of destroying a target at fifteen hundred meters with one shot, a feat that had required an average of thirteen attempts during World War II. Guided antitank missiles in the arsenals of both sides also made their first major impact on the modern battlefield, doubling the range at which a tank could be hit and knocked out even by infantrymen. The result was that the fighting devoured tanks and ammunition at startlingly high levels. Though Israel eventually prevailed, in just over two weeks of fighting it lost the equivalent of three years' worth of U.S. tank production.

Starry's guide was an Israeli general who had commanded a reserve armored division during the fighting on the Golan Heights. He took them to the eastern front, where Baer and Starry visited the Israeli command post at Kuneitra.

The landscape was still scorched and pocked by the recent fighting, and littered with the charred hulks of Soviet-made tanks, destruction that climaxed in what came to be known as the Valley of Tears. There the Israeli 7th Brigade had withstood wave after wave of advancing Syrian tanks.

As the Israeli officer talked them through the battle, pointing out the various attack routes and the sites of the fiercest fighting from their vantage point atop the Golan Heights, Starry could suddenly see it all clearly: a withering artillery barrage announcing the attack in true Red Army fashion, tanks advancing relentlessly in Soviet-style echelons, the sky abuzz with combat aircraft, and the outnumbered but better-trained defenders with their backs against the wall in a last-ditch defense.

There on the Golan Heights, Gen. Don Starry experienced an epiphany. It was the Fulda Gap nightmare that had troubled so many of their deliberations at Fort Knox, brought suddenly into terrible three-dimensional focus.

The Fulda Gap was the solar plexus of the NATO defense in Central Europe. The "gap" itself was actually a wide north-south bowl on the border between West and East Germany, bordered on the north by the rugged Knüllgebirge and to the south by the highlands of the Hohe Rhön. For four hundred years invading armies in Europe had thus traveled through the natural gateway between them, from the Prussian Black Hussars heading west in 1759 to Napoleon's army marching east on Russia in 1812.

From the Fulda Gap a succession of valleys spilled sixty-two miles directly into Frankfurt, West Germany, home to the 7th Army and its 3rd Armored Division. Of the five or so invasion routes the Soviets might choose to attack Western Europe, the Fulda Gap was thus the most likely, and the tenuous position and vulnerabilities of vastly outnumbered American forces in West Germany somehow seemed to crystallize at that point.

For months after the Golan Heights visit, Starry pondered the lessons of Yom Kippur with his staff at Fort Knox and with Gen. William DePuy, who had taken over at the Army's new Training and Doctrine Command (TRADOC) at Fort Monroe, Virginia. Everyone sensed the implications for the U.S. Army were profound.

Somehow, the Israelis had prevailed against odds much like those the allies faced in Europe. Warsaw Pact tanks now outnumbered those of NATO by more than two to one, and recent intelligence spottings of the new T-64 meant that Warsaw Pact forces had skipped ahead a generation in tank modernization while the U.S. Army was mired in Vietnam.

Against the demoralized U.S. 7th Army in Germany of six and one-third divisions—which the Army had bled nearly dry of experienced personnel and equipment during Vietnam—the Soviets had arrayed thirty-one divisions along the East-West border. That included ten tank divisions in East Germany alone, with two tank divisions each in Poland, Hungary, and Czechoslovakia. While Red Army divisions were somewhat smaller than their U.S. counterparts and included many older tanks, the Soviets also had proximity very much in their favor. West of the Ural Mountains lay another sixty Soviet divisions, while the entire Atlantic Ocean separated the U.S. 7th Army from reinforcements.

While the situation in Europe was bleak, by most calculations the Israelis should also have surrendered in the first week of the Yom Kippur War. Most assumptions on force ratios and their impact on the outcome of battles were taken from studies done in the 1950s, complete with charts telling commanders at which point the numbers assured victory for the attackers, and at which force ratio the defenders would win.

Prompted by the Yom Kippur War, Starry had his staff conduct a historical study, and they discovered numerous examples where the larger force was actually badly mauled by a smaller army. The key seemed to be a commander who managed to seize the initiative and wring from it every ounce of advantage. Throughout history, such commanders had fought and won against seemingly overwhelming odds, from Alexander the Great and Genghis Khan to Robert E. Lee.

The common thread uniting these tacticians seemed to be armies with an ability to outmaneuver and deceive their foes, exploiting tactical opportunities before an enemy could react. Given advances in technology and the vast amounts of territory that an individual soldier could then control, up from ten square meters in ancient times to forty thousand square meters per soldier in the 1973 war, that probably meant giving subordinate commanders much greater independence and latitude in deciding how to fight their part of the battle.

As he pondered these findings, Starry kept returning to the incredible accuracy and lethality of modern weaponry, which he had seen evidenced in the Golan and Sinai. In less than two weeks both sides had lost more tanks than the United States had in all of Europe.

After studying the Yom Kippur War, both Starry and DePuy recognized that the old industrial-mobilization model of warfare the U.S. Army had long ago adopted was bankrupt. Long before the country could bring its industrial might to bear on a future war in Europe, the American commander in Europe was likely to face a decision between being run off the continent or escalating to the use of nuclear weapons.

Yet the concept that America was a sleeping giant that could afford to awake to peril deliberately and somewhat clumsily was deeply ingrained in the military psyche. It shaded nearly every decision concerning the fundamental "readiness" of U.S. forces: how many divisions they needed, how many and what kind of weapons and munitions they should stockpile, and how trained and ready to fight they had to be on any given day.

Starry had no idea how they were going to deal with the follow-on echelons of Soviet tank forces in Central Europe when it looked doubtful that the Army could blunt even the first wave. The Israelis had relied on a superior air force for the deep attack coupled with better-trained soldiers at the front, and that seemed like a good place to start thinking.

Starry had also left the Golan Heights with an idea of how they could use that rare testing ground to help shape weapons then under development, especially the new tank, armored personnel carrier, and attack helicopter. The Syrians had made good use of their night-fighting capability, and he decided to write that requirement into plans for the new tank, personnel carrier, and attack helicopter.

Even more importantly, the Yom Kippur War had suggested a new doctrine to both Starry and DePuy, one that brought scant consolation to an Army still staggering from Vietnam, the same Army that had been badly mauled in the initial stages of virtually every fight it had joined in the past century. The Army would very likely have to fight and win the *first* battle of the next war. That would have to be the departure point for the Army's new doctrine, and Starry and DePuy both knew that it changed everything.

15: Bloodless Battles 1973

BRIG.Gen. Paul Gorman knew he was about to have a family mutiny on his hands, and even as he listened to the voice on the other end of the telephone, his mind raced frantically for a way out of the predicament. Gorman's wife, Ruth, had just finished unpacking their household goods and arranging the furniture at their new quarters at Fort Carson, Colorado, where in 1973 he was set to serve as assistant division commander of the 4th Infantry Division, and the kids were looking forward to finally spending a full year in one school.

For much of the previous year his family had lived out of temporary quarters in Los Angeles, while Gorman testified in the Pentagon Papers trial of Daniel Ellsberg. U.S. District Court judge W. Matt Byrne had finally dismissed all charges against Ellsberg, whom Gorman and Jack Galvin had worked with writing the classified study years earlier. The whole dismal affair was just one more indication of the debilitating grip that Vietnam continued to have over all their lives.

And now Lt. Gen. William DePuy, his former division commander in Vietnam when both were with the 1st Infantry Division back in 1966, was asking what Gorman thought about picking up everything and moving back east to work for something called TRADOC.

"Sir, I think that is one of the worst ideas I have heard in a long time," replied Gorman, knowing that if he couldn't talk his old boss out of this, DePuy's three stars were going to decide the issue. One-star brigadier generals, Gorman figured, were easier to jerk around than platoon sergeants.

"Well, you're going to come anyway," said DePuy.

Though Gorman had occasionally run into DePuy when they both served in the Pentagon a few years back, their relationship had stayed on strictly professional terms. He considered the wiry general one of few authentic tactical geniuses in the Army. He also knew from serving under him in war that he could be a difficult and abrasive boss. In his desperation, Gorman decided on bluntness.

"Look, sir, I have a major problem on my hands. My wife has just gotten our family unpacked in the first permanent quarters we've had in a long time." It came out almost plaintively. "I'm just going to have a hell of a time disengaging here."

DePuy began describing the wonderful accommodations at Fort Monroe, Virginia, home for the new TRADOC headquarters. Fine schools were nearby and good waterfront for boating and swimming at the mouth of the Chesapeake Bay, DePuy stressed. The selling job was merely a formality. Gorman knew from the tone in his former division commander's voice that this was not a request. What he didn't know was how he was possibly going to break it to Ruth and the kids.

For sheer drive, bureaucratic savvy, and toughness, few officers in the Army were the equal of Lt. Gen. William DePuy. As one of the original architects and practitioners of search-and-destroy tactics in Vietnam, DePuy did not apologize for the Army's conduct of the war. In truth, however, he was deeply troubled by what he had seen of the Army's performance, both as a division commander and inside the Pentagon. Characteristically, Bill DePuy thus maneuvered himself into an almost unique position to change the Army.

During a stint as assistant vice chief of the Army beginning back in 1969, DePuy had developed a small cadre of officers into the key force planners in the Army. The group was initially established at the behest of former defense secretary Robert McNamara. Unlike many of his contemporaries, DePuy neither despised nor resisted McNamara's systems-analysis approach to management. He felt that the old General Staff management style still prevalent in the Army, where critical decisions were often made on the intuition of senior officers with precious little empirical data, was outdated.

Unless the Army armed itself with the techniques and terminology of modern program management, DePuy also believed, they would always remain at a disadvantage when confronted by the charts and computer printouts of McNamara's "whiz kids," who were rising through the Pentagon's systems-analysis shop into high-level civilian positions.

DePuy thus became an ardent believer in scientific program management, surrounding himself as assistant vice chief with bright, hardworking, and likeminded disciples at the colonel and lieutenant-colonel level. Officers who fell out of his favor were fired with regularity, as Jack Galvin could have attested as far back as 1966. General officers sitting on promotion boards at the time even confessed to secretly giving extra points to his numerous victims out of sympathy. Those who flourished under DePuy's mentorship, however, were mentioned with not a little envy by their contemporaries elsewhere in the Pentagon: Max Thurman, Louis Menetrey, Max Noah, John Woodmansee Jr., John McGiffert, Robert Montague, Colin Powell. All of them would reach the general-officer level, as would thirty of DePuy's subordinate officers. An astonishing seven would achieve four-star rank.

While the Army was focused primarily on extricating itself from Vietnam, DePuy had been given the task of reorganizing the Continental Army Command (CONARC). The huge umbrella organization for the continental armies and the Army's schools and training centers was proving too unwieldy and inflexible to cope with the massive demobilization.

Armed with a basic outline, DePuy had gone on the offensive, using the considerable force of his personality, his grasp of systems analysis, and an intuitive understanding of the personalities and politics at work within the Pentagon. In an unprecedented blitzkrieg of an organization famous for the recalcitrance of its entrenched bureaucracies, DePuy engineered a major reorganization of the Army in the space of a week. Many of the key players whose turf was invaded never really knew what hit them.

DePuy's plan called for splitting CONARC in two, giving the troops and operational bases to the new Forces Command. The Army's training centers and schools he lumped under another command. With the Army in a state of seismic flux, DePuy understood that it was the head of this second command who would have unprecedented latitude to cross traditional boundaries to effect lasting change in the Army. Almost no one was surprised when Creighton Abrams chose DePuy to lead the new command in the spring of 1973 and awarded him a fourth star. DePuy even chose the name of the new organization: Training and Doctrine Command.

In the harshest way possible, Vietnam had taught them all that the Army clearly had woefully inadequate training. And beyond the industrial-mobilization model of World Wars I and II, which assumed that short of nuclear Armageddon the country with the most factories would eventually win, they had precious little in the way of unifying doctrine. Training and doctrine. That was the train that ran through virtually everything the Army did.

It was no accident that DePuy insisted on recruiting Paul Gorman as TRADOC's deputy chief of staff for training. He knew that Gorman had recently worked on training innovations at the Army Infantry School at Fort Benning, and the man was one of the most capable battalion commanders DePuy had ever seen. He had handpicked Starry and Gorman, just as he had seeded his headquarters staff with trusted aides from his programming shop. That was the way Gen. William DePuy always prepared for a long and difficult campaign, especially one with two fronts: training and doctrine.

DePuy was still preoccupied with the lessons of the Arab-Israeli war. As staggering as the lethality of the battlefield was, he was equally impressed by the fact that the better-trained and more tactically proficient Israelis eventually carried the day against momentous odds. U.S. Army training still reflected the old mobilization doctrine, where officers were trained for jobs two rungs from where they stood on the command ladder on the assumption that in a war they would likely be promoted to make way for the huge influx of green draftees. Because of the need for an extremely high state of readiness, Israeli training tended to focus soldiers' attention on preparing to fight tomorrow. For Israel there would be no second chances.

Somehow the Army would have to adopt a training philosophy and regimen that would also prepare its soldiers in peacetime to fight and win the first battle of the next war. It was a fundamental change with sweeping implications, many of which he could not even begin to foresee.

Already DePuy and Starry were working on a rough draft of a new doctrine that would stress the need to win the first battle of any future war. In terms of training, DePuy was depending on Gorman. Gorman had his own stubborn streak, and indeed the frequent clashes between them would lead Gorman more than once to tender his letter of resignation. None were accepted by DePuy. On one key point, however, they were in total agreement: the Army's basic school system, including the Infantry School at Benning, was badly skewed toward theory and sterile classroom education as opposed to hands-on training.

Gorman had never forgotten taking over as 1st Brigade commander in the 101st Division in Vietnam three years earlier, only to discover to his horror that almost none of his soldiers even knew how to properly zero their weapons so that their sights and barrels were in correct alignment. Worse, when Gorman tried to explain the critical importance of the procedure, they looked at him as if he had personally dreamed it all up just to make their lives more miserable. Soldiers even told of being trained to carry their rifles in their right hand when covering the left side of a trail, and in their left hand when covering the right side, as if troops under combat stress were all suddenly ambidextrous.

Not only had many of these soldiers gone through training at Fort Benning without learning the barest fundamentals of combat, but when Gorman wrote back to the Infantry School from Vietnam for some field-worthy training techniques in the basics of fire and maneuver, he had received a stack of complicated lesson plans designed for a classroom. Returning to Benning after Vietnam in September of 1971, Gorman had had fire in his eyes.

Under Westmoreland's direction, Gorman had set up his own brainstorming group to explore innovative training approaches. At his direction, the Combat Arms Training Board (CATB) looked at training experiments being conducted throughout American industry and in the military, as well as at research from various think tanks and academic institutes.

Some of the most interesting work in the field that they had unearthed, however, was being done at the Human Resources Research Organization (HumRRO) in Alexandria, Virginia. If the Army could somehow create a training environment where its soldiers could see the direct result of their actions in terms of exposure to fire, the analysts at HumRRO believed, they would internalize those lessons much faster than a classroom lecture.

That jibed perfectly with Gorman's outlook, distilled during two combat tours. Based partly on the HumRRO research, Gorman's group created a training video directed specifically against the rote memorization and classroom approach then favored at Army schools.

In the video a father is seen holding a baseball and explaining the game to his young son, who is wearing a glove. This is a baseball, the father explains, and it is made up of so many yards of string, wrapped into a ball of such and such diameter, covered by a cowhide wrapping with so many stitches. All the while the camera focuses on the young boy's increasingly furrowed brow as he impatiently pounds his fist into his glove. Enough already, his expression says, throw me the ball!

The pedantic father in the video was a direct swipe at the Army's branch schools and training centers, and Gorman and the rest of the training-board members took the analogy a step further: they developed a crude ball for the game of simulated combat called SCOPES (Squad Combat Operations Exercise Simulation).

Essentially SCOPES was nothing more than a weapons sight whose optics could be adjusted to approximate the range of various weapons. Both sides in the game of army were equipped with SCOPES and asked to wear numbers, and a "hit" was registered by a firer simply reading the number of his target to a referee or "controller." Though cumbersome and awkward, prehistoric really, it was by far the most realistic field training system ever put into the hands of Army troops.

The Berlin Brigade, which was conducting urban-warfare training at the time, was chosen to test the new system. By shipping them SCOPES instead of a stack of classroom lesson plans such as Gorman received from Benning while in Vietnam, Gorman and the Combat Arms Training Board were essentially throwing them the ball.

The response from the officers and noncoms of the Berlin Brigade had been a resounding recommendation that SCOPES be adopted for training Army-wide. In the "learning by doing" training environment promoted by SCOPES, where casualty avoidance became its own reward, units quickly internalized lessons on using cover and concealment and suppressing enemy fire. Gorman and the other officers at the training board had given this novel training approach a name—tactical engagement simulation—and subsequent tests seemed to reinforce the experiences of the Berlin Brigade.

Two findings in particular interested Gorman. First, compared to more conventional training, these combat simulations developed units that clearly learned how to avoid casualties. In early head-to-head comparisons, the differences in casualties were as high as 40 percent. Secondly, the more realistic training revealed that the entry-level proficiency of the average Army unit was frighteningly low. In the early stages of the combat simulations, most units were simply *wiped out*. Thomas Scott, an analyst who observed the comparisons for the U.S. Army Research Institute for the Behavioral and Social Sciences, was alarmed enough by what the tests revealed, in fact, that he warned of global repercussions.

"If the tactical proficiency of most small combat units is as poor as that of the test units, the degree of unpreparedness for combat has serious implications," he wrote at the time. "Without at least moderately proficient small units, larger units cannot be effective. . . . Ill-prepared tactical units can only weaken the deterrent effect of U.S. ground combat forces." Gorman and the others at CATB knew they had stumbled onto something with disturbing implications, but they were not certain exactly what it all meant.

That was the background and baggage that Gorman brought with him to TRADOC when DePuy appointed him deputy chief of staff for training in the fall of 1973. As Gorman would soon learn, in the intervening year while he was in Los Angeles testifying at the Ellsberg trial, the institutional resistance to the training reforms he represented had predictably coalesced. Many senior commanders, Gorman knew, viewed the costs associated with simulated combat as money thrown away on playacting and toys for the troops, or worse.

The depth of that resistance became clear sometime later when DePuy sent Gorman to the Pentagon to brief his training ideas to a gathering of retired four-star generals. As he stood before the assembled eminences, reciting the early SCOPES results and giving anecdotal evidence from the Berlin Brigade, Gorman noticed a number of the heads in the audience begin to wag. Before he could finish his presentation, one gnarled old visage whom Gorman immediately recognized rose above the crowd on unsteady legs.

"Am I to understand that you declare casualties in these exercises?" asked the retired general.

"Yes, sir."

"Damn you," the old man snarled, pointing a bony finger at Gorman as if he actually meant it as a curse. "You're teaching American soldiers to die!" With that the general stormed out of the briefing room with a number of his colleagues, and Gorman slunk back down to TRADOC headquarters.

If he was ever going to win DePuy over to his ideas on training reform and overcome such institutional resistance, Paul Gorman knew that he would have to back his arguments up with far more conclusive empirical data. DePuy was not a man to be swayed by anecdotes and homilies, yet if Gorman could convince him of the validity of the training reforms, probably no man in the Army was more likely to find a way to see them implemented regardless of the opposition.

Gorman found some data in a classified paper written by an Army colonel on Henry Kissinger's staff at the National Security Council. After seeing early results of air combat in Southeast Asia, most of which were still top secret, Jack Merritt had written a memo to his boss arguing that the Defense Department had better start reexamining both the selection and training of its fighter pilots.

Data from the first four years of the air war in Southeast Asia only proved what combat pilots knew intuitively all along: in contrast to the successes of the Korean War, when their ranks were filled by many combat-seasoned pilots from World War II, U.S. pilots initially fared miserably in Vietnam. Between 1965 and 1968, both the U.S. Air Force and Navy lost one fighter for every two North Vietnamese MiGs downed.

What caught Merritt's and Gorman's eyes, however, were the figures from the second half of Vietnam. After a lull in fighting during 1969, the Air Force continued to loose aircraft in aerial combat at a ratio of roughly one to two. Between 1970 and 1973, however, the Navy had improved its kill-loss ratio *by a factor of five*, notching twelve enemy kills for every loss.

The difference couldn't be explained away by any breakthrough in weapons design or equipment, because the Navy flew the same F-4 fighters that were the workhorse of the Air Force. How then to account for the fact that Navy fighter pilots had apparently become not only far more lethal, but also far more likely to survive in combat?

The Navy felt the difference could be traced back to the establishment in 1968 of the U.S. Navy Postgraduate Course in Fighter Weapons, Tactics and Doctrine. The pilots simply dubbed it Top Gun. In response to their poor initial showing in Vietnam, the Navy had essentially designed a graduate course in dogfighting for its air-to-air fighter pilots. Selected pilots who entered the course were pitted against expert instructors flying aircraft similar to the enemy's. After each simulated dogfight, instructors took the student pilots through detailed after-action reviews of what had really happened up there, versus what the younger pilots *thought* had happened.

When Top Gun graduates began reaching the Navy's fleet in Southeast Asia in the spring of 1969, they revealed many of the attributes of combat-seasoned pilots, namely a dramatically increased ability not only to kill but to survive in battle. Gorman recognized in the simulated combat training conducted at Top Gun a far more sophisticated version of the Army's experiment with SCOPES. The Air Force, Gorman knew, was even then preparing to take the experiment with tactical-engagement simulation a step further.

In its classified "Red Baron" study, the Air Force had meticulously reconstructed each of the 625 air-to-air engagements between Air Force pilots and enemy MiGs during Vietnam. While the report identified some shortcomings in their equipment, the most obvious thread that ran through each account was a woeful lack of realistic training. Because the MiGs were much smaller and harder to spot than the F-4 Phantom and relied on ground-control intercept radars and thus attacked from different angles than the U.S. pilots were used to seeing in training, the vast majority of American pilots who were shot down never even saw the aircraft that hit them.

The Air Force's response had been to establish that year a squadron of "Aggressor" aircraft to act as sparring partners for operational wings. The pilots flew small training aircraft similar in size and performance to the MiG, and they were steeped in Soviet tactics and doctrine. There was even talk that the Air Force wanted to establish a massive training range that, along with the Aggressors to replicate the air-to-air threat, would have simulated Soviet surface-to-air missile batteries to evade and realistic targets to bomb and strafe. The maverick band of Air Force fighter pilots who were pushing such a revolutionary training range—where the service could train not just its air-superiority pilots, but also pilots in ground-attack, command-and-control, and electronic-countermeasure aircraft—wanted to call it Red Flag.

What if they could actually pass along the lessons of combat in such training? Given what Gorman knew about the horror, confusion, and complexity of battle, it seemed far-fetched that they could even come close to approximating the stresses of battle in a training environment, but what if? It would be comparable to throwing combat-seasoned pilots and troops into the first battle of any future war.

Paul Gorman sensed that all the data was leading him to the edge of some important truth about military training. He was reminded of an adage about the mighty Roman legions, who were said to train so that their drills were bloodless battles, and their battles bloody drills. The Air Force's Red Flag would be the next crucial step in developing a bloodless battlefield. If they were able to duplicate the Navy's success with Top Gun on a much larger scale, he would have his proof.

Ironically, even while Paul Gorman and others were contemplating the import of the Red Baron report, many of the faces behind those grim statistics on downed pilots were gathering in Las Vegas for a massive celebration. Back in 1967 at the officers' club at the Ubon Air Base in Thailand, a group of Air Force pilots involved in the time-honored tradition of drinking and chumming had established the Red River Valley Pilots Association. Membership was open to every pilot ever to hop the Red River en route to Hanoi, and those who belonged were known simply as the River Rats.

By 1973 the annual gatherings of the River Rats were already legendary within fighter-pilot ranks. One year the Navy chapter hosted the event near Miramar Naval Air Station, complete with a golf tournament and an open bar at every fourth hole, as well as an air demonstration by a formation of F-4s flying at treetop level. As they blew over the heads of the River Rats on the fairway, one of the aircraft had peeled off and flown solo into the clouds, a maneuver universally recognized among pilots as the "missing man" formation.

While they met every year, it was understood from the beginning that the River Rats would never hold an "official" reunion until the members still missing from their ranks had been released from prisons in North Vietnam. The vast majority of the POWs held by North Vietnam were Air Force and Navy pilots. On March 29, 1973, the last of those 591 known POWs had lifted off in C-141s from Hanoi's Gia Lam Airport, bound for Clark Air Force Base and freedom.

In August of 1973, the River Rats were thus finally gathering for their official reunion. Ever since the return of the POWs, they had been cheered and embraced wherever they traveled in the country. While the war had ripped at the fabric of American society, the public clearly felt that the return of the POWs marked a final chapter. The healing could finally begin.

Thereafter, the August 1973 reuniting of the River Rats with their fallen brethren was simply referred to as the Reunion. Hotel lobbies and hallways in Las Vegas were crowded with thousands of flight suits and echoed with glorious shouts of recognition as men dropped their luggage and clasped to themselves friends who in some cases were last seen disappearing in fireballs over a distant jungle.

During the massive banquet on Saturday night there was a full bottle of wine at each seat, and Vegas headliners such as Wayne Newton, B. B. King, and others were shuttled in by limousine to entertain the raucous crowd for free. During "Tie a Yellow Ribbon," a song that had skyrocketed to popularity as the country's unofficial Top 40 dedication to the POWs, the former prisoners in the audience tied their yellow napkins together and paraded onstage in a thumping line dance that was both a chorus line and a primal rite of exorcism.

For the finale the River Rats had arranged a ceremonial ringing of the Liberty Bell. Forged back in Bangkok in the late 1960s, the brass bell had been cast in a mold like the Philadelphia original, complete with a crack down its side. The River Rats had lugged that bell halfway around the world and carried it to every annual meeting, pledging never to ring it until the POWs were finally released. The ballroom quieted expectantly for that long-awaited moment, and the bell was struck . . .

Only the sound was all wrong. They had never tested it, and instead of a peal worthy of sweet liberty, the bell emitted a jarring, hollow clanging. As that din spread, the ballroom was momentarily quiet. More than a hundred of their friends and colleagues had died in captivity in Vietnam, and 1,284 were still listed as missing in action. In nine years 304,000 of their countrymen had been wounded in Vietnam. Of a total of 3 million American men and women who had served in Vietnam, 58,183 would never return alive. Vietnam. Vietnam. Vietnam. As the pilots and their families stood listening, remembering those for whom that bell so dreadfully tolled, some of them already sensed that the discordant note would resonate their entire lives.

16: Red Flag 1978

FROM the ridge some fifty miles inside the borders of a restricted training range roughly the size of Switzerland, just north of Nellis Air Force Base, Nevada, the only visible movements in the morning sun were the furtive shadows of a formation of F-4 Phantoms as they streaked across the valley floor. Yet no one had to tell Lt. Col. Chuck Horner that they were not alone.

Indeed, ever since the formation had refueled over a southern-Nevada dust bowl called Texas Lake, then crossed through "Student Gap" into contested airspace, the games had begun in earnest. The formation was immediately bombarded by warning signals, and Horner could tell from the nervous chatter over the radio that his young pilots were reeling from sensory onslaught.

An alarm tone blared in his own headset, telling him that his F-4 was being tracked by a surface-to-air (SAM) missile battery, and blinking warning lights indicated that enemy fighters were "painting" their formation with multiple radars. Ground control kept shouting directions and MiG coordinates as Horner tried to digest them and keep track of his own attack cell, coordinating their time over the target while his rear-seater's head whipsawed back and forth checking their "six" for Aggressors and then ... the electronic jamming started.

As Horner eased closer to his wingman and tightened up the four-aircraft formation in an effort to burn through the nauseating distortion, he subconsciously began the combat pilot's trick of recalculating his priorities. Traveling at 250 feet and 600 miles an hour, he quit looking over his shoulder and mentally blocked out the SAM warning indicator in his cockpit. Even if those threats weren't simulated, their biggest concern at that altitude would be antiaircraft guns, and Horner fully understood that the only thing real about this mission was the live bomb underneath his belly and the very real ground below.

The distinction, however, was obviously lost on some of his younger pilots. "Smokey SAM" rockets—the white smoke trails simulating a surface-to-air missile launch—were now streaking into the air as they approached the airfield that was their target that morning. Later at a debriefing, camera film and radar information from the manned SAM sites would indicate whether or not they represented a clean "kill." Suddenly one of Horner's pilots began jinking back and forth at dangerously low altitude in an effort to break the lock of the SAM radar.

"This is flight lead, number four," Horner called into his radio. "Level off."

"But I've got a—"

"I said knock it off!"

Horner watched as the pilot rocked his wings, the fighter pilot's signal for capitulation, and returned to course. The formation was flying through what officials at the Red Flag training exercises sometimes called the "shadow of death," and the young pilot had just used up one of a Red Flag pilot's ten lives. Horner was determined to see that the only true casualty in this simulated war was a little fighter-pilot pride.

Distilled down to its barest essence, the message of the final Red Baron reports and the Air Force's experience in Vietnam was that it took a pilot roughly ten combat missions before he was experienced enough to rate a reasonably good chance of survival. Beginning in 1975, the Air Force had spent hundreds of millions of dollars on this radical experiment to give its pilots that chance prior to the outbreak of the next war.

Vast ranges had been set up with targets and threat simulators layered across the desert floor to resemble an attacking Soviet formation, with tanks and antiaircraft platforms on the forward edge of battle, Soviet second-echelon forces with mobile surface-to-air-missile protection just behind, and deep-strike targets in the rear such as airfields and railroads heavily defended by longer-range SAMs.

Over those ranges roamed the Aggressors, the squadron of pilots emulating Soviet tactics that Horner's former instructor Boots Boothby had formed back in 1973. At Red Flag the Aggressors flew defensive patrols, pouncing on attack cells with their small, maneuverable F-5 aircraft, a realistic proxy of the Soviet MiG-21. For many pilots who had no combat experience and had yet to fly against the Aggressors, Red Flag exercises represented not only the first time they saw an entire strike package of aircraft assembled in the air, but also the first time they flew against opponents in dissimilar aircraft with the maddening buzz of electronic jamming for distraction.

Pilots with ground-attack missions had to coordinate attack routes and midair refueling schedules with other attack cells, everyone relying on coordination with friendly air-superiority fighters and directions from command-and-control aircraft. Red Flag thus amounted to the largest, most sophisticated simulated battlefield in the world, and just as the initial months of war had in the past, it revealed glaring deficiencies that the Air Force was loath to confront.

Already Red Flag training exercises had killed so many pilots that there was talk of Washington shutting it down. Horner had been struck by a sobering memo sent out by Gen. Robert Dixon, the usually bombastic commander of Tactical Air Command. In it he implored commanders to strictly adhere to safety rules and rein in their pilots' freelancing, or they could jeopardize the entire training experiment that Red Flag represented.

Within the tactical-air community they even had a name for the attitude that fighter jocks brought to Nellis: Nevada Freestyle. Fighter-pilot egos being what they were, every squadron came to Nellis where the exercises were held determined to whip the Aggressors in the air, bull's-eye the target, and pull out grinning. Only they had never faced training like Red Flag.

That was why each of the five Red Flag exercises held annually began with the visiting pilots being read the riot act on rules of engagement, all of them written in blood. The warnings were backed up with video taken from the ranges of aircraft literally skipping off the desert floor trying to evade SAM sites, or in the less lucky instances blasting craters in the local landscape.

Yet on nearly every rotation, the pilots whose landings ultimately failed to equal their number of takeoffs continued to grow. In the first few years after it opened in 1975, more than thirty pilots had died flying their airplanes into the ground trying to avoid lock-on from a SAM sight or an Aggressor aircraft. Near midair collisions occurred with startling regularity. Confronted for the first time by a determined enemy, realistic threat indicators, and the complexities of a full-up strike package of aircraft, younger pilots especially were finding themselves overwhelmed or "task saturated." At that point the unlucky ones, in fighter-pilot parlance, "ran out of airspeed, altitude, and ideas at the same time."

Chuck Horner figured it was up to combat vets like himself to remind young pilots that if they tried to digest every threat warning at once and did-n't prioritize them, they might very well miss the one that tells them they're only one foot above the ground. At that point, all the other problems were the wrong ones to worry about.

"What the hell were you jinking so low for?" Horner asked the pilot after the morning sortie, walking down the air-conditioned corridor of Building 201 at Nellis for their debrief. As the deputy commander for operations at the 4th Tactical Fighter Wing, Horner had led the squadron out from their home at Seymour Johnson Air Force Base, South Carolina. Already the hall-way was lined with framed and autographed photos from units that had ro-tated through Red Flag, and the amphitheater where the debriefings were held was plastered with plaques bearing fighter-squadron insignia.

"Well, that SAM site had me locked on," the young pilot began, sounding as if he already knew he wasn't going to like where this was going.

"Look, guys, if you're down in the dirt, the chance of the ground killing you if you hit it is *one hundred percent*," Horner said, still walking. "The chances of an antiaircraft gun killing you is probably ninety percent. The chances of a SAM killing you is maybe ten percent. Remember that."

Horner felt that he had a personal stake in making Red Flag work. Like the idea of establishing a dedicated Aggressor squadron as a Soviet-style sparring partner for Air Force pilots back in 1973, Red Flag had been pushed up through the bureaucracy from the bottom by a group of young pilots who re-ferred to themselves as the Fighter Pilot Mafia.

The actual concept for both the Aggressors and Red Flag could be traced to a rough-edged visionary named R. "Moody" Suter, whom Horner had be-friended at the Fighter Weapons Center at Nellis. Col. Richard Suter was a notorious note-taker who during his extensive travels had questioned pilots at many bases about their combat experiences during Vietnam. Rather than a computer, however, Moody used an assortment of smudged bar napkins to collect his data.

The idea for Red Flag had crystallized for Suter in a long drinking session at the Nellis officers' club. Later he came to the Pentagon to work with Chuck Horner and Col. Bill Kirk in the Air Force intelligence shop, and the three of them pitched the concept of a sort of super combat-training area to anyone who would listen.

After seeing those early briefings and then flying in a Red Flag exercise for the first time, however, it was easy to wonder whether they had created a monster. During the debriefing in Building 201 following Horner's morning mission, for instance, each flight lead stood up and tried to re-create what had happened to his flight. They were followed by Aggressor pilots and SAM operators, who called out the aircraft they believed were casualties during the mission. Because the only proof of a kill in an air-to-air encounter was camera film, which was sometimes inconclusive, arguments soon broke out over "kill" claims.

No one wanted to be chided mercilessly that night at the officers' club as a notch on an Aggressor's gun stock, so the briefings often degenerated into shouting matches, the participants waving their hands to emulate two aircraft locked in a dogfight. Every fighter pilot knew the routine, had played it out in countless bars over countless drinks practically since the days of first flight—he with the biggest watch and loudest voice wins. The Navy pilots called it First Liar to the Blackboard Wins. Whatever the outcome of the debriefings, however, in their hearts most of the visiting pilots usually knew they had not fared well in their initial encounters at Red Flag.

On his way to the officers' club that night, Horner marveled at the transformation that had taken place at Nellis since he taught at the Fighter Weapons School back in 1967. From a hot-tarmac scorpion trap and trailer park, Nellis had blossomed into a desert rose. It was by then the largest air base in Tactical Air Command, with nearly ten thousand employees and two of the busiest runways in the world. With the addition of Red Flag to the Fighter Weapons School, the Aggressor squadrons, the Tactics and Training directorate, and the Thunderbirds air-demonstration team, the base certainly lived up to the claim on the billboard at the main gate: "Welcome to Nellis Air Force Base—Home of the Fighter Pilot."

As he was drinking within the familiar confines of the Nellis officers' club with his squadron, Horner noted some of the familiar names etched on the bar top. Steve "Stormy" Ritchie, 414 FWS, the Air Force's first ace of Vietnam; George "Baby Huey" McCarthy; Lloyd "Boots" Boothby; the Fightin' 522nd Fireballs. As usual the bar was flooded with women, who gravitated to such watering holes, smiling into the eyes of pilots as if they were hanging on every word, a look that spelled lucky tonight.

A boisterous crowd of Aggressor pilots were laughing among themselves and carrying on loudly at one end of the bar, their sleeves rolled up and flight suits zipped down practically to the navel to reveal their signature checkered scarves. Since Boots Boothby inaugurated the first Aggressor squadron back in 1973, the training they offered in dissimilar aircraft tactics had proven so desperately needed that the concept had been expanded to four Aggressor squadrons, two of which were located at Nellis.

With the rapid expansion and influx of new and less experienced Aggressors, however, many pilots felt that they had lost the initial cadre's spirit of "Be Humble, Be Tactful." Word on the Aggressors now was that on the road or at home, they always swaggered into the bar wearing gold-lamé gloves and silver flying suits, striking sparks. Humble these guys definitely were not.

Horner had flown against the Aggressors plenty of times and thought they were probably the best air-to-air pilots in the world. They knew their small, maneuverable aircraft better than any other pilots in the Air Force, and maybe they sometimes used that to unfair advantage in training. He might have done the same thing. And if they got in his face with their smirk of superiority to gloat about it afterward, Horner decided he would rip their lips off.

Some of the resentment growing in the pilot ranks against the Aggressors had little to do with them personally. It was just jealousy over their logging as many as forty to fifty intense training sorties a month, something unheard of for pilots in operational squadrons. Unwilling to cut active-duty squadrons, Air Force leaders had absorbed the cuts of the Carter years by continually trimming the operations and maintenance accounts, which meant that pilots who needed an absolute minimum of fifteen hours of flying time a month just to stay current in their aircraft were typically getting ten or even less. The average airplane that had flown twenty-three sorties a month in 1969, for instance, was flying only eleven by 1978.

Given those cutbacks, and the fact that the skills and mental acuity needed in what amounted to a knife fight at supersonic speeds were notoriously perishable, it was hardly surprising that for every hundred thousand hours flown seven airplanes were crashing. At Red Flag, which was specifically designed to stretch the outer edge of a pilot's performance "envelope," they were discovering in tragic fashion that those boundaries were not what they should be. Meanwhile the Aggressors, who were revealing those weaknesses, were too often laughing about it later at the bar.

Whenever he looked at a boisterous group of Aggressors, however, Horner was reminded of nothing so much as himself as a young, cocky captain. Resentment of the Aggressors was only a symptom of what was ailing the Air Force, he knew, just as were the alarming accident rates at Red Flag.

If you put thirty fighter pilots in a briefing room and told them only one was likely to make it back from a suicide mission, each would look around the room and shake his head, voicing sympathy for the other twenty-nine unlucky bastards. Yet behind that fighter-jock machismo, Horner knew that many of his young pilots were badly scared, wondering who among them would fail to return home to their families from this Red Flag rotation. In that sense the exercises had become a far more realistic simulation of actual combat than anyone had intended. Some of the pilots were calling home every night just to reassure wives who were worried sick.

Yet Horner had vowed not to lose anyone on this exercise, and he planned to keep that promise. Mary Jo had always said she would divorce him if Horner ever started acting like a colonel, and he realized that it had finally happened. Maybe Chuck Horner would call his wife when he got back to quarters that night.

After the two-a-day missions of Red Flag, Horner was too tired and preoccupied to wonder at the deeper meaning behind it all, the cause of the problems that had become so evident on the training ranges north of Nellis. Yet he had glimpsed the roots of the malaise a decade earlier in Thailand. The first casualty of a war that made no sense was integrity. It was there in the white lie—"I released my armament at forty-five hundred feet on a forty-five-degree angle"—that became blacker and bolder over time, until somewhere along the way the Air Force had fallen into the habit of lying to itself.

The fact that a lot of young pilots were finding themselves overwhelmed at Red Flag came as no particular surprise to some of the veteran pilots who had trained them. A number of the handpicked Aggressor pilots and those at Nellis's Fighter Weapons School had transferred from Homestead Air Force Base, Florida, where young pilots received their final training before being assigned to operational squadrons. After Homestead, those veteran pilots understood that the Air Force had begun lying to itself in ways that could get a man killed.

The overriding preoccupation with statistical measurements of success that pilots had seen bloom in Vietnam—a bureaucratic concern with sortie rates over what was actually accomplished on a mission—had become deeply embedded in the Air Force's culture. Wing commanders' careers were increasingly judged on their ability to maximize the numbers: on-time takeoffs, sorties flown, aircraft repaired.

Only, after years of declining budgets and steady cuts in operations and maintenance accounts, sortie rates throughout the tactical air forces were dropping like an aircraft in the clutches of a "floating leaf fall," the unrecoverable tailspin all pilots dreaded. In an effort to generate more flights with less money at Homestead, someone had the brilliant idea of sending the aircraft up with less fuel. That cut fuel costs and refueling times on the ground, increasing sortie rates. Of course, it also meant that the students didn't get nearly as much training time in the air, but some things didn't show up on the view graphs and statistical charts tracked so meticulously back at Tactical Air Command headquarters.

Routinely instructors would return from training flights that they graded as "noneffective" because the student hadn't accomplished the training goal, and the wing commander would override them. One instructor recalled being forced to graduate a student who had failed six consecutive training missions. The message was clear: regardless of the circumstances, the numbers would be served.

Students and instructors alike were also growing concerned that they were being asked to fly unsafe airplanes. Pressured to rate aircraft as "mission capable" on increasingly tight budgets, maintenance shops were taking dangerous shortcuts. When problems did develop with an aircraft, it was often difficult to pinpoint who in the centralized and multitiered depot maintenance system had actually worked on it.

Pressured to keep aircraft flying and sortie rates up, pilots were also severely reprimanded and in some cases dismissed for overstressing an aircraft—putting too much gravitational force, or "g forces," on it during aerial maneuvers. Thus even some instructor pilots routinely erased the readings on the onboard "g-meters" in their cockpits before returning to base. That kind of fibbing could also cost a pilot his life.

At night in the officers' club bar at Homestead, the instructor pilots often gathered to commiserate on the sorry state of affairs, even going so far as to talk among themselves about simply refusing to fly. It was mostly just the drink talking, though a few of the more angry ones wrote letters of complaint over their bosses' heads to the Tactical Air Command headquarters. Others vowed just to quit the Air Force altogether.

The wing commander at Homestead, Col. Sam Johnson, was a well-respected pilot who had spent years as a POW in North Vietnam. Many captains at Homestead, however, felt that his response to the problems on the base was simply to increase the pressure on them and the volume of his tirades. Indeed, ruling by fear and intimidation had become a popular command style throughout the Air Force, with a generation of officers typecasting themselves in the mold of Curtis LeMay, the bombastic general who was said to have once replied to a warning that he was smoking a cigar so close to an aircraft that was refueling that it might blow up, "It wouldn't *dare*."

As the crossroads of the fighter-pilot community, Nellis was an even better vantage point from which to recognize the problems plaguing the Air Force. There were pilots there who had been at Holliman Air Force Base, New Mexico, for instance, when a disgruntled captain who was quitting the Air Force wrote a letter to the local newspaper about the routine falsification of dive-bombing scores. Pilots were routinely writing themselves up as having completed a "dive toss" maneuver without ever even activating the "dive toss" bomb-delivery system. They jokingly called it "dive lie." An inspector general's investigation also revealed that pilots were falsely logging in that they had completed midair refuelings with aerial tankers, despite the fact that Strategic Air Command listed no tankers in the area.

Even within the confines of the elite Fighter Weapons School at Nellis, pilots were not immune to the corrosive effects of a bureaucracy that had seemingly come to worship and take comfort in statistics, as opposed to the uncomfortable truth they were originally designed to reveal. It started with small things: pilots who reported takeoff times more than fifteen minutes over schedule, and thus officially late, were being called back from the tower and asked if they *really* had that time right. Couldn't it have been fourteen minutes and fifty seconds, just under the fifteen-minute ceiling? Stories abounded at the bar of pilots being told by an overtaxed and pressured maintenance shop that an aircraft in for repairs was ready to be taken up again, only to have junior sergeants run up on the flight apron to whisper urgently that they would never fly in that airplane if it were *their ass* on the line.

A young instructor at the Fighter Weapons School was the first to step forward to say that he'd had enough. After one too many implicit invitations from the command post to lie, one wink too many from a maintenance shop on which his life depended, Capt. Ron Keys sat down at a typewriter and angrily poured his frustrations into an angry and eloquent letter to the commanding officer of Tactical Air Command.

One more angry letter from a disgruntled captain threatening to quit hardly qualified as major news in the Air Force. Indeed, experienced pilots were leaving the service in droves, and at 1979 retention rates the Air Force stood to lose seventy-five out of every hundred pilots by their eleventh year of service. Word around Nellis was that after pouring out his frustrations, Keys had actually wadded the letter up and thrown it away, and that someone had retrieved it out of the trash can and sent it for him.

Soon, however, nearly every pilot at the Weapons School had a copy of the letter, the crumpled lines clearly visible on the Xerox copies, and within weeks Ron Keys's letter was spreading through the tactical Air Force, carried by Weapons School students returning to their units and pilots passing through Red Flag. Nellis Air Force Base, after all, was the mecca for the fighter-pilot faithful, the crossroads where ideas such as the Red Baron report, Aggressor squadrons, and Red Flag had originated, then bubbled up through the Air Force hierarchy. Only this time what rose was a primal shout of frustration and disappointment that was soon known throughout the tactical Air Force simply as the "Dear Boss" letter.

Some months after writing the letter that had touched such a raw nerve, Ron Keys was told to report to Tactical Air Command headquarters at Langley Air Force Base, Virginia, for a discussion with the new commander. On a given week, captains will rarely talk even with the colonel commanding their wings, much less generals. The idea of a captain conferring with a four-star general was ludicrous, and in the learned view of some observers it undoubtedly spelled doom for Ron Keys's career.

After Keys returned to Nellis, however, it was rumored that Tactical Air Command had begun an investigation into the improprieties at Homestead Air Force Base, and that the author of the "Dear Boss" letter had been selected for the investigating team. Against all odds, it seemed the boss had gotten the message.

17: Sky Blazer 1978

WHEN Gen. W. L. "Bill" Creech took over command of Tactical Air Command in 1978, he couldn't have been more different from his bombastic predecessor, Gen. Robert Dixon, another of the Air Force commanders cast in the Curtis LeMay mold. Creech was a handsome, fastidious man whose uniforms always seemed freshly pressed, and whose hair, which many privately suspected he dyed jet-black, was never out of place. Also the butt of comments and imitations was his high, nasal voice, which Creech never raised. All in all, he was the antithesis of the blustery, cigar-chomping, tantrum-throwing generals who had long been the favored role models in the combat-pilot ranks.

To some of the barnstormers of the Korean War era, something was not quite right about Creech's finicky attention to appearances and aura of constraint, and despite a stellar war record that reached back to the Korean War and included 177 combat missions during Vietnam, some mistook his manner as a sign of meekness. Often that was the last mistake of their Air Force careers.

Had his own career gone by the numbers, Creech would have been ushered out of the Air Force, and certainly he would not have reached four-star status at his relatively young age. Under regulations, a severe heart attack he'd suffered a few years earlier was grounds for automatic retirement. Air Force chief of staff Gen. David Jones, however, had changed the retirement policy and kept Creech in the active force, just as he had bucked protocol years earlier to make Creech one of the fastest-rising stars in the Air Force, designating him for a two-star general's job when he was only a colonel.

Creech's wife, Carol, used to joke that each time General Jones passed her husband in the hall, Bill Creech ended up with two more weeks' worth of work. While his colleagues were out on the golf links or home with their families on weekend nights, Creech's fastback Mustang could usually be found parked outside his office, his light sometimes the only one burning in the building. Creech had helped Jones engineer a difficult agreement with the European allies to build hardened shelters for U.S. aircraft that would reinforce NATO in a crisis; had turned around a troubled air base in Madrid, Spain; had deftly handled troubled weapons-development programs as head of Electronic Systems Division. Whatever it took, Bill Creech always seemed to get results.

In truth, Gen. David Jones himself was not a man enamored with traditions or what he saw as arbitrary policies in a bureaucracy already choking on them. Some critics even accused Jones of never meeting a command he didn't try to reform, and he admittedly was not one to wait for something to break before trying to fix it. Thus even as a four-star he made the military bureaucracy uneasy.

In that sense David Jones recognized in Creech a kindred soul, and he sent him down to Tactical Air Command specifically to shake it up. Together, the two men would have a profound impact not only on the Air Force, but on the nation's entire military organization.

Along with command of the bombers and tankers of Strategic Air Command (SAC), control of the massive tactical air forces was the most coveted four-star job in the Air Force. Bill Creech inherited an operational fiefdom with 3,800 aircraft, 115,000 full-time employees, and 65,000 uniformed personnel scattered over 150 separate installations around the world. He had a discretionary budget in the billions, and assets under his control that would dwarf all the U.S. airlines combined. And despite the fact that in terms of modernization and personnel the Air Force was generally in better shape than the other services in the anemic 1970s, Creech found TAC to be an overcentralized and thoroughly dispirited mess.

On any given day, half of the planes in TAC's $25 billion inventory were not combat ready because of some malfunction, and 220 aircraft were outright "hangar queens," unable to fly for at least three weeks for a lack of spare parts or maintenance. Training sorties were dropping at the rate of 8 percent a year, and frustrated pilots—each trained at a cost of roughly $1 million— continued to desert the service in droves. If present trends continued, the Air

Force was staring at a shortage of over 2,100 pilots and 400 navigators by the end of 1980.

Studying TAC, Creech was reminded of a stint he had served in the Pentagon briefly back in the 1960s during Robert McNamara's tenure, when he watched as the former Ford Motor Company president planted the initial seed of centralized management. Just as its tenets had overtaken Detroit and business-school curricula across the country, Creech believed the principles of centralized management—eliminating duplication, realizing economies of scale, consolidation for the sake of efficiency—had spread like kudzu vine in the loamy soil of the military bureaucracies, sprouting regulations and statistical imperatives along the way. Combined with declining budgets, they were choking off the more fragile flowers of teamwork, cooperation, and simple pride in a job well done.

Creech's seminal vision for leadership, however, was not formed in the executive suites of American industry or in the vast Pentagon bureaucracy. Rather it was crystallized at twelve thousand feet and supersonic speeds, in the rarefied atmosphere of soaring barrel rolls and precision, wingtip-to-wingtip aerial acrobatics that he had orchestrated as the leader of the Sky Blazers air-demonstration team.

Given the aircraft and the training of the mid- to late 1950s, when Creech led the Sky Blazers, aerial demonstration was the riskiest type of flying short of combat. On average, even experienced teams crashed two aircraft a year, killing pilots like clockwork and making occupations like Grand Prix auto racing and bullfighting seem absolutely tame in any statistical comparison. During the four years that Col. Bill Creech led the Sky Blazers, however, they never had an accident.

That experience influenced Creech profoundly. Flying around Europe to various air shows, with no generals to look over their shoulders or bureaucrats to check their figures, the team members enjoyed unusual autonomy and responsibility. Because at times everyone in an aerial-demonstration team except for the leader flies looking at his partner's wingtip, following each other's every move in an exact and dangerous polka, absolute trust and honesty became a bylaw. Anyone who got drunk until the wee hours at the officers' club the night before a show risked killing not only himself but everyone else on his team.

For the same reason the ground crew responsible for working on the precision aircraft took their bows alongside the pilots and were afforded the same respect. The whole purpose of aerial-demonstration teams being to act as goodwill ambassadors for the Air Force, pride in appearance and a professional demeanor also went with the territory.

Even while he climbed into command positions in ever-larger units and organizations, Creech's essential viewpoint was that of a Sky Blazer. In his experience good things were not accomplished by tens or even hundreds of thousands of people, but rather by teams of five or ten people, all striving together for a shared goal. That concept flew in the face of conventional wisdom in the late 1970s and was instinctively resisted by the military bureaucracy. Yet that one overriding vision drove every change Creech was about to make at Tactical Air Command.

Col. Chuck Horner sensed early and acutely that perhaps he was not an officer in the mold of his new boss at Tactical Air Command. Where Creech was slim and ramrod straight, with never a hair out of place or a button seemingly unshined, Horner could somehow manage to appear rumpled even in freshly pressed blues. Though he wasn't proud of it, Horner also had to fight a sometimes losing battle to keep his temper in check. Creech had never lost his temper in a room full of people in his entire life.

It was part of the Creech creed, laid out in four rules of leadership that he passed along at the regular commanders conferences he began holding. All of them were pass/fail criteria, and Creech made it clear there would be no appeals for officers who broke one of his canons. He simply would not countenance lying; any integrity violation; abuse of power; and he would not tolerate public displays of temper.

When he was a young captain, an abusive and alcoholic commander had pushed Creech to the point of nearly quitting the Air Force. Instead Creech had stood up to the man and as a result suffered the kind of fitness report usually reserved for rapists and bank robbers. That experience explained why instead of shouting at Ron Keys for writing the "Dear Boss" letter, or having him fired, Creech admired the young captain for having the guts to stand up to what he felt was a corrupt and sorry system. Creech wasn't about to let any of his commanders rule by intimidation.

"Gentlemen, command must be reasoned," Creech told his assembled colonels at the initial commanders conference. "Once you've lost your temper, you've lost your power of reasoning, and you are being controlled by your emotions. It is all right to put steel in your voice, but if you're going to get mad, get up and leave the room instead."

Horner and many of the other commanders sat listening with teeth gnashing and mouths agape, the fighter-pilot brethren gathered to hear their fearless leader and suddenly finding themselves listening to a four-star version of Mr. Rogers! What absolute crap! They were supposed to lead the warrior elite on the precepts of the Golden Rule, doing gently unto others as you would have done to you?

That night while a number of commanders clustered around Creech's table at dinner, Chuck Horner sat in a corner with another pilot he knew, both of the men charter members of the Bar Stoolers, an informal club of hard-drinking, hard-charging fighter pilots. The two of them got bleary-eyed drunk lamenting what appeared to be the end of the Air Force as they knew it. More than once when he looked up from his drink, Horner could have sworn he caught Bill Creech watching them out of the corner of his eye.

After that, it was seemingly impossible for Chuck Horner to avoid Creech at the commanders conference dinners. Horner would circle the room, wait and go through the buffet line last, anything to avert having to take part in the toadying that surrounded any four-star general. And always Creech would call him over to an empty place saved at his table for Horner.

On one night of particularly boring conversation, Horner felt a pressure building directly behind his eyeballs as he listened as first one colonel and then another solicited the general's views on the overarching political issues of the day or suggested morale-building innovations designed to win kudos from the general.

Goddamn it, Horner thought as the pressure built and his vision practically swam, we're not politicians, we're freaking fighter pilots! The premier practitioners of drinking and chumming and daredevil flying! As he finished off his drink, Horner realized there was a lull in the conversation and that Creech was looking at him, giving Horner his turn to ask a question on the overarching blah blah blah. Instead Horner thumped his glass down on the table.

"Hey, did you fellas hear the one about the two French whores . . ." As he plowed ahead with his off-color joke, Horner was undaunted by the sickly look on the faces of his fellow officers. To hell with them! For whatever reason, however, General Creech was smiling, not so much at Horner as at the expressions on the other officers' faces. And the next night as he hurried past the general's table with eyes downcast on his plate, Horner heard Creech's distinctively nasal voice and his spirits sank. "Chuck, come over here and sit down," Creech called. "We've saved you a seat."

Even those officers who railed against Creech's proposed changes, and initially they were legion, had to eventually admit that much of what he stressed made sense. Colonels visiting Langley for the commanders conferences no longer had to change into dress uniforms, but rather were encouraged to stay in their flight suits and leather flying jackets. Flight jackets, Creech insisted, were a treasured uniform. Likewise, wing commanders who had felt pressure to spend their days behind a desk managing were encouraged to start flying more. A leader's place, said Creech, was in the air.

A senior maintenance sergeant's place was not shuffling spare parts orders in a rear-area maintenance control center, but apparently out on the flight line turning wrenches, and it didn't matter if it was thirty degrees below zero at Minot Air Force Base, North Dakota, in the dead of winter. That was the message behind one of Creech's first major reforms, which was the breakup of massive two-thousand-person wing maintenance operations into much smaller squadron repair teams. Good things were accomplished by small teams.

Not only were repair teams accountable only for their squadron's aircraft but for the first time young crew chiefs were allowed to paint their names on the side of their individual aircraft just like the pilots. Squadron decals and insignia, previously banned from aircraft, began showing up on fuselages again and on shoulder patches and baseball caps worn by the maintenance personnel.

In the first two years under the new system, with some of the most tightly constrained budgets in a decade, the number of TAC's aircraft that qualified as mission capable increased by 10 percent, and the average fighter was logging eight more hours a month of flight time. On one of his regular tours of operational bases, Creech asked a young sergeant about the rapid turnaround that followed the reforms toward crews' "owning" a particular aircraft. "General," the young man replied, "when was the last time you washed a rental car?"

Squadron commanders were given far greater latitude to design their flying schedules, and any squadron that met its monthly sortie goal for flying training missions was allowed to take an extra three-day weekend. The vise grip that declining budgets were putting on operations and maintenance accounts was also relieved somewhat when Creech made the difficult decision to deactivate seven squadrons, transferring their assets and personnel to poorly equipped and undermanned units. We are not going to make everyone a little sick, he explained, just to retain a whole that is less than the sum of its parts. Creech also made clear that no commanders would be punished for failing an operational-readiness inspection if they could prove the failure was caused by factors outside their control.

Horner and other commanders couldn't help but notice, however, that while the merciless browbeatings of previous reigns at Tactical Air Command had ceased, Creech was in his temperate and reasoned fashion giving an inordinate number of officers the ax. After the Homestead investigation, for instance, the wing commander's name disappeared from the brigadier generals promotion list. The leadership of the Aggressor squadrons at Nellis was also purged. A series of crashes of F-4s during Aggressor training prompted Creech to request the gun-camera films, and he discovered that Aggressors were positioning themselves on the tail of the much less maneuverable F-4s and taunting them into ever tighter turns in an attempt to escape, finally provoking "GLOC"—g-induced loss of consciousness. The Aggressors, Creech told the commander at Nellis's Fighter Weapons Center, were badly in need of some adult supervision.

While Creech expanded Red Flag, he made it clear that the days of Nevada Freestyle were over. While the barnstorming ethos of the Air Force he had joined in the 1950s may have been tolerated in an era when fighter pilots were lone hunters flying $50,000 prop aircraft, by the late 1970s the service was entering a new technological era of precision-guided bombs, airborne command-and-control, beyond-visual-range missiles, and "look down, shoot down" radars. The Air Force had only recently begun deploying the new F-15, for instance, a twin-engine, Mach 2.5 air-superiority fighter costing nearly $30 million.

Creech had fired a young pilot out at Holloman Air Force Base, New Mexico, who almost lost his F-15 while putting on an unscheduled air show over his hometown of Plano, Texas. That had inspired a write-in campaign on the young pilot's behalf seemingly by everyone above the third grade in Plano, including entire elementary-school classes, but Creech refused to reconsider his decision. They weren't spending $30 million on aircraft for pilots to impress their hometowns or each other.

Creech knew that the roots of Nevada Freestyle reached far deeper than just the ranks of impetuous young pilots, a fact confirmed when he read the collateral investigation report on an aircraft accident in Germany. The brigadier general who had led the flight had already explained to Creech that his wingman had gotten spatially disorientated in bad weather after making the long cross-Atlantic flight and had ejected from his aircraft. Creech had taken him at his word. Only the investigation report revealed that the general was leading his twelve-ship formation in a flyby at the base, putting on a little air show after more than a twelve-hour flight. Creech called the general's office.

"I was just reading your collateral report on the accident," Creech said, his voice even and measured as ever. "Is all this true?"

After a moment of silence that spanned a long and distinguished Air Force career, the general admitted that it was.

"You lied to me," said Creech. "You know that, don't you?"

"Yes, sir, I know."

"I'll tell you what I want you to do. Hang up the phone, walk out your office door, get out of your uniform, and mail your request for retirement to the deputy for personnel. Your other option is a general court-martial. Do you want an hour to think it over?"

"No, sir, I let you down. I'm on my way out the door right now."

While his ironhanded handling of the incident caused some disgruntlement in the pilot ranks, Creech regained that ground after a far more tragic accident in which a Thunderbird flight lead drove his aircraft into the ground, followed in split-second succession by three other aircraft in his flight. It was the third major accident for the Thunderbirds that year, one more example of Nevada Freestyle in the minds of many, and it lead to a movement inside the Pentagon to disband the flight team forever.

To save the Thunderbirds, Creech had driven from Langley to Washington, D.C., to personally promise the Air Force leadership and Congress that if the Thunderbirds suffered so much as one more accident, he would hand in his resignation. He had then gathered the Thunderbirds together to talk in a very reasoned way about the value of adult supervision, and there had been steel in his voice and new admiration in his audience.

At the conference-room table the visitors couldn't help but notice a decrepit old chair with stuffing bursting through torn seams and a block of wood strapped to one leg where it was missing a roller. Creech had imported it from a grease-smudged and grimy maintenance hangar he had visited, and the command's chief of logistics was forced to sit in it at meetings until Creech judged the command was sufficiently far along on his "Proud Look" program to spruce up every facility in Tactical Air Command, beginning with a fresh coat of paint. Ever since his days as a Sky Blazer, Creech couldn't remember seeing a shabby-looking outfit that was worth a damn.

When they heard that Tactical Air Command was spending money painting the backs of stop signs, the General Accounting Office, Congress's investigative arm, sent a team down to Langley to find the crazy general behind the scheme. What they found instead was a command in 1979 that was flying 11 percent more sorties than the year before despite funding cuts, and seeing rapid improvements in retention and mission-capable statistics. Creech told the GAO investigators that for the price of a single F-15 he could paint every building in Tactical Air Command's vast empire, which is exactly what he intended to do.

Not that the changes Creech made came easy to the Air Force, especially the old guard. When he heard that Creech was visiting his air base, for instance, Col. Chuck Horner felt the same sinking feeling he always got when the general saved him a seat at the commanders conference dinners. Before Creech arrived, Horner drove the route they would take from the flight line to the base headquarters. At the first building they were scheduled to visit, he parked his car and walked inside and to the men's room.

Horner could visualize everything. The first thing Creech would do on entering the building would be to take his hat off. Horner checked that there were hat hooks outside the bathroom. Then Creech would want to comb his hair in a mirror. Horner went into the bathroom and checked out the facilities. If Creech decided to use the bathroom and found graffiti plastered on the stall, Horner knew there would be hell to pay.

Later as he was driving General Creech onto the base, Horner noted with some horror an empty can of Coke on the sidewalk that hadn't been there earlier. Without even thinking what he was doing, he pulled the car over to the curb.

"Excuse me one second, sir," Horner said, and then walked around the car to pick up the stray litter, which he knew would stand out like a trash dump to the fastidious Creech. Holding the sticky can in his hand, Chuck Horner felt his face redden as it occurred to him how out of character he was acting. What if his old pals could see him now? What would Skinny Innis say for Christ's sake, or the Bar Stoolers, seeing one of the true brethren on litter patrol like some damned anal retentive? That's when it occurred to Horner. He's cloned us! Walking back around the car shaking his head, Horner couldn't let go of the thought. We're all becoming fucking Creech clones.

18: Borderline 1978–79

SOMEWHERE in the distance, the bell of a streetcar trilled as Jill McCaffrey walked toward the post from their house in a suburb of Schweinfurt, West Germany. The upstairs windows of some of the houses were flung open, and thick comforters were draped outside to air. As she continued down the narrow, clean-swept streets, Jill admired the tidy flower gardens and fresh-scrubbed look of the buildings. With their bustling railway stations and cobblestoned streets filled with prosperous shoppers, German towns and villages exuded an undeniable old-world charm.

While the first year in Germany back in 1976 had been difficult, neither Jill nor Barry McCaffrey wanted to think about leaving now. During the past three years Jill's German had steadily improved, and their small circle of German friends continued to expand. By 1979 the family had come to call West Germany home. The children loved the holidays and vacations spent exploring the capitals of Europe. They knew the family wasn't rich, but not many of their friends back in the States could boast of spending Christmas in Rome one year and then in Paris the next. After six years being away from commanding troops, in West Germany Barry was also clearly falling in love with being a soldier again. As for Jill, the war years had left her with a lingering bitterness and distrust of nearly all things civilian, especially back home. West Germany suited her just fine.

Certainly there was plenty to do in Germany to keep her busy. In just a few years, the proportion of women and families had skyrocketed on Army bases. In Germany it was becoming common to see pregnant soldiers strolling around base in uniform, and the befuddled wives of young enlisted men were easy to spot around town in their clunker cars with the signature green license plates, so obviously overwhelmed at finding themselves overseas and probably away from home for the first time. More than 60 percent of soldiers were now married, up significantly since the end of the draft, and many were married to other soldiers or were single parents.

Indeed, the *From Here to Eternity* Army of their parents' era, when all Army life centered around barracks where bachelors spent most of their free time, was apparently gone forever. Predictably the Army's support structure for families and women had lagged far behind. Jill McCaffrey and some of the other officers' and senior enlisted men's wives pitched in to help where they could, operating as the social workers the Army apparently didn't yet realize it needed.

As she strolled onto Ledward Barracks, a former Luftwaffe post that now housed the 1st Brigade of the 3rd Infantry Division, Jill flashed her ID card at the gate sentry. Opposition had been growing in West Germany over the government's announced plans to deploy U.S. long-range nuclear missiles in Europe, and security had been tightened after a series of terrorist attacks on U.S. installations.

As she walked by a barracks, Jill's pace quickened even before she heard the inevitable whistles. Soon the call was taken up as soldiers leaned out from a bank of yawning windows, and Jill resisted the temptation to start running. "Oh, baby! You're looking fine!" "Hey, pretty mama, come back here to daddy . . ." Jill McCaffrey kept her eyes straight ahead.

• • •

"Just state your name, son," Lt. Col. Barry McCaffrey instructed the soldier, but the young man continued to stammer, obviously either intimidated or confused by the reenlistment ceremony. As a battalion executive officer in the 7th Army's 3rd Infantry Division in West Germany, McCaffrey was proud that his unit had one of the highest reenlistment rates in Europe. Chronic recruiting problems were reaching a crisis point in 1979, and with the Army shrinking below its authorized strength for lack of recruits, commanders were told to reenlist their personnel or face losing their slots.

McCaffrey had only two criteria for reenlistment: Will the soldier fight if it comes to that, and is he currently a felon? If the answers were yes and no respectively, McCaffrey would sign them up. Yet this was the first time he could remember reenlisting a soldier who apparently couldn't state his own name.

By the end of the reenlistments it was getting late, and while Sgt. Maj. Robert Poole closed up shop, McCaffrey grabbed his large four-cell flashlight and reflecting sunglasses, pulled his field hat with the lieutenant colonel's insignia close over his eyes, and strolled out toward the barracks. The patrols were a little ritual that he and Poole had started, just to remind the troops who the bosses were.

Many of the soldiers were great kids, and McCaffrey enjoyed just stopping by and shooting the breeze with them. Other times they had broken up knife fights in the barracks and had once stumbled on a soldier locked in the latrine and nearly dead from a heroin overdose. McCaffrey knew he struck quite a figure with his prematurely graying hair and mirrored glasses, but if trouble started—and it could start at any time—McCaffrey figured to get the bastards right between the eyes with the flashlight while they were still wondering what to make of him. In 1979, officers in the U.S. Army were sometimes reminded of a comment attributed to the renowned British general, the duke of Wellington: "I don't know how the enemy feels about these soldiers, but they sure scare the hell out of me."

In truth, the patrols gave Barry McCaffrey a rare chance to be alone with his thoughts. Sometimes the very fact that he was still policing a dingy barracks in Germany seemed stunning to McCaffrey, when so many of his friends and cohorts were walking the halls of power in Washington, D.C., apparently on a fast track to greater things. After the war, the vogue for promising officers of his age was toward staff jobs in the Pentagon or scholarships in government or academia, anyplace where the great matters of the day were decided. No one would mistake Ledward Barracks for such a place.

Already Barry McCaffrey had applied for a White House Fellowship while at West Point, just missing the cut. Shortly after arriving in Germany he was pulling together a second application, encouraged by friends who had won the coveted fellowships in the past that the second time would be the charm, when Robert Elton stopped by his office one evening. Elton was by then a full colonel and chief of staff of the 3rd Infantry Division. The two had become close back in the early 1970s while working on the creative-leadership team as part of the Modern Volunteer Army effort, a bonding experience if ever there was one.

When he heard what McCaffrey was up to, Elton had put the question bluntly: What do you want to be, Barry? It was a better question than McCaffrey cared to admit. Did he want to be at the center of power, pondering weighty matters in the shadow of the great men of the day, or did he want to be a soldier? He should make a decision, Elton told his younger friend, because the Army was in trouble, and it needed good soldiers as much as at any time in its history.

After Elton left his office, McCaffrey sat alone thinking about what he had said, and pondering the eight-page application in front of him. "Describe, in 300 words or less, your life's ambition, what you hope to accomplish or achieve in your lifetime, and what position you hope to attain."

In 300 words or less, your life's ambition . . . As he read that, McCaffrey sensed that his life was at another crossroads. It recalled a snowy night at Andover nearly twenty years earlier, when as a teenager he had sat alone pondering his future.

That the Army was still in considerable trouble in 1979 was undeniable. The rot that had begun with the war had continued to spread, even reaching within the granite battlements of staid West Point to blacken the reputation of the Military Academy itself. When McCaffrey left in 1976, the campus was rocked by a massive cheating scandal. Fifty cadets from the class of 1977 were expelled and as many as three hundred implicated in a scandal that sparked congressional inquiries and national media attention.

Like the rest of the Army, West Point was struggling to cope with an influx of young Americans who, in terms of social makeup and basic values, were unlike any cadet classes ever before seen on the campus. The Academy was finding that the traditional military values they taught were more at odds than ever before with the thinking of this new "me generation." Perhaps they should have all seen it coming. Vietnam, Watergate, the assassinations of the late 1960s, all had served to cut a new generation of Americans adrift, severing the ties that once bound them to institutions like West Point, or for that matter the Army itself.

With the end of the draft, the proportion of black recruits in the ground forces was also ballooning, on its way from 12 percent in the early 1970s, or roughly in line with the eligible population of American youngsters, to a peak of 37 percent in 1979. While the number of black officers had increased nearly twofold during that time, it still lagged far behind those numbers. Whereas Barry McCaffrey's class of 1964 had graduated only three black cadets, West Point in the mid-1970s had more than three hundred black cadets, and nearly four hundred Hispanics and Asian Americans.

The number of women joining the Army continued to increase as well, and just three years after McCaffrey had been chewed out by the superintendent at West Point over his paper on integrating women into Army ranks and abolishing the WAC, 118 female cadets had entered the Academy with the plebes of 1976, the first women cadets in West Point's history. For months the instructors had been forced into a crash course on how to deal with the influx of female cadets on campus, including instruction on female menstrual cycles and biological rhythms. They were preparing them as if for an invading army, a fact that struck many of the instructors as laughable.

The night Elton told him the Army was in a disorienting flux, McCaffrey had thought about many of those things, and in the end he came to the same conclusion he had reached at Andover many years earlier. The next morning the soldier who cleaned the office of the battalion executive officer carried out with the trash an application for a White House Fellowship. Barry McCaffrey wanted to be a soldier again.

In the three years hence, McCaffrey had been offered Pentagon staff jobs and promotions to brigade staff, but had turned them all down to stay with line troops at the battalion level. On a visit to Germany, his father had even joked about it. In his experience, retired general Bill McCaffrey told his son, any soldier who stayed in one place so long either had a drug problem, a girl-friend, or some racket on the side. Barry didn't even ask in which category his father felt he belonged.

As he got older, Barry McCaffrey found himself seeking out his father's advice more and more, where as a young man he was just as likely to reject it outright. Sometimes after a family dinner as the women cleared the table and retired into the kitchen, the McCaffrey men would sit for long hours talking about the Army. Young Sean loved to sit in on these sessions, listening to his grandfather's stories about World War II and Korea, and both his and Barry's tales of Vietnam.

In truth, the talks around the table after dinner were therapeutic for Barry McCaffrey. Listening to his father recount tales of World War II and Korea, hearing his stories again of whose wife would routinely drink too much and cause a scene at the officers' club in Panama back in the thirties, of putting on a formal dinner for Gen. George Catlett Marshall in a captured casino in

Italy during World II, of helping Gen. Douglas MacArthur plan the famed Inchon landing, all gave Barry a reassuring sense of the great pendulum of time on which the Army's fortunes rode. Sometimes Barry McCaffrey had an almost overwhelming sense that the Army was coming unraveled, but his father always took the long view that the American people would help it right itself in the end. And somehow his stories made Barry McCaffrey believe it.

From his little outpost on the frontier between East and West, however, McCaffrey was sometimes amazed that everyone couldn't see what seemed so blatantly obvious to a lowly lieutenant colonel. Everything he had learned throughout his career told McCaffrey that military power was a tool of ideological struggle, and in the years since Vietnam the military balance had shifted dramatically in the direction of the Warsaw Pact.

The Soviet Union was already beginning to exploit that leverage. You could read it almost daily in newspaper reports of Soviet adventurism worldwide; it was there in the Moscow-supported coup in Afghanistan, in Soviet support for Vietnamese aggression in Cambodia and Kampuchea, in the increased use of Cuba as a proxy to seed communist insurrections in the Caribbean and Central America, in stepped-up Soviet activity in Ethiopia and Somalia and elsewhere in the Horn of Africa.

Yet from the vantage point of the barbed-wire scar that ran the 836-mile length of Germany, those appeared as distant sideshows. Nowhere was the fundamental struggle between East and West in higher contrast, especially for an American wearing Army green. Soldiers who manned U.S. outposts along the border told stories of hearing explosions echoing along that no-man's-land at night. Everyone knew that it was probably just an ill-fated bird, or perhaps a fox, that had stumbled into the fence separating East and West, with its deadly SM-70 mines spaced at differing heights, falling at about the level of a man's head, groin, and legs. Legend had it that the mines had originally been developed by SS-Sturmbannführer Erich Lutter to guard against escape from Nazi concentration camps.

It wasn't hard to recognize from the western side that they now imprisoned an entire country of 17 million people, though occasionally young East Germans and even some families dared the odds with escape attempts. Over the years hundreds would fail to make it to the other side, which was why if you had all night to sit awake at a lonely guard post listening to distant explosions, you could fear what the morning light had to reveal along that particular stretch of fence.

Sometimes at night after the children had gone to bed, McCaffrey would tell his wife that if things continued as they were, he worried that within a few years the Army's growing weakness would tempt the Soviets into a war in Europe. That or the Europeans would capitulate to the Soviets' obvious superior strength without ever firing a shot. Already a wave of leftist terrorist attacks had caused near panic in West Germany, and massive and often violent demonstrations were being mounted against the proposed stationing of additional U.S. nuclear weapons to counter similar deployments by the Soviets in Eastern Europe.

If it did come to war, the two-hundred-thousand-strong U.S. Army in Europe could well be swept off the continent before the country could adequately mobilize to reinforce them. The previous year, for instance, the Defense Department had held the largest mobilization and deployment exercise since World War II, called Nifty Nugget '78, and the results had been disastrous.

The mobilization and logistics on which U.S. forces had always relied had been steadily transferred into the reserve forces since the inception of Total Force back in 1973, and the exercise proved the reserves were woefully inadequate to the tasks. There were also shortages in air- and sealift, in mobilization plans, and especially in interservice coordination.

As part of one such exercise, the families and dependents of U.S. soldiers in Europe were mobilized to be sent home. McCaffrey's son, Sean, then fifteen years old, had come to him and said that after his mother and sisters were on the boat home, he wanted to come back and fight beside his father. Barry was touched and told Sean that he could pin lieutenant bars on him right then, and that the boy had the right sparks in his head to make a fine soldier.

When the time came, however, would Barry really want Sean to follow him into the Army? It would be nothing like the Army he had joined fifteen years earlier. It was much better off than in 1973; they had diffused some of the racial tensions and rid themselves of the worst criminals. Yet the ranks were still riddled by drugs, and statistics showed that drug offenses were still rising. McCaffrey guessed that half his soldiers were probably smoking dope. On the front lines, it also seemed that warnings that an all-volunteer force would require the services to scrape the bottom of the recruitment barrel were coming true.

Nearly half of the new recruits in 1979, for instance, were rated as CAT IV, the lowest mental category the military accepted. Many of the best sergeants that had formed the backbone of the Army before Vietnam had departed since the war. Some of those who remained would have been the rejects in an earlier era, and McCaffrey knew that nothing could turn the bright young recruits off faster than having one of those blockheads dogging them from day one.

Such as it was, however, the 7th Army in Europe was the cream of the crop, manned and equipped to a higher state of readiness than any other units in the Army. Sometimes McCaffrey had to remind himself that he truly loved living in West Germany, and that the children especially looked forward to their traditional holiday trips around Europe.

That Thanksgiving, however, the McCaffreys decided to stay in Germany, and the entire family dressed in its Sunday best for a special dinner given at the battalion mess for officers and enlisted soldiers and their families. The unique sense of community that had drawn both Barry and Jill to the Army in the first place was especially strong at overseas postings, and both had looked forward to spending the holiday with their friends on post.

Barry wore his dress uniform with its fruit salad of battle ribbons and decorations: two Distinguished Service Crosses, second only to the Medal of Honor in recognition of valor in combat, the two Silver Stars, the Bronze Star with "V" device with three oak-leaf clusters, the three Purple Hearts. Jill had also worn her Sunday best and had outfitted little Tara and Amy in matching yellow dresses. As she and the girls positioned themselves on one side of the long row table, Barry sat down on the other between two young soldiers.

"Anyone want eggnog?" he asked, and the two girls and Sean all shouted yes. Barry got up smiling and walked to the punch table across the room, heedless of the derisive looks the soldiers were casting at his chestful of ribbons. As soon as he was gone, one of the enlisted men turned to his buddy and exclaimed loud enough to terrify Barry McCaffrey's two little girls and shock Jill into stunned silence:

"Hell, if I'd have known I'd have to sit next to some motherfucking general, I wouldn't have bothered coming to this gig."

Even though Sundays were an officially designated day of rest in West Germany, with all shops and department stores closed by law, Brig. Gen. Jack Galvin found it impossible to take naps on Sunday afternoons even in sleepy Mainz on the banks of the Rhine River. As the assistant commander of the 8th Infantry Division, Galvin headed a special task force in charge of preparing the defense of the nearby Fulda Gap. In 1979, that was not duty that brought peace of mind.

If he closed his eyes, Galvin's thoughts would often take the route unbidden. It was usually at night, and his mind's eye would follow the river valley out of Frankfurt, climbing higher and higher through the dark countryside until in a few short hours there it was: the electrified fence, the guard dogs, the probing searchlights.

Galvin knew something about the Warsaw Pact forces arrayed on the other side of that fence, where they were and how they practiced for war. In the event of an invasion he would be responsible for rushing American troops to plug the Fulda Gap. In truth, Jack Galvin refused even to take his shoes off on Sunday afternoons.

Warsaw Pact training bothered him especially. Galvin had spent the last seven years in Europe, and during that time he had pondered their military exercises. Always the exercises were offensive operations with long, punishing attack phases, followed by a short, fig-leaf defense to consolidate gains. Like every military man familiar with the dynamics, Galvin knew that massive armies fought the way they trained.

Sometimes Galvin had to remind himself that the Soviet generals faced some daunting concerns themselves. Their doctrine of massing successive echelons was clumsy and difficult to manage. The active defense the Army was beginning to practice was designed to disrupt those waves. There was also the question of whether or not Soviet "allies" in the Warsaw Pact would actually fight in a war. Maybe they wouldn't, but then again some of his friends in the West German Bundeswehr suggested that the East Germans were even more doctrinaire than the Soviets. What if they did fight?

The deterioration in the balance of military power in Europe was cause enough for alarm. Among the fifteen nations of the Atlantic Alliance, it was known as the "lost decade." While the United States had been distracted by Vietnam and its aftermath for the decade of the 1970s, the once comfortable military advantage enjoyed by NATO had disappeared. By 1979, chronic military inferiority loomed.

The most dramatic evidence of that shift had come with the surprise discovery by intelligence agencies in 1977 that Moscow had perfected guidance technology for its SS-18 intercontinental ballistic missiles (ICBMs) years ahead of forecasts, giving the Soviet Union a potential first-strike capability against Minuteman ICBMs based in the United States. By the end of the lost decade, the Soviets were also ahead of the U.S. in intercontinental ballistic missile launchers, and in submarine-launched ballistic missiles. Only in long-range bombers did the U.S. continue to cling to an advantage.

With the United States' once unquestioned nuclear superiority suddenly diminished, more of the weight of deterrence shifted to the conventional forces. There the trends were even more disquieting, as the conventional forces had suffered most from the relative decline in U.S. military spending under Pres. Jimmy Carter. With 3.6 million troops, the Soviet military was nearly twice the size of that of the United States, and in the past decade its tank and artillery forces had grown by 35 percent and 40 percent, respectively. The Soviets' technological breakthroughs, approach toward nuclear parity, their growing conventional superiority—all were signs of a seismic shift in the complex geography of deterrence, and those rumblings were enough to keep Jack Galvin wide-awake on Sunday afternoons.

Sometimes Galvin wondered that his career had survived Vietnam. Certainly no one was more surprised than he when his name had come out on the promotion list for colonel years back, which led to a job writing speeches for Gen. Andrew Goodpaster, then the supreme allied commander, Europe (SACEUR). He had been in Europe ever since.

They were rising through the ranks, those officers whose formative command years were spent in Korea and especially Vietnam as opposed to World War II. Recently it had even been announced that Gen. Edward Meyer would be jumped ahead of a number of senior officers to become the Army's next chief of staff. Selection of the younger Meyer marked a significant passing of the torch in Army leadership, and Galvin applauded the announcement. He had never forgotten his tour in Vietnam with the 101st, when, as division executive officer, "Shy" Meyer had shown confidence in Galvin's ability to command a battalion in combat when few others had. When Galvin had refused a direct order to mount a nighttime attack outside of artillery protection, it was Shy Meyer who had come to his defense. Galvin wondered, however, whether the political leadership understood the change they were heralding with Meyer's selection to head the Army.

As for Galvin's career, he had been offered the position of assistant commander of the 8th Infantry Division in West Germany by Maj. Gen. Paul Gorman. Sometimes it seemed that whenever his career approached a crossroads, it intersected with that of Paul Gorman. It had taken an almost fatal turn for the worst back in 1966 when Galvin was relieved after nearly killing Gorman with an errant air strike, yet it was Gorman who had later enlisted his help on the Pentagon Papers project, a seminal event in Galvin's understanding of what went wrong in Vietnam.

Along with the rest of the Army's leadership, Galvin knew that Paul Gorman was the key figure in a revolution in Army training that was about to reach a milestone with establishment of the National Training Center (NTC), slated to open in California in 1981. Galvin also knew that the idea to turn 650,000 acres of land in the high Mojave Desert into a simulated battlefield for training brigade-sized forces had met with considerable resistance in the Army.

To some operational commanders in West Germany who were watching their budgets dwindle annually while the enemy on the other side of the Iron Curtain grew ever stronger, the idea of spending hundreds of millions of dollars so soldiers could shoot at each other with harmless lasers seemed like madness. Yet Jack Galvin thought he recognized the work of a visionary.

Of course, Gorman himself was aware that much of the Army remained skeptical about the concept of a massive training center in the California desert, just as he was sure that he had helped convince the one man who mattered most in the person of Gen. William E. DePuy. Their four years together at Training and Doctrine Command (TRADOC) had been every bit as tumultuous as Gorman had once feared, with his letters of resignation flowing in rough proportion to DePuy's refusal to accept them.

Yet DePuy had firmly grasped the implications of Gorman's campaign for a shift in combat training from an emphasis on static firing ranges to freeform, force-on-force tactical engagements such as the Air Force was conducting at Red Flag. From that point on, DePuy had made the National Training Center his own cause, and his tactics and tenacity mirrored those Gorman had seen DePuy display on the battlefield. DePuy worked to penetrate and co-opt the opposition and seize the high ground. When there was opposition, he would flank it with trips to Washington to visit the chief of staff. In all matters concerning the NTC, DePuy deftly aimed for what he sought in battle: victory at whatever cost.

They all understood that changes as radical as the ones they were proposing in training and doctrine would take years to realize, and DePuy said as much in his lectures at the War College. The National Training Center, for instance, would not even open for another two years. The doctrine of "active defense," whose development was overseen by DePuy and Gen. Don Starry, had likewise been ridiculed as too defensive in nature.

Published in 1976, the doctrine, espoused in the official Army handbook *Field Manual 100-5* ("FM one hundred dash five"), warned for the first time, however, that the Army must prepare to "fight outnumbered and win." Because of the lethality of modern weapons, "the first battle of our next war could well be its last. . . . The circumstance is unprecedented: we are an Army historically unprepared for its first battle."

Those who had served at TRADOC understood that subsequent editions would integrate the active defense with deep attack of Soviet echelons when technologies and weapons then in development began entering the arsenal early the next decade. In the meantime, Starry had been named to follow DePuy as head of TRADOC when the wily general retired in 1977. It was something else DePuy had intuitively understood: the first duty of a leader is to create other leaders to carry the torch after he has gone, and few four-stars left more protégés in positions of influence than William DePuy.

In much the same way, Paul Gorman seemed to be grooming Jack Galvin. Of course, the two men never spoke openly of it, just as they never broached the subject of their nearly fatal encounter back near Phu Loi. At a chance meeting in 1979, however, Jack Galvin did run into several former colleagues from those days in the Big Red One, and the bloody Battle of the 25th of August, 1966, had predictably come up in conversation.

With DePuy finally retired and Galvin's career obviously back on track, someone asked, how did Galvin feel about getting fired and DePuy's conduct of that disastrous fight? Galvin thought back to that terrible day, and what had been a shattering blow from which he feared his self-confidence might never recover. Now here his friends were offering him vindication, an opportunity to set the record straight.

The peculiar thing about war was the strength of the bond Galvin still felt with all those men. He always sensed it with Paul Gorman, who had never sent an accusatory glance in his direction, and he felt it with all the men he had fought alongside that day, the living and the dead.

War had even bound him in some inexplicable way to Gen. William DePuy, the hard-charger who without thinking had almost ruined Galvin's career, and whose aggressive nature had led them all into so many dark places. Perhaps some truths were simply better left undisturbed there, as unearthing them would require leveling guilt and assuming innocence in a matter of war.

"Well," Galvin told his old buddies from the Big Red One, "I guess I share as much blame for that day as anyone else." With that, Jack Galvin largely put to rest the awful memory of August 25, 1966.

19: Long Memories 1979

ON a flat, endless expanse of Pacific Ocean that stretched as far as the horizon, Capt. Stanley Arthur watched flight operations from the bridge of the USS *Coral Sea*. The aircraft carrier and her escorts were the only visible occupants of a broad swath of the globe. Far below on the deck, pilots could be seen running to their aircraft, just as Arthur had run to his own countless times during Vietnam, only now there was no emergency. It was just Navy tradition that pilots ran from the ready room to man their airplanes, and in October of 1979 the Navy was trying to hold firm to its traditions as a drowning man grasps a life preserver.

Even from the bridge the roar of jet engines was a constant presence. At the front of the carrier an A-6 Intruder waited at the end of the catapult, its pilot saluting to the catapult officer and then bracing himself. Seconds later the aircraft was hurtling off the end of the deck as if from a slingshot, trailing a stream of friction smoke down the catapult rail. For a moment the bomber seemed to hang suspended over the ocean, then it banked and climbed as the twin retort of its engines sent more deafening white noise washing over the deck.

Watching the flight operations, Stan Arthur experienced the surge of pleasure that he often felt at sea. He was happy to be away from shore, where sailors often had too little to keep them busy and too many opportunities for mischief.

Not that this deployment had gone smoothly. They said that ships had long memories, and many of the *Coral Sea*'s he would just as soon forget. During Vietnam, protesters had thrown buckets of red paint down on her as she sailed out of San Francisco harbor. On this cruise she had come right out of overhaul, and Arthur had been forced to leave the West Coast with a hastily gathered crew that in many cases had not even had time to settle families before leaving. Because the entire Navy was shorthanded, the average length of their deployments had also been steadily increasing, and his men knew they were not likely to see their loved ones for at least seven or eight months, maybe longer. All in all, it made for a bad start.

Part of the problem of keeping the crew motivated was their lagging operations tempo. Strict fuel rationing meant that aircraft would typically fly eleven or twelve days out of a thirty-day sea rotation. If you weren't maintaining or flying airplanes, there wasn't much else to do at sea on an aircraft carrier. People got careless.

Spare-parts shortages also routinely grounded as much as a third of their aircraft. Throughout the Navy, ships and aircraft squadrons coming in from deployments were thus raided for spare parts by those going out, a practice called cross decking. Everyone knew that was just a polite euphemism for cannibalization. Starved for funds, the Navy was feeding on itself.

Commanding any ship in the U.S. Navy in 1979 thus required constant vigilance, and carriers demanded more than most. Arthur was lucky that the *Coral Sea* was recently out of overhaul. For a lack of either adequate maintenance or spare parts, or experienced crew to man engine rooms, a number of carriers were deploying with only three of their four screws turning. Even a fresh overhaul was no guarantee against potential disaster; that much had been proved by the sad case of the USS *Kitty Hawk.*

With the Navy desperately short of experienced petty officers, many enlisted personnel were working at jobs that should have been filled by someone at least two grades above their rank. In the entire Navy, only the nuclear-submarine fleet under the stringent guidance of Adm. Hyman Rickover was fully manned with qualified personnel. The day-to-day and often dangerous work performed by the rest of the Navy was done by sailors who frequently had neither the requisite training nor experience. Many were simply over their heads. In the case of the *Kitty Hawk,* that volatile situation had nearly cost the Navy an aircraft carrier.

As it was transiting the Pacific, the *Kitty Hawk* had experienced what was initially a minor engineering malfunction. In managing the problem, however, the engineering crew had made it worse, allowing water to flood the ship belowdecks. After limping into Subic Bay in the Philippines, the *Kitty Hawk* spent nearly its entire deployment getting rewired and repaired. That incident had followed a similar crisis aboard the USS *Saratoga* in the Mediterranean.

On taking command of the *Coral Sea,* Arthur was thus determined to heed any potential early-warning signs of trouble. In the end, however, dissension found the ship anyway, though at least it occurred in the middle of the Pacific Ocean, where Arthur felt he could deal with it his way. It began after he received a message in his comfortable quarters that the ship's black sailors were forming on the hangar deck in what was beginning to look like a demonstration of some sort. Though racial tensions had dissipated significantly since the early 1970s, when captains sometimes faced near mutinies on board, Arthur felt that the Navy and all the services were being forced by the chronic recruiting shortages to accept more than their share of troublemakers. And whenever there was trouble, too often it tended to polarize along racial lines.

On his frequent rounds of the ship, however, Arthur had made a point to try to get to know sailors and aviators from all the various subcommunities and cliques on board. It was the only way he knew to monitor the pulse of what in essence was a small city of nearly five thousand men. Rather than discipline the perpetrators or have them forcibly dispersed, Arthur thus sent for a black sailor he had gotten to know who was bound to be in the middle of any melee.

"You sent for me, sir?" the sailor said after knocking on the door to the captain's quarters.

"I hear you've got a little meeting going on down on the hangar deck," Arthur said. "What's going on?"

"Well, sir, we just don't feel like we're being treated fairly on this ship."

"You personally? The rest of the black sailors? Who?"

"All of us."

"Look, let's not make this a black-white issue. You know I've got to maintain discipline on this ship, so why don't you tell me what the problem is, and I'll tell you if I can help," Arthur said, laying the options out for the man. "And if I can't, or won't, I'll at least explain why."

Eventually Arthur was able to diffuse the crisis by personally hearing the gripes, which in the end had nothing to do with race. Later when he was alone, listening to the various creakings and groans of the ship, feeling her shudder internally each time an aircraft caught the arresting cable, Arthur mulled the incident over.

It was difficult not to worry about the direction the service was headed. While the Navy continued to weaken throughout much of the 1970s, the Soviet Navy was becoming stronger and more arrogant at sea. Even then the *Coral Sea* was within what Pacific Fleet called a "Bear box," and they were constantly forced to intercept land-based Backfire bombers coming in for a close look. Indeed, the Soviet aircraft often conducted mock attacks on U.S. ships, and Soviet surface ships and submarines had become so aggressive that the Navy instigated negotiations for an "incidents at sea" agreement to avoid a possible international crisis.

While the Navy still held an undisputed qualitative edge in ships and logistics infrastructure over the Soviet Navy, it had shrunk during the 1970s from roughly 900 to 479 ships. The Soviets, meanwhile, had introduced or were introducing a whole new generation of modern warships—Kiev medium aircraft carriers, Kirov nuclear-powered destroyers, Udaloy destroyers, Alfa nuclear-powered submarines—each far more capable than its predecessor.

While Stan Arthur's father would undoubtedly be proud to see his son commanding an aircraft carrier, would Holland Arthur even recognize the Navy he had once loved so dearly? What would his father think of the constant discipline problems, the slipshod operations, and deteriorating infrastructure? A career Navy man, Arthur's father had always been a steady and unflappable presence. There might not have been much flamboyance to him, but he was a shipshape sailor who followed the rules and was devoted to duty. Ever since Stan Arthur was a child, that had been his image of the Navy itself, and suddenly he was acutely aware that it bore little resemblance to the reality of 1979.

After finally leaving the vast tracts of the Pacific behind, the *Coral Sea* sailed through Luzon Strait and into the South China Sea late in 1979. The ship had already passed the Naval Communications Station near the northern end of Luzon Island at San Miguel, and across Subic Bay they could see aircraft approaching Cubi Point, the Navy's most active overseas air station.

The silhouettes of floating cranes and block-long warehouses announced the massive U.S. Naval Base at Subic Bay in the Philippines, the Navy's largest overseas logistics hub and gateway to 7th Fleet operations throughout Asia and the Middle East.

With the help of a small armada of tugboats, Capt. Stan Arthur guided the *Coral Sea* into Subic. Except for the interlude during World War II when U.S. forces under MacArthur had been driven off the island, the Navy had called the Philippines home since 1898, the year it had defeated the Spanish fleet in Manila Bay during the Spanish-American war.

With orders to report to Hawaii to begin a tour on the headquarters staff of Pacific Fleet, Stan Arthur relinquished command of the *Coral Sea* and picked up his wife, Jennie, and his four kids. Hawaii would actually be a return engagement of sorts for Arthur, who was evacuated off the island as a young boy in 1941. Only in the first grade at the time, he had just had his appendix out, and the ship's crossing was a journey he would never forget. Less than two months after they sailed, the Japanese attacked Pearl Harbor.

When Arthur arrived at Pearl Harbor, however, he found Pacific Fleet headquarters on another kind of war footing. Arthur was told to immediately join a secret planning cell responsible for helping to coordinate a military operation with enormous potential risks. A mob of Muslim "students" had just overrun the U.S. embassy in Tehran, Iran, seizing every American in the compound.

20: A Hollow Force 1979

AS the aircraft circled the wooded complex of Camp David, Army chief of staff Gen. Edward "Shy" Meyer listened distractedly while Deputy Defense Secretary W. Graham Claytor explained the lay of the land. A former Southern Railroad man, Claytor pointed out the empty tracks that in summer used to deliver swarms of sweltering Baltimore tourists to the cool of the Maryland mountains. On November 24, 1979, however, the gray smoke drifting from some of the chimneys on the mountainside cast a wintry pall over the scene. It matched perfectly the mood of Shy Meyer on his first visit to the presidential retreat.

The Joint Chiefs of Staff were gathering at Camp David to discuss next year's defense budget with Pres. Jimmy Carter and his national security team. Carter had come into office vowing to cut the military budget by $5 to $7 billion, and while the budget had actually grown somewhat during his first three years in office, the steadily declining value of the dollar against currencies in foreign countries where the military operated, inflation in the high teens, and wildly escalating fuel costs had all conspired to make the Carter years some of the leanest in modern times in terms of defense buying power.

Having only been appointed chief that June, Meyer's visit to Camp David marked his first full budget conference with the president and the other chiefs. For weeks he had struggled to compile a clear depiction of the Army's capabilities so that no one would be confused should the Army be called on in an emergency. As he entered the conference room of Camp David's main lodge, Meyer was thus weighted by the burden of the messenger who knows he is bearing bleak news at absolutely the worst time.

For Pres. Jimmy Carter, November 1979 marked the beginning of what would prove the most difficult period of his life. Earlier that month, Carter had been awakened by the news that radical Iranian militants had seized a hundred hostages at the American embassy in Tehran in the wake of his decision to allow the former Shah of Iran into the United States for cancer treatment, thrusting the administration into the worst international crisis of its tenure.

For the first time in anyone's recollection, a host government had failed to step in to protect foreign diplomats, and indeed Iran's religious leader Ayatollah Ruholla Khomeini even praised the captors as heroes of his revolution. Just four days before the Camp David meeting, Khomeini had threatened to try the hostages as spies if the Shah was not returned to Iran, going so far as to mock Carter for lacking the guts to intervene militarily.

In response to erroneous reports that U.S. soldiers had defiled holy sites in Saudi Arabia, an angry Moslem mob had also recently attacked and burned the U.S. embassy in Islamabad, Pakistan, killing a Marine guard and forcing nearly one hundred members of the mission to flee to the roof of the burning building, where they were eventually rescued. Pakistani mobs had also attacked the U.S. consulate in Karachi, destroyed the American library in Lahore, and burned the American Cultural Center in Rawalpindi.

Even as the chiefs met at Camp David, their staffs back at the Pentagon were hurriedly studying how best to back up Carter's recent threat of military action if the captives in Iran were harmed, and the Army's secret Delta Force commando team was preparing an emergency and probably suicidal assault plan if the Iranians began killing the hostages. Though businesslike, the mood in the Camp David conference room was understandably somber. Gen. David Jones, chairman of the Joint Chiefs of Staff, opened with a brief overview of the defense budget request.

Shy Meyer was next. When asked to brief the president on the Army's prime mission of reinforcing its forces in Europe with ten divisions in fourteen days, Meyer responded that they had neither the divisions ready to deploy nor adequate lift to get them to Europe. Only four of the ten active divisions in the United States were capable of deploying overseas in an emergency, and the wholesale transfer of critical support and logistics functions into the undermanned reserves as part of the Total Force concept meant that troops could not be sustained in combat anywhere beyond a few weeks.

The tight funding of the Carter years had exposed the ambitiousness of two of the most crucial decisions made by the late Creighton Abrams in the early 1970s—establishment of the Total Force concept with its unprecedented reliance on reserve forces, which were typically treated as stepchildren at the budget table, and expansion of the Army to sixteen active and eight reserve divisions during a period of budget and manning shortfalls.

Meanwhile, chronic drug and alcohol problems persisted in the Army, the number of high school graduates recruited in 1979 had been the lowest since the all-volunteer force began, and for the first time the Army had experienced a manpower shortage because of its inability to recruit even marginally qualified soldiers.

"Mr. President," Meyer summarized after glancing in the direction of Defense Secretary Harold Brown, "basically what we have is a hollow Army."

After answering a few perfunctory questions from Carter, Meyer yielded to Adm. Thomas Hayward, chief of naval operations, who briefed for the Navy. The picture he painted of an undermanned and demoralized Navy was equally as grim as Meyer's. The service was short twenty thousand petty officers, its most skilled enlisted crew members, and spare parts and equipment were so sparse that the Navy was routinely "cross decking" everything from support equipment to aircraft. The shortage in personnel also meant that sailors were routinely forced to stay out at sea for eight-to-ten-month cruises, and sometimes even longer. When ships finally did return to home port, the number of sailors opting out of the service ballooned.

Though he realized the situation he described was alarming, Hayward was ready to administer the shock treatment. After serving as chief of naval operations for sixteen months, the former 7th Fleet commander and jet pilot was speaking directly to his commander in chief for one of the first times during his tenure. Hayward was convinced that Defense Secretary Harold Brown kept them away from the president purposely, knowing that the bleak news they would bring would make it harder to rationalize inadequate defense budgets. The message Hayward wanted to leave with the president was that the armed forces weren't just hollow, but were becoming so inept and demoralized as to be downright dangerous. If anyone needed proof, Hayward was ready to offer up the case of the USS *Canisteo*.

Earlier in the year, the front-line support ship *Canisteo* became the first active-duty ship in anyone's memory to cancel a scheduled deployment because her captain decided it was unsafe to sail. The ship was simply short too many key crew, including experienced chiefs, boiler technicians, and machinist mates. Despite calls to punish the captain from some voices in Congress and inside the Office of the Secretary of Defense, Hayward had supported the captain's decision. He still vividly remembered the case of the *Kitty Hawk*, when an inexperienced engineering crew had turned a minor problem into a crisis that threatened one of their precious aircraft carriers.

The *Canisteo* was just the most obvious symptom, Hayward believed, of the worst malaise to afflict the Navy since he'd joined the service during World War II. Their bases were crumbling, ships were rusting, and privately his subordinates were telling Hayward that as many as half the people in the Navy were on drugs.

Meanwhile, the Russians were becoming increasingly aggressive. What most worried Hayward was a nagging sense that the Navy rank and file had begun to believe that the Soviets were better than they were. What he wanted the commander in chief to understand before they left Camp David was that Hayward couldn't make the Navy feel good about itself again if they were continually underfunded and underappreciated.

As Meyer listened to the Navy briefing, he was stunned to realize that another service was in as much trouble as the Army. This was not generally admitted even within the halls of the Pentagon, and certainly the briefings depicted a U.S. military establishment in far worse shape than was generally acknowledged to the media and in congressional testimony. Meyer felt that lack of essential honesty and the breakdown in communication was exactly what had failed all of them—the civilian leadership, the military, the whole damn country—during Vietnam.

The other services' briefings were far more upbeat, with the chiefs essentially telling Carter that their forces were willing and able to perform whatever mission the president tasked them with. Listening, Meyer felt his resolve hardening. It was the same can-do attitude that he remembered from the

1960s, when he was privy to discussions in the upper reaches of the Pentagon as the assistant to Army chief of staff Gen. Harold Johnson.

Something in the very nature of the military man had led the leaders to salute and say, "Can do," even when they clearly couldn't do or knew they shouldn't do. Admirable in battle, that heroic stoicism served them poorly in critical councils with civilians, and Meyer was convinced that fundamental failure to communicate had cost the country dearly in Vietnam and during its aftermath. At Camp David he vowed that come what may, he would continue to be brutally honest in stating the problems of the Army. The question in his mind was whether it was too late.

One month later, on December 27, 1979, even while the national Christmas tree remained dark as a symbol of the loss of freedom for the hostages, and with Carter a virtual hostage inside the White House, the Soviet Union invaded Afghanistan in a boldly planned and elegantly executed military operation that put them on the threshold of the world's oil supply. Afghan president Hafizullah Amin—who the Soviets insisted had "invited" them in—was assassinated and replaced by a leader handpicked by the communists. Any lingering doubts that Moscow was intent on exploiting America's weakened position around the globe disappeared in the waning days of the lost decade.

As he strode out of his doorway on the Pentagon's E Ring for the short walk to the secretary of the army's office months later, Shy Meyer knew that it might well prove his last act as chief of staff of the Army. He also recognized the irony in his predicament: to uphold what he saw as his responsibilities under the Constitution, he was about to thwart the direct wishes of his civilian master.

The call asking him to report to Army Secretary Clifford Alexander Jr.'s office had not been unexpected. In the spring of 1980, all of the service chiefs were testifying on the administration's proposed defense budget before congressional committees. That morning under pointed questioning, Meyer had essentially repeated the warning he had delivered to President Carter months earlier at Camp David. The U.S. Army, Meyer told the assembled congressmen, was in many respects a hollow force.

For an administration that was desperately trying to counter charges of "weakness" in the midst of an election campaign and a foreign-policy crisis, Meyer's testimony was hardly welcome. Thanks in large part to the continuing hostage crisis and the Soviet invasion of Afghanistan, a Harris survey revealed that between mid-December 1979 and April 1980, Carter's popularity had already done an alarming reversal, from a 66 to 32 percent approval rating to a 65 to 24 percent *disapproval* rating. The last thing administration officials felt they needed was one of the Joint Chiefs talking publicly about a "hollow Army."

Not that Meyer believed the administration had ignored the warnings of the Camp David meeting. Indeed he saw it as a turning point. The events of late 1979 had clearly opened Carter's eyes to the dangers of an increasingly assertive Soviet Union and a steadily weakening military. The administration's current $157.5-billion military budget represented an increase of $16 billion over the previous year's outlays, and after Camp David the five-year plan for defense spending proposed by the administration had jumped dramatically.

Responding to the invasion of Afghanistan, Carter had also used the State of the Union address to Congress on January 23, 1980, to issue a policy later dubbed the Carter Doctrine by newspaper reporters. The president declared that any attempt by an outside force to control the Persian Gulf would be regarded as a direct assault on the vital interests of the United States.

To address the strategic paradox of declaring vital national interests in an area of the world that had no interest in hosting American military forces, Defense Secretary Harold Brown pushed through establishment of a two-hundred-thousand-troop rapid-deployment force whose equipment would be stored in prepositioned ships in the Persian Gulf area. The Carter administration's just-released fiscal year 1981 defense-budget request included money not only for enough equipment to outfit three Marine Corps brigades, but also the ships to store it in.

Yet knowing all of this, Meyer was still undeterred in his congressional testimony. It had taken the United States its first defeat in war and a lost decade to come to the sorry pass its armed services found themselves in at the beginning of 1980. A reversal of fortune might require some equally cataclysmic event and consume as much time, if it could be engineered at all. Meyer had his doubts. In the meantime, he intended to honor the vow he had made at Camp David.

"Shy, I want you to rescind the statements you made on the Hill today," Clifford Alexander said after closing the door to his office. An awkward moment of silence followed as the two men eyed each other and Meyer framed his answer.

They had worked together for the three years of Alexander's tenure as secretary of the army, during which Meyer had served in the Pentagon as the Army's deputy chief of staff for operations, and now as chief. Meyer admired Alexander, one of the few black men ever to reach such a high-level position in the defense establishment, and he credited him with helping to force the Army to take a hard look at the institutional racism hidden in some of its policies.

On the issue of his constitutional responsibility to level not only with the administration but also with Congress, however, Meyer was not about to yield to Clifford Alexander or anyone else.

"Sir, I can't do that," Meyer told Alexander. "I'm certainly willing to hand in my resignation, but I took my oath to the Constitution, not the president or this administration."

Meyer had thought long and hard about the issue before accepting the job as Army chief of staff. The year before he even delivered a series of lectures on the subject to military schools in Great Britain, explaining that what made the U.S. military unique was its oath of allegiance not to a monarchy, individual leader, or political party, but rather to the laws and ideals expressed in the Constitution. As a young cadet at West Point, Meyer had heard how that loyalty to a law rather than an individual broke with ancient military tradition and was credited with helping the young nation avoid even the threat of a military coup. After Vietnam, Meyer and many other officers of his generation had studied their oath of allegiance anew.

In Vietnam, they had been sent to war without a declaration of war by Congress, and Meyer and many of his friends had been left to fight on for years without the support of the American people. As deputy chief for operations, Meyer had recently critiqued and helped edit a seminal book out of the Army War College on the lessons of Vietnam entitled *On Strategy*. Written by a bright young colonel named Harry Summers, it put the failures of Vietnam in historical perspective, and its findings were much on Meyer's mind.

Warning of disastrous results that have historically followed a failure in civil-military relations in Washington, Summers wrote that "what we are faced with is the obverse of the problem President Kennedy faced when he issued an order in 1961 directing the Joint Chiefs of Staff to be 'more than military men.' Just as the military need to be aware of political, economic, and social issues, so our civilian leadership must be aware of the imperatives of military operations."

To the extent that it was within his power, Meyer had vowed to make the civilian leadership aware, and that included Congress, the representatives of the people. Because the last thing the administration needed was a separation of powers battle with Congress and the Army in the midst of the Iranian crisis, Meyer was also still the Army's chief of staff when he walked out of Clifford Alexander's office.

In choosing the fifty-one-year-old Meyer the year before, Jimmy Carter had reached well beyond the top tier of senior generals whose frame of reference was rooted in the old Army of World War II. He wanted younger blood and fresher ideas in the chief of staff of the Army's office. Gen. Edward "Shy" Meyer recalled the adage that it is prudent to beware what you wish for.

He had harbored no ambitions for the chief of staff's job. Yet the fact that Shy Meyer didn't really want the top position in his service even when it was offered the previous year had come as a terrible realization for a career Army man. Meyer sensed already that his best memories of the Army lay behind him in those years spent commanding soldiers in the field, talking with them and laughing at their antics, earning their fierce loyalty.

A charismatic and intelligent presence, tall and rangy in the mold of a Jimmy Stewart, Meyer had found that command came naturally. That special fellowship between men of arms was the reason he had come to love the Army, not the congressional hearings and endless bickering over budgets that characterized Pentagon duty. Having already spent four years in the building as the Army's powerful deputy chief of staff for operations, Meyer also thought he recognized the chief's job for what it was: an opportunity to preside over the demise of the Army as he knew it and wanted it to be.

Nor should it have been his to accept or deny. Everyone knew the logical candidate for the job was Gen. John Vessey Jr., a popular and widely respected soldier who had climbed from buck private to four-star general. Yet as commander of U.S. forces in Korea in 1977, he publicly opposed President Carter's announced intention to withdraw combat forces from South Korea, a position widely believed to have cost him the chief's job. Soon after Meyer accepted the job, he graciously made Vessey the *vice* chief of staff. Thus the administration had its first harbinger of Meyer's leadership style and independence.

Before accepting the job as chief, Meyer had driven from Washington, D.C., to his hometown of Saint Marys, Pennsylvania, for his father's eightieth birthday. Meyer knew of a grotto near the church in Saint Marys, and he went there and knelt down alone to pray.

Both times before going to war in Vietnam he had talked the decision over with his wife, Carol, who had had to stay behind with their five young children. Meyer had wanted to speak to her before deciding on the chief's job, but Carter and Defense Secretary Harold Brown asked him not to discuss the offer with anyone. Edward Meyer would have to decide alone whether to assume responsibility for an Army that was in dire trouble, and that had precious little support in the Congress, the administration, or, as far as he could tell, in the nation as a whole.

If he said no, Meyer knew that he would have to retire. You didn't turn down an offer of the top job in the Army by the president of the United States and stay in uniform. Meyer also had a clear vision of the direction he felt the Army needed to be led, grounded in his airborne experiences in Vietnam, and in his reading of the crises cropping up around the world with alarming frequency. He would spell it out in a White Paper the following year.

"The most demanding challenge confronting the U.S. military in the decade of the 1980s is to develop and demonstrate the capability to successfully meet threats to vital U.S. interests outside of Europe, without compromising the decisive theater in Central Europe," Meyer's *White Paper 1980* would read. "Our capabilities to project combat power worldwide must be improved."

The more responsive mobile force he pictured, however, was totally at odds with an Army in 1979 that was stumbling over the fundamentals of recruiting qualified soldiers and training and equipping them adequately. Shy Meyer had a vision all right; what he hadn't been able to see from his vantage point in the summer of 1979, kneeling in a small grotto in Saint Marys, was any possible way to realize it.

In the end, he had been bolstered by the realization that being chief of staff of the Army was not a job that any one man could accomplish. Meyer began to see it as matter of pointing the right people at the worst problems and hoping for the best. Certainly many fine soldiers had stuck with the Army through the dark days of the 1970s, and indeed for those who had persevered it had become a point of considerable pride. In 1979, West Point classes from the mid-1970s were already holding parties to celebrate completing half of their obligated service, and thus being halfway out of the Army. You couldn't really blame them, given the service they had inherited, but in accepting the chief's job Shy Meyer was keeping faith with those who, for whatever reasons, had long ago stubbornly decided that they were in for the duration.

Meyer hadn't forgotten the briefing he'd received from Bob Elton and Barry McCaffrey on the *Leadership for the '70s* study back in 1972, when he commanded the 82nd Airborne. He had even chided the enthusiastic young captain at the time, telling the obviously mortified junior officer, "McCaffrey, your boss tells me you step on your dick all the time." Now in a position to act on their recommendations, however, Meyer called in Brigadier General

Elton and told him to begin implementing as many of the ideas as he could, and he tasked his brain trust to come up with a solution for the command merry-go-round and the constant turbulence caused by the individual-replacement system.

As chief, one of Meyer's first edicts was to declare that the length of command tours would rise from an average of two years to a minimum of three years. For an Army that had rotated officers through command every six months during Vietnam, it was an unprecedented nod in the direction of command stability over flexibility of movement and advancement for officers. Not surprisingly the move presaged considerable grumbling in the officer corps. Each command tour was seen by the officer corps as a step up the ladder of promotion, and the idea that they would be stalled in their climb for three years was not a popular one. Meyer could hardly attend an Army ceremony or function without the wives of lieutenant colonels and colonels grilling him about why he was trying to stabilize the Army at the expense of their husbands' careers.

Trying to stabilize the enlisted ranks in an undermanned Army where turnover in companies and platoons averaged 15 to 20 percent *each month* was a far more difficult task, yet Meyer was determined. He still remembered returning to Vietnam and the 1st Cav Division in 1969, after being away for three years, and seeing the havoc wrecked by the constant officer shufflings and the individual-rotation system, even in what was one of the proudest divisions in the Army. Every military history book he had ever read stressed that men at war fight and die not for abstract ideals or flags, but for each other. He was intent that the next time U.S. soldiers went to war they would know the men they fought alongside.

Meyer favored the British regimental system, under which soldiers and young officers joined a regiment with a home post and could count on serving with familiar faces when they rotated overseas and returned home as a unit. Because it was less expensive and far less complicated to rotate individuals in and out of positions rather than whole units, however, huge institutional resistance to the idea existed not only in the Office of the Secretary of Defense, but also throughout the personnel structure. They continued to favor an individual-rotation system, as if war-fighting was just another form of shift work.

Under Meyer's direction Elton and others involved in personnel changes came up with the idea for experimental "cohort units." Soldiers in these units would bond together during basic training and serve in the same unit for their entire three-year tour. Efficiency would be sacrificed in the name of cohesiveness. If the experiment worked, Meyer planned to institute the idea Army-wide.

Later, Meyer called into his office Walt Ulmer—who along with Mike Malone had risked his career and shaken up the Army hierarchy a decade earlier with the scathing *Study on Military Professionalism*. Ulmer was commanding a division in Europe when Meyer promoted him to lieutenant general and gave him command of the III Army Corps at Fort Hood, Texas, and told him to establish a center for leadership excellence, applying everything on empowerment and participatory command that he had learned and written about in his seminal study. Furthermore, he was to report directly to Meyer and no one else, who might disagree with or try to thwart his program. Ulmer had a hard time keeping the smile off his face during the tirade.

In terms of training and doctrine, Meyer felt the Army was at least on the right track. During the 1970s, Training and Doctrine Command (TRADOC) had earned a reputation as one of the best-managed commands in the Army, and the succession of protégés of retired general William DePuy had begun. TRADOC commander Gen. Don Starry was again revamping *FM 100-5*, the Army's basic fighting doctrine, with an eye toward exploiting the capabilities of a new generation of weapons finally poised for production, including a new tank, infantry fighting vehicle, attack helicopter, and artillery system. Meanwhile, the National Training Center so stridently pushed by both DePuy and Gen. Paul Gorman would be ready for ground-breaking at Fort Irwin, California, in roughly a year.

While he had the knack of inspiring others, however, it was easy in that first year for Shy Meyer to worry that he was presiding over an Army in decline. Certainly he knew that new weapons, improved doctrine, and better training grounds would eventually prove hollow victories if they could not reverse a receding tide of quality recruits into the Army.

Given the Army's size and voracious appetite for new recruits, which far outpaced that of the other services, some experts noted that as went Army recruitment, so went the all-volunteer force. By the end of 1979 the all-volunteer force was looking more and more like an abject failure. Warning signs were such that the Army had even lobbied Congress unsuccessfully for a return to peacetime registration for the draft.

What most concerned Meyer and others was not just that the Army was 15,400 soldiers short of its authorized strength in 1979 because of recruiting shortfalls. Rather it was how hard they had to scratch to make even those dismal numbers. On standard military aptitude tests between 1977 and 1980, close to half of all the Army's male recruits scored in the lowest mental category the service allowed. Thirty-eight percent were high school dropouts. That raised serious questions about whether the soldiers the Army was recruiting would be capable of exploiting the capabilities of a host of very expensive, high-tech weapons systems the service was poised to buy that were based on sophisticated computers, laser range finders, and thermal imaging.

A testing error in 1979 had hidden the full scope of the recruiting short-falls from the Army for a year, but there was little doubt in anyone's mind that the Recruiting Command was stymied and in disarray. A full-scale recruiting scandal, for instance, revealed that recruiters were routinely falsifying high school diplomas, concealing police records and medical information, furnishing word lists for tests, and hiding the fact that many applicants had dependents. By September 1979, 5 officers and 187 noncommissioned officers were relieved from duty because of the recruiting scandal, including 82 persons who held supervisory positions.

The personnel experts could quote chapter and verse to Meyer on the reasons behind the worsening problems with recruitment, from a 10 percent decline in military pay relative to civilian pay between 1975 and 1979, to the demise in 1977 of the Vietnam-era GI Bill. Perhaps unsurprisingly, even the number of career soldiers who chose to reenlist was plummeting, from close to 83 percent when the draft ended to 69 percent by 1979. Put simply, the Army was hemorrhaging talent that it was increasingly unable to replace.

Yet every man and woman in uniform, and especially those who had fought in Vietnam, knew the Army's personnel problems went much deeper than just a lack of adequate pay or incentive packages. They were a living reminder of the scar Vietnam had left on the American psyche, and somehow in its collective consciousness the nation still seemed tentative about a reconciliation. Given the events of late 1979, it was difficult to imagine what else it would take to convince the American people how dangerous was the path they had chosen.

Meyer had decided at Saint Marys that he could not bear the weight of the Army's burdens on his shoulders alone. Years earlier Gen. George Forsythe had stressed that the Army itself needed to change, to repackage itself and its message to connect with a new generation of Americans the like of which the country had never before seen. At the time Forsythe had been denied the means to take that message to American youth, and he had found the Army leadership ultimately unwilling to take steps to reform itself. If there was one thing that didn't daunt Shy Meyer, however, it was change.

Meyer had taken the job of chief with the idea of pointing the right people at the worst problems, and in the case of the recruiting crisis Meyer chose another protégé of retired general William DePuy. The man was intense, tireless, and possessed of a tough and analytical mind that recalled his mentor. Selecting him to tackle perhaps the worst long-term problem facing them all was a natural choice. Meyer felt Max Thurman was probably the most capable soldier in the U.S. Army.

21: All You Can Be 1980

"**HOLD** it! That guy's a wimp! There are no wimps in the Army!" As the projectionist dutifully stopped the film and the lights came up in the screening room at the N. W. Ayer Inc. advertising agency in New York, the advertising executives cast sidelong glances at one another. Having worked with the wiry, frequently abrupt general for months, they were becoming accustomed to Maj. Gen. Max Thurman's outbursts.

"Max, he's an *actor*," said N. W. Ayer chairman Louis Hagopian.

"Well, from now on we're not going to use anyone in the spots who isn't actually in the Army," Thurman replied, ignoring the slack-jawed expressions of his audience.

"And by the way, the Army is big and strong, with a thick neck," said Max Thurman, smiling. "Whatever you do, don't pick any snotty little guys with glasses like me."

A devout Catholic who had never married, the forty-eight-year-old Thurman approached each assignment in the Army with the fervor and devotion of a Trappist monk. His brother Roy was also a general and bachelor. Those who lived lives less devoted to duty and to very long hours had reason to avoid the Thurmans.

The sessions with the advertising agency had underscored that point. At the very first meeting at the Army Recruiting Command in Chicago, the agency executives had tried to explain some of the complexities of the advertising business to this neophyte. Instead, Thurman had done most of the explaining.

The advertising executives felt like hostages in that conference room during the around-the-clock marathon. Whenever an executive asked for a break to use the bathroom or to smoke a cigarette, Thurman invited him to leave but insisted that the meeting would continue in his absence. By the time the ad executives had staggered out of that conference room, there was little question that the center of gravity for the Army's recruiting efforts had shifted from the Pentagon to Chicago. Gone was the cushy relationship that the agency had long enjoyed with the civilians in Washington who had formerly controlled the Army's recruiting account.

The agency could take some comfort in the knowledge that Thurman had somehow convinced the Defense Department to increase the Army's advertising budget. Already, however, the executives at N. W. Ayer were discovering that it was the hardest $65 million they were ever likely to earn.

Since taking over Recruiting Command in November of 1979, Thurman had undertaken a crash course in the advertising business. Total immersion was very much his style. Already, he privately believed he could do the job of the ad agency suits in his spare time.

His friends in uniform—and he had relatively few others—would sometimes chide Thurman about the *Vogue* and *Glamour* magazines strewn about his home. Flipping through the dog-eared pages, however, Thurman would grill them about dozens of advertisements whose corners he had turned down. What message do you think the advertiser is trying to get across to women who look at this? What do you think our Army advertisements stressing duty, honor, and country say to a seventeen-year-old? What if a seventeen-year-old today doesn't give a damn about duty?

Thurman's education in the image business had begun in his first weeks on the job with a Pentagon briefing by a team of advertising consultants. An analyst and programmer by nature and experience, Thurman was always in search of hard data, and the figures from the Defense Department's annual Youth Attitude Tracking Survey had just been compiled. As usual, the brightest young Americans of recruitment age ranked the Army behind all the other service branches except the Marines in terms of desirability. With an Army that had a far-larger appetite than any other branch, requiring about two hundred thousand recruits a year, Thurman needed to know why.

To begin with, the consultants told him bluntly, the Army still had an image problem. When Thurman's generation thought of the service, they conjured up images of the liberation of Europe in World War II, of "Willie and Joe" cartoons and MacArthur at Inchon. Teenagers in 1980 were more likely to flash back to napalmed civilians, fraggings, dope addicts, and race riots. After nearly a decade, Vietnam still cast its long shadow over the Army. Furthermore, the consultants explained, if the Army wasn't willing to change the "product" it was marketing, the glibbest ad campaign in the world wouldn't help.

At the time Thurman had practically sputtered in indignation at the idea of "repackaging" an institution that had two hundred years of history and tradition, one to which he had devoted his life. Later, however, his analytical mind kept rolling their comments against a backdrop of troubling numbers and view graphs. Since 1977, Thurman had worked as the Army's director of program analysis and evaluation, keeping track of how many recruits had flunked out of school, how many fell behind standard in the self-paced training program, how many reenlisted after their first tour. All of the numbers pointed to a burgeoning crisis in personnel.

With an inadequate advertising budget, steadily lagging salaries, and no GI Bill for enticement, recruiters were meanwhile arguing that they needed to lower quality standards still further to make their quotas. Because the service was enlisting a historically high percentage of blacks, every time Army leaders raised the issue of the lagging quality of its recruits with Congress, they opened themselves up to charges of racism. So dire had the situation become the previous year that Thurman had finally accompanied then chief of staff Gen. Bernard Rogers to Capitol Hill to all but beg the Senate to reinstate the draft.

One typical commentary on the Army's calls for a renewal of the draft was published in *The Progressive:* "Uncle Sam does want you—if you're white, bright and ready to fight. And that may be why he's thinking about putting the draft back to work: The U.S. Army is short on white men with managerial or technical know-how."

With the administration remaining adamantly opposed to the draft as a solution, Thurman knew that, after seven years of an all-volunteer force, they still did not know how to entice nearly enough good people to join the Army, or in truth to take care of them once they were in. So, after studying reams of magazines and research data, Thurman concluded that their message was all wrong. Teenagers didn't care about duty or abstract appeals to patriotism. They cared about adventure, upward mobility, getting an education. A crucial step to enticing smart kids into the Army, Thurman decided, was to somehow get the GI Bill reinstated. Yet it had been killed as part of cost-cutting measures three years earlier, and administration officials saw red if they even heard the term *GI Bill.*

Always in search of hard data to back up his intuition, Thurman had succeeded in getting a study on the issue commissioned, and the Rand Corporation was already working on it. Meanwhile, he and Shy Meyer were making frequent trips across the Potomac as the lone voices lobbying Congress for an educational-benefits package, and given the weight of their dismal recruiting numbers, Thurman felt they were starting to make headway. With the "repackaging" of the product thus under way, Thurman turned his attention to his sales force.

He called Mary Kay of Mary Kay Cosmetics and listened to her advice on motivating a sales force for direct sales. He read women's magazines, spoke with advertising executives, quizzed marketing experts. The son of a North Carolina lumber salesman, Thurman found that he was at ease in a world of sales quotas and accounts payable and due. He had a degree in chemical engineering and an analytical bent honed by his years working for Gen. William DePuy, first in the Pentagon when in the early 1970s Thurman was considered by some the most powerful colonel in the Army, and later at TRADOC under both DePuy and Gen. Paul Gorman.

What Thurman discovered after visiting his recruiting regions around the world was a demoralized command that had been totally co-opted by its noncommissioned officers. In other Army branches such as infantry, armor, and artillery, officers had to apprentice before being promoted up through the ranks. At Recruiting Command lieutenant colonels entered laterally with no experience other than a brief school course; the assignment was an unglamorous pit stop on the road to a "real" command. For master sergeants tired of being jerked back to Europe or Korea every few years because of the acute shortage of noncommissioned officers, however, extended recruiting duty was a sweet deal. All they had to do was make their quotas.

Because many high school administrators forbade recruiters from school grounds, another holdover of Vietnam-era animosity, even those recruiters with initiative were sometimes reduced to rummaging through trash bins behind schools searching for student rolls. More common was the situation Thurman found at Newburgh, New York, where the territory included Brooklyn. Recruiters at Newburgh would simply drive the streets of ghettos such as Bedford-Stuyvesant, pulling potential recruits from the trash-strewn sidewalks and off basketball courts during school hours. When Thurman asked how many high school graduates he netted with that technique, the officer in charge responded with what Thurman soon realized was a standard about-face: "Well, what do you have to say about that, Sergeant Major?"

At another recruiting station, a kid who had scored CAT IV, or in the lowest mental category the Army allowed, was asked how he had nevertheless logged a nearly perfect score on the word exam. "Well, sir, the old sarge gave me a dictionary and told me I'd better go home and memorize it before the test." What it turned out the old sarge had given him was an advance copy of the test itself.

While speaking in San Diego at the annual dinner for recruiters and their wives in the southern-California region, Thurman had an inspiration on how to force his officers to once again assume accountability for recruiting. He was looking down from the podium on a happily foaming sea of formal dresses and dress uniforms, everyone having a good time celebrating a year of failure. That's when Thurman, an old artilleryman, thought of the Gunners Badge.

"Is there any noncommissioned officer here that comes from field artillery?" he asked, and watched as three or four hands were raised in the audience. Thurman singled out a sergeant first class.

"Can you describe for me what the recruiting service's equivalent for the

Gunners Badge would be?" Thurman asked, referring to the standard qualification test and graduation badge that every officer had to earn before commanding a field artillery unit.

"General, that would mean having to put a guy in boots," said the sergeant, using the recruiter's term for signing up an enlistee.

"That's right, Sergeant. Which is why within thirty days of tonight, every officer from the grade of captain and above will have to put a man in boots or leave the recruiting service."

There was an awkward silence, during which Thurman noted the uncomfortable looks passing between his officers. Soon, however, the many non-commissioned officers in the audience who had taken much of the blame for recruiting failures began cheering and applauding.

In place of a Gunners Badge, Thurman established the Mission Box, a card that everyone in the recruiting service had to carry on his or her person at all times. On it was written that person's recruitment quota for the month, determined after careful evaluation of census records documenting the recruitment-age youth in his or her region. The mission was broken down into high school graduates, upper-mental-category recruits, women, and non-high-school grads. No substitutions were allowed. Whenever Thurman visited a command, he made a point of asking to see everyone's Mission Box.

As recruiters began focusing their attention on the largely unexplored territory of high schools, many recruiting stations began relocating from inner-city ghettos to the suburbs. Thurman also succeeded in having recruiting service established as mandatory duty. Not only would the best soldiers from each of the Army's various branches have to serve three-year recruiting tours but they would then return to the field to serve with the soldiers they had recruited. Having introduced the principles of management by objective, Thurman had thus given everyone a direct stake in the outcome.

The former commander of an artillery battalion in Vietnam during Tet and the division artillery for the crack 82nd Airborne, Thurman sensed the momentum in his once demoralized command shift. He knew the signs. The spirits of his best soldiers improved as they rose to the challenge of a clear goal and scored some impressive successes. Many of the others found excuses to leave the command. The next crucial step was to give the ones who stayed a new image to sell.

During a New York transportation strike in March of 1980, Thurman met with the creative team from N. W. Ayer in a motel in Stamford, Connecticut. He wanted them to come up with four separate advertising treatments for the Army's new ad campaign to present at a crucial meeting of the Pentagon's Advertising Policy Council. In the past only one treatment had been required, but then little had been the same with the Army account since Thurman had taken over.

On the issue of four treatments, Thurman was characteristically obstinate. The men on the Pentagon's Advertising Policy Council knew him by reputation as an analyst who did his homework, presenting various options and weighing each dispassionately. For him to pitch a single ad campaign, Thurman knew, might signal that he had been co-opted by the advertising agency.

Not that Thurman had any doubt about which campaign he would recommend. On the Thursday before the Monday-morning meeting with the Ad Policy Council, he even traveled up to New York to review the last rushes of the campaign. Substituting real soldiers for models gave the spots an authenticity that was unmistakable, at least to Thurman's eye. Yet there was something missing.

"Hold it! There's no song! Where's the music!" As the lights came up in the screening room, the advertising executives once again cast glances at one another. At that preliminary stage, with four alternative campaigns still under consideration, no one had thought that a complete score was needed. What if the ad council chose "The Advantage of Your Age, Join the Army" or "Join Tomorrow's Army Today" or "Army, We'll Show You How." Thurman, however, was adamant. They needed a song for the favored ad campaign, and they needed it before the Monday-morning presentation.

On Friday, a New York musician named Jake Holmes was commissioned to write the theme song for the campaign. That Saturday they scored and recorded it, and on Sunday it was juxtaposed with the video images. On Monday morning at seven A.M., three hours before the Advertising Policy Council meeting, Louis Hagopian and his creative team from N. W. Ayer gave Thurman an advanced screening.

As the lights went down in the Pentagon briefing room, a montage of young soldiers' faces paraded across the screen—men, women, blacks, whites, Hispanics—all of them real soldiers involved in the exciting work and apparent high adventure of a high-tech Army. It was only a rough stand-in for the finished creative work that would take months to produce, but against that melting-pot backdrop pounded the exultant chorus of a song with a deceptively simple message: "*Be!* . . . All you *can* be!"

For once there were no interruptions, no shouts to turn up the lights or stop the projector. Indeed, throughout the entire screening Max Thurman was uncharacteristically quiet. Even after the screening was over his darkened silhouette remained still. Only when the lights came up did the others in the room realize that the man many considered to be one of the toughest and most dispassionate generals in the Army had tears streaming down his face.

22: Storm Clouds 1980

EVEN on a blustery spring day with the cherry blossoms in flower and the oppressive blanket of summer heat still only a threat, all the news on April 16, 1980, seemed to mire Washington, D.C., in an almost tangible funk. The government had just reported that industrial output had plunged 0.8 percent the previous month, another sign that a recession was looming. Over 250,000 auto workers were jobless in the heartland. World oil prices had doubled since the Iranian revolution began, and the chief executive of the largest bank in Maryland predicted that interest rates could climb as high as 30 percent.

The Soviets had consolidated their hold over Afghanistan by pouring nearly one hundred thousand troops into the country, and Japan added its name to the list of countries planning to boycott the summer Olympics in Moscow. Soviet foreign minister Andrey Gromyko was traveling to Europe in an attempt to exploit a growing rift in NATO over a U.S. plan to station additional nuclear missiles on European soil. Start II was in trouble. The Cuban boat lift continued to wash up on the shores of southern Florida.

Meanwhile, campaigning around the country on a vision seemingly frozen in another time, Ronald Reagan was promising an America once again self-assured and prosperous, admired by its friends and feared by its adversaries. In April 1980, that message found considerable resonance in American audiences.

It was day number 165 of the Iranian hostage crisis.

After finishing his newspapers, Gen. Shy Meyer prepared to leave for what was likely the final briefing on operation Eagle Claw to rescue the hostages. Descending from his second-floor office on the Pentagon's outer E-ring, Meyer took a right at the familiar eighth corridor, with its portraits of the former chairmen of the Joint Chiefs of Staff. Halfway down the hallway at a guarded entrance he stopped. After showing his ID to the guard, Meyer was ushered through to the inner sanctum of the Tank, or the National Military Command Center.

As he took his seat at the conference table, Meyer noticed that the only people filing in were the other service chiefs or their representatives, and the commanders in the joint force tasked with rescuing the hostages. There was Adm. Thomas Hayward, chief of naval operations; Gen. Robert Barrow, commandant of the Marine Corps; Gen. Robert Mathis, vice chief of staff of the

Air Force; Army general James Vaught and Air Force general Philip Gast of the Joint Task Force; and Gen. David Jones, chairman of the Joint Chiefs.

During the small talk that preceded the meeting, Meyer turned around to a seat against the wall and slapped Col. Charlie Beckwith on the knee. The two men knew each other well. Two and a half years earlier, Meyer and General William DePuy had engineered the creation of the secret Delta Force counterterrorist unit that Beckwith had built from scratch, which would now be responsible for freeing the hostages. The move was controversial at the time, given the continued unpopularity of Special Forces in the aftermath of Vietnam. The rise in international terrorism and the increasing use of hostages as a tool of extremists, however, had convinced both men of the need for an elite force modeled after Britain's famed SAS, or Special Air Service.

Meyer knew Beckwith well enough to sense that he would have been far more comfortable conducting survival training in the signature green beret of a Special Forces officer than sitting here in a coat and tie amidst an irascible bunch of generals. While Meyer's familiar gesture helped put Beckwith somewhat at ease, it did little to dispel the obvious tension in the room.

As chairman, Gen. David Jones began the briefing.

"As you all know, we have been working hard to develop a means to rescue the hostages from Tehran. We have been working the problem since November. Now I think we have a sound plan that is going to make the job a lot easier—"

Slap! All eyes turned to the sudden thunderclap as Shy Meyer's hand hit the table and he practically rose out of his seat. Once again Meyer sensed that they as well as the president were about to get the can-do treatment and be asked to make recommendations without having the dangers and risks involved fully explored. "Hold it, David! I'm not going to sit here and listen to you tell everyone how this is going to be a cakewalk."

If no one else registered surprise, Beckwith, who was in the Tank for only the second time, was stunned by the outburst. He was even more surprised when Jones seemed to placate Meyer and calm him down.

"Shy, no one meant to imply that this is going to be easy," said Jones. "It's not a simple plan. But at least now we've had time to rehearse it."

In the crucible of a national crisis, underlying tensions between the services that constantly simmered were once again boiling hotly to the surface. The military command system was unified mainly only at the top, requiring the Joint Chiefs to respond to many crises by hastily throwing together a "joint task force" of units from separate services that had never trained together, inevitably leading to confusion over procedures and command-and-control. It was the same system that had failed them in Vietnam, and some of the men in the room were discovering that it had changed little in the interim.

Perhaps no one was more frustrated by those failings than Shy Meyer. At the validation exercise held for the Army's Delta Force just that summer, observers from both the British SAS and West German GSG-9 counterterrorism units had given Delta high marks, but stressed that it needed to be a joint force with a full spectrum of capabilities, including its own dedicated lift and intelligence assets. The cohesion important to any military unit was absolutely crucial to commando units involved in surgical strikes and rescue operations, with their greatly magnified risks, stress, and tempo of operations.

Meyer knew, however, that establishing a joint special-operations force would require that each of the services give up a measure of control over their own Special Forces units. For that reason it had been opposed by the men in that room, or more specifically by the "iron majors" on their staffs who were charged with reminding each chief of how every proposal affected his individual service. The idea had predictably been bartered down like most bold recommendations to a lowest-common-denominator "statement of intent" guaranteed not to offend or threaten any service.

While Delta Force and the rest of the Joint Task Force had spent four months training, the incredible security demands of the operation had dictated that much of that training be conducted in separate, compartmentalized pieces. A full-up dress rehearsal, it was feared, would attract the notice of Soviet satellites or spies. Though he understood the precautions, Meyer was still worried about the way forces had been cobbled together for Eagle Claw.

Although few in the room knew it, Meyer had already threatened Jones with his resignation on more than one occasion. Too often Meyer felt that he was consulted too late or not at all on critical matters, and that his concerns were not reaching the president's ear. Meyer knew that the chairman did it out of frustration with the meaningless minutiae that seemed to consume most meetings of the Joint Chiefs. Jones thus liked to operate in small, informal groups outside normal channels. Privately, Meyer referred to it as rule by "adhocracy." That style caused Meyer and the other chiefs considerable heartburn. On this final briefing on the hostage rescue attempt, Meyer was thus determined to vent his concerns.

"I'm worried," he told Jones and the others. "How will the operation be controlled here in the Pentagon and on the scene at Desert One? Exactly who is going to be charged with making the decisions at each level?" Another question nagged at Meyer, but he filed it away.

Having served on the JCS since 1974, first as the Air Force chief of staff and now as chairman, David Jones knew what it was like being pestered by a host of voices from the White House demanding detailed tactical information during a crisis, each one "speaking for the president." He shared Meyer's concerns and promised to raise the issue with the president at a White House briefing that evening.

The fact that Meyer was willful enough to always speak his mind was one of the reasons the chairman of the Joint Chiefs liked having him around. Jones reasoned that Meyer's intensity played off well against his own more even-keeled style. Both men were tall enough to see eye to eye with each other but rarely did, clashing often and heatedly, many times over Jones's conduct of the Joint Chiefs. Yet Jones never seriously considered accepting the resignations that Meyer had offered.

To an extent even Meyer was unaware, the highest-ranking uniformed officer in the land shared his conviction that the JCS organization he led and the fragmented military force structure it professed to control were all but unworkable. The military command structure had changed little since 1947, when the National Security Act created both the Office of the Joint Chiefs of Staff and a Defense Department headed by a civilian secretary of defense. The Key West Agreement of 1948 had laid out the broad roles and missions of each service within the national security framework.

The problems of streamlined command and the services' apparent inability to work harmoniously together had been hotly debated ever since those early post–World War II days and had been the subject of a number of commissions. The issue struck at the heart of service tradition, however, as well as each service's claim on the defense budget. With each service chief having an equal voice and thus a de facto veto in discussions among the Joint Chiefs, meaningful reform of the system from within the Pentagon had proven impossible. Jones was beginning to believe it would always prove so.

The failings of the Joint Chiefs system were clear enough to Jones in the day-to-day sessions on budgets and spending priorities. Especially egregious were the "iron majors" who stood behind each of the chiefs at these meetings, each one temporarily assigned to the Joint Staff with the primary task of informing his or her chief where to stand firm for the good of his individual service. Promotion of the iron majors, which still rested in the hands of their parent service, depended on how persuasive they were.

Jones had tried to buck the iron majors by suggesting that the chiefs should all have aides from a *different* service advising them, but had been rebuffed. In fact, the idea had gone over like a hand grenade in a crowded foxhole. To get around the gridlock of full JCS meetings, Jones thus frequently arranged smaller discussions outside normal channels. Though things were easier to accomplish in this fashion, any of the chiefs or their aides who were not included were invariably furious.

Because the services worked and trained together relatively infrequently, cobbled-together operations like Eagle Claw frequently led to friction over clear command-and-control. Jones was still uncomfortable with the fact that on-site operational control during the mission would shift from Air Force colonel James Kyle on the ground at an interim staging point in the Iranian desert, dubbed Desert One, to Army colonel Charlie Beckwith during the actual rescue in Teheran. From what he had already gathered about the strength of Beckwith's personality, Jones worried that the command picture out in the Dasht-e-Kavir desert might become muddled.

The demand for absolute secrecy had also badly hamstrung all preparations for the mission. Ever since one of the peripheral players had gotten drunk in a bar in Langley, Virginia, one night, spilling a little too much of what he knew to what turned out to be a local newspaper reporter, Jones had been obsessed with avoiding leaks. He could think of no better way to get everyone killed, including the hostages.

Yet the lack of a full-up dress rehearsal was a glaring void for such a complex rescue operation, which included Air Force aircraft and pilots, Navy helicopters with Marine pilots flying off an aircraft carrier, and an Army rescue team. Jones would have felt better if the Air Force had complete responsibility for the airlift portion of the operation, but it hadn't been practical to put Air Force helicopters on the Navy carrier in the area.

Task Force commander Vaught was finishing his brief on the mission background. Essentially, Eagle Claw called for six Air Force C-130 aircraft to depart Masirah Island off the coast of Oman, carrying Delta Force and enough fuel to refuel eight helicopters from the USS *Nimitz* at Desert One. From that interim staging site in the remote desert, Delta Force would proceed in the helicopters to an overnight hideout near Tehran and camouflage the aircraft. The next night trucks hidden in the outskirts of Tehran would transport the rescue team into the city. Once there, Delta was to free the hostages and move them to a soccer stadium near the embassy compound. There the helicopters would reappear from their bed-down point outside Teheran, transporting Delta and the freed hostages to a nearby airfield that had been secured by an airborne Ranger force. The entire force would then be extracted aboard MC-130s and two C-141 air transports, with the helicopters being left behind.

It was an extraordinarily complex plan, with a thousand of the lurking "unknown unknowns" feared by every military planner, but with a little luck the Joint Task Force commander believed they could pull it off. Though he didn't bring them up, Vaught was most concerned about the helicopters, which were then aboard the USS *Nimitz*. Everyone involved in the plan had agreed in advance that six of the RH-53D Sea Stallion helicopters was the absolute minimum needed to accomplish the mission, and the operation plan called for sending two extra helicopters to the Desert One staging site as backup.

Yet just days earlier, Vaught had received a report from one of his men who had visited the *Nimitz* that the Number 7 helicopter had made only a few flights before breaking down and was even then unflyable due to an ongoing parts shortage, and that Number 8 was likewise grounded and waiting for parts. Meanwhile, the other helicopters were being flown on training runs that were only half the duration of what would be required for Eagle Claw, and apparently the mechanics responsible for maintaining them had no idea of the importance of the mission they were being prepped for. Vaught had almost gone through the roof the previous month, when his request for a personal on-site inspection of the helicopters aboard the *Nimitz* had been denied. Sneaking one Army general aboard an aircraft carrier was somehow viewed as an insurmountable operational security risk.

With the lives of the hostages and the pride of the nation riding on Eagle Claw, they were unable to keep eight helicopters flying for a lack of spare parts! Perhaps there was no greater testimony to the chronic malaise afflicting the entire military than that single fact.

Delta owned a state-of-the-art satellite communications radio for secure communications, for instance, but they had run into considerable trouble trying to locate similar radios for the other Joint Task Force elements. There had been a shortage of night-vision goggles for the training of air crews, and when they had initially scoured the inventory for Air Force Special Operations MC-130 tactical transporters with an in-flight refueling capability, only seven had been located worldwide.

After Vaught finished briefing, Jones invited Col. Charlie Beckwith to walk through his assault plan for the embassy compound.

Once again Beckwith outlined the ground assault plan that had filled his waking moments and subconscious dreams ever since he had been awakened more than five months earlier by a message that U.S. embassy personnel had been taken hostage in Iran.

A slab of a man with blunt edges and a frequently blasphemous style, Beckwith was something of a legend in the Army. As a Special Forces commander in Vietnam running behind-the-lines reconnaissance and hunter-killer missions as part of Project Delta, Beckwith had taken a .51-caliber machine-gun slug in the stomach. At the point of being abandoned in emergency triage as a lost cause, Beckwith had summoned the strength to grab the nearest nurse and impart a memorable message: "Now let's get one thing straight here. I ain't the average bear, and I didn't come here to pack it in. Goddamn it, let's get on with it."

Though he eventually lost twenty-three pints of blood, his gallbladder, and nearly two feet of small intestine, Beckwith hadn't packed it in. Later he had gone on to incorporate the lessons of Vietnam into the Army's infamous Ranger training regimen and had used his early experience as an exchange soldier with the British SAS in the jungles of Malaya to help create Delta Force from scratch.

Beckwith explained for the Joint Chiefs how his team would get from Desert One to its hiding place outside Tehran, and then to the embassy to free the hostages and escape the following evening.

Perhaps sensing something in his delivery, Meyer asked how Beckwith and his team were going to handle the stress through a thirty-six-hour mission. "What kind of condition will you and the operators be in when you go over the wall?" Meyer asked.

Beckwith explained how the team planned to rotate during the day spent in hiding outside Tehran, 50 percent on alert and 50 percent standing down. What he didn't tell the general was that after eight or nine false starts in the previous few months, with Delta put on deployment alert only to be called off at the last moment, Beckwith himself was wound so tight he was practically humming.

Beckwith also wanted to go ahead with this plan enough not to mention that his Special Forces bullshit detector had been twitching in the red almost from the beginning of the crisis. Human intelligence, the foundation of all special operations, was nonexistent in Tehran at the start of the planning stage. At the initial command meeting inside the Pentagon, Beckwith's demands for key information on which to develop a tactical assault plan had been met with blank stares until the CIA representative had asked to see him in the hall. There he told Beckwith that the Agency didn't have anyone inside Iran.

That problem was largely behind them. Over the months the CIA had either placed or activated a deep-cover Iranian source close to the hostages. Delta, meanwhile, had done some of its own snooping. In an incident that had prompted considerable mirth within the Delta team, an intelligence operative in Tehran had even gotten his picture taken arm in arm with one of the Iranian militants while he was casing the embassy compound. Still, Beckwith felt the CIA was parting with information only reluctantly.

He also couldn't understand how the leadership could throw a task force together for this kind of specialized mission and appoint an Army general with no Special Operations experience. Command-and-control was also murky. Army major general James Vaught was Task Force commander, but Air Force major general Philip Gast, a special assistant to the Task Force, had recent experience in Iran.

Probably nothing about the proposed mission bothered Beckwith more than the selection of the Marines to fly the helicopters. They had been chosen to replace Navy helicopter pilots who couldn't hack the overland flight regimen, yet except for recent rehearsals, this mission was like nothing the Marine pilots had ever attempted either. Beckwith believed it was no coincidence that the man General Vaught had gone to for a recommendation on replacements for the Navy pilots was Marine Corps general Phillip Shutler, the director of operations for the Joint Staff. Each of the services thus grasped firmly to a piece of the action in one of the most complex and high-risk operations in modern military history, and Beckwith was left with a twitching bullshit detector and an overriding desire to get this thing done. Beyond answering the generals' direct questions, he kept his mouth shut.

Around three-thirty P.M. the JCS briefing adjourned. While he was gathering up his notes, Meyer remembered the question that was nagging him that he hadn't had time to ask. That was typical, Meyer felt, of JCS meetings. Even Dave Jones sometimes complained in private that the depth of the discussions in these high-level meetings was almost inversely proportional to the importance of the subject. Given all the collective airborne experience in the room, however, Meyer's question was probably too elemental to worry about. Still, no one had ever given a detailed rundown of the weather in the Persian Gulf region.

Ironically, had he asked, no one would have recalled hearing major concerns about seasonal dust storms that gathered force as they rolled over the desert floor in that part of the world like hurricanes over open ocean. Somehow, the subject never really came up. Yet a storm was gathering that was about to touch every life in that fast-emptying briefing room and blow through the vast empire they oversaw.

23: Desert One 1980

THEY had gone into combat having been thrown together only months before, and what little trust existed between them had been twisted by the strains of a mission that was fast reaching its tolerances in timing and bad luck. Caught in an unexpectedly fierce dust storm on the night of April 24, 1980, two of the Marine air crews had aborted and never even made it to Desert One. Charlie Beckwith was in the jump seat behind the pilot and copilot of the last of the required six RH-53Ds to land, waiting for an answer to his shouted question of when his men could load up. Already they were nearly an hour and a half late.

Having agonized at Desert One as each of those precious seconds ticked by, Beckwith was close to losing it. It was bad enough that his men would likely land at their hideaway after sunrise. Now the senior Marine commander, Lt. Col. Ed Seiffert, seemed to be ignoring him.

With the deafening racket of the rotor blades masking the pounding in his head, Beckwith brought his hand up and rapped Seiffert's helmet with the palm of his hand, hard. Before his copilot could jump out of his seat to start a brawl, Seiffert took off his helmet and turned toward Beckwith.

"There's no guarantee, Colonel, we'll get you there during darkness," he yelled.

"I know that," Beckwith shouted.

"Okay. You've got permission to load."

Beckwith, dressed in jeans, a black field jacket, and a woolen Navy watch cap, was out the door and yelling at Delta Force to load up. All of the Marine helicopter crews were badly shaken by the harrowing flight through the sandstorm, and at least two of the crews at Desert One had already suggested aborting the mission. Whether the Marine pilots ever truly believed the mission would actually be launched was a question mark in Beckwith's mind, and he felt their resolve weakening badly. Of course, Beckwith hadn't just flown through a vertigo-inducing sandstorm at night under radio-blackout conditions.

The scene in the darkened desert outside was a whirling maelstrom of sand and deafening noise, everything washed in the blinding prop blast of four C-130s and six massive helicopters, engines running. In the middle of the landing area a busful of frightened Iranians huddled under guard, and just to the south flames from a burning fuel truck flickered in the night.

From the first moment, the imponderables that lurked in any combat mission had whipsawed Eagle Claw mercilessly.

As soon as the first C-130s had landed, Maj. Jesse Johnson had had his hands full. The roadblock teams he was in charge of were not even in position when a Mercedes bus with headlights glaring had driven right into the perimeter. Almost before that crisis was in hand, a gasoline tanker truck had approached the landing zone from the west, failing to respond to warning shots. One round from a light antitank weapon had settled the issue, though the driver had escaped in a small pickup truck that had been following. All this on a road that intelligence reported was normally deserted.

The Air Weather Service team on which the Joint Task Force relied had confidently predicted clear weather conditions in the area for a forty-hour window. Somehow, they had never warned the Task Force planners of potential dust storms in the area and had totally failed to pick up two suspended dust clouds that had wreaked havoc with the helicopter formation. The reaction of the helicopter crews to that unexpected emergency, meanwhile, exposed serious failings in a communications network that had been patched together from the equipment, procedures, and jargon of too many different services.

All of which meant nothing, Beckwith knew, if he could get his men on six airborne helicopters and under way. Approaching the final two aircraft as they loaded up, however, Beckwith was approached by the pilot of the Number 2 helicopter. The message he delivered changed everything. They had flown for nearly two hours with a flashing light in the cockpit warning of a hydraulic malfunction. When pilot B. J. McGwire reported to Lt. Col. Ed Seiffert, the senior Marine commander on the scene, that he had lost his second-stage hydraulic pump, the decision had been made to abort.

"The skipper told me to tell you we only have five flyable helicopters. That's what he told me to tell you," the pilot shouted to Beckwith.

"Jesus Christ Almighty!" The impact of the message hit Beckwith like a blow. Immediately, he ran to find Col. James Kyle, the commander at Desert One.

"That goddamn Number 2 helo has been shut down! We only have five good choppers—you've got to talk to Seiffert and see what he says," Beckwith yelled, knowing the Marine commander would be in no mood to see him again. "You talk their language—I don't."

As Kyle sprinted for Seiffert's helicopter, his heart pounding, he heard Beckwith mutter something about the Marines having finally found an excuse to quit.

At that point the fate of the hostages, the president of the United States, and, to an extent none of them could have fathomed, the fortunes of the U.S. military depended on the next decision made by three officers at Desert One.

Aboard the senior Marine commander's helicopter, Air Force colonel James Kyle put the question bluntly. Could the Number 2 helo be safely flown with one hydraulic pump?

Marine Corps lieutenant colonel Ed Seiffert had been thrust into the position of helicopter flight leader unexpectedly when his senior officer had aborted on the way to Desert One. He might have decided that the critical importance of the mission outweighed the obvious risk involved in ordering a helicopter to fly with one hydraulic pump. He did not.

"No! It's unsafe! If the controls lock up, it becomes uncontrollable," Seiffert shouted. "It's grounded!"

Air Force colonel Kyle was ostensibly ground commander at Desert One, but he couldn't order the helicopter to fly. Among pilots, an abort decision is all but sacrosanct. If it had been a problem with one of the C-130s, Kyle would at least have been in a better position to judge the seriousness of the malfunction for himself. Kyle knew little, however, about the RH-53D. Had he known more, he might have decided to talk to the pilot of Number 2 personally about his willingness to fly and perhaps raise Task Force commander General Vaught on the satellite communications radio to get him involved in the decision. He did not.

The final and most fateful decision would fall to Beckwith, who was waiting outside the helicopter, the wind nipping at his clothes and the high-pitched whine of the helicopters screaming in his ears like banshees. The sense of impending doom was palpable. No matter how frantically they moved, it seemed to have been stalking them since Beckwith landed on this godforsaken patch of desert. Seiffert's decision was written all over Jim Kyle's face when he exited the helicopter.

After passing along the discussion with Seiffert, Kyle wanted to know if Delta could reduce its force enough to allow the mission to continue with only five helicopters.

"Charlie, this is as tough a decision as you probably will ever have to make," Kyle recalled telling Beckwith in his book, *The Guts to Try.* "History will be our judge. Can you cut down your force by about twenty men?"

Beckwith's mind raced over what Winston Churchill once called the "terrible ifs." Some of his men were responsible for two or three jobs as it was. What if he cut one who was the linchpin in all their careful planning? What if other helicopters broke down tomorrow or were taken out by small-arms fire, stranding them all in Tehran? The balance between success and potential disaster had been precarious to begin with on this mission, and each man he cut could tip the scales. Beckwith could risk it all, go against the instincts that were telling him that the unfathomables on this mission had somehow eaten irretrievably into his margin of error. He did not.

"Ain't no way, Jim. No way! You tell me which one of those 130s you want me to load up. Delta's going home."

While they were waiting for final instructions from the command bunker, the order was given to load the helicopters and C-130s up for extraction. Some of the C-130s, whose engines had been running for more than seven hours, were getting dangerously low on fuel. The only glimmer of hope in any of their minds was that if they could cover their tracks and get out undetected, they might get a second chance at a rescue.

Minutes later, even that fragile hope was vaporized in a sudden fireball. Somehow one of the helicopters had drifted sideways upon takeoff, slamming down on top of a fuel-laden C-130. Flames leapt hundreds of feet, followed by secondary explosions and hissing missile trails as grenades and Redeye rockets began cooking off in the inferno.

Stepping back and shielding their eyes from the burning pyre and the death it tragically contained, everyone could now see the naked failure of Desert One illuminated in searing detail. In that harsh light, the scene at the refueling site already had a nightmare quality. Each of them felt the wave of almost nauseating disappointment and sadness that would soon ripple through the military and the entire country. Sent to rescue a nation held hostage, they would be returning from the Iranian desert empty-handed and with blood on the saddle.

Inside the Joint Chiefs of Staff's Special Operations Division, the question hung uncomfortably in the air. Gen. David Jones had just informed the White House of the abort decision, and national security adviser Zbigniew Brzezinski wanted to know whether the mission could proceed with five helicopters. The specter of White House interference on a key tactical military issue was suddenly in the room, not quite real yet menacing nonetheless.

Shy Meyer and Marine commandant Gen. Robert Barrow sat against one wall, and Adm. Thomas Hayward, chief of naval operations, stood nearby. All eyes were on David Jones as he relayed Brzezinski's question.

"It's a no go," Meyer said aloud. "We all agreed ahead of time that six helos was the drop-dead point." Everything would had to have gone right for the mission to stand a good chance of success, and apparently nothing had. It was far too risky a plan, Meyer felt, to attempt on a shoestring.

Essentially, only two people at that point had both the authority and possibly the inclination to override the abort decision. One was Pres. Jimmy Carter, and the other was Jones. Jones nodded his agreement to Meyer's assessment and gave Brzezinski his answer. Minutes later Carter himself called Secretary of Defense Harold Brown at the Pentagon for the latest report on the mission's progress. At Brzezinski's urging, he asked Brown for the opinion of the commander in the field. When General Jones confirmed that the commander's decision was to abort, Carter said simply, "Let's go with his recommendation."

Carter had kept his promise to Jones not to micromanage the operation or second-guess his military advisers, and knowing what the president must have been going through, Jones's admiration for the man had never been higher. It was shared by the other officers in the command center. Carter's ordeal, however, had just begun. At 5:58 P.M. Jones called the president back to inform him of the accident with casualties at Desert One.

With no more decisions to distract the men in the Pentagon's operations center, the atmosphere in the room became oppressive. The finality of what they had just witnessed was numbing. The military had been mired in the aftermath of Vietnam for most of a decade, and though they all understood the operation was risky, their desperate play for redemption had just blown up in all of their faces. Little was said as the generals finally took their leave of each other late in the evening, filing out into the mostly deserted halls of the Pentagon to be alone with their thoughts. Their failure was final, but the looks on their faces said nothing would be the same again.

Gen. David Jones believed that the problem with Washington, D.C., was that no one had time to sit back and reflect. Long-term strategy always seemed to fall victim to the shrill impertinence of the morning headlines and the next block on the scheduler's calendar. He had seen critical National Security Council meetings broken up so the president could keep a photo opportunity with the Future Farmers of America.

The debacle at Desert One helped convince Jones, however, that it was time to try to do something about the apparent inability of the military services and the Pentagon's command structure to operate as a smoothly functioning whole. If he didn't have time to reflect on the problem, Jones was determined to assign someone who could. Though the senior members of the Joint Staff strongly volunteered their services, Jones knew where their efforts would lead. The iron majors would manipulate any study and nudge the corporate body away from major change. Instead Jones convened the independent Chairman's Special Study Group, a collection of retired generals and admirals, and charged them with studying the organization and function of the Joint Chiefs of Staff.

While he was on his way to Newport News, Rhode Island, early the next morning to speak to the Navy War College, Gen. Edward Meyer heard Carter on the radio announcing to the nation the failure of the rescue mission. The terse statement left no doubt that the president had slept little the night before. After praising the courageous men who had given their lives in the effort, Carter took full responsibility and blame for what had happened. Shy Meyer knew better.

The tragedy at Desert One heightened Meyer's conviction that the Pentagon needed a joint special-operations force that reported directly to the Joint Chiefs of Staff, yet he knew that under the present structure the chiefs could never collectively agree to the idea. And it went far beyond that.

Desert One was a microcosm of the kind of conflicts Meyer believed they would face in the decade to come, and on it were writ large so many of their failings: the inability of the services to operate in harmony as a team, equipment shortages and breakdowns, communications problems, lack of clear command authority, poor training. All of it had been distilled down into a few tragic hours at Desert One, and the dregs they were left with were all the more difficult to swallow for their bitter potency.

Though it infuriated Carter and the Defense Department's civilian leadership, Meyer continued to warn of a "hollow Army," and in the wake of Desert One, he found an increasingly receptive audience on Capitol Hill. Soon, the other members of the Joint Chiefs turned up the volume on their own warnings. Gen. David Jones was quoted in *The New York Times* comparing the United States and the Soviet Union to two ships in a "strategic bathtub." "In the next couple of years, we'll hit the bottom of the bathtub," Jones warned. Air Force chief of staff Gen. Lew Allen, Jr., warned a congressional panel that "the Soviets have a momentum in every area, from strategic nuclear to projection forces to naval forces."

Congress reacted by approving intact Jimmy Carter's amended fiscal year 1981 defense budget, which the president had bolstered from $158 billion to $173.9 billion. Included was an 11.7 percent across-the-board increase in basic military pay, and an increase in enlistment bonuses that improved military compensation by an average of about 17 percent for the year. Combined with an 14.3 percent increase that would be granted the following year, military pay would increase by roughly one-third in just two years.

The initial educational package for Army enlistees Shy Meyer and Max Thurman had pushed for so long was also approved later that year, raising the maximum amount of educational benefits to $20,100. In a major reversal, Congress also enacted legislation in 1980 limiting to 25 percent the proportion of new recruits who scored in the lowest mental category, and to 35 percent the proportion of new Army recruits who had not completed high school.

During the next year's Super Bowl, the Army's "Be All You Can Be" commercial would premiere and help kick off the new pay and incentive packages, and in one of the most concentrated advertising blitzes ever, it would saturate the airwaves. Soon high school and college bands across the country to whom Gen. Max Thurman had thoughtfully sent sheet music would start playing it, and even Doc Severinsen and crew would hop on the bandwagon. "Be All You Can Be" became a catchy theme song for the military resurgence to come. And as went Army recruiting, so went the all-volunteer force.

In the Navy it was still said that ships have long memories, and after 108 days at sea in support of Eagle Claw, the crew of the *Nimitz* had the 11,500-mile trek back to the east coast of the United States to reflect on their nearly nine-month deployment. Despite the largest homecoming celebration since World War II, led by President Carter and his wife, the crew members who walked off the *Nimitz* onto Pier 12 at the Norfolk Naval Base nonetheless found children who were in a different grade in school and wives going on a year older. Many never walked back aboard a Navy ship.

The ship that replaced the *Nimitz* in the tense Persian Gulf area, the USS *Dwight D. Eisenhower*, would return only after the Navy's longest deployment since World War II—251 days. At one point the crew toiled at sea without a port call for 152 straight days. As for the *Nimitz*, after a shipyard overhaul later in the year, she would deploy for sea trials, during which an EA-6B prowler would crash on her deck during a night landing, killing fourteen crewmen and injuring forty-eight others. Though an investigation of the crash was inconclusive as to the cause, it would reveal that some of the flight-deck crewmen tested positive for drug use.

Shortly after the *Nimitz* crash, an investigation Adm. Thomas Hayward had launched into drug use in the Navy would conclusively reveal that after any accident or on any given day, roughly half of Navy personnel who were twenty years old or younger were likely to test positive for drugs. Despite the strident objections of Defense Department civilian personnel, who warned of class-action suits and a devastating impact on an already beleaguered recruiting command, Hayward thus instituted a controversial new policy on drug use in the Navy that would have seemed unthinkably draconian only a few years earlier. He called it "zero tolerance." In a no-nonsense video that was required viewing for everyone in the Navy, Hayward described the Navy's new policy this way:

"For those of you using drugs these days, on liberty, at home, on the base, aboard ship, in your squadron, at work, my message to you today, my friends, is 'Heads up.' We're out to help you or hammer you—take your choice. . . .

"The most prompt, effective way we can get our arms around this problem is through you, through the peer-group pressure that you can apply. All it takes is your accepting one simple set of standards: 'Not here'—'Not on my watch'—'Not on my ship'—'Not in my Navy.' "

Originally the zero-tolerance policy, under which everyone in the Navy was subjected to spot urinalysis tests and searches by dog teams, was intended only for officers. Enlisted personnel caught with drugs were to get a second chance. The master chief of the Navy, however, came to Hayward and personally asked that the chief of naval operations make no exceptions for enlisted personnel. The chief petty officers in the fleet wanted to use zero tolerance to reverse the peer pressure young sailors felt to try drugs. At that moment, Admiral Hayward may have been the first person in uniform to see clearly a way out for the military in its long and difficult flirtation with drug use.

The events that unfolded so quickly in the wake of Desert One made clear that the debacle had served as a sort of national catharsis. Long-repressed guilt over Vietnam and the scorn heaped upon the military in its aftermath were somehow purged by pictures of mullahs picking over the remains of U.S. service members in the Iranian desert. If there was such thing as a silent majority that was uneasy with the country's strained relationship with a military obviously in dramatic decline, it was silent no more. Indeed, the voice they found in the wake of Desert One was deafening.

"America the Gulliver Mired in Impotence Again," proclaimed a headline in *The Washington Post* days after the tragedy.

"An apt metaphor—the modern-day equivalent of the tiny Lilliputians snaring the mighty giant with their tangle of threads. We felt the same way during our long years in Vietnam. . . . Expressions of humiliation, depression, remorse were [once again] commonplace across America yesterday. . . . That charred American wreckage and those burned American bodies lying now on the Mideast sands are another monument to another disappointment."

Desert One was the low-water mark, though that scream of national frustration would carry through the election year, hitting a crescendo on November 4, 1980, the one-year anniversary of the kidnapping. At seven-thirty P.M., the television networks called the presidential election. Jimmy Carter conceded that the hostages had become almost an obsession, and with all of them still held captive on election eve, he was overwhelmingly defeated. The irony was that despite his troubled relationship with the military and the tragedy of Desert One, Carter would leave office consoled by the fact that so little of the blood of U.S. service members had been spilled on his watch.

Throughout the year, Ronald Reagan had continued to campaign on a vision seemingly frozen in time, promising an America once again self-assured, admired by its friends, and feared by its adversaries. America was ready to believe. Even as Reagan rode that wave of the faithful into the White House, however, few could have guessed that the high-water mark would carry them through the largest peacetime defense buildup in the nation's history.

Part III

24: Central Command 1981

0 N an early-summer day in 1981, a familiar south-seas breeze was rattling the flag rigging outside Pacific Fleet headquarters as Capt. Stanley Arthur threw his bags in the car for the trek to the airport. Pacific Command headquarters sat atop a hill on Camp Smith overlooking Pearl Harbor, where ships and submarines of 7th Fleet rested at their moorings. The sunken hull of the USS *Arizona* still lay where Japanese torpedoes had sent it forty years ago.

A memorial to the nearly 2,400 men who had died in that December 7 attack had been built on the *Arizona*. Beyond the harbor and the volcanic crater rose Oahu's two rugged mountain ridges, between them a lush central plain of sugarcane and pineapple plantations. It wasn't the view or time-worn memories of his family on Hawaii in 1941, however, that most occupied Arthur's thoughts. Rather, it was the question of where this trip to Florida would lead.

The journey had probably begun on that awful night back in April of 1980, when Arthur had sat with the head of Pacific Command and other members of a special planning cell, monitoring message traffic from ships involved in the hostage rescue attempt and watching as the operation began to fall apart with each successive cable. When it was finally over, Adm. Robert L. J. Long, commander and chief of Pacific Command, or CINCPAC, had stood up and left them all with a message before walking out of the room.

"I want you to go back through the planning of this from day one," Long had instructed them. "Let's take another look and see if there wasn't something we should have seen from out here. I don't want to let go of this thing without going back and trying to understand what went wrong."

Since coming to Pacific Command from the *Coral Sea,* Arthur had found

Long to be a precise and demanding boss with a keen intelligence, as was befitting a nuclear submariner who was one of the Pentagon's four true warlords, between whom the U.S. military divided the world into operational spheres of influence. As CINCPAC, Long was responsible for a broad swath of the globe that stretched from the west coast of the United States all the way to the Indian Ocean. His forces included not only the Navy's 7th and 3rd Fleets in the Pacific, but also substantial Air Force and Army forces permanently stationed in Hawaii and Korea. The head of Pacific Command had ostensibly had authority over conduct of the Vietnam War. Long's counterpart at Atlantic Command, headquartered in Norfolk, Virginia, was responsible for an area of operations that ranged from the Norwegian Sea south to the Horn of Africa and included both the Caribbean and the Mediterranean. The Pacific and Atlantic Commands were always headed by a Navy four-star.

The Pentagon's other two geographical commands were always commanded by an Army four-star, including U.S. European Command headquartered in Stuttgart, West Germany, the largest and most truly unified of the overseas commands. Because the CINCEUR was also "dual hatted" as the head of allied forces in NATO, he was referred to as the supreme allied commander, Europe, or SACEUR. The final geographical command was U.S. Southern Command, headquartered in Panama and responsible for Central and South America.

One unalterable fact struck Arthur and everyone else who studied that arrangement on a map. The one spot in the world that was most incessantly blinking on all of their threat warning radars fell along a fault line between Atlantic, Pacific, and European Commands. And far from having cooled since the failed rescue attempt, the Middle East in 1981 seemed ripe for meltdown.

While the embassy hostages had been returned by Tehran, taking Western hostages in the region was fast becoming a cottage industry. The 1980 invasion of Iran by Iraq had also seriously shaken already skittish U.S. allies in the region, leading a senior member of one ruling Arab family in the Persian Gulf to retort to a newspaper reporter, "God help us if one of them wins." Libyan leader Mu'ammar al-Gadhafi was also becoming increasingly bellicose, his actions threatening to bring him into direct confrontations with U.S. Navy forces in the Gulf of Sidra. Meanwhile, Israeli forces were poised for an invasion of Lebanon to oust forces of the Palestine Liberation Organization (PLO).

As a result of those developing crises and the backlash created by the Desert One debacle, new secretary of defense Caspar Weinberger had recently followed through with the Carter administration's announced intention to form a Rapid Deployment Joint Task Force (RDJTF), which would be responsible for contingency planning for the Middle East. Initially it would consist of a small headquarters of fewer than three hundred people at MacDill Air Force Base in Florida and depend on forces based in the United States and equipment being marshaled aboard prepositioned ships at Diego Garcia in the Indian Ocean. That prompted many experts to question whether it was rapid, deployable, or even much of a force.

However, since the mid-1970s, civilians within the Carter administration who favored establishing a new "unified" command with responsibility for the Middle East and other contingencies had encountered stiff bureaucratic resistance from the military services. It had taken the crises of recent years even to get something as modest as the RDJTF in place. And as Stan Arthur well knew, nowhere was that resistance stronger than in Navy ranks.

The aggressive new secretary of the navy, John Lehman, was arguing that Navy forces in the Persian Gulf region should continue to report directly to either the Atlantic or Pacific fleets, rather than some layered bureaucracy in Florida. He called the location of the new command in Tampa "absurd." All of which helped explain why Arthur was approaching his first visit to the RDJTF headquarters with some trepidation, having just been named as the Navy's component commander to the new task force.

On the long flight over the Pacific and across the breadth of the country, Arthur ruminated over the Navy's reluctance to embrace the new task force. Of course the service had a wide streak of independence, but it went deeper than that.

Because none of the countries in the Middle East deigned to allow permanently stationed U.S. forces on their territory, Pacific Fleet had long supplied the U.S. presence in the region, and they did it 365 days a year. That was one reason why Long had chosen Arthur, a Pacific Fleet planner with experience in the Desert One operation, to represent the Navy on the RDJTF. With their forces already patrolling the Middle East on a nearly permanent basis, however, Navy leaders were churlish about ceding even planning authority in the area to an upstart joint task force in Florida headed by a Marine Corps general.

Entering the conference room of the RDJTF, located in a complex of trailers on the south side of MacDill Air Force Base, Arthur was introduced to Gen. P. X. Kelley, the cigar-chomping commander of the new task force. Kelley was a respected soldier known for speaking his mind and letting the consequences be damned. His résumé also bespoke an unusual amount of joint experience for a Marine Corps general, from his service as a military liaison with the British Royal Marines in the early 1960s, to a stint at the Air War

College and two years as the chief, Southeast Asia Branch, of the Plans and Policy Directorate of the Joint Chiefs of Staff.

Many senior officers in the Marine Corps predicted that Kelley was destined to become not only the next commandant of the Corps but also quite possibly the first Marine to chair the Joint Chiefs of Staff. After being introduced to Kelley, Arthur and the lieutenant commander he brought along as his aide took their places at the table. Immediately, Stan Arthur knew the Navy was in trouble.

Representing the Air Force was Lt. Gen. Larry Welch, the head of the 9th Air Force, who from his headquarters at Shaw Air Force Base, South Carolina, commanded all U.S. fighter bases east of the Mississippi River. Behind and around him milled a retinue of less senior Air Force generals. The Army component commander, commander of the 18th Airborne Corps, was equally well chaperoned. A number of Marine Corps two-star generals clustered around Kelley, including the commander of the 1st Marine Expeditionary Force from Camp Pendleton, California.

Across from this assembled constellation of stars, representing the Navy, sat Stanley Arthur, who commanded a desk at Pacific Fleet headquarters. Though he had been approved for promotion to rear admiral, Arthur still wore the four stripes of a Navy captain. Beside him sat a lieutenant commander who, before being recalled to active duty, had most recently been spotted tending bar at a ski resort. No one had to ask which service came to this joint party most reluctantly.

Certainly Gen. P. X. Kelley didn't need the sight of a slightly squirming Navy captain to alert him that some powerful interests viewed the RDJTF as a major threat. When he had first begun this crusade a few years earlier, one vice admiral in the Navy had gone so far as to practically accuse Kelley of being a traitor. In general, that about summed up the initial enthusiasm for the idea of a new, joint force with key responsibility for the Persian Gulf region.

Part of the problem was that the services felt that the idea had been foisted on them by civilians such as former national security adviser Zbigniew Brzezinski and former defense secretary Harold Brown. Reaction within the Marine Corps and Navy to the proposal to store three brigades' worth of equipment at Diego Garcia in the Indian Ocean had been almost universally negative. Many within the Marine Corps viewed the MPS force as a threat to the "Gator Navy," or the fleet of amphibious ships dedicated to forced-entry assaults over the beach. Navy officials recognized it as a pillar of the RDJTF and thus saw it as a threat to their operational autonomy in the area. On some days back in 1979, Kelley could be heard shouting through the Navy Annex that for once the Defense Department wanted to lavish them with new equipment, and he couldn't get anyone in the Navy or Marine Corps to show any interest.

With the pronouncement of the Carter Doctrine and the debacle at Desert One, however, the effort to establish some military entity with primary responsibility for the Middle East gained an irreversible momentum. After being named the first commander of the RDJTF in 1980, Kelley assumed the attitude that the services could either hop on board or get the hell out of the way. Having seen the writing on the wall, the Air Force and Army were strongly on board, and Kelley was bringing the Marine Corps along. That left the Navy and its powerful admirals, whom Kelley privately suspected of harboring suspicions about this whole concept of "civilian control" of the military.

If anything the RDJTF's early exercises and planning sessions revealed just how radical was their vision of a lethal, rapid-reaction force that could be based in the United States and quickly deployed halfway around the world, and how far they were from realizing that vision. Throughout the Cold War, the United States had primarily depended on a strategy of containment of communism by forces deployed on the periphery of the Soviet Union. With no forward-based ground forces to act as a deterrent, the Middle East exposed glaring deficiencies in the United States' strategic air and sealift. In his low moments, Kelley believed that the greatest contribution of the Rapid Deployment Force might just be to prove conclusively that the United States was a rapid-deployment basket case.

Yet on most days Kelley was invigorated by the excitement and challenge of standing up a new command from scratch. The sometimes gruff, always outspoken general would tell anyone willing to listen that the status of the RDJTF would inevitably be upgraded to a full-fledged unified command with four-star status. Thus he referred to himself as "a CINC in waiting."

After attending his first briefing at MacDill Air Force Base and a number of exercises around the world, Stan Arthur was inclined to agree with Kelley. Even after the outspoken Kelley left to become commandant of the Marine Corps, and Army general Robert Kingston took his place, interest in the RDJTF remained strong at the highest levels of the Pentagon. Whether their troops were training in Egypt on "Bright Star" exercises or in the high California desert at the Army's new National Training Center, senior service leadership always seemed to be on hand, including members of the Joint Chiefs of Staff. Practically the only service chief that Arthur didn't see was his own. In fact, Arthur rarely saw a Navy flag officer take any interest in the RDJTF.

When he returned from these forays to Pacific Command headquarters in Hawaii, Arthur always warned that the RDJTF was destined to become a unified command, and that if the Navy didn't take notice, they would be left figuratively on the outside looking in on a key new command. Admiral Long disagreed, however, as reportedly did the most senior leadership in the Navy.

Then Vice Adm. Stan Arthur couldn't let it go, however, and his repeated warnings became something of a standing joke with the staff at Pacific Fleet.

"What are they feeding you on these trips?" he was chided more than once, but Arthur was undeterred.

"No, I'm not kidding you. Mark my words. Within a year this outfit is going to be headed by a CINC."

"It'll *never* happen."

Arthur's colleagues at Pacific Fleet headquarters would continue to kid him right up until January 1983, when the Rapid Deployment Joint Task Force officially became the unified Central Command, and Vice Adm. Stan Arthur was named commander, U.S. Naval Forces, Central Command. In a strange twist of fate, Arthur would be named to the position a second time seven years later, with the country on the brink of war in the Middle East and the Navy's reluctant embrace of the new command having come full circle.

25: Killer Accountants 1982

DOWN the hallway of Building 201, home of Red Flag headquarters, the walls were crammed with photographs and squadron insignia from units that had already been through one of the five-a-year war games by 1982. Inside the dimly lit auditorium, the semicircular rows of theater seats were filled with jumpsuit-clad pilots in the midst of a mission debrief. On a slide screen significant events from that morning's strike were listed by unit. A young Aggressor pilot was finishing up confirmation of a possible kill.

After a few purges to reign in the more blatant hotdoggers, the Aggressors that Boots Boothby had helped found had once again emerged as one of the prized training tools in the Air Force. Their expertise in kicking down the "Green Doors" to intelligence information had even led to the establishment of a "petting zoo" for enemy weapons systems at Nellis, where pilots visiting Red Flag could get touchy-feely with the actual Soviet and Warsaw Pact model antiaircraft weapons that would likely be trying to kill them in a war.

Standing on a dais, the Red Flag operations director asked a young flight lead from the visiting Blue Force to explain exactly what had happened to his formation out there in the desert.

"Well, sir, I think we pushed a little early, and unfortunately that drew the Red air," the pilot responded, referring to the Aggressor pilots, who roamed the ranges of the Great Basin. "Most of us were killed, sir. But we'll take it like men."

The quiet laughter in the auditorium just died down as a second flight lead stood up. The pilot explained that he, too, had been killed. While a command-and-control aircraft was screaming in his ear about a MiG at his six, the pilot explained, a surface-to-air missile site had taken him out.

Outwardly, Red Flag had changed only moderately since Brig. Gen. Chuck Horner had led his unit from Seymour Johnson through an early rotation nearly five years earlier. The couches and chairs in the snack-bar lounge were new, as were the two Astro Fighter video games and the beer machine labeled "Aircrew Debriefing Fluid," all part of Gen. Bill Creech's ongoing Facilities Excellence Program. It was already common to hear Tactical Air Command personnel returning from other service installations complaining of how *seedy* everything seemed.

Horner was passing through Nellis in 1982 after being tapped to serve as commander of an Aggressor-style force of "enemy air" on one of the exercises conducted in the Mojave Desert to test the Rapid Deployment Joint Task Force. He was serving as the commander of the 833rd Air Division at Holloman Air Force Base, New Mexico, but the exercise gave Horner a chance to return to his old haunts at Nellis Air Force Base, and to get a look at Red Flag headquarters.

A mural in the lounge depicted an Air Force strike on the Paul Doumar Bridge in North Vietnam. Horner knew that bridge and remembered the pilots he had flown with in Thailand on just such raids. Pete Van Huss. Roger Myhrum. Boots Boothby. Would they have willingly stood up as young pilots and admitted that they screwed the pooch in a training exercise? Would Horner have? More likely they would have denied it to the bitter end until the matter was finally settled over drinks at the officers' club in an epic battle of He With the Biggest Watch and Loudest Voice Wins.

Red Flag was helping to change the fighter-pilot culture. The increasingly sophisticated electronic and video tracking systems out on the ranges were steadily eliminating doubt about *what* happened, allowing Red Flag officials to jump right into discussing *why* it happened. In the process the exercise controllers, most of them lieutenant colonels or colonels nearly Chuck

Horner's age, said that the younger pilots were becoming far more willing to own up to and learn from mistakes than the older pilots had ever been.

The realism of the Red Flag exercises had also dictated needed changes in their tactics, lessons that were traditionally learned only in combat and paid for in blood. Horner remembered the disastrous tactics they had followed on the first strike against the SAM site on the Black River, and the friends like "Black Bart" Barthelmous and Jack Farr who never made it back.

At Nellis they were still talking about the furor created after TAC commander Gen. Bill Creech read an article about Red Flag in *Armed Forces Journal*. A young captain who had just returned from a Red Flag exercise was asked what he had learned. "I learned you can't survive in combat," the pilot replied.

That had been a Monday morning. By Wednesday the commanding officers of Nellis and other major Tactical Air Command (TAC) units were strapped in their aircraft and winging toward TAC headquarters at Langley, Virginia, for one of General Creech's notorious "commanders conferences." The subject was the problem at Red Flag as revealed by the comments of a young captain to a reporter from *Armed Forces Journal*.

After reviewing the script for a ten-mission rotation at Red Flag, Creech thought he recognized the problem. The syllabus was designed to replicate the first minute of the first hour of the first day of World War III.

In trying to confront pilots with the most demanding scenario they were likely to face, Creech believed, they were teaching bad tactics. The simulated surface-to-air missile (SAM) sites out on the Nellis ranges, for instance, continued to play in an exercise whether or not they had been targeted by an attack bomber. That forced pilots trying to avoid the SAMs to go in low and kick up dirt on every mission, exposing themselves to even more deadly anti-aircraft fire, much as Horner and his friends had found themselves tragically exposed in the Black River Valley. "You're screening videos at the Red Flag debrief showing these kids getting shot down three different times on one mission," said Creech in a measured tone that was somehow still sharp enough to make a listener wince. "And we wonder why they're coming home saying they want a way out of this chicken-shit outfit."

Creech reminded his commanders of what they already knew: TAC was spending a considerable portion of its largess under the Reagan defense buildup to stockpile precision-guided munitions, which were roughly as accurate from 15,000 feet as from 250 feet. Practically every week, Creech told them, he had to run up to Capitol Hill to lobby for the expensive weapons against an emerging and increasingly powerful Military Reform Caucus, whose members generally argued that the military was overreaching its technological grasp. With the media running scores of stories about costly new weapons that didn't work as advertised, the Caucus members were arguing that the services should buy higher quantities of less sophisticated weapons.

Yet in many ways the emphasis on precision munitions was a natural fit with Creech himself: everything about the former Sky Blazer was precise to the point of fastidiousness, and for a man who couldn't stand to see a dirty maintenance bay or disheveled uniform, there was an almost irresistible elegance to a bomb that could ride a laser beam through an open window. Creech was damned if he was going to fight for them tooth and nail, however, only to see his pilots carry them into the next war dodging treetops.

From then on, Creech had told his commanders, they were to start holding special Red Flag exercises to develop realistic tactics and carefully sequenced attack plans for the first *two weeks* of a war, beginning with electronic jammers and F-4G Wild Weasels to take out high-altitude SAMS, then working up to high-altitude bombing runs. Whenever possible, the lessons from those exercises were to be incorporated into the standard Red Flag rotations to prove to pilots that they could roll back and prevail over a layered air defense such as the Warsaw Pact possessed.

Seeing Red Flag again, Chuck Horner wondered if his old friend Moody Suter would even recognize the exercises. Any major project in the Air Force, or in any service for that matter, had a thousand fingerprints on it. That was how change occurred in an organization so massive and far-flung. Yet Horner knew that Suter's prints were indelibly on Red Flag, and that it was as much his creation as anyone's in the Air Force.

Meanwhile, the free-form style of training against an expert opponent that was pioneered at Nellis and Red Flag had been expanded into virtually every area of TAC's business, largely by Creech. When he inherited Red Flag and the Blue Flag command-and-control exercises, Creech had significantly expanded both, while introducing Green Flag for electronic countermeasures, Copper Flag for U.S. air-defense forces, and Checkered Flag for rapid deployments to overseas bases. It was funny, because Moody, with his cowpoke drawl and aw-shucks manner, couldn't stand to be in the same room—or on the same side of the country for that matter—as Gen. Bill Creech.

Horner had been concerned about this exercise with the Rapid Joint Deployment Task Force ever since he had been chosen to lead the Red Force, or enemy air component. He would have been far more comfortable leading a unit of F-15s from his base as the aggressor force. Yet his orders were to form a pickup team of Air Force pilots from Holloman, Marine Corps pilots from El Toro Marine Corps Air Station, California, Navy fliers from Fallon Naval Air Station, Nevada, and an Air National Guard unit out of Indiana. Five years earlier Horner had had his hands full keeping a cohesive unit of young pilots alive under the unaccustomed strains of Red Flag–style training. Trying to replicate that experience with a team culled from scratch sounded like a prescription for disaster.

Yet Horner needn't have worried. In the first Sunday-morning briefing, the young pilots fell into the drill almost effortlessly. Horner had fully expected to spend most of the meeting just establishing common procedures and deciding who would serve as flight leader on the next day's mission. Instead, one flight lead volunteered to serve as mission commander the next day, and the others quickly agreed. Far from worrying about common procedures, they began hashing out an air tasking order that would best replicate a viable enemy threat. Horner was unable to hide his surprise.

"Sir, we've all done this before at Red Flag," the mission commander responded, the other pilots nodding their heads. It was one more advantage of Red Flag that they hadn't foreseen when the exercises were nothing more than a slide show that he and Moody Suter and others in the Fighter Pilot Mafia were pushing inside the Pentagon in the early 1970s. Because the Air Force invited not only pilots from other services to participate, but also units from allied countries, they were coming up with a common way to fight. Horner contrasted it in his mind with Vietnam, when they had to divide target areas into artificial boxes to keep Navy and Air Force pilots from shooting each other down.

On Monday morning, Horner taxied his F-15 for takeoff on what had become one of the busiest runways in the world. The flight line was bustling with military aircraft. There were scores of the new-generation F-15s and F-16s, as well as just about every other fighter aircraft in the U.S. arsenal. Horner allowed himself to marvel at how far the Air Force had come in a few short years.

Signs of the change Horner had been noticing since returning to Nellis were no further off than all of the F-15s and F-16s lined up nose to tail on the flight apron, their squadron insignia now proudly displayed on the fuselages. The Air Force was rapidly replacing older F-4s, F-105s, and A-7s with a new generation of aircraft. Already the Air Force was on a pace to increase its inventory of F-15s and F-16s by more than 150 percent in Reagan's first term alone, for a total of over 720 new aircraft.

Though in some ways the F-15 Horner was sitting in was easier to fly from a stick-and-rudder standpoint than the F-105 and F-4, it represented a dramatic technological leap. The fact that he was flying at all was pure Creech: "A leader's place is in the air."

Gazing at the cockpit, with its seventy-five different displays and three hundred switches—eleven on the control stick alone and nine on the throt-tle—Horner thought of the capabilities at his fingertips: a much improved "look down, shoot down" radar, Mach 2.5 dash speed, and enough computer power and sensors to expand exponentially the area a pilot could reach out and touch, be it for navigation, threat tracking, or targeting.

Yet without enough hours in the cockpit or the realistic training of Red Flag, pilots would never be able to exploit that technology. Bolstered by full budget coffers, however, the Creech reforms had taken firm root in Tactical Air Command. Between 1981 and 1983, peacetime operating stocks and wartime spare parts in the Air Force were on schedule to increase by about 60 percent, and TAC aircraft were approaching a mission-capable rate of 85 percent. Despite the emphasis on more realistic training, the peacetime crash rate had dropped since Creech took over TAC from one for every thirteen thousand flying hours to one for every fifty thousand. Aircraft that were flying an average of just eleven sorties a month in 1978 were now averaging twenty-one sorties. The swing in the Tactical Air Command's fortunes was dizzying.

The changes in Air Force leadership as epitomized by Creech, the rapid advancements in technology and training—all of it was combining to change the style of the Air Force in a way that was fundamental yet somehow difficult to put your finger on. Chuck Horner felt it most acutely on exercises like this, when he worked closest with the young pilots.

Sometimes Horner had to check a temptation to tell them to lighten up and have some fun, so earnest did this new generation of young pilots seem. Thinking back to his own wild antics as a young fighter jock, Horner knew that the old barnstorming ethos of the Air Force he had joined was quickly disappearing and was being replaced by something else. The young pilots were more disciplined, more openly inquisitive than Horner and his generation had been, and undoubtedly smarter. In a sense, Creech had cloned them as well. To the casual observer expecting the hell-raisers of yore, this new generation of fighter pilots they were training came off as more soft-spoken and studious, almost like well-mannered accountants. Horner knew, however, there was one crucial difference: these accountants would slit your throat in a heartbeat.

26: A Parting Shot 1982

THOUGH his relationship with Defense Secretary Caspar Weinberger was chilly by January of 1982, Gen. David Jones hadn't intentionally planned on upstaging his civilian boss. It was just that, on the eve of his retirement, Jones was finally ready to launch his carefully planned campaign to reform the Joint Chiefs of Staff (JCS). He knew the odds, and that over the years meaningful reform of the joint system had eluded such men such as Pres. Dwight Eisenhower, Gen. Maxwell Taylor, and Defense Secretary Robert McNamara.

As he and Weinberger entered the Rayburn House Office Building on Capitol Hill, Jones also understood that it would take a dramatic parting shot to shake the four service pillars on which the JCS stood, a foundation that had proven impervious to the rattlings of would-be reformers for more than three decades.

The closed hearing of the House Armed Services Committee was actually a routine session called to allow the men to present the administration's proposed fiscal year 1983 defense budget, and Weinberger was in his element. A former California legislator and Harvard alumnus who had served as Richard Nixon's director of the Office of Management and Budget, Weinberger had proven an absolute pit bull in lobbying for increases in the defense budget. Jones knew Weinberger felt that Jones's reform efforts would be a needless distraction from the main business at hand.

By tenaciously sticking to a few key debating points on the nature of the Soviet threat and the dilapidated shape of the U.S. military, Weinberger was well on his way to building a consensus for the largest peacetime military spending spree in U.S. history. In their first year, Weinberger and Reagan had proposed a $6.8 billion supplement to Carter's already revised 1981 budget of $173.9 billion. Even after Congress cut 1 percent from the total request, that still represented an almost unheard of 25 percent nominal increase over the previous year's defense budget.

Weinberger then boosted Carter's 1982 defense request of $195.7 billion up to $222.2 billion. Trimmed back 4 percent by Congress, that was another 20 percent increase in Pentagon budget authority. Now the 1983 defense budget request of $259.8 billion was to be one more installment in a buildup that would account for more than $330 billion in real growth in military spending between 1981 and 1985.

Given the long, lean years of the 1970s, Jones publicly supported those increases, though he also voiced his preference for a more gradual, sustainable buildup. Privately, he and many others inside the Pentagon worried that, flooded with so much money so fast, the military's procurement system could flounder. Yet they were equally worried that the first few years of Reagan's term could represent a window of opportunity that might well slam shut in 1984.

Jones's concerns about the steepness of the spending increases were heightened, however, by Weinberger's "hands-off" management style. There was simply not enough money even in the administration's projected budget to satisfy every item on the services' various wish lists, yet Weinberger and his deputies seemed loath to get into the trenches with the services and do the dirty work of setting meaningful priorities between their programs. Meanwhile the unified CINCs in the field, the true warfighters, had little direct say in the budgeting and procurement process.

As Weinberger recited the various programs and improvements under way to the members of HASC in outlining the proposed budget, the scope of the buildup was staggering. A major portion of the spending increases was earmarked for modernizing the strategic nuclear force, including money for a new MX intercontinental ballistic missile; a new B-1 bomber force, to be followed in rapid succession by a new Stealth bomber; new nuclear submarines with the improved Trident II missile; and a new cruise missile.

There were corresponding plans to expand to a six-hundred-ship Navy, replace conventional weapons systems such as front-line tanks and aircraft that were nearing obsolescence, improve airlift and sealift, and develop new air defenses. Meanwhile, "readiness" stocks of spare parts, ammunition, and fuel would continue to receive rapid and badly needed infusions.

While Jones always found Weinberger to be a consummate gentleman, he also knew that the distance that existed between them went much further than just disagreements over budgeting priorities. Ronald Reagan had upheld the tradition that the chairman of the Joint Chiefs of Staff served a fixed term and was not subject to replacement as were political appointees, but it was no secret that Weinberger would have liked to pick his own chairman, and preferably one who hadn't supported SALT II, cancellation of the B-1 bomber, and the Panama Canal treaties.

Jones found it ironic that Weinberger wished Jones had deviated more from former president Jimmy Carter's position on those issues, yet couldn't seem to understand when Jones disagreed with Weinberger's own position during National Security Council meetings. It was as if the man had a blind spot. Jones also knew that of all their disagreements, few were likely to prove as contentious as the one he was about to make public.

After Weinberger finished his presentation, Rep. Bill Dickinson, the ranking minority member and a hawkish Alabama Republican, gave a warm welcome to David Jones. Having served on the Joint Chiefs of Staff since 1974, first as Air Force chief of staff and then as chairman, Jones was a familiar presence to Armed Services Committee members. After the pleasantries were over and he had thanked the Committee, however, Jones made it clear that he would be going out with a bang.

"The FY 1983 *Military Posture* statement describes in detail the geostrategic situation and the military balance," Jones read from his prepared statement. "This year, I have departed from my normal practice of providing a personal overview of that statement so that I might focus attention on what I consider the most important contribution I can make to improving our military posture in the years ahead. . . .

"Unfortunately, the way the joint system is organized does not provide for optimum effectiveness," said Jones, going on to list the reasons he found the present organization at the top of the Pentagon unworkable. In truth, in the two years since the Desert One debacle, Jones's frustration with the joint system had only grown.

As the chairman and a coequal with the other chiefs, Jones found that every proposal seemed to get watered down for the sake of unanimity. It was also next to impossible to persuade the services to relinquish the requisite control to effect anything resembling a more joint structure.

Jones had, for instance, floated a proposal for a badly needed joint transportation command to coordinate mobilization and deployment of forces in a crisis, only to see the idea sabotaged when language was placed in the Defense Authorization bill specifically prohibiting such a joint command. Someone had surreptitiously gotten to a friend in Congress and had the prohibition inserted into law. Jones suspected John Lehman, the aggressive secretary of the navy appointed by Reagan, who had taken the service's traditional commitment to naval autonomy to such extremes that even Weinberger would comment that as far as Lehman was concerned, the Navy was a completely separate country.

Then there was the Joint Staff itself. The study by the Special Study Group, which Jones had tasked with critiquing the Joint Chiefs of Staff shortly after Desert One, was nearly ready for publication, and it confirmed what Jones already knew: less than 2 *percent* of officers who served on the Joint Staff had ever had any "joint" experience at all. For instance, the present J-3 on the Joint Staff, the critical officer in charge of operations, was a three-star general who had spent virtually his entire career in the Army's air defense branch, and thus knew nothing about joint operations, and precious little even about the other Army branches.

With Joint Staff duty seen as something to be avoided, the average tenure on the Joint Staff for generals and admirals was about a year. That, Jones said, was analogous to having a Congress made up entirely of freshmen.

While the congressmen nodded politely from the front of the room to Jones's unexpected diatribe at what was supposed to be a standard budget presentation, one person in the sparse audience was sitting up in rapt attention, a look of disbelief on his face. Archie Barrett was only a junior staff member, newly hired to a House Armed Services subcommittee, yet he instantly understood what perhaps no other civilian in the closed hearing room realized: for the first time in history, a sitting chairman of the Joint Chiefs of Staff had broken the code of silence that ruled that cabal as surely as it did the Mafia, publicly criticizing in the strongest terms the internal workings of the system that he presently headed.

Barrett understood because he had just written a book on efforts to reform the Joint Chiefs of Staff. A recently retired Air Force lieutenant colonel, with an undergraduate degree from West Point and a doctorate from Harvard, he had spent his last two years in uniform studying the subject of defense reorganization on the staff of former secretary of defense Harold Brown. Before retiring, Barrett spent a year at the National Defense University compiling his files on reorganization for a book that was now still in galleys. Knowing the history, Barrett thus understood that Jones's testimony was unprecedented.

The struggle between the services, Barrett knew, went back at least as far as the Spanish-American War of 1898, when the Army and Navy had to deploy and fight together for perhaps the first time as a truly integrated expeditionary force. The internecine wrangling that ensued was so contentious that the Army commander refused even to allow the Navy to be represented at the formal surrender.

While the ensuing decades brought some efforts toward centralizing and coordinating military authority, the Joint Chiefs of Staff began meeting regularly only in 1942, driven by the necessities of World War II. Yet even during World War II the war effort was divided into separate theaters that were fought largely along service lines.

In the immediate aftermath of the war, serious debate began about whether the services should be unified under a centralized national military establishment. The Army, ever dependent on air and naval power not only to fight a war but to deploy to one, was the most receptive to an integrated military structure. The air-power arm of the Army, still attached to the Army at the end of World War II, wanted most to become a separate service. The Navy was different. Historically independent, autonomous to the point of having its own air force, naval fleet, and army in the form of the Marine

Corps, the Navy steadfastly resisted attempts to subjugate its forces to a unified command.

The result of the furious debate that ensued after World War II was the landmark National Security Act of 1947. It had established a separate Air Force; formalized into statute the Office of the Joint Chiefs of Staff, to include the chiefs of staff of the Army and the newly created Air Force, as well as the chief of naval operations; consolidated military departments into a Department of Defense headed by a civilian secretary of defense; and created the National Security Council. In 1949, the National Security Act was amended to include a four-star chairman of the JCS to be a "coequal" of the other chiefs, and in 1952 the commandant of the Marine Corps was added to councils on matters related to his service. His position as an equal member of the Joint Chiefs was codified only in 1978.

Archie Barrett had read many of the twenty or so studies on JCS reorganization that had been conducted since that landmark 1947 legislation, and most pointed to the same problem: rather than a truly unified military establishment, what was created was a loose confederation in which massive service bureaucracies dominated the JCS system, the unified commanders in the field, and with the frequent support of Congress, the civilian secretary of defense. With the services' ability to steer work toward home-state shipyards, airplane factories, and military bases, the powerful service chiefs often locked arms with key members of Congress to form an impenetrable barrier to major reform.

Yet for the first time an acting chairman had publicly vilified the very system he was supposedly leading. Though the implications were hard to fathom, Barrett sensed an opportunity in that stunning break with tradition. The question was, what could a lowly congressional staffer on the House Armed Services Subcommittee on Investigations do about it, especially one with little seniority and only recently hired by lame-duck chairman Rep. Richard White, who didn't plan on running for reelection the next year?

After David Jones dropped his bombshell at the closed hearing, two events suggested an answer. First, David Jones went even more public with his criticisms in an article entitled "Why the Joint Chiefs of Staff Must Change," which was first published in February 1982 in an obscure magazine called *Directors and Boards*. Weeks later, it was reprinted in *Armed Forces Journal*, a trade magazine well read in military circles.

That article was followed the next month by an equally scathing critique of the JCS system in *Armed Forces Journal*. "The JCS—How Much Reform Is Needed?" called for even more radical reforms than Jones advocated, including establishment of a separate National Military Advisory Council of senior uniformed leaders with no ties to the services to advise the president on strategic matters. To nearly everyone's astonishment, it was also penned by a sitting member of the Joint Chiefs of Staff. The difference was, Gen. Shy Meyer had more than a year to go before his retirement when he also broke the Joint Chiefs of Staff's unspoken code of silence.

Rep. Dick White was a congressman at the end of his career who didn't know much about defense reorganization, and Archie Barrett was arguably an expert in defense reorganization but only a lowly staffer and a neophyte in the ways of Capitol Hill. Both of them understood in the spring of 1982, however, that it was time for Congress to do what Congress does best. They decided to hold hearings.

"What I would like to do is not have this be a Dave Jones crusade," Jones told the House Armed Services Investigations Subcommittee on April 21, 1982, leading off as one of the first of more than thirty witnesses in what would become five months of hearings. Jones went on to explain for the congressmen present the reforms he felt were necessary. His suggestions seemed all the more radical for coming from a sitting chairman of the JCS.

To put an end to rule by committee and advice factored down to the lowest common denominator, Jones suggested making the chairman the president's principal military adviser as opposed to the entire JCS. For the many times when the chairman needed a substitute to sit in his stead, Jones favored appointment of a four-star deputy chairman to the JCS. To loosen the grip of the iron majors, the Joint Staff should serve only the chairman, and joint duty should be mandatory for promotion rather than a career dead end. Finally, the commanders in chief of unified commands in the field should have more authority over the service component commanders ostensibly under their command.

After so many years as a joint chief, Jones was convinced that the kind of fundamental changes he envisioned would have to be forced on the Pentagon from the outside. There was simply no other way to overcome the internal bureaucratic inertia present when so much was at stake for so many powerful interests. That conviction led him to go public just before retiring, knowing full well that some if not all of the chiefs would view it as a betrayal. Jones knew that with his testimony he was opening perhaps the most fractious split in the history of the Joint Chiefs of Staff.

All of the service chiefs stepped before the brightly lit semicircle of the Investigations Subcommittee to testify, though it was Gen. Shy Meyer who insured that the reform effort would not merely prove a "Dave Jones crusade."

In a way, they made strange allies. The two men had never discussed coming forth together with their ideas on JCS reorganization, and while they liked each other personally, Jones's exclusive management style continued to grate on Meyer as well as the other chiefs.

By calling for radical reforms such as a National Military Advisory Council divorced from the chiefs, however, Meyer had suddenly made Jones's proposals look more moderate. With a year and a half yet to serve on the JCS, his outspokenness was also purchased at a far higher price than that of David Jones.

The list of more than thirty individuals who followed Jones and Meyer in testifying, gleaned from Arch Barrett's Rolodex, read like a roll call of the men who had shaped the country's military fortunes over the past thirty years. It included all former chairmen of the JCS, several of the former defense secretaries they advised, service chiefs both present and past, as well as some of the commanders in chief of unified commands. There were former JCS chairmen Gen. Lyman Lemnitzer, Adm. Thomas Moorer, and Gen. Maxwell Taylor; former Air Force chief of staff Gen. Curtis LeMay, former defense secretaries Harold Brown, James Schlesinger, and Elliot Richardson.

Had he been more experienced, Archie Barrett might have known that much like defense lawyers, staff members calling witnesses for a hearing were supposed to know at least in general terms what their positions would be, if for no other reason than to insure the hearings didn't take a direction his member of Congress was uncomfortable going. Instead, the testimony was full of surprises. Former defense secretaries such as Jim Schlesinger and Harold Brown, men on whose judgment presidents had relied in making decisions on which the fate of the nation rested, testified in essence that the watered-down advice they received from the highest military officers in the land was often irrelevant, or worse.

"The subcommittee might be better advised to advocate a bold stroke than to err on the side of caution," former defense secretary Elliot Richardson advised.

"The JCS system has become a laughingstock in the Pentagon," said Robert Komer, the former undersecretary of defense for policy and head of the pacification effort in Vietnam. "I think structural reform of the Joint Staff as well as the JCS is long overdue." Others who lent their voices to the side of reform included the legendary Curtis LeMay and Gen. Brent Scowcroft.

The arguments against reform, however, were equally weighty. Most of the previous chairmen advised against Jones's proposed reforms, as did most of the active service chiefs. Chief of Naval Operations Adm. Thomas Hayward felt personally betrayed by Jones's comments, coming as they did just when the services' fortunes seemed to be rising. To no one's surprise, perhaps the most vociferous objections to the proposed reforms were offered by retired Navy admiral Thomas Moorer, the former JCS chairman who had served under Richard Nixon.

"In our bureaucracy we spend millions rearranging furniture, changing letterheads, changing phone numbers, just because somebody makes a study and then wishes to change the organization," Moorer said in a thinly veiled swipe at David Jones. He insisted that upgrading the Joint Staff would only hasten an already apparent trend toward the services rewarding desk work over operational skill. "I say if it works, don't fix it."

Even though he would not be running for reelection the next year, Dick White decided after the hearings to have Archie Barrett draw up a modest military reform bill. Given the unprecedented increases in the defense budget, and stories beginning to emerge on waste in the military-procurement system, interest in military reform was growing. The JCS Reorganization Act of 1982 thus found a receptive audience and was easily passed by voice vote in the House in October of 1982. It just as quickly died in the Republican-controlled Senate, where the gatekeeper for major defense legislation was a powerful, prodefense Republican from Texas named John Tower, chairman of the Senate Armed Services Committee.

The long hearings and fall legislative session of 1982 had taught Archie Barrett two valuable lessons. If the first major reorganization of the defense establishment since 1947 was to stand a chance, then it would likely be up to some member of Congress on the House Armed Services Committee to keep the issue alive on Capitol Hill. Given the events of 1982, it also seemed likely that the final battle would have to be waged in the far more conservative confines of the Senate Armed Services Committee.

In a November 1982 article in *The New York Times Magazine* entitled "What's Wrong With Our Defense Establishment," recently retired David Jones passed along this warning: "After serving on the Joint Chiefs of Staff longer than anyone else in history, and under more Presidents and Secretaries of Defense, and being a student of military history, I am convinced that fundamental defense deficiencies cannot be solved with dollars alone—no matter how much they are needed. . . . There is reason to believe that, faced with a contingency requiring a major joint operation, our performance would be below the level we should expect or need." It would be less than a year before a series of remarkable events in the waning months of 1983 proved Jones tragically prescient.

27: Semper Fi 1983

THE rhythmic pounding of his footfalls, the quickening expulsion of breath, usually it helped relax him. Col. Tom Draude pushed himself still harder along his jogging route in the heights above Pearl Harbor, waiting for the exertion to take him past that familiar barrier beyond which his thoughts obeyed orders. He still had a ways to go.

The Corps had come so far since the 1970s. There were images of the confused midshipmen he had taught at the Naval Academy in the early 1970s, ashamed to wear their uniforms off-campus. If anything, Camp Pendleton afterward had been worse. Thefts. Murders. Staff duty officers wearing sidearms to the barracks for protection against assault, never a night without trouble finding Draude at home at the end of a phone.

The grandson of Irish immigrants and a devote Catholic, Draude also recalled his own deep confusion in those years when prominent members of the Catholic clergy continued to denounce the war in Vietnam and those who fought it. The nuns had led him to believe military service was a vocation not unlike the priesthood—service rendered unto others, beliefs for which you were willing to sacrifice.

Yet with sacrifice they had put all that behind them. A Corps that could fit inside a telephone booth. That's what former commandant Gen. Louis Wilson had said he was willing to have back in 1976, as long as they were good Marines. God bless him. That had been the point when they turned back the mob that had threatened to overwhelm the Corps in the 1970s, that and the hundreds of "expeditious discharges" that followed as commanders jettisoned their troublemakers, and recruiters somehow reconnected with the great American middle class. What were left by October of 1983 were damn good Marines.

Draude thought about his daughter Loree, who would graduate from high school in a couple of years, standing with her class in cap and gown, head peeking out from a stacked necklace of Hawaiian leis. But headed in what direction? Tom Draude hoped she would follow in his footsteps at the Naval Academy. What they needed were more good kids.

Draude slowed his pace after hearing what sounded like music, and then almost subconsciously he jogged toward the noise. It was a beautiful fall morning on Oahu, where he was serving as the inspector for the Fleet Marine Force, Pacific. This early on a Sunday, only a few people were out as

Draude trotted into a shopping center where a man was playing bagpipes on the sidewalk. As the man finished his tune, Draude caught his breath.

"I don't suppose you can play the 'Marines' Hymn' on that?" Draude asked.

"I sure can," the man said with obvious pride. "You know, it's the only service song you can play on bagpipes."

"Have you heard the news this morning from Beirut?"

The man's smile faded.

"Well, could you do me a favor? Play it for about two hundred Marines who will never hear it again."

The man started into the familiar refrain, and it seemed to Tom Draude that the hymn might have been written especially for the bagpipes.

> *From the Halls of Montezuma,*
> *To the shores of Tripoli,*
> *We fight our country's battles*
> *In the air, on land and sea.*

Draude thought about some of the young Marines who had died making him a better officer. He could still remember the kid who had joined his company in the midst of a firefight, and all he had asked in exchange for his willingness to lay his life on the line was that someone know his name. Funny, but now Draude couldn't forget their names or their faces. Before sleep, he prayed for each of their souls. That night his prayers would be especially crowded.

Without even thinking, Draude came to attention and saluted as the bagpipes wailed, and when the song was over, he wiped his eyes on his sleeve. "God bless you." Draude was a devout man, and it was something he frequently said in parting. He never meant it more, however, than at that moment. Then Tom Draude jogged off toward home, this time at a slower pace.

October 23, 1983, sent a reverberating shock through the tight-knit fraternity of the Marine Corps, where there are no "ex-Marines," only former Marines and those still in uniform. In an instant the day registered permanently on the collective psyche of the Corps. The jolt had reached Col. Mike Myatt at the end of a jangling telephone at four A.M. that same Sunday morning. Myatt was serving on the Joint Staff, one of four colonels working directly for the new chairman of the Joint Chiefs, Gen. John Vessey, Jr. Late-night telephone calls were not unheard of for members of the Chairman's Staff Group, but just the same it was a disoriented Myatt who fumbled to answer the phone before it woke his wife, Jill.

"Mike, you need to get down here right away," said a voice that he recognized immediately as the general in charge of his staff group at the Pentagon. "The Marine barracks has been blown up."

Still trying to shake off the sleep as he drove his pickup through the empty, darkened streets of the capital, Myatt wondered at the message. He hadn't thought to ask which barracks had been bombed. Could the general have meant the Marine barracks at Eighth and I streets at the Navy yard in Washington, D.C.? Myatt reached for the dial of the truck's radio and muttered under his breath after remembering that it had been broken for months.

When he arrived at the Pentagon shortly before dawn, the scene at the national command center was hectic. Myatt immediately learned that it was the Marine barracks in Beirut, Lebanon, that had been bombed. The potential for devastation was suddenly clear to him. After being subjected to periodic sniping and mortar attacks, most of the 350 men of the Battalion Landing Team headquarters element in Beirut had been consolidated under one fortified roof, a building on the Beirut airport grounds that had earlier been occupied by the Israelis. Ever since Marines had been deployed to Beirut the year before as part of a multinational peacekeeping force, the Joint Staff had debated what many saw as their increasingly vulnerable position and ambiguous mission.

As Myatt well knew, his boss, General Vessey, had unsuccessfully argued against sending them to Beirut in the first place. The main problem in the minds of many observers in the Pentagon was that the Marines were on a "peacekeeping" mission, with commensurate rules of engagement that precluded even loading their weapons. Yet there was demonstrably no "peace" to be kept in Beirut.

The initial report indicated that six Marines had been killed, which would have made the bombing the largest single loss of life since they had deployed to Lebanon. The next dispatches put the death toll at twelve, then twenty-five, and forty. Initial battle-damage assessments were always unreliable, something Myatt remembered from Vietnam. All of their hopes in those early hours after the disaster hung by that thread, everyone praying that they were just hearing exaggerations made in the inevitable fog of a war zone. After the projected death toll topped one hundred Marines and kept climbing, however, the atmosphere in the command center turned to one of stunned disbelief.

By the time General Vessey arrived, it was clear that no one was more visibly shaken than the chairman himself. He had enlisted during World War II, rising in the last forty years to become the nation's senior general, and earning a reputation as a "soldier's soldier" along the way. Since taking over as chairman the previous year, Vessey had also gone a long way toward healing many of the divisions left in the wake of David Jones's tumultuous reign.

While Jones's frustration with the JCS system had led to a style the other chiefs viewed as exclusive, Vessey leaned in the other direction. Whenever possible, he strove to include the other chiefs in all deliberations. Never was that more evident than the day after the barracks bombing, when for the first time in memory Vessey brought all four service chiefs with him to the White House to brief President Reagan personally on details of a top-secret plan for a possible invasion of Grenada.

Unlike Jones, Vessey was also convinced that whatever reforms were needed in the JCS system, they could be accomplished from within. Many times Mike Myatt heard the chairman try to push internal reforms through the Pentagon's recalcitrant bureaucracy by arguing that they had to actively combat the perception that the military was incapable of meaningful change on its own.

Vessey's appointment had also muzzled a key proponent of JCS reform, Army general Shy Meyer. Meyer had personally chosen Vessey to be his vice chief of the Army, and the two generals were close. In hearings before the House Armed Services Committee that both Vessey and Meyer had since attended, Meyer had largely backed off of his earlier calls for radical reform of the JCS. That change of attitude had infuriated proponents of reform on the committee such as Arch Barrett, who recognized in Meyer's defection a potentially fatal blow to the tenuous reform effort.

The string of events that began with a terrorist's truck bomb in Beirut, however, was about to shift the momentum once again in favor of major reform of the military command structure. After reviewing the latest classified reports of the bombing, Vessey departed the Pentagon for a National Security Council meeting at the White House that would last almost the entire day. With President Reagan and nearly all of his national-security and foreign-policy officials present, the atmosphere was predictably strained.

The deployment of the Marines to Lebanon had exacerbated an acrimonious rift between some of those present, with JCS chairman Vessey and Secretary of Defense Caspar Weinberger having argued strenuously against it, and Secretary of State George Shultz and National Security Adviser Robert McFarlane in favor. To some observers the clashes between Weinberger on the one side and Shultz and McFarlane on the other—a clash not only between their views on the uses and limits of military power, but also in their personalities—recalled earlier acrimonious power struggles between the Brzezinski-Vance and Kissinger-Schlesinger national-security teams. If one side or the other was unable to gain the upper hand with the president, the resulting tug-of-war could give national-security policy a haphazard appearance as it lurched first one way and then another.

The NSC meeting had been planned to discuss the deteriorating situation in Grenada, where CIA reports indicated that roughly eight hundred American medical students were in danger of being taken captive by a radical faction that had just overthrown the prime minister.

But before Vessey got into details of a hurriedly assembled Pentagon plan to rescue the American students and restore democratic order on Grenada, however, he first updated those present on the latest reports from Beirut.

At 6:22 A.M. local time, someone had driven a yellow Mercedes truck down Beirut's main airport highway, turned left into the four-story headquarters building of the Battalion Landing Team, 24th Marine Amphibious Unit, and detonated thousands of pounds of explosive in a suicidal blast that brought the entire building down. Casualties were high, but exact numbers were unknown.

Everyone in the room knew the subtext. A multinational force of U.S., French, and Italian troops had originally been sent to Beirut in the aftermath of the June 1982 invasion of Lebanon by Israeli Defense Forces. While the primary aim of Israeli forces was to destroy the Palestine Liberation Organization, which was headquartered in Beirut and led by Yasir Arafat, the operation prompted a move by Syria of major forces into Lebanon's Bekáa Valley, where they clashed with the Israelis. The fight between those relative titans, meanwhile, had toppled an already tenuous truce between local Lebanese factions, including Christian militias whose leaders dominated the government and generally sided with Israel, and Muslim factions allied with Syria and Iran.

In a sense, the Marines were victims of their own success in that earlier intervention. Despite objections by Weinberger and Vessey to that deployment as well, the first multinational force had succeeded in securing Beirut and supervising the departure of the PLO. It had then quickly departed the country itself. Israeli forces remained on the periphery of Beirut, however, and Syria in the Bekáa. When Christian strongman and president-elect Bashir Gemayel was assassinated along with many of his lieutenants in September of 1982, his militias retaliated by slaughtering approximately seven hundred unarmed Palestinians in the Sabra and Shatila refugee camps, while Israeli troops stood by outside the gates.

The world outcry prompted by that atrocity had persuaded Reagan to agree to the deployment of a second multinational force. Thus it was into that increasingly volatile cauldron of vengeance, reprisal, and ancient hatred—Christian against Muslim, Arab against Jew, Sunni against Shiite—that a second force was sent to oversee the withdrawal of Syrian and Israeli forces and the restoration of authority to the fledgling Lebanese government. But the Syrians and Israelis did not withdraw despite the efforts of Shultz to secure their departure, and the longer the multinational force stayed the more it came to be seen as simply one more, and not the most heavily armed, antagonist in a country rapidly descending into anarchy.

The day after the bombing of the Marine barracks, Marine Corps commandant Gen. P. X. Kelley was dispatched to Beirut. More than two hundred Marines were dead at last count. The question that Mike Myatt couldn't get out of his mind as he waited for further word at the Pentagon, the question that haunted them all, was not unlike the one that he had agonized over in a rice paddy at Ap Chinh An nearly two decades earlier, his hand gripping the dog tags of other young Marines who had been entrusted into their care and had died needlessly. How could this possibly happen?

That was a question the Senate Armed Services Committee was eager to put to Gen. P. X. Kelley on his return to Washington later in the week. The commandant appeared alongside Bernie Rogers to explain to the assembled senators how the peacekeeping mission in Beirut had somehow led to the largest single loss of life in a military operation since Vietnam. And in one of the most tense and confrontational Senate hearings since that war, the dream that P. X. Kelley would become his service's first chairman of the JCS died a very public death.

"Sir, I have never in my entire life worked for so many masters as I have in the past week!" Kelley blurted after being pressed by Sen. Carl Levin at one point. Suddenly the spacious hearing room was silent. Many aides had heard Kelley to say, "I have never worked for so many *bastards* . . ."

"Did you say 'masters'?" Levin responded.

"I said masters. I did not say the other word, Senator."

P. X. Kelley's penchant for speaking his mind caught up with him that day. Clearly affected by what he had seen in Beirut, Kelley was convinced in his heart that Congress was unfairly putting him on the spot even though as a service chief he was ostensibly out of the operational chain of command. Something in the public posturing and hand-wringing by some members also angered Kelley, as if they were surprised to find that Marines sent to a foreign war zone were inherently in danger. French troops had also been killed in a similar blast, and in Kelley's mind the French had taken the news with an equanimity befitting a world power that sends its troops into harm's way fully realizing the risks. Privately, he also suspected that some members who opposed the defense buildup were using the tragedy as a way to get at Ronald Reagan.

Yet it was all part of the agonizing process by which the United States publicly confronts the consequences of its military actions. If there was something inherently unequal in the forum of a Congressional hearing, where those in uniform have to answer for their actions and atone for their culpability in front of television cameras and much professed righteous indignation, that, too, was part of military tradition, and P. X. Kelley knew it.

The problem was that Kelley had just returned from a place whose laws bore no relation to Capitol Hill protocol, or the ordered universe of Washington, D.C. At no time was that more obvious to him than in a private meeting he had attended with two members of Congress who had suggested that the Marine Corps could put the disaster behind it faster if the commander in Beirut was immediately court-martialed. Kelley had declined their request for a sacrificial lamb with a shake of his head.

Inevitably, the finger of blame reached out first toward the colonel in charge of the Battalion Landing Team. The commander on the scene always bore direct responsibility for the safety of his men, if not for a policy that placed them all in an untenable position. Kelley was not going to rush that process, however, for he understood that at that moment no act of Congress, nor all the powerful men and women in the capital pointing their accusing fingers together, could touch the soul of Marine colonel Tim Geraghty.

The loud clanking of bulldozers, rooting in the shadowy rubble under harsh arc lights, filled the night. What had once been the multistory barracks building was by then an expanse of heaped concrete and debris, steel reinforcing rods twisted everywhere into grotesque sculptures. Even the trees glistened like blown-glass figurines in the floodlights, the force of the nineteen-ton blast having vaporized the building's windows into a fine, molten spray. Site of the largest nonnuclear explosion in history.

Through the lighted doors of a nearby aircraft hangar, forklifts could be seen carrying pallets stacked with metal body containers. Two hundred and forty-one Marines were dead or dying. At the site a shout went up and the bulldozers stopped momentarily. Marines crowded around an unearthed pocket. They saw the body of a gunnery sergeant who had been crushed from the waist down. Before the Marine died, he had taken his dog tags off and put them between his teeth, something he knew a corpsman would otherwise have to do. Then the gunnery sergeant had placed his .45 pistol to his head. At that point he must have passed out from the pain.

The work had gone on like that for days without stop, and after the body was removed the bulldozers just started back tearing through the ghastly rubble. One of the Marines who had helped unearth the gunnery sergeant stood by watching it start up again and felt his shoulders start to shake involuntarily.

"Are you all right, Slate?" The voice seemed to come out of nowhere, but when the Marine turned, Col. Tim Geraghty was standing right next to him, a look of concern etched on his face.

"Are you okay?" Geraghty asked again.

Geraghty had been a constant, calming presence on the scene since the initial blast. His frustration with the restrictive rules of engagement and the Marines' vulnerable position at the airport, subject to fire from the surrounding hills, was well known to his men. Many had heard him shout at U.S. embassy personnel in Beirut—who short of war or a declared national emergency were still technically in charge—complaining that their restrictions were endangering his men. Geraghty was a respected commander, and everyone had assumed that he was a shoo-in for general. Suddenly the Marine felt that it was he who should have been asking if Geraghty was all right.

"Yes, sir, I'm fine," he said.

Perhaps they should have seen it coming earlier that summer, when the Lebanese stopped waving. At the time they entered the war-torn city in the wake of the refugee-camp massacres and the assassination of Gemayel back in 1982, both the Muslims and the Christians had initially welcomed the Marines, always waving to them on the streets as they passed. As the summer of 1983 wore on, however, the Marines had come to be increasingly seen as allies of the Christian militias, whom they were helping to train. Especially in Muslim-dominated neighborhoods, where heavily armed youths crowded the sidewalks, the waves were gradually replaced by sullen stares. Soon after, the sniping and mortar fire had begun.

Still the rules of engagement generally precluded keeping magazines loaded in weapons, a rule many Marines simply disregarded. Unfortunately, these apparently did not include the Marines guarding the gates of the compound on the early morning of October 23, a bit of insubordination that might have saved a lot of lives.

Everything seemed to be driven by politics rather than sound military principles. Fire teams stationed at "whisky posts" along the runway, for instance, were required to come out and salute each time a VIP vehicle drove by. When the Marines pointed out that the practice singled out the VIP cars for snipers, the orders eventually came down not to stop the inane practice, but rather for the Marines to salute *every* vehicle. Soon hunched-over fire-team members were dashing out of their whisky posts into the open to salute their own dump trucks.

Yet, even so, how could the Marines have failed to take greater security precautions, and to get their concerns about the rules of engagement addressed by the chain of command? Certainly there was ample warning after April 10, 1982, when the U.S. embassy in Beirut was destroyed by a similar terrorist bomb that killed sixteen Americans. And why was intelligence that indicated a growing terrorist threat apparently ignored by the Marines on the ground?

The person chosen by the secretary of defense to answer those and other questions in the immediate aftermath of the bombing was recently retired admiral Robert L. J. Long, Stan Arthur's former boss at Pacific Command. Whether Long's experience and frustration watching the Desert One debacle unfold from Hawaii played any part in his thinking is unclear. What is undeniable, however, is that the report issued by his commission was one of the most stinging condemnations of the military command structure ever.

Of course from a purely military standpoint, the Marines should never have occupied the compound in the first place. By definition, however, peacekeeping missions were not purely military operations. The Marines, for instance, knew that they were going to be shot down upon from the surrounding hills. Because the highlands overlooked Israeli positions, however, the State Department believed occupying them might give the impression that they were protecting the Israeli Defense Forces, and thus taking sides. Even after the sniping and mortar attacks started, Marines were not allowed to aggressively patrol in the hills.

Far more damning was the fact that the Marines on the ground appreciated all too well that the Muslims had come to view them as enemies, but their strenuous objections to the restrictive rules of engagement had been diluted or simply ignored as they trickled up and down a lengthy and convoluted command chain. From Beirut that chain ran out to ships offshore in the Mediterranean and the commander of CTF 61, the amphibious task force to which the Marines were attached; to the commander of the 6th Fleet, headquartered in Gaeta, Italy; to the commander in chief, U.S. Naval Forces, Europe, headquartered in London; to USCINCEUR Gen. Bernie Rogers at SHAPE headquarters, Mons, Belgium; to the Pentagon and the defense secretary's office.

"Beirut was a classic example of where the situation on the ground changed dramatically, and the people in charge did not change the mission, the rules of engagement, or the setting," Long said after the commission's report was released. "Certainly the rules of engagement were not as clearly articulated as they should have been in terms of hostile intent, and they didn't evolve because the chain of command was too long to be sensitive to threat changes."

Admiral Long did not spare Geraghty in his criticisms. In the view of the commission members, the commander had clearly failed to take adequate security measures. Soon after the Long Commission's report landed like a thunderclap at the Pentagon's doorstep, President Reagan would hold a press conference accepting blame for the incident, noting that he felt the commanders involved had suffered enough. Eventually Navy Secretary John Lehman would issue a nonpunitive letter of instruction, which under the circumstances was probably the least he could do. There would be no stars for Tim Geraghty, who would retire soon after, but by then he was beyond the reproach of Washington.

While the circumstances surrounding the bombing of the barracks were being sorted out, most of those at the site itself spent the days and nights banding together and digging themselves out. For a week, TV reporters at the site deliberately panned their shots in especially wide arcs so that worried parents and wives back home could hopefully catch a glimpse of their loved ones. A wire-service reporter handed some Marines his company-issue American Express card, which could be used for long-distance calls home, and told them they had five days before he reported it missing.

Mostly what the Marines in Beirut wanted, however, was just to collect their fallen comrades and go home. Even in this, however, the grim luck of October 1983 held. The Marine Amphibious Unit that was already under way to relieve them, they were told, had been unexpectedly diverted on October 25 to Grenada. At that time, most of the Marines couldn't have told you whether it was a country or a tropical fruit.

28: Urgent Fury 1983

THE hulking figure of an Army major general standing alone on the bridge of the helicopter assault ship was an incongruous sight. Loaded with seasick pills, he was on loan from a heavy-mechanized division based in Georgia and configured to fight in the desert sands of the Middle East. By his own admission the general, a comer in the Army who was destined to become that service's powerful deputy chief for operations, was feeling about as welcome on this Navy-run show in the Caribbean as a case of the mumps. Yet from his perch on the bridge of the USS *Guam*, Maj. Gen. Norman Schwarzkopf could literally see the object of all their desires.

The flagship *Guam* was sailing off the coast of Grenada on the late morning of October 26, and the dormitory building at Grand Anse that held the bulk of the American students they had been sent to rescue was clearly visible beyond a fingernail of white beach. Nearly everything that had hamstrung Operation Urgent Fury to that point—especially a veil of absolute secrecy and a lack of time to plan and gather adequate intelligence—had been driven by the need to quickly secure the safety of those students and avoid an Iranian-style hostage situation. And more than twenty-four hours into the operation, with nearly three thousand crack American troops already on the island and hundreds more pouring in by the hour, the students in the dormitory off the bow of the *Guam* were still at the mercy of Cuban and Grenadian soldiers.

Schwarzkopf knew that the coup de main they had planned for Urgent Fury, a single fell stroke that was meant to swiftly overwhelm an enemy and seize all objectives, had failed utterly. He had only been briefed into the plan two days earlier in Norfolk, Virginia, headquarters of the Navy-run Atlantic Command with responsibility for the Caribbean. Though his initial welcome from CINCLANT (commander in chief, Atlantic Command) Adm. Wesley McDonald was cool at best, Schwarzkopf had partially mollified the feisty admiral at the time by pointing out that he had served a tour on the staff of Adm. Robert Long at Pacific Command.

The plan Schwarzkopf was briefed on called for nearly simultaneous assaults on the main objectives on the island. The Marines were to take Pearls Airfield and a military garrison at Grenville on the northern end of the island; the Army Rangers were responsible for seizing the Point Salines airfield under construction by Cuban workers on the southern tip, as well as the nearby True Blue campus where the American students were thought to be held; and Special Operations forces including SEAL teams and Delta Force were to rescue the British-appointed governor-general at his residence near the capital of St. George's on the westward side of the island, as well as capture the radio station and Richmond Hill Prison above the city.

A Navy SEAL team that had been sent to scout the Point Salines airfield had been lost in high seas the night before the invasion, which meant the Rangers had parachuted into the area yesterday morning totally blind. Even as they descended, the Rangers were taken under heavy fire, and a vicious firefight with hundreds of dug-in Cubans had ensued at Salines. When they finally did secure the airstrip and the True Blue campus, the Rangers learned to their shock that most of the students were at another campus two miles away called Grand Anse.

The Special Operations forces fared even worse. Their helicopters ran into equally intense antiaircraft fire around St. George's, and two Army helicopters crashed into the ocean. The only team that got through were the lightly armed SEAL sent to rescue the governor, who once they landed soon found themselves surrounded and outgunned. At least the Marines had met only light resistance in the north and had quickly seized all of their objectives.

As he ruminated over the operation's dismal start, Schwarzkopf knew that not all of their problems could be explained away as the inevitable glitches of a hurried combat operation. Some participants seemed to believe that the island was simply not big enough for the Marines and Army both.

A bear of a man and a decorated veteran of Vietnam, Schwarzkopf had both a mercurial temper as well as a thoughtful streak. As he related in his autobiography, *It Doesn't Take a Hero*, Schwarzkopf had been astounded the night before when Atlantic Command in Norfolk had ordered them to provide a "body count," and the naval staff had dutifully broken it down into 13 for the Army and 133 for the Marines. Schwarzkopf was technically only an Army adviser to the Task Force commander aboard the *Guam*, Vice Adm. Joseph Metcalf. In a burst of temper, however, Schwarzkopf had advised the staff that a bullshit competition over body count between the Army and the Marines was the last thing they needed. If Vietnam had taught them nothing else, it had at least taught them that.

Pondering the student dormitory from the bridge of the *Guam* on the second morning of the invasion, Schwarzkopf noticed nearly a dozen helicopters below on the flight deck. With Army paratroopers still stalled at Point Salines at the southern tip of the island, and the Marines to the north at least a day away by land, pressure had been mounting from Washington to hurry up and rescue the students. Quickly Schwarzkopf walked inside the ship's command center and got permission from Admiral Metcalf to use the helicopters to ferry Army Rangers and airborne troops from Point Salines to the dormitory to rescue the students.

Schwarzkopf then called the Marine colonel in command of the helicopters to come to the bridge, where he explained the plan. The man flatly refused.

With the lives of the students potentially hanging in the balance, the colonel stated categorically that he had no intention of flying Army soldiers in Marine helicopters. Only after Schwarzkopf threatened the colonel with a court-martial for disobeying a direct order did he relent. Later that afternoon, 224 students were rescued at Grand Anse by Rangers ferried to the beach aboard Marine helicopters. When he heard the story about the earlier trouble with the helicopters, Admiral Metcalf, to his credit, officially made Schwarzkopf the deputy commander for Urgent Fury.

Metcalf and Schwarzkopf received another unpleasant surprise the following day at Point Salines, when the *Guam* relayed an urgent message from Atlantic Command that the Joint Chiefs of Staff wanted a reported terrorist training camp at Calivigny barracks captured that afternoon. That was pushing ahead the scheduled phasing of the operation, yet when a message was sent back that the 82nd Airborne would occupy the barracks by the end of the next day, CINCLANT reiterated the JCS orders that it fall into their hands *that afternoon.* In the hurriedly assembled assault, two helicopters collided at the landing zone, wounding nearly two dozen soldiers, many of them seriously. When they did arrive at the Calivigny barracks, the Rangers found it deserted.

As a fuming Schwarzkopf climbed to the *Guam*'s bridge from the hospital bay later that evening, having just visited with a young soldier who lost a leg in the accident, he wondered what son of a bitch had ordered the attack. To the list of trip wires to his vaunted temper, Schwarzkopf added, after Urgent Fury, unnecessary interservice rivalry and interference by higher command in combat operations.

As Gen. David Jones had predicted a year earlier, the largest joint military operation since Vietnam left each of the services and many of the key participants with difficult questions to ponder. For instance, how could a military force deployed at least nominally to rescue American students arrive not only ignorant of their whereabouts, but also apparently in very real danger of bombing the very people it had been sent to rescue?

According to a source with access to the classified after-action report on Grenada, a State Department official aboard the *Guam* was dumbfounded to see that the Grand Anse campus where many of the students were housed was marked as a potential military target. Apparently years before it had served as a police academy. Critical intelligence on the students' whereabouts that could have been gleaned from State Department sources or even from a medical-school prospectus was ignored. The students, meanwhile, were left at the mercy of Cubans and the People's Revolutionary Army for nearly thirty-six hours.

The most glaring deficiency in Operation Urgent Fury, however, was the continued inability of the services to work together as a cohesive team. Had the Rangers been supported by the Navy guns and aircraft just off the beaches, for instance, they might have broken through earlier and not required massive reinforcement. Yet because no Army representatives had attended naval planning sessions prior to the operation, they did not know the procedures or communications channels needed to call in naval fire support. Without Army liaisons or Air Force forward air controllers aboard the aircraft carrier *Independence*, its aircraft were meanwhile not allowed to fly south in support of Army troops.

In the most tragic example of this lack of interservice coordination, a Marine liaison team that was attached to the 82nd Airborne accidentally called in a Navy air strike on the unit's tactical operations center, wounding seventeen men and killing one. So incompatible were the communications systems between Army ground forces and the Navy ships, in fact, that one frustrated Army officer called back to North Carolina from a phone booth to try to coordinate naval air support.

Special Operations experts would have their own questions about the operation. Lightly armed SEAL teams were trained experts in covert reconnaissance, but were questionably used to try to rescue the governor-general. Both the SEAL team and Delta Force suffered casualties and had to be rescued by Marines.

Finally, the national press wondered why they had been nearly totally blocked from covering the invasion. Initial plans to introduce reporters onto the island on the first day had been scrapped as the operation descended into chaos. Blocking media coverage of the largest military operation since Vietnam undoubtedly exacerbated the residual antagonism between the press and the military.

Yet for all its missteps, Urgent Fury accomplished its goal of rescuing roughly a thousand American students without injury and paving the way for free elections on the island within months. The operation received a major publicity boost when the first of the rescued students to get off the plane at Charleston Air Force Base stooped down to kiss the tarmac. The cost in American lives was eighteen U.S. servicemen killed, ninety-three wounded, and sixteen missing. As if to underscore the point that the American public had reconciled with the military that it had so long spurned, crowds waving American flags and bands greeted many of the returning soldiers. For many Vietnam veterans such as Norman Schwarzkopf, it was the first time they had been welcomed home from a war.

Ronald Reagan called Urgent Fury a "brilliant campaign," and Caspar Weinberger went so far as to refer to it as a model for future military operations undertaken on short notice. In matching that ebullience, the Army awarded nearly nine thousand medals for valor and achievement during the Operation, far more than the number of soldiers who actually landed on Grenada.

Many analysts, however, saw in Urgent Fury a familiar litany of shortcomings, including a muddled chain of command, an inability of the services to work in concert, a lack of appreciation for the proper uses of Special Operations forces, and poor intelligence. The services' after-action reports on the operation began to reveal many of those shortcomings, and the Long Commission report on Beirut was released criticizing the Pentagon's command structure, reviving interest in the moribund military-reform effort. If anything, the events of late 1983 seemed to prove conclusively just how far the armed services had yet to travel on the long road back to redemption.

29: Politics 1984–85

THE shock absorbers of the dark blue limousine groaned as it sped through the pockmarked streets of the capital, the weight of the extra armor giving it a mushy feel over the inevitable bumps. At Fourteenth and F streets the car pulled over outside the National Press Club, discharging Secretary of Defense Caspar Weinberger and his aides. Maj. Gen. Colin Powell knew that his boss was about to make a case for nothing less than a new paradigm for the future use of American military force.

Since becoming Caspar Weinberger's senior military assistant in 1983, Colin Powell had come to look on Weinberger as one of his great mentors. As his senior aide, Powell was responsible for playing the honest broker before all of the competing interests that vied daily for a piece of Weinberger's time, and Powell was undeniably good at it.

Powell had first met Weinberger back in the early 1970s while working as a White House Fellow at the Office of Management and Budget, where Weinberger was earning the sobriquet "Cap the Knife" for his budget-cutting zeal. Powell's actual boss at the time was Frank Carlucci, later named Weinberger's deputy secretary of defense. The fellowship and his acquaintance with those two men had irrevocably altered Colin Powell's career.

While not always agreeing with Weinberger's decisions, Powell had never met anyone who was more sensitive to the need to make a credible case for his views before the American public. That was one reason why Powell took more than the normal interest in the speech Weinberger was set to deliver on November 28, 1984. Earlier that year, Powell had accompanied Weinberger to the Middle East, where they had flown out to the USS *Trenton* to talk with the Marines who were finally withdrawing from Beirut. Some observers saw in the withdrawal of the Marines from Lebanon after the bomb blast and the failure of the peacekeeping mission tragic parallels to an earlier withdrawal from Saigon. With the crippled skyline of Lebanon clearly visible in the distance, Weinberger had told the Marines on deck how proud he was of them, and of his sorrow at their losses. Caspar Weinberger had obviously been deeply moved by that experience.

"The outcome of decisions on whether—and when—and to what degree—to use combat forces has never been more important than it is today," Weinberger told the gathered journalists and television cameras at the National Press Club. ". . . Some on the national scene . . . reject entirely the question of whether any force can ever be used abroad. . . . On the other side, some theorists argue that military force can be brought to bear in any crisis. . . . Neither of these two extremes offers us any lasting or satisfactory solutions.

"The first—undue reserve—would lead us ultimately to withdraw from the international events that require free nations to defend their interests from the aggressive use of force. . . . The second alternative—employing our forces almost indiscriminately and as a regular and customary part of our diplomatic efforts—would surely plunge us headlong into the sort of domestic turmoil we experienced during the Vietnam War, without accomplishing the goal for which we committed our forces. Such policies might very well tear at the fabric of our society, endangering the *single*-most critical element of a successful democracy: *a strong consensus of support and agreement for our basic purposes.*"

Weinberger went on to detail six "tests" that should be passed before the country committed its forces to combat. The country's vital interests need be at stake, he said, and the United States willing to commit enough forces to win decisively. Both the political and military objectives should be clearly defined, and the military forces sized to achieve them. There must be a reasonable assurance that the American people would support the action. Finally, U.S. forces should be committed only as a last resort.

Colin Powell had read an advance copy of his boss's speech, though he had no major part in crafting it. The speechwriters on staff had even warned that "six" was too awkward a number, and that the secretary should keep his prerequisites on the use of force to a manageable three. Caspar Weinberger was determined, however, and once the secretary set his mind on something he was not a man easily dissuaded.

Perhaps it was a good time to reflect soberly on the proper uses of military power and to revisit the lessons of Vietnam. Certainly the country was feeling resurgent as it gradually shook off the mantle of defeatism that it had worn since Vietnam. A renewed sense of manifest destiny, however, held perils as well as promise.

Personally, Colin Powell had reservations about the utility of a "when-to-go-to-war doctrine" that could be applied to every crisis. Each contingency would likely be unique. The questions, however, were good ones. Have all diplomatic and nonviolent avenues been explored? Is the political objective clearly defined and understood? Are the risks acceptable? If all the answers were yes, and unambiguous objectives could be given to the armed forces that were firmly linked to political aims, then and only then was force to be considered. Certainly inserting those proud Marines as a buffer in a five-faction civil war in Lebanon, complete with terrorists, hostage-takers, and spies in every camp, would not have qualified.

Working at the center of power in Washington, D.C., was opening Powell's eyes to the political and public relations side of the national-security equation. Sometimes he felt that vital part of their business was not always fully appreciated by those in uniform. In the military's sometimes hyperdefensive response to criticisms in the press over Grenada and the latest acquisition scandal, for instance, Powell saw troubling reminders of the Vietnam "circle the wagons" syndrome.

A free press naturally looked for scandal or the sensational angle, Powell was coming to believe. The answer was not for the military to withdraw into its shell. They needed to have the confidence to stand up, admit mistakes when they made them, and try to get their side of the story out. There was a good story to be told about the resurgence of the military, yet somehow it was being obscured by a crush of negative headlines and the reactions of an overly defensive military. If you didn't handle the story right, Powell believed, you could win the battle and lose the war.

On Friday nights, Weinberger frequently walked around the office and apologized to everyone personally for keeping them working so late. That was part of a gracious manner that seemed to place him in a different era. After he was gone, Colin Powell sometimes sat around and reminisced about his days in the field with his junior aide, Navy captain Ronald "Zap" Zlatoper.

The younger man would talk about flying off the deck of carriers in the Mediterranean, sometimes marveling at how far the Navy had come in just a few short years. As a squadron commander in the late 1970s, Zlatoper vividly remembered having to write the parents of sailors who had died of drug overdoses on overseas deployments. Routine catapult launches were occasions of deep dread, when Zlatoper would break into a clammy sweat for fear that a stoned or incompetent sailor was about to send him to the bottom of the ocean.

Yet morale in the Navy had improved radically. It was now common to see groups of sailors milling around outside of a head, their names having been chosen randomly by the last digit of their social security number, all waiting for their turn to dutifully if somewhat uncomfortably fill their sample jar under the watchful gaze of a master-at-arms. Since 1980, when surveys revealed that 47 percent of Navy personnel tested positive for marijuana or hashish, and 11 percent for cocaine, the highest of any service, drug use had dropped dramatically. With the other services having adopted similar programs and strict urinalysis testing, drug use had dropped in the armed services from 26 percent to 16.2 percent in 1982 and was still rapidly falling. For the military, former CNO Admiral Hayward's "zero tolerance" policy was clearly a masterstroke.

Zlatoper had harbored his doubts. Like many Navy officers, he initially feared the policy was too draconian and worried that a mix-up might ruin his career. But there was no arguing with the results in the fleet. Zero tolerance, pay raises, the rapid improvement in their recruiting fortunes, strict observance of a six-month maximum for deployments—all of it had returned a badly missed equilibrium to their ranks. Between 1978 and 1983, overall retention throughout the Navy's ranks had grown from 31.4 percent to 46.3 percent. Instead of worrying about potential maintenance disasters or averting near mutinies, the Navy was now talking about war-fighting again.

For his part, Colin Powell would talk about his days as an assistant division commander of the 4th Infantry Division, Fort Carson, Colorado, or the dark days of the early 1970s, when he traveled to Korea and turned around a demoralized battalion during one of the most satisfying years of his career. Zlatoper always sensed during those talks that Powell would still rather be out in the field commanding troops than playing a power broker in the Pentagon.

Powell already sensed that duty in Washington was destined to pull him away from commanding front-line troops and upward into the highest councils of power. Some of his cohorts referred to him derisively as a "political general," as if there were any other kind. Powell was coming to understand that politics was the theater in which the military operated, to be ignored at their own risk. Politics was the way the Defense Department itself worked. It was the way foreign policy was formulated. It was how the military got approval for its policies. Politics touched everything.

After having suffered through what seemed like endless hours of congressional testimony, Caspar Weinberger sank back in his limousine's upholstery. Not for the first time since becoming the defense secretary's military aide, Zap Zlatoper wondered at the older man's stamina. It was something he and Colin Powell frequently remarked on.

Though everyone in uniform was used to working late hours, Weinberger was seemingly tireless. Typically the sixty-seven-year-old secretary of defense arrived at the Pentagon at seven-thirty A.M. having already read four newspapers, his driver carrying two oversize briefcases of paperwork that Weinberger had worked on the night before at home. Days were a string of scheduled meetings broken only by the crisis du jour, and at night Weinberger frequently left his office late in a tuxedo to attend whatever social function had been penciled onto his calendar.

Days before congressional hearings were never typical, however, as Weinberger insisted on spending nearly twice as many hours in preparation as the testimony itself consumed. The imperturbable demeanor that was his hallmark depended on Weinberger's not being surprised or caught off guard during questioning.

As the limousine glided through the streets of the capital, Weinberger's voice broke the silence.

"How do you think it went?" Weinberger asked his aide without raising his head, always eager for feedback on what he considered one of his most vital duties.

"Fine, sir," said Zlatoper, who marveled at his boss's dogged ability to drive his standard message home no matter how unreceptive the audience. "Only, frankly, Mr. Secretary, you really didn't answer the chairman's first question."

"Oh, I know I didn't," said Weinberger, his face wrinkling into a knowing smile. "But they didn't need to know the answer to that question. I told them what they needed to hear."

In late 1984 what Weinberger believed Congress needed to hear, indeed had heard for nearly four straight years of unprecedented growth in the defense budget, was that America must continue apace with its costly rearmament program to deter the Soviet behemoth.

With the country's deficits growing ominously, however, the budget debates even within the administration were becoming increasingly unpleasant. Certainly Weinberger was well aware of his reputation in Congress, especially among Democrats, for being uncompromising to a fault.

"You give every appearance of being an inflexible ideologue who has lost any sense of rational proportion when it comes to assessing the defense needs of this country," Sen. Donald Riegle, Jr. (D-Mich.), had charged in a particularly acrimonious budget hearing the year before. "By your fanatical insistence on defense increases that are larger than needed, larger than we can afford, I believe that you are damaging our national security."

Weinberger, however, felt that his mission to restore the strength of the U.S. military was simply too important to be subjected to the laws of give-and-take that normally governed Capitol Hill. If Congress was going to reverse or slow the defense buildup, it would have to do so without his or the administration's complicity. Weinberger wasn't going to provide Congress the cover of his equivocation. So far the tactic had worked spectacularly. To date the Reagan administration had gotten almost everything that it wanted for the Pentagon, with Congress tinkering only around the edges of the annual defense-budget requests.

The danger of Weinberger's approach, of course, was that in continually stonewalling he risked eventually becoming irrelevant to the debate. At some point Congress was bound to put the brakes on the defense buildup, if for no other reason than that the accompanying deficits were threatening to bankrupt the country. Without input from the secretary of defense on where the inevitable cuts should come, pork-barrel politics were likely to dominate the discussion instead of national-security priorities.

Potentially, there was also a considerable price to be paid for Weinberger's adamant refusal to countenance an end to the defense buildup he had so painstakingly engineered: in developing their five-year spending plans, the services relied on the Office of the Secretary of Defense for budget guidance. Weinberger's optimistic projections of continued real growth in defense spending with no end in sight, an optimism that flew in the face of mounting evidence that the buildup was losing steam, allowed the armed services to continue spending billions of dollars launching new weapons developments that most budget experts predicted they would be unable to afford in the distant "out years."

This practice of "buying in" to multibillion-dollar programs with up-front expenditures was an old Washington game. If a service could get Congress to commit enough money early to a new weapons system, often by making wildly optimistic promises in terms of performance and cost, a program inevitably developed a constituency and thus a life of its own. At that point, when contracts were let and jobs were at stake, weapons programs were almost never canceled.

Certainly no one could deny that Weinberger had enjoyed a remarkable run. While his intransigence infuriated many members of Congress, he had defied nearly all conventional wisdom within the capital beltway. In the decades since World War II, never before in peacetime had the Pentagon's budget grown in real, after-inflation terms for more than three years running. Yet between fiscal year 1980 and fiscal year 1985, the number of dollars devoted annually to defense more than doubled, from $142.6 billion to $286.8 billion, and in November of 1984 the defense budget was still rising by roughly 10 percent a year. Indeed, Weinberger saw in Ronald Reagan's landslide reelection earlier that month a clear mandate for the continued defense buildup.

Weinberger was a Harvard-educated lawyer and had been chairman of the California Republican Central Committee when he was tapped by then-governor Ronald Reagan to become state finance director. Though he had served with the federal government in the 1970s both as the head of the Office of Management and Budget and as the secretary of health, education and welfare, it was not Cap the Knife but Cap the shrewd attorney who journeyed to Capitol Hill at regular intervals to sell Ronald Reagan's defense buildup. Sitting behind him at most of those sessions was either Zap Zlatoper or Colin Powell.

Weinberger approached each congressional hearing as if he were entering a trial court. After exhaustive preparation he invariably arrived early, milling about before the press photographers and cordially shaking hands while engaging in polite banter with the members of the committee. Once the hearings were under way, Weinberger always led off with a prepared statement, usually outlining the considerable threats to U.S. interests worldwide. Whenever possible, charts and graphs were used to back up his points. And once the tough questioning started, Weinberger was focused and unflappable, a master at the politician's trick of answering not the question he heard, but rather the one he wanted to hear. In such a way had he shepherded America's largest peacetime defense buildup.

The charts of what the Pentagon had purchased with the considerable largesse of Reagan's first term were impressive. After the "hollow force" days of the late 1970s, each of the services had begun restocking depleted spare parts and refilling munitions bins. Based on funding between fiscal years 1982 and 1984, for instance, service inventories for war-reserve munitions were scheduled to grow by an aggregate of roughly 40 percent.

The force structure and modernization figures were equally dramatic. Between 1980 and 1984, the Navy had increased its force structure from 479 battle-force ships to 525, including four World War II–era battleships that were taken out of mothballs and equipped with modern electronics and Tomahawk cruise missiles to go with their massive sixteen-inch guns. The Air Force had added two full wings of roughly seventy-two aircraft each and had another on the way.

All of the services, meanwhile, had gone on a long-delayed buying spree in order to rapidly modernize aging arsenals. Between 1981 and 1984, the Army funded 2,929 new M-1 Abrams tanks, 2,200 Bradley Fighting Vehicles, and 171 AH-64 Apache attack helicopters; the Air Force, 270 F-15 and F-16 aircraft; and the Navy, 400 F-14 and F-18 aircraft. The strategic nuclear triad had also been rapidly modernized with the procurement of the Peacekeeper Intercontinental Ballistic Missile, the Trident submarine armed with Trident II missiles, and the B-1B bomber.

In selling that unprecedented buildup to Congress, Weinberger brushed aside criticisms that he was throwing too much money at the Pentagon too fast. Likewise he downplayed the seriousness of the "spare-parts horror stories" that had begun circulating in the early 1980s over $700 hammers and $400 toilet seats, as well as "waste, fraud, and abuse" charges revolving around defense contractors kenneling their pets and entertaining at posh retreats at government expense.

Usually, Weinberger would insist, it was the Pentagon's own audits that had revealed the overcharges. "I've been a little disappointed that having discovered the bank robbery, we stand accused of having made it," Weinberger had chided the Senate Armed Services Committee the previous year.

Evidence that the toilet seats and dog kennels were only symptoms of a floundering acquisition system, however, was growing by the mid-1980s, as delivery began on the unprecedented bow wave of new weapons that had swelled before Reagan's spending juggernaut like water before a ship's hull. In the manufacture of sophisticated weapons that push technology to its limits, even the most successful programs invariably experience teething problems. Under normal schedules, however, many of those are worked out during lengthy development cycles, attracting relatively little attention.

Anxious to capitalize on a rare window of opportunity during Reagan's first term, however, the Defense Department had feverishly embraced a whole host of "concurrent" weapons developments, with accelerated schedules and overlapping development and production phases. That pushed many of the problem-plagued weapons into the field and out into the open, where congressional investigators and the press were anxiously waiting.

Frustrated by their inability to slow the pace of Weinberger's defense buildup and concerned about the Pentagon's apparent rush to field a host of sophisticated and ultraexpensive new weapons, congressional reformers and oversight committees had already begun tightening their checks and balances on the system. In 1983, for instance, Congress established an independent director of Operational Test and Evaluation in the Pentagon to provide a final pass/fail exam for new weapons. The idea was to ascertain whether new weapons in fact worked as advertised and lived up to the performance requirements the services had set in selling them to Congress in the first place. At that point, many weapons became victims of the services' own overly optimistic projections.

The result was a steady drumbeat of negative headlines, as one major weapons program after another ran into serious trouble in the mid-1980s. For instance, one of the most concurrent programs of the decade, the Air Force's B-1B bomber, was besieged by problems from its very introduction. By signing production and development contracts on the same day, the service delivered the first aircraft in just five years. To do that, however, the General Accounting Office revealed that the Air Force had cut testing, restricted operational training, and fielded aircraft prematurely.

The result was an aircraft that had not only normal teething problems such as leaking fuel bladders, but also critical subcomponent malfunctions. The B-1B's electronic countermeasures (ECM) system, for instance, failed repeated tests and would eventually take years and hundreds of millions of dollars to address, some would say never adequately. That raised serious questions of whether the B-1B could even perform its fundamental mission of penetrating Soviet air defenses for nuclear-bomb delivery. "The Air Force was simply faced with a choice of doing the job properly or staying on schedule. It chose the latter," a GAO investigator commented on the B-1B program.

Meanwhile, pressure created by a highly concurrent schedule for the Air Force's MX "Peacekeeper" missile would lead personnel at the contractor to try to bypass standard testing of components in a desperate effort to regain lost time. That would lead to nine criminal investigations of contractor Northrop Electronics, for everything from falsifying test results to double billing and time-card fraud. At one point, investigators would find that critical navigation parts for the doomsday weapon were being mailed untested through a secret post-office box.

Overwhelmed by the negative publicity, the services were retreating into a siege mentality and heavy-handed tactics. When live-fire tests of the new Bradley Fighting Vehicle revealed problems of crew survivability, for instance, the Army initially responded by trying to have the colonel who conducted the tests transferred. Later the Army conceded that his proposed improvements made the Bradley a safer and better vehicle.

Perhaps the most damaging case of all was the Army's DIVAD (Division Air Defense) antiaircraft gun. Congressional investigators discovered that during operational tests conducted by the Army, testers had placed special radar reflectors on targets to help DIVAD's radars acquire them; had repeatedly flown target drones in front of the gun at low altitudes and suicide speeds without taking evasive action; and had even placed gas cans in a stationary helicopter target to produce a dramatic secondary explosion for the cameras.

In 1984 the criticisms on the DIVAD were already reaching such a crescendo that the next year Weinberger would be forced to abort the program after $1.8 billion had already been spent, making it one of the most costly weapons cancellations in Pentagon history. Not only did the public drubbing the Pentagon was taking over that host of troubled weapons programs inevitably begin to drown out Weinberger's well-crafted message for continued increases in defense spending, but it obscured from the American public much of the progress the armed services were making in distancing themselves from the "hollow forces" of the 1970s. And in the constant drumbeat of "waste, fraud, and abuse" there were those in Congress who thought they detected once again the faint heartbeat of serious military reform.

30: Windmills and Reformers 1984–85

IT was well past midnight, and the voices behind the closed doors of room S407 could be heard echoing down the deserted hallways of the Capitol. There were no television cameras or reporters present in those early-morning hours in October 1984, and many of the congressmen and senators gathered at the long table to work out the 1985 Defense Authorization Bill were stabbing at nearly full ashtrays and shifting restlessly in their chairs. Their agitation was visible, no one wanting to push this thing until actual blows were struck.

"It's getting late, and I think we should table this," said Republican senator John Tower of Texas, referring to the rider on reforming the Joint Chiefs of Staff that the House Armed Services Committee had attached to the defense authorization bill. Tower looked across the conference table directly at the man everyone in the room knew he had outmaneuvered. "We really shouldn't be addressing this on an authorization bill in the first place."

Though a short man, Tower was a consummate politician and a presence when in his element. Certainly he hadn't risen to become the powerful chairman of the Senate Armed Services Committee (SASC) on the strength of his warm personality or softball tactics. A brainy, partisan politician with an acerbic bent, he kept a tight grip on his committee by commanding respect rather than loyalty. Tower had been a key hawk on increases in defense spending in support of Reagan's buildup, and a number of those present knew that he harbored a deep ambition to one day become secretary of defense. With plans to retire soon from the Senate, Tower was not about to go out having alienated his key constituencies in the Pentagon and White House by forcing unwanted reforms on them.

After twenty-three years in the Senate, John Tower of Texas was also an expert enough tactician to know when he had won. The only question remaining was how much humiliation Rep. Bill Nichols needed to endure before accepting that he had lost.

Nichols was seething. A conservative Democrat from rural Alabama, he made for an unlikely military reformer. He had first come to Congress in 1966, a George Wallace Democrat from one of those Southern districts that tended to stick loyally with their pols. In two decades on the House Armed Services Committee (HASC), Nichols had risen to become chairman of the Investigations Subcommittee a few years earlier after Dick White retired. It was the same subcommittee that had held hearings in the wake of former JCS chairman Gen. David Jones's surprise call for reforms in 1982.

More recently, Nichols had chaired exhaustive hearings on the bombing of the Marine barracks in Beirut, as well as spare-parts procurement scandals. An Army veteran who had lost a leg in World War II to a land mine, Nichols had personally visited Beirut, and he had seen and heard enough to believe that the Pentagon's command structure had let those Marines down in Lebanon. As witnesses had also pointed out in the hearings, crises requiring a joint military response in the past decade were a list of infamy—Vietnam, *Mayaguez*, *Pueblo*, Desert One, Beirut. As details continued to emerge on Operation Urgent Fury in Grenada, even that "victory" had written on it many of the problems that had doomed other operations to failure.

If he was increasingly committed to meaningful reform of the Pentagon, however, Nichols retained the low-key demeanor and almost courtly style familiar in Southern politicians. His anger was thus all the greater because Bill Nichols would never treat a respected colleague the way John Tower was treating him.

Tower had assured Representative Nichols that the Senate staff was working on its own military-reform package, and that they could work out a compromise in conference. After hearing through back channels that Tower might be stalling, Nichols had attached his Joint Chiefs of Staff reform measures to the defense authorization bill, knowing that Tower could thus not easily sidestep the issue at the last moment as he had in the past.

As chairman of the House/Senate Conference, however, Tower controlled the agenda on the hundreds of amendments that are part of any major authorization bill. Each time the JCS reform measure came up for discussion, Tower had simply placed it at the bottom of the stack with assurances that they would get to it later. Now they were in the final hours of the conference, and Tower's strategy was revealed to everyone. It had all been a ruse.

Nichols looked up and down the long conference table. On the opposite side sat the entire Senate Armed Services Committee. The Republicans had a clear though not overwhelming majority, and Nichols knew his opponent well enough to wager that Tower had his committee firmly in line behind his opposition to the reforms. On either side of Nichols sat an equal number of representatives from the larger House Armed Services Committee. By now Nichols heard considerable grumbling on both sides of the table, everyone wanting to finish this thing and go home.

Nichols cast a glance at Archie Barrett, his aide on the Investigations Subcommittee staff who had gone to work for him after the retirement of Dick White, and who was largely responsible for writing the reform bill. He wasn't ready to give up, and with a shake of his head Nichols tried one last time to argue the case for strengthening the power of the chairman of the Joint Chiefs and the Joint Staff.

Watching a year's worth of hearings and preparation disappear down this unexpected trap, Arch Barrett was speechless. When he was studying legislative affairs for his doctorate at Harvard, Barrett had learned about House/Senate conferences held at the end of each legislative session to work out compromises between competing legislation. He knew the chairmanship of these conferences rotated each year between the two bodies of Congress. No one ever mentioned, however, the pivotal importance the chairman had in controlling the agenda, and it was an oversight he was coming to rue. John Tower was teaching both him and Bill Nichols a lesson in politics that they would never forget.

"Arch, you better take what they're offering, 'cause no one wants to stay much longer." Looking up, Barrett saw that it was the HASC staff director speaking in his ear. What Tower was offering amounted to a few token reforms, the legislative equivalent of face-saving scraps.

"Arch, this thing's going to crumble *soon.*"

Behind the senators on the opposite side of the table, Barrett could see Jim Locher sitting against the wall. His counterpart on the Senate staff refused to make eye contact. It was Jim Locher who Tower had assured them was studying serious military reform for the Senate Armed Services Committee. Barrett got up to suggest to Nichols that it might be time to fold their hand.

That two relatively faceless staff members such as Arch Barrett and Jim Locher were at the center of the defense-reform debate might have surprised observers unaccustomed to the workings of Capitol Hill. The whole concept of unelected professional staff was a recent development begun in earnest only after the Legislative Reorganization Act of 1946. In 1900, for instance, congressional employees numbered fewer than three hundred. To combat the ever-expanding staffs of various agencies in the executive branch, and to keep pace with the volume and overwhelming complexity of modern legislation, Congress had steadily increased the number of its professional staff members since World War II, until by the early 1980s they numbered more than nineteen thousand.

Though chartered to act primarily as clerks, translating the policies of the elected members of Congress into reports and legislation, in truth staff members accounted for much of the expertise in Congress. There were simply too many arcane subjects for each member of Congress to master, even within the realm of his or her chosen committees. The more expert a staff member was on a critical issue of the day, or the less astute his or her member of Congress, the greater the staff member's incandescence in the peculiar solar system of Capitol Hill. In the end, however, the best ones kept sight of the fact that theirs was always a reflected light.

Across the room, Jim Locher knew better than to even open his mouth. The SASC staff director had made it perfectly clear that his input would not be appreciated. Locher had advised Senator Tower not to get involved in this reform business in the first place. Everything about it spelled trouble, something Locher was well qualified to judge.

A West Point graduate with an MBA in management from Harvard, the thirty-eight-year-old Locher had spent nearly a decade inside the Pentagon working in the Office for Program Analysis and Evaluation, the former spawning ground for McNamara's systems-analysis whiz kids. He had witnessed firsthand the dismay of defense secretaries who felt the advice they received from the Joint Chiefs was frequently marginal at best, understood the frustration of former chairman Gen. David Jones over his inability to get the service chiefs or the Joint Staff to operate independently of their individual services.

Yet Locher also understood the enormity of the challenge. A few members of Congress and their staffs were trying to reform the largest bureaucracy in the free world, one that had successfully resisted similar efforts for nearly four decades. Jones and Gen. Shy Meyer were retired, and while their stunning criticisms of the JCS while they were sitting members may have opened a brief window for reform, Locher believed that it had since slammed shut. The present Joint Chiefs of Staff and the Pentagon leadership were all firmly unified in their opposition to reorganizations or reform.

Given the strong ties between members of the Senate Armed Services Committee and the military, Locher also doubted they wanted any part of the acrimonious controversy that a serious military-reform battle would surely provoke. As a former enlisted sailor, Tower had strong ties to the Navy, by far the service most resistant to reforms. Republican senator John Warner of Virginia was a former secretary of the navy with major naval bases such as Norfolk in his district. Jeremiah Denton of Alabama was a retired Navy admiral, and Strom Thurmond of South Carolina a retired Army general.

Both Sen. John East and Sen. John Glenn had served in the Marine Corps, and as they said, there were no ex-Marines, only former Marines. Marine Corps commandant Gen. P. X. Kelley had emerged as a vociferous opponent of reforms. Republican senators Dan Quayle and Phil Gramm, meanwhile, could be counted on to solidly back the White House, which was sure to oppose reforms as a backhanded swipe at Caspar Weinberger's stewardship of the Defense Department.

Though less predictable, archconservatives such as Sen. Barry Goldwater certainly seemed unlikely firebrands for military reform. Even James McGovern, the staff director of SASC and Locher's direct boss, was a former Naval Academy graduate who was aghast at most of the reform proposals.

Locher knew all that, advised Senator Tower against becoming involved in a major reform effort, and still he had been directed to study the matter earlier that year. Privately, he thought Tower believed a thorough review of the issue would vindicate the status quo and act as a foil to the constant proddings toward reform by the House Armed Services Committee. Instead, when Locher's findings seemed to validate the need for reforms that went even further than those proposed by the HASC, Tower abruptly lost interest in the effort. It was at that point that SASC staff director James McGovern had first started making life hell for Jim Locher.

Some sources said that Navy Secretary John Lehman personally called McGovern and asked him to squelch the study. Certainly every time Locher showed signs of picking up with his defense-reorganization inquiry, McGovern would dump a new load of work on his desk. Already Locher was facing such a backlog that his three research assistants were beginning to bend under the burden, and still McGovern piled it on. The message was sent, in the way those things were made clear on the staff, that Locher's study on reform was a dead issue. Before the House/Senate Conference had begun, McGovern had all but stuffed a gag in Locher's mouth. At least they couldn't say that he hadn't warned them.

When the meeting in S2407 finally broke up and a furious Bill Nichols retreated with the scraps on reform that Tower had tossed him, not many members stayed around for the traditional backslapping. For his part, Arch Barrett was devastated. Collecting his papers and preparing to leave, he turned to see the kindly face of Rep. Ike Skelton, a Harry Truman–style Democrat from western Missouri who was a major voice for reform on the House Armed Services Committee.

"We won a great victory here tonight," Skelton said, smiling.

Barrett shook his head ruefully, sure that the kindly congressman was trying to cheer him up after a humiliating defeat.

"No, I'm serious," Skelton insisted. "Modest as it was, that was the first JCS reform that's passed Congress since 1958. We've broken the dam."

Thinking back on that night in S2407, Sen. Barry Goldwater thought that if they had stayed a little while longer, an actual fight might have erupted. Not that the thought overly concerned him. The irascible old man of Arizona politics had been grinding the sausage of governance in similar smokehouses for thirty years, and in his frequent experience the more blood and gristle left on the floor the better the final product.

Still, the tensions in the room that night were memorable, all the more so because the antagonists were both experienced members. As a rule the older members of the two Armed Services Committees shared a collegial rapport and more often than not banded together to put freshmen in their place. This latest showdown on military reform had been between two seasoned members not known for radical stances, however, and still it had gotten wild in there. That intrigued Barry Goldwater.

When the seventy-five-year-old Goldwater assumed the chairmanship of the Senate Armed Services Committee two months later, his appointment caused little alarm in the Pentagon. After all, he was the self-proclaimed granddaddy of the conservative movement, a noted hawk on defense who was also close with his predecessor John Tower. Both men shared in common a painful electoral loss to Lyndon Johnson. In Tower's case it had been a campaign for the Senate seat eventually inhabited by LBJ. When Johnson vacated that seat to run as vice president with John Kennedy, Goldwater had traveled to Texas and campaigned for John Tower on an exhausting whistle-stop along the panhandle.

It was Goldwater's 1964 campaign as the Republican nominee for president against Lyndon Johnson that had forever solidified his image in the collective consciousness. Much was made of his performance at the Republican National Convention of 1964. "Extremism in the defense of liberty is no vice," Goldwater had proclaimed, and he meant it. Lyndon Johnson successfully played off fears of a hip-shooting reactionary with his hand on the nuclear trigger. In a particularly memorable commercial run by the Democrats, a picture of a young girl picking flowers in a field was supplanted by one of a nuclear mushroom cloud. The advertisement didn't even mention Goldwater by name. It didn't have to.

The reality, of course, was far more complex. Irreverent and salty, Goldwater had made a career out of saying exactly what he thought, frequently on the Senate floor. In a deliberative body where speechwriters could haggle for hours over the political ramifications of an adverb, that candor and bluntness won him grudging respect and a large measure of tolerance.

As Michael Barone noted in *The Almanac of American Politics*, Goldwater's fundamental belief in less government and aggressive defense harked back to the Taftish Republicans of the 1940s. He was neither a close confidant of Ronald Reagan nor a darling of the New Right, the supply-siders, and most certainly not the Moral Majority. Goldwater went his own way in a town where a premium was placed on consensus, and thus his ascension to the chairmanship added an unknown quantity to the already volatile military-reform mix.

Intrigued by the contentious showdown between Tower and Nichols over the issue, Goldwater scheduled one of his first meetings as the incoming SASC chairman with retired general Andrew Goodpaster, the former Supreme Allied Commander, Europe. Along with an impressive cast of defense experts, Goodpaster had been studying military reorganization for the Center for Strategic and International Studies (CSIS), a moderate-to-conservative Washington think tank.

Among others, participants in the CSIS study included Sen. Sam Nunn, the ranking minority member on the Senate Armed Services Committee, and a man Goldwater considered to be one of the most capable in Congress regardless of party affiliation; Rep. Les Aspin, the chairman of the House Armed Services Committee and a key backer of reform; Gen. Edward "Shy" Meyer, who after leaving the Pentagon had once again renewed his calls for JCS reform; and Gen. David Jones, who had continued agitating for major reform of the Joint Chiefs since relinquishing the chairmanship. Perhaps not surprisingly, the CSIS study stressed that reorganizing the Pentagon's command structure was imperative.

As Goodpaster briefed him on the findings of the CSIS study, which was soon to be published, Goldwater harked back to his own experiences in the military. After serving in the Air Force during World War II, Goldwater had risen to the rank of general in the Air Force reserve. Jim Locher, who had been invited to the Goodpaster briefing, noticed that every time Goodpaster laid out a problem, Goldwater would nod his head and add an anecdote from his own long experience with the military. Shortly after, Goldwater received a briefing by Col. Ted Crackel, who had spent years studying reform and compiling another soon-to-be-released study for the Heritage Foundation, a more conservative think tank in Washington, D.C.

After the briefings, Goldwater grabbed Locher's arm, and the staff member could feel the older man's excitement in his grip.

"Jesus Christ, Jim, this is something we should have done fifty years ago!" Goldwater told him, setting a reform agenda as the Committee's top priority.

Goldwater began sketching out a year-long campaign for military reform. When Congress reconvened in January, Goldwater was going to establish a bipartisan task force and make Sen. Sam Nunn an equal cochairman with himself. They could never collect the necessary votes on an issue this emotionally charged, he said, if an eventual vote broke down along party lines. Locher was to drop everything else immediately and devote himself to finishing the comprehensive defense-reorganization study that he had begun under Tower, to serve as the blueprint for an eventual Senate bill.

Goldwater lacked the inclination to sort through the endless details of a reform bill of such mammoth proportions and complexities, but for that he had Jim Locher. What he brought to the effort was political savvy and an indomitable personality. Knowing that Jim McGovern would subtly work to thwart the effort, Goldwater took the unusual step of circumventing the staff director and ordering Locher to report directly to the task-force chairmen, and no one else.

"By God, there's a real problem here, and I'm going to devote my last two years in the U.S. Senate to doing something about it," Goldwater said, and Locher didn't doubt it for an instant. The distinguished gentleman from Arizona knew better than anyone that the odds were heavily stacked against them, and that a conservative Republican with major military bases in his backyard would have to be crazy to provoke a public battle with the Pentagon. He just didn't give a good goddamn.

What many people failed to understand about Barry Goldwater was that he had first put on a uniform as a fourteen-year-old boy in a Virginia military academy, and as far as Goldwater was concerned, he had never taken it off. When he died, Goldwater planned to be cremated in his uniform and have his ashes scattered over the Grand Canyon. Tilting at the windmill of military reform, Goldwater would be fighting one last grand battle in a long campaign that had known its share of hopeless causes. The military-reform effort had found its Don Quixote.

Col. Ted Crackel's report on defense reorganization was not published by the Heritage Foundation as scheduled. Just before the paper was to go into print, Heritage president Ed Feulner reportedly received a late-night phone call from Navy Secretary John Lehman. The next day the project was canceled.

John Lehman vigorously denied charges that he had created a special branch in the Navy Office of Legislative Affairs to kill the JCS legislation, though he later conceded meeting on an occasional basis with other DoD officials opposed to the reforms to track their progress and strategize. Certainly it was no secret inside the capital beltway that the dynamic Navy secretary had taken it on himself to lead the antireform effort.

Nor was Lehman known for his restraint. Because "a coalition of civilian armchair strategists, who don't really understand the Pentagon bureaucracy," were mistakenly pressing for JCS reform, argued Lehman to a *New York Times* reporter in 1984, nothing less than civilian control over the military was in jeopardy. If these strategists had their way, the result might be a "Prussian-style general staff." "It's a terrible, terrible move, terribly pernicious," Lehman told the *Washington Post*.

When John Lehman took up the antireform standard in 1985, he was at the pinnacle of his power, and arguably one of the most influential men in the capital. Charismatic, brash, intellectually combative, he had in his first four years almost single-handedly redefined the role of the civilian service secretary. During that time the Navy had prospered in relation to the other services.

During Reagan's first term, for instance, the Navy experienced the greatest growth in both force structure and military strength of all the services: from 479 to 523 deployable battle-force ships between 1980 and 1984, or a 9.2 percent growth in force structure, versus 3.2 percent for the Air Force and none for the Army. His success led one senior official to quip that to be fair, Lehman should probably be rotated to serve as secretary for each of the services.

Yet in his visible and increasingly vitriolic opposition to proposed JCS reforms, Lehman was steaming into dangerous political waters with the Navy in tow. Win or lose, he was bound to make powerful enemies in the effort, and memories in Washington, D.C., tended to last far longer than the tenure of even the most durable service secretaries.

A stridency had also crept into Lehman's tone, especially when he addressed subordinates in the uniformed Navy. With an uncompromising streak of independence, and an intellectual arrogance that brooked little internal disagreement or argument, it was almost as if Lehman was coming to reflect in exaggerated form the darkest tendencies of the Navy itself.

Certainly the Navy secretary's leadership style and his aggressive opposition to powerful reformers in Congress were causing considerable nerves on the Navy staff, where Vice Adm. Stan Arthur took over in July of 1985 as the director for Aviation Plans and Requirements on the staff of the chief of naval operations. Because his first love was always naval aviation, Lehman assumed an even more active role in aviation affairs than normal, though in truth he involved himself in all Navy matters to an extent unprecedented for a service secretary.

Stan Arthur had watched with interest as John Lehman rose to become one of the most powerful and controversial civilian service secretaries in history. They had first met over lunch back in the mid-1970s, when then-commander Arthur was working in the assignment shop in the Naval Annex in Virginia, and Lehman was a young go-getter with the Arms Control Agency in Washington. The Navy Plans staff in the Pentagon had called Arthur and asked him to set up a summer training cruise for a naval reservist "J.G.", or lieutenant junior grade. Needless to say the tour they mapped out, which included jet-pilot refresher training at Kingsville, Texas, and carrier duty in the Mediterranean, was a reservist's dream.

"Jeez, do you guys know what you're doing?" Arthur had asked at the time.

"Don't worry," the voice at the other end of the line had replied without hesitation. "Someday, this guy's going to be secretary of the navy." As Stan Arthur had discovered to his shock in 1981, someone in Navy Plans had known exactly what they were talking about.

Since the Navy Department was created in 1798, service secretaries had traditionally confined themselves primarily to administrative and management duties, leaving strategic planning and operational concerns to the uniformed military. John Lehman was a traditionalist, however, neither in temperament nor background. Besides being an active naval reservist and aviator, he had written a book about aircraft carriers and had a Ph.D. in international relations. He was even related to Princess Grace of Monaco, a fact that added greatly to his mystique.

Though Lehman's autocratic and frequently domineering style left bruised feelings everywhere in his wake, in 1983 he was deftly engineering expansion of the fleet to six hundred ships and fifteen carriers, and he was using the Maritime Strategy as the theoretical underpinning of that expansion. Originally developed as Sea Strike by former chief of naval operations Adm. Thomas Hayward and his staff at Pacific Command, the plan called for the 7th Fleet to attack the eastern flank of the Soviet Union and deny the Soviet navy sanctuary. Under John Lehman's dynamic salesmanship, the Maritime Strategy had been expanded, with Navy leaders envisioning the service simultaneously fighting a two-ocean, global war against the Soviet Union, including attacks on mainland Soviet targets from the Norwegian Sea. The Navy deftly sidestepped critics who charged that its ships simply could not survive long in the Norwegian Sea, close to the Soviet coastline and within reach not only of land-based bombers but also of antiship missiles.

Chief of naval operations Adm. James Watkins called the Maritime Strategy his number-one priority, stressing that it would not only ensure that the White House understood the relevance of the Navy but also restore a sense of common purpose to a divided and demoralized force. In that regard the Maritime Strategy was serving much the same purpose as the Army and Air Force's new "AirLand Battle" doctrine for waging war. Massive organizations on the scale of the armed services needed a common direction to focus the efforts of their many disparate commands, and war-fighting doctrine supplied that unity of purpose. The difference was that while AirLand Battle by definition required a closer coordination between the Army and Air Force, the Maritime Strategy codified the Navy's strong streak of independence, calling on a global fleet built around fifteen aircraft carriers to take the fight to the Soviet Union from the open ocean.

While the Navy married its fortunes to the Maritime Strategy, a number of critics questioned why the Pentagon was investing what many considered a disproportionate amount of capital on a six-hundred-ship navy, when the main threat to the United States was arguably 180 Soviet divisions on the Eurasian land mass.

Even in the realm of naval aviation, Lehman's strategies had been controversial. The effort to reach a six-hundred-ship fleet had seriously depleted other accounts. The Navy was not buying precision-guided munitions at anything like the rate the Air Force was, for instance, and its aviation arm was rapidly aging. Young naval aviators new to the fleet, for instance, were still flying the A-6 Intruder that Arthur remembered from Vietnam, the aircraft in some cases having logged more birthdays than the pilots. The gamble seemed to be that once the Navy purchased the aircraft carriers, the Congress wouldn't dare refuse them the funds to outfit them with modern aircraft.

Yet the dilemma Lehman presented in 1985 went far beyond the details of any single program. There was no question in Arthur's mind that Lehman had kept the Navy focused on the future and had been successful beyond most of their dreams in leading the charge for a six-hundred-ship fleet. Arthur had also doubted Lehman's decision a year earlier to create Strike U, a Red Flag–like training area for Navy strike aircraft, believing it was overkill in reaction to a fiasco in Syria, when two Navy aircraft were downed while striking lightly armed targets. He had since come to see that Lehman was right.

On an emotional level, the service also broadly supported Lehman's opposition to proposed military reforms. While the reformers might couch their purposes with "motherhood" terms like *jointness* and *efficiency*, the service sensed that the true agenda was to somehow single out the Navy and pull it in a different direction, getting back at the service that had most prospered during the Reagan defense buildup. If anything, Lehman's headstrong opposition to reforms inflamed that us-against-them sense of defensiveness in the Navy.

Still, Stan Arthur and many other officers on the Navy staff were worried about a potential backlash to Lehman's uncompromising resistance to reform. Watching his boss, Arthur was reminded of a man who couldn't take the smallest step backward for fear of losing face. He believed Lehman had decided that if he ever started backing up, then the intellectual foundation on which he had engineered the Navy's comeback would somehow come tumbling down. What Lehman didn't seem to realize was that he wasn't going to be around forever. And far from grooming leaders who would take his place, Lehman was if anything driving them away with his autocratic style.

Stan Arthur was not the only one to notice a serious talent hemorrhage at the upper reaches of the officer corps. Respected leaders such as retired admiral Thomas Hayward, the former chief of naval operations who had initially embraced Lehman's leadership, were privately warning that he was destroying the Navy's ability to think for itself. Lehman made it clear that the Navy was going to do things his way, and some of their best people were leaving rather than occupy high-level positions of irrelevance. Lehman was failing in one of the first and most pivotal responsibilities of military leadership, which was to groom future leaders. What if when the backlash comes, Stan Arthur worried, the Navy finds it has forgotten how to fight its own battles?

31: A Palace Coup 1985–86

ON a Saturday morning in early October 1985, a handful of Blackhawk helicopters lifted off the helipad at the Pentagon across from Arlington Cemetery, hovered for a moment as they gained altitude, and then joined up in single file heading along the Potomac River. From the air, Washington, D.C., emerged as the ordered, European-style capital that L'Enfant had originally envisioned nearly two hundred years earlier, its symmetrical grid broken by broad avenues and uncluttered vistas connecting the monuments and the various centers of power. The shadows of the helicopters flitted across the broad span of Memorial Bridge that joined the hillsides of Arlington Cemetery to the Lincoln Memorial, commemorating America's greatest wartime commander in chief.

Though nearly exhausted, Jim Locher was feverishly wondering about this weekend retreat to Virginia. He had finally finished his Congressional Staff Study, *Defense Organization: The Need for Change*, all 645 pages of it, and Barry Goldwater had organized this getaway as a final chance to sell it to the nine senators on the Senate Armed Services task force that he had formed under his and Sam Nunn's chairmanship. Fifteen prominent experts had also been invited to share their reactions to the report. As far as Locher could tell, the task force could go either way. Indeed, they had labeled the effort a staff study rather than a "committee report" precisely because Goldwater wasn't at all sure they could get the entire committee to vote to release it.

For the past week, both Goldwater and Nunn had been giving speeches on the Senate floor that Locher and his aides had helped them prepare, blasting the military as an opening salvo to the study's release. With the Joint Chiefs and the Pentagon united firmly in opposition to reform, many senators were extremely uneasy about joining a crusade led by a few members of Congress and a handful of professional staff. The speeches were sharp, frontal attacks designed to overcome that sense of caution.

"If we have to fight tomorrow, these problems will cause Americans to die unnecessarily!" Goldwater had thundered. The press immediately picked up on the speeches, *The New York Times* reporting on them under the headline "Two Key Senators Join in Assault on the Military." The fight over defense reorganization and military reform had been joined in earnest, with both sides finally out in the open.

Rumors had been circulating for months suggesting that Goldwater had become enfeebled, the implication clearly being that his mind was going as well as the aging body that had required hip surgery a few years earlier, forcing the senator to walk with a cane and sometimes use a wheelchair. Supposedly Goldwater was now a patsy being manipulated in the reform effort by the Democrats, with Sam Nunn the behind-the-scenes puppet master.

Locher had to smile at that one. Goldwater tended to see things in broad strokes, and he certainly didn't have the grasp of complicated minutiae on many of these matters that Sam Nunn commanded. But Goldwater had a vision of how to wage this battle, and Nunn had always seemed deferential to it and to his committee chairman. If Goldwater was crazy, as some said, he was crazy like a fox.

It had been Goldwater's idea to send early copies of their work to Robert McFarlane, the president's National Security Council adviser and a former Senate Armed Services professional staff member. McFarlane had seen right away that the administration was on a collision course with the Senate Armed Services Committee. There was no love lost between McFarlane and Caspar Weinberger, and the NSC adviser had seen a way to give the administration cover on the effort and neutralize Weinberger's opposition in a single stroke.

McFarlane had convinced President Reagan to appoint his own blue-ribbon Commission on Defense Reform that past summer. It was headed by David Packard, a respected former Defense Department official and the successful businessman of Hewlett-Packard fame. Initially Weinberger had strongly opposed the idea and, when it looked as if Reagan was going through with it anyway, had argued that the commission should focus only on defense acquisition, and not reform of the Joint Chiefs of Staff and the Pentagon command structure. Weinberger was somewhat assuaged after his former deputy Frank Carlucci was named as a commission member. The impression that the Packard Commission was almost exclusively focused on defense acquisition remained with the press and the public, despite the fact that Packard had wide latitude to pursue his own agenda.

David Packard and his fellow commission members such as Brent Scowcroft had regularly visited Barry Goldwater to learn what the SASC was doing. From Locher's take on those meetings, it seemed likely that the Packard Commission would generally endorse the main thrust of their reform effort. Insomuch as Weinberger had been strangely quiet on the reform issue as of late, McFarlane's plan also seemed to have worked.

Outside the beltway and even among members of Congress, however, many people continued to believe that the reorganization and reform effort was mostly about $700 hammers and procurement "waste, fraud, and abuse." That was the story that had kept the effort alive, and ultimately a vote on the complex reform package could hinge on that vague sense that something was wrong at the Pentagon and thus needed "reforming." Those who had worked closely on the effort, however, wondered if the press and the country at large would wake up to discover one day that they had been talking all along about the most fundamental reorganization of the military command structure in forty years.

After the helicopters landed at Fort A. P. Hill in Virginia, just north of Richmond, and the participants got squared away in their quarters, Locher briefed his report. First he outlined the familiar litany of problems, ranging from rule by committee on the JCS; a tendency on the part of the services to denigrate joint-duty assignments; service parochialism that stood in the way of smoother interservice coordination; and the relative neglect by the services of functions not central to their prime mission, such as airlift and close air support by the Air Force, sealift by the Navy, and special operations by all of the services. Fundamentally, however, the reform effort was about the inability of the command structure to coax smoothly coordinated teamwork out of the services on joint operations.

Locher shifted to the study's recommendations, which in scope went far beyond the more modest proposals on JCS reorganization that the House Armed Services Committee had been pushing for years. Locher began with the most radical suggestion. The Joint Chiefs of Staff should be abolished outright, the study concluded, and replaced by a Joint Military Advisory Council consisting of a chairman and a four-star military officer from each service. This was in effect former Army chief Gen. Shy Meyer's proposal re-stated, and Locher hoped it would once again serve the same purpose of making their other proposals look moderate in comparison. In his mind, they were going to need a decoy to draw the inevitable fire that opponents would launch at them. A small band of more radical military reformers led by Sen. Gary Hart were providing some of that cover, causing the services to expend their political ammunition fighting Hart's proposal for creation of a sort of superservice he called the National Defense Staff.

Other recommendations in Locher's report included making the chairman the principal military adviser to the secretary of defense and the president, ending the committee approach, which constantly watered down JCS recommendations; establishing a deputy chairman to act in the chair's stead when he wasn't present; placing the Joint Staff under the exclusive direction of the chairman; and strengthening the hands of the CINCs of unified commands in the field, having them report directly to the chairman, with clearer authority over their component commanders and more input into Defense Department decisions on budget matters.

Following Locher's presentation, the task force members and experts debated each chapter of the study and the recommendations. Gen. David Jones was there in a place of honor and, not surprisingly, fully endorsed the study's general thrust. For Jones, Fort A. P. Hill marked the culmination of a fight begun nearly five years earlier, and one that had brought him considerable vilification from many of his former comrades-in-arms. With an arch-conservative such as Barry Goldwater now leading the reform effort, however, Jones was as hopeful as he had ever been about the prospects for truly meaningful change. Adm. Thomas Moorer also spoke, and Nixon's former JCS chairman just as predictably obstreperously opposed nearly all the suggestions in the report.

Having recently retired and joined in the reform debate as a member of the Packard Commission, Gen. Paul Gorman shared his own insights gained from serving as the unified CINC of Southern Command in Panama. The man whom some in the Army were calling the "father of the National Training Center" had come to believe that recent years had seen a striking growth in the level of interdependence among the services, driven in large part by modern technology. Thus he fully supported measures strengthening the "joint system"—the chairman of the JCS, the Joint Staff, and the unified commanders in the field—at the expense of the individual military departments.

After dinner that night, the group reconvened for one last time. Former defense secretaries Harold Brown and James Schlesinger spoke. Between them, these two civilians had been at the helm of the Pentagon during one of the darkest decades in its history and had seen its operations from the inside as the services felt their way through the end of Vietnam, the first stumbling years of the all-volunteer army, the "hollow force" years, and over critical chasms such as Desert One. Both strongly commended the report and unequivocally endorsed its recommendations.

Sensing momentum from their comments, Goldwater worked the other outside experts after the former defense secretaries were finished. Then he asked his colleagues on the task force to speak. Some of them were still hesitant, but in their comments reform proponents such as Locher and David Jones sensed that the senators' reservations were weakening.

As the men boarded the Blackhawks for the short flight back to Washington, D.C., the next day, Goldwater sensed that his getaway at Fort A. P. Hill was a watershed. Flying down two days earlier, the task force members had primarily associated military reform with a few headstrong colleagues and their professional staff members. In this quiet, informal setting, away from the political undercurrents that charged congressional hearings and nearly every discussion inside the capital beltway, they had come to see it through very different eyes. They would hold hearings on the report to give the service chiefs a chance to condemn it, and of course the recommendations would have to be written into legislation. Still, the next windmill that Goldwater could already see looming on the horizon was the crucial vote in the full Senate Armed Services Committee.

On February 5, 1986, during the second day of deliberations on the reform bill by the full Committee, Barry Goldwater saw the opposition's end-game strategy finally laid bare. It was to be death by amendment, and Sen. John Warner had clearly been designated as executioner. As Warner excused himself from the Committee room once again, Goldwater had no doubt that his friend had an open line going to the Navy Department. Every time they started discussion of another aspect of the reform bill, the former secretary of the navy left the room and came back a few minutes later with fifteen proposed amendments. Goldwater was willing to bet that half the Navy staff over at the Pentagon were standing by to write those amendments that were threatening to gut his reform bill.

It was one hell of a state of affairs, Goldwater felt, that the enemy had turned out to be the second-ranking Committee member from his own party. The way things looked, Warner might well win. The vote on the first measure had been a near thing, ending up ten for and nine against. From that point on they had gotten bogged down in Warner's endless amendments.

John Warner could have been cast by Hollywood to play the part of the Virginia gentleman who had made it to the U.S. Senate with his courtly manners intact. In Washington, he was far better known for his affable personality and for being married to Elizabeth Taylor than for his intellect. His reputation in that department suffered from Warner's occasional lapses into cliché-ridden pomposity. Nor had his service as secretary of the navy under Richard Nixon left any question on where his true sympathies lay.

Watching Warner return to the Committee room with another batch of ready amendments, Goldwater was reminded of a dinner party he had attended at Warner's impressive horse farm out in hunt country near Middleburg, Virginia. Elizabeth Taylor had stood up and started in on a seemingly endless political speech that was embarrassing her husband. Rolling his eyes, Warner had asked Goldwater to try to get her to quiet down. At which point Barry Goldwater had walked up to Elizabeth Taylor, whacked her on the ass, and told her to sit the hell down.

Friendships aside, Goldwater decided as Warner introduced fifteen or so new amendments to the reform legislation that it was just about time to give Warner a few hard raps, and anyone else who hoped to render his bill stillborn by amendment.

When the Committee adjourned after spending the entire afternoon debating the amendments, Goldwater pulled Jim Locher aside.

"What are we going to do about this?" he asked his young aide.

"Senator, I'm not sure."

"Well, you spend the night thinking about what we can do to put pressure on them to cut this crap out."

The next morning when he arrived at work, Locher visited Goldwater's office and handed him a list of eight or nine measures, any one or two of which he said could signal to the Committee members and the Pentagon Goldwater's seriousness. They included halting all Pentagon requests for budget reprogrammings; stopping all planned budget hearings; freezing promotions as well as nominations for civilian appointments in the Pentagon; and halting the strategic home-porting plan, a pet project of John Lehman's that called for dispersing the fleet to numerous bases around the country to guard against a surprise nuclear strike by the Soviets. Home-porting also had the not inconsequential advantage of spreading Navy largess into the districts of far more members of Congress, thus exponentially expanding the service's political base during budget battles. Because many of the Committee members had proposed bases in their districts that would be affected by the plan, Goldwater suspected this measure might prove particularly effective. Last he had checked, there were no Navy bases in Arizona.

"That's great," Goldwater told Locher, then handed him back the list. "Do it."

"Which, sir?" Locher had asked, expecting Goldwater to choose two at most.

"Do them all. We're going to close down this committee until that reform bill is reported out. Until that time, I don't want another piece of paper moving out of this committee."

When the full Senate Armed Services Committee gathered later that morning, Goldwater read them the riot act.

"This committee is going to meet on this bill until we hear every amendment argued, and every emotional appeal is debated. And if this bill is the only thing this committee gets done this year, including the defense authorization, then it'll be worth it," Goldwater told his colleagues. If once the bill was reported out and the amendment tactics continued on the Senate floor, Goldwater added, then he promised to hold all other Committee action in abeyance until the bill passed the full Senate.

No one was going to bulldoze the powerful members of the Senate Armed Services Committee into voting one way or another on a revolutionary piece of legislation. There was no longer any question, however, of nicking it with amendments until it died the death of a thousand cuts. For the next two weeks the votes on each successive measure hovered around even, with Goldwater usually providing the critical swing vote.

Gradually, however, after countless hours of debate, and with the cries for relief beginning to sound from the Pentagon, the reform camp picked up another vote. And then another. When the reformers reached fifteen votes, the opposition collapsed. On May 7, 1986, the Senate voted 95–0 in support of the reorganization bill.

"Only Goldwater could produce this," one senator said from the floor as the Senate was deciding to name the bill after the distinguished gentleman from Arizona. "If anybody else had been the one who had been advocating this reorganization, every military man and woman at the Pentagon would have been down our backs as 'communist sympathizers.' "

Reflecting back on the past year as the Senate vote was recorded, Barry Goldwater felt that he had never had so much fun in all his life. He was eager to volunteer to anyone who asked that it was the best goddamned thing he had done in thirty-five years in the Senate.

As his colleagues on the floor rose in unison to pay tribute to that accomplishment, the crusty old warrior wiped at his eyes from his wheelchair. The man might have been right about anyone else trying to push something as radical as that reform package on the Pentagon, but Goldwater had noticed a funny thing. After receptions where generals would frequently bend his ear about how misguided the reforms were, a junior ranking aide would invariably come up in private and earnestly thank Goldwater for his reform efforts. They all had stories like that—Jim Locher, Arch Barrett, everyone who had joined the crusade. Far from thwarting the Pentagon or those in uniform, Goldwater felt at that moment as if he was keeping the true faith.

The House/Senate conference that convened behind the doors of S2407 in early September of 1986 was a study in contrasts to the tension-filled meeting chaired by Senator Tower less than two years earlier. While Congress was out for its August recess, Arch Barrett, Jim Locher, and their aides had worked sixteen-hour days, seven days a week, hammering out the final compromises on the Goldwater-Nichols Defense Reorganization Act. The legislation consumed more than nine hundred printed pages, but their work was nearly done.

The chairmanship of the conference had rotated back to the Senate, SASC chairman Barry Goldwater presiding. The House delegation had been trimmed down to a handful of representatives who knew the issues and supported the reforms. They included HASC chairman Les Aspin, who had been a driving if behind-the-scenes player pushing for Goldwater-Nichols. Though it was unusual for staff to sit at the conference table with the members of Congress, Arch Barrett occupied a place of honor beside Rep. Bill Nichols.

Barrett was explaining the house position on a certain measure when, in midsentence, he was startled by a loud *crack!* Looking up, he was staring into the glowering face of Goldwater, which was hovering over the cane the senator had just stamped on the floor.

"I think we've heard enough on this," Goldwater said. "The Senate is going to concede to the House on this measure." With that, Goldwater slowly panned left and right down the Senate side of the conference table. There were no dissenters.

The sense of urgency in the room was still very real. The conferees were all anxious to have Goldwater-Nichols in front of Ronald Reagan as quickly as possible, leaving them time to mount an override campaign before the holiday recess should the president veto the bill. Except for the provision to eliminate the JCS in favor of an independent advisory committee, the final bill was close to the recommendations contained in Locher's study, including the provisions for JCS reorganization that had always been central to the House Armed Services Committee's reforms.

Though the bill was complex beyond the understanding of all but Congress's most devoted defense experts, the unmistakable thrust was in the direction of more "jointness." The chairman of the Joint Chiefs, the only member not dual-hatted as chief of a military service, would become the principal uniformed adviser to the secretary of defense and the president. Commands to and requests from the unified CINCs were to be channeled through the chairman, essentially putting him directly in the operational chain of command.

The Joint Staff of well over a thousand officers was to be under the exclusive direction of the chairman, eliminating the reign of the iron majors, and representing a fundamental shift in power within the Pentagon from the massive service staffs to the chairman's Joint Staff. Service in a joint assignment, either on the Joint Staff or elsewhere, would be necessary for promotion to flag or general rank and thus a required stepping-stone for the services' best officers. A joint curriculum was to be established at each of the services' Command and Staff Colleges and War Colleges, and officers would be required to complete a joint-duty assignment following graduation.

The Pentagon's true warlords, the commanders in chief of the unified commands, meanwhile, were to have broader authority over their subordinate commands and joint task forces. A four-star vice chairman would also be added as a sixth member of the JCS, both to assist the chairman and to represent the voices of the CINCs in internal discussions on budget matters and resource allocation.

Congress's triumph with Goldwater-Nichols was also key in breaking down the services' ironclad resistance to the establishment of two new unified commands. The legislation overrode the restrictions against a joint transportation command that had been placed into law years earlier to thwart David Jones's attempts to integrate global air, land, and sea assets under a single commander. In 1987, Transportation Command (TransCom) was established on a direct recommendation of the Packard Commission report. Its mission: coordinate strategic deployments, merging the Air Force's Military Airlift Command (MAC), the Navy's Military Sealift Command, and the Army's Military Traffic Management Command under a four-star Air Force general, who was also dual-hatted as the commander of MAC. Reformers had argued the need for such a coordinated approach to mobilizations since the disastrous Nifty Nugget exercise of 1978 and the helter-skelter deployments to Grenada.

As a follow-on to his work on Goldwater-Nichols, Jim Locher would be instructed by Senators William Cohen and Sam Nunn to study the establishment of a unified command to coordinate the training and equipping of the services' special-operations forces. Such a coordinated approach had been strongly advocated by former Army chief Gen. Shy Meyer and others ever since the debacle at Desert One.

Ever reluctant to cede control of their own forces, however, the services had strongly opposed the idea. In 1987, Special Operations Command was created, to be headed by a four-star Army general. In an unusual move, Congress bestowed on the commander budget-approval authority independent of the services. The new position of assistant secretary of defense for Special Operations and Low Intensity Conflict was also established in the Pentagon, a post that would later be held by Jim Locher himself.

After the Packard Commission had released its report in June, the danger of a Reagan veto of Goldwater-Nichols was diminished. As expected, Packard had endorsed their key reorganization proposals, while suggesting changes that would put the services' vast acquisition bureaucracies under more direct oversight of the Office of the Secretary of Defense and a newly created undersecretary of defense for acquisition. Many observers saw that as a veiled criticism of Weinberger's laissez-faire style in managing the services' acquisition systems.

In a direct rebuttal of the practice of "concurrency" then so prevalent in defense acquisition, Packard also strongly promoted a slower "fly before you buy" approach that called on the services to carefully prototype new weapons, testing them and working out problems and inadequacies before an all-but-irreversible decision to begin production was made. Though the policy was hardly a guarantee against "waste, fraud, and abuse" or teething problems in new weapons, it did promise to slow somewhat the feverish pace of weapons development that had characterized the early 1980s.

In many ways, Reagan's endorsement of the Packard Commission and Congress's passage of Goldwater-Nichols were the high-water mark of an activist era of both unprecedented defense spending and pioneering defense reform. Unquestionably, however, the era was passing, as was the rare consensus between the White House and Congress that the country's military forces needed radical revitalization. By the end of 1986 much of the job seemed done, and that same year the tide of defense spending began a steady reversal that would continue well into the next decade.

Many of the key players also soon passed from the national scene. John Lehman would retire early in 1987. Lehman's farewell dinner would be hosted by Marine Corps commandant Gen. P. X. Kelley, the man who had helped him lead the opposition to the Goldwater-Nichols reforms. Tellingly, the top admirals of the U.S. Navy all declined their invitations to Lehman's farewell. P. X. Kelley would retire the same year, as would Caspar Weinberger. Barry Goldwater retired shortly after passage of the legislation bearing his name. Bill Nichols would die of a heart attack in 1989. It would be years before the country or the participants themselves fully understood exactly what had been purchased with their arduous labor and the sacrifice of national treasure that they had overseen.

By the time Arch Barrett, Jim Locher, and a few key aides had finished working out the final details of Goldwater-Nichols, it was nearly midnight on a Friday night in mid-September 1986. The members of Congress had long since gone home. The staff were working in the Rayburn House Office Building and had already arranged to have a friend in the clerk's office in the Capitol return to officially accept the bill that night. After countless months of working practically around the clock on the legislation, they were numb with exhaustion.

"Well, I guess that's it," Barrett said, gathering up the massive document. "You guys don't have to stay. I'll just walk this over to the clerk."

Jim Locher glanced over at his aide Rick Finn, who had been in on the effort from the beginning. He in turn looked at the House and Senate legislative counsels who had helped draft the bill. All of them shook their heads and rose as a group to escort the landmark Goldwater-Nichols legislation over to the Capitol en masse.

Once again the halls were deserted, and their footsteps echoed hollowly down the passageways. Each was lost in his thoughts. All of them wondered how the myriad and in some cases quite radical ideas they were about to commit into law would actually play out in practice, knowing that the stakes could be the future security of the country and the lives of American service members.

As the group handed over Goldwater-Nichols to the clerk, they each felt that they were witnessing a historic moment. Barrett and Locher exchanged glances, and quiet congratulations were offered. Maybe it was the deserted Capitol building, or maybe it was just the exhaustion. Yet at that moment, there was an undeniable feeling that the kitchen staff had just staged a coup, and no one in the palace had yet awakened to the fact.

32: Reveille 1984–86

DRIVING his Subaru south down Interstate 5, a college fraternity brother from the University of Washington at his side, Sean McCaffrey studied the wide-open expanse of the Pacific Northwest. Away to the right the snow-capped Olympic Mountains seemed to spring out of the bottomless blue well of Puget Sound, and far to the southeast the peaks of the Cascades were visible. After four years in West Germany and another at Carlisle, Pennsylvania, where his father attended the Army War College for a year, the western

United States seemed somehow able to shrink people and even cities into an altogether different perspective.

Sean was taking his fraternity brother to Fort Lewis for one of his mom's home-cooked meals. Having traveled around the world and lived within the shadow of an Army base practically his entire life, Sean McCaffrey knew that he was something of an oddity at his fraternity and on the University of Washington campus. Washington State in general was politically liberal, and Sean frequently heard his friends tell stories of how their fathers had avoided Vietnam and the draft. Some of their parents even still smoked pot.

"Have you ever been on an Army post?" Sean asked his fraternity brother as they neared Fort Lewis.

"Never."

"Well, most of it's buried underground on account of the three or four air-raid drills they have every day."

"No shit?"

"Yeah," said Sean, wondering how far to take it. "And they're gonna issue you a uniform at the gate."

"Are you serious?"

"Sure, and you'll have to carry a sidearm while you're on base." Sean glanced over and saw that his friend was actually buying it all. Holy Christ! Finally Sean couldn't help but crack up. Having grown up in the Army, he had just assumed that the country with arguably the most powerful armed forces in the world would have more than just a passing knowledge of it. Yet as far as he could tell, the average American knew absolutely nothing about the military. That seemed like either a blessing or a curse, though Sean Mc-Caffrey wasn't sure which.

Finishing school on his ROTC scholarship, Sean knew he would be committing to four years in the Army. The prospect didn't daunt him. While he might kid with his fraternity brothers about studying to be a pitchman for Victoria's Secret, in a way Sean felt as if he had joined the Army at birth. Already he had traveled farther and seen more of the world than practically anyone he knew at school.

Those long discussions around the dinner table while he was growing up had also left their mark, Sean sitting quietly after the dishes had been cleared and listening to his father's and grandfather's stories about far-flung postings and desperate battles. As he got older, Sean sensed an almost unspoken understanding between his grandfather and father that they would not exert any pressure on him to choose an Army career. Yet their lives had always seemed like great adventures full of heroic deeds to Sean, and privately he yearned for that sense of adventure in his own life.

When Sean and his fraternity brother arrived at Fort Lewis, Jill McCaffrey was obviously delighted to see them. Returning to the United States after four years in West Germany had been difficult on everyone, and especially Sean, who had been in his senior year in high school at the time. Practically the entire family had cried on the plane coming back from Europe. Her son was obviously happy at the University of Washington, however, and in truth Jill found herself feeling more comfortable in Washington than she had felt anywhere else in the United States for a very long time.

Part of it was meeting Sean's friends and seeing the other students when she and Barry visited the University of Washington campus. They seemed so normal. Compared to the angry and hostile students in the late 1960s and early 1970s, incited by Vietnam to hurl insults and worse at anyone connected with the military, the students in the 1980s seemed blessedly polite.

Whatever it was that Jill had discerned in the expressions of the civilians she met during and immediately after Vietnam—whether it was disgust or merely condescension toward anyone associated with the military—by the mid-1980s it was gone. Tentatively, Jill found herself reaching out beyond the tight-knit military fraternity, embracing the community beyond the gates of the Army post in a way she hadn't dared since the war. For the first time in more than a decade of self-imposed exile, Jill McCaffrey felt as if she was home again.

If Barry was reticent about encouraging Sean toward an Army career, a caution she knew he had inherited from his father, Jill McCaffrey believed that her son had always wanted to go into the service. Though not for everyone, it was a choice she could warmly support. When Sean had prepared to go off to college, Jill had thus given him a little motherly advice about choosing a potential wife. You're going to need an independent and strong-willed wife, cautioned Jill, because Army life will take some coping.

For the most part, Jill believed that the Army offered a wonderful lifestyle for a family. Even after all these years she still enjoyed the travel and sense of close-knit community, though increasingly she also enjoyed settling down during longer tours. That was in keeping with the Army's new policy, however, which stipulated at least thirty-month command tours for officers.

The Army had also been forced by necessity to pay far greater attention to its support system for families. In the decade since the draft had ended in 1973, for instance, the proportion of enlisted men in the Army who were married had nearly doubled from one-fourth to nearly one-half. Those married soldiers seemed much more mature to her than their bachelor counterparts who had hung out the windows shouting catcalls and whistling whenever Jill walked by back in Schweinfurt, West Germany. As far as Jill

McCaffrey was concerned, a lot of positive changes began taking place in the Army ranks as more and more soldiers got married.

Col. Barry McCaffrey had typically been working late in his office as the chief of staff of the 9th Infantry Division when the new division commander walked in the door in civilian clothes shaking his head. Maj. Gen. Robert RisCassi had been biding time until his official change-of-command ceremony, getting the feel of Fort Lewis. Barry knew that RisCassi had spent a few years away from front-line troops since serving as an assistant division commander in Europe in the late 1970s.

"The damnedest thing just happened to me," RisCassi said, obviously bemused.

"Yes, sir?"

"On my way here I passed by a group of young soldiers in my civilian clothes. And without having any idea who I was they all came to attention, saluted, and said, 'Good evening, sir.' Can you believe that?"

RisCassi's incredulity at discovering a group of young soldiers who would politely salute someone just because he was older and looked as if he was probably an officer was understandable. Sometimes McCaffrey himself found the rapid turnaround in the Army's recruitment fortunes dizzying. He had first heard about it from a Recruiting Command briefer while at the Army War College in 1981, when "Be All You Can Be" was saturating the airwaves, the new pay increases and educational packages were taking hold, and Pres. Ronald Reagan seemed to appear in photo opportunities with the military at every opportunity, the commander in chief taking such obvious pride in whipping off salutes to his troops.

McCaffrey had seen the figures, but still hadn't believed that recruiting could turn around so fast until he had come to the 9th Infantry Division. By the mid-1980s every field commander who had struggled during the 1970s just to man units knew the statistics, and they were staggering.

Compared to the last three years of the 1970s, for instance, the proportion of new recruits with at least a high school diploma had jumped from 62 to an unprecedented 85 percent by 1983, higher than the national average and more than ten percentage points higher than the Army's average level even during the draft. The CAT IVs, or those who scored below average on the Armed Forces Qualification Test, had registered a corresponding drop from 44 to 20 percent, while those who scored above average had risen from 18 to 31 percent.

McCaffrey and other front-line commanders were well aware that the turnaround had occurred in the nick of time. The Army was embarked on one of the most ambitious modernization efforts in its history. Bolstered by the rapid rise in the defense budget, the service was now in the midst of fielding or nearing introduction of the new M-1 Abrams tank, the Bradley Fighting Vehicle, and the Apache and the Blackhawk helicopters. Together these laser-guided and computer-driven weapons represented a dramatic leap from the electromechanical age to one dominated by the microchip. While far more lethal than their predecessors, these weapons would also demand a new level of technological sophistication that was totally at odds with an army whose ranks and efforts were dominated by low-aptitude soldiers requiring constant remedial training.

A collateral benefit of the rapid rise in the quality of recruits was also immediately applauded by commanders in the field: soldiers with high school diplomas and higher aptitudes were more likely not only to successfully complete their initial tours, but also to reenlist once they were completed. That cut down on training demands and led to a force whose experience level was steadily rising. At a relatively constant end strength, for instance, the Army had to recruit 157,000 new volunteers in 1980. In 1982 and 1983, that number dropped to 117,000 and 118,000, respectively. If those retention trends held, the Army of the 1980s was destined to become older, gaining in both maturity and experience through the decade. It would in fact resemble what the framers of the all-volunteer force had originally envisioned more than a decade earlier: a truly professional army.

Though the significance of those improvements was obvious even on Recruiting Command flow charts, the true impact was most dramatic in the field. In five years, Barry McCaffrey had gone from a battalion commander in West Germany who was forced to limit his hurdles to reenlistment to felony convictions, to a brigade commander at Fort Lewis who was threatened with lawsuits and inspector-general investigations for being too stringent in setting standards for reenlistments. With so many bright, motivated soldiers suddenly eager to reenlist, Barry simply saw no reason to keep soldiers whose records were studded with Article 15s for barroom brawls or repeated drug convictions.

During division parades at the 9th Infantry Division, McCaffrey loved to stand on the parade grounds and watch as the soldiers marched by in lockstep. In a sense it recalled similar formations on the Plain at West Point when he was a young cadet. Watching the troops wheel in unison to the marching band, their starched colors flapping in the wind, he wondered what it was about these fifteen thousand soldiers that distinguished them from a group the same size five years earlier. Instead of the mournful sound of taps that seemed to pervade the "hollow force" days, the Army was once again blowing reveille for the sense of purpose and pride so obviously back in its step.

McCaffrey knew that stunning reversal had to do with discipline and trust and the culture both within the Army and in society at large. Barry McCaffrey also had a keen sense during those moments of how many long years it had truly taken the Army to claw itself back to this point. But why now?

That was the question that perplexed many officers, serving as the grist for frequent discussions between McCaffrey and his colleagues. Perhaps it was in the dynamics of organizations as large as the Army that they sometimes seemed to move like a glacier, and at other times like an avalanche. Yet what had happened to so dramatically alter the Army's recruitment fortunes in the space of just a couple of years? Nearly everyone had an opinion.

Some officers credited the rapid rise in military pay as well as the defense budget, and Pres. Ronald Reagan for helping bring overt patriotism out of the closet where it seemed to have been shut for so much of the 1970s. According to this argument, that proved to those in uniform that the country valued them once again.

Others pointed to the increase in educational benefits, logically concluding that the best way to attract smart kids was to equate the Army with incentives to higher education. Recently, Congress had enacted the Montgomery GI Bill, rewarding enlistees for their initial three-year tour of duty with $10,800 toward a college education. Still others credited Recruiting Command under Max Thurman for its more scientific approach to recruiting and for the "Be All You Can Be" commercials, which were fundamentally altering the Army's image.

Barry McCaffrey believed all of those things were important, yet suspected that even more elemental forces were at work. The sheer speed of their reversal of fortune suggested as much. Barry thought back to the dismal days following Vietnam, and his father's assurances that the pendulum had always swung thus for the Army after a war, in victory as well as defeat. While sometimes Barry could scarcely see a way out from the depths that were plumbed after Vietnam, William McCaffrey had always been serenely confident that the American people would help the service right itself in time.

After staring into the abyss of Desert One and its humiliation at the hands of the Iranian mullahs, the country was once again confronting an obviously hostile world with renewed confidence, and unabashedly embracing the military and such core ideals as patriotism. Barry reasoned that the pendulum had finally swung fully in the Army's favor once again.

One of the friends that Barry discussed the issue with, as well as the distance the Army still had to travel, was Col. James "Binney" Peay III, who commanded 9th Infantry Division's artillery while Barry commanded the division's 3rd Brigade. A former senior military aide to JCS chairman David Jones, Binney Peay seemed almost the opposite of Barry. Where Barry was by nature outgoing and gregarious, full of humorous or snide quips, Binney Peay seemed reserved and thoughtfully introspective, though his sometimes aloof demeanor masked a relentless inner drive. Certainly they seemed like unlikely friends.

Like McCaffrey, however, Peay had also served two combat tours in Vietnam, the first as an artillery battery commander with the 4th Infantry Division during the bloody Tet Offensive of 1968. Shortly after returning from his first tour Peay had deployed to the streets of Chicago during the violent demonstrations against the war at the Democratic National Convention. Later in 1972, he was with one of the last units of the 1st Cavalry Division to withdraw from Saigon, knowing that their cause was lost. Though Barry knew those experiences affected Peay deeply, through it all Binney Peay kept his belief that most Americans had never really broken faith with the military, but rather had gone silent in confusion over so many of the tumultuous events of the late 1960s and 1970s. Thus he tended to view the early 1980s as the country rediscovering its voice.

What McCaffrey and Peay spent most of their time talking about, however, was upcoming war games scheduled for units of the 9th Infantry Division at the Army's National Training Center (NTC), which had opened for business in 1982. The next year, Training and Doctrine Command had released the Army's long-awaited new doctrine, commonly referred to as Air-Land Battle. It called for fast-paced, offense-oriented maneuver warfare coordinated with deep strikes to defeat a superior enemy at the front and counter his echelon forces. With the 9th Infantry Division acting as a high-tech testbed for the concept of mobility and agility, and its reputation as an elite new division led by some of the Army's most aggressive officers, it was considered a prime candidate to test the new tenets of AirLand Battle.

In many ways the 1982 version of FM 100-5, the official designation of the Army's doctrine manual, was a direct repudiation of the dogged, "pile on and slug it out" doctrine of attrition that had dominated Army thinking when McCaffrey joined nearly two decades earlier. Instead, the 1982 version of FM 100-5 admonished commanders to "move fast, strike hard and finish rapidly." Above all it capitalized on what were seen as American strengths in individual initiative and technology as represented by a new generation of weapons, filtering into the Army arsenal, that could move faster and shoot farther than their Soviet counterparts.

"Agility—the ability of friendly forces to act faster than the enemy—is the first prerequisite for seizing and holding the initiative . . . ," stated the Air-Land Battle document. "This must be done repeatedly so that by the time the enemy reacts to one action, another has already taken place, disrupting his plans. . . . It is this process of successive concentration against locally weaker or unprepared enemy forces which enables smaller forces to disorient, fragment, and eventually defeat much larger opposing enemy formations."

Officially begun in 1976 as a letter by retired general William DePuy soliciting input for the doctrinal equivalent of a "pot of French soup," AirLand Battle was galvanizing the Army. The revolution it clearly represented dominated conversation in officers' clubs and barracks throughout the service. To McCaffrey and Peay and other officers of their generation, it seemed as if for the first time since Vietnam, the Army, too, was talking about fighting again. And for the first time, soldiers such as Barry McCaffrey and Binney Peay were not only talking about the challenges of fast-paced maneuver warfare, but they also had a revolutionary new kind of training ground on which to test those concepts and themselves.

33: National Training Center 1985–86

WITH only a sliver of moon, night in the high desert is pitch-dark and surprisingly cold. The vastness that stretches out for a thousand square miles can swallow an entire brigade-sized task force of twenty-five hundred men and more than seven hundred vehicles with hardly a trace. Whole units were known to get lost; it happened all the time. Yet hidden at the bottom of a shallow gully, where long-forgotten waters had carved a trough in the cracked desert floor, the occupants of a scout jeep knew exactly where they were. That was something the Soviet-style Opposing Force, which called the National Training Center home, prided itself on. One of many things.

The "OPFOR" called themselves the 32nd Guards Motorized Rifle Regiment in Warsaw Pact parlance, and their scouts were there to identify the defensive positions of the visiting Blue Force before their main-force regimental attack, which both sides knew would be coming at first light. Already they had passed through the Blue Force security perimeter around 0300 in the morning, the guards obviously asleep. That wasn't unusual. With the training rotation nearing the end of the two-week mark, the fatigue that had begun weighing on the Blue Force the very first day was now an elephant's foot. They needed to enforce stricter sleep schedules.

In the distance the scouts heard the unmistakable gnashing of approaching engines, the sound carrying clearly in the quiet desert night. One of them raised a pair of night-vision goggles to his eyes while the other started the scout vehicle's engine. Time to leave the Blue Force with one more lesson to ponder on their way home.

Through the night-observation device the desert sprang into an almost liquid green relief, like sunlight filtered to the bottom of a deep lagoon. The dark contours of boulders and depressions took shape against luminous desert sands. An armored convoy was just visible coming down the road they were watching, a Blue Force unit shifting position for tomorrow morning's attack.

The stunt they were about to pull was dangerous, but if it didn't get them "killed" or captured, it could make the scouts heroes of the next day's battle. If they were taken out, another OPFOR scout team was nearby, the importance of having redundant eyes on the battlefield one of the patented tricks of a trade the OPFOR was mastering like no other unit in the U.S. Army.

Waiting for enough tanks and trucks to go by to kick up a sufficiently dense cloud of dust, the OPFOR scouts gunned their vehicle quickly into a break in the line and simply joined the convoy. While one drove, the other stared through the night-observation device. By carefully noting the detours the convoy took and the terrain, the OPFOR scout was able to note likely minefields and promising avenues of approach for the next day's attack. Some of the barriers erected by the Blue Force combat engineers looked hastily thrown together and ineffective, a point the scouts relayed. Another sure sign of fatigue.

As the convoy slowed, the lead vehicles began to disperse, and the scout with the night-vision goggles realized that the hulking shapes he had seen all around were not large boulders, but rather massive vehicles and tents under camouflage netting. The night goggles, which were sensitive to heat, turned hot air into flickering flames that appeared at the top of one particularly large tent, with other bright spots all around its edges. Stovepipes and generators. They had stumbled onto the Blue Force's Tactical Operations Center, or TOC, its command-and-control nerve center. A well-placed artillery or commando strike to lead off tomorrow's attack would decapitate the Blue Force. In the dust cloud created as the convoy braked and dispersed, the OPFOR scout vehicle veered off into the night, the scout speaking into his radio all the while.

A few hours later the scout vehicle sat atop a bluff overlooking the Blue Force positions in "Death Valley." Behind them the ridge line was tipped with fiery magenta. So as not to chance giving away their position, the OPFOR scouts had taken the windshield out of their vehicle where it might have refracted the morning sun, another signature bit of fieldcraft. Already lights were blinking in the valley below, part of the MILES laser-engagement system pioneered by Gen. Paul Gorman. The flashing lights indicated a Blue Force vehicle that had been "destroyed" by enemy saboteurs the night before. Time to sit back and enjoy another spectacular sunrise in the high desert.

Their binoculars were trained on a huge smoke cloud that hung draped over the desert floor, laid there to simulate a smoke barrage by the observer-controllers who acted as referees at the National Training Center. On a "deliberate attack," the OPFOR liked to get in close before giving away its main avenue of attack, probe the soft spots in the Blue Force defenses identified by the scouts, and break through to their rear before they had a chance to regroup.

Both scouts saw it even before the crackle of gunfire reached them from the valley floor. The hazy shapes of tanks that had been modified by fiberglass to closely resemble Soviet armor began appearing through the smoke cloud, spewing dust trails, their hulking shapes somehow turned into something graceful and fearsome by motion and speed. Col. Jerrell Hamby was leading another full-up regimental attack of the "32nd Guards," more than 170 vehicles bearing down with their turrets wagging back and forth like the snouts of hunting dogs hot on a scent. In the after-action reviews that followed every battle, the Blue Force commanders always said that the full-up regimental attack was a significant emotional event.

"What were you thinking at this point?" the observer-controller asked at the after-action review (AAR) the morning after the battle. This self-discovery technique was increasingly being adopted at the NTC to avoid the judgmental finger pointing that had dominated early after-action reviews. The Blue Force commander sat tight-lipped at the head of his officers nevertheless, the embarrassing details written on a battle review board for all to see. He wanted desperately not to believe what he was hearing, and not to have to hear about it in front of his own men.

People had gotten lost. He had left his tactical operations center unprotected. The time it had taken the brigade staff to translate orders into battle plans and filter them down to the front-line units had far exceeded the recommended ratios in the manual. Thus the ranks were confused about the commander's intent, the invisible will of leadership needed to guide the many disparate elements of a combat maneuver brigade in cohesive action. The result was another rout by the vaunted OPFOR.

The person most directly responsible for dishing out those hard lessons was OPFOR commander Col. Jerrell E. Hamby, who was fast becoming the most feared man in the Mojave Desert. Visiting commanders had been known to put a bounty on his head, offering leave to any soldier who took out his command tank during an engagement. Hamby had molded the Army's first-ever dedicated aggressor force into the ultimate sparring partner. The esprit de corps of his crack 32nd Guards was already legendary within the Army.

Hamby had served as an enlisted Marine in Korea and, after earning a commission in the Army, had gone on to become a decorated Army combat soldier in Vietnam, where he was awarded the Silver and Bronze Stars for valor, as well as a Purple Heart. That same dedication Hamby had once shown to fighting the enemy had been directed toward providing a top-notch opponent for units visiting the NTC. Tragically, Hamby would later be killed in a training accident at the NTC, and a memorial in his honor still stands on a high desert bluff overlooking the training grounds he once roamed.

Besides being steeped in Soviet fighting doctrine at the OPFOR academy, the OPFOR soldiers carried Soviet weapons and wore Soviet-style uniforms with signature black berets and red stars. Indeed, since the OPFOR practically lived in the field, putting as many as fifteen times the miles on their tanks as the typical Army unit, many observers suspected they were the best Soviet-style motorized rifle regiment *in the world*. Certainly the originals didn't benefit from the level of realistic training that was the reason for being of Col. Jerrell Hamby's desert rats. And in contrast to visiting units, who had never operated over the vast distances at the NTC, the OPFOR fought each battle on its home field.

The charter of the OPFOR at the National Training Center was simple: Find any structural weakness in a visiting Blue Force unit and pry into that fissure relentlessly until you either crack the brigade wide open or the Blue Force patches up the problem. If "the enemy" hasn't paid enough attention to countering your reconnaissance forces, or his guards are nodding off for lack of sleep discipline, make him pay. If he is unaccustomed to the vast distances at the NTC and thus leaves his logistics lines exposed, make him pay.

If his casualty evacuation system is weak or his maintenance turnaround times slow, make him pay, and pay and pay. It might as well have been an OPFOR mantra.

The confidence level of Blue Force commanders at the NTC suffered noticeably from those continual debits. Indeed, for all the self-discovery techniques meant to soften the blow, what they actually discovered, indeed what virtually every unit that had visited the NTC had confronted, was undeniable evidence that they were not as good as they thought. In many cases, the preponderance of the evidence indicated that the units were not very good at all.

One of the earliest units to have rotated through the NTC, for instance, was a battalion of the 4th Infantry Division (Mechanized), from Fort Carson, Colorado. Observing that exercise was the assistant division commander for operations and training, Brig. Gen. Colin Powell. Confident that one of his division's hottest battalions would give the Opposing Force all it could handle, Powell had stood appalled as they were routed time and again. Pressed for details after his return on how the 4th Infantry Division had fared in the desert, an obviously humbled Powell would reply succinctly, "We stepped on our foreskins."

Watching the image it had held of itself wither in the unforgiving crucible of the NTC, the Army predictably went through a stage of denial and disbelief. Some commanding generals simply accused their officers of incompetence. After a typically dismal rotation of a brigade from the 2nd Armored Division, both battalion commanders were summarily relieved of command upon their return. Others followed, until word got out in the officer corps that a two-week rotation at the National Training Center could prove a "bet your bars" proposition.

In truth, for all the strides the Army had made, it was still uncomfortable with self-criticism, and the lessons being force-fed to units out in the high desert were apt to make anyone testy. The level of animosity in the after-action reviews in those early rotations was thus often palpable. Actual fistfights between the visiting units and the OPFOR were not unheard of out in the desert. Though the Army had lost the arrogance of the perennial winner in Vietnam, it had yet to fully shake the last vestiges of the "zero defects" mentality that admitted no mistakes, and that was totally at odds with the reality units were experiencing at the NTC.

Initially, the handpicked observer-controllers—who were meant to act as referees as well as the mentors and institutional memory at the NTC—aggravated the problem. Accustomed to the old Army Training Test, where evaluators simply gave units one-way critiques of their performance, they were notorious for brutalizing the units who stumbled through early rotations at the NTC. That only tended to make already defensive commanders even more reticent to admit their mistakes, however, and the trainers at NTC began realizing that if the commander was unwilling to honestly confront his unit's mistakes and obvious faults, junior officers were certainly not going to step forward.

Eventually, a unit's own chain of command was made primarily responsible for critiquing its performance, and no one else would sit in judgment. A hard rule was also established that units were not to be rated or compared to one another, and commanders at the NTC fought in Congress to continue to use the training ground to test the readiness of Army units. With roughly nine out of ten units being badly mauled by the OPFOR, it became increasingly apparent that whatever weaknesses were being revealed by this revolutionary new training, they were pervasive throughout the entire Army.

Observer-controllers began to see themselves as mentors more than judges, there primarily to prod learning along. "What were you thinking here?" Thus the after-action reviews began to take on the feel of a group therapy session for a somewhat dysfunctional family, with junior officers increasingly questioning the decisions and actions of their superiors that had just gotten them destroyed on the battlefield.

Though they did not yet realize it, that willingness of junior officers to openly question their superiors, and of superior officers to admit mistakes in front of their subordinates, was beginning to fundamentally change the culture of the Army. An organization that would once have considered such behavior little short of insubordination began to encourage self-criticism in an effort to get at the truth. Officers who thrived in that environment were those who rededicated themselves to learning their craft, who liked to get down and mix it up with the troops intellectually, and who led from the front physically. Others had reason to fear the National Training Center.

If many officers were initially surprised that the free-play, force-on-force training exercises conducted at the NTC revealed so many cracks in their armor, it was the same painful lesson hammered home in the initial months of past wars, when at places such as Kasserine Pass in North Africa and the Ia Drang Valley in Vietnam the Army paid for its unpreparedness in blood. At the NTC the coin for that enlightenment was not carnage, but a certain lost bravado.

As the buses carrying the soldiers of the 9th Infantry Division passed through Barstow, California, a desert way station roughly midway between Los Angeles and Las Vegas and all the way to nowhere, Barry McCaffrey and Binney

Peay knew that the next few weeks would come as close to actual combat as many of their troops had ever experienced. An entire generation of junior officers and NCOs had come of age in the decade since the last Army troops withdrew from Vietnam.

Most of the soldiers stared longingly out the window at the assorted taco stands and windowless honky-tonk bars of Barstow, ripe with the promise of dark booths and cold beer. At its essence a soldier's life is about learning to savor the everyday things that average citizens take for granted—dry socks, a lover's touch, falling asleep on the couch in front of the TV. Already many of them sensed that after the next twenty days in the desert, they would walk across broken glass for a burrito and cold beer.

They were on the final, thirty-five-mile stretch of blacktop that dead-ended at Painted Rocks, a pile of boulders outside the gates of Fort Irwin where visiting armored units had painted their insignia going back to the tankers of Gen. George Patton's 4th Armored Division, which made the California desert its last stop before North Africa. The buses passed lonely gas stations hawking "genuine" Indian artifacts. Indeed Fort Irwin had something of the feel of an old frontier outpost. It was totally isolated, surrounded by hostile desert, and if there were no Indians roaming the territory, there damn sure was Hamby and his vaunted OPFOR.

Col. Barry McCaffrey had thought long and hard about the OPFOR. As the buses pulled into the Dust Bowl, where his units would spend three days requisitioning much of their equipment for the exercise, McCaffrey wondered again if he had overlooked anything. They had spent weeks preparing, studying the scenario for going to war that the NTC had drawn up to put their slice of the battle into the context of a larger conflict, poring over the fighting manuals, studying the Soviet doctrine that drove OPFOR operations.

The Soviet's doctrine of massing tank echelons was effective but unimaginative, and McCaffrey felt their centralized command-and-control system was a serious weakness. In that sense, he was convinced that the OPFOR's success had more to do with expert execution than brilliant tactics. As a test bed for high-mobility warfare, his 3rd Brigade of the 9th Infantry Division was there specifically to test whether the Army's new AirLand Battle could counter those Soviet blunt-force tactics with speed and agility, and the technology to see farther and strike deeper behind the front lines than the enemy. Compared to typical armor units, for instance, the 3rd Brigade had the advantage of a significantly beefed-up command-and-communications system and night-vision capability. It also had "remotely piloted vehicles," small unmanned reconnaissance airplanes used for seeing deep behind enemy lines.

Walking among his men during preparations in the Dust Bowl, McCaffrey found them sky-high. Of course some had forgotten to leave paychecks with their wives or to pay their bills, but his junior officers would have to cope with those real-world problems in an actual deployment. In truth McCaffrey's own intensity was the topic of much discussion. Anyone who rises to the brigade command level in the Army is nearly guaranteed to be a driven, type A personality, and Barry McCaffrey definitely qualified. McCaffrey was an operator at heart, and if a lever was around, he could be counted on to pull it. The sense of purpose and drive that had awakened in him as far back as his earliest days in the Army with the 82nd Airborne had become an overriding trait.

McCaffrey might not be the commander you'd choose to have to impress during a readiness inspection at home base, but few were more likely to give OPFOR commander Col. Jerrell Hamby a run for his money. Because this represented a special rotation to test the concepts of AirLand Battle, everyone also realized that some of the Army's most senior generals would be observing it from the bluffs that rimmed the desert.

Not surprisingly, preparation for this exercise had been intense. Nothing focused the mind of a unit and intensified home-based preparation like the challenge of a visit to the NTC to match up against the OPFOR. Aggressive brigade commanders had been known to covet assignments simply because they would include a rotation at the NTC. In the months prior to deploying to Fort Irwin, units typically spent weeks in the field honing the various pieces of the combat-arms puzzle that they would attempt to assemble as a brigade-sized whole in the vast reaches of the NTC. Victory dinners were held where troops performed skits depicting them walloping a hapless OPFOR.

Much of the time in the Dust Bowl was spent "bore sighting," or carefully calibrating the MILES weapons scoring system. The brainchild of Gen. Paul Gorman, MILES was the basis for the suspension of disbelief at the NTC. Every weapon had one of the MILES laser transmitters clamped to its barrel, coded to correctly reflect its range and lethality against a range of weapons. A complete weapons hierarchy was keyed into MILES, so that a soldier firing a machine gun, for instance, could not take out a tank.

Even the probability-of-kill of such weapons as hand-held Dragon antitank missiles could be keyed into the system for added realism. Whenever a blank round was fired from a weapon bearing MILES, the noise triggered the transmitter, which sent its pulse downrange to the receptors that adorned every soldier and vehicle. A high whine, accompanied on vehicles by a blinking light, indicated that for someone the battle was over. At that point, only an observer-controller could rekey the system, putting the system or the soldier back into the game for the next battle.

Nor did the detailed realism stop there. To keep pace with the more fluid operations under AirLand Battle, the 3rd Brigade had reconfigured its separate logistics units handling medical, supply, and maintenance into a single entity. McCaffrey knew that for the first time, his logisticians would be operating in a tactical "war zone" at the NTC. This piece of the puzzle was little stressed in most home-based training. If they went on the attack, the support commander would have to keep up and plan for the increased fuel that would be consumed. Defense would mean a shift in their needs toward greater stocks of ammunition and barrier equipment. If his tanks broke down and the support unit couldn't quickly get them back into the battle, McCaffrey would have to face the three-to-one odds of the OPFOR regimental onslaught shorthanded. And if the OPFOR broke through his lines and caught a critical supply convoy by surprise, the battle could be over before it started.

While visiting units were busy putting the finishing touches on their preparations in the Dust Bowl, the OPFOR liked to do a regimental pass and review, give the Blue Force something to think about before they took off for the unknown recesses of the desert. This was their turf, and they wanted to let the visitors know it. It was time for the games to begin. McCaffrey figured they were ready.

Lima Lima Michael Foxtrot. Lost like a motherfucker. It had been more than twelve hours since 3rd Brigade had heard from one of its scout platoon leaders, and without that input they were temporarily blinded. Up to that point Barry McCaffrey felt that for the better part of the exercise they had fought well against the OPFOR, many engagements ending in a virtual standoff. The expanded night-vision capability had helped them counter the enemy's reconnaissance forces and increase the tempo of their operations, and his brigade's ability to see deeper and move faster had led to a number of high-speed flanking maneuvers that had succeeded in keeping the OPFOR's main force off-balance.

Always they aimed to avoid direct confrontations, hit the enemy where he wasn't concentrating or expecting an attack. Through it all McCaffrey's confidence in the Army's new AirLand Battle doctrine had steadily grown. It allowed them to seize the initiative and innovate, something McCaffrey felt played to American strengths. If things went well, they could use AirLand Battle to counterbalance the clumsy weight of superior Soviet forces, turning it against them with jujitsu.

But now things were not going well. McCaffrey tried to clear his head of the fatigue. It had grown every moment since they'd left Fort Irwin for the ranges more than a week and a half ago, a black hole of weariness seemingly capable of bending time itself, slowing everything down until even getting out a complete sentence was sometimes an effort. At the NTC, it was as pernicious an opponent as the OPFOR itself.

In isolation every task of a combat-maneuver brigade seemed relatively straightforward. Putting it all together on a precisely sequenced timetable, trying to coax coordinated action and timing out of widely dispersed recon elements, artillery batteries, forward armored units, aircraft, logistics support, all under the haze of sleep deprivation with the OPFOR dogging every move you made, it just seemed . . . If only he could get a moment to himself to gather his thoughts . . .

What was he thinking about now? It seemed like every other minute the observer-controller who was shadowing him like an alter ego wanted to know. While the O/C's observations were often helpful, he was beginning to get on McCaffrey's nerves. The thought he couldn't escape was that without input from his lost scout platoon, he couldn't direct Binney Peay's artillery batteries to blunt a possible attack. McCaffrey also knew that the fast-paced, swirling warfare that they were practicing had presented considerable challenges to Peay's artillery, whose situational awareness of the battlefield had to be precise.

Coordinating all of those elements with the Air Force, which would be responsible for holding enemy echelons down in the rear while armored forces probed for his center of gravity up front, was also trickier than it had seemed in the manuals. That was the "air" half of AirLand Battle, and it was already obvious that the new doctrine would require even closer coordination with the Air Force than was traditional for more stationary ground forces that fought mainly during the day. Observer-controllers told stories from the live-fire range, for instance, where commanders had correctly called in successive strikes on advancing targets first by air and then artillery, and a one-minute lapse in the schedule nearly had Air Force F-16 pilots flying through a "friendly" artillery barrage.

Suddenly the command radio network came alive, the intricate algorithm that dictated who could talk to whom temporarily obliterated by scores of nervous voices all speaking at once. McCaffrey's light attack battalion had blindly stumbled into the main force of the 32nd Guards in Death Valley. The battle damage assessments shouted over the net seemed wildly exaggerated at first, which was not unusual in the heat of battle. The thing to do was to fall back and regroup. One by one, however, the voices dropped off the net as their tanks and vehicles were taken out by the OPFOR.

In twenty minutes it was all over. An entire battalion of roughly six hundred men had been wiped out, just like that. It was a lesson that McCaffrey and the 3rd Brigade would not likely forget. The fast-paced maneuver warfare promoted in AirLand Battle was effective but risky. If synchronization broke down or any element collapsed, especially situational awareness and the ability to see the enemy deep on the battlefield, then it was just a way to get yourself killed twice as fast as before.

The tactical operations center was quiet as McCaffrey gathered up his charts and looked for his driver to take him to the after-action review. Though he despised losing and would let his men savor the taste, McCaffrey was philosophical. In the 3rd Brigade perhaps only he and Binney Peay and the handful of other veterans from Vietnam fully grasped the message of the National Training Center and thus understood its true worth. An army learned far more from its defeats than it ever did from victory.

At least one of the generals who sometimes stood on the bluffs of the NTC watching units experiment with AirLand Battle also understood that with its potential came commensurate risks. War was inherently a risky proposition, never more so than when troops were outnumbered. He had made that point at countless briefings and during lectures to nearly every Army War College class of the last four years. Gen. Donn Starry also understood, however, that historically the battle was won by the side that seized the initiative. What he saw at the NTC were units learning to do just that, and starting to believe in themselves in the process.

Ten years earlier, on a bluff not unlike the one on which he was now standing, Starry had first begun to comprehend that the old American style of warfare, based on the industrial-mobilization model of massed forces and brute-force annihilation, was essentially bankrupt. The vantage point then had been the Golan Heights, and the desert the battle-scarred Sinai in the wake of the 1973 Arab-Israeli war. The lesson, however, had held: the increasing lethality of modern weaponry and the necessity to fight outnumbered and win the first battle of any future war demanded a new style of warfare, something more deft and elegant, and ultimately more deadly. Something like what he was beginning to witness at the National Training Center.

After succeeding Gen. William DePuy as head of Training and Doctrine Command in 1977, when the controversy surrounding the new "active defense" fighting doctrine had been at full boil, Starry had initiated a second iteration of *Field Manual 100-5* almost immediately. In his mind the 1976 version of the doctrine was always meant as something of a stopgap measure, to teach commanders how to fight fluidly at the forward edge of a battle. The next edition had needed to address the deep counterattack and maneuver in an enemy's rear area.

One of those who had worked for him at TRADOC was Jack Galvin, who served as a deputy in charge of training after returning from Europe, where he had worked for Paul Gorman. The flashing lights in the valley Starry was observing were concrete testament to the worth of Gorman's brainchild, the MILES system. To write the new doctrinal manual, Starry had enlisted the services of a bright lieutenant colonel at the U.S. Army Command and General Staff College at Fort Leavenworth, Kansas, named Huba Wass de Czege. The result was the 1982 version of *FM 100-5*, or AirLand Battle doctrine.

If anything, the development of technology in the intervening years since the Yom Kippur War had reinforced the vision expounded in AirLand Battle. Starry knew from his time at the head of Training and Doctrine Command that the military was on the brink of developing "synthetic aperture" radars, originally designed for nuclear-weapons targeting, that if applied to conventional command-and-control systems could revolutionize ground warfare the way earlier radars had turned the tide for the Royal Air Force in the Battle of Britain and forever changed air warfare. This key piece of the AirLand Battle puzzle, the ability to bring the extended battlefield into clear focus for the tactical commander, was the closest thing to a magic bullet Starry had ever seen. Victory in the next conflict might well go to the side who won the information war.

Starry's former TRADOC boss Gen. William DePuy had always said that it took roughly ten years to develop a new weapons system or doctrine, and another five to get them comfortably out into the hands of soldiers in the field. As in so many things, the tough old general—whom Starry considered perhaps the greatest soldier of his time—was close to the mark. The problem was that none of those charged with shepherding the Army through the changes lasted that long. Starry was himself poised for retirement, Paul Gorman would retire in another year, and DePuy had left the Army back in 1977.

Far below the bluff on which he stood, Starry could make out the distinctive silhouettes of some of the Army's new M-1 Abrams tanks on which he had worked so hard in the early 1970s at the Armor Center along with the M-1 program manager, Brig. Gen. Robert Baer. With its unmatched speed and a laser range-finder combined with a computer-stabilized gun that could fire accurately even on the move, the M-1 was a bulwark of AirLand Battle. Though its turbine engine was a gas guzzler, it also made the Abrams so fast and quiet that it was already earning the nickname from soldiers of "whispering death."

The sight brought to mind the M-1's namesake. In the months before the end when Creighton Abrams knew he was dying, he had given Donn Starry a little pep talk. During those final months the general had preferred to hold court on the white-columned porch of stately Quarters 1 at Fort Myer. From a grassy knoll across the street known as General's Row, the heights of the Virginia shoreline dropped down across Arlington Cemetery in a clear sweep to the Potomac far below and the monuments beyond. The silent army of headstones in between, lined up row upon row, were soon to embrace a standard-bearer into their ranks.

Somehow Abrams sensed that the Army was on the right track when few others could see it, and his old mentor had entreated Starry to stay the course and not give up. Staring out over the vast expanse of the National Training Center a decade later, the shadows of clouds sweeping across a broad desert valley where armored units maneuvered, Donn Starry knew that both Abrams and DePuy would have loved the view.

Part IV

34: A Defining Struggle 1989

PERHAPS it was possible to wait your entire life for a day you never really expected to see. When November 9, 1989, actually arrived, however, Gen. Jack Galvin was far too anxious to revel in it. A wide arc of sixteen national flags flapped in unison outside his office, another wintry workday at Supreme Headquarters Allied Powers Europe (SHAPE), in the pan-flat countryside outside of Mons, Belgium. Inside the gates of the modern, sprawling complex, pockets of men and women in clashing uniforms could be overheard discussing in a tongue mother to none of them the extraordinary events of the day. There was nothing typical about November 9, least of all for the supreme allied commander, Europe (SACEUR).

Galvin had a direct line open to U.S. European Command, in Stuttgart, West Germany, which he also commanded. His four-star deputy there reported a tense situation developing at Checkpoint Charlie in Berlin, entrance to the American sector under the Four Powers Agreement that still governed the city. After the Berlin Wall was erected in August of 1961, U.S. and Soviet tanks had faced off briefly across the divide at Checkpoint Charlie in one of the most dangerous moments in four decades of the Cold War. That event and nearly thirty years of daring escapes across the wall were chronicled in the small museum that abutted the checkpoint.

Earlier in the afternoon of November 9, 1989, East German leader Egon Krenz had announced that he was opening the border, and East Berliners were reportedly flocking to the crossing point in droves. Soviet border guards and East German security police had apparently failed to receive the order, however, and were turning the civilians back in confusion.

The doctrinaire East German military was an unpredictable element in the anxious showdown. If it was encouraged to crack down by the Soviet military forces garrisoned in East Berlin, Galvin worried, a powder keg could explode. At that moment he asked himself the same questions that had troubled NATO deliberations for two years: Will the Soviet military really let this happen, or is this the step to the brink that might cause it to turn violently against democratic reforms? Certainly no icon of communism was more pregnant with symbolism than the Berlin Wall.

Finally, Stuttgart sent word from intelligence agents in East Berlin that the Soviets were staying in their garrisons. An intense sense of relief flooded through Jack Galvin. At 11:17 P.M. the captain of the East German border police shrugged his shoulders and the gates to the West swung free.

Cameras caught hundreds of East Germans as they burst through with a single cry, their faces illuminated in the harsh, unfamiliar glare of television lights. "Remember the ninth of November!" shouted a middle-aged man over the noise of the crowd. An obviously stunned East German woman was stopped by a *Newsweek* reporter soon after on West Berlin's fashionable Kurfürstendamm shopping promenade. "There's so much color," she marveled. "So much light."

Jack Galvin had returned to Europe in 1987 after serving in Panama for two years as commander in chief, U.S. Southern Command (SouthCom). There once again his career had intersected with that of retired general Paul Gorman, whom he had followed as CINC SouthCom. Though Galvin didn't know it, his old boss had recommended him highly for the job in Panama. Perhaps nowhere in modern society was the art of mentoring more honored than in the military, and throughout his career—fighting in Vietnam, working on the Pentagon Papers, serving in Europe in the turbulent late 1970s—Galvin had learned much from watching the quiet-spoken and self-effacing Gorman. The torch of Army leadership he carried, Galvin believed, was far brighter for being passed by Paul Gorman.

Having spent seven years in Europe in the 1970s, Galvin was fluent in German language and politics, and in retrospect he believed he could pinpoint the moment of conception that was leading to the birth of a reunified Germany. In an impassioned speech at the United Nations, Soviet leader Mikhail Gorbachev had proclaimed that the satellite nations of Eastern Europe could go their own way without threat of a Berlin blockade or a repeat of Prague in 1968. "Freedom of choice is a universal principle," Gorbachev had proclaimed, and Hungary and Poland had quickly tested his sincerity. Czechoslovakia and now East Germany had followed suit.

Ever since arriving in Europe to take over as SACEUR in 1987, Galvin had been likewise testing Gorbachev's sincerity on a number of arms-reductions proposals, from intermediate and short-range nuclear forces to the Conventional Forces Europe (CFE) treaty. As yet he had found no reason to question the Soviet leader's veracity. In those negotiations, the Warsaw Pact had for the first time begun accepting the concept of disproportionate reductions to address the vastly superior numbers of Soviet weapons.

Stunned by the rapid movement on arms control after so many years of stalemate, Galvin and other NATO leaders had asked themselves in those negotiations if they were somehow being tricked, and each time events in Eastern Europe seemed to suggest that the talks were already lagging behind the historic changes taking place. In NATO people had begun speaking in terms of an "acceleration of history."

Watching the Berlin Wall come down, Galvin began to allow himself to believe that the chains were indeed finally being broken. In the euphoria that followed, however, as East Germans poured into the West driving their clunky Trabants and Western journalists flocked to the newly accessible East, the speed with which the dissolution of the Warsaw Pact was accepted as almost a preordained conclusion was wondrous. Reports in many media depicted a hollow society rotten at the core, concluding that it was destined all along to simply topple from the burden of its own clanking weight with little outside interference. As if it wasn't every bit as much in the nature of such societies to explode throughout history as well as implode.

Perhaps it was human nature, Galvin thought, this tendency to belittle a vanquished foe as hardly worthy of the fight. Yet as NATO's contacts with military officers in the Soviet Union and former Warsaw Pact increased in the months following the crumbling of the Wall, Jack Galvin was if anything struck by how much greater the danger had been than many of them had realized. As an assistant division commander in 1979 in charge of defending the Fulda Gap with a demoralized army, Galvin could literally remember being afraid to drop his vigilance long enough to take a nap on Sunday afternoons. Had he known then what he discovered in 1989 and 1990, he might have slept in his boots at night.

Despite charges over the years that NATO forces consistently overestimated the enemy threat, Galvin had discovered that the opposite was in fact true. NATO intelligence had significantly underestimated the Warsaw Pact forces. That had become obvious during the Conventional Forces Europe (CFE) negotiations, when the Soviets for the first time had made a good-faith effort to account for their forces arrayed against NATO. To reach approximate parity under the agreement, for instance, the Warsaw Pact would have to destroy upward of one hundred thousand tanks, artillery pieces, and armored combat vehicles, roughly ten times the number NATO nations would have to eliminate. In one of the more shocking discoveries, it would be revealed that Moscow's nuclear arsenals had peaked at roughly forty-five thousand warheads, twice the number of U.S. estimates of the time and one-third larger than assumed under the SALT I and SALT II agreements.

Equally chilling were detailed plans, documents, and war reserves discovered as NATO officers began exploring Eastern bases after German reunification in 1990. Not only had the Soviet bloc seriously contemplated an invasion but their level of readiness for such an assault far exceeded that presumed by Western intelligence. East Germany's secret Stasi police force, for instance, had even preprinted new street signs and maps for Western cities. Düsseldorf's fashionable shopping street Königsallee, a boulevard noted for its furriers, jewelers, and designer fashions, was to be renamed Karl Marx Allee.

Investigators also found cellars full of cash that East Germany had printed for immediate distribution in an occupied West Germany. Other cellars containing weapons, vehicles, and railroad equipment were also discovered, as were ammunition stocks for the 160,000-man East German military that were greater than the West German Bundeswehr had stockpiled for its 500,000 troops.

As late as 1985, updated Stasi documents detailed a strategy for overwhelming 12,000 allied soldiers in West Berlin with 32,000 communist troops. Written in cooperation with Soviet officers, the plan called for quickly seizing Berlin's most important structures, including the Brandenburg Gate and the Reichstag building where the legislature met. There were also indications that the communists had prepared lists of West Berliners to be arrested, including intelligence agents, police, politicians, and journalists.

Whenever Galvin spoke with military officers in Poland, Hungary, and Czechoslovakia after the crumbling of the Wall, asking them whether they would really have gone through with the attacks if ordered by their Soviet masters, they invariably shook their heads as if the question itself was a display of American naïveté. Of course they would have fought.

On the wall of his office at SHAPE, Galvin displayed a desk-sized map outlining a Warsaw Pact battle plan. In the spirit of reunification, it had been given to one of his West German officers by an East German counterpart. On it, his U.S. VII Corps was shown in great detail, defending forward at the Fulda Gap. Depicted in large, red arrows, Warsaw Pact forces are shown converging in a pincer move on Wiesbaden, roughly one hundred miles behind American front lines. When asked where the Warsaw Pact had planned for its own defense, the East German had answered, smiling, citing the diamond center of Belgium: "Antwerp."

The confluence of factors that led top Soviet officials to conclude after more than forty years that they could not win the Cold War was complex and shrouded in the sometimes inscrutable Soviet character. Galvin did not intend to press them on the issue. A number of observers believed his delicate handling of the Soviet capitulation during this period qualified the thoughtful general as one of the Army's premier soldier-statesmen of the modern era. Certainly there was none of the rancor or bluster of the exultant victor in Galvin's manner.

He remained at heart a writer, the thoughtful author who had published books such as *The Minute Men* on the first battle of the American Revolution, and *Three Men of Boston* on political events leading up to that war. Whenever his career had seemed stalled or at a dead end, Galvin had always fallen back on his writing talent. That's how he had come to work with Paul Gorman and Daniel Ellsberg on the Pentagon Papers back in the late 1960s, and later he gravitated to SHAPE as a speechwriter for Gen. Andrew Goodpaster, the SACEUR in the mid-1970s. Now the conclusion Jack Galvin intended to write as the supreme allied commander at the end of the Cold War was about also winning the peace.

In discussions with his Soviet and Warsaw Pact counterparts, however, Galvin did learn of the Soviet's deep unease about U.S. and allied military developments in the 1980s. They commented on NATO's command-and-control capabilities and the United States' strategic mobility, flexed during annual Reforger (Return of Forces to Germany) exercises. The Soviet generals always monitored the exercises closely, saw the development of fluid Air-Land Battle doctrine to counter their own echelon forces, witnessed the evolution of satellite and communications technology that allowed NATO to piece it all together.

Always the Soviets came back to the allies' evolving command-and-control capabilities, something the Defense Department had spent roughly $25 billion a year on during the defense buildup of the 1980s. The Pentagon rightly viewed it as a force multiplier to counter larger Soviet forces. When the pilot of a Warsaw Pact MiG-23 aircraft was forced to eject over Poland early in 1990 and the aircraft continued into NATO airspace, the Soviets admiringly noted how NATO interceptors scrambled out of the Netherlands in time to meet it at the border. Often thereafter they commented on how quickly Galvin's forces were able to distinguish that aircraft from all the thousands of others that made up the air clutter in Central Europe, then track it to a precise interception.

The failure in Afghanistan and the accident at the Chernobyl nuclear plant in Ukraine in 1986 had also made a profound impact on the Soviet psyche, the latter providing the most tangible evidence of the potential devastation of a nuclear war. There were also comments about former president Ronald Reagan's Strategic Defense Initiative, and concerns especially on the part of Gorbachev that attempting to match such an ambitious technological effort would bankrupt the Soviets. In the end, the revitalization of U.S. military forces during the 1980s had succeeded not only in deterring aggression, but ultimately in deterring Soviet military ambitions as well.

As the festivities signaling the approaching reunification of Germany intensified in 1990, Gen. Jack Galvin found himself sitting at home one night watching TV with his wife, Virginia, and some friends visiting from Louisville, Kentucky. On the screen they watched a moving scene at the Brandenburg Gate, the spiritual solar plexus of the great divide that had separated East from West for decades. The wall and the guard towers that had marred the beautiful arch had been torn down, and the broad avenue Unter den Linden was once again open and mobbed with crowds celebrating under a sparkling shower of fireworks.

Looking around at his friends, Galvin saw that everyone in the room was reduced to tears by the spectacle. They were Americans crying in Belgium over German reunification, but the moment seemed to transcend national boundaries. It was as close to a victory celebration as Galvin would come. Already there were questions about the future of NATO, calls in Europe for a vast reduction of U.S. military forces, and protestations for a peace dividend at home.

Even while the Berlin Wall was still crumbling the previous December, Galvin had watched with interest as his former Southern Command in Panama rushed troops into the country to unseat dictator Manuel Noriega in an operation that might well presage others in what was being termed the "new world order."

The Panama operation had been led by the head of Southern Command, Gen. Maxwell Thurman, the former William DePuy disciple whom Galvin and many others in the Army greatly credited for helping to turn the all-volunteer force around a decade earlier. Even in 1990 "Be All You Can Be" remained the theme song behind the Army's wildly successful recruiting campaign, which was attracting 97 percent high school graduates. Max Thurman liked to joke that the Army wouldn't dare drop "Be All You Can Be" as long as he was alive.

Indeed, Panama was just the first indication that disorder seemed a far more likely characteristic of the uncertain era ahead. JCS chairman Gen. Colin Powell had recently contacted Galvin and requested that the aircraft-carrier battle group assigned to the Mediterranean under his control be diverted to the Persian Gulf. Iraq was massing troops near its border with Kuwait, and apparently the commander of Central Command, Gen. H. Norman Schwarzkopf, wanted an extra presence in the region.

For Cold War warriors who for much of their adult lives had manned the battlements of communist containment, from guard duty at the Fulda Gap and the Korean DMZ to desperate combat in Vietnam as young men, it was a striking moment. As a young lieutenant, Colin Powell had commanded a platoon in defense of Fulda and had returned with his twenty-two-year-old son in 1986 after replacing Galvin as commander of VII Corps in West Germany. Norman Schwarzkopf, who had followed Galvin as commander of the 24th Infantry Division in the early 1980s, had spent a tour of duty as a lieutenant in Berlin. Jack Galvin was in Europe still. In NATO the talk was of an acceleration of history, and maybe that's what it meant. These men represented an entire generation of soldiers who had just won the defining struggle of their age, and there wasn't even time to celebrate.

35: Burden of Duty 1990

STATE Highway 144 spans the dense pine forest of coastal Georgia like a trestle, a blacktop causeway knifing through the marshy lowlands in the direction of Fort Stewart. The sleepy summer heat and the sunlight flickering through the tunnel of trees mesmerizes, but the shoulders along the narrow roadway are sandy and treacherous. Certainly it wouldn't do for the new commander of the 24th Infantry Division (Mechanized) to veer off into the scrub pines on the way to his new assignment.

Maj. Gen. Barry McCaffrey thought about a story he had heard about Jack Galvin. It seemed that on taking command of the 24th years earlier, Galvin had become so mesmerized by that long straightaway that the military police had clocked him speeding coming onto the post and had given him a ticket. Welcome to Fort Stewart, General.

Reporting to work as the division commander in June of 1990, McCaffrey was in fine spirits. It was a day every career Army officer dreams about, placing him in an elite group of only eighteen division commanders in the entire

Army. Soon that number would drop as the Army shrank to adjust to the end of the Cold War. Many generals look back on the assignment to lead a division as the pinnacle of their days commanding troops. After that, only a select few would ever go on to command an entire corps, an echelon further removed from front-line forces. Most could look forward to retiring or ending their careers in a staff job.

Jill McCaffrey was happy for her husband and pleased to be back in the South. Though an Army brat, she had been born in Georgia, and the rural South had always been a welcome host to the military. In its conservatism and stubborn sense of tradition it was not unlike the Army itself.

Jill's rapprochement with the society outside the gates of all military bases was long ago complete. She could trace the split back to the traumatic party at their cramped apartment near Walter Reed Hospital twenty years earlier, when she was just getting used to her maimed husband's being whole again and Barry's service friends were spitting on the Army on their way out, not caring whom they hit. Whatever forces had so bedeviled the country back then seemed to Jill to have long ago disappeared from the landscape. She and Barry were even tentatively trying to reestablish some of the friendships torn asunder that awful night.

More than twenty-five years earlier, on a road not unlike Highway 144, she and Barry had traveled together in an old LeMans to his first Army assignment with the 82nd Airborne. How full of promise and excitement the journey had seemed then, before their lives entered the dark era of Vietnam. With Barry poised now to fulfill the promise of division command, those years were a distant memory. The way ahead seemed more certain. Now her son, Sean, was a young lieutenant and hotshot paratrooper with the 82nd Airborne, and her daughter Tara an Army nurse, both eager to start on their own adventures.

While Jill had thrilled to the unpredictability of Army life as a young woman, she had come to better understand the sacrifice in the intervening years. Already her family was scattered around the country, and with two children in the Army she understood that they would likely be separated for the rest of her life. Jill McCaffrey would never live in a town with her children and grandchildren gathered around her. Sometimes when she met families with generations living within blocks of each other, she felt a melancholy overtake her. The Army had been good to her family, but it exacted a price.

Yellow "tank crossing" road signs marked the outskirts of Fort Stewart. They passed white clapboard buildings dating back to World War II, freshly painted and framed by the green lawn of the parade ground. In contrast, the modern barracks buildings in red brick looked like college dormitories. All in all, Fort Stewart had a campus feel to it, another indication of the vast face-lift of its facilities the Army had conducted in the affluent 1980s.

The base commander's house was located on a scenic cul-de-sac, and as they passed through the front door, Jill, Barry, and their youngest daughter, Amy, all noted the plaque listing former commanders of the 24th. It was certainly esteemed company. There indeed was the name of Gen. Jack Galvin, now the supreme allied commander, Europe, one of the most prestigious positions for anyone in uniform, and a man Barry respected greatly. Jill also recognized the name of a man she had first seen in Berlin when she was a starry-eyed young teenager, and he a dashing lieutenant and general's aide. Former 24th Division commander Gen. H. Norman Schwarzkopf had also gone on to greater things.

One of the first things Barry McCaffrey told the assembled officers of the 24th Mech was that they would be fighting a war within ninety days. He had said much the same thing after assuming his first command in the 82nd Airborne in 1965, and for the same reason. In times of uncertainty, it was important to focus a unit's attention on its primary mission of war-fighting, even if the possibility seemed remote indeed to a heavy division stationed in south Georgia.

The fact that a bellicose dictator in Iraq had amassed the fourth-largest army in the world was one of the reasons McCaffrey had coveted the 24th Mech practically above all other division assignments. Any division command was an honor, and he hadn't lobbied for it. But this division was in his prayers. As Central Command's heavy force in waiting, the 24th Mech was configured and outfitted to fight not in Europe but rather in the deserts of the Persian Gulf, right down to the "chocolate chip" desert camouflage paint on its tanks and armored vehicles.

Having spent much of 1989 in Brussels as part of the U.S. military delegation to NATO, McCaffrey also understood clearly that the threat in Europe that had consumed Army thinking for much of his career was waning fast. For all of his education in international security relations, and there had been plenty of it, McCaffrey had totally missed the call on events in Europe and the dissolution of the Warsaw Pact.

Every commander in uniform having studied it, they all knew that the Soviet system dominating Eastern Europe was cruel, overcentralized, and corrupt, but over the decades it had proven resilient and had become a familiar villain. If there was some mental hesitancy to let it go, then there was perhaps consolation in the fact that those in uniform had plenty of company in their general failure to predict the remarkable speed of the Warsaw Pact's unraveling.

That McCaffrey had been sent to a "joint" assignment in NATO was partially a reflection of the imperatives of Goldwater-Nichols. After furiously fighting the reforms, the active-duty leadership had since honored military tradition by saluting their civilian masters and making what most critics judged a good-faith effort at implementing Goldwater-Nichols.

Under the legislation, anyone promoted to general or flag rank must first have completed a joint curriculum at one of the War Colleges, followed by a joint-duty assignment. That remained one of the most controversial aspects of the law, as the services were loath to relinquish their most promising officers who were arguably at the height of their command skills. Unquestionably, however, the services could no longer treat joint duty as an afterthought or receptacle for deadwood.

Less than a month after taking command of the 24th Mech, McCaffrey and nearly a thousand of his officers deployed for a joint command-post exercise organized by Gen. H. Norman Schwarzkopf, the four-star commander in chief at Central Command. Centcom's operative war plan was designated 1002-90, and it called for a deployment to counter a Soviet invasion into Iran. Given the tenor of world events, however, Schwarzkopf had instructed that the command-post exercise in the summer of 1990, code-named Internal Look, depict an Iraqi invasion of the Arabian Peninsula.

In a sense, command-post exercises flowed from the force-on-force training pioneered at Red Flag and the NTC, only they were designed primarily to stress command staffs at the brigade and division level and above. Computers simulated the movement of enemy and friendly forces, as well as the "fog of war." Even so, the exercise caused considerable grumbling among the officers, many of them apparently believing there were better ways to spend their time than living out of tents and working twenty-hour days for a week running a war game.

Weeks prior to the beginning of the exercise in mid-July, Central Command's message center began issuing fictional dispatches about a huge Iraqi force of three hundred thousand troops and over three thousand tanks massing at its southern border. Planning for the worst is the essential business of unified command staffs, and this was undoubtedly a classic "worst-case scenario." When the war game began, however, Central Command's message center also began sending intelligence bulletins about the real-world situation in the Middle East. The problem was, the worst-case scenario and the real-world events were virtually indistinguishable.

Even while the command staffs were wrestling with Internal Look, Saddam Hussein was publicly threatening war on Kuwait and the United Arab Emirates. Convoys of Iraqi troops and trainloads of tanks began moving south into southern Iraq at the same time, including two divisions of Iraq's vaunted Republican Guard. Those movements were so similar to the ones briefed as part of the Internal Look exercise that Central Command briefers sometimes confused reality with the fiction they had carefully scripted for the exercise.

About that time the officers of the 24th Infantry Division began looking differently at Maj. Gen. Barry McCaffrey. Their new boss was undeniably intense and bright, personable and articulate with the troops, and sheer hell on the staff. He was just the kind of ambitious and hard-charging SOB who could make life unnecessarily difficult around a peacetime garrison. Yet McCaffrey had predicted that they would be going to war within ninety days, and already some were discerning the distant beat of war drums. At Fort Stewart, the comment increasingly heard was that if it came to war, this decorated war hero McCaffrey might be just the kind of guy you'd want to follow into a fight.

By the end of July, the Central Command staff was confident that its satellite imagery from the Middle East was showing an Iraqi army in battle formation on its southern border, and it predicted an invasion. If Central Command was asked to respond, the 24th would surely be called. Though that implied a questionable clairvoyance on the part of McCaffrey, it made him wonder. He never did mention to his officers that the same thing had happened when he predicted in 1965 that his company of the 82nd would be going to war within six months.

Even as he knew Iraqi forces were massing near the Kuwaiti border, however, McCaffrey saw reason for confidence. Some believed that the United States had applied the right army to the wrong war in Vietnam. If the national command authority handled this right, that would certainly not prove the case against Iraq, which relied on Soviet doctrine, Soviet weapons and massed tank forces, and Soviet-style command-and-control. AirLand Battle doctrine had been devised to counter just such a force, and the National Training Center had for years offered a high-fidelity replica of the kind of desert battlefield they could expect to find in the Persian Gulf. Winston Churchill once said that World War II was won in the classrooms of U.S. military schools in the 1920s and 1930s. Well, Barry McCaffrey had been to the Army War College, and this was a textbook example straight from his thesis: the defense of Saudi Arabia.

McCaffrey was not home the night of August 2, 1990, shortly after Iraq invaded Kuwait, when his wife received a phone call from Lt. Sean McCaffrey.

Jill knew that her son had been devastated that his battalion didn't take part in Operation Just Cause in Panama the year before. He was so much like his father as a young man that Jill was sometimes taken aback. Pictures of Sean in uniform were so reminiscent of his father as a young man that the two could be mistaken for each other. Jill could remember Barry in the 82nd, so despondent about possibly missing combat that she had prayed he be sent. She also remembered Vietnam. No matter how disconsolate the boy sounded, there would be no prayers for Sean McCaffrey's being sent to war.

"Mom, is Dad around?" Sean asked over the telephone, obviously fishing for news. "Have you heard of anything weird going on?"

Jill McCaffrey told her son that his father was working late as usual, but she had no news to report. Even if there was, they both knew that operational security dictated they not discuss it. Army families, however, tended to develop their own shorthand. Later that night, Sean McCaffrey's phone rang. This time it was Jill who was obviously affecting nonchalance.

"Oh, by the way, Sean, are you the Division Ready Brigade this week?" she asked, referring to the unit in the 82nd that was kept on a state of constant alert.

"Yeah, we are."

The silence on the other end of the phone was all the news that Sean McCaffrey needed to hear, and it encapsulated a mother's remembrance that the debt of duty that the Army exacted could come due at any time.

"I see," Jill McCaffrey finally said. "Well, I'll write to you."

36: A Gathering Storm 1990

LT. Gen. Chuck Horner was airborne in an F-16 fighter, on his way to Washington, D.C., for an accident review board, when he was instructed to return to 9th Air Force headquarters at Shaw Air Force Base, South Carolina. The day before, Iraq had invaded Kuwait, and rather than occupying contested parts of northern Kuwait such as the Rumaylah oil field or Bubiyan Island, as the common wisdom had assumed, Hussein had overrun the entire country. As commander of 9th Air Force, which included all U.S. fighter bases east of the Mississippi River, Horner was Air Force component commander for Central Command. He had been expecting the call.

Having languished at 9th Air Force for three years, Horner figured that his reputation had finally caught up with him. Even as a three-star, he still had a penchant for stretching the norms of general-officer behavior at least until they squealed a little. After all these years, Horner would still prefer drinking and chumming with a fellow member of the Command Bar Stool Association than sitting around a table of wise men discussing the overarching political implications of blah, blah, blah.

Someone in the Air Force must have finally decided he was a potential embarrassment, Horner figured, so the 9th Air Force was a way to put a decorated combat veteran gently out to pasture. Well, Horner was surprised he had climbed as far as he had. It was like what his father-in-law, who knew absolutely nothing about the military, had remarked when first told that his daughter's husband had been awarded a coveted third star: "Well, I guess that means you'll be staying in for the full twenty, eh?"

Horner never quite understood what retired TAC commander Gen. Bill Creech had seen in him in the first place. Certainly Horner was never one of the ramrod-straight and buttoned-down types who were molded in Creech's image. Yet for whatever reason, Creech had shuffled him around to various commands, grooming Horner just as he had groomed the other generals now running the Air Force, testament to the oft-stated Creechism that the first duty of any leader was to create more leaders.

After serving in various staff positions under Creech, Gen. Larry Welch, for instance, had migrated over to Strategic Air Command and had then become chief of staff of the entire Air Force, spreading Creech's gospel of decentralization and empowerment. The entire Defense Department and a large chunk of American industry had more recently embraced those same principles under the rubric of Total Quality Management, or TQM. Having benefited from that philosophy for over a decade, the fighter community tended to display a confidence in their abilities that bordered on arrogance.

Meanwhile, the present Air Force chief of staff, Gen. Mike Dugan, was a fighter pilot who had worked at TAC headquarters under Creech, as had Gen. Mike Loh, the vice chief of the Air Force. Horner had seen it coming a decade ago. Creech had cloned them all.

Since he got to fly fighters and run a crack command, Horner tended to view 9th Air Force like a velvet prison. He didn't really care about climbing any higher. People like him were often passed over in peacetime. Many of his fellow Bar Stoolers and fighter-pilot brethren had long since fallen by the wayside. In wartime, however, things could quickly get more interesting for the Chuck Horners of the military.

When Horner arrived at MacDill Air Force Base in Florida, Central Command staff was in near pandemonium. The same Republican Guard divisions that had spearheaded the invasion of Kuwait were heading south toward the border with Saudi Arabia, bringing their logistics support forward for what Schwarzkopf had to assume was an invasion into the West's oil-producing underbelly. Horner had already put two tactical fighter wings on alert, and he asked the Central Command staff if they needed any help. When he was told no, Horner retired to an office upstairs with a yellow pad and pencil and basically scribbled some ideas down while waiting for the crap to hit the fan.

It did just that around eleven P.M. that evening, while Schwarzkopf was being briefed on a draft operations plan for the defense of Saudi Arabia. Having served so long as the Central Command air-component commander, Horner knew Schwarzkopf well, and the man was undoubtedly wound even tighter than usual. Understandably so, thought Horner, given that he was supposed to brief the president the next day. The problem was that while the staff had a good handle on the ground forces part of the brief, Horner thought the air portion was disastrously sketchy. Apparently Schwarzkopf agreed, and he promptly blasted off on one of his patented harangues. By his own admission, Schwarzkopf was pressuring his staff mercilessly, determined not to be led into repeating the mistake the military had made in Vietnam of giving cavalier promises and "sugarcoating the truth" in an effort to please the commander in chief.

For those senior officers of Schwarzkopf and Horner's generation, the memories of Vietnam were weighing heavily again. Lyndon Johnson picking bombing targets from the White House, the disastrous escalation of the war by increments, overconfident generals constantly predicting victory just around the corner—all of it had since become part of service lore. Now on the cusp of possible war, it was suddenly real again for the senior commanders such as Schwarzkopf and Horner. This time, however, history would be judging them.

In the midst of a Schwarzkopf outburst over the air operation, Horner interjected his own vision of an air campaign, reading off his scribbled notes. The CINC immediately liked what he heard. Some of the Central Command staff wondered at Horner's ability to conceptualize a complex defensive air campaign on a yellow notepad. What they didn't realize, however, was that he had done it all before.

One of the commands Creech had sent Horner to in the early 1980s was the 23rd Region of the North American Aerospace Defense Command. As part of the "flag" series of training exercises that had begun with Red Flag and been expanded by Creech into nearly every aspect of Air Force business,

Horner's command had run Copper Flag exercises to test the continental air defense of the United States. Long-range Air Force F-111 and B-52 bombers acting as enemy air would fly out over the Atlantic, then turn around and launch a mass raid on the East Coast. Horner's staff was responsible for mounting the defense, coordinating the input of AWACS airborne early-warning aircraft and radar ground stations, then vectoring fighter aircraft for rapid intercepts. Essentially what Horner had done on his yellow pad in Central Command headquarters was outline a Copper Flag exercise, only substituting "Saudi-theater air defense" for "continental-theater air defense."

After hearing Horner out, Schwarzkopf told him to gather the staff and put together a more detailed version of the plan he had just outlined. Then pulling him aside, Schwarzkopf told Horner that he would be coming along to help brief the president at Camp David the next day. An old softball teammate from his days at the National War College would also be there, and Chuck Horner looked forward to once again seeing the man who had since become the youngest chairman in the history of the Joint Chiefs of Staff.

The group of men who piled into golf carts on the helipad at Camp David early on August 4, 1990, were well known to each other. Chuck Horner fell in beside Schwarzkopf and Gen. Colin Powell, chairman of the Joint Chiefs of Staff. Leading the group was Secretary of Defense Dick Cheney, who's soft-spoken demeanor belied a tough and forceful personality.

Inside the conference room of the main lodge, they met with Pres. George Bush and his inner council of advisers, including Secretary of State James Baker, National Security Council adviser Brent Scowcroft, Vice Pres. Dan Quayle, White House chief of staff John Sununu, and CIA director William Webster. Except for the three generals in uniform, everyone else was dressed casually for what would prove the key council on whether to deploy U.S. military forces to confront Iraq in the Middle East.

President Bush made it clear from the beginning that he didn't believe the Iraqi aggression could be allowed to go unchallenged. When it came his turn to speak, Schwarzkopf thus briefed the room on what the United States would face in the Persian Gulf. Besides its nine-hundred-thousand-man army with sixty-three divisions, the Iraqi arsenal included some of the best weapons money could buy on the open arms market.

Saddam had nearly six thousand tanks, over one thousand of which were modern Soviet T-72s; thirty-five hundred pieces of artillery, much of it excellent South African 155mm heavy artillery; and an air force that included modern Soviet MiG-29 fighters, Su-24 bombers, and French Mirage fighters.

While not having much of a navy, Iraq also possessed Chinese and French antiship missiles, specifically the French Exocet, which had wreaked havoc with the British during the Falklands and had crippled the Navy's USS *Stark* when it was fired upon by a reportedly confused Iraqi pilot during the war with Iran.

Everyone in uniform perceived weaknesses in Iraq's military, especially in its centralized command and a clearly outclassed air force. But in sheer size, it ranked behind only the armies of China, the Soviet Union, and Vietnam. Of major concern was the Iraqis' ability and willingness to use chemical weapons on the offensive, which it had displayed in the Iraq-Iran war. Essentially, Saddam Hussein had mass and initiative on his side, and battle-hardened Iraqi troops who had earned the respect of military men in the only way armies truly can: by having fought and won a brutal war.

After assessing the threat, Schwarzkopf outlined the defensive plan 1002-90 and the troop-deployment timetable Central Command had sweated over during Internal Look. The Division Ready Brigade of the 82nd Airborne, roughly four thousand soldiers, could be sent immediately as a line in the sand, but the lightly armed paratroopers would clearly be little more than a dangerously exposed trip wire.

Within two weeks, Schwarzkopf said, he could have a brigade of Marines in the theater. By the end of the first month, heavy forces needed to seriously thwart the Iraqis on the ground would begin to arrive. Schwarzkopf stressed that he would require roughly three months to get the full defensive package of 1002-90 in place, knowing full well that it would seem like an eternity to the men gathered around the conference table at Camp David to discuss a crisis that was only three days old.

Schwarzkopf also showed a slide of what would be required to kick Iraq out of Kuwait. Central Command would essentially need to double its force, pulling at least six additional divisions out of Europe and the United States, an unprecedented logistical effort that would take eight to ten months. There were shocked expressions around the conference table at this timetable. The burly commander also stressed that with so much of their support in the National Guard and reserves, a deployment this size would require a politically charged reserve call-up.

After Schwarzkopf sat down, Chuck Horner spoke. Though the Iraqi Air Force had 1,127 aircraft, many were not the most modern. With the United States' superior training and pilots, he confidently predicted that the Iraqis would be chased from the sky in a matter of days. With Saudi Arabian air bases available, and Navy carriers in the Persian Gulf area and Red Sea, Central Command could quickly mount combat sorties in the region numbering several hundred a day.

Horner also noted that the scenario favored the use of airpower. Unlike the jungles of Southeast Asia, the desert offered few places for massed forces to hide, especially from sophisticated precision-guided munitions. Even during Iraq's war with Iran, the Iraqis had not suffered greatly from air bombardments due to an ineffective and strangely reticent Iranian Air Force. After Horner finished outlining the air campaign around nine A.M., he and Schwarzkopf were excused from the room. The other principals, however, were asked to stay behind.

When the option of going strictly with airpower was raised after Horner's confident assessment, Colin Powell made it clear he was strenuously opposed to an air-only option. Airpower had never won a war by itself in the past, he emphasized, and it would be inadequate to fully protect the Saudi kingdom. Also, something in the air-only option reeked of gradualism and a school of thought that wars could be fought with half measures, which clearly disturbed this particular chairman of the Joint Chiefs.

When George Bush had chosen him for the position in 1989, the president made the fifty-two-year-old Powell not only the youngest chairman in JCS history, but the first black. Goldwater-Nichols and this burgeoning crisis would combine with Powell's forceful personality to make him one of the most powerful. He was also the first chairman of the Joint Chiefs whose fundamental frame of reference was not World War II or even Korea, but rather Vietnam and all that had come after. And Colin Powell had been thinking a lot about exactly what his responsibilities were at that moment.

Powell never lost sight of the fact that he had no troops directly under his command except the Joint Staff nor an official place in the operational command chain. By law, the chairman of the Joint Chiefs served simply as the chief military adviser to the defense secretary and the president. His power lay in his access to and influence with these men. The chairman even needed a letter from the secretary of defense in order to send instructions to the commanders in chief in the field. Colin Powell had such a letter.

Powell knew that some of his colleagues considered him a "political general," and the thought still irked somewhat. He considered himself first and foremost an infantry officer, skilled in the use of military power as a tool of national security. Yet he was convinced that his military advice would only prove relevant to the civilian leadership in that room if it reflected the political context in which it was given. And Powell did not believe in giving irrelevant advice.

If anything, Powell sensed at that moment that his experience in Washington and knowledge of the men in the room was a critical asset. Having served as national security adviser in the Reagan White House and as former defense secretary Caspar Weinberger's chief military aide, Powell had an unusually close relationship with George Bush. Cheney and Powell, meanwhile, had forged a good relationship during the tense weeks of Operation Just Cause in Panama.

Indeed, if time eventually proved this to be a war council, then Colin Powell liked the national security team that was in place. National Security Adviser Brent Scowcroft was a retired Air Force lieutenant general. A naval aviator who had been shot down in World War II, President Bush had his own wartime frame of reference to draw on, and he saw clear parallels between the present crisis and the reaction of nations to the burgeoning Nazi threat in the late 1930s. Bush's obvious conviction that the Iraqi aggression could not go unchallenged was the starting point for their deliberations.

Powell continued to advise strongly against a piecemeal deployment. If the president wanted to defend Saudi Arabia, Powell believed that they should go into it with an unambiguous commitment and the decisive force outlined in 1002-90, as well as with a clear understanding of the risks involved and the time required to get the force into the Persian Gulf.

As for the U.S. military, Powell believed it was as ready as he had seen it during his long career.

It had taken nearly twenty years, but the Army had recovered from Vietnam and its aftermath on the strength of some courageous leadership along the way and with considerable assistance from the American people. Thinking back on men such as retired general William DePuy and the late Gen. George Forsythe, Powell realized that those who stood up at the darkest moments often made the greatest sacrifice, while others reaped the rewards. It was often that way with the Army. If it came to war with Iraq, the nation might well owe those men a debt of gratitude.

Certainly Colin Powell was keenly aware of the debt that he owed to the black soldiers who had come before him. In his spacious Pentagon office hung a painting of Henry Ossian Flipper, the first black graduate of West Point, who was shown leading a patrol of "buffalo soldiers," black cavalrymen so named by the Cheyenne Indians they fought against.

The racial tensions that Powell had seen rip at the fabric of the Army beginning in the late 1960s in Vietnam had long ago subsided. Even the racial consciousness-raising sessions had gradually been abandoned, commanders finally convinced they were simply no longer needed. Their ranks were nearly drug free, and the soldiers were demonstrably the best educated ever.

Indeed, the educational paper chase had become an overriding characteristic of the entire all-volunteer force in the 1980s. With the number of enlistees with high school diplomas approaching 98 percent, many of them enticed into service by the GI Bill's promise of college tuition, the military had established a de facto linkage between education and advancement. No law stipulated that even young sergeants had to complete a couple of years of college, but increasingly those who didn't were falling behind their cohorts and being passed over for promotion.

Meanwhile, all of the services were riding a wave of weapons modernization effected during the Reagan buildup. Though the only true test of both weapons and soldiers was the one being discussed that morning at Camp David, Colin Powell was as confident of the Army's readiness as Chuck Horner had clearly been of the Air Force's.

Powell well remembered Horner from their days as students together at the National War College. One of the advantages of the joint service schools was that familiarity between officers of the various services, and Powell approved of the emphasis on joint military education in Goldwater-Nichols. He recalled playing on the softball team with Horner and Gen. John Yeosock, Central Command's Army-component commander, as well as Air Force general Hansford T. Johnson, the commander of Transportation Command. Unless Colin Powell misread the direction of the discussion at Camp David, they were about to be teamed again, and this time in the big leagues. It was a point he reiterated to President Bush and his advisers seated at the long conference table.

The risks and scope of the proposed operation were enormous, and to an unprecedented degree the weight of the decisions that shaped it would fall on the shoulders of Colin Powell and Norman Schwarzkopf. Not only had Goldwater-Nichols made Powell alone the principal uniformed adviser to the president and secretary of defense, but it had de facto placed him and the Joint Staff at the top of the operational chain of command. Schwarzkopf, meanwhile, would have unprecedented latitude to control events in the theater of operations. This would be no Vietnam, with the field commander constantly wrestling for control of his service component commanders, and the command chain diverted through a faraway commander in chief in Hawaii.

Yet was placing so much emphasis on the judgment of the chairman a dangerous concentration of power in a national crisis, as many had warned? By strengthening the JCS chairman and the commander in chief in the field, had two competing power sources inadvertently been created that might engage in a destructive tug-of-war? Would the powerful service chiefs rebel against being out of the command chain and being relegated to seconding voices in JCS deliberations? On the afternoon of August 4, 1990, the theoretical concerns that had perplexed the framers of Goldwater-Nichols were suddenly very real.

Later that same Saturday afternoon, Powell phoned Schwarzkopf in Tampa. The chairman wanted him to join a delegation that was preparing to leave for Saudi Arabia almost immediately to brief Saudi king Fahd on just what the United States could offer. The next morning when he arrived back in Washington, Schwarzkopf wanted to know if the U.S. government was ready to commit forces. He was clearly shocked at how much had been decided so quickly.

"Yes," said Colin Powell. "If King Fahd gives his permission."

Sometimes it seemed to Colin Powell that one of the most influential decisions he had made since taking over as chairman was to change the office letterhead. Instead of having it continue to read "Joint Chiefs of Staff," he changed it to "Chairman, Joint Chiefs of Staff." He said it half-jokingly, and to those unfamiliar with the internal workings of the Pentagon, it sounded laughable. To Powell, however, that change in letterhead symbolized nothing less than being able to put his recommendations in writing and direct the operations of the Joint Staff without having to get anyone else's okay.

In fact, Powell felt that assigning the sixteen-hundred-person Joint Staff specifically to the chairman was perhaps the most important structural change associated with Goldwater-Nichols, and one that had gone a long way in correcting many of the ills in the JCS system that Congress had identified. By making such joint assignments mandatory for general-officer candidates, the law also insured that the chairman had the pick of the litter in terms of officer candidates.

Being the principal military adviser with direct access to the civilian leadership and having a large staff of crack officers at his disposal not only facilitated rapid response and clear decision-making channels, but it had significantly elevated the Joint Staff as a player in contingencies.

Nor was the apparent ease with which the generals took to the lectern during press briefings accidental. Goldwater-Nichols had made mandatory for all those promoted to general the six-week General Officers Course called Capstone. It was the culmination of a long educational trail followed by every officer with an eye on promotion. Indeed, a 1988 study by the Center for Creative Leadership had found that 88 percent of one-star, brigadier generals held master's degrees, as compared to only 19 percent of upper-level managers in major U.S. corporations.

For general officers, Capstone was designed not only to prepare them to work in a joint environment but also to emphasize how the military fit in as only one cog in the complex machinery of national security strategy. Presentations were given to participants at the National Defense University in Washington, D.C., by senior representatives of the State Department, the National Security Council, the national media, and Powell himself.

The instructors at Capstone also taught officers how to brief civilian audiences who might not have a detailed understanding of military matters. That was a direct nod to the imperative of building and maintaining public support for any military operation, and a refutation of the jargon-laced and often amateurish "Five O'clock Follies" that so many of the generals remembered seeing as young officers in Saigon.

Never was Powell's ability to speak with the single voice of the chairmanship backed by the Joint Staff more critical than in the days just after the Iraqi invasion. Immediately, the Joint Staff had gone into its crisis-management mode. Reading off of Schwarzkopf's list of priorities as outlined in 1002-90, a crisis action cell coordinated closely with Transportation Command, trying to hone a time-phased force-deployment data scheme, or "Tip Fiddle," matching the forces to deploy, available air- and sealift, and the people needed to route them to the Persian Gulf.

The Joint Staff was also in constant communication with Central Command headquarters at MacDill, which held hastily called meetings even while Schwarzkopf traveled to the Persian Gulf to help brief King Fahd. The first painful reality that set in during those discussions in Central Command's cramped planning room was the need to quickly split the staff if given the order to deploy, forcing commanders to manage a massive mobilization as they simultaneously shifted headquarters from Florida to Saudi Arabia.

Even lacking a formal order, the U.S. military establishment had begun a subtle but unmistakable transformation in those tense days of waiting, making the first tentative steps in shifting from a mammoth peacetime bureaucracy to a focused if sometimes unwieldy instrument of force projection. Nearly every major support command and those fighting units high on Central Command's wish list of forces began forming round-the-clock crisis action teams in anticipation of a potential thumbs-up.

The 7th Marine Regiment at Twentynine Palms, California, began preparations for a full-scale deployment under the guise of a planned exercise. Squadron leaders at the 1st Tactical Fighter Wing at Langley Air Force Base, Virginia, which would have only twenty-four hours from a thumbs-up to liftoff, began tracking down pilots on temporary duty rosters and hurrying aircraft maintenance cycles. The 82nd Airborne at Fort Bragg began canceling softball games, a sure sign to observers in Fayetteville that the United States was contemplating war.

Inside the National Military Command Center in the Pentagon, meanwhile, the Joint Staff had carefully reviewed Central Command's operations plan. The only thing missing was an order to execute from the president and the secretary of defense, who was in Saudi Arabia. At that point, the center of gravity for the entire operation would shift to Central Command. Schwarzkopf would become the "supported" commander in chief, and all other commands the "supporters." Given the right word from an Arab king, that vast military machinery would lurch ahead onto the uncertain ground between the best-laid plans and a worst-case scenario.

Late in the afternoon of August 6, Lt. Gen. Chuck Horner and the rest of the U.S. delegation led by Cheney and Schwarzkopf were quietly walking from the Saudi Royal Palace in Jidda to a waiting convoy of Mercedes Benzes, King Fahd's astounding "Okay" still reverberating in their ears. The group of men were sobered by the enormity of the mobilization they were about to unleash.

Chuck Horner was glad that his tactical fighter wings at Langley and Shaw had been kept on alert, despite grumblings from Tactical Air Command that it had been adversely affecting readiness. Wait until oil climbs to $40 a barrel, Horner had ruefully joked, and you'll see real readiness problems. Until the moment of King Fahd's formal invitation, however, the massive deployment they had been contemplating had still seemed like a remote possibility, and the past few days like an extension of the Internal Look exercise. All that was about to change.

As they approached the cars, Schwarzkopf turned from Cheney to Horner. "Chuck, get them moving," was all he said.

Everyone sensed the irreversibility of that moment. They were about to set into motion a system so massive and complex that many of its individual elements had never been tested together. For all the collective experience in that room, as the Pentagon's newest war-fighting command Central Command itself was still something of an anomaly. No one had ever tried to so quickly deploy a force that large halfway around the world, not in the initial phases of World II, Korea, or in Vietnam. The threat of imminent attack would infuse everything with a wilting sense of urgency.

As the senior man present after Schwarzkopf, Horner was put in charge as commander in chief of CENTCOM forward. For a moment Chuck Horner's vaunted sense of confidence deserted him. This was too big! Already he knew that his 9th Air Force must be preparing to deploy from bases up and down the East Coast. The thought of hundreds of aircraft being launched into the skies over North America filled his consciousness, and he didn't even know where he was going to direct them to land.

There's no way we can do this! Instinctively, Horner reached for that familiar place where every experienced fighter pilot retreats when events are threatening to spin out of control, and his thoughts began to prioritize themselves. From past exercises, Horner knew some officers high up in the Saudi military, and in the Middle East personal relationships counted for plenty. It was time to get reacquainted. Everything else was in God's hands.

37: A Line in the Sand 1990

THE quickest arrows in Chuck Horner's 9th Air Force quiver were already preparing for launch on August 7. At Langley Air Force Base, Virginia, the 1st Tactical Fighter Wing's unofficial motto was "First in, best dressed," and armed security guards were already suspiciously eyeing badges on the flight line. The F-15C air-superiority fighters cordoned off were being armed with live ammo—four AIM-7 and four AIM-9 air-to-air missiles, nine hundred rounds for the 20mm cannon—and the security guards waved even crew members away. Dangerous territory at the best of times, a flight line of forty-eight fully armed fighters during an emergency force generation is an especially edgy place to be.

Though it is taken for granted that U.S. warplanes are mobile, scrambling fighter squadrons in less than twenty-four hours for deployment to a bare airstrip halfway around the world was the mobilization equivalent of brain surgery. Yet eighteen hours after receiving the go signal, the first aircraft of Alpha squadron announced their departure with a deafening roar, the F-15s hurtling down the runway and banking sharply skyward.

They might actually have left sooner, but Tactical Air Command (TAC) decided to hold the start so that weary pilots would not face a night landing on the other side of the world. That and a number of unforeseen delays caused TAC to abandon the timing portion of the time-phased deployment plan altogether, a ripple that would be felt throughout the airlift schedule. Even with the delays, however, the 1st Tactical Fighter Wing had the first fighter squadrons launched for Saudi Arabia, a point of considerable pride. They were soon followed by many others.

So far the deployment, which was so young that it hadn't yet been given a name, had gone much like one of the Checkered Flag overseas deployment exercises that the wing conducted annually, or the quick-reaction deployments to U.S. bases that they practiced each month. The training revolution that had begun with Red Flag more than a decade earlier was beginning to pay real-world dividends. This time, however, the planes that began flocking to the air from bases up and down the East Coast had live missiles under their wings, and there was some confusion about exactly where the pilots were heading and what they would find on their arrival.

Watching from Riyadh as one squadron after another touched down after the exhausting overseas flight, Chuck Horner said a silent prayer of thanks to all the Checkered Flags and Blue Flags and the operational-readiness inspections that Bill Creech had force-fed the Tactical Air Force, getting them in the habit of deploying quickly as a way of life. The Air Force had promised Schwarzkopf five squadrons in place at the end of a week, and while the rest of the deployment was already behind schedule, they had actually delivered more than *double* that projection.

The problem was suddenly where to base over two hundred advanced fighter aircraft, with more flowing in daily. Despite the Iraqi threat, the region was still sensitive to the presence of U.S. military forces. Even the Saudis were suddenly skittish about all of these warplanes invading their airspace. They were understandably worried that a bunch of crazed American fighter pilots would start buzzing their camel herds and blowing the tents off sleeping bedouin tribesmen. Thinking back to his own shenanigans as a young fighter pilot on deployments to Tripoli for gunnery practice, Horner figured the Saudis had a point.

As acting Central Command commander, he took the attitude that they were guests in Saudi Arabia, to operate at their host's discretion. He gave the Saudis his word that not one airplane would fly that wasn't on his daily tasking order, which he submitted for Saudi approval.

Chuck Horner had been thinking a lot about Vietnam, the only frame of reference for an operation this size. He vividly remembered Takhli, and the arrogance of a U.S. military that had poured into Thailand and South Vietnam with an attitude that clearly communicated a message of, "Okay, you

little brown shits, get out of the way, we're going to show you how it's done."
Horner knew that Schwarzkopf was sensitive to the same memories. That
was a mistake they did not plan to repeat.

Each night Horner held a war council, and he stressed that everyone present was an equal partner. If a Kuwaiti major wanted to say something,
Horner counted him as the military representative of the Kuwaiti emir, and
thus all but equal to himself. At Schwarzkopf's direction, they had very early
assumed a command system where the military forces of each country were
under their own commanders, with the actions of the allied forces coordinated at the top in these war councils.

With ten of his squadrons in place, along with the air wings of the aircraft
carriers USS *Independence* and USS *Dwight D. Eisenhower*, which were already on station in the area or closing fast, Horner felt a critical first panel of
Desert Shield had fallen into place. At that pace, in a little over a month the
tactical airpower in the Gulf region would be roughly equivalent to the force
deployed in Europe during the Cold War. Even by the end of the first week,
Chuck Horner was already confident that the United States ruled the air.

The problem was that Iraqi ground forces kept pouring into Kuwait unabated. Already a brigade of the 82nd Airborne and some Saudi border police
were staring down nine Iraqi divisions, or roughly 130,000 soldiers, 1,200
tanks, and 800 artillery pieces capable of firing toxic-chemical shells. Tensions had increased significantly after Iraq sealed its borders, trapping more
than 13,000 Westerners in the country, including some 6,500 Americans and
Britons, and the United States had announced a naval blockade. Under international law that was an act of war. Schwarzkopf had directed Horner personally to make sure each night before he went to bed that every commander
in the region knew what to do in the event of an Iraqi attack.

Unfortunately, many of Horner's air bases were vulnerable to being overrun in the first hours of any major Iraqi assault. At one meeting, Horner
turned to his roommate in Riyadh, Lt. Gen. John Yeosock, the Army component commander, and asked him point-blank what kind of protection the
Army could provide his squadrons. A cigar-chomping Pennsylvanian with few
pretenses and a blunt sense of humor, John Yeosock reached into his pocket
and smiled, pulling out a tiny penknife.

"Sean, I've got too much to live for to die out here. See, my wife has these
absolutely huge knockers and—"

"Give it a rest, will ya, John," Lt. Sean McCaffrey replied, gripping the
stock of a portable antitank rocket launcher and peering into a stretch of

trackless desert north of Al Jubayl, Saudi Arabia. Sean knew the humor was meant to bolster his spirits, reflecting the bawdy sense of machismo for which the 82nd Airborne was rightfully famous. Just then, however, McCaffrey was contemplating the hundreds and perhaps thousands of Iraqi tanks that he knew were out there somewhere in the featureless expanse.

They had been in the desert for six days. The phone call McCaffrey had been expecting after the conversation with his mother had come just after ten P.M. the previous Monday, the voice on the other end of the line proclaiming an Alpha Company telephonic alert. Sean McCaffrey had picked up the phone before the second ring. Every soldier in the 82nd Division's ready force was on two-hour recall and had to sign out on a roster where they could be located at all times. After ringing off and calling the next name on the roster, Sean had gathered his already-packed rucksack much as his father had twenty-five years earlier. On his way out, Sean had left instructions in an envelope on the apartment counter for his girlfriend, Debbie.

Sitting in the desert with a bunch of unwashed paratroopers, he could hardly avoid thinking of her. They had been carrying on a long-distance romance for over a year now. Since she had been scheduled to fly down to Fayetteville for a visit from the West Coast, Deb might even then be finding out that he was gone. Operational security, however, had made warning her of the deployment impossible.

Jill McCaffrey had once cautioned her son that if he planned on making the Army a career, Sean had better find a strong-willed and independent woman who wasn't too "clingy." From what Sean already guessed about this mission, he figured to learn a lot about how that search was going before ever seeing the inside of the apartment or his girlfriend again.

If the Iraqis attacked, the plan called for the 82nd Airborne to bloody their nose, then retreat in a series of hit-and-run fallback movements. Those who survived as far as the coast were to try to swim their way out to Navy ships. Every kid in the outfit understood the chances lightly armed paratroopers had against tank divisions, and they had even put a name to their exact role in what was being called Operation Desert Shield. They were "Iraqi speed bumps."

To those with long memories for these things, such as his grandfather William McCaffrey, the 82nd's position was uncomfortably reminiscent of U.S. forces in Task Force Smith, which were routed and nearly wiped out in the early days of the Korean War. Sean McCaffrey figured they would put up one hell of a fight if it came to that, but he wasn't going to sleep easy until his father or someone else showed up leading one hell of a lot of tanks.

• • •

Given the constant rotations that are so much a part of military life, the crisis inevitably caught key players in a game of musical chairs. Someone was always just leaving or reporting to a critical assignment. As luck would have it, when the music stopped in August of 1990, Maj. Gen. Mike Myatt happened to be standing in front of an empty chair at the head of the 1st Marine Division.

The palm-tree-lined roads of Camp Pendleton, hard against the southern-California coast, were already snarled with convoy traffic. Artillery and automatic-weapons fire echoed in the canyons and off the sides of craggy blue mountains, many of Pendleton's 175 separate fire ranges having suddenly erupted with extra activity. Even units scheduled on the ranges the next day could be found outside their barracks conducting "snap-in" drills, repetitiously aiming their empty rifles and practicing the correct breathing technique for firing, all of it reflecting the Marine Corps's obsession with the fundamental art of putting a projectile downrange on a target.

Marines from the 1st Marine Expeditionary Force from Pendleton and nearby Twentynine Palms had just received the expected word to begin flowing to Saudi Arabia. For all the Marines knew, they could be fighting almost immediately upon landing. It was already abundantly clear that the Wednesday-night miniskirt contest at Ralph and Eddie's outside Camp Pendleton was not going to be the same for some time.

Myatt's change-of-command ceremony was scheduled for that month, but he had already canceled the participation of elements of the 7th Marine Expeditionary Brigade at Twentynine Palms, which would be the first units scheduled to arrive in Saudi Arabia. The entire Marine Corps was organized into flexible packages and command cells that could be quickly expanded in building-block fashion in a contingency. Thus the initial Marine Expeditionary Brigade sent to the Gulf would be steadily expanded into a Marine Expeditionary Force, the largest of the packages. Their tanks, stored in the dehumidified hulls of ships anchored off Diego Garcia in the Indian Ocean, were the United States' best hope for a quick insertion of heavy mechanized forces into the Saudi Arabian theater.

Though his close-cropped hair was grayer, Mike Myatt had changed little since he'd served as a colonel on the Joint Staff and aide to former chairman Gen. John Vessey, Jr., during the Beirut-bombing tragedy. At Camp Lejeune, North Carolina, the Marine Corps still held annual observances to the men lost that day, a constant reminder of the risks of their profession. As for Myatt's being within a size or so of fitting into the first uniform he had worn in the Corps, that was part of the pride of keeping in fighting trim that especially marked Marine Corps officers.

Thinking back on Camp Lejeune, and the awful summer of 1973 he spent there trying to quell race riots, when the ranks were riddled with drugs and the remnants of the Project 100,000 dropouts, Myatt marveled at how thoroughly the Corps had regained its pride and confidence. It was a prime reason he had hungered to return to commanding troops at Pendleton after serving two years in a staff job at Marine Corps headquarters in Washington, D.C. In a sense, returning to Pendleton was like coming full circle for Myatt. It was here as a young boy that he had first watched his cousins cutting the hair of Marine recruits, dreaming of one day, too, sitting in the same barber chair.

Yet they had taken a proud Marine Corps into Vietnam as well, and Myatt had watched as circumstances conspired to slowly unravel it before his eyes. The disruptive officer rotations, helter-skelter replacements, attrition-warfare tactics—he had joined many of his generation of officers in cursing those policies from the foxhole. As young platoon and company commanders, however, they had been isolated from the wartime pressures that had led to some of those decisions. Now it was their turn.

Myatt was heartened upon learning that his assistant division commander would be Brig. Gen. Tom Draude. The two men went back a long way, including serving as advisers together in Vietnam, and later as instructors at the Naval Academy just after the war. As luck would have it, the man who was slated to become the commander of the 1st Marine Expeditionary Force, and who would thus be the senior Marine Corps commander in the Persian Gulf, was also in the midst of changing jobs. Lt. Gen. Walt Boomer had just arrived on base after driving across country with his wife. Word had it that he had first heard about the invasion of Kuwait somewhere in the Midwest over his car radio.

For all the bustling activity at Pendleton, the equipment necessary to transform the Marines into a potent fighting force still lay anchored halfway around the world. Despite the careful planning and exercising, the concept of Maritime Prepositioned Ships was still unproven in an actual emergency. What if much of the equipment failed to work? Because the ships were owned by commercial carriers and operated by the Military Sealift Command, Myatt could only hope that someone had gotten them the word in time. What if, when the Marines arrived in Saudi Arabia with Saddam's divisions breathing down their necks, the ships weren't there?

The lights in the headquarters and support buildings of the 24th Infantry Division had burned late into the night from the moment Iraq had invaded

Kuwait. The division was adjusting to the habits of its commander, leaning far forward in the saddle.

Typically, Maj. Gen. Barry McCaffrey had not waited for someone to officially invite him to get his forces moving. He figured that Iraq might even invade Saudi Arabia before the 24th could get there.

If crossing into Saudi Arabia was ever on Saddam's mind, and the disposition of his forces south said that it was, then the Iraqis had a clear window of vulnerability to exploit in August and September. Should Iraq take eastern Saudi Arabia while the 24th was in transit, they would probably have to unload somewhere on the Red Sea coast and traverse the Saudi Arabian land mass. Barry chose not to dwell on the implications of such an invasion for his son, Sean.

When news came that the Saudis had approved a deployment, McCaffrey had simply assumed that the 24th would be the first heavy division called. After all, they were Central Command's heavy force in waiting, and the only division in the Army custom-configured to fight in the desert. McCaffrey thus issued instructions to get the division "ready brigade" moving to port in Savannah, and to load so that they could be fighting as they came off the ship. Thus while Central Command was trying to prod other units into faster action, and the Navy's Fast Sealift Ships were still closing on Savannah, the 24th was already on the move. That kind of assertiveness would later prompt General Schwarzkopf to label Barry McCaffrey his most aggressive and successful ground commander.

One of the first steps McCaffrey took in the early days of the deployment was to call in Brig. Gen. William Holland, commander of the Georgia National Guard's 48th Infantry Brigade (Mechanized), which was supposed to "round out" McCaffrey's division under the Total Force concept. Though neither man yet knew it, their meeting was the prelude to one of the most enduring controversies surrounding Desert Shield.

Ever since Total Force had been established in 1973 at the behest of the late Creighton Abrams, the Pentagon had continued to delegate key, and in some cases nearly wholesale, support and transportation duties to the reserves. Fully 70 percent of the Army's combat-service support resided in the reserves, as did 60 percent of the Air Force's strategic airlift units and 93 percent of the Navy's cargo-handling battalions. The Military Traffic Management Command, responsible for manning the ports, air bases, and railyards during a deployment, depended on the reserves for 100 percent of its Terminal Transportation Units. That's why during his brief to President Bush on August 2, Norman Schwarzkopf had made the point that the size of the mobilization being considered made activation a foregone conclusion.

As notices to report to active duty went out to the first fifty-thousand reservists, the public was responding viscerally, closing ranks behind the commander in chief. In a way that deployment of the professional army had not, the reserve call-up also brought home to American communities the unmistakable realization that the work-a-day fabric of their lives was being rent by this national emergency. Reservists were generally older than their active-duty counterparts and they stayed in one place, and many had extended families and close ties to the community. In one Air Guard C-130 transport crew activated for Desert Shield, the average age was fifty-four. Unexpectedly, husbands and wives, even grandfathers and grandmothers, were being taken away from their families, and employees from companies that depended on them.

The reserve activation thus carried heavy political baggage, and while he never questioned the military's stated need for the reservists, President Bush was not entirely happy with being forced into the decision. He knew the activation involved Congress directly in the deployment. By proclaiming a national emergency, Bush could by law call up to two hundred thousand reservists to active duty for up to 180 days, at which point Congress would have to agree that a continued state of emergency existed or the president would have to bring the reservists home. Calling the reserves thus hastened the debate in Congress and around the country over the duration, purpose, and ultimate wisdom of Desert Shield.

It was just such a contentious public and congressional debate that Lyndon Johnson had hoped to avoid back in July of 1965, when he had announced to the country that the massive deployment he was ordering to Vietnam would not require a reserve call-up. The misery that flowed from that fateful decision to send the armed forces off to fight a war without the will of the country mobilized behind them had consumed the final years of Gen. Creighton Abrams's life. Never again, the former Army chief of staff had vowed, would the Army go to war without the reserves, and thus the will of the American people behind them. Here, then, was the legacy of the last U.S. commander in Vietnam, as the willful Abrams reached out seventeen years beyond the grave to force the president's hand on the reserve mobilization.

Of course the reserve call-up foretold by Total Force did not insure public support. Rather, it insured early participation in any major mobilization of a broad swath of the American public and body politic and consequently guaranteed that debate over whether the country supported a military action would be joined early and vigorously. Thus it was a double-edged sword for both the president and the military.

In the early weeks of Desert Shield, however, those larger issues surrounding the reserve call-up were greatly obscured by a brewing controversy that confronted Barry McCaffrey and a number of other division commanders. Defense Secretary Cheney's published instructions implementing the reserve call-up permitted only the activation of support units, ruling out immediate deployment of National Guard combat brigades meant to augment their understrength divisions under Total Force's "round-out" policy.

While understandably the pride of the reserves, National Guard combat-maneuver brigades of up to two thousand reservists were by far the most ambitious aspect of Total Force. In general, reserve combat units tended to be far smaller and thus easier to integrate into active-duty ranks. Nearly everyone had assumed that the full-up round-out brigades, which trained for only an average of sixty days a year, would need time for some postmobilization workups before they were truly ready for combat.

Having just returned from observing the 48th Infantry Brigade at the National Training Center, McCaffrey meant to stress that point. He had been forced to augment the 48th's artillery battalion with active-duty units for training, for instance, because they were not even certified to fire live rounds in proximity to actual troops.

"Look, Bill, you're going to be under enormous political pressure to say things from a strictly Guard point of view," McCaffrey told Gen. William Holland, the commander of the National Guard's 48th Infantry Brigade, whom he had come to respect in their time working together. "Now don't you dare do anything but use your honest military judgment."

Both of the men understood the sensitivity of the issue. The active-duty Army had a long history of belittling the capability of "weekend warriors" in the Guard and Reserves. Many Guard proponents were rightly convinced that the front-line role of the round-out brigades had not only helped them counter that bias, but was also critical in the National Guard's ability to wrangle new equipment out of the active Army.

Personally, McCaffrey had always felt his spirits lifted after spending time with citizen soldiers who took time off from meaningful careers to step into uniform each month. Given the Army's reliance on the reserves for support under Total Force, he was going to depend heavily on those men and women in the months to come. Yet suddenly not only lives but national security was at stake, and he believed the 48th would need a minimum of three months, and probably longer, to prepare for the complexity of maneuver warfare on a brigade scale.

The advice he gave to Holland was thus the same that McCaffrey himself had once received from Gen. Colin Powell. Don't agonize over or try to decipher the political dimensions of a crisis situation, but rather trust to your principled military judgment. When the order to deploy did arrive, the active-duty 197th Infantry Brigade (Mechanized) from Fort Benning, Georgia, was chosen to round out the 24th Mech.

Later that year, the 48th would finally be activated and sent to a special rotation at the National Training Center in preparation for possible deployment to Saudi Arabia. Though there would be some controversy over the rigors the 48th Infantry Brigade was subjected to in what amounted to the longest training rotation ever at the NTC, Army trainers there would find the brigade so ill-prepared that Holland was relieved of command on a bluff overlooking the Mojave Desert training ground. A number of observers believe that General Holland's career was an early and unheralded casualty of Desert Shield, a position with which Barry McCaffrey would concur.

Anyone running across McCaffrey in Garden City port near Savannah, Georgia, in early August of 1990, however, recognized that time—whether to prepare a National Guard round-out brigade or for anything else—was a luxury this general didn't believe he could afford. Those who realized that his son's unit was a stretched-thin trip wire in the Saudi Arabian desert understood why. But then as a division commander possibly on the eve of war, McCaffrey had more than ten thousand soldiers to think about, each one of them a son or daughter, husband or wife.

Even as the first ships transporting the 24th began steaming out of port, and Fort Stewart and nearby Hunter Army Airfield outside of Savannah began the unmistakable transformation from bustling military bases to ghost towns, Capt. Marie Rossi climbed into bed determined to bring up the issue of her engagement ring with her husband.

The need for both of them to fill out wills before deploying from Hunter Army Airfield—her as commander of a transport helicopter company and he as a Special Forces helicopter pilot—had prompted the most matter-of-fact discussions about how their belongings should be distributed if something happened to either one of them. Nights were different. Each time Marie turned off the lights the reality of their pending separation was there waiting in the dark. The journey was too frightening to explore in any one conversation, so they tried it a passageway at a time, usually lying in bed. That night Marie opened with her engagement ring.

Holding it up in the bedside light, a diamond in a simple Tiffany setting, Marie turned to her husband. "You know, I don't want to leave my ring behind."

Andy Cayton smiled at her, and Marie was reminded of why she had married this man. Tall and lanky, with a firm jaw and brown hair and mustache, he looked every bit the part of the rakish Special Forces helicopter jock. Privately, Marie was miffed that he seemed so damn eager for this deployment. As a Blackhawk helicopter pilot with the Army's elite "Night Stalkers" Special Forces unit, Andy Cayton would be all but guaranteed some of the most dangerous missions imaginable if it came to war. It was one reason she was so reluctant to part with the most tangible reminder of their lives together.

When he smiled and reassured her that it would be all right to leave the ring for the short time they would be gone, reminding her how easy it would be to lose in the field, Andy revealed the earnest sweetness that had so attracted Marie back in Korea. They had first met in 1986, when Warrant Officer 2nd class Andy Cayton had given Capt. Marie Rossi her first checkout flight as a new CH-47 helicopter pilot with the 213th Black Cats, 8th Army, South Korea.

While some had snidely joked about female pilots being weak links in Korea, none of it had especially bothered Marie. In her experience in the Army, if you showed you could pull your weight as an equal, then the respect you were due would eventually follow. If women had to earn the respect from a skeptical audience, rather than having it automatically bestowed as it was on so many of her male counterparts, well, that was life. After coolly navigating a few flights through "Indian Territory" along the mountainous DMZ in central Korea, where the reward for a wrong coordinate could be a surface-to-air missile, the jokes had quickly subsided. Marie had even gone on to become the first female pilot to command a CH-47 in South Korea.

It was difficult to say when Andy's admiration had transferred from her stick and rudder skills to Marie's winning smile. Korea was a hardship tour, with plenty of loneliness to go around, but Marie had certainly not planned on a romance. There were even some hazy concerns about fraternization between a senior officer and a warrant officer, a special career path chosen by helicopter pilots who simply wanted to stay in the cockpit. On their off hours, however, members of the unit had little to do except to drink and pal around at Wango Tangos or Mr. Kim's, and at some point the last ones left drinking and chumming together had been Marie Rossi and Andy Cayton.

After four years and considerable assignment wrangling, they had finally decided to get married just that past June. Immediately, both wondered why it had taken them so long to make the leap. The day after the small ceremony in a square in historic Savannah, Rossi had assumed command of an entire CH-47 helicopter company of more than two hundred people based at Hunter Army Airfield, which like the 24th Infantry Division was attached to the XVIII Airborne Corps.

Without her husband's constant encouragement in those first anxious weeks of company command, Rossi would have felt overwhelmed. Ever since they first started dating in Korea, he had been there for her, offering support when she was afraid of failing a physical training test or was reeling from the myriad responsibilities of company command, from phone calls in the middle of the night about soldiers arrested downtown, to complaints of a lack of toilet paper in the bathroom.

If anything, her husband was a little too quick to brag on her, which made Rossi uneasy. As a Southerner from North Carolina, Cayton's manners sometimes seemed excessively deferential to a woman who had grown up in the brasher environs of New Jersey. More than once in Korea she had upbraided him for trying to carry her flight bag, a typical gesture. Still, it was part of the sweet nature that had attracted Rossi to her husband in the first place. Now she faced the sudden prospect of deploying a helicopter unit to a faraway desert in a country where women were not even allowed to drive cars, and Rossi knew she was going to miss her husband's pep talks.

Not that her predicament was particularly unique. Though at times it seemed as if the public at large had taken scant notice, the role of women in the all-volunteer force had continued to evolve in the 1980s to the point where they accounted for 11 percent of the active-duty Army, compared to just 1.5 percent at the end of the Vietnam-era draft. In all, 223,000 women were in the active-duty armed forces, and 41,000 women service members would eventually deploy to the Persian Gulf.

Despite a history stretching back seventeen years, the all-volunteer force was very much a peacetime work in progress. This first major mobilization was thus exposing some of its idiosyncrasies. The exact role of women in a war zone was a prime example. Back in the "hollow force" days of the late 1970s, when the services were having trouble attracting even marginally qualified recruits and serious consideration was given to abandoning the all-volunteer concept and returning to a draft, the Army had relied heavily on women soldiers to fill its depleted ranks. Yet women were still prohibited from serving in combat units.

There was a fundamental contradiction, however, in excluding women from combat in an organization where, especially in the upper reaches of the service, promotions were traditionally bound to rotations through combat units. In the Air Force, women thus comprised 12 percent of the officer corps, but only 4 percent of the service's lieutenant colonels, 2 percent of its colonels, and 1 percent of its brigadier generals.

Privately, Marie Rossi's ambition was to one day reach the level of light colonel, a rank that she knew few women aviators in the Army had ever achieved. As for the combat exclusion, no one had to tell Capt. Marie Rossi or thousands of other women in uniform that modern warfare had seriously blurred the lines between the front and the rear in a combat zone.

Nor was it just the significant presence of women that made the all-volunteer force deploying to the Persian Gulf different from any the country had fielded in past national emergencies. Personnel officials had long taken for granted that it was a somewhat older force. Compared to the latter stages of Vietnam, when the average age of those sent to the war was just nineteen, the average age of U.S. troops deploying for Desert Shield was twenty-eight. A higher percentage of those more mature service members were married, and like Marie Rossi and Andy Cayton, many were married to other service members. For those two-career service couples with children, that was creating some wrenching partings in August of 1990, as children were being handed off to grandparents and godparents around the country. There were also a total of more than thirteen thousand single parents in the armed forces.

Even without having to worry about children, Rossi felt the added burden of having to brace herself for a difficult journey while at the same time worrying whether her husband would return from his own. Both of them knew that his was the far more dangerous path. That was one of the reasons she was suddenly balking at leaving her engagement ring behind.

The ring was almost a private joke between them. For the longest time, Rossi had insisted that she didn't even want an engagement ring. She had even convinced herself she meant it. When Cayton finally went ahead and bought her one anyway, Marie loved it instantly, and her joy had been impossible to hide. Andy remarked many times afterward that he wished he'd bought it for her earlier. Now she just couldn't see leaving it behind.

Finally, however, her husband convinced Rossi that it would be a foolish risk to take the ring along.

"You know, if something did happen to me, and it won't, I want you to know that it would be okay if you remarried," said Andy Cayton, and suddenly their conversation had taken a turn down another unexplored passageway. "I wouldn't want you to be lonely."

"Well, I don't know if I'd want to," Marie said.

"Just so long as you know how I feel. Only make sure he's at least as kind to you as I've been."

That sweetness of his was coming through again, and Marie Rossi's eyes glistened as she looked at her husband for a moment. "I guess it would be okay for you to remarry, too," she said. "But I wouldn't want you to ever forget about me."

Marie didn't know why she had said that, and for a moment it frightened her a little. Andy Cayton just laughed at the notion, however, and she felt better. He could always do that for her.

"Marie," Andy said, "there's no way in the world I could ever forget about you."

38: Band of Brothers 1990

BY mid-August the scene at the port of Al Jubayl was reminiscent of a set from *Lawrence of Arabia*. Thousands of bodies, many of them living out of temporary sheds hastily constructed on the docks themselves, swarmed on the massive quays in sweltering 105-degree heat, anxiously unloading the five massive ships of Maritime Prepositioned Squadron 2 from Diego Garcia. With major trouble only four hours up the road, the frenzied Marines on the dock knew they would be vulnerable until they could lay hands on the equipment the ships carried.

Some of those dockside knew each other and the unload drill from an exercise the previous year in Thailand called Thalay-Thai, and from annual Bright Star exercises in Egypt. That familiarity was one more unspent dividend that had accrued from the Defense Department's huge investment in worldwide military exercises.

Ever since former commandant Gen. P. X. Kelley had first latched onto the maritime prepositioning concept back in the early 1980s, the idea of sequestering so much precious equipment away in the hulls of ships had remained controversial. Of course, there was the roughly $5-billion price tag to consider. Yet if the Marines' ability to quickly project so much combat power in his path would just give Saddam Hussein pause for the next few weeks, then it would have been money well spent. Every day that Iraq delayed attacking from that moment on, the United States would get stronger and Saddam Hussein weaker.

While the MPS ships were unloading the equipment for his first troops to arrive in-country at Al Jubayl, Lt. Gen. Walt Boomer traveled 450 kilometers southwest to the Saudi Ministry of Defense Building in Riyadh, the in-country headquarters for Central Command. As component commander for all

Marine Corps forces, he needed to work out the battle order to funnel his Marines north to relieve the vulnerable 82nd Airborne. Even more important, Boomer wanted to get a feel for his Air Force and Army counterparts. How these very different men related to one another and to the commander in chief would determine much about how their respective services meshed in the months to come.

If it hadn't been for a fraternity brother at Duke University who talked him into naval ROTC, Walt Boomer would probably never even have found his way into the military in the first place. His mother had grown up in Norfolk, Virginia, and thus approved of the move at the time. Naval officers, she used to tell him, were true gentlemen. When Walt finally confided in her that he was thinking of joining the Marine Corps instead, his mother had said only over her dead body. Luckily, before passing away she came to love the Marines Corps nearly as much as Walt Boomer did.

Yet in two combat tours in Vietnam, Boomer had seen a series of policies that he felt bordered on the immoral wreak havoc on the Corps. He had witnessed firsthand the corruption inherent in body-count tactics, seen his share of micromanagement from Washington, and watched as officers rotated through command and learned their jobs on the backs of their Marines. Like the Air Force general he was about to meet, Walt Boomer had been thinking a lot about the lessons of Vietnam.

The nerve center for Desert Shield was located in a subbasement of the Saudi Ministry of Defense Building, five stories below ground level. Technicians were busily constructing a command center modeled after Central Command's original in Tampa, including a war room, intelligence center, communications room, a small auditorium, and offices for the staff. Surveying the hectic scene reminded Boomer that Central Command was a true anomaly. It was a war-fighting headquarters that had never before fought a war, and whose actual headquarters was located within the shadow not of the bad guys, but of Disney World.

After he settled in at Riyadh, Boomer found his Army counterpart, Gen. John Yeosock, solid and unflappable. In that respect the Pennsylvanian was a rougher-edged version of Boomer himself. While Yeosock and his staff would be more involved in planning a potential ground campaign, Schwarzkopf had decided against making either Yeosock or Boomer the single ground-force commander with authority over both Army and Marine Corps forces. That role Schwarzkopf essentially reserved to himself.

The command situation with Chuck Horner and the air forces, however, was far different. Boomer had only met Horner for a few minutes during Internal Look and knew nothing of the man's reputation. As the acting commander of Central Command forward, Horner was bearing much of the weight of the early deployment on his shoulders; and watching as he put out one fire after another with a minimum of posturing, Boomer felt himself warming to the man.

Finally, Horner pulled the Marine Corps component commander aside and the two men got their first chance to size each other up. On the surface, they could hardly have been more different: the irreverent, slightly rumpled, and frequently profane fighter pilot, and the straight-backed, laconic Tennessean and infantry officer. These opposites, however, had to immediately decide a question that had bedeviled their respective services throughout the Vietnam War.

The issue was control of allied aircraft in-theater by a single air manager. During Vietnam, each of the services had retained operational control of their aircraft. This led to many divisive arguments over targets and priorities, and frequent lapses in coordination of the air war. Those lapses were indelibly etched in the minds of both men.

One of the few times air operations in Vietnam were placed under a single manager had been for Operation Niagara to relieve Marines besieged at Khe Sanh. Then MACV commander Westmoreland eventually had to threaten his resignation to overcome objections by the Joint Chiefs to a single Air Force manager for the air operations. Both the Marine Corps commandant and Army chief of staff at the time reportedly feared setting a precedent that could lead to their losing control of their own airpower. Such a potentially divisive split now hung in the refrigerated air in the basement of the Saudi Defense Ministry.

In designating Chuck Horner as the single joint-forces air-component commander, Schwarzkopf had already flexed some of the considerable muscle that Goldwater-Nichols had imbued him with as one of the Pentagon's true warlords. The military called it "combatant commander command." What it amounted to was ultimate control over the component commanders and their forces to a degree unparalleled in the past. A geographical commander in chief, according to the Goldwater-Nichols legislation, has "authoritative direction over all aspects of military operations." Both Horner and Boomer would come to see the unambiguous authority given Schwarzkopf as critical to shielding them from the kinds of power plays back home that had undercut their counterparts during Vietnam.

As recently as the mid-1980s, Schwarzkopf's predecessor, Marine Corps general George Crist, complained that he had to practically plead for service support to conduct the Earnest Will tanker reflagging operation in the Persian Gulf, finally taking his case to the secretary of defense. As CINC of

Southern Command in the mid-1980s, Gen. Jack Galvin also found to his consternation that SouthCom's component commanders had a stronger ear for what their services were telling them than for what he was asking them to do. Years after Grenada, for instance, Galvin was forced to buy commercial radios that contractors typically used at construction sites just so his Air Force, Army, and Navy component commanders could talk with one another.

By appointing Horner as the single manager of the air war, Schwarzkopf had bypassed squabbling over operational control of air assets that had dragged on for years during Vietnam. Horner and the other component commanders, however, had to make it work. The issue was not a petty one. Because of the need for the Marines to deploy quickly and relatively light, Marine Corps doctrine emphasized an unusually close coordination of Marine air and ground assets, substituting airpower in place of heavy artillery. As Chuck Horner and Walt Boomer stood eye to eye, both of them knew that many lives were at stake.

"I want you to understand that the only thing that matters to me is that we all do the best we can to win this war," Horner said. "Everything else is bullshit. Service sniping, who owns what, all the rest of it is just crap."

The arrangement Horner had in mind was for the Marine Corps to sign over operational control of its F/A-18s, AV-8Bs, A-6s, and all its other aircraft to use as he saw fit in a potential strategic bombing campaign of Iraq. As the time neared when the Marine Corps might need its air arm to support troops fighting on the ground, it was understood that Marine pilots would be allowed to refocus on supporting their own troops.

Considering the threat to Marine Corps forces even then convoying to the Kuwaiti border, it was a radical proposal that the Marine Corps had strenuously resisted in the past. Though he couldn't refuse a direct order, Boomer could certainly oppose Horner's suggestion, taking his arguments to Schwarzkopf, or if need be even back channels to the commandant of the Marine Corps. Already, Gen. Al Gray had reportedly expressed his consternation that the early deployment of fighter squadrons was lopsided in favor of the Air Force, and that the Corps's F/A-18 fighters needed to support his Marines were not given high enough priority for scarce Air Force refueling tankers. In some quarters within the Marine Corps, opposing Horner's suggestion would be considered nothing less than Boomer's duty.

Yet as the two men spoke openly about the huge responsibility they felt, voiced concerns that Washington would try to micromanage any war, shared their willingness to resign before seeing the lives of their people risked needlessly for political expediency or service competition, they kept finding themselves on common ground. Horner insisted that whoever "owned" the aircraft, if the Marine Corps needed them, there would be no arguments. Intuitively, Boomer trusted him. That was the bedrock foundation of the understanding he carried back to Al Jubayl to set up a forward Marine Corps headquarters.

Not that his staff liked it. No sooner had Boomer set up a forward headquarters than a major on his staff came in shaking his head over the air-tasking order issued that day by Horner's staff. "Sir, do you know what the Air Force is doing to try and screw us today—"

Before he could go any further, Boomer cut the man off. "Major, get out of here and go find something important to work on, because that's not going to happen. General Horner and I have an understanding."

Though his voice was stern, Walt Boomer didn't really hold it against the man. That was the way majors were taught to think. It occurred to him, however, that if given a chance, the iron majors could still stir up plenty of mischief.

Behind Chuck Horner's, Walt Boomer's, and John Yeosock's uniforms lay vastly different service cultures, and three men who could hardly have seemed less alike in temperament or style. Yet somehow they had stared across that gulf with a sense of recognition and brotherhood, all of them tracing their scars and convictions on war back to the same troubled upbringing as junior officers.

By contrast, Chuck Horner's initial talks with the Navy component commander about managing air assets were disastrous. When Vice Adm. Henry Mauz Jr., commander of the 7th Fleet in the Pacific, was dispatched to the Persian Gulf to take over as the Navy component commander in the first days after the invasion, some observers saw it as a clear sign of the Navy's long-standing ambivalence toward Central Command and joint operations.

While the Army, Air Force, and Marine Corps component commanders were all at the three-star level, the normal Navy component commander— NAVCENT in military vernacular—was a one-star, Rear Adm. Bobby Sutton. As the potential size of a deployment that would eventually grow from six ships to one hundred and twenty became apparent, the Navy had upgraded its senior commander on the scene by dispatching Mauz, a three-star vice admiral with a background in the surface Navy of destroyers, frigates, and cruisers.

Ironically, of all the services the Navy remained the most familiar with operations in the Persian Gulf. It had engaged in numerous showdowns with Libya during the 1980s, including the joint Air Force–Navy bombing of

Tripoli. The Earnest Will tanker reflagging and escort effort in 1987–88 had been largely a Navy operation. When this present crisis passed, it would surely be the Navy that supplied the continuing U.S. presence in the volatile region.

Ever since his own P-3 aircraft had flown into Saudi Arabia from Japan on August 15, Mauz had been under considerable stress, along with the other Central Command leaders. Representing the first major U.S. presence on the scene, the aircraft carriers *Eisenhower* and *Independence* had established defensive "air caps" over the Persian Gulf beginning in the initial days of the deployment.

Using the powerful radars of his Aegis cruisers, designed to provide a protective radar umbrella around aircraft-carrier battle groups, Mauz had set up a layered air-defense network in the Persian Gulf of successive "wedges" patrolled by naval combat aircraft from the carriers. The Navy had also been responsible for enforcing a naval blockade and coordinating the participation of a number of allied navies. Over many years of exercises, the Navy had already worked out common tactics, signals, and secure communications links with many of those allied navies.

However, under Maritime Strategy, which dominated Navy doctrinal thinking for much of the 1980s, with its emphasis on fighting the Soviets in the open ocean, the Navy had paid relatively little attention to coordinating operations with the Air Force or Army. The communications systems on Navy ships, for instance, could not receive the detailed Air Tasking Order (ATO) issued each day by Horner's staff in Riyadh. These included critical information on each day's flying activities, including takeoff and landing times, air refueling tracks, the quantity of fuel to be transferred, altitudes to be flown, as well as assigned targets. In one of his early meetings with Chuck Horner, Mauz thus suggested dividing airspace into separate sectors to be patrolled independently by Air Force and Navy aircraft.

Suddenly Horner was back in the cockpit of his F-105 again, risking his life over North Vietnam to bomb truck parks while being waved off of real targets because they were inside the Navy's "route package." His reaction was visceral and startling.

"Fuck that! Don't ever talk to me about it again, because we're not going to do it! I'll resign first," Horner shouted, and then gave Mauz his back.

Perhaps the misunderstanding was inevitable. Hank Mauz was not an aviator and had served his tour in Vietnam in patrol boats as part of the riverine force. While the Army and Air Force component commanders and their staffs were located side by side in the Ministry of Defense Building in Riyadh, where the CINC himself would soon be based, Mauz continued to operate from his flagship, a direct reflection of the arm's-length approach to Central Command and joint operations that the Navy had long ago adopted. Whatever the reason, Horner and Mauz had stared across the same gulf of service culture and experience as the other component commanders and had utterly failed to connect.

When Schwarzkopf's aircraft landed at the Riyadh military airport in late August, Horner and Yeosock were there waiting for him on the flight apron in sweat-stained uniforms. As soon as Schwarzkopf was settled into the second-floor office and adjacent bedroom in the Ministry of Defense Building that would serve as his home for the next nine months, Horner briefed him on Instant Thunder. His "Black Hole" gang in the air operations center in the basement had been massaging the plan tirelessly.

Initially, Horner had been angered on hearing that a plan had been developed in the Pentagon by Col. Jack Warden, a noted strategist on the Air Staff in the Pentagon who had written the seminal book *The Air Campaign: Planning for Combat*. He told Schwarzkopf that the last thing they needed was a repeat of Vietnam, with Washington picking air targets. Since then, however, Horner's top planner, Brig. Gen. C. Buster Glosson, had expanded on the plan for retaliatory air strikes with the help of two of Colonel Warden's officers. Together, they made the air campaign Central Command's own.

The four-phased campaign called for attacking centers of gravity in Saddam's overcentralized command-and-control network, including command bunkers where Saddam Hussein would most likely try to orchestrate a war; a phase-two assault on what were generally considered "strategic targets" such as munitions plants, weapons labs, oil refineries, bridges, and railroads; a phase-three emphasis on decimating the Republican Guard in Kuwait; and a phase-four offensive ground campaign whose straightforward assault into the teeth of Iraqi forces was dictated by what planners still felt were inadequate ground troops.

Schwarzkopf thought it was the best air-campaign plan he'd ever seen, and he intimated as much to Colin Powell during a conversation over their secure phone link. During the early days of September, however, Horner received his own call from the Pentagon informing him that Air Force chief of staff Gen. Michael Dugan was coming to the Gulf for a visit and wanted to receive the same briefing on the air campaign that Horner had given to Schwarzkopf. Dugan was another in a long line of senior Air Force leaders who had been groomed by Bill Creech at Tactical Air Command in the early 1980s.

Horner was immediately wary. It was exactly the type of request that exposed a component commander's split allegiance. The primary role of the service chiefs under the Goldwater-Nichols reorganization was to prepare the service budgets, develop doctrine, and to supply well-trained and equipped forces to the commanders in the field. Their input in terms of operations came when they sat at the table as the Joint Chiefs, and Colin Powell took great pains to insure during Desert Shield that hardly a day went by when he didn't talk with each of the service chiefs, either individually or as a group.

Everyone understood that the service chiefs were not used to being out of the chain of command, and that each of them was still maturing into his new role under the Goldwater-Nichols reorganization. Suddenly being out of the loop in the largest military mobilization in two decades was obviously taking its toll.

Horner guessed that behind General Dugan's request for a briefing on the air campaign was the old insatiable craving for detailed tactical information that every senior military leader felt in time of war. He also knew that Schwarzkopf would not be thrilled with the idea of getting one of the service chiefs involved in their operations. Yet the Air Force was jumping through hoops to give Central Command everything it requested. Snubbing the chief of staff would do nothing to enhance that spirit of cooperation. Anyway, Mike Dugan was an old friend and fellow fighter pilot, one of the true brethren. Horner decided to support the briefing request.

Predictably, Schwarzkopf was adamantly opposed.

"Look, Chuck, not even the operations guys on the Joint Staff know about this plan. It's Powell, me, you, Buster, and the Black Hole crew. We're the only ones read in."

"But, sir, the chief has requested it . . ." Horner's exasperation was clear in his voice. Probably because he had been the acting commander forward before Schwarzkopf arrived, Horner was probably closest to the CINC of all the senior staff. Yet he found Schwarzkopf too volatile for anyone to get truly close to as a friend and was wary of pressing him now.

"I really feel we need to brief General Dugan," was how Horner worded it.

After a moment of silence Schwarzkopf relented. "All right, but you can brief Dugan, and only Dugan. No one else."

When Dugan arrived in Riyadh with five of his senior generals, Horner had to tell them that only the chief could hear the briefing. Lt. Gen. Jimmie V. Adams, the deputy chief of staff for plans and operations, was predictably bent out of shape at what he perceived as a snub. He, too, was feeling the insatiable craving, which was exactly why Horner had been wary of the briefing request in the first place. In the end, only Dugan heard the detailed plan for

Instant Thunder, and after the chief and his entourage left, Horner was relieved to get back to the business of planning a war.

Until he was awakened in the middle of the night a few days later by an irate and shouting CINC. Schwarzkopf had received a copy of a front-page article in *The Washington Post* dated Sunday, September 16, 1990. It was based on interviews with Dugan and his senior staff by reporters who had accompanied them on their flight back to Washington, D.C. Schwarzkopf was livid. Both of them knew that Horner had nothing to do with the interview, but he had pushed the briefing and Schwarzkopf needed someplace to vent his anger at the Air Force. After reading the copy under the headline "U.S. to Rely on Air Strikes If War Erupts," Horner could understand why.

"The Joint Chiefs of Staff have concluded that U.S. military airpower—including a massive bombing campaign against Baghdad that specifically targets Iraqi president Saddam Hussein—is the only effective option to force Iraqi forces from Kuwait if war erupts, according to Air Force chief of staff, Gen. Michael J. Dugan.

"Although U.S. ground and naval forces would play a substantive role in any military campaign, Iraq's huge army and tank force means 'airpower is the only answer that's available to our country' to avoid a bloody land war that would probably destroy Kuwait, Dugan said. That view, he added, is shared by the other chiefs and . . . Schwarzkopf."

It was a stunning performance! In a stroke, Dugan had anointed himself spokesman for the JCS and the CINC, then pitched their classified offensive air campaign into the public domain in a way that promoted airpower and seemed to denigrate the contribution of the other services.

Michael Dugan was a decorated command pilot with three hundred combat missions to his credit, and he had a stellar reputation as an accessible and likable general. It could not have been easy for him to reach the highest rank in his service and suddenly find himself outside of the command loop in the largest deployment of air forces in two decades. Yet having succumbed to the insatiable craving for detailed tactical information and a direct part to play, Dugan had so obviously become drunk on that potent nectar.

Reading the article, Chuck Horner was struck by how many times Dugan said "I," as if to say that "I'm in charge." After detailing the target list that Horner had briefed him on, for instance, Dugan had this to say to reporters: "That's a nice list of targets, and I might be able to accept those, but that's not enough."

Chuck Horner loved Dugan, but the chief of staff still didn't get it. It wasn't up to him to decide their target list. Horner couldn't imagine what it must be like to be in Dugan's position under these new rules. War may be hell, but for a four-star fighter pilot to be out of the operational loop during the kind of crisis for which he's prepared his entire life was far from heaven.

When days later Mike Dugan was relieved of command by Defense Secretary Cheney and publicly humiliated, some observers believed that Goldwater-Nichols had claimed its first victim. All Horner knew for sure was that the General Dugan who climbed aboard that airplane back to Washington and said those things was not the same Mike Dugan he had known as a young captain, when they were both red-hot fighter pilots and the world was a far simpler place.

39: War Council 1990

A S his Blackhawk helicopter continued its long journey south on November 14, 1990, Barry McCaffrey looked out over a vast and featureless landscape. Convoys snaking across the desert floor raised dust clouds that could be seen to the horizon, revealing the vast force that was still stacking up behind the 24th Infantry Division. Days earlier President Bush had announced that they were increasing the size of the deployment by 150,000 troops, bringing the total number of U.S. forces in this barren desert theater to roughly 400,000. Unless he was mistaken, the summons McCaffrey was answering along with the other commanders was to discuss an offensive plan for war.

Three hundred miles north of their original entry point of Ad Dammām harbor, McCaffrey's 24th Division was acting as a blocking force for the stream of troops that continued to pour into Saudi Arabia. Everyone understood that Transportation Command had been late meeting Central Command's needs, and that they had been extremely lucky that Iraq had not attacked in the vulnerable early weeks. Yet it was equally apparent that Desert Shield was not destined to be another "Nifty Nugget," the disastrous mobilization exercise of 1978, nor was it characterized by the disjointedness and lack of interservice coordination evident during the Grenada invasion.

Most of them credited Transportation Command (TransCom), the Pentagon's newest unified command that owed its creation to the Goldwater-Nichols reforms, with bringing off one of the most intense surge deployments in military history. Accountability was often a scarce commodity in an organization as massive as the U.S. military, and in that respect even the fact that so many players had pointed accusatory and demanding fingers at TransCom in the early weeks of Desert Shield was a victory of sorts. For once they all knew where to point.

The shadow of McCaffrey's Blackhawk skimmed across an uneven desert below. Somewhere down there was Sean. The thirst for adventure and excitement at the prospect of combat had come through clearly in the boy's letters. They were so alike, father and son, and that alone was cause enough for concern on the eve of war. Barry McCaffrey understood more acutely than ever his father's reluctance to encourage his own Army ambitions.

His father had apparently written the boy, warning Sean to surround himself with friends in the foxhole, to always take someone with him on recon patrols, to post guards every night for a thousand nights and more, or on the thousand and first something bad would happen. Bill McCaffrey had never forgotten the Mary Ann tragedy of 1971, when North Vietnamese sappers had broken through the weak security perimeter of the Americal Division, nearly wiping out the 196th Brigade. Both Barry and his father also understood that Sean was the type to volunteer for all the hazardous-duty assignments, and that the price of war's folly was always exacted most heavily on the young.

So much now depended on the plan, and the lessons it revealed about what they had all learned since Vietnam. McCaffrey had no doubt that Schwarzkopf was about to brief them on an offensive plan for war, and that placed them on history's darkest precipice. In that sense hundreds of thousands of their countrymen were lined up behind the handful of men filing into a former officers' club in Daharan on November 14, the latest in a long line of torch bearers.

"Because, let's face it, the prestige of the United States military is on our shoulders. But more importantly, the prestige of the entire United States of America rests on our shoulders," Schwarzkopf was saying, looking out over his assembled senior officers at the "Desert Inn" at Daharan.

The men accepting that burden stared back at their commander, intense expressions reflecting the depth of their shared sense of purpose and experience. For many of the twenty-two generals and admirals present it was an epiphany.

Behind Schwarzkopf stood the fifteen-foot-wide map of Kuwait and Iraq whose large arrows revealed for the first time to all of them the battle campaign for Desert Storm. The first three phases were an air blitz against Iraq and Iraqi forces in Kuwait whose intensity was unmatched in modern warfare. The final phase was a ground campaign with the Marine Corps attacking up the middle to hold the enemy in place and a swinging "left hook" flanking maneuver by both the Army VII Corps and XVIII Airborne Corps to crush them against the sea. Together with Schwarzkopf's impassioned speech, that map answered a lot of questions.

Revealed for the first time in its entirety, the operation was in many ways a direct refutation of the painful memories that haunted them all. There would be no gradualism or conceded sanctuary. They were going to hit the enemy hard, wherever he lay, and with everything they had. Rather than plodding, attrition-style warfare, they were going to adhere to the tenets of AirLand Battle, substituting to the extent possible maneuver speed and superior technology for casualties. There would be no body counts of enemy dead. The only thing that counted was the annihilation or surrender of the Republican Guard.

And the men and women they led were not nineteen-year-old draftees commanded by twenty-two-year-old sergeants with shake-and-bake training. They were older, more mature professional soldiers and volunteers, led by a seasoned noncommissioned officer corps, many of them having trained in the demanding crucibles of the National Training Center or Red Flag or Strike U. Not so much as a beer was to be found in the rear areas, much less a gnawing drug epidemic. Rather than reeling from a merry-go-round of individual replacements and helter-skelter officer rotations, meanwhile, their units had bonded and coalesced during months together in the unforgiving desert. No one was going home until the job was done.

"We're not going into this with one arm tied behind our back," Schwarzkopf recalled emphasizing for the sake of the Vietnam veterans, which accounted for practically everyone present. "We're not going to say we want to be nice as we possibly can, and if they draw back across the border, that's fine with us. That's bullshit! We are going to destroy the Republican Guard."

Knowing glances swept around the room as Schwarzkopf spoke. John Yeosock cast a look at his friend Chuck Horner. The briefing held no drama for the four component commanders, yet only they understood the full subtext behind it. The plan for an offensive ground campaign had sparked a major controversy between Central Command and Washington.

For weeks Yeosock and Schwarzkopf had worked with a planning team from the Army's School for Advanced Military Studies (SAMS), an elite year-long program at the Command and General Staff College that focused on the art of campaign planning. SAMS had been established back in 1982 under the auspices of Huba Wass de Czege, a protégé of retired general Don Starry and the author of the original AirLand Battle doctrine released that same year by Training and Doctrine Command. Inside the Army, SAMS graduates were referred to as the "Jedi knights."

Colin Powell had already received a briefing on the new "left hook" plan, prefaced by Schwarzkopf's insistence that he could only carry it out with an additional Army corps. Both of them understood that such a massive escalation would require a unequivocal mandate from Congress. After some agonizing, Powell had assured Schwarzkopf he would get his extra forces. "If we go to war, we will not do it halfway," Powell promised Schwarzkopf.

True to his word, Powell and the national command authority had responded with the announcement of a near *doubling* of the Desert Shield force. Congress had also extended the administration's reserve call-up authority, even paving the way for activation of the three National Guard round-out brigades, which were being diverted first to the National Training Center to verify their combat readiness.

Everyone understood that the presence of Gen. Fred Franks at the briefing was due directly to that doubling of force, and that his VII Corps was even then being dispatched by their commander in Europe, SACEUR Gen. Jack Galvin. Galvin had called the deployment a reverse Reforger, and instructed his commanders to answer any phone call from Central Command with a "Yes, sir, now what's the question?"

Having worked on the campaign plan from the beginning, Yeosock felt the significance of that moment. Schwarzkopf had identified the Republican Guard as the enemy's center of gravity, making their mission unambiguous. In his mind the American military best understood missions and time lines that framed operations with a beginning and an end. That clarity of purpose was noticeably absent from Yeosock's memories of Vietnam.

The trouble in the ranks that had characterized those years was also happily missing. Despite the miserable conditions in the desert, the all-volunteer force that the Army had been boasting about to scant notice was passing its first major mobilization with aplomb. Yeosock had fewer discipline problems in the force of roughly 250,000 Army troops under his command in Saudi Arabia than he had suffered as a squadron commander in the 3rd Cav in 1973, commanding 1,000 troops.

Listening to the forceful briefing, Horner felt admiration for Schwarzkopf. The CINC was under intense pressure, some of which Horner felt was self-inflicted, and his mercurial temperament had whipsawed wildly in recent weeks. Yet to Horner, Schwarzkopf's adamant refusal to be pushed into a premature ground campaign that could needlessly cost lives made the CINC a hero. Having fought the battle for that support, Schwarzkopf was now conducting the briefing shades of George Patton. Horner believed that the air campaign he had helped devise, which was the most intense in history, would prove decisive.

Vice Adm. Hank Mauz knew that if the Navy was going to be relevant to the war and the air campaign outlined on that map board, he was going to have to take a step the service had avoided for the better part of two decades: operate its precious aircraft carriers in the relatively constrained waters of the Persian Gulf. Carriers typically operated from open ocean, surrounded by a layered defense of long-range interceptors, missiles, and close-in Gatling guns. Besides increasing the threat from mines, the Persian Gulf would seriously crimp those concentric layers, cutting down reaction times in the event of an aircraft or missile attack. Unless Navy aircraft wanted to rely almost solely on land-based air refuelers, which would seriously limit the number of targets they could attack, for almost the first time they were going to have to float the queens of the blue-water Navy into the confines of a relative bathtub.

Walt Boomer was mulling over the Marine Corps's unenviable mission. His two divisions would be responsible for attacking into the teeth of Iraqi defenses at the Kuwaiti border, keeping them occupied while the Army delivered the decisive "left hook." Given their reliance on resupply from the sea, the Marines were a natural choice to attack up the coast. Their advance toward Kuwait City would also pave the way for Arab forces in the coalition, who were to liberate Kuwait. If the Marines were to flank the Iraqis to avoid a slugging match, however, it would have to be from the sea with an amphibious assault.

From his seat, Mike Myatt glanced over at Barry McCaffrey. Their divisions had been positioned side by side for months now, and they had met and talked together often. Myatt had come to think a lot of the intense, driven Army general. He would have preferred to keep McCaffrey's heavy tanks by his side during the attack up the coast, where he counted eleven Iraqi divisions in the path of his Marines with their older M-60 tanks. In all, there were twenty-six divisions and roughly 450,000 Iraqi troops in the Kuwaiti theater.

Myatt's mind kept going back to something the CINC had said earlier about training and preparing their troops for the worst. To do any less, Schwarzkopf had said, would be a disservice to the parents who had given each man in that room the privilege of commanding their sons and daughters. Some critics were claiming that the military was falsely painting the enemy "ten feet tall," but Myatt didn't see it that way. Their own leaders had once disparaged the Viet Cong and North Vietnamese, and it had cost many of the men in that room dearly. Perhaps along with so much else, they had left that arrogance back in Vietnam.

"There isn't going to be anybody else in this thing except us," Schwarzkopf was concluding the briefing. "There are no more forces coming. And for our country we dare not fail. We cannot fail, and we will not fail. Anybody in here who doesn't understand that, get out of the way. Any questions? . . . Okay, good luck to you. You know what needs to be done."

As the assembled officers gathered up their papers, Barry McCaffrey sat for a moment stunned. So they were actually going to play to their strengths and the enemy's weaknesses, substituting tactical savvy for the blood of American soldiers. Even as his mind raced over an unprecedented logistical challenge, what the war colleges would call a potential war stopper, McCaffrey was confident. The briefing had been a revelation. He turned to his friend Binney Peay with glistening eyes.

"That's it, Barry," said Peay. "That's what we'll do."

40: The Gulf 1990

"WE may very well have to drive Saddam Hussein out of Kuwait, and that's where you come in, Marines!" President Bush told his Thanksgiving Day audience, and the cheers thrown back at him from the thousands of troops gathered at the 1st Marine Division command post were deafening and emphatic.

Mike Myatt looked over at George Bush, then out at the troops gathered to hear him speak at the desert command post. Dressed in a casual blue work shirt and khaki slacks, Bush was smiling broadly at the rousing reception, the commander in chief so obviously invigorated by the raucous spirit of his troops.

Ever since Myatt had learned earlier that month that the 2nd Marine Division that was meant to replace his own division was instead going to reinforce, and that everyone was staying until the job got done, morale had skyrocketed.

The issue of rotation dates and replacements had dominated many of the discussions between him and Tom Draude, both of whom still carried the scars of the individual-replacement system in effect during Vietnam. Both men could still recall how the helter-skelter replacements had continuously ripped at unit cohesion, thrusting individuals into their companies in the midst of fighting before anyone had even learned their names.

Of course, all of the services had long ago put a spoke in the command merry-go-round officers had ridden to Vietnam on, when ticket-punching was a priority and Myatt had four battalion commanders in the space of a year. Likewise the success of the all-volunteer force meant that their all-important noncommissioned officer corps was staffed with seasoned sergeants typically with eight or nine years of experience.

No Marines were going to die fighting as strangers in their own units if Desert Storm was launched. Marine Corps commandant Gen. Al Gray had even assured them that to the extent possible combat replacements would be by entire units, as opposed to throwing individuals into a new unit in the midst of the fighting. After months of training together and sharing the considerable deprivations of the Saudi desert, the cohesion of units in the 1st Marine Division was as good as Myatt had ever seen. Now they didn't have to worry about the distractions of rotation dates either. Bush had tapped into that sense of shared purpose and determination in his speech, everyone convinced that the way home now was through Kuwait.

Just how the Marines were going to attack into the teeth of Iraqi defenses without suffering prohibitive casualties, however, was the topic of much heated discussion in late November, and soon after Bush's visit Lt. Gen. Walt Boomer swung by the 1st Marine Division's command post to air it out again.

The problems were daunting. Though the Marines were the supporting attack, until the Army's swinging hammer blow could descend on the Republican Guards from the far western desert, they would bear the brunt of the ground fighting in Kuwait. Yet not only were they badly outnumbered by the Iraqis and outgunned by their artillery, but the Iraqis were also frantically digging defensive barriers and obstacle belts, something they had become expert at during the Iran-Iraq war. Attacking outnumbered into well-fortified positions was a blueprint for disaster.

The natural solution for Marine Corps planners was an amphibious assault, flanking the Iraqis from the sea. Boomer had a 32,000-man amphibious force afloat in the Persian Gulf that was eager to participate in any fray. Establishing an amphibious beachhead somewhere on the Kuwaiti coast along the path of the 1st Marine Division also solved a difficult support problem. Marine Corps doctrine had never envisioned a major land campaign of the distances facing the 1st and 2nd divisions, and Boomer's logisticians were telling him they probably couldn't support a land attack stretching their support lines all the way from Al Jubayl to Kuwait City.

Thus Boomer had from the beginning included an amphibious assault in their plans. In early October, they had begun rehearsing major amphibious operations during exercises in Oman. Central Command had even invited the press to those rehearsals to give Saddam Hussein something else to worry about.

The problem was, the Marine Corps may have done its public relations job too well. Intelligence showed that at least three Iraqi divisions, and perhaps more, had turned and dug in along the Kuwaiti coast to repel a potential landing. Saddam Hussein's troops were also mining many of the beaches and water approaches. A contested beach landing under such a scenario risked very high casualties.

Boomer wanted to discuss that intelligence with Myatt, Draude, and other of his senior commanders. In the constellation of forces arrayed in the Persian Gulf region, any weapon as potent as a 32,000-man Marine amphibious force had a gravitational pull all its own. For those assembled officers, it was almost unthinkable that those Marines would just be left to float offshore.

As the latest intelligence findings were recited, however, all of them began to cast worried glances at one another. The subtext of the briefing was lost on no one. Certainly Boomer understood it. The Pentagon was in the midst of a massive post–Cold War drawdown that would resume as soon as this threat had passed. If in the largest mobilization of U.S. military forces since Vietnam it was deemed too risky to mount an amphibious assault—essentially the raison d'être for the Marine Corps—no sooner would they all return to Washington, D.C., than the people with say in such matters would start asking why the hell the country needed a Marine Corps in the first place. Published reports said that Marine Corps commandant Gen. Al Gray was lobbying Colin Powell hard for an amphibious landing, insisting that it could deliver a strategic coup de main against Iraqi forces in Kuwait.

Once upon a time, however, each of the men in the 1st Marine Division's command post had cursed the powers that be from their besieged outposts up and down northern I Corps in Vietnam, and their seeming indifference to the plight of the lowly grunt. That was why they took an almost perverse pleasure in enduring the same deprivations as their troops in the desert in contrast to the generals who had operated out of air-conditioned rear bases in Vietnam. They would likewise share in the dangers if it came to war. Now that they held the power, the old memories simply would not abate.

"If we're seriously considering conducting a landing just to say we did a landing, then shame on us," Tom Draude blurted in the midst of a heated exchange. "If we'd risk a Marine's life just to improve our political standing, then we're not worth these stars we're wearing."

It had just come out, and for all Draude knew he had just scuttled his career. When he looked across at Walt Boomer and Mike Myatt, however, rather than anger on their faces he saw that both of them were nodding their heads in agreement.

"We're in total agreement then," said Boomer, who promised to go back to his planners and explore every other option. "There's no way we're going to conduct an amphibious assault just to prove to the world we can do it."

Not long after, Walt Boomer was told that Gen. Al Gray, commandant of the Marine Corps, was planning to make his third trip to the Gulf to review "his" troops. They all owed a lot to Gray, who had recognized the promise of the maneuver-style warfare promoted in the Army's new AirLand Battle doctrine, and had seen the new tactics reflected in the Marine Corps's own doctrinal manual *Warfighting. Field Manual 1.* The new emphasis on fluid, flexible warfare was perhaps the greatest leap in thinking for the Marine Corps, which had always prided itself on the ability to outtough any enemy in a slugging match.

Yet in these repeated trips to the Gulf, Boomer sensed that the commandant was forgetting that this wasn't his fight. The Dugan affair had already shown how a senior general in a war zone who was not in the operational chain of command could muddy the waters, and two trips should have been enough. After mulling over the issue, Boomer decided to take a step that would have been practically unthinkable prior to Goldwater-Nichols, when component commanders in the field closely monitored the wishes of their service chiefs back home. Boomer had a talk with Schwarzkopf, and it was soon announced that General Gray would not be visiting a third time after all. Boomer took no pleasure in the incident, and it could conceivably cost him. Yet Gray should never have asked for the third trip, Boomer thought. *He should have known better.*

Flying over the waters of the Persian Gulf on December 1, 1990, Vice Adm. Stan Arthur noted warships spread out in a wide fantail, the distinct superstructures of warships unmistakable even at a distance. They were part of what had long since become the largest naval operation since Vietnam. Arthur was assuming command of Navy forces in Central Command from

Vice Adm. Hank Mauz, who was due to rotate back to the United States.

At the moment of that change of command, Arthur would take the reins of the most powerful armada ever assembled, to eventually include 6 carrier battle groups, 2 battleships, a 31-ship amphibious task force, 13 submarines, and over 550 combat aircraft.

The helicopter alighted on the deck of the USS *Blue Ridge*, the amphibious command vessel and flagship that served as headquarters to the Navy component commander. After showing him around, Mauz led Arthur into his quarters to bring him up to date on planning for naval operations.

After a rocky start, Mauz felt they were operating fairly smoothly with Central Command planners in Riyadh. Coordination of the international naval embargo was working well. The inability to electronically receive the Air Force's massive daily tasking order remained a major irritant, and the ATO was being flown out to the fleet. Otherwise, Mauz believed they were on a relatively even keel in responding to Central Command's needs, and he related a very positive visit to the fleet by Schwarzkopf. Mauz made no secret, however, of the rough going he had experienced with Chuck Horner.

Later, as he was setting himself up aboard the *Blue Ridge* and preparing to fly to Bahrain for his official change-of-command ceremony, Stan Arthur took stock of the tactical situation. Nearly everything about it felt dangerously out of kilter.

Predictably, some aviators were grumbling about being shortchanged in their operations by Air Force planners in Riyadh, but that didn't especially concern Arthur. It was in the nature of the crisis that the contribution of carrier aircraft and the Navy itself was perhaps greatest in the early stages, when they were the first on the scene with major combat punch. Their stock would undoubtedly rise again when the Arabs inevitably asked the U.S. forces to leave and a remaining military presence was needed. And they would certainly hold up their end if it came to war. With no major enemy navy to defeat, however, and with the Air Force and Army having months to pour in forces uncontested to air bases and ports in the area, the Navy naturally shifted to more of a supporting role.

What was more peculiar about the Navy's position was that Arthur or Mauz were even there in the first place. Arthur had long been scheduled to take command of the 7th Fleet in the Pacific and had been as surprised as everyone else at the decision to pull the 7th Fleet commander all the way from headquarters in Hawaii to serve as the Navy component commander. The normal commander of Naval Forces, Central Command, Rear Adm. Bobby Sutton, was deemed too junior for such a large-scale deployment. Yet it was Sutton who had established the interpersonal relationships at Central

Command and had participated in its exercises and planning.

Arthur could trace the genesis of their dilemma back to the summer of 1981, when as the Navy's first component commander to the Rapid Deployment Joint Task Force, and later to Central Command, he had sat as a captain amidst a constellation of two- and three-star generals from the other services. The Navy's reluctance to come to Central Command's joint table in those early days was coming back to haunt them.

If he was surprised at becoming commander, U.S. Naval Forces, Central Command (NAVCENT) for the second time in his career, Arthur was flabbergasted to find himself isolated out on the *Blue Ridge* while his Army and Air Force counterparts were sitting next to Schwarzkopf at Central Command headquarters in Riyadh. That again went back to the autonomy the Navy had prized in the past. Serving as the Navy commander under former Central Command commanders in chief Gens. P. X. Kelley and Robert Kingston, however, Arthur had always operated by their side, whether in Tampa or on deployments during exercises. He was convinced that was where a component commander belonged.

On his first trip to Central Command headquarters in early December, Arthur decided that his major order of business was to look into relocating himself in Riyadh, and to smooth over quickly any remaining rough edges in the Navy's working relationship with air-component commander Gen. Chuck Horner. However, as soon as he was briefed by Schwarzkopf on the offensive campaign plan, Arthur realized it was too late to relocate ashore. Hostilities could erupt in a matter of weeks, and he didn't want to get caught in a headquarters move in the midst of trying to run a war.

As for introducing himself to his Air Force counterpart, Arthur thought back to what Mauz had told him about the disagreement with Horner. With so many pilots from different services and allied nations flying so close together, determining friend from foe would be one of their greatest challenges. Some sort of modified sector approach was probably a legitimate suggestion, especially from an admiral from the surface navy who was sensitive to the possibility of repeating the *Vincennes* debacle, when one of the Navy's Aegis cruisers had misidentified and shot down an Iranian airliner with the loss of hundreds of innocent civilians. With five hundred combat missions in Vietnam under his belt, however, Arthur also understood the extreme sensitivity among pilots of his and Horner's generation toward the issue of separate "route packages" for Air Force and Navy fliers.

When he found Horner, Arthur introduced himself to the man who would be running the air war. Though Horner was the taller of the two, both men were going to gray and had put on a few pounds since their days of roaming the skies over Hanoi and Haiphong. Chuck Horner clasped Stan Arthur's hand.

"God, I'm sure glad you're not one of those ramrod-thin guys," Horner said with a smile. "You're a round belly like me."

Stan Arthur had to laugh at this introduction. Here was another of the true brethren after all.

"You're right," said Arthur. "We're going to be just fine."

41: Peace on Earth . . . 1990–91

DESPITE the distractions of a touring Bob Hope show and the promise of real turkey in the Christmas mess, the sense of expectancy that marked the holidays in the Persian Gulf was as tangible as a held breath. Ducking under the tent flap of the "Campus Cathedral" on Christmas Eve, Brig. Gen. Tom Draude sensed it immediately. The crowd of Marines that had gathered for midnight mass was so large that they had been forced to roll up the sides of the tents to accommodate the overflow.

Listening to the service, Draude glanced at the crowd of glistening faces, from senior officers down to privates. As the assistant division commander he was one of the few people in the cramped audience who knew of the war plans already being put into place, and after Vietnam he grasped clearly the implications. Looking out over the troops, he couldn't stop himself from wondering which of those faces would be in their prayers after the battle to come. Which ones?

Days before, many of them had listened over Armed Forces Radio as President Bush gave a forceful speech to the nation about the United Nations' decision to back the use of force to liberate Kuwait if Saddam Hussein failed to leave by January 15. President Bush had spoken to all of their concerns in that address: "In our country, I know that there are fears of another Vietnam. Let me assure you, should military action be required, this will not be another Vietnam. This will not be a protracted, drawn-out war."

Bush had gone on to distinguish the situation in the Persian Gulf from America's great military misadventure, including a different opposition whose forces and resupply routes were more exposed; a coalition effort backed by the United Nations; and a highly motivated all-volunteer force that he had become acquainted with while in the Persian Gulf over Thanksgiving.

Certainly in approving Powell's and Schwarzkopf's insistence on a massive deployment before a shot had ever been fired, in not flinching from the politically charged step of calling up the reserves, and in his promise to "never, ever agree to a halfway effort," George Bush seemed to have taken to heart many of the political mistakes associated with Vietnam. Yet as many had predicted, and as the system intended, the announcement to greatly increase the deployment to open an "offensive option" had fully engaged Congress in the debate.

The Senate Armed Services Committee had convened a pivotal series of hearings that some were already comparing to the Fulbright hearings of 1966, which brought initial opposition to the Vietnam War out into the open. Indeed, during the ongoing Senate hearings of 1990, a long parade of respected statesmen and former soldiers were urging restraint and caution, and asking that the economic sanctions be given more time to work, a policy supported by the powerful SASC chairman Sen. Sam Nunn (D-Ga.). While Bush had avoided a showdown on the issue by agreeing to dispatch Secretary of State James Baker to Baghdad, a separation-of-powers battle was still looming over whether the president would even consult Congress before starting a war.

Tom Draude and other officers who could still remember Vietnam, however, were comforted by the stacks of mailbags from the United States. There were personal letters with ribald photos of wives in pinup poses, and "Any Marine" letters from elementary-school classes and concerned citizens from across the land. There were Merry Christmas and Happy New Year cards. There were letters from people who said they couldn't support a war, yet who backed heart and soul the service members who might be asked to fight it. Perhaps most important, there were so many Americans who now understood the difference.

When the time came for the Marines to offer each other a sign of peace during the Christmas Eve ceremony, everyone turned to clasp one another with handshakes or embraces. Peace be with you. God bless you. The irony of evoking the Prince of Peace on the eve of war was not lost on Tom Draude, yet neither was the poignancy of that moment. Somehow, he felt closer to God than if he were kneeling in prayer at St. Peter's.

• • •

Barry McCaffrey figured that anyone who would sign up to be an infantry officer probably had equal measures of both the romantic and the fool, and he had decided to indulge the former on Christmas Eve. After choosing that moment to reveal the battle plan to the assembled officers of the 24th Mech, he had left little to chance.

On the linen-covered tables before each commander lay an aluminum briefcase. Walking them through the enclosed battle plans, McCaffrey saw the enormity of the operation begin to register on their faces, each reaction a mirror image of his own to Schwarzkopf's briefing back on November 14. These officers, who had been weaned on armored maneuvers in the relative sandbox of the National Training Center, were suddenly confronted with an operation equivalent in scope to Patton's march across Europe.

After the plans were locked safely away again in the briefcases, china and crystal settings replaced them on the tables, and a catered French meal was served. Soon a small brass band began playing Christmas music, led by a beautiful woman who was both a singer and instrumentalist. At other times, Specialist Michelle Khani could also be found toting an M16 rifle as a soldier of the 24th Mech.

Her presence was just one more indication to McCaffrey that this was unlike any army the United States had ever sent to war. Roughly one thousand women in the 24th had endured some of the worst field conditions he had ever experienced, and while a higher percentage of women than men had been unable to deploy from Fort Stewart because of various medical problems, McCaffrey had yet to have a commander bring a problem concerning female soldiers to his attention. Some of his hard-bitten commanders even volunteered that the female soldiers had a calming influence on the men, who seemed to behave better and were less likely to show cases of nerves around women.

Regardless, Michelle Khani had become something of the sweetheart of the 24th, and as she led the band in singing traditional Christmas carols, McCaffrey had the sides of the tents rolled up. They were situated on a mesa hundreds of feet above the desert floor, and the lights of an unknown town shimmered in the night like a far-off galaxy. Each officer also received from the division commander the gift of a piece of petrified wood, along with McCaffrey's promise that what they were about to accomplish would be remembered for a thousand years. For a moment at least, sitting atop that mesa like Ozymandias on his throne, it was indeed possible to believe.

In the rear area of the nearby XVIII Airborne Corps, WO Andy Cayton and Maj. Marie Rossi were also exchanging Christmas gifts, though they worked

hard at not talking about the war. Both of them knew Rossi would be heading west soon with the 24th Infantry and the rest of the XVIII Airborne
Corps, though her destination was top secret. Regardless, this was likely the
couple's last private moment together until after they returned home to Savannah. Andy silently noted Marie's bare hand, recalled telling her to leave
her diamond engagement ring at home.

As a Special Forces pilot with the Army's Night Stalkers, Cayton had unusual freedom of movement. He had wrangled an assignment to brief his
wife's commander on flying conditions in the desert just for the promise of
this night. The apartment was on loan from an intelligence officer and friend
of Cayton's, and it had come with a Filipino servant to cook them Christmas
Eve dinner.

Just as the sand seeped into every open pore and cranny in the desert,
however, so did the talk of war intrude on every conversation. Rossi knew her
husband's missions would take a very dangerous turn at the outset of any
hostilities. For his part, Cayton could tell that something was bothering his
wife that went beyond the usual frustrations of any company commander in
the field, where everyone was invariably miserable and more than happy to
tell you about it. Certainly the fact that she could lead a helicopter company
yet was barred by Arab law from so much as driving a car also grated, but
Cayton sensed there was something else.

It turned out the Army had tried to take away Marie Rossi's command. As
the sands ran out on Bush's ultimatum to Iraq, Rossi's unit had been redesig-
nated from a transport to a combat-support company, and someone had noticed that her command slot was officially designated as a male-only
position. With war looming and women accounting for 6 percent of U.S.
forces deployed to the Persian Gulf region, the combat-exclusion rule, which
was easily overlooked or papered over in peacetime, was becoming an increasingly controversial issue.

Typically, Marie Rossi had resisted what she considered any special treatment based on her being a woman. If the Army wanted to pull her and the
other female pilots out of the cockpit, Rossi told her commander, then it
must want to remove all of the enlisted women from the unit's ranks as well.
The contradiction was clear: enlisted women soldiers and crew members
would conceivably be in as much danger as the pilots, and Rossi knew the
unit could not afford to replace them at the last moment. Eventually, the
matter was dropped.

Marie Rossi could see the concern in her husband's face grow as she told
him the story, and she knew how to deal with it.

"Well, what if I asked you not to fly just because I'm worried about you,"
she asked Cayton.

"I can't do that."

"That's right, and neither can I," said Marie, and they both laughed at their mutual stubbornness. "As far as that goes, I want my air medal, too."

42: Air War 1991

"CHUCK? You're not saying anything."

Air Force chief of staff Gen. Merrill McPeak, offering some unsolicited advice over a secure communications link to the Black Hole in Riyadh, caught the silence on Chuck Horner's end of the line.

"No, no, General, I'm just writing down some of your ideas," Horner lied.

"No, you're not. You're telling me that I'm not in charge," said McPeak, yet there was no rancor in his voice.

"General McPeak, believe me, I want to hear what you have to say."

"No, you don't. You're the one in charge," said McPeak, who caught himself before the insatiable craving for tactical information and input that had consumed his predecessor Mike Dugan took hold. McPeak signed off. He had reiterated that Horner should feel free to ignore any unwarranted queries from the air staff in the Pentagon, which had been instructed to funnel their inputs and questions through the chain of command beginning with the Joint Staff.

In fact, the initial plan for the most intensive and nontraditional air campaign in history was already being put in place to launch Desert Storm. It outlined an integrated, nearly simultaneous attack by a strike force of 668 allied aircraft on over a hundred Iraqi command, control, and communications facilities, air-defense sites, airfields, Scud launchers, and nuclear and chemical-weapons facilities.

In many ways it was a typical rollback of a layered enemy air-defense network that the Air Force practiced regularly at Red Flag exercises. Stealth F-117s and cruise missiles were tasked with taking out heavily defended air-defense command centers in Baghdad, effectively blinding the centralized command-and-control of Iraq's air-defense network. Air Force F-15 Eagle and Navy F-14 Tomcat air-superiority fighters would fly combat air patrol to engage Iraqi interceptors, while Air Force EF-111 Raven and Navy EA6B Prowlers provided electronic countermeasures and jamming, and Air Force F-4G Wild Weasels suppressed enemy radars, sending HARM missiles down their beacons. Those support aircraft would be followed by a massive multinational strike force.

Yet traditional delineations between "strategic" and "tactical" targets and aircraft were also totally obscured by Horner's centralized control over all aircraft in theater, a result primarily of the Goldwater-Nichols reforms strengthening the authority of the CINCs. Horner's imaginative staff of air planners had Army Apache helicopters firing the first shots on a key Iraqi radar for instant damage assessment, typically considered a "strategic" mission, and later Strategic Air Command B-52s conducting the "tactical" mission of pounding the front-line enemy forces. At the suggestion of Gen. Jack Galvin, a composite wing from the United States Air Forces Europe would also be hitting targets in northern Iraq from Incirlik Air Base in Turkey.

Even before the United Nations deadline of January 15 arrived, Schwarzkopf passed preliminary attack orders to Horner and other senior commanders. On January 12, after extensive hearings in the Senate Armed Services Committee, both houses of Congress had approved the president's use of force following what was the most somber and eloquent floor debate in memory. The distraction of a constitutional showdown over the War Powers Act was thus averted, and Congress atoned for the Gulf of Tonkin Resolution of 1964, when it delivered then president Lyndon Johnson what one critic warned was a "predated declaration of war" in Vietnam after only hours of largely perfunctory debate. The actual order to execute arrived by secure fax late on the night of January 15, signed by President Bush and Defense Secretary Cheney. Desert Storm would commence at 0300 local time, on the morning of the seventeenth.

In the early-morning hours of January 17, Chuck Horner was pacing the Black Hole, so called for the top-secret planning that had been conducted there over the past four and a half months. Large screens in the Tactical Air Control Center displayed intelligence from Air Force AWACS (Airborne Warning and Control System) and Navy E-2C Hawkeye aircraft, U-2 and TR-1 long-range reconnaissance aircraft, unmanned drones, satellites, and powerful ships' radars. At that moment 160 tankers were in the air, refueling aircraft for the attack runs into Iraq. From Tehran to Turkey to southern Saudi Arabia, Chuck Horner had a God's-eye view of everything flying in the Middle East.

On the surface the situation was indistinguishable from countless war games he had played over the years. Only this time, Horner realized, those are real people out there, and we're really going to kill them. Or they will kill us. Doubt was nagging at Horner in those moments before the malignant breath of war was finally released.

Nothing concerned him more than the wing of F-117 aircraft that he was sending against the most heavily defended targets in Baghdad, naked except for their "stealth" cloaks. Suddenly all of the newspaper and magazine articles questioning the effectiveness of this unproven technology were eating at his confidence. If they had missed something important, then his friend Col. Alton Whitley and the entire 37th Tactical Fighter Wing would fly into a deadly maelstrom.

If the view from the Black Hole was God's eye, in those final moments Chuck Horner felt anything but godly. Before the night was over, people would die on his orders, and their blood would be on his hands just as surely as that of the people he himself had killed in war. How will I stand before God so besmirched, thought Horner, and dare to say, "Look what I've done"? *You can't* . . .

A silence descended over the Black Hole as the clock edged toward H hour. Upstairs, one of Horner's aides was monitoring the live television broadcast of CNN reporting from Baghdad. Bernard Shaw was telling his fellow correspondent that they had heard no jets when Peter Arnett broke in: "Now the sirens are sounding for the first time. The Iraqis have informed us—"

At that moment the transmission was abruptly cut short. One of the first sites on Horner's target list was the telecommunications building in Baghdad. Horner's aide sent word down that CNN had just gone off the air. A deafening cheer went up in the Black Hole, some of the staff noting that the time was exactly three A.M. Put it aside, thought Horner, and just do your job the best you can. The war had begun, and he had his airmen to worry about.

High up in the coastal mountains near the Red Sea, the Nighthawk pilots of the 37th Tactical Fighter Wing had walked quietly from their briefing room into the night air at Khamis Mushait Air Base, and immediately the wing's support personnel knew that the night's mission was for real. The pilots, quieter and more preoccupied than usual, had all taped over their rank insignia and removed their identification patches. Many were snapping live ammo clips into the sidearms they carried in shoulder holsters, adjusting and readjusting the harnesses over their G suits. Col. Alton Whitley zipped a small American flag into his flight suit, much like the one he had carried when he flew the first operational flight of the F-117 eight years earlier.

As a wing commander with combat experience, Whitley had for days been telling his men that it was all right to feel scared at that moment. He had only to think of his wife, Ann, and the boys, and the fear and anxiety would wash through him as well. Yet he knew something his younger pilots didn't. A few years earlier commanding Red Flag training exercises at Nellis, Whitley saw in the poise and confidence of the young pilots finishing that program that Red Flag training had lived up to its initial charter. He had only to think back to his days as a lieutenant flying F-100s in Vietnam to realize that the young pilots he now commanded were starting from a point it had taken him harrowing combat missions to attain. The wild card in all their calculations, however, was the F-117 itself. As one of the original Nighthawks— which the F-117 pilots called themselves because they only came out at night and no one knew who they were—Whitley probably had more experience with the F-117 than any other pilot in the service. He had tested it against numerous threat systems and configurations, pored over more test data on its stealth characteristics than he cared to recall, logged so many hours in its cockpit that his tailbone often ached, and he secretly carried a "whoopee cushion" on every mission to ease the discomfort. Yet in his heart Alton Whitley wasn't sure stealth would work.

In many ways the F-117 epitomized much of the high technology on which so much depended in those crucial hours. During the 1980s, it had indeed been the prototype for a whole generation of weapons that were produced rapidly and at great cost, and that aggressively stretched the boundaries of technology. Every pilot understood, however, that a complex synergism of systems and situations was at work in an actual war that were impossible to duplicate in peacetime. For every advance in the arms race, there inevitably came an enemy reaction. If Iraq's onetime Soviet sponsors had reacted in response to stealth in some way not yet revealed, then the pilots on that flight line at Khamis Mushait were dead men.

Alton Whitley thought about his early days of the F-117 program. Back in 1982, he had become the first operational Air Force pilot to fly the supersecret F-117A stealth aircraft; that made him a pioneer in one of the most closely guarded weapons programs since the Manhattan Project of World War II. For years in the early 1980s, Whitley had commuted each week from his home in Las Vegas to the top secret Tonapah airbase deep in the Nevada desert. On Monday mornings Whitley would kiss his wife and their two children good-bye and board a chartered passenger jet at Nellis Air Force Base, and return on Friday afternoons. Ann understood that she could never ask where he had been. As for the children, for all he knew they thought all fathers only appeared for two days at a stretch.

Whitley himself was part of a long heritage dear to the military, a son of the conservative South who had grown up in a family of modest means. His father had served as an Army corporal in World War II, and spent most of his life as a textile worker. Though neither of Whitley's parents had attended college, they were determined that Alton and his brother would have it better. It was during his ROTC stint at Clemson University in South Carolina during the mid-1960s that Alton Whitley had first thought about joining the Air Force. With the Vietnam War in full swing, flying over the jungles of Southeast Asia had seemed more appealing than trudging through them. There had never been a question of somehow trying to avoid service.

In the early days of the F-117 program, Whitley had traveled often to Lockheed Skunk Works plant in Burbank, California. There he had met the feisty wizard behind the legendary Skunk Works. A small man with the personality of a dynamo, Ben Rich had run Skunk Works like a benevolent dictator.

At the time, Ben Rich had told a prophetic story of one of the earliest stealth experiments, when a scale model of the F-117 was being tested for its radar signature. Rich and the other observers who monitored the tests from inside the building had been horrified when the stationary model appeared on the radar screen as a clear signature. Just as suddenly, however, it disappeared. It turned out that a bird had landed on the model in the midst of the tests. The story underscored, however, just how novel the technology was that they were all betting so much on.

The awareness of that fact colored the comments heard on the flight line as the pilots prepared to board their aircraft for their flight to Baghdad. Of course it was spoken with the lighthearted bravado of the true brethren, but the laughter that followed had the hollow ring of gallows humor. Whitley heard it himself and subconsciously concurred. "Goddamn, sir," said one of his pilots, "I sure hope this stealth shit works."

Whitley had scheduled himself in the second wave of aircraft over Baghdad, and a hundred miles into Iraqi airspace he sensed that he had done himself no favors. Their mission was to blind Iraq's air-defense system, whose command center was situated in Baghdad. Theoretically at least, an F-117 pilot would slip in under radar undetected and could thus focus longer on the task of putting his weapon on a target without taking evasive maneuvers. Combined with the accuracy of the weapons-delivery system, that capability explained why during the war only the F-117 would be allowed to strike targets in central Baghdad, where the coalition hoped to avoid collateral damage to civilians.

Over the horizon, Whitley could see an orange glow like the promise of a harvest moon. That was strange, because Chuck Horner's planners had deliberately chosen a night with minimal lunar illumination. At eighty miles the light on the horizon appeared as a vast charcoal grill, smoldering with red embers, small fires, and tiny sparks. By the time he was within forty miles, Whitley could make out the whole fireworks show, with the spewing streams of tracers and surface-to-air missiles. At that moment he felt like the hiker on a mountain trail who comes along five minutes after the guy who kicked over the hornet's nest.

Feeling his heart pumping wildly, Whitley purposely started drilling himself on his attack sequence, adjusting his navigation headings, checking altitude, and adjusting for the symbols on his heads-up display that told him to fly left or right to correct for crosswinds. Willing him to look up from his cockpit on the approach over the city, however, Whitley's mind screamed a chilling and unbidden message. No freaking way in hell, he thought, are you going to make it through this.

Coming in over Baghdad with the autopilot cued on the attack run and the bombs armed, Whitley felt the aircraft buffeted and jolted sickeningly from the explosions of nearby flak. Tracer streams poured into the night air in front of his canopy and off to the side, many of them seemingly fired wildly. They were flying across a shooting gallery, but the trigger pullers were apparently firing blindly. As opposed to the unimaginative "bomber stream" tactics that characterized the early years of Vietnam, the aircraft were coming at their targets from different directions and on different tracks to confound air-defense gunners. Time to take care of business, thought Whitley.

From the infrared picture on his display he spotted his target and matched the crosshairs precisely over the aim point. Depressing the target-designator button with his fingertip, Whitley sent a continuous, pinpoint laser beam at the target that the bomb would, in theory, glide down as if on a rail. At the right moment he hit a red button on the top of his control stick, heard the weapons-bay doors pop open and the huge bomb release with a resounding *thunk!* Lightened, the F-117 banked up into the night sky.

The F-117s flew thirty sorties over a heavily defended Baghdad that first night without losing a single aircraft. The Iraqi air-defense headquarters in Baghdad was destroyed by an F-117 that dropped a laser-guided bomb down the air shaft of its hardened concrete structure. In western Iraq, an air-defense-sector operations center was taken out by an F-117 bomb flown through the hole made by a previous bomb. In a press conference a few days later, Chuck Horner would astound the public by showing video of an F-117 taking out the headquarters of the Iraqi Air Force with another GBU-27 dropped down an air shaft, the bottom floors and windows of the building clearly billowing out at the moment of impact. Overall, the F-117s would fly only 2 percent of the combat sorties throughout Desert Storm, which was roughly equivalent to their representation in the vast allied air armada assembled in southwest Asia. Yet F-117s would attack more than 40 percent of the strategic and most heavily defended targets hit during the war.

Because in wartime the standards by which weapons are judged are absolute and unambiguous, it is a truism that the same weapons system can cast a vastly different shadow in wartime than in peace. In wartime success is everything and cost is no object, while in peacetime success is relative to expectations, and cost is often *the* object. For Col. Al Whitley and the rest of the Nighthawks of the 37th Tactical Fighter Wing, however, the true beauty of the F-117 that was revealed on January 17 was that in war as well as in peacetime, the stealth fighter cast hardly any shadow at all.

It was indicative of the communications breakdown between Riyadh and Navy ships in the Persian Gulf that when the *Ranger* carrier battle group contacted the USS *Blue Ridge* with a question about exactly when the war was to start, Adm. Stan Arthur didn't have a ready answer. Because they were unable to receive the voluminous air-tasking order electronically, the four carriers in the Persian Gulf were flying the computer discs aboard by hand, then duplicating the tasking order for the other ships in their group. After reviewing the copy, one of the war planners aboard the *Ranger* had thoughtfully raised the issue of whether the 0300 H hour was Greenwich mean time or local time. No one aboard having ever started a war before, it was not a rhetorical question.

With no direct communications between the carriers and Riyadh, the carrier-battle-group commanders had to ask the *Blue Ridge* for clarification. Stan Arthur had been frustrated for weeks by his inability to interface with the ongoing planning in Riyadh. Constantly he seemed behind, unable to keep pace with the tempo and flow of decision-making out of Central Command headquarters, and unclear on a number of issues with life-and-death consequences. The most glaring example of that disconnect would come when Arthur received the critical rules of engagement *after* the war had already started and his aircraft were in the air, only to discover that Iraqi tankers he thought they were free to sink were specifically excluded from the target list.

Chuck Horner had assured Col. Dave Eberly that the first combat missions should be easier than everything his pilots had done to prepare for them, and on the first mission that was essentially true. When he walked out of the briefing room with his flight gear in tow a few days into the air war, however, Eberly was suddenly not so sure. He shivered in the chill January air. The assistant commander of the 4th Tactical Fighter Wing thought back to the muggy August night in North Carolina when this journey had begun five months earlier, and Eberly had assured his wife that he'd be back in time for their son's Parents Day weekend at school in early September. How naive they had all been.

Dave Eberly was undeniably worried about that night's mission. By virtue of their advanced night-targeting and navigation systems, the F-15E Strike Eagles of the 4th Tactical Fighter Wing had been tasked with high-risk missions such as hitting heavily defended airfields and communications sites, as well as Scud missile launchers. Theirs had been one of the first aircraft shot down in the war, and Eberly lost his wingmates Maj. Tom Koritz and Lt. Col. Donnie Holland. That night the target area was farther north than anything they had flown against, and intelligence described it as heavily defended. Already the area had earned the nickname SAM's Town. While he was thinking about the briefing, Eberly ran into his boss, Col. Hal Hornburg, a silver-haired Texan who commanded the 4th Provisional Wing that had been assembled in the Gulf.

As the commander and assistant commander of the wing, both men had flown missions on the first night of the war, emphasizing the Air Force's "lead from the front" creed. A forward-air controller during Vietnam, Hornburg had commented that he saw more flak that first night than during an entire year in Vietnam. Both of them understood that they wouldn't ask any of their pilots to fly missions like the one scheduled for that night unless they were willing to lead the way. Before Eberly went out to his aircraft, Hornburg patted him on the back and wished him luck.

"You know," Dave Eberly told Hornburg in parting, "this one's worth twenty years of flight pay."

Scanning the iridescent cathode-ray tubes and a heads-up display in his darkened cockpit, Dave Eberly was viewing a key link in the technological revolution that was, during Desert Storm, fulfilling the old promise of decisive airpower. The F-15E Strike Eagle had a synthetic aperture radar that supplied TV-quality images at night of the ground below. The LANTIRN targeting and navigation system that was mounted in pods underneath his fuselage included a terrain-following radar for navigation, and a wide-angle, forward-looking, infrared radar (FLIR) and laser-designator for tracking targets. Behind Eberly sat his weapons-system officer, or "whizzo," Maj. Tom Griffith, who was monitoring four video screens displaying radar, weapons selection, and enemy radar tracking.

While Eberly's predecessors such as Chuck Horner had roamed enemy territory outside of their own ground radar coverage during Vietnam, operating in hunter-killer teams and using flares for night illumination to detect enemy convoys, Eberly had an unprecedented amount of information at his fingertips. There was a direct link to airborne AWACS command-and-control aircraft, which could track anything flying in his sector, as well as information from the developmental Joint STARS aircraft that had been rushed to the Persian Gulf at Schwarzkopf's request. Utilizing its powerful synthetic-aperture radar with a 155-mile radius, Joint STARS could track virtually anything moving on the ground, from enemy convoys to mobile Scud missile sites. Framers of AirLand Battle doctrine had long viewed this kind of "look deep, see deep" technology as a key link to the style of maneuver warfare they were promulgating, with its emphasis on deep strikes to disrupt the massing of enemy echelon forces.

Each time pilots passed into Iraqi airspace they felt the same rush of adrenaline, akin to the thrill of robbing banks every night. This mission was no different. Eberly's aircraft was the third in over the target, and as they began their approach, he could see the Roman-candle flashes of surface-to-air missiles launching, burning daggers probing for his soft underbelly in the night. As he banked for his own run on the target, Eberly noted with a sense of pride that no confused or excited screaming came over the radio net as they had all heard from the old tapes of pilots crossing the Red River for the first time back in Vietnam.

"Dave, we've got one on our right side back here," Tom Griffith's voice came over the headset. Eberly swiveled his head in time to see the growing embers of not one but two surface-to-air missiles on his right side. He banked hard left into the black nothingness to avoid the missiles, his stomach churning from the violent maneuver and fear. The whine of the two Pratt & Whitney engines turned into a high-pitched howl, and after a moment Eberly turned right back over the target area and directly into the path of the third missile, which he never even saw.

The shock of the impact was profound. Like swinging on a rope vine as a kid, caught up in the giddy sense of motion and then suddenly hitting the tree. Eberly knew he was alive, but everything was numb. Immediately his hand reached up for the ejection lever. As a young fighter pilot Dave Eberly had always fantasized about flying a crippled aircraft home, getting it out of a tight spot à la John Wayne. Yet something was wrong in that cockpit, something unfamiliar and menacing, and Eberly knew he and Griff had to get out of there.

•   •   •

Chuck Horner took the call in his command center in Riyadh, Col. Hal Hornburg relaying the news that Dave Eberly had been shot down. Having lost two aircraft and now his vice commander and director of operations in only a matter of days, Hornburg was obviously shaken. Horner and Buster Glosson both assured him that their tactics were sound, that he should press on and not dwell on the loss. That's what you did in a war.

Though their losses were historically light in those early days, each one came as a blow. Chuck Horner knew Dave Eberly well and had hired Hal Hornburg to command his old unit at Seymour Johnson. Donnie Holland, a friend who was killed on one of the first missions, was an older pilot who had desperately wanted to get in the cockpit of an F-15E as a weapons-systems officer. Horner had personally interceded on his behalf, and now the man was dead. Soon Horner would have to talk to Holland's wife and tell her that if he hadn't interfered, her husband might still be alive.

Bill Creech had said it years ago concerning training at Red Flag, and it applied to any extended air campaign. You didn't have to run it as if every mission were being conducted on the first minute of the first hour on the first day of a war. Horner was determined to manage the air war with attrition as a driver, backing off whenever casualties threatened to get out of hand, or circumstances allowed. Thus after the first week and following the loss of Eberly, as well as six RAF Tornadoes on low-level attack runs, he directed that all coalition aircraft start operating at safer medium altitudes.

Their success during the first week in crippling Saddam Hussein's command-and-control system made the decision possible. By the sixth day of the war, electronic emissions from the radars controlling Iraqi surface-to-air missiles that could target them at medium altitudes had dropped 95 percent. Many missile sites were simply leaving their radars off for fear of being targeted by a Wild Weasel. At the end of the second week, even Saddam's backup communications were destroyed to the point where he was using messengers to hand-carry dispatches to his troops in Kuwait.

In the meantime, Horner had the twin problems of Iraqi Scud missiles and Saddam's strangely dormant Air Force to worry about. On the second day of the war, Iraq had launched seven Scud missiles at Israel, recalling Saddam's veiled threat to "burn half of Israel" with chemical weapons. Though it turned out that the missiles carried conventional warheads and were notoriously inaccurate, the Scuds were effective as terror weapons against civilian populations, and their use threatened to bring Israel into the war and possibly rupture the coalition. While that battle was being fought diplomatically in Washington, Horner diverted an increasing number of his sorties to the frustrating hunt for Mobile Scuds.

They had already targeted every known Scud site in western Iraq in the first days of the war, destroying thirty-six fixed launchers. However, the remaining mobile launchers, essentially an eight-wheeled truck utilizing predetermined launch pads, were devilishly difficult to locate. By the time sensors detected a launch, and the coordinates were relayed to pilots in the air, the trucks had often packed up and retreated to various hiding places. Luckily, the Army's Patriot antimissile batteries, which had never been battle-tested and were originally developed to target aircraft, were apparently proving at least somewhat effective in intercepting the Scuds.

Later, a furor would erupt over whether the Patriot missile was the high-tech wonder that Central Command was depicting to the public, or a fraud. The controversy offered a glimpse at the distance between perception and the reality of weapons performance, and how it is often obscured by the fog of war. Initially, the Army claimed near-perfect success for the Patriots, stating that they had intercepted 45 out of 47 incoming Scuds. Later reports indicated that because the Scuds were already breaking up by the time they were intercepted, the warheads of many of the "successfully intercepted" missiles were not touched. Some experts questioned whether any Patriots had truly been successful.

Perception vs. reality. Was the Patriot the near-perfect missile originally described by the Army, or the failure alluded to by its critics? As in so many matters of war, the truth was ambiguous. In fact, the Patriot was originally designed as an antiaircraft missile and had been modified to provide antimissile defense for critical military targets such as airfields, not blanket defense for an entire city. In the point-defense role, pushing a warhead even partially off its course might prove effective. At least initially, the perception was also that the Patriot offered a viable defense against Scuds for the people of Israel, and that perception had the very real effect of helping keep Israel out of the war.

From a purely military standpoint, the question of Iraq's Air Force was of greater concern to Horner. Iraq had essentially ceded the skies to the allied aircraft, leading to concern that Saddam might be hoarding his Air Force for an "Air Tet," or some sort of mass suicide strike that might have a major psychological impact on the coalition, or public support for the war.

Shooting down Iraqi aircraft was not the problem. Though some of the Iraqi aircraft were state-of-the-art, for U.S. pilots who had grown up in the cockpit sparring with the vaunted Aggressors, or earning their advanced degrees in aerial combat from schools such as the Navy's Top Gun or the Air

Force's Fighter Weapons School, the Iraqi pilots were no competition. On the first night of the war, the Iraqis had sent twenty-five fighters into the air, and within ninety minutes Air Force F-15s had shot down four of them and another was driven into the ground. By the end of the first week, the Iraqis had lost fourteen fighters in aerial combat to zero casualties for the allies.

Shortly after Horner began ordering the attack of the aircraft on the ground in their hardened shelters, much of the Iraqi Air Force began flushing to Iran. No one knew for sure what Iraq had in mind with this maneuver. Perhaps Saddam Hussein simply assumed he could retrieve the aircraft once the war was over, or maybe in some secret deal Iran was providing a safe haven. Whatever Saddam had in mind, Horner responded by establishing "barrier patrols" of F-15s to intercept any Iraqi aircraft making for Iran. Sometime after giving that order, Chuck Horner received the phone call he feared might lead to his resignation.

After a high-speed chase, one of their F-15s had destroyed two Iraqi aircraft. When the U.S. wing commander checked the coordinates of the wreckage, however, he discovered that it was twenty miles inside the borders of Iran. Suddenly Horner could see it very clearly. Some diplomat in Washington was going to throw his hands up in despair of this international incident, and they were going to establish a buffer zone around Iran, just as they had around the border of China during Vietnam. Of course Saddam would move his aircraft to that buffer zone, and Horner's pilots would be out there risking their lives while the enemy was once again granted a safe haven. *Never again . . .*

At that moment, Horner decided that he would argue against any such buffer zone with all the logic and reason he could muster, and if the chain of command couldn't be swayed, he would resign. It's what we always felt our leaders in Vietnam should have done, Horner thought, and the thinking of it hardened his resolve.

"Sir, we just shot down two of theirs inside Iran," Horner told Schwarzkopf over the phone. "I'm sorry. It was a mistake."

"Well, that happens," Schwarzkopf replied, apparently unfazed. After relaying the news to Colin Powell, Schwarzkopf called back and assured Horner that the chairman hadn't made a fuss. In the end, the Iranians apparently put out word that their air defense forces were not to fire on American aircraft venturing across the border in pursuit of Iraqis.

The incident afforded Horner a brief moment of reflection amidst his wartime worries, and he felt renewed confidence that they were going to do this thing right. Already his air blitz had blinded Iraq to two Army corps that were snaking inexorably west on Tapline Road in massive convoys, and in a matter of weeks they would be in position to deliver the pincer blow on the Republican Guards in Kuwait. In the meantime, heavily defended strategic targets such as bridges that had taken the Air Force years and countless sorties to destroy during Vietnam—every fighter pilot of Horner's generation remembered the notorious Dragon's Jaw bridge—were falling in a matter of hours to a combination of stealth technology, precision-guided munitions, and enemy defense-suppression techniques.

As those prime targets fell in the first few weeks of the air war, Horner was able to devote an ever-increasing number of sorties to pounding the Iraqi forces in Kuwait with a goal of destroying 50 percent of their tanks and artillery. The number was not chosen at random. Historically, military units that suffered levels of attrition approaching half their combat power collapsed. If nothing forced them into a costly ground campaign prematurely, Horner was confident he could slowly strangle the Iraqi military from the air.

43: Eve of Destruction 1991

THE Blackhawk helicopter passed over a convoy heading west during the long flight to Riyadh a week into February, and Barry McCaffrey thought ruefully that more of his people than he cared to think about had died on Tapline Road. Shifting the entire 24th Infantry Division five hundred kilometers along that vital east-west artery in just ten days had proven a monumental logistical challenge.

It had taken nearly 70 convoys of 150 vehicles each, driving around the clock and sorting through nightmare traffic jams as the VII and XVIII Corps crossed paths, the heat melting the tread off recapped tires. A number of his soldiers had perished in traffic accidents along the way. Yet for all the typically American faults, of which you could probably write volumes and put impatience and impertinence somewhere near the top, McCaffrey had a new admiration for the American eagerness to dare great feats.

If he was pensive that day, it was because McCaffrey was flying to Riyadh to help brief Secretary of Defense Dick Cheney and Gen. Colin Powell on whether the 24th was ready for war. Thinking about what he was going to say made him feel like Grant's captain, asked for his opinion by the great general on the eve of battle.

They were ready. After completing the swing west, the division commanders had spent thousands of hours in constant rehearsals for the attack, walking through it in elaborately constructed sand tables just as they had learned to use back at the National Training Center. After more than five months in the harsh desert climate, meanwhile his tanks registered an operational readiness rate of 98 percent, his Bradley Fighting Vehicles 97 percent, and his TOW vehicles 92 percent. The readiness of his helicopters, including the much maligned Apache, was 100 percent.

The story of how a notorious hangar queen like the Apache, the subject of a recent 60 *Minutes* exposé and a critical General Accounting Office report the year before, was metamorphosing into a reliable high-tech wonder during Desert Storm provided yet another example of how the same weapon could cast a vastly different image in war than in peacetime.

The Apache was one of the highly concurrent weapons programs developed during the 1980s, when the bloom was on the Reagan defense buildup and weapons were being rushed to the field with little testing. In April of 1990, GAO officials told Congress that because key Apache parts failed so often, the helicopter couldn't perform all of its assigned missions half the time, and a third of the time it couldn't perform *any* missions.

With no distractions and no maintenance personnel off on leave or at various service schools, however, McCaffrey's Apache maintenance shop and others in the Persian Gulf had surged from an average of two and a half hours a day of wrench-turning time on the helicopter to up to twelve hours a day. The Army was also airlifting up to three times as many spare parts to Apache battalions as would be the case in normal deployments, and because there was little threat to logistics areas from Iraqi aircraft, the 24th Division's maintenance depot was pushed forward where aircraft needing relatively minor repairs could be turned around faster.

GAO investigators were sent to visit the Persian Gulf, a move that angered many commanders, and they endorsed all of the measures. They later pointed out correctly, however, that while the Army had less than half of its entire inventory of 660 Apaches deployed for Desert Storm, in many critical support areas it was using 100 percent of its capability, emptying spare-parts bins and slashing flying hours for Apaches not deployed to the Persian Gulf in half. In the European scenario for which the aircraft was primarily designed, they noted, the Army would not have five months to raise the Apache's readiness, and it might well need its entire fleet.

Besides the fact that he could count on nearly all of his Apache forces, however, the issue concerning the high-tech gunship that most interested Barry McCaffrey was not even mentioned in all the reports and exposés. The Army didn't talk publicly about the range or protection level of its weapons, actually preferring that potential enemies who monitored the press underestimate their capabilities. The whole idea of the Army classifying such information was that they would prove just how good their weapons were when it mattered most.

Given their nighttime targeting and navigation systems and accurate Hellfire missiles, however, mobile Apache forces could maneuver well outside the range of enemy tanks and destroy them with relative impunity night and day. Given the 24th's mission of striking three hundred kilometers deep into the enemy's rear to block the retreat of up to a half million Iraqi soldiers through the Euphrates River Valley, that capability was suddenly the only issue in the Apache saga that mattered.

All of the senior commanders were present for the briefing, which began early on Saturday morning and ran most of the day. Chuck Horner, John Yeosock, Walt Boomer, and Stan Arthur led off with their individual assessments, each stressing that they were ready for the ground war. The sense of camaraderie between these four component commanders, forged under months of incredible stress and stoked by Schwarzkopf's furious temper, was solidly fused by February 9.

When Walt Boomer briefed the Marine Corps battle plan, it still included an amphibious assault to relieve pressure on the Marines on the ground attacking into the teeth of Iraqi fortifications. After General Powell asked some pointed questions about expected casualties, Boomer conceded that the beaches were heavily defended, and that the Iraqis had mined the approaches. Listening to his friend describe the Iraqi shore defenses, Chuck Horner had a nightmare vision out of the Pacific campaign of World War II, with the bodies of Marines floating in a surf laced by machine-gun and heavy-weapons fire. Clearly, both Powell and Cheney also had concerns about an amphibious assault. In truth, Walt Boomer had long since begun to share them.

As the day wore on, Gus Pagonis outlined the massive shift of two Army Corps westward, which had been completed in the allotted three weeks and drew strong praise from Powell and Cheney. Lt. Gen. Fred Franks, commander of VII Corps, presented next, and the deliberate attack plan and insistence that he would need the division being held in reserve in order to succeed highlighted a brewing controversy. From the beginning, Schwarzkopf felt that Franks's attack plan was plodding and overly cautious. In fact, he had been leaning hard on Yeosock on that very point, stressing to the Army component commander that VII Corps's mission was to slam into the Republican Guard with "audacity, shock action, and surprise."

Schwarzkopf considered Barry McCaffrey his most aggressive ground commander, and McCaffrey's turn to brief came next. McCaffrey gave a detailed assessment of the 24th's attack plan and was characteristically upbeat. After he was finished, Cheney broke in to ask McCaffrey how he anticipated the battle unfolding.

After the 24th severed the Euphrates River Valley, McCaffrey said, he hoped that the Republican Guard divisions would bolt for Baghdad, trying to come right over his positions.

"If they do, will you be able to handle them?"

"Absolutely. No problem."

"Okay, General. Now tell me what you're worried about," Cheney said.

McCaffrey hadn't expected the question, and for a moment it took him aback.

"Well, sir, my son's life is at stake in this battle to come," McCaffrey said. "You also should understand that I've been wounded in combat three times. I have no illusions about what ground warfare is all about. So I hesitate to say this, but I'm not worried. The division has rehearsed its plan. The plan is logistically supportable. We're fully modernized. Our soldiers are the best in the world. And I feel uncomfortable saying this, but I don't think these guys we're fighting are very good. My guess is that we'll destroy the Iraqi Army in ten days to four weeks."

McCaffrey knew that he sounded gung ho and optimistic, but it was his honest assessment. Still, it wasn't entirely true that nothing was worrying him. "Sir, I will say that I expect the Twenty-fourth to take anywhere between five hundred to two thousand casualties in that fighting. I suspect it will be closer to five hundred."

Some experts were predicting the bloodiest day for the U.S. military since the Normandy landing. McCaffrey knew from his phone conversations with Jill that back at Fort Stewart they were already holding blood drives and assembling chaplain teams to begin the grim process of notifying thousands of families that their loved ones were gone. McCaffrey could sense that bubble of horror poised to descend over his post back home, and he resolved to make a trip out to where the 82nd Division was located to visit Sean before the ground war started.

• • •

The final decision on whether or not to conduct an amphibious assault was made aboard the USS *Blue Ridge*. Schwarzkopf had requested another briefing on the assault plans, which was given by Stan Arthur because the 32,000-man Marine force afloat was under Navy command until it hit shore. It was also up to the Navy to maneuver its ships to support an amphibious landing, a risky venture given that the amphibious assault ship USS *Tripoli* and the Aegis guided-missile cruiser USS *Princeton* had been badly damaged after striking mines.

Arthur explained that they would be forced to destroy some of Kuwait City, because the spot the Marines had chosen to go in was overlooked by apartment buildings occupied by the Iraqis. Though the Marines could undoubtedly get through the beach defenses, which were relatively shallow, they would certainly endure casualties. Finally, the Iraqis had mined the approaches, and there was little chance of clearing those mines before the G-day timetable of somewhere around February 21–26.

After listening to Arthur's assessment, Schwarzkopf wheeled deliberately in his chair and addressed the question that was on all of their minds to Walt Boomer, who was sitting at the other end of the conference table.

"Walt, can you accomplish your mission without an amphibious assault?"

The seconds ticked away while Boomer considered his answer, and the lengthening silence seemed almost to draw the air out of the room. For a Marine Corps general, especially one confronting the tactical problem of those Iraqi fortifications, the allure of that amphibious force remained powerful. Attacking over beaches is what the Marine Corps did, and no one was more eager to prove that point than those Marines sitting in ships in the Persian Gulf.

Perhaps much the same kind of decision had confronted the Screaming Eagle commander who ordered eleven assaults up Hamburger Hill in Vietnam decades earlier, at a cost of nearly four hundred American dead or wounded. Because that's where the enemy was and that was what airborne troops did. But there were going to be no Hamburger Hills during Desert Storm.

"We can make it without the amphibious assault," Boomer said finally, breaking the silence that for him had seemed to last forever. "But we've got to make them *believe* we're coming ashore." Boomer went on to stress that his forces would need good weather for air support, and eventually he would ask for a few extra days to reposition his troops on the Kuwaiti border. Schwarzkopf readily agreed to both requests, despite the fact that the pressure from Washington to launch the ground war early was already beginning to make him crazy.

• • •

"Listen up, you cocksucker!" Chuck Horner shouted into his phone at Brig. Gen. Steven Arnold, berating the G-3 operations officer at Army headquarters. Unsatisfied with Horner's targeting list, Arnold had apparently been sending out snide message traffic to the effect that the coalition could win this war if only the Air Force would do what the Army asked. Horner was incensed. The Army had yet to jump into this freaking fray, and his pilots had been fighting and dying for a month! The conversation went downhill from there.

The pressure in Central Command headquarter cells was reaching critical mass. With only days to go before G day, ground commanders were getting understandably anxious, and Horner was dealing with the competing demands of a handful of corps commanders, each picking specific targets and asking for top priority. While Schwarzkopf was the final arbiter of each day's targeting list, Horner was being blamed by corps commanders, who didn't think the Air Force was concentrating heavily enough on pounding the Republican Guard.

The frayed tempers between Horner and the Army staff and corps commanders had been exacerbated by the fact that Horner's roommate and friend, John Yeosock, the Army component commander, had been medevaced to Germany for an emergency gallbladder operation. In the brief command vacuum Arnold had apparently begun sending his sniping message traffic. With the right word, Yeosock would have squelched the carping from his staff before Horner blew his lid, something he knew he could never have explained to Bill Creech.

The pressures to start the ground war early were also reaching a fever pitch. With the Soviets floating initiatives that some in Washington believed could lead to an unsatisfactory peace, members of the National Security Council were clamoring for an early window that would put the launch in the middle of a storm front. However, both Walt Boomer and Binney Peay of the 101st Airborne needed clear weather for their aircraft and were arguing for a postponement. The issue even prompted a rare shouting match between Schwarzkopf and Colin Powell.

While Horner admired Schwarzkopf for steadfastly resisting being hurried and putting the lives of his soldiers first, the intense pressure was not making the volatile CINC any easier to work with. Just a few days before the ground war was set to begin on February 24, Chuck Horner was thus in a dark mood when he returned to his room past midnight and found a nurse standing there. It was the closest he'd been to a woman in nearly seven months, but what caused his face to slacken was the apparition just behind her. There, white as a ghost and sitting with an IV drip in his arm while he watched television, was John Yeosock.

When Horner stammered his surprise that the gruff Army general was back only days after major surgery, Yeosock pulled a fat cigar out of his mouth and, with a lopsided grin, lifted up his shirt to proudly show off his still-oozing incision. At that moment, Horner sensed that his recent troubles with the Army were over.

44: Ground War 1991

WITH the winds picking up on February 24, the horizon where the desert met the sky blurred into a dirty brown haze. The mood at the division command post for the 24th Infantry, near the town of Ansab in western Saudi Arabia, was somber and edgy. The Marine Corps and other select units had already launched their initial jabs into the teeth of Iraqi forces to stand them up, and all of XVIII and VII Corps were waiting to uncoil their surprise left hook. You could almost clock the minutes until H hour by observing what soldiers decided to throw away in those last hours, and how many officers stopped by to say final good-byes. No one wanted to be weighted down with extra baggage, emotional or otherwise, where they were going.

Barry McCaffrey had already spoken by phone with General Schwarzkopf, who had called the previous day and wished him Godspeed. The week before Barry had flown out to the 82nd Airborne on his western flank to visit with Sean. The boy was upbeat and excited. Just seeing and hearing Sean had done him good, but Barry had decided it would be better not to think about what lay ahead for Sean. Even as he waited on February 24 for their launch hour the next morning, McCaffrey knew that the 82nd had already crossed the border.

When Army headquarters called and asked if the 24th Mech could launch fifteen hours early, it was almost a relief. The Marines were advancing faster than anticipated, and Schwarzkopf wanted to make sure that McCaffrey's division was in place in time to plug the Euphrates River Valley against possible reinforcements from the north, or Iraqi forces retreating from Kuwait. That was exactly what McCaffrey intended to do.

At three P.M. on February 24, the "Victory" Division crossed the Iraqi border in a blinding sandstorm. Even bunched up tighter than usual because of the poor visibility, it was a massive, three-pronged juggernaut of over 1,700 tracked vehicles, 6,500 trucks, nearly 100 helicopters, and 26,000 soldiers. McCaffrey attached his command cell of four armored vehicles to one of the brigade tactical command posts. He also kept two helicopters at his disposal to move forward as the advance and the weather allowed.

McCaffrey's Apaches had been scouting the area just inside the Iraqi border for weeks, reporting that the area standing between the 24th and its first-day objectives was deserted. Before nightfall, the division had reached all of those assembly points inside Iraq, and McCaffrey pushed his commanders to keep going. At darkness the winds died down temporarily, then kicked up again intermittently in howling rainstorms. Still they advanced.

In the middle of the night the lead elements entered a land of rough-hewn hills, with steep cliffs and treacherous gulches. The rain and dust blinded tank drivers, who picked their way with infrared night sights and handheld Global Positioning System navigation devices. The weather grounded helicopter battalions, but the division pressed on without them. The landscape was soon dotted with overturned tanks and other vehicles that drove blindly into ditches and tumbled down wadis. The cavalry unit assigned to pick a path through what became known as the Great Dismal Bog lost many of its vehicles. McCaffrey pushed them through a night march of endless exhaustion, which for him recalled the torturous months of Ranger School. Only this time it was not an infantry company stumbling ahead in the dark, but an entire mechanized division.

By dawn the next day the weather had cleared, and by early afternoon McCaffrey was ordered to consolidate his forces. The 24th had already pushed more than sixty miles inside Iraq, far outpacing the VII Corps on its right flank led by General Franks, and Schwarzkopf was worried that if it got too far out in front, the 24th might have to face a Republican Guard counterattack by itself.

Later Schwarzkopf complained in his biography that he felt as if he were driving "a wagon pulled by racehorses and mules."

Later in the day, however, McCaffrey was given the okay to proceed. By late afternoon on the second day, all three brigades had reported enemy contacts, but after short engagements many Iraqis were surrendering. Again the winds picked up, and by nightfall they were slogging through another howling rainstorm, the worst yet. Still McCaffrey drove them through another all-night advance.

As Barry McCaffrey crested a rise that second night near the edge of the Euphrates River Valley, he saw that the entire division was engaged in a running gun battle. The flaming wreckage of hundreds of trucks and armored vehicles floated on a vast sea of darkness, over which muzzle flashes from artillery and tanks swept like lightning squalls. At first McCaffrey tried to convince himself that the thunderous explosions nearby were from their own artillery, but intuitively he knew they were enemy incoming. Surely here was the giant battle against hardened Iraqi forces that he had anticipated all along. Only the morning would reveal the true extent of the horror that had descended at last.

We really didn't kill these people, Capt. Linda Suttelhan thought to herself as her armored personnel carrier drove through a landscape of utter destruction the next morning. She was in the command cell for McCaffrey's 1st Brigade, by then spearheading the advance into the Euphrates. This is just the set of some twisted movie about the end of time, staged not far from where some believed time began for mankind in the Garden of Eden. The bodies out there—some burned black as charcoal, others headless or bent obscenely into broken-doll poses—were only props. Over and over again, Suttelhan could hear her driver mutter in a voice that was on the verge of tears, "It's just not right. It's just not right."

Suttelhan tore her eyes away from the surreal scene, the still-burning skeletons of vehicles and lines of POWs walking in the opposite direction and flashing peace signs, one of them wearing a Grateful Dead T-shirt, all of it mesmerizing as an auto wreck in slow motion. Suttelhan knew she was not supposed to be there. Her job as an intelligence officer for a combat brigade was clearly barred to women. After what they had all witnessed that morning, however, it would be hard to argue that anyone was meant to be in a place like this. She was still an officer, however, and one of her soldiers was on the brink of losing it.

"Look, Harold, I know this looks bad. I know it. But this is war, and there's a bigger picture than what we can see here."

"But, ma'am, I just had a baby I haven't even seen yet, and we're over here killing these people. It's just not right."

"Well, either we kill them or they're going to kill us," Suttelhan said, trying hard to convey her sense that they were in the right, but feeling inadequate to the task in the face of so much mute death and destruction.

As they drove across an overpass, Harold suddenly shouted in a different voice, "Get down!"

The deafening explosion seemed to erupt all around them, shaking their armored vehicle in a violent grip. Suttelhan kept her mouth open as she had been instructed to minimize the effect of blast pressure, sure that they had triggered a land mine and would die. Only their track somehow kept going. As it turned out, an Iraqi truck hidden under the overpass was hit by one of their own Bradley Fighting Vehicles just as they passed overhead. After that, Suttelhan heard very little from her driver.

They were leapfrogging to rendezvous with forward elements of the 24th Infantry Division's 1st Brigade under Col. John LeMoyne. Arriving, Suttelhan dismounted from her track and went over to where LeMoyne was standing with his executive officer. As they turned to greet her, Suttelhan saw the face of war.

They looked like different men. She hardly recognized LeMoyne, whose eyes burned almost feverishly out of deep sockets, his once-handsome face stretched into a mask of creases and hollows by nearly forty-eight hours of fighting without sleep. When he talked, the words came out agonizingly slow, as if he had to wrestle with each one.

"Deuce," said John LeMoyne, referring to this woman by her position as the brigade "two," or intelligence officer. The lines around his mouth relaxed into what might have been a smile. "It's good to . . . see . . . you."

They had paused for a couple of hours to refuel LeMoyne's brigade task force of six full battalions, practically the first time in more than two days that the 1st Brigade had stopped long enough for anyone to dismount their vehicles. After the previous night, bouncing over unseen ditches in the gear-gnashing confines of the tracked Bradley Fighting Vehicle, chilled by a cold rain and hot flashes of danger, just standing safely on the ground in warm sunlight was a sweet reprieve. Now as adrenaline subsided, the fatigue was a presence as real as gravity, a black hole of exhaustion capable of warping time and waking thought. Yet the night march had paid off.

At many of the enemy outposts they had overrun, the Iraqis hunkered down against the elements had simply surrendered in astonishment, mouths gaping at this deadly vision materializing out of a nearly impenetrable sandstorm. The advanced thermal sights on their M-1 tanks and Bradleys, whose supercool lenses were sensitive to any heat signatures in their fields of vision, gave the U.S. forces a decided advantage at night. Because of its computer-adjusted laser targeting system, the M-1 could fire accurately on the move, often from a distance of thirty-five hundred meters or more, outside the range of the front-line Soviet T-72 tanks it was fighting. The secret armor of the M-1A1s, hardened by depleted uranium, was also proving impervious to many enemy weapons.

The M-1's turbine engine was living up to its reputation as a voracious gas guzzler, and the advance was in danger of outrunning its fuel lines. Yet the turbine also made the M-1 whisper quiet and remarkably fast. More importantly, in deadly combat the rival T-72 was clearly no match for the M-1A1, proof once again that some critical truths about weapons only reveal themselves on the battlefield.

LeMoyne had perhaps been most worried about Iraqi artillery during the night fight. A number of times, the stomach-churning reverberations of enemy ranging rounds had crumped off near his command vehicle. The 1st Brigade's artillery experts were able to track the trajectory of the incoming rounds with Q-36 and Q-37 counterbattery radars, however, and each time LeMoyne had responded with a battalion-sized barrage on the corresponding map grids. One incoming invariably invited scores of outgoing. Not once were they targeted twice by the same Iraqi artillery position. In the morning light, they had overrun four Iraqi artillery units that had been either completely destroyed or abandoned because of the accuracy of their counterbattery fire.

After the 1st Brigade had finished refueling, LeMoyne ordered them to remount and resume the advance into the Euphrates. Cresting the ridge before the descent into the river valley, he told his driver to stop. Spread out before him over a long, sloping draw was nearly the entire brigade of more than a thousand vehicles. It was exactly the kind of swift, deep flanking attack that retired general Don Starry had once envisioned from the Golan Heights as his mind was helping concoct AirLand Battle. LeMoyne knew that few men had seen its like since the North African campaigns of World War II.

Continuing down the slope, LeMoyne noticed that the force in front of him had split in a large Y as if to avoid some impassable barrier, and as his Bradley dipped into a shallow wadi he saw why. Directly in their path was a small sheep herd and some bedouin shepherds, undoubtedly terrified by these massive war machines descending on their camp. Despite the fatigue, the lack of sleep, and the combat stress, the brigade had the discipline to heed LeMoyne's direction to keep a lookout and give a wide berth to bedouins so as not to frighten them unnecessarily.

As the soldiers passed, they waved and saluted at a shepherd standing at the edge of the herd with two young boys. By the time the commander's Bradley passed, the shepherd was saluting back with a smile, and LeMoyne returned both. Earlier he had seen the same troops dismount their vehicles and give their food away to hungry Iraqi POWs, some of whom were so surprised at not being executed that they rewarded their cringing benefactors with a scraggly kiss on the mouth. God bless these soldiers, thought LeMoyne.

• • •

It was the damnedest thing Barry McCaffrey could imagine. The handful of vehicles that comprised his division command post were sitting in the middle of the desert somewhere to the rear of 2nd Brigade. While McCaffrey talked with LeMoyne and his other brigade commanders over the communications net, scores of Iraqi soldiers kept approaching his command post to surrender.

With each new report from his forward commanders, McCaffrey's sense of relief grew. The casualty figures simply defied even the most wildly optimistic projections. So far the 24th had destroyed two massive logistics complexes, twenty-five aircraft, more than three hundred armored and wheeled vehicles, and more than one hundred artillery pieces. They had captured over four thousand Iraqi prisoners, with the number growing each time McCaffrey looked outside his command post. They were three hundred kilometers deep into the enemy's rear, and they had reached the Euphrates River Valley not in the projected four to five days, but in two.

Instead of a bubble of horror of five hundred to two thousand dead soldiers, however, preliminary reports indicated that the division had to date lost fewer than ten soldiers killed in action, scant consolation to their families but a profound relief to McCaffrey. After reporting his progress to headquarters, Barry used his satellite communications system to call Fort Stewart, Georgia, where his wife, Jill, had set up an informal group of senior officers' wives called the Sisterhood to help the families of younger service members cope with the many months of anguished waiting and uncertainty. Given the lethality of the battlefield, their light casualties were a miracle that had to be shared. Barry McCaffrey had seen a lot of combat and fought in some great units, but he had never seen an equal to the army that was even then pushing down the Euphrates.

45: Inferno 1991

LISTENING to the message from the commander of Task Force Ripper, it occurred to Mike Myatt that his and Tom Draude's propensity to lead from the front was about to catch up with them. Despite a breakdown in intelligence that had at the last moment forced the Marines to send a captain back to Washington, D.C., to get reliable imagery of the Iraqi obstacle belts, the first day's attack through those fortifications had gone better than anticipated.

In fact their advance was moving so far ahead of schedule that Myatt was forced to link up with his forward command post to keep his communications lines intact. Already he had lost contact with Walt Boomer's command post farther to the rear. Looking at Tom Draude and listening to the latest intelligence on their vulnerability, however, Myatt understood instantly that it was a mistake for both of them to be there.

The sputtering roar of the oil fires thrummed in their ears like some great misfiring engine. It was nearly midnight in a small crop of trees called the Emir's Forest, an oasis just on the edge of the Al Burqan oil fields. The choking smoke from the hundreds of burning oil wells that the Iraqis had ignited turned day into night, and night into something altogether sinister and eerie. The black cloud smothered even the reflection from the fires, so there was flame and heat and deafening noise, but without light. And there was the smell and threat of violent death. To Myatt and the others, it seemed like Dante's inferno incarnate.

"They're going to come out of the flames, that's what my Kuwaiti interpreter said, and he's so spooked I believe him," the commander of Task Force Ripper was saying over the radio. Advancing forward, Ripper had captured a massive Iraqi bunker complex and apparently a document outlining an enemy counterattack out of the Al Burqan oil fields. Myatt hadn't believed any force could survive in that inferno. Suddenly he wasn't so sure.

"Sir, I know where your command post is, and I know you assume no one could live in those oil fields. But there's no one between you and where they're supposed to come out."

"Yeah," said Myatt, thinking it over. "You're right."

After signing off, Myatt looked at Tom Draude and then his executive officer. It was a foolish risk to have both the division's commander and assistant commander in such a spot.

"How in the hell did I get myself in this position?" said Myatt. "Tom, I'm going to have to send you back to the rear."

As the assistant division commander, Draude had asked Mike Myatt from the beginning to be allowed to take the division command post forward into the battle. Now, however, Draude thought about the nagging premonitions of death that had haunted him for weeks. Many experts had been predicting U.S. casualties of twenty thousand or higher in a ground war, and Draude was convinced that the bankroll of personal luck that sustained every soldier in combat had in his case been seriously depleted by Vietnam.

Even after sealing the envelope on his final letter to his daughter before the ground war, Tom Draude had realized that the heavy sense of fatalism hanging over him had crept into his letter. Perhaps of all his family, Loree Draude best understood that her father was exactly where he most wanted to be, premonitions of death notwithstanding. At his strong urging, she had graduated from the University of San Diego on a Navy ROTC scholarship and was even then struggling to earn her wings as a Navy pilot at Pensacola. Tom Draude knew how difficult that male-dominated world would be for his young daughter, and he felt both proud and partly responsible for her ambition to fly fixed-wing jets. The last thing Tom Draude had wanted was to distract Loree with worries about his safety. Before mailing the letter, he had thus scribbled a simple message to his daughter on the outside of the envelope. "I'll pin your wings on."

Now here was Mike Myatt giving him an honorable out just when his premonition seemed all too prescient. And Tom Draude simply couldn't take it.

"Sir, please don't send me to the rear."

Sensing the conviction in Tom Draude's voice, Myatt agreed instead to order a light armored vehicle company from one of their forward task forces back to provide perimeter security, and to lay in an artillery strike on the likely assembly points for any counterattack. Then they would just have to sweat out the night. For Myatt, the intelligence on a possible counterattack was the first piece of bad news in a day that had exceeded their expectations.

At first, the stormy weather had seemed like an ill omen to the Marines, who relied heavily on their air cover and had lobbied hard before the start of the ground war for a seventy-two-hour window of good weather. On top of the storm, they had to worry about the northwest wind, which the Marines had observed for months in the desert. That made it likely that they would be assaulting the two belts of Iraqi fortifications without air cover and with the smoke of burning oil wells and possibly deadly chemical gases in their faces.

Near the start of the ground war, however, the wind had inexplicably changed direction. For the first time, it began blowing from the southeast, back into the faces of the Iraqis. With the help of that cover, the penetration of the two mine belts and fortifications had gone just as they had rehearsed it for months. To everyone's relief there had been no reported use of chemical weapons, and many of the Iraqi firing positions at the barriers had been abandoned. The first day's casualty figures for the 1st and 2nd divisions was thus an astounding one Marine killed in action.

Like McCaffrey, Myatt was also finding that their counterbattery radars worked with devastating effect at silencing the feared Iraqi artillery units. Given the circumstances, Myatt had pushed his units ahead of schedule, and indeed, it was the speed of their advance that prompted Schwarzkopf to accelerate the entire timetable for the ground war. Yet that aggressiveness had also landed Myatt and Tom Draude directly in the path of a potential counterattack at the edge of the burning Al Burqan oil fields.

Around two-thirty A.M. a hulking figure walked into the command post and introduced himself to Myatt's executive officer. Capt. Eddie Ray, Company B, 1st Battalion, Task Force Shepherd, was reporting to augment the defense of the division CP. The man was obviously irritated to be there, and he spoke up directly to Myatt after the mission was explained.

"Sir, tomorrow morning you're going to have to exchange another company for mine. My men and I are scheduled to take the lead in tomorrow morning's attack north." B Company had been held in reserve all day, and now this mission had apparently drawn it farther to the rear.

Myatt had turned on hearing Captain Ray's tone, which suggested defiance and irritation, if not outright insubordination. A broad-shouldered young black man, he was built like a linebacker. This captain was obviously not daunted by the presence of two generals, so it seemed unlikely he'd be afraid of anyone else. Eddie Ray would do just fine.

"Okay, Captain, I'll see what I can do about that tomorrow morning," Myatt said. After Ray left the command post, Mike Myatt exchanged a smile with Tom Draude and his staff and retired for a few hours of much-needed sleep.

In fact, Eddie Ray had played offensive guard at the University of Washington, joining the Marine Corps in frustration when an injury ended all hope of a professional football career. Ray knew he had taken a chance with his tone in the command post, but plenty of officers would prefer to be back with the division command post rather than leading an attack, and Ray wanted everyone to realize he wasn't one of them.

After the battle of Khafji weeks earlier, Ray had seen Myatt expose himself to potential enemy fire as he climbed a berm to get a better sense of the just-fought battle. Ray was gambling that if anyone would understand an officer's desire to lead from the front, it would be this scrappy general. The division commander wouldn't even be in this fix if not for his own aggressiveness. Anyway, from Ray's first inexplicable decision to join the Corps in the midst of a pleasurable career of partying at the University of Washington, he had always gambled on his impulses.

With the draft relegated to ancient history, military commanders no longer saw screen idols, pop stars, or famous professional athletes join their ranks, as they had in World War II, Korea, and to a lesser degree even in Vietnam. No Clark Gables were in the Air Force, nor Elvises in Germany, and no Muhammad Alis were forced to choose between joining Desert Storm or going to jail. The sense of an egalitarian society whose sacrifices were shared by all was an integral part of national service, and it had been lost with the abolition of the draft. Yet many senior commanders in 1991 wouldn't have traded the days of the draft military for the gains of the all-volunteer force, and Eddie Ray went a long way toward explaining why.

Even while Ray was positioning his company in a defensive perimeter around Myatt and Draude's command post, a debate was raging in the United States over whether African-Americans would shoulder a disproportionate share of the ground war's casualties. Due in large part to high enlistment rates in the 1980s, the very real fear that the all-volunteer force would become a haven of the dispossessed and disenfranchised had finally been dispelled. With the services having the luxury of becoming increasingly selective, their recruits were nearly all high-school graduates, and studies showed that nearly half of active-duty recruits came from areas of above-average incomes.

It was equally true, however, that the lure of a tight-knit and supportive community, relatively free of drugs and institutional bigotry, was an especially strong lure for many minorities. While blacks represented 12 percent of American society at large, for instance, they accounted for more than 20 percent of the armed services, and almost 30 percent of all Army troops. Blacks also reenlisted for second tours at a rate much higher than their white counterparts (63 percent versus 37.6 percent in the Army). What was considered a powerful catalyst for upward mobility in peacetime, however, could also be viewed by some as an unfair burden during war.

Only Eddie Ray didn't see it that way. A product of the mean streets of South Central in Los Angeles, son of a hardworking truck driver, Ray had seen plenty of people shot at before ever being sent off to war. Football had been his escape of choice from the life of gangs and drugs that snared many of his friends and cousins. Groups of teenagers used to throw bricks at him during his jogs around the neighborhood because Eddie refused to join their gangs. Where Ray came from, those who didn't get out usually went under.

When his football career at the University of Washington was cut short by injury, Ray had enlisted in the Marine Corps on impulse, finishing his college degree at night and eventually enrolling in officer candidate school. Attending mandatory seminars in the Marines on race relations and substance abuse, listening to the anger and confusion of young recruits forced for the first time to confront issues of bigotry and drug abuse, Ray had begun to see the Marine Corps in a different light. There had been no whites in his home of South Central, but plenty of drugs. There had been lots of partying and athletic adulation at the University of Washington, but few other blacks and a sense of alienation. What he found in the Marine Corps was a place where issues such as drug abuse and alienation were at least tackled head-on. What the Marine Corps found in Eddie Ray was someone searching for a home.

Ray was asleep on the ground beside his armored vehicle when something woke him up. Visibility told him that somewhere the sun was coming up, though a grimy blanket of smoke had smothered any dawn over the Burqan oil fields. There it was again, the distant thunder of artillery against the constant sputtering of the burning oil wells. The sound must have wakened him.

Assuming that it was their own, Ray radioed the battalion fire-support coordinator and gave him the coordinates for the division command post. The impacts sounded too close for comfort, and if they were firing near this grid, he wanted it shut down. Even as the coordinator offered assurances that they had nothing firing near his position, Ray saw an artillery shell explode no more than a hundred yards away.

"Well, that's bullshit! I've got impacts inside my perimeter! Somebody's fucked up—" Suddenly Eddie Ray was facedown in the dirt, a Marine's natural reaction to the nearby crackle of machine-gun fire. The sound was coming from deeper inside the Emir's Forest, where he had placed an infantry company as forward lookout. Ray hopped inside his LAV-25 armored vehicle, which had a 25mm chain gun capable of piercing light armor, and instructed the driver to head toward the sounds of fighting.

As his vehicle approached the forward positions, Ray passed by a Humvee from the infantry company speeding in the other direction. The driver screamed that enemy armored vehicles were approaching up ahead, and Ray ordered them back to the rear command post. At that moment, he saw the silhouette of an armored track begin to emerge from the trees a few hundred yards ahead, its weapon poking through the branches. It was clearly not one of their own.

"Gunner, I've got an APC at my three o'clock, about two hundred yards. Do you see it?" Ray spoke into his headset, then saw the 25mm chain gun swivel in its turret.

"Got it."

"Fire."

The first round of high-explosive munitions fell short, the impact kicking up in front of the enemy armor. The second three hit dead center, and Ray saw a fireburst and then smoke. By that time he had already spotted a second Iraqi armored vehicle approaching.

"Got another one ten degrees to the right, about the same distance. See it?"

"Got it."

"Fire."

In the excitement the gunner had locked onto the first track again, however, sending a second burst into the already burning Iraqi vehicle. By this time enemy fire was impacting in the trees all around Ray's vehicle, chipping bark and sending tree limbs cluttering down behind his head. That was close, he thought, even as he redirected the gunner onto the second target and took it out. Then Eddie Ray noticed the puff of smoke downrange.

"Enemy Sagger! Back up!"

They had rehearsed it a hundred times, and Ray's head jerked forward as his driver slammed the vehicle into reverse and mashed the accelerator. The telltale smoke of the launch he had detected meant a missile was already in the air, bearing down on them. In that fleeting moment before impact he hoped for total destruction and not to be maimed or slowly burnt alive.

A blast tore at the ground at exactly the spot where they had been parked. At the same moment Ray realized he hadn't even bothered to turn around to insure that they didn't back up into a tree.

"Stop!"

Ray reoriented his vehicle behind a tree and directed other LAV-25s from his company into position as they came up. During a brief lull in the fight, Ray pulled his vehicle back and circled the division command post to get a better idea of their tactical situation. It wasn't good. The scene was one of chaos, with mortar rounds exploding near the command post, and everyone grabbing weapons and running to join the fray. The only thing standing between at least an Iraqi armor brigade and 1st Division's command post and its two senior generals was Ray's company.

At that moment Eddie Ray made the decision for which he would later be awarded the Navy Cross, his service's highest award for valor and second only to the Medal of Honor. To Ray there seemed little choice. If they lost even a little ground, the Iraqis would roll right over the division command post. After returning to their forward line of defense, Ray thus ordered the nineteen LAVs of B Company to charge a force three times its size.

"All right, move out on my vehicle," Ray ordered over his command net. "All at once now. Nobody gets through us."

• • •

At the division command post, Mike Myatt's executive officer was screaming over his radio for additional helicopter support.

"I've got to get more Cobras, we're in a real fight up here!" shouted Col. Jerry Humble.

"Everyone's in a fight," the dispatcher said. The Marines were fighting off three Iraqi counterattacks in a series of battles up and down the coast, constituting the largest armor battle in Marine Corps history. How bad could the need be back at the division command post?

"Well, we're in a *real* fight!" Humble shouted, pulling up the tent flap and holding the radio receiver out to catch the sounds of Eddie Ray's nearby battle.

"*Jesus Christ!* We're committing every available Cobra."

Humble had wanted to put Mike Myatt and Tom Draude in a vehicle and withdraw them to the rear, but when he tried to find their drivers, he discovered that the aides had all picked up weapons and joined the firefight. In all, the battle raged around the command post for most of the day, delaying Myatt's advance forward by twenty-four hours. An investigation would later show that the nineteen armored vehicles of Capt. Eddie Ray's B Company, 1st LAI Battalion, destroyed fifty enemy armored vehicles in the fighting that day, many at very close range. They also took 250-plus Iraqi prisoners.

Toward the end of the day, a clearly exhausted Eddie Ray returned to Mike Myatt's command post to brief the general on the fight in the Emir's Forest. The scene by then was one of massive destruction and death. Yet despite extremely heavy fire, B Company had not lost a single man, a remarkable achievement that Ray credited to their superior gunnery. The Iraqis, he told Myatt, were simply not very good shots.

After Ray was finished, Myatt thought how different he sounded from the night before.

"I know I promised to get you out of here last night," Myatt said, "but I'm afraid you're not going anywhere. I'm keeping you with me."

There was no protest from Eddie Ray.

The counterattacks of February 25 constituted the last attempt of the Iraqi military to seize the initiative. The next day the Marines swept up the coast, and by February 26 they had completely encircled the capital. Iraqi forces in the city had retreated hastily before the Marine onslaught, stuffing their vehicles with whatever plunder they could lay hands on and heading north on Highway Six. The Marines' orders were to hold in place until a vanguard of Arab forces could reach them from the south and enter Kuwait City first.

Driving up the coast in the shadow of an unnatural dusk was like traveling across some ghastly slave planet, the flames from oil wells flickering against a coal black sky as bands of prisoners under guard walked through a landscape of twisted machinery and destruction. Stopping his converted Bronco to talk with his commanders, Myatt learned that many of the Iraqi artillery positions they had overrun had been pointed out to sea. The tracks where the Iraqi gunners had tried unsuccessfully to shift them around at the last moment were still clearly visible in the soot-covered sand. In that sense, the amphibious assault that never came was a success after all.

They had orders to capture the still heavily defended Kuwaiti Airport, but before attempting it Myatt had his Marines isolate the perimeter and then use their psychological-operations unit to try to get the Iraqis to surrender through the night. They took it the next morning after relatively light resistance.

It had been much the same in all their operations. They were there to defeat the enemy, not fight him head-on. Myatt had pushed his commanders to continually search for a flank, exploit some weak spot where they could get in behind the enemy. If they could bypass and isolate a force on the battlefield and still achieve their objective, all the better. Mike Myatt had never forgotten Operation Oregon and the bitter lesson of Ap Chinh An, when his company had repeatedly been ordered to attack across a minefield into the teeth of dug-in Viet Cong forces. Their battalion had lost half as many killed and wounded trying to take that small hamlet as two Marine divisions lost in liberating Kuwait.

On February 27, with Arab forces in the coalition rolling into Kuwait City to a tumultuous welcome, Gen. Walt Boomer stopped by Mike Myatt's command post after visiting the city. The 1st Marine Division was on standby to continue its attack north, but both men suspected a cease-fire was imminent. Intelligence estimated that of the forty Iraqi divisions in the theater at the beginning of the war, twenty-seven had been destroyed or captured. After the destruction both men had witnessed, it was difficult to imagine how Saddam Hussein would survive the debacle.

"Mike, you've got to see what I've just seen," Boomer said with a shake of his head. "Take your commanders with you."

The city of Kuwait looked to have been ravaged by a swarm of malevolent locusts. Entire city blocks had been stripped clean down to the street signs and house numbers, and most of what was left was charred or debased. The once luxurious beachfront was an ugly scar of barbed wire, pillboxes, and bunkers.

Scattered debris covered the city, much of it the apparent result of a wanton vandalism whose only apparent aim was to defile. The city's ten major hospitals had been turned into morgues. Doctors reported that many executed Kuwaitis bore signs of torture and even lacked eyes and fingernails. The dead were everywhere.

Yet what most struck Mike Myatt and his commanders was the grateful jubilation of the Kuwaitis. Everywhere they went the people stopped to thank them, and though the Kuwaitis had nothing, they insisted on foisting gifts on the Marines, from tiny Kuwaiti flags to candy bars. The women cried, embracing them. When Tom Draude went into one hotel, he and his officers were approached by a Kuwaiti couple whose twelve-year-old daughter asked permission to kiss each one of them on the cheek. To be an American in Kuwait that day was to be lauded as a savior. Watching the bedlam, Mike Myatt thought of a saying the Marines had. For those who have fought for it, freedom has a flavor the protected will never know. The almost unbearably sweet taste of that day would linger the rest of their lives.

46: Partings 1991

DESPERATE to escape the advancing 1st Marine Expeditionary Force, the Iraqi III Corps had piled all the bounty it could loot from the city onto tanks, trucks, buses, ambulances, and stolen cars and begun fleeing north toward Basra. The revolutionary advance in battlefield intelligence that the Joint STARS aircraft represented—the ability to track and target ground movement deep in an enemy's rear area with radar—paid off when that massive convoy traffic was revealed as a jumble of small crosses on the Joint STARS video downlink.

When word of the retreat reached the Black Hole, Chuck Horner and Brig. Gen. Buster Glosson realized that the only aircraft with a good chance of stopping the Iraqis at night in bad weather were the new F-15Es of Col. Hal Hornburg's 4th Provisional Wing at Al Kharj. The Strike Eagles' state-of-the-art LANTIRN targeting and navigation pods were designed specifically for such conditions.

The problem was that most of Hornburg's air crews had already flown missions as long as five and six hours that same night. After flying in combat for forty days straight, many of the pilots had already begun to sport the thousand-yard stare that every commander fears. Glosson called Hornburg nevertheless, emphasizing that many of the Iraqis on Highway Six were the same ones who had committed the atrocities in Kuwait City. His instructions were simple. Stop them at all costs.

Within ninety minutes, Hornburg had turned Strike Eagles loose on their second straight mission of the night, only this time they were briefed on the target locations in the air by the Joint STARS. Swooping in unseen out of the night, guided by LANTIRN, they had hit the front of the convoy with cluster bombs just before it reached Mutla Pass. Then they hit the rear, effectively trapping more than a thousand vehicles. At first light the next morning the weather cleared, and Horner hit the column with everything they had.

By the time reporters entered a liberated Kuwait and traveled out to Highway Six, the scene of destruction was unimaginable. For miles the four-lane highway had been blasted into a junkyard.

By February 27, the footage of the "Highway of Death" had produced a clamor for a cease-fire, the White House eager to avoid any impression of wanton killing. Colin Powell called Schwarzkopf to talk about a possible cease-fire. The CINC wanted one more day to finish his destruction of the Republican Guard, which the VII Corps was leading, but later in the day Powell called a second time with news that the controversy over wanton killing was becoming intense. Even the British and French were getting anxious for a cease-fire. Agreeing on a time, Schwarzkopf called Chuck Horner, John Yeosock, Stan Arthur, and Walt Boomer with the news. After a one-hundred-hour ground war, Desert Storm would cease at five A.M. on February 28.

Chuck Horner decided to pay a visit to Col. Hal Hornburg. Following the losses of the first few days and the change in tactics to primarily midaltitude attack runs, the 4th Provisional Wing had lost no more aircraft. Hornburg had also learned to his profound relief that assistant wing commander Col. Dave Eberly had survived after ejecting from his aircraft and was presumably alive somewhere in an Iraqi prison.

The two veteran pilots talked about what had happened in Desert Storm. In Vietnam, Hornburg had flown an old Cessna "Birddog" as a forward air controller, and he remembered well the days of calling in targets that because of bureaucratic inertia and planning snafus wouldn't be hit for days, after the enemy had long since disappeared. Because Washington wouldn't allow pilots to pick secondary targets on the spot in those days, they would bomb empty jungle.

Yet on Highway Six they had identified moving targets at night in a storm, loaded the right munitions on aircraft that had been buttoned down for the night, and within hours their bone-tired pilots were sweeping out of a night sky to thwart the plunderers of Kuwait. War was the most tragic, wasteful, counterproductive labor known to man, thought Horner, but as war-fighting went, that was phenomenal.

Both men knew that before long the analysts and academics would be dissecting Desert Storm and would use the results to argue yet again whether airpower could actually win wars. Not everything had gone well. There had been serious intelligence disconnects, problems with reliable bomb-damage assessment, and though they had clearly cut down on the Scud launches, there was little reliable evidence that they had actually destroyed any mobile launchers.

Yet in 41,309 strikes over a forty-day air campaign, they had severely crippled the communications links between Baghdad and its field army, immobilized the vaunted Republican Guard, and destroyed roughly half of Iraq's armor and artillery before they could be brought to bear on American ground soldiers. Equally important, they had completely blinded Iraq to the massive westward movement of allied ground troops for the surprise left hook that flanked the surprised Iraqi defenders.

And much of the technology had worked better than either man had dared hope. The day after the first air strikes, a concerned Hal Hornburg had called the Black Hole to inquire about his friend Al Whitley. The two were former neighbors and had commuted together back in the mid-1980s while attending the National War College. Hornburg had seen the flak over Baghdad that night, knew that Whitley and the rest of the F-117s were flying through it naked except for unproven stealth technology. Yet despite attacking 40 percent of the strategic and most heavily defended targets, they had lost no F-117s during the entire air campaign. Horner had finally called Al Whitley and admonished him personally for flying too many missions himself.

For Chuck Horner, the point was never about whether airpower could win a war on its own. Nor was it conceivable that Saddam Hussein could ever have won the war. Except for the air campaign, however, he might have inflicted thousands of casualties on the Americans and claimed victory even in defeat. What mattered all along was helping win this war with as few casualties as possible, and in that the air campaign they had orchestrated and executed had proven decisive.

"How did we do this?" Horner said, looking over at Hal Hornburg. The subtext needed no explanation. Tactics that anticipated the threat, pilots trained to fight on the first day of a war, technology and tactics that leveraged lives, unprecedented operational-readiness figures for their aircraft. Above all, the synergism that was created by the combination of all of those things. "How did we make all this come together?"

Both men looked at each other. The answer was there in the emphasis on high technology and precision-guided munitions, just as it was there in the port-o-toilets the Air Force used in the desert while the Army was digging holes in the dirt. The name came to their lips almost at the same moment, and they shook their heads in unison. "Creech."

As he watched carrier flight operations from the Persian Gulf, it occurred to Adm. Stan Arthur that the pilots no longer ran across the flight deck. For as long as he could remember, pilots hearing the "man your airplanes" order always dashed out of the ready room, as if manic motion would somehow get them launched off the flight deck faster. At some point, this new generation of brash, inquisitive young pilots and sailors had had the audacity to question why and had not settled for the standard answer: because that's the way the Navy has always done things. Later they had simply stopped running. It might seem like a small thing, but Stan Arthur wasn't so sure.

After watching the young sailors during Desert Storm, he had no doubt that they were much better than he had been at their age. Against their grasp of strategy and doctrine, and the level of realism in their training, so much of what Arthur had done at a comparable stage in his career now seemed like rote busywork.

For instance, as the antisurface-warfare commander, Adm. Zap Zlatoper briefed him on the Battle of Bubiyan, where his pilots sank a large portion of the Iraqi Navy in a night operation. Intelligence revealed that Iraq would try to flush its Navy patrol boats to Iran, much as it had its Air Force. Those boats had been helping to lay thousands of mines and represented a future threat to international shipping in the Persian Gulf.

One of Zlatoper's A-6 Intruders had caught the flotilla sneaking out of the Bubiyan Channel late at night. Pilots given rough coordinates had scrambled off the carriers at night and had located and destroyed nearly all of the moving targets. During the entire war, they had officially destroyed more than one hundred Iraqi vessels. Both Zlatoper and Arthur knew only too well that even if their training as young pilots had allowed them to react so quickly to such a difficult night mission, by the time permission to attack the boats had cleared channels the enemy would have long since disappeared.

As hard as Arthur pushed his crews, they had responded by wanting to go further. The accepted wisdom was that you could run flight operations for seventy-two continuous hours maximum. After that, you had to shut the system down for twenty-four hours to restock parts, conduct critical maintenance, and let everyone have a rest. Even under combat conditions and stress, however, Arthur's carriers had routinely worked through the seventy-two-hour mark.

Arthur thought back to the order from Chuck Horner to change the mission profile from low-level to medium-altitude attacks, out of range of the antiaircraft guns that had claimed the most kills. That put the Navy aircraft at a relative disadvantage to the Air Force, because they lacked the extensive stockpile of precision-guided munitions to bomb accurately from those heights. Still, it was the right thing to do.

That was another way they had changed, Arthur knew. During Vietnam, they had never really made that adjustment in tactics to fit the threat scenario. Someone either hadn't had the good sense to change tactics, or they didn't know any other way. In the Persian Gulf, their training had afforded them the flexibility to adapt on the spot, within a matter of a few days.

Yet commanding naval forces during Desert Storm, Arthur had begun to question some of the ways the Navy had always done things. The reluctance to cooperate in joint operations, which he had witnessed since the early days of the Rapid Deployment Joint Task Force in the early 1980s, had created serious frustrations. And given the apparent fading of the Soviet Union from the world stage, along with the vaunted navy that had for so long been the focal point of their war planning, it was difficult to imagine operations in the future that wouldn't be joint service.

In his discussions with Schwarzkopf and Yeosock, Arthur also came to believe that many logistics and sustainment challenges involved in maneuver warfare that the Army found daunting were second nature to the Navy. They were used to supporting large, mobile forces over long distances. What the Navy lacked was the ability to interface adequately with the other services, and a common language to work closely with them. Just as soon as he took up residence as 7th Fleet commander in Yokosuka, Japan, Arthur planned on brainstorming with his staff on exactly those problems.

Something else was bothering Stan Arthur. Because of the constant rotation of carriers and his impending departure for Japan, he would never get the chance to address all his fighter squadrons to tell them what an excellent job they had done. Knowing what he did about the ways of Washington, D.C., he guessed that the public-affairs battle over who had made the greatest contribution to Desert Storm would soon be fully joined, and under the circumstances he worried that the contribution of his Navy pilots would be denigrated.

From his headquarters in Japan, Arthur would thus compose a congratulatory message and arrange for it to be read at a gathering after the war that most of the Navy pilots were sure to attend. Still, given the already tremendous pressures of the military drawdown, and the likely level of pilot frustrations, Arthur had nagging misgivings about the 1991 Tailhook Convention where his message would be read.

After the cease-fire was called, Barry McCaffrey flew out to the 82nd Airborne Division's base of operations to field-promote Sean to the rank of captain. Though they had taken enemy fire, his son's unit had seen little heavy fighting. Sean joked that the only time he'd fired his weapon in anger during the whole deployment was when a patrol he was leading got lost one night.

Despite the humor, however, Sean had conquered the same fears that were common to all soldiers on the eve of battle. Both McCaffreys relished the chance to stand in the desert together while Barry McCaffrey pinned captain's bars on his son's collar.

On his way back to the 24th Infantry, Barry McCaffrey learned that Col. John LeMoyne's brigade was in a major battle with two Republican Guard battalions. The cease-fire statement had reserved the right of allied forces to return fire if attacked, which had apparently happened. Schwarzkopf had also insisted that the Iraqis not withdraw heavy weapons from the theater, concerned that they would soon be turned on Kurds in the north of the country. Suddenly, however, McCaffrey's division was engaged in a battle that threatened to plunge the coalition back into all-out war.

McCaffrey directed his Blackhawk pilot to fly directly for the command post of one of the engaged battalions near the Rumaylah oil fields just south of Basra. As the helicopter skidded down in a swirl of dust, he jumped out and then into the back of the Bradley Fighting Vehicle of Lt. Col. Chuck Ware. Shouting to be heard, Ware confirmed that on confronting an apparently outmanned scout company, Republican Guard tanks on Highway Eight had begun maneuvering into position, eventually opening fire with Sagger missiles. In a pincer move reminiscent of an NTC exercise, Colonel LeMoyne had responded by using two armored battalions to fix the enemy, and another supported by Apaches to flank them.

As the Bradley drove toward the fight, McCaffrey could see miles and miles of burning Iraqi tanks and armor, with ammunition exploding nearby. Catching movement out of the corner of his eye, Ware ordered his driver to stop. Bypassing an enemy who could plug you from the vulnerable rear was one of the greatest dangers in the kind of fast-paced maneuver warfare that characterized Desert Storm. Ware and his men began to round up and disarm scores of Iraqi prisoners, and at one point he turned around to see Barry McCaffrey motioning at a large group of Iraqi soldiers with a rifle, yelling directions. It was time, he felt, to get the division commander back to the rear.

In roughly four hours of fighting in the Rumaylah oil fields, the 24th Mech destroyed seven hundred Iraqi vehicles and took three thousand prisoners. They lost one M-1 tank in the engagement and had one soldier wounded. For Barry McCaffrey it was the damnedest sight he'd ever seen. On one of the canal banks on the Rumaylah, some of his soldiers found thousands of pairs of empty boots, aligned like ghostly sentries. From the footprints in the muddy ground it was clear that the owners had retreated barefoot into the swamps toward Basra. Days later news came of rioting in that city against the regime of Saddam Hussein.

Standing on a rise in the middle of the Iraqi desert, Maj. Gen. Binney Peay watched as the helicopters of the 101st Airborne darkened the sky like a dense flock of blackbirds. Soldiers leaned out the doors of the crowded helicopters, flashing victory signs and thumbs-up at Peay and the other troops standing atop the hill they had dubbed forward operating base Cobra. It looked every bit the largest air assault in history.

They had a saying that no battle plan survived the firing of the first shot, and Desert Storm had proven no different for Peay and the 101st. In fact, it hadn't even survived the first weather report. The storm had delayed their start, but as soon as it lifted, the 101st launched its 165-mile air assault and had actually moved into the Euphrates earlier than expected to beat a second storm.

The story of the assault from the beginning had been one of brief fights to dispel dug-in Iraqi troops, and then Iraqi surrender. Apache pilots returning from the Euphrates for refueling had told much the same story of carnage and a routed enemy. Even before the ground war had begun, an entire Iraqi battalion had surrendered to some of Peay's helicopters. Talking to their officers, he had recognized the face of an enemy whose heart was no longer in this fight. At the time of the cease-fire, one of his biggest challenges was just coping with the number of Iraqi prisoners.

One of the 101st Airborne helicopters flying to the Euphrates Valley in those days immediately following the cease-fire was piloted by Maj. Marie Rossi. She had been tasked with extracting some of the Iraqi POWs in her massive CH-47 Chinook. Though no women pilots had been in the forward-echelon attack companies, Rossi's combat-support company had been attached to the 101st throughout the hundred-hour war, ferrying supplies to the division over enemy territory.

It had been an exhilarating four days, but Rossi felt overwhelming relief that it was finished. She had constantly been worried for her husband, who as part of the Night Stalkers had been conducting perilous air search-and-rescue missions for allied pilots downed behind enemy lines. Privately, she was a little angry that Andy Cayton had seemed to be enjoying the dangerous thrill of combat. All she longed for was for them both to be safely home. Now that this fight was over, Marie hoped he had war out of his system.

Rossi had been so disturbed by her husband's stories that she hadn't even mentioned that his wife had become a minor celebrity. A camera crew from the media pool had interviewed Marie before the ground war about being a female pilot and company commander in a theater of war. The networks back home had all picked up the interview, and CNN had run it repeatedly, and nearly everyone in the battalion had commented about how well Marie came across. Andy Cayton would just have to wait until they got home to learn about his wife's newfound stardom.

The prisoners were not assembled at the base camp in the Euphrates where Marie had been directed to land. By the time they were finally located and loaded up, and she had refueled the Chinook, it was already late afternoon. As she flew into the POW camp on the outskirts of Rafa, Saudi Arabia, the buildings of the dusty town were silhouetted in stark relief by the dying rays of the sun.

After the prisoners were unloaded, she left immediately. Rising from the POW compound, the twin rotors giving the Chinook a slightly lurching gait on liftoff, Marie Rossi saw that the desert landscape was already illuminated by a nearly full moon. Andy would be upset. He had warned her against flying at night, something it had taken even the Night Stalkers months of practice to master in that featureless and unfamiliar land. Rossi had silenced him, however, with the admonishment that as a company commander she had to lead by example. Anyway it was only a short hop to their rear-area base.

The heading took them directly toward the moon hanging low over the horizon. Flying into the light of the moon must have blinded them, however, because an unlit radio antenna suddenly appeared directly in their path. Maj. Marie Rossi and her copilot noticed it at exactly the same time, could see it all clearly in that final moment. Then the Chinook struck the antenna with a wild gnashing of metal, and they were plummeting into the darkness.

Purely by chance, WO Cayton had caught part of his wife's interview on television in the rear area, just before he had launched on a mission to land a special-operations team on the roof of the American embassy in Kuwait City. He was walking by a television tuned to CNN, and there was Marie's disarming smile, the easy confidence he loved about her coming across clearly for the television cameras. She hadn't even mentioned the interview the day before the ground war started when they stole a few hours together at the Rafa Airport. That was just like her. Marie was always uncomfortable with how much he bragged on her. Thinking about it had only made him ache for her more.

Cayton was back in King Khalid Military City in Saudi Arabia, switching an aircraft, when someone said he had unannounced visitors. Walking in the room, he was surprised to see Capt. Billy Sutherland, a good friend from Marie's unit. Then he turned reluctantly from Billy's stricken face and saw Marie's colonel and a chaplain, and Andy Cayton knew. Even as he felt the pain and the shock come on, he could see her clearly, the picture alive and still unsullied by grief. Marie standing surrounded and dwarfed by a group of men in her unit, that big old smile telling you that she thought it was so neat that these were her people, and that she could take care of them. A perfect lady.

Two days later Cayton flew home in a giant C-5A Galaxy transport, its only cargo the four caskets containing his wife and her crew. Only the Chinook's door gunner had survived the accident. Though the C-5A crew was based somewhere in California, they had seen Marie on television, and each of them mentioned to Cayton the profound impression his wife had made on them. Other than that, they let him keep mainly to himself during the flight back.

After the networks and CNN realized that Marie Rossi had been killed, they reran the interview repeatedly, and the outpouring from around the country was overwhelming. By the time Cayton escorted the casket to Marie's hometown in New Jersey, the family was receiving hundreds of letters of consolation each day.

On March 11, 1991, at Arlington National Cemetery, Maj. Marie Rossi was buried with full military honors. The country was already making preparations for the triumphant return of its armed forces when the familiar echo of a rifle salute sounded over those hillsides, three separate volleys from a seven-man firing party. Somewhere a bugler sounded taps, the notes floating like a collective thought above the large group of mourners gathered in a corner of the cemetery, a rhapsody of unbearable sadness.

The scene seemed incongruous in those weeks of celebration, with victory parades and martial music soon to follow, just as similar gatherings had once stood separate and apart from the antiwar demonstrations of Vietnam. While the homecomings defined moments in the collective mood of the nation, the huddled mourners in Arlington bespoke war's one true constant.

Hearing it, Andy Cayton simply could not reconcile himself to all the talk of a war that had somehow been won at remarkably light cost. Many of his friends had been among the fourteen crew members killed when their Special Forces AC-130 Spectre aircraft was shot down by a missile during the battle of Khafji. Marie's copilot had been the best man at their wedding. And then there were the tens of thousands of Iraqis, few of whom had seemed eager for that fight, now buried in mass graves out in the trackless desert. There would be no full military honors for the Iraqis, yet Cayton had learned the honor of adversaries who had shared a common battlefield.

As Marie Rossi had hoped, combat had forever lost its allure for Andy Cayton. He watched as the honor guard removed the American flag from his wife's coffin and, with crisp, snapping motions, folded and carefully passed it down the line in a series of carefully choreographed movements. The last guard in line held the flag aloft in a perfectly formed triangle and slowly lowered it until his face was covered just below his eyes. Then he executed a sharp left face, handing the flag to the undersecretary of the army.

Andy Cayton could remember that night in their bed in Savannah so long ago, when Marie had been so reluctant to part with the diamond engagement ring he'd bought her. Now she was taking it away forever. *Don't you ever forget me* . . . There was a folded flag, and someone was speaking quietly in Cayton's ear, though the voice sounded distant and remote compared to the voices of hurt and anger inside his head. "On behalf of the president of the United States and a very grateful nation . . ."

Epilogue

ON Christmas Eve of 1991, exactly one year after attending the most memorable midnight mass of his life inside a tent in the Saudi Arabian desert, Tom Draude was pacing the reception area at the Dover Air Force Base Port Mortuary, awaiting the body of a fallen Marine. The remains of Lt. Col. William Higgins were due in on a flight from the Middle East, where the former chief of the United Nations Observer Group in southern Lebanon had been kidnapped and murdered by an Iranian-backed terrorist group.

The assignment was a solemn start to a holiday season that already found Tom Draude in a pensive mood. The aftermath of war always brought turmoil to the military, and the upheavals of the post–Cold War period were proving especially profound. With the military in the midst of a restructuring that would see it shrink by at least a third in a very few years, Tom Draude would be leaving an unsettled Marine Corps when he retired after his final year in uniform.

To occupy himself while he waited on Higgins, Draude decided to tour the Port Mortuary. The facility was housed in a sprawling, one-story building covering forty-two thousand square feet, far larger than Draude had imagined. All military casualties that passed through the East Coast stopped at Dover, his tour guide explained, leading Draude into a cavernous room where an astounding array of dress uniforms from each service was neatly displayed, along with every official medal, badge, and campaign ribbon.

Each body that passed through Dover was first conclusively identified, if need be with the help of the Armed Forces Institute of Pathology at Walter Reed Hospital. After embalming and whatever reconstructive work was necessary, the bodies were clothed in a dress uniform from the applicable branch of service. Those who were promoted or honored posthumously would carry the correct rank and medal to the grave. The 1st Marine Division troops killed during the ground war had passed through Dover, as had Army major Marie Rossi.

The issue of the sacrifices of women during the Persian Gulf War was actually much on Tom Draude's mind. He had agreed to sit as the senior active-duty military representative on a fifteen-member Presidential Commission on Women in the Armed Services, whose charter was to decide whether the rule excluding women from combat jobs should be lifted.

The role of uniformed women in a war zone was one of those wrenching social issues that periodically forced the military not only to search its tradition-bound soul, but also to bare it to public scrutiny. Certainly with a daughter soon to graduate as a naval aviator and who wanted to fly combat jets, Draude had agonized over the matter of women in combat more than most.

Forty-one thousand female troops had served in the Persian Gulf, and the largest ever deployment of American women to a war zone had been a defining moment. The Pentagon had leaned heavily on women recruits to fill its depleted ranks when the all-volunteer force was in trouble in the 1970s, but had never fully come to grips with the contradiction of denying them jobs in combat units in an organization where promotions were tied to such service. Now many of the women who had deployed to the Persian Gulf were every bit as reluctant to return to the old system of implied second-class citizenship in the military fraternity as blacks had been after Vietnam.

Draude knew that if readiness and unit cohesion were the only considerations, then Harry Truman would never have ordered the military to integrate blacks into its ranks decades earlier. That had proved disruptive for a considerable time, yet the military eventually benefited from doing what was right. A year earlier, the first black chairman of the Joint Chiefs had orchestrated one of the most lopsided victories in U.S. military history, and the bravery of black Marine captain Eddie Ray had very likely saved Tom Draude's life during Desert Storm. He was at least open to the idea that a policy of greater inclusiveness for women might one day make the military stronger.

What most infuriated Draude was the insistence of many who endorsed the combat exclusion that somehow Desert Storm didn't count. In their view it was apparently not difficult enough a test to qualify as a useful gauge in deciding whether women were suited to combat. Remembering the many months in the desert, the drive through the minefields and the battle of the Rumaylah oil fields, knowing that five women soldiers had been killed and two captured during Desert Storm, Draude objected to the idea that the war had been some sort of walkover.

While at the Port Mortuary, Draude on an impulse asked his tour guide how many casualties they had anticipated from Desert Storm. Dover had prepared for between five and ten thousand killed in action, quite possibly many more.

"What?" Draude remembered the crowd of faces that had surrounded him during midnight mass exactly one year earlier, could easily juxtapose them with the legion of empty uniforms in the room before him. There were women's uniforms as well as men's in that silent army of Dover.

"Yes, sir, that's what we were told to expect."

In one of his last acts as an active-duty Marine, Tom Draude voted for lifting the combat ban on female aviators. Finding his way to that deceptively simple middle ground on an issue polarizing military ranks was his legacy to the Corps and his daughter, both of whom he loved.

"I was a has-been in the Air Force," Gen. Chuck Horner, commander in chief of U.S. Space Command, was telling an audience of disbelieving cadets at the Air Force Academy in late 1992. Sitting nearby on the dais was Marine Corps four-star general Walt Boomer, whom Horner liked to point out as having been formerly stuck in a nondescript job with a Marine Corps reserve division. John Yeosock was so politically incorrect that at a fund-raiser back in the summer of 1991 to support the Washington victory parade for Desert Storm, he had worked the room of society elites by blowing cigar smoke in their horrified faces. "And if you've ever seen Adm. Stan Arthur, you know that he's hardly the image of a lean, mean warrior!"

The introduction predictably drew laughter from the audience. It was indeed an unlikely band of brothers who had served as the component commanders for the Persian Gulf War. Unquestionably, however, the experience had favorably impacted on their careers. While Yeosock had retired with three stars, the rest had ascended near the top of the military pyramid with their fourth stars, the highest rank attained by any living general or flag officer. Walt Boomer and Stan Arthur were vice commandant and deputy chief of naval operations respectively, the number two positions in their services. Horner had moved on to become CINC of the joint-service U.S. Space Command, headquartered in Colorado Springs.

The last time Boomer and Horner had seen John Yeosock was at the Air War College at Maxwell Air Force Base, Alabama. Mostly that's how they ran into each other, speaking at the service schools and war colleges about the lessons they had learned working together in the Persian Gulf. In that sense they were the apostles of "jointness," and some of the strongest proponents in uniform of the reforms that had gone under the rubric of Goldwater-

Nichols. Indeed, the synergism that had resulted from each of those men and their respective services working in tandem, with unambiguous command lines and generally uncontested areas of responsibility, was one of the characteristics that so distinguished the Persian Gulf War.

While the camaraderie between the component commanders of Desert Storm had remained strong, the pressures of rapidly shrinking the military had inevitably caused strains as the services jockeyed for position in the budget battles back in Washington, D.C. Their friend Stan Arthur probably had it the toughest. The Navy was still contending with the corrosive effects of the Tailhook scandal, as well as its reputation for fierce independence in the face of change.

Privately, Stan Arthur felt the Navy was partially paying for the Lehman years. With his intellectual arrogance and fierce opposition to the Goldwater-Nichols reforms and the move toward joint operations that they represented, Lehman had been adept at making enemies. Despite tremendous institutional resistance and many a roaring argument and bitching session, however, Stan Arthur and a number of like-minded officers were managing a dramatic change in course, with the Navy announcing a new doctrine that committed it firmly to joint operations in the future. In the wake of Tailhook, the Navy was also proving the most aggressive service in opening jobs formerly banned to women, including service aboard aircraft carriers. So in crisis and adversity there was also catharsis.

For his part, Chuck Horner worried about what would happen to the Air Force when they retired, all those officers who had lived through Vietnam and its aftermath. How do you pass along the hard-earned lessons to someone who hadn't lived through it all? Certainly in the coming years the Air Force would need that commitment to excellence that was the creed of Bill Creech, and all those who mentored at his shoulder. With the country hungry for a peace dividend and turning its attention elsewhere, the signs of strain in the service were already everywhere apparent.

That thought occurred to Chuck Horner while he was on the telephone one day after returning from a business trip. He was talking to a friend and a junior officer who had gone to work for the Military Airlift Command.

"John, I was flying on one of your airplanes the other day, and I noticed where someone had leaned back in their seat and left these dirty old boot prints on the ceiling of your airplane," Horner said.

"You noticed what?"

Horner knew he sounded like some raving anal retentive, but he didn't give a damn. Everyone in Air Force blue could mouth slogans such as "total quality management" and was happy to faithfully repeat the rhetoric about pride in ownership. Somehow Chuck Horner had to make the man see how it all came down to a pair of dirty footprints on a ceiling.

After a presentation on joint operations at the Air Force Academy, Chuck Horner and his wife, Mary Jo, invited Walt Boomer over for dinner at their quarters. Of all the friendships forged during those many tense months in Saudi Arabia, the one between Boomer, the laconic Tennessee infantryman, and Horner, the outgoing and sometimes profane fighter pilot, seemed one of the most unlikely. Yet it was Horner's very irreverence that Boomer liked about the Air Force general, just as Horner was drawn to the Marine's self-effacing demeanor and no-nonsense toughness.

Over dinner and stories, Horner and Boomer found themselves simply shaking their heads in unison at the memories. So much had happened since Desert Storm, yet the emotional attachments that had formed during the war were enduring. Horner could remember standing on the flight line at Al Dhafra during the change-of-command ceremony after the war, tears running down both his and the base commander's faces, and neither of them knowing exactly why.

Thinking back, it occurred to Horner and Boomer that the last time the fellowship of component commanders had been complete was at the victory parade in Washington, D.C., in the summer of 1991. They talked about how overwhelming the public outpouring had been that day. Each of them knew that war was nothing to cheer about, yet somehow it hadn't seemed like jingoistic chest-thumping at the time. At least that's not how they chose to view it in retrospect. For those men at that moment, the nation had seemed remarkably healthy and whole. They commented about it among themselves. It wasn't just us. The American people learned from Vietnam, too.

Only minutes into one of his weekly meetings with the staff of Pres. Bill Clinton in the spring of 1993, Lt. Gen. Barry McCaffrey sensed the tension in the White House. As the chief military assistant to Gen. Colin Powell, McCaffrey had been acting as the Pentagon's unofficial ambassador to the executive branch for nearly a year. While the woman from the new Clinton administration team he was briefing that morning was outwardly polite, McCaffrey saw clearly that her teeth were on edge. There was no need to ask her why.

Much to the White House's dismay, President Clinton's critical early weeks had been monopolized by the issue of gays in the military, sparked by the military's vehement opposition to his proposal to allow open homosexuals into uniform. All of the Joint Chiefs of Staff opposed lifting the ban, as did the Veterans of Foreign Wars, the American Legion, the Retired Officers Association, and according to a USA Today–Gallup poll, a 50 to 43 percent plurality of the American public.

Clinton's apparent misreading of the depth of the military's unease with open homosexuality in the ranks only underscored concerns about this first Vietnam-generation president and commander in chief. Never mind that the shift from a draft to a professional army back in 1973 had presaged the day when relatively few of the country's civilian leaders would list military service on their résumés. Coming so early in Clinton's term, the controversy over gays in the military had reopened wounds inflicted during the campaign over his avoidance of military service.

On the same day Barry McCaffrey was briefing the White House staff, Clinton was thus announcing a compromise on gays in the military designed to stem the hemorrhage of political capital over the issue. It called for the services to stop asking potential recruits about their sexual orientation while the Senate Armed Services Committee held hearings, and the Pentagon studied the issue of lifting the ban for an additional six months. The compromise did little, however, to quell speculation over a serious rift developing between the commander in chief and his troops. Inadvertently, Barry McCaffrey had stumbled directly into the center of that controversy.

The irony was that of all the national-security issues that brought McCaffrey wide-awake in the still of night, and they were myriad, homosexuals in the military hardly registered. For nearly the entire year since receiving his third star, McCaffrey had acted as Colin Powell's senior aide and troubleshooter. There had been trips to Moscow for high-level discussions with members of the Russian military over a variety of security concerns, and journeys to Bosnia to weigh the five-alarm risks of U.S. military involvement in what amounted to civil war fueled by ancient ethnic hatreds. There was the ongoing negotiation of the largest military dismantlement since Vietnam.

Those were the issues that brought McCaffrey regularly to the White House to brief Clinton's National Security Council staff, which he personally considered one of the most talented he had ever seen assembled. It was not to warn of the threat uniformed gays posed to national security.

Not that the issue of gays in the military was trivial. Given the constant tension between individual freedoms and group responsibility in American society, it exposed the dichotomy between the civilian world, where the rights of the individual were rightfully given precedence unless they infringed on others, and a military where those rights were routinely subjugated to the good of the group in ways both petty and profound.

Service members adhered to an autocratic society where rank governed, everyone wore the same uniform and cut their hair to like guidelines, privacy was routinely invaded by means varying from open toilets to random urinalysis, and entrance and acceptance was denied for reasons as arbitrary as age, weight, height, eyesight, and, in cases such as membership in the Communist Party or the Ku Klux Klan, even political affiliation. For the majority of service members who voluntarily signed on to that group ethic, the idea of adjusting themselves to an openly homosexual lifestyle was undeniably jarring.

Yet if a compromise led to a policy forbidding recruiters from questioning potential recruits on their sexual orientation and ended the periodic witchhunts for homosexuals in uniform, then, Barry McCaffrey believed, Clinton would have provoked healthy change. In his opinion, the questioning was an unneeded invasion of privacy. Either way, when the national debate ended and the president gave his final order, the military would salute and carry it out. Period.

As McCaffrey left the strained briefing and the oppressive atmosphere in the White House and walked outside into a crisp, sun-splashed morning in the capital, he felt his spirits lift. Though he and Jill had lived the existence of true Army vagabonds for their entire adult lives, Washington was as close to a hometown as they had known. Barry had proposed to her for the first time in the officers' club of the nearby Bolling Air Force Base, and now his father had retired next door in Alexandria, Virginia.

As he was walking toward the gate, McCaffrey passed a woman heading the opposite direction on the walkway. She looked to be in her midforties, and he assumed she was a White House staffer.

"Good morning," McCaffrey said with smile.

The woman took a sidelong glance at the nation's most decorated active general and dismissed him without breaking stride.

"I don't talk to the military," she said.

Barry McCaffrey's feet slowed as her words settled in with stunning impact. They were there all along, the memories a nerve suddenly laid painfully bare. There was his brother-in-law Dave Ragin, killed in ambush in 1964 and buried in Arlington Cemetery just across the river; there was the lawn of nearby Walter Reed Army Hospital, across which Barry and other patients of Ward One once stumbled after another night of trying to drink away all memory of being whole; there was McCaffrey's small apartment in nearby northwest Washington where in one night in 1969 former cadets and classmates had carelessly shattered friendships that might have lasted a lifetime. Even the sun-splashed sidewalk that swam before his eyes resembled the one he had once walked like a plank, stopping first to vomit up the fear of his return to Vietnam.

As McCaffrey approached the front gates of the White House, even they became part of that dark tapestry. His father had once ringed those same gates with buses to block antiwar protesters from ransacking the White House, in a time when the country seemed intent on tearing itself asunder and the sight of a uniform was enough to provoke derision and hate. The thoughts collected like filament to the magnet of the woman's rebuff, so that between the saying of it and McCaffrey's stopping dead in his tracks from the crushing weight, there was only an instant. Dear God, Barry McCaffrey thought, it's starting all over again.

From his office at West Point where he was teaching a course in international security, retired general Jack Galvin read in the national press about McCaffrey's apparent snub at the White House. First *U.S. News and World Report* had picked up on the story, and then *The Baltimore Sun*. The incident had since worked its way into the political lore of the capital, imbued with dark symbolism by reporters and critics such as Ross Perot, who pointed to the snub as a sure sign that the White House was viscerally antimilitary. What Jack Galvin couldn't understand was the strange silence on the obviously divisive incident emanating from the Pentagon.

Outside his second-floor window in the social studies department, Galvin could look out on the emerald green swath of the Plain, across which formations of cadets gathered in clumps of dark gray. The West Point chapel was silhouetted on a rise beyond the stone buildings and statues that ringed the parade ground like some medieval cathedral lording over a quiet parish seemingly bypassed by time. He could just make out the statue of MacArthur that overlooked the Plain, the inscribed words of his farewell address at West Point challenging all who dared join the long gray line never to falter.

To the untrained eye West Point had a timeless quality, with little having outwardly changed since Jack Galvin had studied there as a cadet in the 1950s, or later in the 1960s when he'd taught as an associate professor in the English Department. When he and his classmates had driven out of West Point's gates in those days, however, they had known the enemy they would confront around the world, understood in the clearest terms the threat it posed to their way of life. They were quite simply the defenders of democracy and freedom.

For all of West Point's timeless traditions, Jack Galvin knew that the Military Academy was no more impervious to change than the world outside its gates. The cadets whom Pres. Bill Clinton was scheduled to address as part of graduation ceremonies that summer would drive off campus into a far more uncertain world. The alliances that had proven so successful in deterring World War III were failing to deter the same kind of internecine warfare in the former Yugoslavia that had plunged Europe and the United States into World War I.

Until reliable new formulas for deterrence could be found, the likelihood that the West Point class of 1993 would be sent into harm's way had probably increased dramatically. At such a time, the country could ill afford a divisive rift between the man on whose shoulders the weight of those decisions would fall and the young men and women relying on his judgment.

Jack Galvin decided to place a call to the Pentagon and have a personal talk with his friend Barry McCaffrey.

On a wall in Barry McCaffrey's Pentagon office hung a framed copy of Martin Luther King's "I have a dream" speech. Somewhere was the plaque Barry had received from the National Association for the Advancement of Colored People (NAACP) the year before, honoring McCaffrey's leadership in the march for civil rights. It was the first time a commander at Fort Stewart had received the award. The military had tackled racism, drugs, and the end of the draft and emerged the stronger for it. Barry McCaffrey knew they would do the same with sexism, the roles of women and homosexuals in uniform.

On another wall hung MacArthur's speech to McCaffrey's West Point class, and reading it again, he could still recall the legendary general's frail voice gathering strength so long ago in the cavernous mess hall, the words somehow bridging the distance between an idealistic yearling and a weathered general and war hero. Now to find that the bridge ran both ways.

"Duty, honor, country. Those three hallowed words reverently dictate what you ought to be, what you can be, what you will be . . ."

Barry McCaffrey saw what his duty required. He hadn't leaked the story about the White House snub to the press. However, worried that it might be symptomatic of a growing antipathy between the White House and the military, he had repeated it to a few civilians in the Pentagon, and the story had subsequently been relayed to the White House.

The irony was that the White House had quickly put to rest McCaffrey's fears. Deputy National Security Adviser Sandy Berger had phoned McCaffrey at home after hearing about the incident. That would be the woman's last day, Berger assured him, if they knew who she was. The White House would simply not tolerate anyone who showed disrespect for the military. McCaffrey told Berger that the whole incident was forgotten.

Only not by the press. The media somehow got hold of the story and would not let go, following up with a series of wild anecdotes on the same theme. Suddenly Chelsea Clinton was rumored to have refused to ride to school with a military driver, and Hillary Rodham Clinton had banned uniforms in the White House. Both stories were untrue. Many of the anecdotes were undoubtedly fed to the media by disgruntled officers in the Pentagon, some of whom displayed an antipathy to the commander in chief every bit as egregious as the mystery woman had shown to Barry McCaffrey.

When that rancor surfaced openly at an Air Force banquet in the Netherlands—where Maj. Gen. Harold N. Campbell publicly chastised Clinton's "womanizing," "draft dodging," and "pot smoking"—the senior military leadership grasped the seriousness of the affront immediately. A professional army whose leadership openly denigrates the civilian atop the chain of command is a danger to the democracy it is pledged to protect. At the urging of Clinton's senior military advisers, Campbell was relieved of duty.

In McCaffrey's case, many commentators blamed the antimilitary bias on an especially young and inexperienced White House staff, yet no one under thirty in the White House or elsewhere had ever treated McCaffrey with anything but the utmost respect. That was the generation he had led to war in Desert Storm, and that had turned around the fortunes of the all-volunteer force. No, McCaffrey had since come to see the whole incident of the woman's snub and his visceral reaction to it for what they were: one more residual scar from Vietnam.

That dark stain on the American psyche was still capable of casting an unexpected shadow over their lives, reaching out over a space of decades to darken even a sunny day in Washington in 1993. Perhaps it would always be so. As the furor over the snubbing incident grew, however, so did Barry McCaffrey's unease.

Colin Powell, whom McCaffrey considered the most savvy man in uniform in the ways of Washington, D.C., and a man of unimpeachable integrity, told him the whole controversy would blow over. The chairman had also assured President Clinton personally that there was no problem between the military and the National Security Council staff or others in the White House. Powell had gone so far as to delay his planned retirement to put to rest rumors of a growing schism between the White House and the military.

In the midst of the controversy, McCaffrey's aide told him that Gen. Jack Galvin was on the line. There were few men who ever wore the uniform that McCaffrey respected more.

"Barry, what are you guys doing down there?" Galvin asked, obviously disturbed.

"Well, sir, the chairman and I just thought this whole thing would blow over."

"Oh, no, Barry, I don't agree. By your silence, you're not just acquiescing that the incident took place. You're lending credence to the idea that there's a sense of animosity between the uniformed military and *your* president!"

While McCaffrey was still contemplating what Galvin had said, and wondering what to do about it, Adm. William Crowe called. The former chairman of the Joint Chiefs, whom McCaffrey had served during a previous Pentagon tour, was also concerned about the brewing controversy. That was enough for McCaffrey.

After talking with Crowe, he looked up the number of a *Washington Post* reporter. He wasn't going to deliver a paid political announcement for anyone, but as a soldier of the republic, Barry McCaffrey was damned if he would be used as a wedge between his commander in chief and the armed forces.

The photograph of Barry McCaffrey and Pres. Bill Clinton taking a Sunday-morning jog together appeared in *The Washington Post* on April 6, 1993. They were in Vancouver, British Columbia, for a summit with Russian president Boris Yeltsin. Clinton, wearing a University of British Columbia sweatshirt, was shown waving to reporters while McCaffrey jogged beside him in an Army T-shirt with his arms at waist level, the constriction of movement in his wounded arm barely perceptible.

At a dinner for Yeltsin the night before, Clinton had pulled McCaffrey aside. With the future of Russia still very much in doubt, it was a critical first meeting for the two world leaders. Yet the president of the United States stopped what he was doing long enough to tell McCaffrey he knew how badly the incident at the White House must have made the general feel. The man's warmth was genuine. If Clinton was masking some visceral animosity toward the military, then McCaffrey was a poorer judge of character than he thought.

McCaffrey felt it was a national-security team equally as respectful of the military as the one he'd dealt with during the last year of the Bush administration. He was quoted making that very point in a front-page article in *The Washington Post* headlined "Turning About-face Into Forward March." McCaffrey said he was discussing the snubbing incident for the first time with a reporter because he felt it had given the administration a "grossly unfair rap." Thus was the whole affair finally put to rest in his mind.

• • •

In May of 1993, Binney Peay stopped by McCaffrey's office. The two old friends had come a long way since struggling together at the National Training Center a decade earlier. After returning from Saudi Arabia, Peay had received his fourth star and was promoted to vice chief of staff, the number two man in the Army. McCaffrey had just been promoted to the influential position of director for strategy, plans, and policy for the Joint Staff. A fourth star and the coveted position of commander in chief of Southern Command was in his immediate future.

Both men knew that nearly all outward signs of the direction in which the military was headed were troubling. Indeed, the entire Pentagon was buzzing about the negative trends in everything from military readiness to recruitment. The quality of military recruits was dropping for the first time in a decade, and according to a survey of high school seniors conducted annually by the Pentagon, interest in a career in the military was also dropping. Because the turnaround of the all-volunteer force had been a key to the reforms that had revolutionized the American military during the past two decades, those declines were especially worrisome. The parallels to the grim days of malaise and the "hollow force" of the late 1970s were disturbing.

After Peay left his office, McCaffrey ruminated over the meaning of it all. In that day's *New York Times* a powerful senator had called on the United States to begin bombing the Serbs immediately. It occurred to Barry McCaffrey that in Sean's few years in the Army, his division had parachuted into combat in Panama and gone to war in Desert Storm, and the boy had been stationed as part of a peacekeeping force in the Sinai. Somalia and potentially Bosnia and Korea beckoned. Unless McCaffrey was mistaken, the chances Sean would be asked to put himself in harm's way in the future were increasing. Truly, his son was now the prodigal soldier.

As the Army seemed to reel from the tumultuous changes it was undergoing, Barry tried to pass along to Sean his unshakable faith in the society from which the American military drew its strength. Similar talks with his own father after Vietnam had once evoked for Barry the inevitable pendulum of time on which the Army's fortunes rose and fell. Desert Storm had been an unsustainable peak, perhaps the finest fighting force the world had ever known. Now, once again they were on a downward pitch, trying to maintain their equilibrium while America focused its energies elsewhere.

The cycle repeated after every war, and always in the past the military had righted itself only after historic debacles, at Kasserine Pass in World War II, on the Korean Peninsula with Task Force Smith, in the Ia Drang Valley in

Vietnam, and in the blackened sands of Desert One. If the officers at the helm did not discover some way to break that cycle, McCaffrey knew that the pages yet to be written in that cautionary tale might one day be stained with Sean's blood.

Yet if there were dips and peaks, with each swing of the pendulum there was also the progression of time. The Army of 1993 was not the "hollow Army" of 1979, and not every crisis on the horizon was another Vietnam. While that war might always be with them, it had spawned a revolution in the American military. The final challenge for Barry McCaffrey and the others in his unique generation of officers would be to sustain in victory the lessons that they had purchased at such cost in defeat. Judgment awaits the next inevitable breakdown in human discourse, when the pendulum pauses and momentum is lost, and soldiers once again decide matters by war.

Notes

Chapter 1: Duty, Honor, Country

The description of the 4th Class Plebe system at West Point is taken from interviews at West Point by the author, and from his article "Plebe Reprieve," *Government Executive* magazine, December 1992. MacArthur's seminal speech to the West Point class is inscribed on the monument in his honor at West Point, and a copy hangs on the wall of Gen. Barry McCaffrey's office. Kennedy's speech is repeated in *Long Gray Line*. The much documented propensity of the Army to lose its initial battles in earlier wars is from an interview with Army Chief of Staff Gen. Gordon Sullivan; also from *America's First Battles*, Stofft and Heller.

Description of Barry McCaffrey's battle at the DMZ is from interviews, and from citation for his first Distinguished Service Cross. Michael Herr's *Dispatches* also gives an excellent description of the DMZ, and *America Takes Over* (Boston Publishing) outlines this phase of the northern border campaign in detail.

Chapter 2: Barnstormers

Description of Rolling Thunder campaign—including detailed account of the first attack on surface-to-air missile sites—from John Morrocco's *Thunder from Above* (Boston Publishing Company). Also from interviews with participants. Statistics of death among Navy fighter pilots in early 1960s and the number of Korean War aces from Tom Wolfe's *The Right Stuff* (Bantam Books). Curtis LeMay's command of operations during World War II from Mark Perry's *Four Stars* (Houghton Mifflin). The reaction of Army Chief of Staff Harold Johnson to LBJ's failure to activate the reserves is reported in *Four Stars*. Details of the initial deployment announced by President Johnson also in *The American Experience in Vietnam* by Clark Dougan and Stephen Weiss (Boston Publishing).

Chapter 3: I Corps

Detailed analysis of Marine Corps operation Starlite from *America Takes Over—1965–1967*, The Vietnam Experience series, Edward Doyle and Samuel Lipsman (Boston Publishing Company). Operation Oregon is discussed in detail in *The U.S. Marines in Vietnam: 1966* (History and Museums Division, USMC) by Jack Shulimson. Also from interviews with Gens. Tom Draude and Mike Myatt.

Chapter 4: Find, Fix, Destroy

The story of the Big Red One in 1966 from interviews with Gen. Jack Galvin. The terrible cost endured by some units of the division as a result of the baiting tactics involved in search and destroy is detailed in *Mud Soldiers* by George Wilson (Macmillan), as was Army Chief of Staff Harold Johnson's comment that the American public would not long endure the kinds of casualties being inflicted on the division in 1966.

A detailed discussion of the Battle of 25 August, 1966, DePuy biographical facts, and his part in the formulation of search-and-destroy tactics come from *Changing an Army*, an oral history of Gen. William DePuy (U.S. Army Center of Military History).

Chapter 5: Red River Rats

Historical facts on establishment of Nellis from *Red Flag* by Michael Skinner. Number of air casualties in Vietnam from Morrocco's *Thunder from Above* and *Rain of Fire* (Boston Publishing). The situation of Air Force operations in Thailand in 1967 is described in interviews with Gen. Chuck Horner and Col. Lloyd "Boots" Boothby.

Accounts of the Stennis Hearings, McNamara's increasing disillusionment with the air campaign, the horrific casualties in the taking of Hill 875, and methods for avoiding the draft are contained in *The American Experience in Vietnam* by Dougan and Weiss (Boston Publishing).

Chapter 6: Prodigal Soldier

The descriptions of McCaffrey's return to Vietnam from interviews with both Barry and Jill McCaffrey. Figures on inequalities in the draft, and the propensity for deferments to go to children of the middle class, are from the Brookings Institution's *Blacks and the Military*, Binkin and Eitelberg.

Anecdotal descriptions of Vietnam during this period are taken from interviews. Michael Herr's *Dispatches* gives an excellent description of operations by the 1st Air Cav in Vietnam, as well as the jungle area near the Cambodian border. Details from the Tet '69 operation from *The American Experience in Vietnam*, Dougan and Weiss (Boston Publishing). Further details on 1st Cav operations in 1969 from *Vietnam Order of Battle* by Shelby Stanton. Particulars of the battles of February 19 and March 9, 1969, from interviews, as well as Barry McCaffrey's official citations for the Distinguished Service Cross and Silver Star.

Chapter 7: Wounds

Description of Barry McCaffrey's time in Ward 1, Walter Reed Hospital, is garnered primarily from interviews; detailed descriptions are also found in the Pulitzer Prize–winning *Fortunate Son* by the late Lewis B. Puller, Jr. (Grove Weidenfeld).

Accounts of the peace marches of 1969, and President Nixon's response to them, were taken from the *The Vietnam Experience*, as well as *The New York Times* on November 14–19, 1969. The rapid expansion of the officer corps during World War II is outlined in *The Professional Soldier* by Janowitz.

Chapter 8: A Pitiless Folly

Galvin's description of second tour from interviews, and article in *The Washington Post*, July 25, 1992, by Barton Gellman: "Retiring NATO Chief Survived Rocky Start."

Westmoreland's feelings that the Army's personnel problems were directly related to the decision not to call up the reserves are outlined in an article in *The Baltimore Sun*, December 26, 1971. Convictions of the Army provost marshal and other infractions were listed in a *New York Times* article by Lucian Truscott. Westmoreland's letter to the commandant of the Army War College in 1970 is included in *The Study of Military Professionalism*, Ulmer and Malone. Events surrounding the briefing of Westmoreland on the report are from interviews with both Ulmer and Malone.

Army AWOL rates are from an article in *Congressional Quarterly*, February 19, 1972. Westmoreland's optimistic assessment of Army morale is found in the annual Army Posture Statement and repeated in an article in *The Boston Globe*, January 13, 1972, entitled "All's Well with the Army."

Chapter 9: Yankee Station

Events described in this chapter taken from interviews with Adm. Stan Arthur. Details on typical alpha strikes late in the air campaign by carrier-borne Skyhawks are contained in *Rain of Fire* by John Morrocco (Boston Publishing).

Chapter 10: Coming Home

Figures on the number of troops withdrawing from Vietnam in 1971–72 are from *The American Experience in Vietnam*. Statistics on fraggings are from *Congressional Quarterly*, February 19, 1972. Racial tensions and the suspicions with which troops viewed new officers in the early 1970s are related in an article in the *Saturday Review*, January 1972.

Gen. William McCaffrey's propensity for taking the long view of the Army's fortunes was noted in *The Long Gray Line* by Rick Atkinson; also from interviews with Gen. William McCaffrey.

Creighton Abrams's belief that Westmoreland's search-and-destroy tactics had been misguided are recounted in *Four Stars* (Houghton Mifflin) by Mark Perry.

Abrams's comment about Westmoreland leaving him a "goddamn mess" in Vietnam is chronicled in *Thunderbolt* (Simon & Schuster), a biography of the late Creighton Abrams by Lewis Sorley. Weekly hamlet evaluation meetings in Saigon are detailed in interviews with Gen. William McCaffrey and Gen. David Barrato, as well as in "Withdrawal Pains—The War in Indochina," *Newsweek*, June 7, 1971. Statistics on senior officer versus junior officer and enlisted casualties; the effect of the helicopter on command and control; the "Hamlet Evaluation" system; and the muddled chain of command come from *The Pentagon and the Art of War* by Edward Luttwak.

Chapter 11: Days of Rage

Colin Powell's experiences in Korea in 1973 are from an interview with the general. A description of Gen. Hank Emerson, "Gunfighter," is contained in Col. David Hackworth's autobiography, *About Face* (Simon & Schuster). Figures on the recruitment of black cadets at West Point are from a 1970 article in *Army Times*.

Data on the experiences of the Army with high school dropouts versus high school graduates is from *America's Volunteer Military—Progress and Prospects* by Martin Binkin, The Brookings Institution. The higher incidence of death in combat for Project 100,000 personnel and the USMC's problems with recruit quality are quoted from *Semper Fidelis, the History of the USMC*.

Chapter 12: All Volunteer

Most of the details on the ending of the draft—including the Army's plan to double the number of women in the service between 1972 and 1977—are contained in the report *Ending the Draft—The Story of the All Volunteer Force*, written by Gus Lee and Geoffrey Parker for the Human Resources Research Organization (HUMRRO), under contract to the Department of Defense.

The story of Gen. George Forsythe's efforts in charge of the Modern Volunteer Army is taken largely from a printed interview with the general as part of the Oral History series, Army Center for Military History; also from an interview at West Point with his son, Col. George Forsythe. Forsythe's key contribution to the Modern Volunteer Army effort was also stressed in interviews with Gens. Colin Powell and Barry McCaffrey. Specifics on the Gates Commission and Nixon's plans to end the draft are contained in *Ending the Draft* by HUMRRO. Figures on the Army's AWOL incidence, or absence without leave, are from *Four Stars* (Houghton Mifflin) by Mark Perry.

Press accounts of the Project Volar experiment are taken from *The Detroit News*, January 16, 1972; *The Kansas City Times*, December 27, 1971; *The Wall Street Journal*, December 17, 1971; and *The Washington News*, November 15, 1971.

Figures on the crisis in recruit quality are from *Ending the Draft*. General Forsythe's blistering critique of Nixon's support of the all-volunteer Army is from an internal memo he wrote at the time, supplied to the author by his son.

Descriptions of the atmosphere at West Point in the early 1970s from interviews with McCaffrey and Gen. David Barrato. The incident of Sy Bunting's departure from West Point is taken from interviews with McCaffrey and detailed in a January 3, 1973, article in *Family Magazine*, which also includes figures on the number of officers who resigned from teaching assignments. Other figures from "West Point Cadets Now Say, 'Why Sir?' " in *The New York Times Magazine*, July 5, 1970.

Chapter 13: Last Act

Details about Creighton Abrams's seminal year as Army chief of staff in 1973 from *Thunderbolt* (Simon & Schuster) by Lewis Sorley. General disfavor with the idea of ending the draft among the officer corps is recounted in *Ending the Draft—The Story of the All Volunteer Force* (HUMRRO), also from interviews.

The alarming state of the Army in the early 1970s is documented in numerous books and articles at the time and confirmed in many of the author's interviews. Articles referenced for this section include "The Troubled U.S. Army in Vietnam," *Newsweek*, January 11, 1971; "The Neglected and Troubled 7th Army," *Newsweek*, May 31, 1971.

The U.S. military's debacles in early battles in major wars, such as Kasserine Pass, Task Force Smith, and Ia Drang Valley, are outlined in great detail in *America's First Battles*, Stofft and Heller.

Creighton Abrams's visit to the Command and General Staff College is outlined in *Thunderbolt*, also from interviews with Col. Mike Malone. Statistics on the racial makeup of the early all volunteer force are quoted from *Blacks and the Military* by Martin Binkin (Brookings Institution). The unusual relationship that developed between Secretary of Defense James Schlesinger and Army Chief of Staff Creighton Abrams, and their discussions on the correct size of the post-Vietnam Army, are outlined in both *Four Stars* and *Thunderbolt*.

Details on the shift of responsibilities to the reserves as part of Total Force come from several sources. Many of the figures on the shift of support, including studies of reserve call-ups during the Korean War, are contained in the author's article in *Military Forum*, February 1988, entitled "The Total Force at 15." A thorough look at this pivotal policy is also contained in *Twice the Citizen: A History of the U.S. Army Reserve, 1908–1983*, Crossland and Currie, Office of the Chief Army Reserve. That Creighton Abrams engineered Total Force intentionally to insure that U.S. forces could not be sent to war again without a reserve call-up was confirmed in interviews with Gen. Donn Starry and Col. Harry Summers.

Chapter 14: Epiphany

Details of Gen. William DePuy's pivotal role in reorganizing the Army are contained in *Changing an Army*, an oral history of Gen. William DePuy, U.S. Military History Institute. The extraordinary number of his protégés to reach four-star status is mentioned in the general's obituary, which ran in *Army Times* in 1992. Details on the Yom Kippur War of 1973 from newspaper clips, particularly *The Washington Post*, October 1973.

Gen. William DePuy's "pot of french soup" letter soliciting input on a new Army war-fighting doctrine is recounted in *King of the Killing Zone* (Berkley Books) by Orr Kelley. The fundamental shift in Army doctrine from the old "sleeping giant" industrial model to fast-paced warfare designed to win the first battle of any future conflict is outlined in "The Army's Training Revolution 1973–1990" by Anne Chapman, Office of the Command Historian, U.S. Army Training and Doctrine Command; and "From Active Defense to AirLand Battle: The Development of Army Doctrine 1973–1982" by John Romjue, U.S. Army Training and Doctrine Command. Also from interview with Gen. Donn Starry.

Chapter 15: Bloodless Battles

The revolution in military training is recounted in a paper Paul Gorman prepared for the Institute for Defense Analysis, 1990, entitled "The Military Value of Training." Figures and statistics on air losses also from an unclassified summary of the Red Baron Project, I & II. Gorman's seminal role in that revolution is discussed in *Changing an Army: An Oral History of Gen. William DePuy* (U.S. Military History Institute).

Details of the final official release of American POWs in Vietnam from news accounts, including "Last GIs Leave South Vietnam" on March 30, 1973, *The Washington Post*; also from *The American Experience in Vietnam*, Dougan and Weiss, Boston Publishing Company. The first official party of the River Rats as they welcomed home the POWs was described by Col. Boots Boothby, who arranged it.

Chapter 16: Red Flag

Description of Red Flag training and philosophy reported from interviews conducted by author during numerous visits to Nellis Air Force Base for Red Flag rotations, as well as with Gen. Chuck Horner and Col. R. Moody Suter, considered by many to be the father of Red Flag. The casualty figures for early rotations are taken from *Red Flag: Combat Training in Today's Air Force* by Michael Skinner. The decline in Air Force aircraft sortie rates and in pilot retention by the late 1970s are outlined in "Four-Star Management," *Inc. Magazine*, January 1987, and in the Air Force's 1979 Posture Statement.

The scandal at Homestead Air Force Base and the "dive toss" incident were largely recounted by Col. Bill Schwetke, former director of Red Flag and the Fighter Weapons School at Nellis, confirmed in interviews with Generals Horner and Creech.

Chapter 17: Sky Blazer

Background on Gen. Bill Creech and the revolution at TAC from an interview with Creech; also "Four-Star Management," *Inc. Magazine*, January 1987, and "How TAC Increased Productivity 80% from 1978 to 1984," *Government Executive* magazine,

May 1985. Statistics on sortie rates and aircraft maintenance from "Four-Star Management."

Chapter 18: Borderline

Statistics on the growing number of married soldiers by the late 1970s from *America's Volunteer Military* by Martin Binkin (Brookings Institution). Statistics on the number of black recruits in the Army are from *Blacks and the Military,* Brookings Institution. Details on escapes over the East German border are from the author's article "Dark Anniversary: Twenty Years of the Wall," *Overseas Life* magazine, September 1981. The fiasco of the Nifty Nugget exercise is explained in the declassified summary "An Evaluation Report of Mobilization and Deployment Capability Based on Exercises Nifty Nugget–78 and Rex–78," June 30, 1980, prepared by the Office of the Secretary of Defense. Its dire implications are partially spelled out in the preface of the Army's Annual Posture Statement for 1979. The shift in the strategic balance during the "lost decade" in Europe, and USSR gains in missile-guidance technology, are explained in depth in *The Carter Years* by Richard Thornton.

Chapter 19: Long Memories

Most of the information about the declining readiness of the Navy is gathered from interviews with Adms. Stan Arthur, Ronald "Zap" Zlatoper, and Thomas Hayward. Statistics also from *The Post–World War II Navy* and *American Naval History,* both from the Pentagon library. An in-depth explanation of improvements in the Soviet Navy and naval capabilities is contained in *Command of the Seas* by John Lehman, Jr. The Navy's operations at Subic Bay, the Philippines, are outlined in "How Important Are Subic and Clark," *Military Logistics Forum,* November/December 1985.

Chapter 20: A Hollow Force

The meeting of the Joint Chiefs with President Carter in November 1979 is recounted in interviews with Gen. David Jones, Gen. Shy Meyer, and Adm. Thomas Hayward. Reference to 1979 as the most difficult year in President Carter's life, and other details surrounding the Iran hostage crisis, are taken from Carter's memoirs *Keeping Faith* (Bantam Books, 1982); also from news accounts, including a series on the fall of the Shah of Iran by *Washington Post* staff writer Scott Armstrong.

Statistics on the "hollow force" from news accounts, including "Nation's Military Anxiety Grows as Russians Gain" by Bernard Weinraub, *New York Times.* Figures on the crisis in recruiting in 1979 from *America's All Volunteer Military* by Martin Binkin of the Brookings Institution.

The canceling of a scheduled deployment by the captain of the USS *Canisteo* because of a lack of trained crew is recounted in "Beached Whale: Supership Docked for Lack of Crew" by *Washington Post* reporter George Wilson. Details of the Soviet Union's invasion of Afghanistan from new reports, including "Carter Hits Soviets on

Afghan Action," *The Washington Post*, December 29, 1979.

Details about Gen. John Vessey's career from his biography on record at the Army's General Officers Management Office; Carter's decision to pass over Vessey as chief of the army due to his comments on the proposed withdrawal from Korea are outlined in *Four Stars*, Mark Perry. Figures on the turnover rate in Army units are contained in the Army's 1979 Posture Statement to Congress. The issue of the quality of Army recruits in 1979, as well as shortages, is discussed in depth in *America's All Volunteer Military* by Martin Binkin of the Brookings Institution.

The recruiting scandals are outlined in the Army's 1979 Posture Statement. Gen. Edward Meyer's desire to shift to a personnel rotation system more akin to the British regimental system from interviews the author conducted with Meyer and Lt. Gen. Robert Elton (ret.), as well as from "U.S. Army May Use British System to Boost Morale" in the November 13, 1980, edition of *The Christian Science Monitor.*

Chapter 21: All You Can Be

The story of the turnaround in the Army's recruiting fortunes recounted in an interview with Gen. Maxwell Thurman. Details also from "Sell, All That You Can Sell" by Paula Span, *The Washington Post* magazine, March 22, 1992.

Chapter 22: Storm Clouds

The final meeting in the "Tank" on Operation Eagle Claw is described from interviews with participants, including Gens. David Jones and Shy Meyer, Adm. Thomas Hayward, and Col. Charlie Beckwith. The role of Meyer in the creation of Delta Force is outlined in *Delta Force* by Charlie Beckwith and Donald Knox (Harcourt Brace Jovanovich).

Chapter 23: Desert One

The attempted rescue of the hostages and the tragedy of Desert One are meticulously explained in *Delta Force*, as well as in *The Guts to Try* (Orion Books) by John Robert Eidson and Col. James Kyle, the commander at Desert One; also from news accounts on April 25 and 26, 1980. Beckwith's biography and background from *The Long Gray Line* (Pocket Books) by Rick Atkinson. The situation in the Pentagon command room, and at the White House, is described in interviews with participants, as well as from details in *Keeping Faith* by Jimmy Carter.

Military pay and education benefits increases are outlined in the services' Annual Posture Statements for 1980. The accident aboard the USS *Nimitz* subsequent to the Eagle Claw operation is taken directly from ship's logs acquired from the Navy. Admiral Hayward's proclamation introducing the "zero tolerance" policy on drug use is taken directly from a transcript of his video presentation sent to all Navy commands. Figures on drug use in the Navy and subsequent improvements from "A Brief History of the Navy Drug and Alcohol Program," Bureau of Naval Personnel.

Chapter 24: Central Command

The explanation of the Navy's reluctance to take active part in the Rapid Deployment Joint Task Force (RDJTF) from interviews with Adm. Stan Arthur and Gen. P. X. Kelly. An excellent explanation of the Pentagon's geographical command structure is detailed in *The Pentagon and the Art of War* (Simon & Schuster) by Edward Luttwak. Details on the early formation of RDJTF from an interview with Gen. P. X. Kelly. The buildup of U.S. weapons and ammunition stores in the Middle East is outlined in the article "Middle East: Laying the Ground Work" by Peter Grier, *Military Logistics Forum*, September 1987.

Chapter 25: Killer Accountants

Description of Red Flag in the early 1980s from interviews with Gen. Chuck Horner and Col. Steve Turner, and others during visits by the author to Nellis Air Force Base. The facilities in this time frame are also described in *Red Flag: Combat Training in Today's Air Force* by Michael Skinner. Incorporation of Red Flag experiences into Air Force attack doctrine is from an interview with Gen. Bill Creech. Figures on the increase of new aircraft in the Air Force inventory as a result of the Reagan-era defense buildup are taken from the document "Improvements in U.S. Warfighting Capability, FY 1980–1984," Department of Defense, May 1984. Sortie rates and improved accident statistics for Tactical Air Command come from "Four-Star Management," *Inc. Magazine*, January 1987.

Chapter 26: A Parting Shot

The closed hearing where Gen. David Jones sounded his historic warning that the Joint Chiefs of Staff was broken is recounted in interviews with both General Jones and Archie Barrett. Figures on defense spending increases and weapons purchases in Reagan's first term from "Downhill Slide: The Defense Budget Roller Coaster" by David Morrison, *National Journal* magazine, February 21, 1987. General Jones's quoted comments to the House Armed Services Committee taken directly from his prepared statement, supplied to the author by General Jones.

Caspar Weinberger's comments on Navy Secretary John Lehman, and other vital aspects of the movement to reform the Joint Chiefs of Staff, are contained in a 1992 study written on Goldwater-Nichols reforms by Linda Flanagan for the John F. Kennedy School of Government, Harvard University. Figures on the number of officers who serve on joint assignments, and their experience level, are taken from the April 1982 "Report for the Chairman, Joint Chiefs of Staff, on the Organization and Functions of the JCS" by the Chairman's Special Study Group.

The historical anecdote about service wrangling during the Spanish-American War from *Four Stars* by Mark Perry. Biographical information on former representative Dick White from Michael Barone's *Almanac of American Politics* (National Journal). Adm. Thomas Hayward's feelings on the reform effort were espoused in an interview with the author.

The vast rise in influence and number of professional staff members in Congress during the 1900s is recounted in *The Almanac of the Unelected*, published by *National Journal*. Transcripts from the noted House Armed Services Committee hearings are available from the committee; details also from Linda Flanagan's study for Harvard's JFK School of Government. Further background on these hearings was supplied in interviews with Arch Barrett, Gen. Shy Meyer, Gen. David Jones, and Adm. Thomas Hayward.

Chapter 27: Semper Fi

Details on General Vessey's assignment as chairman of the Joint Chiefs from various interviews, as well as *Four Stars* (Houghton Mifflin) by Mark Perry. Caspar Weinberger offers a detailed account of events leading up to the deployment of Marines to Beirut, and his strong objections to the idea, in his autobiography, *Fighting for Peace* (Warner Books). The House Armed Services hearing on the incident, and the grilling of P. X. Kelly, is recalled in *Four Stars*; also from an interview with Kelly.

In *The Pentagon and the Art of War*, Edward Luttwak gives an excellent after-action review of the convoluted chain of command that led from the Marines on the ground in Beirut. Description of the bombing from interview with WO Hardy Slate, a Marine on the scene at the time. Adm. Robert Long's scathing views on the Beirut bombing are contained in the Long Commission Report and reiterated in an interview with the author. Other details from *The U.S. Marine Corps in Lebanon, 1982–1984*, published by the Marine Corps historical center in 1987, written by Marine historian Ben Frank.

Chapter 28: Urgent Fury

Details on Operation Urgent Fury are taken from a number of sources, including *It Doesn't Take a Hero* by Gen. H. Norman Schwarzkopf; *Fighting for Peace* by Caspar Weinberger; and *The Pentagon and the Art of War* by Edward Luttwak. Many examples on the disconnects between the services during the operation are contained in "Grenada: Rampant Confusion" by Michael Duffy, *Military Logistics Forum*, July/August 1985. Also from the author's article "Third World Wars," October 1989, *Military Forum* magazine.

Figures on the declining use of drugs in the Navy ranks, and the improvement in retention, from "A Brief History of the Navy Drug and Alcohol Program," Bureau of Naval Personnel. The Navy's growth in force structure compared to the other services in the early 1980s is outlined in "Improvements in U.S. Warfighting Capability, FY 1980–1984," Department of Defense, May 1984.

The emergence of the Maritime Strategy as the driving force in Navy doctrine is discussed in *The Post–World War II Navy*. The Maritime Strategy is also discussed in detail in John Lehman's autobiography, *Command of the Seas*. Other takes on the Maritime Strategy from interviews with Adm. Stan Arthur and Adm. Thomas Hayward.

Chapter 29: Politics

Colin Powell's relationship with Caspar Weinberger was discussed with the author in an interview; also from *Colin Powell: Soldier/Statesman—Statesman/Soldier* (Donald Fine) by Howard Means. Weinberger's speech at the Press Club outlining his views on the use of force, and his meeting with the Marines off the coast of Lebanon, are detailed in Weinberger's *Fighting for Peace* (Warner Books). Improvements in the Navy's fortunes during this time frame from interviews with Adm. Ronald "Zap" Zlatoper, Powell's assistant as chief military aide to Caspar Weinberger, and former chief of naval personnel.

Caspar Weinberger's approach to congressional hearings—and resentment of it on Capitol Hill—are taken from *Fighting for Peace*. Statistics on the largest peacetime defense buildup in the nation's history are taken from "Downhill Slide: The Defense Budget Roller Coaster" by David Morrison of the *National Journal*. Figures on the growth in the military force structure in Reagan's first term are contained in "Improvements in U.S. Warfighting Capability, FY 1980–1984," Department of Defense, May 1984.

The effect of a highly "concurrent" approach to weapons development and production, and its impact on troubled weapons programs such as the B-1B bomber, are discussed in detail in the author's articles "The B-1B: Concurrency Takes Its Toll" and "Unguided Missiles," *Military Forum* magazine, May 1987 and April 1988. Details on the Army's troubled acquisition programs of the mid-1980s are taken from the author's "What's Wrong with the Army?" in *Military Forum*, 1986.

Chapter 30: Windmills and Reformers

Details of the closed-door House-Senate conference from interviews with Arch Barrett, Jim Locher, and Sen. Barry Goldwater. Biographical information on John Tower from *The Almanac of American Politics* by Michael Barone (National Journal). The rise in influence and power of congressional staff members is outlined in "A History of the Unelected," by Floyd Riddick, Parliamentarian Emeritus, U.S. Senate, in the introduction of *Almanac of the Unelected* (National Journal). Backgrounds on the senators and representatives mentioned is from Barone's *Almanac of American Politics*. Sen. Barry Goldwater's interest in military reform was recounted in an interview with the author at his home in Phoenix, Arizona.

John Lehman's strident opposition to military reform was discussed by many participants and outlined in a 1992 study on the Goldwater-Nichols reforms by Linda Flanagan, of Harvard's JFK School of Government. Concerns about Lehman in the Navy's uniformed ranks were verified in interviews with Adms. Stan Arthur and Thomas Hayward, as well as in Lehman's book, *Command of the Seas*. Serious problems created for naval aviation by the drive for a six-hundred-ship fleet are outlined in the author's "Tough Times for Naval Aviation," *Military Forum* magazine, March 1989.

Chapter 31: A Palace Coup

Goldwater's retreat to Fort A. P. Hill to sell the reforms to the Senate Armed Services Committee was related in interviews with Goldwater, Locher, Jones, Barrett, and Gorman. Weinberger's reaction to the effort, as well as to the President's Blue Ribbon Commission, was related in various interviews, including with David Packard.

Details on Sen. John Warner's attempt to derail the reforms recounted by Barry Goldwater and Jim Locher. The final approval of the reforms is also detailed in the 1992 study on Goldwater-Nichols reforms by Linda Flanagan, from Harvard's JFK School of Government. The fact that none of the Navy's top admirals would appear at John Lehman's retirement is recounted in his book, *Command of the Seas.*

Chapter 32: Reveille

Figures on the turnaround of the all-volunteer force are taken from *America's Volunteer Army* by Martin Binkin (Brookings Institution). Background information on Gen. Binney Peay supplied in an interview. The development of AirLand Battle doctrine is covered at length in "From Active Defense to AirLand Battle: The Development of Army Doctrine 1973–1982" by John Romjue (TRADOC Historical Monograph Series).

Chapter 33: National Training Center

Observation on the National Training Center were culled over numerous visits to the training ground by the author (see "NTC: Training As It's Supposed to Be," *Military Forum*, November 1986; and "Desert Showdown," *Government Executive* magazine, September 1992). Special thanks are due to Gen. William Carter III, NTC commander, for insights into the historical evolution of the center; Col. Patrick O'Neal, OPFOR commander, for a history of the OPFOR; Col. George Harmeyer, chief of observer controllers, for insight into the After Action Reviews; and especially to Col. John LeMoyne, 1st Brigade, 24th Infantry Division, who sponsored the author. Information on the late Col. Jerrell Hamby, who died when his jeep overturned at the NTC, was taken off a copy of "The Order of Hamby," still awarded to OPFOR personnel for meritorious duty.

Chapter 34: A Defining Struggle

Gen. Jack Galvin's impressions of the fall of the Berlin Wall from are from interviews. Details on November 9, 1989, also from newsclips, including "The Wall Comes Down," *Newsweek*, November 20, 1989; "Into a Brave New World," *Newsweek*, December 25, 1989.

Disparities in the number of weapons in the NATO and Warsaw Pact arsenals as revealed in the Conventional Forces Europe negotiations are outlined in the author's article "NATO's Turning Point," *Government Executive*, July 1990. The discovery that the USSR's nuclear arsenal peaked at forty-five thousand warheads, far above U.S. estimates at the time, is recounted in an article by William Broad in *The New York Times*, September 26, 1993. The Soviet Union's detailed invasion plans and weapons stockpiles are outlined in "Soviet Bloc Had Detailed Plan to Invade West Germany" by Marc Fisher, *The Washington Post*.

Reasons why the Soviet military believed it was falling behind the West in the arms race are taken from interviews with General Galvin and others. The fact that the Chernobyl nuclear accident and "Star Wars" program factored into that impression was confirmed by former top Soviet officials at a Princeton University conference on the end of the Cold War (see "SDI, Chernobyl Helped End Cold War, Conference Told," *The Washington Post*, February 26, 1992).

Chapter 35: Burden of Duty

Events surrounding the Central Command exercise Internal Look, from interviews with a variety of participants, as well as with key members of the Joint Staff; also from "Operation Desert Storm: War Offers Important Lessons Into Army and Marine Corps Training Needs" by the General Accounting Office. A detailed description is also included in *It Doesn't Take a Hero* by Gen. Norman Schwarzkopf. Churchill's comments on World War II being won in the classrooms of U.S. military schools in the 1920s and 1930s, and a detailed discussion of the U.S. military school structure, from the author's "Schooled in Warfare," *Government Executive*, October 1991.

Chapter 36: A Gathering Storm

The ascendancy to the top levels of the Air Force command of the fighter pilots groomed by Gen. Bill Creech is outlined in "Four-Star Management," *Inc. Magazine*, January 1987.

The briefing by Schwarzkopf and Horner at Camp David is detailed in *It Doesn't Take a Hero*; also from interviews with participants. Colin Powell's objections to a piecemeal deployment or use solely of air power, feelings on the role of chairman of the Joint Chiefs under Goldwater-Nichols, and confidence in the Army were related in an interview; also from *The Commanders* (Simon & Schuster) by Bob Woodward.

The educational paper chase that underpinned many improvements in the all volunteer force, and the Capstone course for general-officer candidates, are detailed in the author's "Schooled in Warfare," *Government Executive* magazine, October 1991; also from "Bringing Home the Storm" by David Gergen, *The Washington Post*, April 28, 1991.

The Joint Staff's active role in the early days of Desert Shield is detailed from interviews in the author's "The Gathering Storm," *Government Executive*, November 1990. The scene in Saudi Arabia surrounding the decision to deploy from interviews with Gens. Chuck Horner and John Yeosock; also from *It Doesn't Take a Hero* by Gen. Norman Schwarzkopf. Deployment of the 1st Tactical Fighter Wing is taken from interviews, and from the author's "Dash to the Desert," *Government Executive*, November 1990.

Chapter 37: A Line in the Sand

That the Air Force's deployment during the first week of Desert Shield far exceeded expectations was recounted in *It Doesn't Take a Hero* by Norman Schwarzkopf (Bantam Books). The anecdote of General Yeosock taking a penknife out of his pocket was related in *Moving Mountains* by Lt. Gen. Gus Pagonis and confirmed in interviews with the participants.

Deployment of the 1st Marine Expeditionary Force from interviews with the participants, including Gens. Walt Boomer, Mike Myatt, and Tom Draude. The controversial decision not to include the National Guard "round-out" brigades in the early deployments is outlined in "Guard Deployment Decision Postponed" by Tom Donnelly and Sean Naylor, *Army Times*, February 4, 1991; and "The 48th Brigade: A Chronology from Invasion to Demobilization," *National Guard* magazine, May 1991. Further history of the Total Force is taken from the author's "The Total Force at 15," *Military Forum*, February 1988. Descriptions of Maj. Marie Rossi and her concerns on deploying to Saudi Arabia were given by her husband, WO Andy Cayton.

Chapter 38: Band of Brothers

Problems earlier commanders in chief had in controlling their subordinate commanders were taken from interviews with Jack Galvin and others; also from "Beyond Rivalry" by Larry Grossman, *Government Executive* magazine, June 1991. Details surrounding Horner's assumption of Marine Corps aircraft from interviews with Horner and Boomer.

Development of the air campaign from interviews, as well as from *Triumph Without Victory* by the staff of *U.S. News and World Report* (Random House). The comments of Gen. Mike Dugan's that led to his dismissal are taken from *The Washington Post*, September 16, 1990.

Chapter 39: War Council

The description of the seminal gathering of commanders on November 14, outlined in this chapter and in the prologue, was gathered from interviews with many participants, including McCaffrey, Horner, Yeosock, Peay, Myatt, and Boomer. A detailed account of the address Schwarzkopf gave his commanders is also recounted in *It Doesn't Take a Hero*.

Chapter 40: The Gulf

The discussion among Marine Corps commanders on the wisdom of launching an amphibious assault was recounted in interviews with Generals Boomer, Myatt, and Draude. One of the published reports that Marine Corps commandant Gen. Al Gray favored the idea was in "Beyond Rivalry" by Larry Grossman, *Government Executive* magazine, June 1991. Adm. Stan Arthur's uneasiness with the Navy's command-and-control position and inability to accept the air-tasking order electronically aboard ship was related in interviews with him and Admiral Mauz.

Chapter 41: Peace on Earth . . .

Taken from interviews. The reference to Ozymandias is from the poem of the same name by Percy Bysshe Shelley.

Chapter 42: Air War

Details and statistics on the air campaign are taken from *Airpower in the Gulf,* James Coyne (Air Force Association). Congress's debate on approving the use of force in the Persian Gulf is discussed in detail in *Triumph Without Victory* (Random House).

The deployment of the F-117 Stealth fighters was described by Col. Alton Whitley. The story of the early days of the F-117 program from interviews with Whitley and Ben Rich, head of Lockheed's famed "Skunk Works." Also from the author's "Black Programs: Too Big to Hide," *Military Forum,* April 1989. The inability of the Navy to communicate adequately with Central Command headquarters—even to the point of not knowing for sure when the war began—was recounted by Adms. Stan Arthur and Zap Zlatoper.

Chapter 43: Eve of Destruction

Readiness rates of weapons in the 24th Infantry are from division records. The different images cast by high-tech weapons in peacetime and in war is detailed in the author's "Weapons Under Fire," *Government Executive* magazine, June 1991. The meeting where the final decision was made not to launch an amphibious assault was described by Gen. Walt Boomer.

Chapter 44: Ground War

The actions of the 24th Infantry Division during the ground war were described in numerous interviews, including those with Gen. Barry McCaffrey, Col. John LeMoyne, and Capt. Linda Suttelhan.

Chapter 45: Inferno

The 1st Marine Division's battle in the Al Burgan oil fields from after-action reports and interviews, including with Generals Myatt and Draude, Col. Jerry Humble, and Capt. Eddie Ray. The condition of Kuwait after its liberation was recounted by the participants, as well as in numerous news accounts, including "Free at Last! Free at Last!" by Bruce Nelan, *Time,* March 11, 1991.

Chapter 46: Partings

Destruction of retreating Iraqi forces on the "Highway of Death" was recalled by various participants, including Col. Hal Hornburg and Lt. Col Steve Turner of the 4th Tactical Fighter Wing. Details on the destruction also from *Airpower in the Gulf* (Air Force Association).

The 24th Infantry's fight in the Rumaylah oil fields was recalled by numerous participants, including Gen. Barry McCaffrey, Lt. Col. Chuck Ware, Col. John LeMoyne, and Col. Burt Tackaberry. Marie Rossi's actions on the day she was killed were recalled to Andy Cayton by her former colleagues, including the sole survivor of the crash.

Epilogue

The number of women who served in the Persian Gulf from *Who'll Fight the Next War?* by Martin Binkin (Brookings Institution). The incident surrounding the reported snub of Barry McCaffrey at the White House was recalled in "Turning About-Face Into Forward March" in *The Washington Post*. The photo of McCaffrey and President Clinton jogging together is from "Clinton's Quick Steps to Better Relations," *The Washington Post*, April 6, 1993. McCaffrey's award from the NAACP for leadership in civil rights is recounted in the *Savannah Morning News*, March 31, 1992.

Index

About the Author

James Kitfield won the 1990 Gerald R. Ford Award for distinguished reporting on national defense. He has covered the Pentagon for *Military Forum*,
and his work has appeared in *Omni, New York Newsday,* and the *Los Angeles
Times.* He lives in Arlington, Virginia.